Development and Nationhood

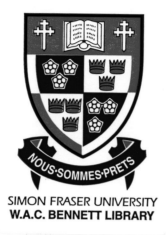

Development and Nationhood
Essays in the Political Economy of South Asia

MEGHNAD DESAI

OXFORD
UNIVERSITY PRESS

OXFORD

UNIVERSITY PRESS

YMCA Library Building, Jai Singh Road, New Delhi 110 001

Oxford University Press is a department of the University of Oxford. It furthers the
University's objective of excellence in research, scholarship, and education
by publishing worldwide in

Oxford New York

Auckland Cape Town Dar es Salaam Hong Kong Karachi Kuala Lumpur
Madrid Melbourne Mexico City Nairobi New Delhi Shanghai Taipei Toronto

With offices in

Argentina Austria Brazil Chile Czech Republic France Greece Guatemala
Hungary Italy Japan South Korea Poland Portugal Singapore Switzerland
Thailand Turkey Ukraine Vietnam

Oxford is a registered trademark of Oxford University Press
in the UK and in certain other countries

Published in India by Oxford University Press, New Delhi

© Oxford University Press 2005

ISBN 019 566760 3

Typeset in Adobe Garamond 10.5/12 by Jojy Philip
Printed in India by Brijbasi Art Press Ltd., New Delhi 110 020
Published by Manzar Khan, Oxford University Press
YMCA Library Building, Jai Singh Road, New Delhi 110 001

To

my father Jagadishchandra, who taught me to argue and
my mother Mandakini, who told me I could always do better

Contents

Preface   ix

Introduction   1

POLITICAL ECONOMY

1. Federalism, Economic Growth, and Economic Stagnation:
    An Interpretive Model of Indian Politics 1947–66   15

2. India: Emerging Contradictions of Slow Capitalist Development   20

3. The Emergency: Past and Future   46

4. The Economic Policy of the BJP   52

5. India: End of the First Republic   62

6. Why is India a Low Inflation Country?   69

7. Does India Need New Politics?   76

8. Death, Democracy, and Decline   84

9. Democracy and Development: India 1947–2002   94

PLANNING

10. Planning by Numbers   107

11. Indian Planning: Techniques, Perspective, and Context   111

12. Is there Life after Mahalanobis?: The Political Economy of India's
    New Economic Policy   122

13. Planning in a New Perspective   133

14. Development Perspectives: Was there an Alternative to Mahalanobis?   141

LIBERALIZATION AND REFORM

15. Capitalism, Socialism, and the Indian Economy   149

16. Economic Reform: Stalled by Politics?   160

17. India's Triple Bypass: Economic Liberalization, the BJP,
     and the 1996 Elections   176

18. What Should India's Economic Priorities be in a Globalizing World 183

19. Has Liberalization Worked in India?   191

NATION AND IDENTITY

20. Birth and Death of Nation-states: Speculations about
     Germany and India   199

21. Towards a Syncretic Vision of India   220

22. Constructing Nationality in a Multinational Democracy:
     The Case of India   222

23. Communalism, Secularism, and the Dilemma
     of Indian Nationhood   232

24. Gujarat and its Bhasmita   264

SOUTH ASIA

25. South Asia: Economic Stagnation and Economic Change   269

26. Economic Problems of South Asia   289

27. Defining a New Vision for South Asia   297

MEASURING THE ECONOMY

28. Demand for Cotton Textiles in Nineteenth Century India   319

29. Macro Econometric Models for India: A Survey   337

30. Power and Agrarian Relations: Some Concepts and Measurements   373

     Index   394

Preface

The Chinese curse—May you live in interesting times—could be the key to the lives of everyone who was around during any of the decades of the 20th century. But having been born in an Indian Native State, watched Independence come at a young age of seven, grown up during the Nehru years, the times were not just interesting but something more, something special. But I left India in 1961 and have never returned to live permanently. Yet I have been engaged with reading about India, thinking about its problems and prospects as well as visiting friends and relations frequently.

India's story is a dual of unexpected surprises and unfulfilled expectations. Who would now believe that in the Lok Sabha, parliamentarians of Independent India lamented that the country could not manufacture razor blades or bicycles and within fifty years the Americans are worried about outsourcing to India. And yet the ambitious plans released on the eve of Independence by the businessmen and radical intellectuals projected growth rates which were not achieved till forty years later. Half the children in India are still malnourished and a quarter of the population is still poor. India was the seventh largest industrial producer in terms of volume of output in 1947 and it is nowhere near that position now. In 1947, Nehru convened a Conference of Asian nations in Delhi since India was a leading country in Asia. Now when they speak of Asia they mean East and South East Asia.

For the first forty years after Independence India epitomized a fog of underperformance combined with a stunning moral arrogance; both aspects which have puzzled the world outside. I know since I have lived abroad for the last forty plus years. Only in the last dozen years has India been taken seriously abroad. It was Information Technology at first but then Bollywood and Beauty Queens also enhanced its reputation. As the 21st century begins, India is taken seriously as a potential economic success though even its well wishers are nervous about the many things which could go wrong. There is for instance as I write this in September in Delhi, a childish display of virulent xenophobia by the Left which behaves in this matter much like their avowed enemies who wear saffron. Horrible criminal acts of systematic violence against minorities await judgement in Delhi for the 1984 anti-Sikh pogrom and the 2002 Gujarat Muslims slaughter following the train carriage burning at Godhra. The destruction of the Babri mosque in Ayodhya is still an unresolved issue. Christian missionaries have been intimidatd and in one instance murdered. In a quieter but no less sinister mode, parents are deselecting female foetuses thanks to the latest developments in medical technology and yet the practice is a continuation of earlier times.

I cannot think about India in terms of economics alone, not even of political economy as it is conventionally thought of. History and ideology and anthropology are all part of the understanding. Economic reform and globalization are as important as communalism and the quality of Indian democracy. Castes and jatis—things we in the Nehruvian days were told were about to decay and disappear—pervade in politics. India is large enough to contain many nations and a failure to recognize the multinational nature of the sub-continent has already caused it to be partitioned twice. India is a nation by assertion but it can be one, in fact, only if the multinationality of its component parts is recognized and woven into a new national fabric. Otherwise there will be more Khalistans, Nagalands, and Kashmirs.

These essays, written over some forty years, engage with all these themes. Living abroad has given me the advantage of distance and detachment but it has also meant that on many issues I have missed the local twists and turns. I am also trespassing on areas other than economics which is my specialization but again here my education in India always encouraged me to roam freely wherever I wished to. Over the years many friends and colleagues far from stopping me from straying outside my discipline have afforded lots of opportunities to try out my ideas. A year visiting the Delhi School of Economics in 1970–1 gave me many friends who watched over me carefully as I rushed in where they feared to tread. Dharma Kumar, André Béteille, Khaliq Naqvi, Sukhamoy Chakravarty, A.L. Nagar. Later still, a US SSRC programme on South Asia Political Economy introduced me to the 'Indianists' of USA, UK, as well as India. Over four years (1979–82) Suzanne and Lloyd Rudolph, Ralph Nicholas, David Ludden, T.N.(Loki) Madan, Philip and Veena Oldenburg, Veena Das, Ashok Rudra tried their best to civilize what they saw as an econometrician given to idle doodling of algebra and diagrams while listening to debates on rituals of dying in early modern India or some such topic.

During the 1990s, my friend Kalyan Banerji gave me the platform in EXIM Bank to launch what has now been a decade long passionate advocacy of liberal economic reform. Ashok Desai invited me to write a fortnightly column for Business Standard during 1996–2001 which sharpened my eye for details as well as for polemics. Isher Ahluwalia often brought me to ICRIER to argue my point as did John Williamson who invited me to participate in a World Bank seminar on South Asia. The late and much lamented Mahbub-ul-Haq became a friend thanks to our mutual friend Amartya Sen. Mahbub inducted me into his South Asia Commission which allowed me to speculate about the region as a single entity. During that time Rehman Subhan, Sartaj Aziz, Khadija Haq also expanded my understanding of the developmental challenges that Pakistan and Bangladesh faced.

Along the way as I have changed my mind on many central issues, I have been engaged in intense but friendly debates with Prabhat Pattnaik, Amiya Bagchi, Arjun Sengupta, Deepak Nayar, Jayati Ghosh, Terry Byers (who is an honorary Indian in any case). My colleagues from London School of Economics John Harriss, Johnny Parry, Christopher Fuller, the late Michael Leiffer, Anthony Smith, Michael Yahuda have at various seminars and workshops taught me a lot. Over the years two friends I.G.Patel and Amartya Sen have watched my activities in this sphere with engaged bemusement. To all these colleagues and friends my grateful thanks for helping me in this amateur passion for Indian political economy.

Oxford University Press has been a very helpful publisher. A veritable army of charming editors has taken on the task of keeping me to my promise of providing the collection. I thank them as well as Kishwar whose editorial skills were deployed with a gentle touch.

MEGHNAD DESAI
November 2004

Introduction

This volume consists of a collection of my writings on South Asia, and particularly on India, over the last 35 years. In many senses, they are in the broad tradition of political economy. Thus, they presume a familiarity with Marxian political economy, venture into political history, and engage in issues of policy. They take up a decidedly non-neutral position about many of the issues under debate. To say that my position is non-neutral is not to say that it has been that way all my life. I do not strain credulity to make it appear as if all my life I have had the same consistent views. Indeed in one vital respect—the feasibility and possibility of socialism in my lifetime—my position has changed radically. This can be attributed to a combination of both my personal trajectory and events over my life. I have been writing more or less continuously over the last 35 years, as the essays in this collection show. These essays are thus more personal than my technical work in economics or econometrics, but at the same time they are very much a product of my professional life as an economist. They are also as much a product of my upbringing in India and my subsequent life as an Indian working abroad. It is best, therefore, to start with some personal background.

My Passage from India

I was born in 1940 in Baroda [Vadodara] in what was then a native state. The Gaekwads of Baroda had established a progressive native state, especially in education. The primary school I went to in Baroda—Madhyavarti—was housed in a splendid red brick structure, perhaps the best educational building I have had the good fortune to work in all my life in India and elsewhere. But by 1950, my father's job had moved to Bombay as native states were absorbed into the Indian Union, and so I spent the next 11 years of my life in Bombay (Mumbai).

Growing up in India during the 1950s was a great experience. Independent India was forging ahead. Nehru as prime minister was an inspiring figure whose speeches were always worth reading. He was shaping our minds as much as the politics of the country. We all thought that casteism, communalism, and religious superstition were evils to be combated. Secularism and socialism were the philosophies we were sure would shape modern India. I certainly imbibed from that atmosphere not only secularism, but an active atheism and a dislike for all the trappings of traditional India, things which today in the West are celebrated as a part of multiculturalism. I thought we would soon see a secular, rational India rather than one full of obscurantist swamis and gurus.

There was in those days a pervasive Left ideology in public discussions. I remember reading Shamlal's weekly column 'Life and Letters' in *The Times of India* every Wednesday with a sense of intellectual adventure. Damodar Kosambi's *Introduction to Indian History*[1] was first reviewed there, and I still think that the channels laid down by Kosambi for the writing of Indian history will endure longer than the chauvinistic nonsense that is becoming fashionable more recently which glorifies India's past in an anachronistic and unhistorical fashion. Some of my teachers at Ramnarain Ruia College in Bombay were known to be members of the Communist Party of India [CPI], others were active in the Praja Socialist Party—Prof Ram Joshi, for example, who later became Vice-Chancellor of the University of Bombay. I also had as a teacher at least one genuine intellectual—Prof G. D. Parekh, who was a Royist [a radical humanist follower of M. N. Roy] and was able to impart real intellectual thrill in his undergraduate lectures on politics. The libraries were well stocked and we were encouraged to read widely. I fully exploited the fact that my classes were in the morning and spent all afternoon in the library of the college. When I had exhausted that source I ventured downtown to the University Library and the library of the British Council.

I specialized in economics because in an Arts college, that was the best passport to job security. The economics we were taught was light on analysis and big on descriptive stuff. So, I learned a lot of economic history and much about 'Indian Economic Problems' as one subject was labelled. Here we read sturdy classics such as Wadia and Merchant, Jathar and Beri, Nanavati and Anjaria—all textbooks descriptive of India's myriad economic problems. In the mid 1950s when I was doing my BA, we were taught no development economics or growth theory.

Things got a bit better at the MA level, which I did from 1958 to 1960. Here in the University Department of Economics [formerly known as the Bombay School of Economics], we had some well-known teachers—Lakdawala, Dantwala, and Brahmanand. I specialized in International Trade taught by Lakdawala and two papers in Fluctuations and Growth taught by Brahmanand. We also had an American Visiting Professor under the Ford Foundation scheme. In my first year, we had Howard Ellis from the University of California at Berkeley, who had co-authored the textbook on development economics with Buchanan and in my second year we had Charles Whittlesey from the University of Pennsylvania, who was a specialist in Money and Banking. These were the heady days of the Mahalanobis Plan and the Bombay economists were flying their own separate flag with C. N. Vakil and P. R. Brahmanand's critique of the Mahalanobis model in their book *Planning for an Expanding Economy*[2] (see my essay in Chapter 14).

In the polemics of those days, Mahalanobis was Left and the Bombay economists were right-wing. It was Left to be for basic capital goods investment, for

---

[1] Asia Publishing House, Mumbai.
[2] 1956, Vohra & Co., Mumbai.

large plans, and for a dominant role for the public sector. It was right-wing to be for agriculture, light industries, and more foreign trade. Bombay was marginalized in the national policy debates, while the Delhi School of Economics and Presidency College, Calcutta were where all the influential economists were. We were aware of this but we were more in a business oriented environment in Bombay than our counterparts in Delhi or Calcutta. Our economics were more applied than theoretical. We were also more open to American influence due to the presence of a senior American economist as well as one junior one. Henry Bruton and Alan Heston were the two junior American economists in Bombay in 1958–9 and 1959–60. Cambridge, UK was more influential in Delhi and Calcutta, though we did read Joan Robinson's *Accumulation of Capital* during my MA in Bombay.

Those were the days of the Cold War and India was a battleground on the cultural front between USA and USSR. The influence of Marxist thinking was pervasive and the Soviet Union fashionable, but the Americans were fighting a subtle battle. I am pretty sure that the Ford Foundation had established a beachhead in this cultural battle by having American economists spend a year in Bombay. We also had newly published American textbooks and journals in our library. Walt Rostow's Marshall lectures appeared in the *Economist*. In those days, the Department of Economics library could afford the air mail edition and so I had the thrill of reading them, as they were delivered, on thin air mail edition pages in my senior MA year in 1959.

In those days, I was much taken by Schumpeter and Hayek and was not sold on Marxist ways of thinking. Like all my fellow students, I had read bits of Marx but in Bombay—the city as well as the University—there were strong non-communist influences. I was, if anything, on the right of the political mainstream and recall going to the founding meeting for the Swatantra Party in the Indian Merchants Chamber building near Churchgate Station. That was the one and only time I heard Jayaprakash Narayan, who was the guest speaker at the meeting. He had come along to support his old ex-socialist friend Minoo Masani and to fly the flag for political liberalism, when any right-wing opinions were being demonized as unpatriotic.

I did not join the Swatantra Party or any other party. I applied to the University of Pennsylvania (Penn) where Charles Whittlesey taught and was lucky to win a full scholarship. I could never have gone to Oxbridge because there were few fellowships available for British Universities in those days. (Things are not much better even today.) My scholarship meant that I had all the tuition fees paid plus my living expenses. I had to work as a Research Assistant for my scholarship and take three (rather than four) courses per semester. This meant that I would have to take course work for at least four semesters before I could finish my requirements and proceed to do my thesis. On this mild condition, I accepted the offer and left India in August 1961.

Various happy accidents followed when I got to Penn. I had hated mathematics at school and left it behind to pursue an Arts degree and you could do economics in those days up to Masters level without maths or statistics. But those happy days of ignorance ended when I was made Research Assistant to Lawrence Klein. I had read his *Keynesian Revolution*[3] but none of his econometric work. I was harnessed to his long-run programme of building up blocks of commodity models and country models and then matching them up to build a global model. I had spent a year at Bombay after my MA, registered for a PhD, and taken International Commodity Agreements as my tentative topic. I found myself working for Klein on an econometric model of the World Tin Economy because there was an International Tin Agreement and I had read something about it while in Bombay. This happy accident meant that unlike most Indian students abroad, I did not end up working on an Indian topic.

By another happy accident, I completed my course work, as well as my thesis, in two years and then Klein got me a job as a Research Officer in the Department of Agricultural Economics at the University of California, Berkeley. My first job was thus to work on problems of the California Dairy Industry. Again, I escaped working on Indian topics (I had written term papers at Penn on Indian topics, but that was all). Berkeley was the place where I was radicalized, taking part in the student demonstrations for civil rights and free speech. The Vietnam war was just hotting up and was controversial with Berkeley in the vanguard of the anti-Vietnam movement. I could have settled down in the USA after my job in Berkeley, but then I needed a Green Card and that made me eligible for the draft. So I left the USA in 1965 and was lucky to land a job at the London School of Economics (LSE). I have since then stayed at the LSE for some 38 years now.

The long and short of this elaborate piece of autobiography is that I never went back to India to work as an economist. Except for one year, 1970–1, when I was a Visiting Fellow at the Delhi School of Economics, I have never spent more than a month in India for these last 30 odd years since 1971. I also ended up working in my professional life on non-Indian topics—macroeconomics of UK and USA, econometric modelling of commodities and developed countries, economic history especially Cliometrics. I lectured on Marxian economics, applied econometrics, and then various courses in economic theory and applied economics. The bulk of my professional work is thus not as an Indian economist, but as an economist born in India.[4]

EXERCISES IN DIASPORIC DISSENT

The articles brought together here are thus by and large what I wrote out of my native interest and engagement with matters South Asian from far away. I have taken part in none of the big controversies which engaged Indian economists during the last four decades—small farms versus large farms debate, measurement of poverty in India, colonial mode of production, agrarian class structure, the size of the home market, plan priorities, etc. My friend Terry Byers has written an excellent survey of these Indian economic debates.[5] He has classified all the

[3] 1950, Macmillan, New York.

[4] Some of my published work has been collected in two volumes of *Selected Essays—Macroeconomics and Monetary Theory, Vol. 1* and *Poverty, Famine and Economic Development, Vol. 2*. Both were published by Edward Elgar in 1995 (Aldershot, Hants).

[5] Terence Byers (ed.), (1998), *The Indian Economy: Major Debates Since Independence*, Delhi: Oxford University Press. See especially the first three essays written by Byers, pp. 1–158.

economists participating in these debates by their birth date and grouped them into cohorts. I am not listed in that essay and quite justifiably, because I was not part of that group. It is in that sense that I am not an Indian economist but an economist born in India. I read a lot of those debates as they were published often in that most excellent vehicle, *Economic and Political Weekly* (*EPW*). I have somehow managed never to publish in *EPW*, but that is by accident rather than anything else.

Yet I would say that all the articles in this collection are responses to the issues which have been at the forefront of attention since the early 1960s. Thus, the earliest of the articles included here (Chapter 1) is a 1968 piece on Indian political economy, 'Federalism, Economic Growth and Economic Stagnation'. This is a succinct summary of where I thought the main contradictions lay in Indian political economy. It started as an evening lecture to the Indian Students Society of the LSE and then developed along more formal lines. I put much more emphasis on regional dimensions of Indian polity—its federal structure—than was done in Indian debates then or even since. I continued this in my New Left Review 1970 article 'Vortex in India'. This piece and its updated version, 'India: Emerging Contradictions of Slow Capitalist Development' (Chapter 2), which was written in 1972 but published in 1975, take a critical look at Left analysis and strategy in India and are quite pessimistic about the prospects of a Left Revolution.

Because I had been radicalized while abroad, my perspective on Indian problems differed from that of my Indian friends. I was much less influenced by theories of imperialism—a big topic among Indian Marxists or by post-colonialism or Third Worldism. I looked at capitalism as the key to understanding all social formations of the twentieth century. For me, India was an underdeveloped, but capitalist economy. It had decades of capitalist development yet to go through before it could have any dreams of a socialist revolution. I was in this respect taking a non-Leninist, but more a classical Marxist approach to Indian political economy.[6] It is not just that the Indian bourgeoisie were too weak to rule and thus had to collude and compromise (as Pranab Bardhan[7] has ably argued), but that the regional heterogeneity by itself meant that a national economy had not yet been created in India. Thus modelling India in terms of national classes was by itself an unwarranted 'speeding up' of the evolution of Indian capitalism as far as the 1960s and 1970s were concerned.

This was not, as I said above, the way the issue was seen in India at that time. During the one year I spent in Delhi, I found that Indian Marxists were deeply implicated in the ruling party's tactics and strategy. They were in fact part of the ideological machinery of the Congress party which manipulated them mercilessly. But they were willing victims of this process. Mrs Gandhi was seen as a progressive person to whose star the CPI wagon had been hitched and while the CPM was in opposition, it was not hostile. Many Left academics were proud of being CPM rather than CPI since it gave them a more revolutionary patina. Of course at that time the Naxalite movement had created an adventurist optimism among some of

[6] I have explained the distinction between a Leninist and a classical Marxist approach in my *Marx's Revenge*, Verso, 2002.

[7] P. K. Bardhan (1984), *The Political Economy of Development in India* (Oxford: Blackwell).

the younger students and faculty in Delhi. I was amazed to hear, for instance, someone complaining that Ashok Mitra, who was then Economic Adviser to the Government of India, had betrayed his Naxalite principles. Now I did not know him well enough then or even since to know the truth of that charge, but I could not understand how anyone in such a high position, in what was after all a 'bourgeois' government, could be expected to have Maoist principles. Having imbibed my Marxism outside India, where one would have to be far away from governments if at all radical, I was uneasy with the cosy accommodation between Indian Marxism and Indian government.

I was also critical of the socialist pretensions of Indian planning. This partly reflected my Bombay background, but it was also clear that Indian planning was failing in accelerating growth or in generating jobs or reducing poverty. It had a statist bias, but that did not imply a socialist policy unless the state itself was a revolutionary or even radical one. The answer to many Indian Marxists seemed even more planning of the type practised, but as I argue in an article written in 1972, 'Planning by Numbers' (Chapter 10), a lot of planning was mere number crunching with only a slender connection to the real economy. On the other hand, I thought that the Green Revolution was a progressive development since it brought capitalism to the Indian countryside. Since India was characterized by an underdeveloped capitalism, any growth of capitalist relations in the countryside was a progressive development in a classical Marxian sense. Again my view (expressed in my 1975 article 'Contradictions', see Chapter 2) was very much a minority view. In those days, some Marxists in India were predicting that the Green Revolution may turn into a Red one. Like the Russian Narodniks, Indian Marxists were dreaming of a leap from what they described as feudal and semi-feudal state of the Indian countryside to a socialist one. This was just delusion and proved to be so.

My stay in Delhi also led to some technical economic work which is reproduced here. There was a project to build a new model of the Indian economy jointly by the Delhi School, led by Prof. A. L. Nagar, and the Institute of Economic Growth, led by my friend Prof. K. Krishnamurty. I did a survey of the then existing models of the Indian economy which is included here as Chapter 29. Another paper is 'The Demand for Cotton Textiles' (Chapter 28) which is a cliometric exercise—the first in Indian economic history I believe—on a statement by Prof. David Morris about the impact of British textile exports on the Indian handicraft sector. I enjoyed this as it took me to the National Archives in Delhi for data gathering on nineteenth century textile trade. The friendship I struck up while in Delhi with Prof. Dharma Kumar led later to my becoming her Assistant Editor on the Cambridge Economic History of India, Vol. 2.

There was a lull during the second half of the 1970s in my writing on India. I did comment on the Emergency in my review article 'The Emergency: Past and Future' (Chapter 11). My analysis was that the Emergency arose out of a crisis of accumulation and that Mrs Gandhi would turn to America in the future to bankroll the Indian bourgeoisie. The Emergency should have laid to rest any illusions that the Congress party could ever be socialist in any accepted sense of the word, but the mainstream of Indian economics continued to run along the same lines as before once Mrs Gandhi was back in power in 1980. But two things happened during the Emergency and the brief and chaotic Janata government. There was a populist movement against the Congress which came from outside the Communist Left, especially from Jan Sangh and the various regional and caste based parties. There was also, through the later half of 1970s, an upsurge among the Dalits and tribals formed loosely as a coalition in Lokayan which was to be a harbinger of the fragmentation of politics in India. These grass-roots developments also took place outside the aegis of the Communist Party Left. Basically, Indian politics had been an elite run phenomenon wherein the elite cleverly bought in lower classes. But by the mid-1970s, the have-nots were no longer happy with the scraps they were getting, while the upper castes and classes, with their higher education, were getting all the jobs in the public sector. Socialism in India had been a massive outdoor relief project for the upper caste elite. The revolt, when it came from below, threw up leaders who soon learnt to use the electoral machine to advance their cause. This is what fragmented the party political structure in the late 1980s and 1990s and ended the Congress and Left hegemony in the Indian political life.

Towards the end of the 1970s I got involved in an exciting multidisciplinary programme on South Asian Political Economy sponsored by the American Social Science Research Council (SSRC) and funded by the Ford Foundation. There was to be cooperation with the Indian Council for Social Science Research (ICSSR) as well since in India all research requires official chaperoning. But I was able to meet 'Indianists' from USA, UK, and of course, India. I began to visit India every year after 1979 (not having been back since 1971) for the next four years. We had a theme on Agrarian Power and Agricultural Productivity which became a book of the same name based on papers edited by Ashok Rudra, Suzanne Rudolph, and myself. We had historians, anthropologists, political scientists, and economists and the atmosphere was intensely intellectual and very friendly. This was a most enjoyable way of doing political economy. I had a chance to revive and deepen my reading of Indian political economy and also broaden my vision by talking to non-economists. My paper 'Power and Agrarian Relations' (Chapters 30) is a response to that challenging seminar.

The full programme of South Asian Political Economy had two more themes. One on Households and Well-being and the other on Order and Anomie. There were again very exciting exchanges among sociologists, Indologists, political scientists, and anthropologists. We met twice, one year apart, for each theme, but unfortunately neither of the two conferences resulted in a published volume. But I made some abiding friendships and learned a lot in those four years, 1979 to 1982. Thus, my understanding of political economy was deepened by having to understand the role of beliefs and ideology, of social institutions and networks. But after that, again my visits to India became infrequent and so did my writing on India in the second half of the 1980s.

CRISIS OF INDIAN SOCIALISM AND RENEWAL OF INDIAN CAPITALISM

A new phase opened up in the late 1980s which has resulted in a steady stream of writings and almost permanent engagement on my part. For one thing, by 1989 it was clear that the Congress *raj* was again in some sort of crisis. In 1989, there was a conference in London at the School of Oriental and African Studies (SOAS) to celebrate 50 years of Indian planning, dating it from the year in which the Indian National Congress established the National Planning Committee. My paper on that occasion 'Indian Planning: Techniques, Perspectives and Context' was critical of the basic assumptions behind Indian planning as I had been critical before. I argued that for one thing, Indian planners had overestimated the surplus drained by the British and hence neglected the task of raising the surplus. They had thought that independence would by itself give them the surplus necessary to develop India and hence the main task—in agriculture, for example—was to make sure that the surplus was distributed correctly. Thus, rather than adopt policies which would enhance the surplus, for example by speeding up accumulation and transforming production along modern lines, Indian planners concentrated on changing relations of tenure and ownership of land in a series of land reforms. They further followed policies which hindered accumulation and restricted technical developments in the manufacturing sector, by limiting the output of modern textile industry while promoting small-scale handicrafts, or retarded the growth of a national market in food grains by restricting the interstate movements of food grains. Planning was thus perpetuating the underdevelopment of capitalism under the delusion that surplus was not lacking, but only its deployment was uncontrolled. But plans were crippled by a shortage of investible surplus as the debacle of the Second Five Year Plan had shown, when it had to be pruned two years after its launch. I have not previously published this paper as it was not welcome at the Conference volume but here it is (Chapter 11).

In 1990, I was invited to Ahmedabad to give the V. S. Desai Memorial lecture at the HL College of Commerce. I took as my title 'Is Socialism Dead?'[8] This was soon after the collapse of the Soviet Empire in Eastern Europe. We in the Labour Party in the UK had suffered three successive defeats at the hands of Mrs Thatcher. The British public had voted for a non-socialist, indeed an anti-socialist alternative to whatever the Labour Party had to offer. This was no isolated trend. The same was happening on the European continent. Left-wing parties were compelled to follow orthodox monetarist policies as in France. Yet there was great surprise among many intellectuals I met in Ahmedabad that I was speculating about the death of socialism. Many thought India could yet salvage socialism.

Then, in 1991, the bottom fell out of the Indian experiment in socialism. After all, the bottom had also fallen out of 'Big Brother' USSR, for so long looked upon by many Indians as an ideal in economic planning matters at least. Having lived abroad, I had imbibed none of this fascination with the USSR. Indeed the dominant strand in British Marxist debates is Trotskyist and so I was well aware of the critique of the Soviet system, not that I was enamoured of Trotsky or Trotskyists. We had our own crisis in the Labour Party after three successive defeats by 1987 and we were looking at new thinking on socialist economics.

The bulk of the essays in this collection are from this period of the 1990s. One theme carried on from earlier days is that of the development of capitalism in

---

[8] This was published in the journal *Contention*, Indiana University Press, Los Angeles (California), 1992.

India. Here my EXIM Bank lecture of January 1993 'Capitalism, Socialism and Indian Democracy' (Chapter 15) is the definitive war cry. I set out my full opposition to all that went before in Indian economic policy and my reasons for its rejection. It excited a lot of debate and many of my Indian Marxist friends were much disturbed by my unreserved dismissal of their ideas. I have continued flying the flag for speedier reform and liberalization ever since. The articles from India Briefing 1995, 'Economic Reforms: Stalled by Politics' (Chapter 16); for the Manmohan Singh Festschrift, 'Development Perspectives: Was There an Alternative to Mahalanobis?' (Chapter 14); and my R.S. Bhatt Lecture 'Has Liberalization Worked in India?' (Chapter 19) are periodic revisits to that central theme as events develop through the 1990s. I was also able to tackle the issue of planning for an open economy in my Sukhamoy Chakravarty Lecture 'Planning in a New Perspective' (Chapter 13). Although Sukhamoy Chakravarty was himself deeply involved in the planning process, his was an open and inquiring mind and he well knew by the late 1980s that the strategy of Indian planning needed rethinking. I know that many would and did disagree with my approach in that lecture which was to use Chakravarty's own early book—his Ph.D. thesis, indeed—in which he had explored the question of planning in an open economy.

Parallel with the crisis of Nehruvian socialism, there was also, starting around the late 1980s, the crisis of Congress as a dominant political party. Thus, I also began to think about another equally important question of Indian political economy. This was the issue of Indian nationalism, or rather conceptions of Indian nationhood. The Nehruvian secular approach had been under great strain in the 1980s as first Mrs Gandhi, and then Rajiv Gandhi, abandoned secularism and replaced it with competitive populism for Hindu and Muslim vote-banks. Thus Mrs Gandhi took to temples and gurus and adopted an increasingly Hindu imagery. Rajiv Gandhi played to orthodox Muslim opinion in the Shah Bano case, denying Muslim women's human rights. He also played soft on the movement for 'shilanyas' for the Rama temple inside the Babri Masjid in Ayodhya which caused trouble later. The resurgence of Hindutva forces was visible to me; even my infrequent visits in the 1980s and the 1990s confirmed this trend. Obviously, the Nehruvian template for Indian nationhood—unity in diversity, secularism, and economic development—was no longer satisfying to the Indian public. Hindutva forces demanded a rethinking of what it meant for India to be a nation.

This issue was totally neglected in political economy debates in the late 1980s. I began by rethinking the history of the partition. My 1990 paper 'Birth and Death of Nation States' (Chapter 20) compares India and Germany in the process of nation formation. Germany was an ill-defined territorial nation, but a cultural nation of some vibrancy in the mid-nineteenth century. I trace the manner in which Bismarck carved out a nation-state by rejecting an inclusive *Grossdeutsch* solution with Austria included and plumped for a smaller more tightly defined Germany—*Kleindeutsch*, dominated by Prussia. The analogy with an undivided India as defined in the Cabinet Mission proposals of 1946 and the partition as it happened was intriguing. This switch from a larger to a smaller India was sudden and meant that Indian leaders, especially Nehru, had to reconceptualize the basis for Indian nationhood. I pursue this theme in 'Constructing Nationality in Multinational Democracy' (Chapter 22). The idea is that India is originally a multinational polity, thus reverting to my stance in my 1968 Federalism article. Language and territory combine with history to define separate nations in India. Religion adds a further complication and this led to partition. But in denying the two-nation theory, Congress and Nehru still had to define Indian nationhood. Nehru did this by institution building and by his writing and exhortation. But the break-up of the Babri Masjid in 1992 and subsequent revival of communalism showed that there was a crisis of Indian nationhood. There was a rival concept of India as a Hindu nation. I trace in my long paper 'Communalism, Secularism and the Dilemma of Indian Nationhood' (Chapter 23) the long twentieth-century history of the three rival conceptions of Indian nationhood. Besides the Nehruvian and the Hindutva ideas there is the notion of India as a loose union of many nations—the multinational polity vision. I trace this back to the Round Table Conferences and the various regional and religious forces operating at the regional and, if you will, 'subaltern' levels.

The implications of this approach are worked out, in some shorter papers: 'Towards a Syncretic Vision of India' (Chapter 21), 'India: End of the First Republic' (Chapter 5), and in my most recent intervention in the Gujarat tragedy, 'Gujarat and its Bhasmita' (Chapter 24). I am very pessimistic about India arriving at an agreed conception of its nationhood peaceably. What does give me hope is that India remains a robust democracy. In my essay for the Hindu/ Encyclopaedia Britannica annual volume 'Death, Democracy and Decline' (Chapter 8), I draw up a balance which is quite bleak since robust as the democracy is, it is also corrupt, implicated with criminality, and incapable of decisive leadership in advancing India in tackling the challenges posed by globalization. In December 2002, I was invited to give the K. R. Narayanan Oration at the Australian National University. I returned to this theme in 'Democracy and Development' (Chapter 9). This is a sort of grand summary of my many writings on economics and politics at least as of the end of 2002. But here I am able to take up a theme I had not articulated before. This is that after independence, Congress took a conservative approach to social reform and a radical one to economic reform. The first perpetuated all the social evils of casteism and communalism and religious superstition that Nehru was fulminating against in my youth, while economic radicalism was just dirigisme to benefit the middle class/upper caste elite and hinder accumulation. This meant that for economic betterment, social groups had to take recourse to the ballot box and manipulate the political process to divert rents their way. The fragmentation of Indian politics, as well the revival of Hindutva, have their roots in choices made at the early outset of India's life as an independent country.

India is of course not unique in many ways. It is always good to place its history in the South Asian context. It is indeed a consequence of my views on nationhood that India, as at present constituted, is something of a historical accident. It could easily have remained what I call *Indica*—the Undivided pre-1947 India. This theme is reflected in the three papers which take a broader South Asian view of India's political economy. 'South Asia: Economic Stagnation and Economic

Change' (Chapter 25) compares the economic performance of South Asian economies and finds them similar. In 'Defining a New Vision for South Asia' (Chapter 27), I pursue a more idealistic vision of an eventual union of South Asia. This was part of a project inaugurated by my friend, the late and much lamented Mahbub ul Haq. He was a great inspiration as much in his work on human development as in his vision of a future union of all South Asian nations.

This then is the collection. Of course in any such collection there are bound to be overlaps and repetitions. There will also be some details which have been rendered obsolete. I have not tried to rewrite or repair any of the articles. They are as they were first written—warts and all.

POLITICAL ECONOMY

1

Federalism, Economic Growth, and Economic Stagnation:

An Interpretive Model of Indian Politics 1947–66

It is fashionable to begin papers such as this by saying that India today is at crossroads or that there is a crisis in Indian Politics. In as much as such a statement can be made about all countries at all times with some degree of truth, this is an empty statement. It is too general and does not help us to know more about the situation or about the person making such a statement. It is much more fruitful, therefore, to start making certain *specific* statements which will tell readers about the model implicit in this paper.

1. The character of Indian politics—its commonly accepted ideals and ac-cepted beliefs about the political process (the way of getting things done and resources allocated)—changed in the mid-1950s. The years from 1947 to 1957 or, at most, to 1960 will be called the Nehru era. The politics of the Nehru era were different from what followed.

2. The change in character was partly brought about by forces inherent in the history of the independence movement and in the Congress party but its fulfilment was hastened by the programme of economic development initiated in the years after independence.

3. This change has led to a slowing down of the growth rate by interfering with the allocation mechanism. From the point of view of the nation/society, this interference is *functional* in the sense that it strengthens the chances of its survival.

4. This change to a political process characterized by growth of state power and

Quarterly Journal of Indian Studies in Social Sciences combined with *India: A Decade of Destiny*, Indian Institute of Asian Studies, Bombay (1967–68).

This is an extended version of a paper read at the Sociology of Development seminar at the London School of Economics. I am thankful to Professor Dore and members of the seminar for several suggestions. I have also benefited from discussions with H. Abdullah, P.K. Chatterjee, and S.B. Scott. The responsibility for any errors is entirely mine.

local leadership represents an Indianization of the set of institutions embodied in the Constitution.

The change I have referred to above has been adequately documented and can be perceived everywhere. The politics of the Nehru era was based on an accepted set of rules of the game—British parliamentary tradition mainly—and accepted set of values. This set of values included nationalism with emphasis on Indian unity and opposition to regionalism, casteism and communalism, secularism, economic planning, economic growth, retention of English as medium of instruction and active concern with international affairs. There were differences of emphasis on many of these points among different parties and factions but a basic consensus was maintained. The new political setup is made up of powerful state level leaders whose coalition (in the Congress party) makes up the federal level decision making process. This setup is based on factions—caste factions, village and district level factions. Linguistic states are based on the idea of maximizing gain to the linguistic group prior to national gain. The new leadership is much more homespun, locally educated and risen from the ranks. The idea that a prime minister of India should be able to write and speak elegant English was taken for granted in the 1950s and in the early discussion of 'After Nehru who?' Today it can be regarded, properly, as a totally irrelevant matter.

How did this change come about? In what follows I have tried to set up a model that tackles this question,

The first building block of the model is the assertion that in India, economic mobility is very low for individuals but very high for roughly homogeneous groups of individuals such as caste groups or linguistic groups. Homogeneity of the group would be defined differently according to the level of aggregation at which we are dealing. Thus, *within* a linguistic state, different caste groups separate themselves as homogeneous but for the country as a whole a linguistic state can be treated as homogeneous. Studies of voting behaviour have shown that caste groups and community groups often try to obtain gain by trading block votes.[1] We have historical as well as contemporary evidence of caste mobility provided by Srinivas, Bailey, and others.[2]

Next we need a concept of dominant and non-dominant communities. Dominant communities are groups which have gained economically in the past. Even the very low growth rate during the British period set up several opportunities in trade, finance, and government bureaucracy which certain groups either by advantage or monopoly of education, native skill, and ingenuity, or due to availability of accumulated savings, took advantage of monopoly. At the beginning of independence these groups were economically dominant. They formed the urban middle class and urban bourgeoisie and upper classes. These groups were also politically powerful in the Congress party. After independence, the cohesion of this group—the temporary alliance they had made—broke up when different parts of the group realized their different and clashing economic inter-

---

[1] Weiner, Myron and Rajani Kothari (1965), *Indian Voting Behaviour*, Mukhopadhyaya.

[2] M.N. Srinivas (1966), *Social Change in Modern India*, University of California Press; Bailey (1958*), Caste and the Economic Frontier*, Oxford University Press.

ests. This set up the basic Right, Left, Centre orientation of national politics in the 1940s and 1950s—the main parties being Congress, Communist, Praja Socialist. The first ten years after independence witnessed in Indian politics the civil war within the dominant group in national parliamentary politics.

Between the first and second General Elections came the formation of linguistic states. This was the first sign that the character of politics was changing. The non-dominant majority was emerging in politics. The non-dominant majority was split up into several states—each state now forming a linguistic community. Within each state there is also a dominant minority and non-dominant majority but we confine our analysis to the opposition of *nationally* dominant minority groups and the groups of *nationally* non-dominant majority which are the heterogenous state units.

I need to explain at this stage the reasons why the non-dominant majority gained ascendancy in the political process over the dominant nationally oriented minority. The transition occurred after the first General Election and the formation of linguistic states in the second half of 1950s is the event which marks the beginning of the transition. There are two reasons for this transition. During the independence struggle the mass movement had already created demands for linguistic states. While the leadership of the Congress party was the nationally oriented dominant community, the rank and file were members of the non-dominant majority and concessions on matters such as linguistic states were essential for gaining mass support. The timing was decided by the events after the first General Election. The results of the first election and subsequent by-elections were not as favourable to the Congress as it wished. On the national front, this led to the adoption of 'the socialist pattern of society' programme to win back dissident factions of the dominant group and a compromise deal with regional groups to ensure success in the second and subsequent elections.

The non-dominant groups fear the process of economic growth would create opportunities which the dominant group can take advantage of much more readily than themselves. Thus economic development may reinforce the initial inequality and result in all or most of the gain of growth going to the already dominant. Such fears have sound historical evidence on their side. In a democratic context, the nondominant majority can, however, try, if not to prevent this division of gains from happening, at least to set up obstacles to such division. They do this by imposing 'tariffs' on the dominant group—encouraging local entrepreneurs, restricting government employment to members of the dominant linguistic group, etc.

The Indian political process becomes less confusing if looked at as a two-tier process. At the national level, ideological differences help explain the party politics both within and outside the Congress party. In our terms, party groups at the national level are factions within the dominant community whose interests clash *vis-à-vis* each other but are homogenous with respect to the rest of the country. At the regional level party allegiances are along caste and community lines. Within each state, we have groups of varying economic and social strength and a party's identification with a dominant group in one state may seem totally at variance with its identification with a non-dominant group in another state or with its national ideology. This is true in general of all the political parties but it is particularly true of the Congress and the Communist Party. The criss-crossing of group allegiances makes party discipline very loose and political decisions hard to understand in the light of party pronouncements.

The variations in the ideological position of a party from one state to another are not, however, purely random. The Swatantra Party in Orissa is an organ of the Swatantra Party different to its counterpart in Gujarat but this can be traced to certain systematic factors. I suggest that these variations can be looked at in terms of two factors: (a) The land-tenure system in the state in the years before independence (b) The degree of economic growth—growth of trade, finance, and industry—in the state in pre-independence years. These two factors should largely account for the class divisions—rural and urban of a state even today.

The political process at the national level now consists of bargaining to get for one's own state a portion of the economic gain—(for example, a steel plant or a refinery). This results in questions of allocation of specific projects and of total planned investment, being determined by political bargaining in the National Development Council and outside.

A number of specific instances of such misallocation due to political bargaining could be cited. In the matter of the location of two oil refineries, one in Bombay and the other in Barauni (Bihar), political agitation in Gujarat and Assam led to the establishment of three refineries, one in Baroda (Gujarat), one in Barauni (Bihar), and one in Noonmati in Assam. The latter two refineries were two uneconomic sized plants which had to be established instead of the originally planned larger unit.[3]

The dominant group wants rapid economic growth in the national context. They are for economic efficiency, location decision based on costs, and free movement of goods and men. The political process impedes efficient allocation by imposing tariffs, slows down economic growth and the lower the growth rate, the more intense is the scramble for a portion of the smaller pie.

There is one more question which must be answered in this model. If the nationally dominant minority was ruling in the first few years, why did it let power slip away from its hands to the non-dominant majority? Why did the growth of state power not get checked? One part of the answer in terms of the election needs of the Congress party has already been given. Much more important, however, is the split in the dominant minority. One partner in the pre-independence coalition was business, mainly big business. The years immediately after independence saw the native business afraid of foreign competition and insecure. But with the initiation of the government economic growth programme, it was strengthened.[4] In the late 1950s, big business questioned the consensus values of the nationally dominant minority—especially the degree of state control which was being advocated. This faction realized that it had everything to gain

---

[3] J.C. Daruvala (ed.), *Tensions of Economic Development in South-East Asia*—especially the paper by Dept. of Politics and Civics, University of Bombay—*Tensions of Indian Economic Development*, Allied Publishers, pp. 70–80.

[4] For the changing attitude of Indian business towards foreign capital, see Kidron, Michael (1965), *Foreign Capital in India*, Oxford : Oxford University Press.

from a weakening of federal government and strengthening of state level leaders. While the movement to regionalism created local entrepreneurs, these entrepreneurs were no threat to the nationally dominant business. The monopoly of credit and finance held by big business was adequate to ensure that they would consolidate their gains and not lose them if local entrepreneurs emerged. The split in the nationally dominant minority strengthened the federalist trends.

The political process results in a low growth rate and has tendencies which may further lower the growth rate. One would like to see if there are limits to this process but I would like to resist any temptation of projecting this model and deriving the consequences of the process in the limit. There is one counteracting force that needs mentioning. The geographical mobility of the skilled workers as a part of economic growth may create high income, vocal groups which are heterogenous elements in a linguistic state and they may influence state or national politics. (There is evidence that the voting behaviour of workers who have emigrated to Calcutta from other states is significantly different from the voting behaviour of Bengal workers and this is an important force in elections).[5] A measure of the importance of this phenomenon can be computed when the details of the 1961 census become available by calculating the 'immigrant' population from other states as a proportion of total population of any state. If this population shows an increase from 1951 to 1961, this force can become important.

I have attempted in this paper to sketch a model which is a helpful way of looking at Indian politics. I have not cited examples and empirical evidence at each point, partly to keep it short and partly because the evidence is easily obtainable and copious. A further step would be to fill out the details with the help of numerous studies of politics at the village, state, and national level, and with studies of the importance of factions in Indian politics.

[5] Weiner and Kothari, *Indian Voting Behaviour.*

2

India

Emerging Contradictions of Slow Capitalist Development

A socialist revolution in India would be an event of fundamental significance to the development of world history. An immense population of 550 million whose rural and urban masses were plagued by abysmal misery and unemployment make India one of the great potential storm centers within world capitalism. Yet the simple fact that India's peasants and workers are massively exploited and oppressed is not enough to guarantee a revolutionary solution since the history of the subcontinent has accumulated a formidable series of devices for containing and controlling the impulse to popular revolt. These range from religious antagonisms which have murderously divided the masses to powerful political machines which yoke them together with their class enemies; from archaic survivals of feudal social relations to the most modern strategies of imperialist penetration. Recently this whole system of domination appears to have strikingly consolidated itself just when serious strains and contradictions were appearing within it.

From the mid-1960s Indian capitalism seemed to be in major trouble. Following defeat in the 1962 border war with China and the indecisive clash with Pakistan in 1965, the Indian government greatly stepped up its military spending so that the military budget nearly quadrupled within the decade. In both 1965–6 and 1966–7 there were famines which impelled the government to import large quantities of wheat from the United States. Inflation accelerated and the balance of payments deficit soared. Under international pressure the rupee was devalued in 1966. In the General Election of 1967, the Congress party emerged with a small majority of 46 seats after 20 years during which it had enjoyed a majority of nearly two-thirds in the Lok Sabha. The Congress party was replaced by coalition of opposition parties of the Left and Right in many of the states. By the end of 1967, 330 million out of a 550 million population were being ruled by anti-Congress coalitions. Two years later the Congress was riven by a bitter national

'Emerging Contradictions of Slow Capitalist Development in India' in R. Blackburn (ed.) 1975, *Explosion in a Subcontinent*, Penguin, London.

split, with many important party bosses opposing Indira Gandhi. At the same time as this crisis in the bourgeois political order there were growing signs of popular revolt. A peasant uprising flared up in the Naxalbari district of West Bengal in 1967, to be followed by a peasant guerrilla movement in the Srikakulam district of Andhra Pradesh under Maoist influence. In Calcutta, the formation of United Front Government led by the Community Party of India (Marxist) was accompanied by the most vigorous strike wave India had ever seen.

The year March 1971 to March 1972 seemed to resolve these different crises in a peculiarly favourable fashion for the established order in India. This was, in fact, an *annus mirabilis* for Indira Gandhi, the dominant wing of the Congress party and the India they represented and led. In March 1971 mid-term elections, Indira Gandhi's Congress party was returned with a two-thirds majority over all her antagonists. The faction which had opposed Mrs Gandhi was virtually elimi- nated. In Srikakulam, the centre of the Naxalite revolt, a candidate for Mrs Gandhi's Congress was elected with a large majority in a high turnout. Following her electoral victory, Mrs Gandhi was able to score an even more impressive military victory over Pakistan, leading to the establishment of Bangladesh and the dismemberment of India's traditional antagonist. This was all achieved while defying the hostility of India's major creditor country, the United States, and by adroitly using the support of the Soviet Union. With such famous victories behind her, Mrs Gandhi was able to inflict another electoral defeat on her opponents and, notably, to oust the Communist Party of India (Marxist) [CPI(M)] from its dominant position in West Bengal. Meanwhile, sectarian warfare be- tween CPI(M) militants and Communist Party of India (Marxist–Leninist) [CPI(M-L)]—Naxalite—militants was used as a cover and an excuse by the government to deploy police and private strong-arm squads to break the Left movement in Calcutta. A *mélange* of murder, torture, and arrests in the cities and in the countryside succeeded in 'pacifying' West Bengal, stamping out most of the peasant unrest, and braking the impetus of the working class movement. The Maoist leader, Charu Mazumdar, was arrested and subsequently died in prison.

With her own internal rivals destroyed and India's external foe decisively humbled, Indira Gandhi appeared to have established an impregnable position for herself. In any moderately stable social system, a string of such brilliant success would suffice to consolidate the political order for many years to come. In the case of India, such a prospect does not seem likely. The diplomatic, military, and electoral triumphs of 1971–2 certainly, reflected a temporary strengthening of Indian capitalism's economic position. But, as we shall see, the long-term pros- pects for Indian capitalism remain bleak, and the very forces which helped to give Indira Gandhi room for manoeuvre in this period will confront her government with grave problems at a later date. The electoral reversal of 1967 had followed two famines and a period of rapid inflation. Consumer prices in 1967–8 were 75 per cent above their level in 1960–1 and food prices had risen by 97 per cent. Only in 1968–9 did the price level fall for the first time in may years. On the agricultural front, food-grains output rose after famine and surpassed the previous highest level of 89 million tons (1964–5) in 1967–8 (95 million tons); this level was maintained in the following year and then rose again in 1970–1 to 107 million tons. The increased food output meant a reduction in imports of wheat from the United States. This, together with the increase in exports following the rupee devaluation of 1966, reduced India's balance of payment deficit in 1968–9 to half its level in the previous two years. This meant a breathing space from her foreign creditors for the first time since large-scale foreign aid started in 1956–7. Meanwhile increased food output naturally alleviated some of the domestic problem confronting the Indian government. An important ingredient in the good harvests of this period was the Green Revolution, whose contradictory impact on Indian society we shall discus below. It was against this background that Indira Gandhi was able to reshape the Congress party and regain its mass support.

Indira Gandhi was to be blessed not only by economic recovery but also by the blunders and failures of her political opponents. The ruling military clique in Pakistan did its best to create an invaluable ally for her in the shape of a powerful Bengali nationalist movement. Domestically, the parties which came to power in the provinces after 1967, whether they are on the Right or on the Left, proved equally incompetent either in defending the interest of the ruling class or in generating massive transformation of the economic or social structure. We shall analyse concretely the record of the CPI(M)-led United Front in West Bengal below. Suffice it to say that it failed to consolidate the proletarian upsurge or use it to launch a wider revolutionary process. It was then forced to face Indira Gandhi's repression at a time when its popular support was ebbing and its strategy in disarray.

The favourable conjunction of good harvests and confusion among her political opponents gave Indira Gandhi just the opportunity she needed to rediscover the original momentum and mythology of the Congress party. In order to find out whether the hopes and expectation rekindled in 1971–2 are likely meet the same fate as those which attended India's birth as a state will require an investigation of the underlying economic and social development since independence. In this way the fundamental dilemmas of Indian capitalism can be seen in proper historical perspective and its future destiny appraised.

ECONOMIC RELATIONS

In the post-independence period, the Indian government relied mainly on state planning to achieve economic growth. Large areas of economic life were naturally beyond the planners' control, and their plans were in any case mainly concerned with preparing blueprints rather than implementing them. In effect, what went by the name of planning are various schemes for mobilizing private and public savings to accumulate capital by taxation, monetization, and credit creation. The failure of successive plans to achieve serious growth, inflationary pressure that arose after 1964, and the bad harvests of 1965–6 led to postponement of the Fourth Five Year Plan which was to have started in 1965–6. There had been repeated talk of revamping the Fourth Plan, recording the priorities towards higher employment and eradication of poverty. The Planning Commission itself was reorganized in 1967, but the Fourth Plan never got off the ground. The result has been that the growth of per capita income has been, on the average, one per cent per annum. But there have been great fluctuations. Per capita income went *down* during the two famine years of 1965–6 and 1966–7. It was only in 1969–70 that per capita income exceeded its previous highest level of 1964–5. Table 2.1 summarizes the record since 1951.

TABLE 2.1
Per Capita Income at 1949 Prices in Dollars

1952	52.21	
1953	53.54	
1954	55.53	
1955	55.86	
1956	55.86	
1957	57.49	
1958	55.76	
1959	58.13	
1960	58.24	
1961	61.16	
1962	61.39	
1963	61.20	
1964	62.81	
1965	65.92	
1966	62.95	(39.84)
1967	62.57	(39.71)
1968	64.27	(40.79)
1969	63.75	(40.46)

Figures in brackets for 1966–9 refer to post-devaluation equivalents. The rupee was devalued in June 1966 from US $20.86 to $13.20 per Rs 100.

Per capita food availability started from the extremely low level of 13.5 ounces per day in 1951. Food-grains output grew up to 1960–1 stagnated for the next three years, and rose in 1964–5; then a famine situation developed in 1965–6 and 1966–7, when output fell below 1961 figures. It was probably back to the 1961 level by 1971. It should always be remembered, of course, that the per capita figures hide the true abyss of poverty of the Indian masses, because of the great inequalities in the distribution of income and wealth. The food-grains record can be seen from these computation (see Tables 2.2 and 2.3).

Growth of industrial production has been more rapid than growth of agricultural production, but has also been very uneven from one year to next. The industrial sector at the time of independence was extremely small. In 1950–1, mines and large-scale industrial enterprises employed only 2.7 per cent of the labour force, while small enterprises and railways employed 9 per cent. In the 20 years since then, the preponderance of agriculture has been reduced from 48 per cent of the Gross Domestic Product to 40 per cent.

TABLE 2.2
Per Capita Availability of Food-grains (ounces per day)

1952	13.53
1953	14.54
1954	16.10
1955	15.66
1956	15.17
1957	15.74
1958	14.39
1959	16.49
1960	15.78
1961	16.46
1962	16.27
1963	15.55
1964	15.82
1965	16.72
1966	14.19
1967	13.96
1968	16.10
1969	14.72

TABLE 2.3
Index to Food-grain Production (1950=100)

1950	100.0
1951	90.5
1952	91.1
1953	101.1
1954	119.1
1955	115.0
1956	115.3
1957	120.8
1958	109.2
1959	130.6
1960	127.9

(cont.)

Table 2.3 (cont.)

1961	137.1
1962	140.3
1963	133.6
1964	136.5
1965	150.2
1966	120.9
1967	123.8
1968	159.0
1969	157.5
1970	168.6
1971	182.7
1972	182.0

TABLE 2.4
Index of Industrial Production (1960=100)

1951	52.0
1952	61.1
1953	59.8
1954	59.3
1955	69.7
1956	77.0
1957	80.2
1958	82.9
1959	98.9
1960	100.0
1961	109.2
1962	119.7
1963	129.7
1964	140.9
1965	153.7
1966	152.4
1967	151.4
1968	160.9
1969	172.4
1970	180.8
1971	186.1

Planning has led to the growth of a state sector, whose role to a large extent has been to build up a cost-free infrastructure for the Indian bourgeoisie by undertaking risky and expensive investments. This sector now produces steel, machine tools, heavy electrical equipment, locomotives, and aircraft. There is also a state monopoly of railways, telecommunications, and some road transport. The state sector, which currently accounts for 40 per cent of all paid-up company capital, has thus created much of the heavy machine-making industry that India lacked at the time of independence.

The private industrial sector is highly concentrated. Twenty family groups controlled 20 per cent of total private capital stock in 1951. This had increased to 33 per cent by 1958. In 1965, the Monopolies Commission found out that 75 leading business groups owned 47 per cent of the assets of all non-government companies. These groups are the Big Bourgeoisie in India. Their investments span trade, finance, and commerce. In 1958 the two largest family groups, Tata and Birla, owned 20 per cent of total private capital stock in Indian companies. Their ownership of banks (until the recent nationalization) gave these dynasties substantial control over smaller and regional institutions set up by the government, to provide industrial capital and by the publicly owned Life Insurance Corporation, both of which regularly invest in the companies of these groups. It should be noted that, in some respects, its high degree of concentration is a symptom of the ultimate political weakness of the Indian Big Bourgeoisie, not its strength. Compared with medium and small business at the regional level, and compared with the interests of rural property, Indian big business has a narrow social base. The degree of capitalization of companies in the modern sector is low: the 20 peak groups control about 1000 companies with total share capital of Rs 3500 million. Diversification of interest means that in each industry the monopoly power of any one group is not very high, but the existence of joint ventures gives these groups collective control over the economy.

The growth of the state sector has been accompanied by the nationalization of credit and financial institutions. Starting with the government take over of the largest foreign-owned commercial bank—the Imperial Bank of India—in the early 1950s and of all commercial banking in 1970, this growth of the 'public sector' has been claimed as evidence of 'socialism' or a 'socialist pattern of society' by the ruling party. What it has really meant is the elimination of obstacle to the growth of the regional bourgeoisie, and the encouragement of an immense growth of government bureaucracy in many regulating activities such as industrial licensing, import licensing, foreign exchange control, state trading, etc. In 1969, the public sector, comprising the federal and state governments as well as their enterprises (excluding railways), employed 10 million people, compared to the organized private sector which employed about 7 million. Between 1961 and 1969, the total number of employees in the public sector grew by 50 per cent— about 3½ million people. One aspect of Indian 'socialism' is job-creation for the petty bourgeoisie.

A related and much-publicized aspect has been an attempt to control Big Business. This is less spectacular than it sounds. The government has carried out inquiries into the affairs of Big-Business houses such as the Birlas and the

Dalmia–Sahu–Jain houses. These are both among the ten largest companies. By nationalizing the banks and creating a public image of hostility to big business, the government has been able to give an impression of radicalism to the petty bourgeoisie and the poor, while at the same time making clear that these credit and licensing policies will foster the growth of all but a few of the largest business houses. This policy and the emergence of linguistic states in the 1950s (on which, see below), have meant the growth of regional entrepreneurs, who, while being large, do not carry the stigma of being Big Business (and who resented the monopoly control of bank credit exercised by the Big Bourgeoisie). In a sense, one could describe the policies of the Indian government since independence—setting up heavy industries, nationalizing credit, and policing the growth of the Big-Business houses and of international companies—as designed to remove the fetters on the growth of capitalist relations. The Big-Big business houses were an obstacle to the government as well as to the growth of smaller business. Congress 'socialism' was a compromise designed to further the interests of the politically influential rural notable as well as the bourgeoisie. The contradictions of this policy are severe and will become serious in the future. The rural property-owner wants high agricultural prices and lavish government assistance to agriculture: the urban Big Bourgeoisie wants low agricultural prices and restrictions on state expenditure. The urban petty bourgeoisie are interested in job-creation for themselves, rather than the economic growth and accumulation that concern the Big Bourgeoisie.

Many government policies are inimical to accumulation. The cost of government inefficiency, wastage, and bureaucracy are paid in terms of inflation and increased taxation which follow the government's budget deficit. It is the rural and urban poor who bear the burden of these policies but do not benefit from the jobs. The Indian state reflects the interests of the rural bourgeoisie and regional business, since the Big Business houses are not big enough to control the state. (They are not big compared to, say, the Zaibatsu in Japan before the Second World War, nor do they have the same close economic and social links with the government that the Zaibatsu enjoyed.) This makes the state adopt contradictory polices towards economic growth, aiding some sections of the bourgeoisie with credit and cheap infrastructural inputs, but hemming in other sections with controls, licenses, threats of nationalization and a wasteful bureaucracy.

If state industrial policy since the 1950s has generally strengthened the bourgeoisie, the aim of its agrarian policy has been to promote capitalist relations in agriculture. Government credit, fertilizer, and procurement programmes have always favoured the rich peasant. Their goal has been to ensure a large marketable surplus for the towns by assisting the rich peasants who are the main suppliers. This has meant a concentration not on increasing output from all farms, but only from those large farms which can generate a substantial surplus. This drive has been accompanied by a growth of sharecropping and of the enormous mass of landless labourers, due partly to landowners' desire to counter land-tenancy reform and partly to the slow growth of the urban sector, which has swelled the number of rural unemployed.

As yet, the predominant mode of production in agriculture is small peasant production. Government land reforms and the land reforms and the reform programmes of the Left concentrate on ending rent exploitation of recent farmers, but have done little to counter wage-exploitation. There is a distinct tendency now towards capitalist agriculture not only in the agriculturally advanced region of Punjab but all over India. A study of large farmers in five other states— Orissa, Andhra Pradesh, Mysore, Tamil Nadu, and Gujarat led Utsa Patnaik to conclude:

A new class of capitalist farmers is emerging: this is a phenomenon common to every region, insofar as every area has been subject to the same forces—albeit operating with varying intensity—of an expanding market and enhanced profitability of agricultural production. The rate at which capitalist development is occurring varies widely in different regions depending on many historical and current circumstances; it may be near zero in some but the reality of the process cannot be denied.[1]

Unemployment has grown steadily over the last 20 years. Open unemployment was estimated at 2.5 million at the end of First Five Year Plan in 1956. It rose to about 17 to 20 million by 1966. By official admission, successive Plans have failed to create enough jobs to absorb even the new entrants to the labour force, much less reduce the backlog of unemployed. In many rural areas, men can find work only about 200 days of the year, but very often only at peak planting and harvesting times.

Given its colonial heritage, India has always been tied into the metropolitan capitalist economies. The Indian bourgeoisie is not, however, purely a comprador class such as characterized China as well as many colonial countries. A part of the bourgeoisie is a merchant capitalist group with firm roots in the Indian caste system. These are the Marwari, Gujarati, and South Indian Chettis, who were the moneylenders and merchants before the British came. The British did create in their image a commercial capitalist group recruited from agents of government and private English trading houses, mainly in the ports of Calcutta, Bombay and Madras. The textile industry was started in the 1860s mainly for exporting yarn to China but moved to manufacturing cloth for the home market in the early 1900s. It was the cotton textile industry and other industry started during and after the First World War by native commercial capitalists which came into conflict with British capitalism during the 1920s and 1930s. This section of the bourgeoisie actively supported the nationalist movement from the late 1920s. By comparison, the jute industry, enjoying monopoly, did not come into similar conflict with British capitalism. The comprador group formed at that time the anti nationalist Liberal party, a rump of which reappeared in the Swatantra party in 1960.

A comparatively large and nationalist bourgeoisie with native industrial capitalism (which, though weak, is of at least hundred years' standing), a native bourgeoisie with a large home market which makes it relatively independent of foreign market but also attractive as a potential source of collaboration partners for foreign capital—this is the Indian bourgeoisie. The Indian government aided the native bourgeoisie immediately after independence by financing the takeover

[1] Utsa Patnaik (1971), 'Capitalist Development in Agriculture', A Note in *Economic and Political Weekly*, 25 September.

of British capital (using India's sterling balances accumulated during the Second World War to pay compensation) and shielding it against encroachment by other foreign capital. Now that the Indian bourgeoisie is less xenophobic about foreign capital and actively seeks foreign collaboration, it finds some of these government policies restrictive. In 1948, foreign investments (mainly British) were valued at Rs 2876 million, being mainly in plantations, foreign trade, and manufacturing. Even this volume of foreign capital is necessarily small in relation to total capital since the entire traditional sector has no foreign investment in it whatever. Bettelheim estimated that foreign capital and Indian capital share control of the modern sector on a 50:50 basis. In the period of 1948–61, gross investment in cash and goods was Rs 2471 million. In the same period, the new outflow of foreign exchange due to repatriation of profits was Rs 7184 million. Collaboration agreements have been on the increase recently.

In the three Five Year Plans since independence, foreign capital's share of total private investment has been successively 13 per cent, 23 per cent, and 24 per cent. There has also been a large flow on public account—up to Rs 58 billion by the end of the Third Five Year Plan and a further Rs 30 billion between April 1966 and March 1969. Total external debt, both public and private, rose from Rs 5 billion in 1948 to Rs 27 billion by 1963. A large proportion of a new aid is now granted for repayment of interest charges on old debts. This aid has come mainly from the USA (20 per cent), the UK, West Germany, France, Italy, Japan, Canada (16 per cent), and USSR (8 per cent). This diversity of sources has given the government a certain ability to take advantage of rivalry between capitalist countries and also of the rivalry between the two blocs. India, however, remains very much in the nexus of international capital.

Let us now sum up. The Indian economy is by no means fully capitalist. Nearly 75 per cent of the population is engaged in agriculture, which remains predominantly pre-capitalist in character, stamped by feudal and customary relations. However, capitalist relations of exchange and exploitation have now achieved a significant penetration of the rural sector, especially in the more advanced regions. There is little division of labour on a truly national scale. Except of engineering and heavy industrial goods, most commodities are traded only locally. There is as yet no national market in food-grains. In this general context, it is clear that India is currently in the throes of slow bourgeois-democratic revolution. It has by no means seen the clear end of this process and doubtless will never do so. A socialist revolution may well overtake it before it can come to fruition, and then accomplish its tasks in an uninterrupted transition to socialism, within the framework of mass proletarian power. But it is important, nevertheless, to be aware of the historical thrust of the present Indian state, however sluggard it may be.

How far do the recent trends in agriculture offer a way out of the record of slow economic growth, mounting unemployment, and international indebtedness? As we said above, the fall in food imports from the US during the early 1970s afforded the government a breathing space in its balance of payments situations; we need to examine, therefore, the origins of this 'Green Revolution'. In fact, the Green Revolution is made up of two phases. One is an Intensive Agricultural Development programme started after 1960–1, which is concentrated in some districts and provides a package of improved seeds, fertilizer, water, pesticide, etc. A second more important phase is the introduction of high-yield-variety seeds (HYV), started in 1964–5 but interrupted by the famine years. Since 1967–8, output of food-grains has gone up from 95 million tons to 107 million tons in 1970–1. The Green Revolution has sometimes been discounted by the Indian Left as a spurious phenomenon mainly due to good rainfall, and/or denounced as helping only big farmers and aggravating the inequalities in the countryside. It is necessary to look at the record carefully.

As far as overall growth of food-grains production is concerned, critics of the Green Revolution have alleged that there is no miracle in the higher output. This, they say, is only the trend that existed before the famines and which is now resumed. From 1950–1 to 1964–5 (itself a high-yield year), the compound growth rate of food-grains output was 2.98 per cent per annum, of which 1.34 per cent was due to expansion of area and 1.64 per cent due to higher productivity. We do not have the area data for more recent years, but the compound growth rates of output between 1964–5 and 1968–9, during 1970–1 and (the forecast level of) 1971–2 were 1.3 per cent, 3.1 per cent, and 3.4 per cent respectively. These were computed for three separate years to show that the answer depends on the year one chooses as the last year. The compound growth rate of food-grains shows some increase over the years but we cannot firmly say that the growth has speeded up. If the 1971–2 figures is confirmed then the growth rate will have been raised. Comparing with the first post-famine year of 1967–8, we get for the three years compound growth rates of 1 per cent, 4 per cent, and 4.2 per cent for the same three years.

The Green Revolution as a matter of high-yield-variety seeds has been confined mainly to wheat and rice. Hybrid strains suitable to Indians conditions are being developed. The progress has been clearly spectacular in wheat, but not so much in rice. Once again there is a lack of data. The only state-wide data available for rice and wheat are for 1968–9 (which was a stagnating year) with some data for wheat for 1969–70, but none for rice. These show, first, an uneven growth-rate of rice and wheat; second, an uneven regional growth in different parts of India. These rates are listed in Table 2.5 below. We see that for wheat, the compound growth rate for yield (output per acre) goes up to 31 per cent in the case of West Bengal, and is as high for Bihar, Gujarat, Mysore, Orissa, and Punjab. The growth rate of total wheat output is given by adding together the growth rates of yield and area, and is 9.4 per cent for 1968–9 and 10.2 per cent for 1969–70. By contrast, the growth rates for rice are very low or even negative. A modest underlying rate of increase was interrupted by bad harvests such as that of 1965–6 and probably that of 1972–3. For the time being only the evidence for wheat is fairly convincing.

There is no doubt that at the present, the package deal of high-yield-variety seeds, fertilizers, water, and credit is benefiting the larger capitalist farmer. In the future, this may mean a demand for these inputs from smaller farmers which the government may find difficult to meet. Much more likely the larger successful farmers will buy out the smaller farmers or lease land from them. If the latter occurs, the tenancy legislation designed to alleviate rent exploitation will work *for*

TABLE 2.5
Compound Growth Rates of Rice and Wheat (% per annum)

	Wheat 1968–9 over 1964–5 yield	Rice 1968–9 over 1964–5 yield	Rice 1968–9 over 1964–5 area	Wheat 1968–9 over 1964–5 area	Wheat 1969–70 over 1964–5 yield	Rice 1969–70 over 1964–5 area
Andhra Pradesh	0.2	–	–1.7	–	–	–
Assam	0.5	–	3.8	–	–	–
Bihar	–0.5	17.7	0.7	13.5	11.8	11.7
Gujarat	–11.9	6.6	–1.5	3.2	7.4	–0.5
Jammu and Kashmir	12.2	18.1	1.3	3.9	17.0	4.1
Kerala	3.6	–	3.6	–	–	–
Madhya Pradesh	4.2	1.6	0.5	0.2	2.4	–0.2
Maharashtra	–2.0	2.2	0.2	–0.8	0.0	–0.8
Mysore	2.0	8.9	3.3	–0.5	4.4	0.7
Nagaland	–2.0	–	-0.6	–	–	–
Orissa	1.6	25.2	-0.2	0.0	20.4	1.3
Punjab/Haryana	1.2	18.0	1.8	5.2	16.8	5.4
Rajastan	–20.5	2.1	5.1	–0.2	1.8	1.3
Tamil Nadu	0.0	–	–0.7	–	–	2.0
Uttar Pradesh	–3.5	3.0	0.5	7.9	2.7	6.8
West Bengal	1.2	30.9	0.9	38.3	19.6	42.4
All India	0.0	5.0	0.2	4.4	5.8	4.4

the larger farmers with a vengeance. At the same time, a section of the urban bourgeoisie will begin to specialize in the provision of rural inputs.

Instead of underestimating the incidence of the Green Revolution, we should look at the inherent contradictions which will attend upon its success. The Green Revolution will spur the accumulation process in the countryside and strengthen capitalist relations. The distribution of cultivated land (owned and leased) may become even more unequal than before. But its most important effect will be to replace the pre-capitalist economic relationships, such as sharecropping, by wage-earning. The encouragement to multiple cropping that the Green Revolution gives will generate a more even flow of labour-demand on the larger farms and lead to the gradual formation of a wage-earning rural proletariat finally divested of all control over means of production such as land. The rural proletariat has been neglected in Indian politics for a long time, since the emphasis was on programmes to alleviate rent exploitation of tenant cultivators. Radical movements have promised landless labourers small bits of land. Without the aid of ancillary inputs, granting of land to the landless will only aid to the takeover of this land (by purchase or lease) by the larger farmers who can survive the competition better. A trend may develop towards organized struggle by the rural proletariat against the larger farmers in areas where the Green Revolution is successful.

Higher output of wheat has also meant a fear of falling prices. In the last two years, the federal government has been forced to reject the recommendation of the Agricultural Price Commission that the procurement price paid by the government for wheat should be lowered. The powerful agricultural interests of Punjab and Haryana, especially, have been able to prevail upon the government not to implement these recommendations. Lower prices are in the interest of the urban petty bourgeoisie and the mass of rural and urban poor who have to purchase food. A conflict of interests is clearly arising here between the rural bourgeoisie and urban petty bourgeoisie. A subsidy to the farmers in the shape of high procurement prices will be a burden on the federal budget which will be borne by the poor. If prices are allowed to fall then the farmers' support of the ruling party may be eroded.

The Green Revolution is, therefore, no panacea for Indian capitalism, though it will alter production relationships rapidly in the countryside. Even more radically than the land reform legislation, it is altering the status of landless labourers and sharecroppers. At this point, it is necessary to look at the relative numerical positions of the various classes in India.

THE SOCIAL STRUCTURE

What is the class structure in India? Bettelheim has attempted a comprehensive analysis in his book *India Independent*. His results can be combined with more recent data to give a picture of the rural and urban class system. Bettelheim classifies the population engaged in agriculture into three classes—*maliks, kisans,* and *mazdoors*. Maliks are the rural bourgeois and peasants. Kisans are in the category generally called middle peasant. A proportion of them are tenants and sharecroppers. Mazdoors are landless labourers and the poorest peasants. The worse-off kisans have much in common with the mazdoor population; together they form the vast rural underclass. The proportion of each category in the rural population in 1954 was as given in Table 2.6.

TABLE 2.6

	% population	% area	Farm size (acres)	% holdings
Maliks	17	52	11.4	35
Kisans	45	36	7.7	35
Mazdoors	38	8	2.9	20

In the cities, the bourgeoisie is defined by Bettelheim as that class which has an income of Rs 10,000 ($2000) or more. He reckons that the large maliks of the countryside and the urban bourgeoisie together comprise 1.5 per cent of the total population of India. Of these, what we have called the big bourgeoisie or national capital would be the core of 75 to 100 largest business houses, which own 50 per cent of all private company assets in India. The non-agricultural bourgeoisie is estimated to be a mere 0.5 per cent of the population, yet it receives 28 per cent of non-agricultural national income. The petty bourgeoisie includes such 'non-industrial wage-earners' as teachers, civil servants, bank and insurance employees, and office workers, as well as the self-employed. They earn more than industrial workers and constitute what is known as the 'middle class' in India. According to the 1951 census, there were 4.6 million industrial wage-earners in India. To the latter should be added 2.1 million self-employed. It is immediately apparent that the urban petty bourgeoisie is a highly vocal group in Indian politics. It tends to form the bulk of the membership of all parties and a large proportion of their leadership. The apparent radicalism of some factions of the Congress party, the Praja Socialist Party (PSP), and even CPI, derive largely from this group. It is not, however, revolutionary and traditionally has no links with the rural proletariat.

The most important points which emerge from any analysis of the Indian class structure are thus:

1. The small size of the classical proletariat, due to the low level of development of the forces of production of urban workers of all types and their families now number perhaps 40 million out of population of 550 million.

2. The preponderance in the towns of the non-industrial wage-earners and self employed—in other words, the petty bourgeoisie. This is not a politically homogeneous group; sections of it have in the past aligned themselves with industrial workers.

3. The overwhelming weight of the rural proletariat and middle peasants. They constitute 80 per cent of the agricultural population and nearly 60 per cent of the total population.

All these figures are subject to one crucial qualification. Uneven regional development in India makes national computations difficult to translate without mediation into correlations of forces.

THE PROBLEM OF REGIONALISM

British imperialism everywhere sought to introduce a market in land in India, but the tenure system differed form region to region. In Bengal, for instance, it was the *zamindari* system in which the *zamindar* owned many villages at a time. Feudal services such as the *corvée* abounded in these parts, and the ownership pattern was extremely concentrated. In other parts of India, notably much of the south, the *ryotwary* system involved a considerable number of owner-cultivators; land distribution was naturally unequal, but it was not heavily concentrated in the hands of a few landlords. These variations in land tenure led to different systems of surplus creation and absorption, and the size of the surplus also differed. In present day India, such regional disparities have greatly aggravated the inherent problem for the revolutionary Left of organizing the rural poor on a national scale. Thus, in *zamindari* regions, landless labourers and middle peasants are nearly synonymous, while in *ryotwari* regions many middle peasants have taken to capitalist farming and are unlikely to combine with landless labourers. Since class composition varies from one region to another, the possibility of alliance of different categories of the oppressed classes necessarily varies with it. Historically, Andhra and West Bengal had serious peasant revolts in the late 1940s; Kerala and Tamil Nadu also have traditions of rural unrest. By contrast, Gujarat, Maharashtra, and Mysore have no history of peasant resistance in the twentieth century. Different regions are also unevenly industrialized. West Bengal, with proximity to minerals and coal, has been heavily developed, and substantial portion of its working class was imported from Bihar, Orissa, and other states. Maharashtra and Gujarat, especially Bombay city, also possess an important industrial base and a cosmopolitan workforce. Elsewhere in India, industry is feebly developed and in large parts non-existent.

On the other side of the basic class-divide, there are critical antagonisms between regional and national capital. Growth of trade and commerce in colonial India meant the creation of jobs and educational opportunities at coastal centres like Bombay, Calcutta, and Madras. This led to the emergence of some consumer industries in these enclaves and hence to the development of a merchant capitalist class which started to invest in industry. This gave these regions a head start over other regions before independence was achieved. Today, these disparities have been accentuated and exacerbated by the later uneven development of India. For there are a large number of bourgeois entrepreneurs whose activities are confined to small regions. These businessmen rely for their labour and market on the local population. Their interests thus frequently conflict with the Big Bourgeoisie, which relies on a national market. For its part, national capital in India derives mainly from early merchant capitalist from Bombay and Calcutta who today control a major part of the industry, trade, and finance, not only in these cities but throughout the subcontinent. Naturally, the regional bourgeoisie of the different states, who arrived later on the scene, have resisted monopolistic control by the Big Bourgeoisie. In the 1950s and 1960s this produced violent struggle for the creation of 'linguistic' states, which mobilized both regional capital and the non-bourgeois opposition parties in such states are Maharashtra, Orissa, and Mysore, often under the influence of the Communists. Here the fight was allegedly waged against Gujarati or Marwari capital, but in fact the unleashing of regional chauvinism often hindered the creation of national class consciousness by the oppressed, and merely helped regional capital in its competition with national capital.

It should, however, be emphasized that despite the recent conflict at the political level, the growth of regional capital has in no way hindered the complementary expansion of national capital. Vigorous temporary clashes of interest between regional and national capital do not exclude an underlying harmony between the two. It can thus be seen that while they intervene in every aspect of political life in India, on balance regional divisions weaken the oppressed classes and the political organizations which seek to lead them much more than they do the ruling class.

Another factor in the uneven regional development was the growth of the education system. British imperialism linked India to the metropolis via trade relations and the coastal areas especially round the ports of Bombay, Calcutta, and

Madras became the intermediate link acting as an agent of the metropolis to the Indian hinterland, and of the hinterland to London. The first universities were established in coastal areas and educated professional class, mainly lower-paid government and commercial clerks, grew up in these areas. These regions also threw up an élite bourgeois group of lawyers who were involved on both sides of the independence movement. The educated petty bourgeois are politically conscious, and take the best government jobs all over India. Their class interests make them side with the national government, but they are coming into conflict with the educated petty bourgeois of the backward regions who see their own state governments as guarantors of a share in the economic surplus.

Lack of a national market in industrial products and the predominance of small peasant agriculture lead to a further tendency towards fragmentation of the class struggle into regions, with inter-regional antagonisms added to class antagonism. A revolutionary movement in a single region thus gets isolated since the objective conditions of alliance with other regions are lacking. Having inherited the administrative superstructure of a nation-state without an underlying base of national economy and national division of labour, the federal government can use this fragmentation and isolation of regional struggles to defeat them. The agrarian unrest in Telengana and the recent sporadic Naxalite activities are examples of such isolated struggles. The Naxalite movement has attracted a lot of attention since its beginning in 1969. Its localization in certain parts of India, especially West Bengal, Andhra, and Kerala, meant that the federal government was able to counter it with the Central Reserve Police and the Army in each state separately. Attempts to link up these separate movements via a 'Great March' or formation of liberated zones met with little success.

Uneven regional development has meant, therefore, uneven and often isolated development of the class struggle in different parts of India. Inter-regional differences in the intensity of class struggle, and the inter-regional rivalry between the politically articulate petty bourgeoisie of different regions have extended to regional factions of political parties: while parties have national labels, they have diverse regional existences. The ruling party has for a long time been a coalition of regional forces; when it is in power it can dispense jobs and patronage, which keeps this coalition together. For the purpose of perpetuating the coalition it has at its service the administrative superstructure and the ideology of nationalism first developed in the anti-colonial struggle, but kept on since then by an appeal to the 'Unity of India' against 'foreign enemies'. The Leftist opposition parties partake of this nationalist consciousness though they differ about the particular foreign enemy the country has to fight. Being out of power they find it hard to perpetuate the coalition of regional interests. Their best chance of coming to power is at a regional level. This makes them victims of all the contradictions of Indian politics simultaneously. The temptation is then to define the class struggle at the regional level alone, but that means recognition of impotence. The peculiar problems faced by the CPI(M) during their tenure of office in West Bengal afford a very good example of the contradictory pressures faced by a regional party. To understand them we need to look also at the history of Communist movement in India.

INDIAN COMMUNISM

There are today two major factions of India Communism: the Communist Party of India and the Communist Party of India (Marxist), generally known respectively as the CPI and the CPI(M). The original party split in 1963–4, when a large number of militants became dissatisfied with its policy of collaboration with the 'progressive bourgeoisie' represented by Nehru, and its subservience to the USSR.

Up to that date, the frequent zig-zags of the CPI could be traced mainly to ideological weakness, the class influences on its leadership, its obedience to political (mis)guidance from Moscow, and its failure to come to grips with the problem of Indian nationalism.

There were isolated workers in India sympathetic with the Comintern from 1920 onwards, and the British government swiftly exercised repression against them (Cawnpore Conspiracy case of 1926 and Meerut Conspiracy case of 1929). A Communist Party was not fully established until 1933. It was to suffer much from Comintern and/or Communist Party of Great Britain (CPGB) tutelage in ideological matters. The main stumbling-block for it was its assessment of the political character of Gandhi and the Indian National Congress. The Comintern, CPGB, and CPI vacillated between claims that Congress's fight for Indian independence embodied a progressive inter-class alliance (although its leadership was bourgeois), and denunciation of the Indian bourgeoisie and the Congress party as a wholly collaborationist and reactionary force. Throughout its early period, the CPI was a peripheral presence in Indian politics.

The Popular Front policies of the mid-1930s brought the CPI into coalition with the more radical forces inside Congress Socialist Party (CSP). Once Popular Front tactics had been decided by the Comintern, the CPI outdid even the CSP in its moderation and desire to stay within Congress. At the outbreak of the Second World War it briefly took a position to the left of Congress in denouncing the War as an inter-imperialist conflict. After Hitler's attack on the Soviet Union, however, it explained that this was now an anti fascist 'people's war' and openly collaborated with the British government, while Congress continued to fight against it for Indian independence. This policy more than any other mistake alienated the CPI from nationalist feeling, and has had the grave consequence of impelling it to take an ultra-nationalist line since then to avert a repetition of 1941. Thus, on the question of India's relationship with Pakistan and the Kashmir issue, the CPI has always been chauvinist and, as we shall see below, it was its response to the Sino-Indian border clashes that ignited the final crisis within the party.

From 1946 to 1948, the CPI leadership generally took a rightist line, in accordance with the post-war diplomacy of the USSR. It praised the Congress party as a progressive alliance of many classes and was content to radicalize it by criticism from the outside. When the Indian naval ratings mutinied in 1946, the CPI promptly played down the revolutionary implications of the event. In 1948, however, the Communist Party of Soviet Union (CPSU) abruptly shifted international course at the inspiration of Zhdanov, and the CPI was launched on a Left course of urban unrest, strikes, and direct attack on government property. This was in line with the Malayan and Philippino rebellions in Asia, and the French strike-waves in Europe. The CPI announced that India was ripe for a revolutionary seizure of power, whereas in fact it did not have any evident mass support for its new strategy.

The only successful militant action during this period was the peasant uprising in Telengana, a region within the present state of Andhra Pradesh which was then partly in Madras and partly in Hyderabad. The Telengana peasant struggle had started autonomously in 1946, while similar rural upheavals were also going on in Bengal, Kerala, and Tanjore. It lasted from 1946 to about 1950, and at one time peasants societies ran many villages in the two districts. Land was forcibly occupied, the landlords were driven off, and many were killed. The CPI nationally had not encouraged the Telengana (or any other struggles) in the 1946–8 period, since it was then pursuing a Right course. Local Communist cadres in Telengana did, however, lead the peasant struggle there. Yet even after the Left swerve of 1948, Party emphasis was officially on urban uprising, and the Maoist inclinations of the Telengana Communists were not wholly approved by the veteran Stalinist Ranadive, then in charge of the CPI nationally. It was only in late 1948 that the CPSU and the Indian specialists in the USSR decided that a rural path might be permissible in India, and Ranadive was replaced by the Telengana group. From 1948 to 1950, the Telengana peasants fought the Indian Army itself, and they had not been defeated by 1950. In that year, however, the CPI suddenly abandoned the struggle, and adopted a parliamentary strategy, supporting Nehru's foreign policy and the 'progressive' aspects of his economic policy.

Thereafter, from 1951 till 1964, the CPI followed an orthodox electoralist path. It formed a 'United Front' with other Left parties in several states in the 1952 elections, when it emerged as the second largest party in the Lok Sabha (Lower House of Parliament) in Delhi, and repeated this performance in 1957 when it also succeeded in forming the first Communist state administration in Kerala, with the marginal help of some Independents. The major success of this period, outside Kerala, was the CPI's role in the movement for linguistic states. A Telugu-speaking state of Andhra was created in 1954, after massive campaigns by a broad movement of big landlords, local bourgeois, peasants and educated petty bourgeois. The Andhra Communists were active in this campaign and they were thus able to show some strength in the first Andhra election.

After this, local units of the CPI everywhere joined in the movement for the creation of linguistic states. In most states, opposition to the Big Bourgeoisie (identified as an alien Marwari-Gujarati clique), cultural revivalism of the regional heritage and the self-interest of the local bourgeoisie and the educated white-collar groups who wanted jobs in a new regional bureaucracy all fused to form a large mass movement. In many states, the CPI tried to lead this coalition. But it did not try to radicalize it or to broaden the struggle against the Big Bourgeoisie to include the whole bourgeoisie. Its objectives were merely parliamentary gains. In Andhra, then in Maharashtra and Gujarat, success of the parliamentary front proved short-lived. As an anti-Congress strategy, these movements had very little hope of long-range success. Once in power locally, the regional bourgeoisies soon settled down to comfortable coexistence with the Congress center (the recent example of the regionalist Dravida Munnetra

Kazhagam (DMK) in Tamil Nadu is striking in this respect). CPI tactics did not seek to educate the masses or to raise the issue of class struggle in non-provincial terms.

Throughout this period, the CPI never had a clear position on the class nature of the Indian government. It vacillated between denunciations of it as a big-landlord-big-bourgeois apparatus that was reactionary *en bloc*, and protestations that there were serious divisions within the bourgeoisie between progressive and conservative currents. Sometimes only the Big Bourgeoisie was denounced as an enemy force, while the progressive bourgeoisie (the 'national' bourgeoisie for the CPI) was praised for its doughty struggle against foreign domination. At other times, the entire Congress party and the national revolution were regarded as progressive. A related problem for the CPI was its fluctuating assessment of the importance of the foreign (British or American) capital in India. In practice, the leadership of the party assumed that this was overwhelming, and therefore the Indian bourgeoisie would necessarily resist it and in so doing be a progressive force. The opposition within the party, on the other hand, saw the Big Bourgeoisie as autonomous partners and not mere pawns of foreign capital, and therefore logically viewed it as the straight forward number-one class enemy of the Indian masses (undoubtedly the correct estimate).

There was also a virtually total neglect of any rural base by the CPI. Except in Andhra and Kerala, its peasant cadre was non-existent. At the same time, its leadership was petty bourgeoisie by its own admission, and a substantial portion of its rank and file was also white-collar workers and professionals. Membership of the Communist-controlled trade-union federation, All India Trade Union Congress (AITUC) was less than a quarter the total the number of unionized workers in India. Its industrial base was thus small. Regionally, the CPI had a following only in West Bengal, Andhra, Kerala, Madras, (now Tamil Nadu) and Punjab. It also had a certain union membership in Bombay city. In other parts of the country, it was a negligible presence.

The long period of extreme Rightism from 1951 onwards hid many ideological differences within the party. In 1962, the trauma of the CPI's isolation during 1941–5 led the party leadership to slide even further to the Right during Sino-Indian Border War. Many of the opposition faction-leaders within the Party were jailed by the Indian government. In the middle of the crisis, the remaining CPI leadership published an ultra-chauvinist resolution entitled 'Unite to Defend the Motherland against China's Open Aggression', whose sentiments were identical to those of any other petty bourgeoisie nationalist party.

When the oppositional faction-leaders came out of prison in 1963 they were naturally resentful of the pro-bourgeoisie positions of the CPI and its complicity with anti-Chinese hysteria. They nevertheless took care not to be labelled a Peking faction, and have always maintained their distance from any orthodox Maoist line. In April 1964, the CPI finally and formally split. Since then a CPI (Right) and a CPI (Marxist) have disputed the heritage of Indian Communism. In 1964, the CPI(R) claimed a membership of 108,000 and the CPI(M) a membership of 119,000. The CPI(R) increased its membership to 173,000 by 1966, while Left defections reduced CPI(M) membership to 83,000 in 1967 and 76,000 in 1968.

No later figures are available for either party. CPI(M) membership is relatively more concentrated in the three states of Andhra Pradesh, West Bengal, and Kerala (70 per cent of the total) than is the CPI(R) membership (only 40 per cent). Both parties are thus modest in size and have members concentrated in a few areas only.

On the electoral front, the CPI(M) did somewhat better than the CPI(R) in 1967, gaining more seats in Lok Sabha. It also played a leading part in the formation of the United Front governments which emerged in Kerala and West Bengal.

THE UNITED FRONT EXPERIENCE IN WEST BENGAL

A government with Communist participation in West Bengal represented a wholly new phenomenon in India's politics, qualitatively far more important than earlier experience in Kerala. For West Bengal is the most industrialized state in the country. Its capital, Calcutta is the largest city in India, with a massive population of 9 million. Its proximity to the area of iron and coal mines has made it a major producer of engineering goods. It also includes large jute mills and tea planta- tions. Much of West Bengal's industry is dependent on the national market, while its tea and jute are exported into the international market. There is still large-scale British investment in West Bengal industry, and domestic owners are part of the Indian bourgeoisie. The phenomenon of the small regional entrepreneur that abounds in Orissa or Maharashtra does not exist in West Bengal. This area saw the emergence of industry comparatively early, for Calcutta was already a major trading centre by the middle of the nineteenth century. The tenure system in the rural hinterland was *zamindari*, making for idle élite class who developed a rich cultural life. Under British rule, a Western school system was soon implanted and there is today a large mass of educated middle elements in the province. Since the beginning of the century this class has had tradition of terrorist activity and belief in the efficacy of armed struggle. The peasantry is extremely poor. *Zamindari* relations have created a vast rural underclass of small peasants and landless labourers. The urban proletariat is made up of migrants from the rural areas of Bihar and Uttar Pradesh, as well as West Bengal. It is highly unionized and has long tradition of militancy.

In the 1967 election there were two United Fronts formed by the two factions of Indian Communism. The CPI along with the Bangla Congress (a splinter from the Congress party) formed one, and the CPI(M) along with the Socialist Workers party, the Socialist Unity Center, and other groupings formed another. For the first time, the Congress party failed to get an absolute majority (gaining only 127 out of 280 seats) and the possibility of the two Fronts forming a government together emerged. This they did in February 1967; Ajoy Mukherjee, leader of the Bangla Congress, became Chief Minister and Minister for Home Affairs.

The presence of the CPI(M) and the CPI(R) secured undoubted changes in the *modus operandi* of the state governments. While neither party tried in any way to implement measures of a revolutionary nature (which would have got them into conflict with their coalition parents and with the Central government), they did materially assist the struggle of the working class in the cities and those of the landless labourers in the country. The bad harvest of 1965–6 and 1966–7 had resulted in a recession in 1966–7. The engineering industries centered in West Bengal were hard hit: employment fell by 300,000 between March 1966 and June 1967. This led to a heightening of strike activity and a novel form of industrial struggle which came to be known as *gherao*. A *gherao* is the barricading by the workers of management in their factory offices, until the workers' demands are met. The UF government did not actively initiate this form of combat, but it did assist it by preventing the use of police on behalf of the employers.

Between March and August 1967, there were 1018 cases of *gheraos* affecting 583 industrial establishments. At one extreme, some of them (15 per cent) lasted between half an hour and four hours; at the other extreme a few (8 per cent) lasted longer than 24 hours. Only 12 per cent of these *gheraos* were 'terminated' by police invention and 16 per cent by search warrants; 31 per cent were ended by setting up bipartite conciliation machinery. Police power was restrained from being deployed against all strikers. The ministry of labour, which had always hitherto been an employers' mouthpiece, this time leaned towards the workers. There was a consistent demand by the Bengal bourgeoisie for Central intervention by Delhi to restore law and order.

In the countryside, the United Front connived at (or probably actively encouraged) the occupation of *benami* land by landless labourers. This is land left surplus after government imposition of legal ceilings on landholdings. In fact, these lands are usually occupied by the landlords to whom they formerly belonged. From then on their seizure by poor peasants and landless labourers was not prevented by the government, where a Congress régime would have mobilized the police to stop them. The United Front also exempted poor peasants from the grain procurement policies, took over the Calcutta tramways (refusing to raise fares), and supported the fight of Central government employees for higher pay.

The Naxalbari revolt led by the CPI(M-L), a pro-Chinese faction, caused the United Front grave problems. However. the Delhi government sent in the Central Reserve Police and the Army to quell this revolt. Both CPI(R) and CPI(M) condemned Naxalite activity as Left adventurism; the CPI(M) was in exchange denounced by the Naxalites as a neo-revisionist sell-out group. In the closing days of the first United Front government there were rumours of a flight of capital from West Bengal and many ministers started to conciliate local business. The government fell by a no-confidence motion in November 1967, but the successor Congress government could not survive for long and Presidential rule was imposed in West Bengal.

In 1969, the United Front (UF) coalition was triumphantly re-elected winning 214 out of 280 seats. This time the CPI(M) emerged as the largest single party in the state, with 80 seats though no majority. The intensity of industrial struggle was now, however, somewhat reduced since the Indian recession had come to an end in 1968. The CPI(M) obtained the Home Ministry and with it, control of the police. Henceforward, Jyoti Basu, the most popular mass leader of the party, was Deputy Chief Minister and Home Minister. The government once again supported major strikes in the jute industry and tea plantations and checked the traditional use of police against the workers. But it did not change the system of urban property taxation or undertake any other economic measures to relieve the desperate situation of the Bengali poor.

The CPI(M)'s Political-Organizational Report for 1968 provides the following theoretical justification of the coalition governments in which it had participated:

The UF governments that we have now are to be treated and understood as instruments of struggle in the hands of our people more than as Governments that actually possess adequate power that can materially and substantially give relief to the people... In class terms, our Party's participation in such Governments is one specific form of struggle to win more and more people and more and more allies for the proletariat and its allies in the struggle for the cause of people's Democracy and at a later stage for socialism.

The document goes on to warn of the 'fake character of the power invested in the state governments' and against the 'reformist delusion' that these governments can give any relief to the people. 'There is an ocean of difference between declaring them [state governments] straightaway as "instruments of struggle" and the direction to drive to utilize them as "instruments of struggle" [*sic*].' Having thus guarded against 'reformism' and 'adventurism', the CPI(M) saw its achievements in two ways.

1. Our Party's firm stand against the use of police against the popular struggles strengthened the democratic forces. The widespread working-class *gheraos* to redress some of their longstanding grievances and demands, peasants struggles in several districts against the evictions and for taking possession of government's 'surplus' and wasteland from the illegal occupation of big landlords, the relief secured by the middle-class employees of the state Government and the civil liberties ensured for their legitimate trade-union activity, etc., were examples of how different oppressed sections of the people were utilising the presence of the UF state Government for carrying on their just struggles and how our Party and others cooperating with it were assisting them in this struggle.

2. The important fact that should not be lost site of is the extremely limited and curtailed powers and resources of the state Governments as they are at present constituted under the present Indian constitution. The devastating effects of the deepening economic crisis on the working class, toiling peasantry and the middle classes today are such that they cannot be removed by the meagre ameliorative relief measures that a state Government can provide, they can only be reduced by a radical and revolutionary change in the entire social set-up. It is increasing awareness of the people and their political consciousness of this time that constitute the acid test of whether the UF state Governments have been utilized as instruments of struggle or not in peoples revolutionary struggles for a revolutionary change.

The CPI(M) claims to be a revolutionary party. It is against any immediate armed struggle, as its condemnation of Naxalite revolt clearly showed. On the other hand, the CPI(M) asserts that United Front government has been utilized by the oppressed classes in their struggle for elemental demands. There is a certain truth in this. But by declining any economic reforms or relief measures, as well as confrontations (armed or otherwise) with the Central government, the CPI(M) had chosen not to initiate any radical—let alone revolutionary—changes from its position within the United Front administrations. While state power is formally limited by the Constitution and factually by Delhi's control of the Army and Federal Budget, there are a number of transitional measures state government could take which would both provide material relief to the masses and help to unleash revolutionary struggles by them. The Congress land reforms programme mild as it is, has never been fully implemented. Ruthless enforcement by a state government of the law on *zamindari* abolition and tenants' rights, wholesale elimination of intermediates and minimum wage legislation for agricultural labour could radically alter the situation in the countryside. A swingeing tax on residential property to finance slum clearance and improvement of Calcutta's public amenities would be another effective measures.

By ostentatiously denying that state governments have any power, the CPI(M) had chosen the luxury of relying on the unaided initiative of the masses for social change. The United Front governments have never tested the limits to which a state government can go in pursuing its policy before the inevitable confrontation with the Delhi government comes. Yet defiance of Delhi in pursuit of local programmes is regularly practiced by provincial Congress governments themselves: in this respect even the first Communist government in Kerala in 1957 was more activist. The verbal Leftism of the CPI(M)—profuse denials that state administrations have any power whatever—in fact concealed a policy of practical rightism and passivity, just as the apparent radicalism of Blum's famous declaration 'We are in office, not in power' served to justify the capitulations of the Popular Front in France in the 1930s.

At bottom, the CPI(M) is pessimistic about the immediate possibility of any revolutionary upsurge in India. Thus it is against armed struggles, which it fears would be quickly isolated and defeated by the Army. It is actually aware that both the CPI(R) and the CPI(M) are significant movements only in three or four states (Andhra, West Bengal, Kerala, and, to some extent, Tamil Nadu). A serious challenge to Delhi by any one of these states would not have any easy chance of success, and the states are not a geographically contiguous area either. Large parts of India, meanwhile, are dominated by mass Rightist movements such as the Jan Sangh. In this situation, the CPI(M) basically purses an inter-class coalition against the Big Bourgeoisie, the large landlords, and imperialist capital. It is ready to use state governments as instruments in the task of building such a coalition, but it is committed to a legal path of 'changing the Constitution from within' in its quest for a 'People's Democracy' in India (not socialism, which is relegated to a separate, more remote future).

Typologically, the CPI(M) might be compared within the world communist movement to the Partei Kammunist Indonesia(PKI)in Indonesia–a Left centrist party preoccupied above all with building up its mass organizations, and masking an opportunist practice with a veil of revolutionary phrases. But popular support in one region, no matter how great, without a correct political strategy, will not ultimately benefit the CPI(M) any more than it did the PKI: West Bengal could well be its Java. Revolutionary vigilance and initiative are the only sure weapons of a Marxist party in the long run. It is to be hoped that the electoral reverse inflicted on the CPI(M) in March 1972, accompanied as it was by a vicious Congress terror campaign, will lead to a fundamental questioning of the party's inherited ideology and strategy.

CONCLUSION

After coming to power in 1969, the CPI(M) faced a new faction, the CPI(M-L), on its Left. The intensity of inter-party conflict between the CPI(M) and the Naxalites increased after the removal of the United Front government in March 1970. Political violence and murders were frequent occurrences. The federal government was able to take advantage of this conflict and, through the Central Reserve Police, mounted a systematic campaign of arrest, torture, and shooting in Calcutta and its immediate vicinities. The uncertainties of the inter-party clash among the Leftist groups meant that no united opposition to police terrorism could be mounted. The 'liberal' forces such as Congress(R) and CPI(R) could connive at police intervention in the interest of law and order, and the CPI(M) was not wholeheartedly against it as long as the police made an indiscriminate practice of arresting and shooting the Naxalites.

After starting and a rural base in West Bengal, the Naxalites faced a systematic campaign by the Central Reserve Police, local police and the Army in parts of India where they gathered support. Through 1970 and 1971 there was a shift towards urban terrorism, especially in Calcutta and in the towns of West Bengal. Naxalites appear as a decentralized phenomenon of autonomous groups of urban educated youth who are unemployed and are mostly between 16 and 25. Their shift of tactics to urban areas and concentration of their attack on the CPI(M) led to further fragmentation of their movement in to several groups. Charu Mazumdar led one of these groups, but many other leading Naxalites such as Kanu Sanyal and many of the Srikakulam leaders were soon imprisoned.

During the course of the Bangladesh struggle, many of the problems and contradictions of the Indian Left became evident. The results of the mid-term elections of March 1971 reaffirmed the national status of Congress(R) and the regional nature of every other party. The CPI(M) survived at the national level due to its strength in West Bengal, and for all practical purpose it may be regarded as a West Bengal party (whereas CPI(R), for example, is mainly a Kerala party). The emergence of the Bangladesh movement almost immediately after the elections caught everyone unawares. To begin with, it combined all the parties in West Bengal (and India) around an anti-Pakistan platform. The attitude of CPI(M) and CPI(M-L) was, however, confused. The CPI(M) saw an opportunity of creating a United Red Bengal out of the Bangladesh situation and therefore accused Mrs Gandhi's government of doing nothing to aid Bangladesh refugees out of fear of such an eventuality. The CPI(M)'s analyses also predicted that the imperialist pressures would prove strong and prevent the ruling party from aiding Bangladesh guerrillas. (This was only after a first month of euphoric forecasts from all Indian parties of imminent triumph of the Bangladesh movement against the West Pakistan Army—forecasts which were quickly belied.) The CPI(M-L) was also actively involved at the outset in aiding the guerillas, hoping to start a Bengali peasant revolution. The Chinese support of Yahya Khan caused grave ideological problems, however, and some factions were caught defending Yahya Khan on the grounds that Mujib and the Awami League were bourgeois stooges and that Yahya Khan by his pro-Chinese foreign policy had taken an anti-imperialist stand. The

Chinese support of Yahya Khan may prove to have had the same impact of the fragmented Naxalite movement as the Nazi-Soviet pact had on Western European parties, or as the Soviet Union joining the allies had on the CPI in 1941. (At that time the CPI took an anti-nationalist and pro-British stand on the ground that the threat to the Soviet Union was the paramount problem. In this sense, the Naxalites have proved as dependent on the Chinese for their ideological stand as the old CPI were on the CPGB and the Comintern.)

In the event, the decision to send the Indian Army into Bangladesh and the short and successful war took everyone, especially the CPI(M), by surprise. In West Bengal, the Congress(R) could now pose as the liberator of Bangladesh and make inroads into CPI(M)'s regional support. The crucial mistake in CPI(M) analysis was regarding the degree of autonomy of the Indian ruling class from imperialist pressures. As we have shown above, while India is very much a part of the international capitalist nexus, the Indian ruling classes are not a comprador bourgeoisie. This relative autonomy will mean that, even *vis-à-vis* the Soviet Union, there is no prospect of India becoming a client state; not at any rate unless the bourgeoisie suffers some massive setback.

One such setback that is often forecast is the emergence of a United Red Bengal. During the course of the Bangladesh struggle it was hoped that a long-drawn-out guerrilla war in Bangladesh and the presence of 10 million refugees could be transformed into a revolutionary war against India and Pakistan. Is there, however, an objective basis for such an alliance? Common language and culture do form a basis for Bengali nationalism, especially among the petty bourgeoisie, as they do in any other linguistic region of India. But the economic interests of the two petty bourgeois groups are in conflict, since a separate Bangladesh will guarantee jobs for the Bangladesh petty bourgeoisie which they may lose in a United Bengal. The dependent status of East Pakistan in the Pakistan economy was, after all, only a continuation of the dependent hinterland status of East Bengal in pre-independence Bengal. West Bengal had all the manufacturing investment, better universities, a better port, while East Bengal was rural, agricultural. The dominant feudal *zamindar* class in East Bengal was Hindu, while the exploited group was Bengali Muslim peasantry. Bangladesh nationalism, while it shares Bengali culture with West Bengal, stands at present in hinterland status as far as its economic life is concerned. In a United Bengal, it could easily stay in that position. In fact, the present friendly relations between India and Bangladesh may be short-lived once the competing interest of the two countries in exporting jute and tea become clear. The manufacturing industry and the trading interests of West Bengal may easily feel tempted to push Bangladesh back into its old dependent status. It is not enough to assert that the exploited masses of Bangladesh and West Bengal will rise. An objective basis of alliance has to be defined.

The greatest setback to the Indian ruling class is likely to arise from its two main contradictions. The first is the alliance between the bourgeoisie and the petty bourgeoisie in a programme of capitalist economic growth with a state bureaucratic 'socialist' façade. In creating jobs for the middle classes and industrial profits for the bourgeoisie, an enormous wastage is incurred. The wastage due to government inefficiency, jobbery, and corruption is added to the wastage due to conspicuous consumption and unplanned and wasteful industrial growth leading to excess capacity and recessions. The inability of the ruling classes to pursue accumulation and growth has been seen in the continuously rising unemployment in the urban and rural areas. The cost of government waste and private wastage is reflected in inflation and rising commodity taxation which have a regressive bias. The bourgeoisie cannot, because of its weakness, pursue unbridled capitalist accumulation. The petty-bourgeois view of socialism and public-sector expansion means a creation of unproductive government jobs and the policing of the Big Bourgeoisie with a paraphernalia of state agencies. In this curious alliance lies the contradiction of the Indian ruling class. Its mass support is in conflict with its class interest. The deadlock results in slow and uneven growth insufficient to alleviate unemployment and poverty.

This slow and uneven growth also strengthens the other main contradictions: uneven regional development and inter-regional antagonism. Slow growth postpones the emergence of a national economy with division of labour on a national scale. In doing this, it also, however, frustrates the possibility of an alliance of the poor across regions. It keeps the class struggle fragmented regionally and diverts the energies of a regional struggle into chauvinistic channels. The example of Bangladesh will be remembered by those engaged in regional struggles, in case sometime in the future the failure of the ruling classes to alleviate working-class problems becomes so extreme that a regional movement can be organized successfully.

If the Green Revolution is successful in permanently increasing the output of food-grains, a national market in food-grains will emerge for the first time. Already surplus food-grain output at harvest time depresses the price and the government procurement programme has to step in to keep prices stable at each year. Sooner or later this situation will mean a national price for all food-grains. The Green Revolution will also lead to the creation of a rural proletariat. In the more advanced agricultural regions of Punjab, rural labour is already being imported from neighbouring states at harvest time. From the creation of a rural proletariat in a sector with a national market, the interdependence of proletarian interest in different rural areas may emerge as an objective fact rather than a slogan.*

---

* I may be allowed to add that I was supportive of the Green Revolution in the early 1970s, see my article in Blackburn (1975), *Explosion in a Subcontinent 'Contradictions of Slow Capitalist Development in India'*, Harmondsworth: Penguin.

3

The Emergency
Past and Future

David Selbourne[1] has written an angry book about India at the time of the Emergency. He is not your day-to-day journalist to fall for cliches of dark days of emergency annihilated by the true dawn of Janata democracy. He knows that the Emergency dates back to the days of the India–China war. As far back as 1961, the Congress party tried to stifle criticism of Nehru by saying that 'those who criticise are traitors' (p.155, footnote). As a witness told him 'what is happening now is, in the question of repression, what from 1949 to 1951, we suffered from Nehru also. For us it is not new' (p. 183). He traces the roots of recent episodes into an on-going pattern of paternalism, hypocrisy, and violence. The politics of Indian illusion—'the familiar alternations of professed innocence and brutal practice' (p. 79), 'the irruption of the misery of the people and its expression in rebellion and struggle' countered by 'both paternalist concern for their welfare, and violence' (p. 83), the professions of socialism, our socialism. Indian socialism in the midst of ban on strikes and cancellation of bonus, the disgraceful record of foreign (especially British) leaders of Social Democracy in praising Mrs Gandhi, the connivance of the Soviet Union and the silent complicity of the USA—are illustrated by him with copious notes, rich with references and quotations. In terms of documentation of the period in the words of the perpetrators of the daily atrocities, the book should be read and preserved. Of its 561 pages, 370 pages comprise the text, selected documents and statistical tables take up 66 pages, and footnotes run to 80 pages.

It makes for a crowded text. Indeed, David Selbourne's desire to support every phrase of his writing by sources, and his almost palpable anger at the world he finds himself in, very often make it hard to find the analytical core of his argument. He also alternates between scenes from daily life—'ankho dekha haal'—which parodies bitterly the vignettes of Beautiful India one finds in tourist brochures and in the foreign press—and straight political reporting. This shifting of perspectives he defends early in the text. 'Different modes of perception can be

[1] David Selbourne, *An Eye to India: The Unmasking of a Tyranny*, UK: Penguin, Orient Longman Ltd., 1977.

brought to bear upon any of the immanent social consequences. One is arrived at by taking the already disclosed path of immediate observation; another, say, by the route of the official blandness of state government surveys. They reach the same destination, that of inescapable conclusion, and (if in a different dialect) speak a common language' (p. 44). I found the eyewitness bits distracting, the constant shifting back and forth puzzling (this is very much a matter of personal taste). It is as if one was trying to listen to an argument being carried on in a noisy train—the bits one can hear are interesting but constantly interrupted by irrelevant but functional noise.

This is, however, a minor criticism. I almost hesitate even to detract this much from the merits of this superb book because the Indian elite has mechanisms of insulation against adverse criticism. Xenophobia is one and a pretension of being able to fault content on account of style is another. The important kernel of David Selbourne's book deserves serious analytical treatment and this is what I shall do in the following pages.

One can begin by asking some basic questions about recent events in India.

1. What caused the Mrs Gandhi government to declare 'Emergency'? Was this just a continuation of the old emergency since 1962 or was it qualitatively a new event?
2. What caused the government to call the elections and risk, albeit by its own miscalculation only slightly, the popular rejection of the government? What forces led to the rejection of the government?
3. What were the collaborationist forces and what where elements that engaged in struggle?
4. What do we learn about the nature of the Indian State from the recent experience?

The social and economic context of post-independence India has to be borne in mind in answering all these questions. Without regressing into the remote past, the following can be stated:

1. A low (at most 1 per cent per annum) and widely fluctuating growth rate of per capita income; an overall economic performance over the last 30 years so miserable that unemployment is continuously increasing the proportion of officially 'poor', already high initially (say 50 per cent) has if not increased, at least not gone down: the achievement of an industrial base large in absolute terms though with considerable wastage—because of, rather than despite—planning, in terms of excess capacity, wrong product mix, income and price distortions, regional imbalances; the growth of a public sector as wasteful as the private one, emergence of the State as the largest employer and of a vast bureaucracy, the top of a which can extort considerable privileges; fluctuating harvests, alternations of famine and shortage of food storage capacity, rural underemployment except when famine relief provides jobs for all.

2. A complete failure on the part of the polity (government, opposition, intelligentsia, Left and Right) to make a dent in the social structure. The task of smashing the Indian (mainly Hindu) traditional society, undertaken by the Benthamite utilitarians but abandoned after the scare of 1857, has been left to the

forces of voluntary action. Illiteracy, repressions of the caste system, the systematic exploitation of and discrimination against women, untouchables, and tribals, the religious and mystical ideological influences—all remain only marginally disturbed. Paradoxically, it was the forces of social conservatism that proved in 1977, as once before in 1857, the obstacle that tripped up the autocracy. Then, as now, deeply held religious convictions of the people were violated by the government and there was a price to pay.

THE RULING CLASS

There are two views about the nature of the ruling class. One view is that it is monolithic—the feudal and kulak elements in the countryside, the national and regional capitalists, and their intellectual hirelings form a monolith, Economic stagnation is a consequence of the unwillingness of this class to redistribute income and purchasing power to an extent which will be sufficient to ensure a home market necessary to realize economies of scale of industrialization. In addition, the ruling class is in thrall to international imperial economic forces and is unable to break out of the status of hinterland. Various shades of differences can be drawn into this picture. The search for a progressive element in the Congress party or in the Indian bourgeoisie, the latching on to even the rhetoric of industrial self-sufficiency and political non-alignment as against a total rejection of the parliamentary road and the adoption of the strategy of armed struggle (albeit in the rhetorical sense) partake of the same basic analysis of the ruling class.

To some extent, David Selbourne would endorse this view. In his first chapter, he refers to 'a stagnant rural economy presided over by the landlords and a minority of rich peasants who can be termed Kulaks', to the agrarian relations being 'a compound of feudal structures of and tenure, large land holdings, precarious tenancy, cruel and extortionate rents, sharecropping, and an army of indebted revolution' (p. 5), 'the client state of the richer bourgeoisie and landlords, which is itself in turn deeply mortgaged. That is, the state itself is encumbered by international indebtedness while struggling to assert its national autonomy, as might a fly in a web; ...' (p. 6).

But David Selbourne is aware that the monolithic view has its shortcomings—the basic one being that there is mounting evidence against it. The Indian ruling 'class' is not so much Janus-faced but like Ravana has at least ten heads all looking in different directions and speaking with different tongues. The class interests of the different factions often clash and the result is continuous compromise on all fronts. Thus Selbourne says, 'India's is a political economy in which the poor are (not unusually) held in a vice-like grip; held not only by the exigencies of poverty and structural destitution, but by functional political necessity. That is, one section of the ruling classes must resist the agrarian revolution which is needed by another for the development of capitalism; has no choice but to hold down the rural poor in preservation of their own political and economic interests. The others seek to build, and partially succeed in building, an indigenous capitalism, while itself held in near thraldom (circumscribed by shortages of resources, insufficient investment and its inherited position within the international division of labour) to the World economy, with its disorderly succession of slumps and recoveries, inflation and recession, and its control of both capital and market' (p. 11).

The picture is thus not so much of a monolith but of a coalition of ruling interests with kaleidoscopic shifts in strength and alignment. There are contradictions between interests of agriculture and industry, within agriculture between feudal and capitalist sections, between national and regional industrial entrepreneurs. Also in the ruling coalition, as a managing agent rather than a partner, is the political element—the professional party politicians and ideologues, with the political muscle of rank and file crowds behind them. No individual group in the coalition is powerful enough to dominate over the rest, much as it may wish to do so. Each needs the others but they all need the managing agency of the politicos who legitimize the economic system by and through the political system.

This leads to ideological confusion and to a confusion of the means to be used to attain disparate ends. Simultaneously the rulers want socialism but would like industrial unions to be curbed, socialist ideologues fall over each other diligently searching for the progressive national capitalist, the limits of radical agrarian vision are set by the notion of giving everyone who wishes a tiny morsel of land. 'The political economy of India since independence has been a battleground; not only a battleground between the classes, but between the shifting economic and political oppositions and compromises within the ruling classes. There has been vacillation and irresolution in reform (and the capacity to 'plan' only a backward and dependent economy). There has been an oscillation between paternalism, parliamentarism and savage reprisal against the people and their organizations, particularly at times of rebellion in the vortex of actual social, political and economic crisis. There has been alternation, in foreign and trading relations, between appeasement of India's paymasters and belligerent assertions of a largely illusory political and economic independence of them.'

Such a system with its house reactionaries has its illusions. One persistent illusion has been that a strong progressive government at the Centre can speed up economic planning and related political legislation for India's drive towards self sufficiency. Leave out the fact that such self-sufficiency may not guarantee any benefit for the poor. A nationalist capitalist/state capitalist economic programme has been high on the agenda of the Left. Progressives look back to the brief period in the mid-1950s when the Second Five Year Plan was launched, 'Socialist pattern of society' was adopted as a slogan, friendship with the USSR was cemented, and non-alignment triumphed at Bandung. Two years later, the exchange crisis forced the economy to begin its long reliance on foreign aid. Thrown off course by the India–China war, pressurized by creditors to alter plan priorities and finally forced to devalue the rupee, the confused rulers dismantled planning. The Congress majority declined to its lowest level in 1967. The myth then gathered power that given once again a large majority and strong progressive leadership, economic progress could resume. From the summer of 1969 to March 1971, all the various conditions were secured one by one. But then these large majorities and progressive leadership failed utterly to deliver the goods—they even failed to achieve completion of the Fourth Five Year Plan! The progressives were faced with massive industrial unrest—the small rail strike in 1973 and the massive strike of 1974. Food prices soared and famines—shortages—recurred after years of the Green Revolution.

GOVERNMENT OF INDIA ACT 1935

The myth was, however, powerful. The progressives knew they were left-wing. In Brecht's famous words, the government rejected the electorate. If only, the explanation went, all this agitation could be stopped, progressive policies could be implemented. Unsure of support from the powerful economic interests of the ruling coalition, the progressives relied on retaining army loyalty by sticking to the Constitution—its amendment procedures and its built-in provision for suspension of democracy. One must not forget that apart from the chapters on Human Rights and the Directive Principles of State Polity, the Constitution is the Government of India Act 1935; Thus under the name of sovereignty of Parliament, the Government of India Act 1935 was brought back into play.

But repression was costly. Agitation, subsiding at first, started again. What is more, the ruling party had its two-thirds majority but like the masses this mob was not trustworthy either. It had to be cleansed of reactionaries so that the next time only 100 per cent guaranteed progressives could be elected. That was clearly one push for elections. But for another, all the repression had not brought the bonanza to the economy. The ruling coalition by its nature could not cut food grain price to transfer investible surplus to the industry. Profits could not be increased sufficiently by cutting real wages either—not by enough anyway to finance accumulation and luxury consumption. What was needed was a new injection of foreign money. The Soviet Union could not bankroll the Indian bourgeoisie. Hence the orchestrated attack on the Communist Party of India (CPI) well advance of the elections. The progressives in power wanted to change horses in harness, by nothing as bloody as the massacre of the Indonesian Communist Party, but by pensioning the CPI off. The new Youth Congress would be anti-CPI, pro-USA.

The creditors, of course, have long had their own powerful myth. This is that if only Indians would stop breeding like rabbits, all would be well. Their demands were anticipated by the Youth Congress and the ruling party. This is where the whole scheme hit a snag. The old simple fables of Asiatic Mode of Production should have been a warning. The peasant would let the State do anything it liked. Dynasties may change and he will be content to pay the tax. But touch him in his private religious, superstitious parts and he reacts. He is a reactionary. Be it biting a greased cartridge as a sepoy or be it undergoing *nasbandi*, he will react. Those who had benefited from social backwardness were finally destroyed by it.

No doubt about one thing: The intelligentsia, long used to State patronage and having come to love it, did not so much knuckle under as swallow the new rhetoric. The older section of the Left collaborated disgracefully. The final agitation was not led by the established Left except perhaps in terms of an electoral alliance. People had to fend for themselves in organizing strikes, boycotts, and protests but that wouldn't have been a bad thing.

David Selbourne deals very little with the kinds of protests organized at the popular level against the Emergency. He deals only briefly in the penultimate chapter with the March 1977 election. He is not so sure that things have changed very much. They have, if only in a negative way. If the Indian ruling coalition runs into a crisis again, it may not retain the political professionals as their managing agents. Of whatever political line, politics have failed their test as dictatorship material.

Next time, the ruling coalition will not go to a politician but to a proper strong man. He only has to be quite sure not to have pretensions about social progress. Leave religion, home, and hearth alone. The constitution permits everything anyway; the precedent has been set by the civilians. When the Emergency comes next time, it will be stronger willed, more single-minded, not confused by radical claptrap. Will the Opposition be prepared then?

4

The Economic Policy of the BJP

The Bharatiya Janata Party (BJP) is the Opposition party in the Indian Parliament and as such forms the shadow government of India. Its number of seats in the Lok Sabha rose from 2 in 1984 to 86 in 1989 and finally to 119 in 1991. The BJP had also formed governments in four states—Uttar Pradesh, Madhya Pradesh, Himachal Pradesh, and Rajasthan. These governments were dismissed by the President of India in December 1992 following the destruction of the Babri Masjid in Ayodhya and on evidence of the implication of the BJP in that destruction. In the recent mid-term elections in these four states plus Delhi, the BJP has been returned to power in Rajasthan and Delhi though it lost Himachal Pradesh and Madhya Pradesh to the Congress and Uttar Pradesh to a conjunction of Bahujan Samaj Party (BSP) and the Samajwadi Party (SP), two Left parties representing the backward castes.

Despite this reversal, the BJP remains the only credible alternative as a national government. Thus its economic polices are of interest to any one interested in the prospects of the Indian economy. As is well known, the Indian economy is undergoing a process of structural reforms, with liberalization and integration into the world economy as prominent themes. Although the pace of economic reform has been uneven, it is clear that as long as the present government stays in power, economic reforms are irreversible. One of the questions at issue in examining the BJP's policy is its attitude to economic reform. As an ostensibly right-wing but nationalistic party, the BJP combines (as any political party does) contradictory elements of liberalization and dirigisme. The policy of the BJP is, however, neither a seamless cloth nor is it frozen in aspic. Factions within the party have differing views and the policy emphasis shifts over time. In this paper, I shall attempt to examine the economic policy of the BJP, discernible from its own documents.

Much of the literature on the BJP, concentrates on its political stance, especially its Hindu nationalism as reflected in its slogan of Hindutva. There has been an upsurge in the study of the BJP and of the Sangh Parivar in general since the Babri

NCSAS Discussion Paper No. 1, National Centre for South Asian Studies (NCSAS) Melbourne, Australia, January 1993.

Masjid's demolition. Important though the issues raised in this literature are—secularism, communalism, nationalism—they are not my concern. In its economic policy, the BJP allows no role for any specific Hindu or Hindutva element. Thus for example it does not espouse any notion of Hindu economics, as some of its followers, for example, champion Vedic Mathematics (Jayaraman 1993). It is possible, therefore, to discuss the economic policy of the BJP without reference to its Hindu 'fundamentalism'.

Sources

Before going into the subject of this paper, it is appropriate to say that there seems to be no available treatment of the economic policy of the BJP to my knowledge. The BJP itself has published a pamphlet, 'Humanistic Approach to economic Development (A Swadeshi Alternative)'. I have also referred to economic policy resolutions at various National Executive Meetings and the Election manifesto for 1991 'Towards Ram Rajya'. Besides these, the BJP regards as a fundamental document, a set of lectures by its past president Deen Dayal Upadhyaya entitled 'Integral Humanism' (Upadhyaya 1965). I have not yet, however, as of now consulted the 1986 Policy Statement.

The Economics of Economic Nationalism

The BJP is a right-wing nationalistic party. Until recently, it tried to maintain an image of a secular rather than a religious party. In the last three years, there has been a real tension within the party among elements which want to emphasize the Hindu face and those who want to maintain a secular nationalistic face. Be that as it may, the BJP is also often labeled a fascist party. It seems, however, that as far as economic thinking is concerned, there is no parallel between corporatism of Italian fascism or the totalitarianism of German fascism and the economics of the BJP. Thus, it would be fruitless to drag in the European literature on the economics of fascism. The economic thinking of the BJP has to be analysed within its Indian context.

In the broader context of Indian economic nationalism, there has always been the Nehruvian left-wing version and the Gandhian right-wing version. The contrast between the two runs across the role of the state, the importance of large versus small industries, the degree of centralization, the reliance on Western as against indigenous models, the modern machine oriented versus the traditional handicraft production, etc. These two strands coexisted uneasily within the Congress, and to some extent permeated official economic policy (for example, in the restriction on machine textile sector to the advantage of the handspinning/weaving sector). During the brief regime of the Janata coalition 1977–9, it was the right-wing Gandhian economic nationalism which was much on display.

There is also another strand of right-wing economic nationalism. This could be labelled the big business economic nationalism. The Swatantra party represented this strand with an acceptance of large-scale industrialization, foreign (western capitalist) model but with an emphasis on the private sector rather than government. The Bombay plan of 1946 was a preliminary version of this strand of nationalism.

It used to be thought that the Jan Sangh, the forerunner of the BJP, represented neither big business nor the Gandhians but the small shopkeepers. It was normal to characterize it as a petty bourgeois party. I am not aware of any hard documentation for this but do remember it being frequently asserted as obvious. It was also very protectionist and used to believe in the virtues of low imports.

What this brief outline of different economic tendencies points to is that a 'right-wing nationalist party' has no precise economic profile. Indeed, being right-wing may mean market oriented and internationalist, which will conflict with being nationalist. Right-wing thinkers sometimes are anti-market and conservative, wishing to uphold the traditional social order. There is, in British terms, a difference between a whig and a Tory, though both are right-wing. Socialists pride themselves in being internationalist but in economic matters are anti-market, protectionist, and nationalist. In their aversion to the entry of foreign capital, a Nehruvian socialist will ride in tandem with a BJP follower.

A separate set of dividers will be along the centralist/decentralist orientation in which again the conventional Right/Left divide does not fit neatly. Gandhians are right-wing decentralist but European fascist were right-wing centralist though recently on the European Left, a fashion has broken out for decentralist communitarian economics. Right and Left divide best along property ownership/redistribution lines with Leftist more keen to abridge private property ownership and use taxation/confiscation to redistribute income and wealth progressively. Right-wing thinkers treat private property as sacrosanct and even if they may deplore inequalities, they would rather rely on voluntary agency to effect redistribution. Gandhi with his idea of private property as trust is very much in the right-wing mould.

The BJP is in this sense an eclectic combination of right-wing and nationalist elements. By the 1991 election, it had acquired an inclusive set of right-wing beliefs and once the economic reforms process was embraced by the Congress government, it also moved decisively in to the anti-internationalist camp. Reading the 'Humanistic Approach', we sense that by 1992, the BJP had staked a claim for the Nehruvian self-reliance, anti-foreign capital ground. While criticizing the licence–permit–quota *raj*, the BJP emerges not as a free market, competitive libertarian party but a conservative nationalist dirigiste party. The best way to substantiate these claims is to follow the published sources.

The key document is the 'Humanistic Approach' pamphlet (BJP 1992c). It brings together arguments put forward earlier in the National Executive Economic Resolution as well as the 1991 Election Manifesto. It is 54 pages long and has 15 sections. It is a document that lays out a general philosophy as well as particular policy options on individual sectors—agriculture, industry, infrastructure, etc. As in all political documents written especially by opposition parties, there is more promise than is likely to be fulfilled, more criticism of the government than spelling out the hard choice that the party may have to face if and when it is in power. But this is the normal course of political rhetoric.

Significantly, the BJP starts off by claiming that its economic approach flows 'from our national heritage and from the concepts of Mahatma Gandhi's *Ram Rajya* and Pandit Deen Dayal Upadhyaya's *Integral Humanism*' (BJP 1992c, p.7 emphasis in the original). Given the attitude of the RSS towards Gandhi about other matters, it is remarkable that the BJP now claims the Gandhian mantle. The influence of Upadhyaya is much more direct. Perusing 'Integral Humanism', a pamphlet embodying four lectures delivered by Upadhyaya, one senses that his ideas are at the origin of the BJP's economics when it says it 'believes in a new social and economic order which is non exploitative, competitive and harmonious and which provides full play to the individual initiative and dignity' (BJP 1992c).

The Upadhyaya pamphlet reveals an interesting and not wholly consistent jumble of ideas. The Indian ideal is said to be holistic and the Hindu way of fourfold goals which form Purushartha Dharma is said to be define individual aspirations. There is an awareness of Marxism and of Western liberalism but a determination to reject both as too partial. There is an aversion to the market oriented system prevailing in the USA, and a conservative critique of capitalism is attempted. In this respect, there is a parallel between Gandhi's *Hind Swaraj* and Upadhyaya's *Integral Humanism*. There is a vague desire for a third way but without any hard economic reasoning to back it up. It may be helpful to quote extensively from the last and fourth chapter of the pamphlet to give a flavour of the ideas.

Both these systems, capitalist as well as communist, have failed to take account of the Integral Man, his true and complete personality and his aspirations. One considers him a mere selfish being lingering after money, having only one law, the law of fierce competition, in essence the law of the jungle; whereas the other has viewed him as a feeble lifeless cog in the whole scheme of things, regulated by rigid rules and incapable of any good unless directed. The centralization of economic power is implied in both. Both therefore result in de-humanization of man.

We want neither capitalism nor communism. We aim at the progress and happiness of 'man', the integral man. (BJP 1992c, pp. 76–7)

The sentiments expressed in the paragraph above are not untypical of many green, 'new economics', small is beautiful followers. Of course, lacking any economic theory of how people behave or how things can be produced, allocated, and distributed, much of this kind of thinking remains on the plane of the rhetoric. As happened with Gandhism, in the practical realm of economic affairs, these schools of thought live with the existing system and are thus conservative though they sound radical.

But such idealistic dressing up can be ignored. Its significance for our purposes is that there is no invocation of any old Hindu philosophy of economics as the correct one, no Vedic production system to worship. Upadhyaya's thought is in line with many conservative and (in my view) muddled thinkers who are terrified by the market as well by planning.

Once we are past the idealist packaging, the BJP's economic policy is said to be based on '(t)he spirit of the Swadesi and self reliance'. Right at the onset 'the growing resentment and resistance of many socially conscious groups and citizens of the county to operations of multinational companies in the country' is recorded sympathetically. 'Integration into a global economy', we are told, 'should not mean obliteration of national identity and predominant sway of powerful economic forces from outside'. Thus, 'India must liberalize, industrialize and modernize—but it must do so the Indian way'.

This message of Swadeshi and the Indian way looks politically attractive indeed, one doubts if the 'left forces' in India would disagree with this outline. However, what is lacking in the document is any appreciation of the economic consequences of following a severe Swadeshi path. Given India's indebtedness as well as the globalization of the world economy during the recent years, it is necessary to understand that a strategy rejecting and restricting the entry of foreign capital imposes severe burden on a domestic economy. (I have outlined some of these problems before (see Desai 1993 and chapter 15)). The BJP's economic programme doesn't face up to this set of constraints and indeed in many ways makes inconsistent demands.

Indebtedness, both domestic and foreign, is clearly a major problem for the Indian economy. The BJP makes great play of criticizing the government for getting into these debts. In a special pamphlet issued presumably in 1992, (but like some other BJP documents carrying no date) 'Towards a Debt Free India' (TDFI), the BJP blames the Nehru–Mahalanobis model. In fact, it is the 1980s' dash for rapid economic growth with foreign borrowing, a tacit departure from the Nehru–Mahalanobis model that caused the indebtedness. This is not a rhetorical point since the Nehru–Mahalanobis model is as much based on self-reliance as the BJP advocates.

The BJP is acutely alarmed about the internal debt as much as the foreign debt. It was the growth of revenue deficit during the 1980s which allowed internal debt to go up from Rs 310 billion in 1980–1 to Rs 1700 billion in 1991–2, or 52 per cent of Gross Domestic Product (GDP). Foreign debt has grown from 10 per cent of GDP in 1980–1 to nearly 40 per cent by 1991–2.

The BJP asserts 'if we decide on a steadfast approach of reduction in foreign loans over the next 5 yeas, it is not a difficult job' (BJP 1992b, p. 9). Of course, a *reduction* in foreign loans still *increases* the foreign debt. If anything can be said about the BJP's policy on debt, it is that it fails to understand that while there is some connection between internal and foreign debt, they require different policies.

Most of the BJP policies are directed towards reducing internal debt. Their general exhortations to convert deficits into surpluses, to liquidate existing debts by selling the holding of private sector equity in the hands of government financial institutions, leasing out surplus land, privatizing of public sector undertakings, etc.[1] But correct as these policies are, how do they reduce foreign debt? The 'Debt Free' pamphlet says.

Instead of writing demeaning letters to the IMF [International Monetary Fund] and the World Bank begging for loans, let the Finance Minister draw up a programme for reducing the debt in a phased manner, cutting down on budget deficits and doing away totally with revenue deficits. Even the American Congress, which represents the richest society in the world, is asking for

---

[1] However, as we shall see below, the BJP is opposed to any cut in agricultural subsidies on water and electricity which they consider to be the 'natural rights of farmers'.

constitutional ceilings on budget deficits, after being burdened with huge debts. The BJP has also called similar ceilings ... (BJP 1992b, p. 110).

It is quite obvious from the quotation that the BJP confuses ceilings on internal debt with those on foreign debt. The reference to the American Congress is rather piquant and it is clear that the deterioration of the US capital account has escaped the BJP's notice. The reduction of internal debt by cutting budget deficits is alright; indeed, the IMF, much reviled by the BJP, insists on it. But the reduction of foreign debt requires cutting of the trade deficit by increasing exports above imports and/or by acting on capital account. It is here that the inflow of foreign equity investment, whether direct or portfolio, is a crucial step. Since much of India's foreign debt was incurred in the form of bonds or shorts run commercial paper, inflow of equity investment may help relieve the payments problem. A foreign debt denoted in equities has its risk shared between the lender and the borrower. The present Indian debt concentrates all the risk on the borrower. This was, however the result of the mistaken belief that the Indian government would be better able to control the influx of foreign money if it borrowed abroad rather than let in foreign multinationals. National autonomy has costs attached to it and neither the Congress in the 1980s nor the BJP in the 1990s is wiling to be able to face up to this hard fact.

It is in the question of entry of foreign capital that the BJP is most in line with the previous Nehru–Mahalanobis type policies. Thus, on foreign capital, 'Humanistic Approach' says:

Opening up of the country to external competition should be on selective basis and strictly keeping in view interests of the domestic economy–industry, materials, local talent and labour force. However, the party realize that there is scope to welcome foreign investment and technology in areas where domestic efforts have been weak–energy conservation, pollution control, coal washery technology to name a few. The BJP's attitude is guided by the following principles:

- Foreign investment should be allowed in high-tech, export-oriented and import substitution areas.
- Consumer goods should not be open for foreign investment.
- Existing multinational companies in the area of consumer goods industries will have to dilute their control within time frame to be evolved. In such cases, preferences will be given to existing Indian employees in transfer of equities. (p. 23).[2]

This set of policy guidelines is of course precisely what was the official Congress policy. The problem with them as in many discussions of the issue of foreign capital in India is that the BJP sees India in a powerful position to be able to choose what type of foreign capital it would like. In the globalized world of the 1990s, countries are competing to attract foreign capital to their shores and this competition includes developed countries like the UK as well as developing countries–China, Vietnam, Malaysia, etc. It is a peculiar mark of insularity of

[2] I should say that in the copy of Humanistic Approach that I was given, the last paragraph has been cancelled out but is still readable. I compared this against other copies with the National Centre for South Asian Studies and the para is retained. I am not sure whether this is a recent modification in the BJP which is being signalled exclusively to me.

such nationalist thinking in India which will not accept this competition as a fact or as applicable to India. Then, of course, Indians complain that foreign capital refuses to come to India!

The solutions proposed to the external debt problem in the chapter on Balance of Payments in 'Humanistic Approach' make this confusion obvious. Thus, despite the fact that the external debt problem is liable to be exacerbated by continuing borrowing from commercial banks or Non-resident Indians (NRIs) on a no risk sharing basis (i.e. as debt rather than equity), the BJP promises that 'the scheme would be drawn to attract substantial portions of (NRI) savings' which it estimates at $100 billion. It also advocates discriminating in favour of industrial units set up by NRIs which can only discourage direct investment by companies which are not NRI yet foreign.

The trade policy of the BJP is vague and exhortatory. Export promotion boards are promised for each export commodity: 'Corporate sector would have to fulfil its export obligation especially if its production is import intensive'. It advocates import restrictions for non-essential imports and thinks this is a rational import policy. The current climate of free trade in which other developing economies are hoping to gain by GATT provisions (Uruguay Round) is clearly not to the BJP's liking. Of course, any trade restrictions actually adopted may violate GATT principles and lead to a denial of Most Favoured Nation (MFN) treatment for Indian exports. The damage caused by such denial of MFN treatment would be serious and worsen the debt problem.

There is a similar lack of consistency in the internal debt reduction policy. Thus, while in the chapter on fiscal policy in Humanistic Approach (BJP 1992c) and in 'Towards a Debt Free India' (BJP 1992b), much is said about reducing the revenue deficit, the proposals scattered throughout 'Humanistic Approach' are to raise government expenditure. A particularly dramatic example of this is also available in the Economic Resolution of September 1991 at the Thiru-vananthapuram meeting of the National Executive of the BJP. It is worth quoting extensively from this document to show how the BJP straddles both sides of the issue:

The government resorted to slogan mongering of liberalization with an ulterior motive to attract foreign loans. It played cruelly with economy of Agriculture Sector by slashing the subsidy and further trying to differentiate between functionally non-differentiable farmer community by restoring the subsidy partially. The Executive Committee not only demand full restoration of subsidy to the farmers and early finalization of agricultural policy which should include among others availability of good seeds in sufficient quantity at reasonable rate, providing water resources, electricity and like at reasonable rate, loans at concessional rates of interest are facilities akin to industries be provided. (BJP, 1991b)

The Election Manifesto for May 1991 'Towards Ram Rajya' (BJP 1991a) says in its Charter of Rights of Kisan:

Ensure abundant supply of water and energy, *the farmers have a natural right on these basic inputs.* (BJP 1991a, p. 12, emphasis in the original).

There obviously seems to be no realization that subsidies on fertilizers, water, and power add to the burden of the large deficit since they amount to selling these inputs at commercially losses making prices and the losses of the public sector agencies selling them will be part on the internal debt. The additional fact that undirected subsidies encourage excess input use as well as having adverse distributional effects is another blind spot.

In the section on taxation measures in 'Humanistic Approach', the BJP is for raising the income tax exemption limit, corporate tax exemption to employment-oriented industries in non-municipal areas, and abolition on octroi duty (with an exhortation to 'persuade state governments to make good the loss to municipalities'). There is not a single revenue raising proposal but only revenue reducing ones.

MARKETS OR INTERVENTION

The BJP combines a rhetoric of attack on the permit–licence–quota *raj* with a large list of measures which involve setting up government boards, subsidies, legal restrictions on corporations, etc. Indeed the balance in the party's thinking is interventionist of the 1960s and 1970s type rather than towards internal liberalization. In no particular order of importance, I list the interventionist policy items from the section on the industrial sector in 'Humanistic Approach':

- A separate Ministry for Handicrafts and Village Industries
- National Artisans Development Bank to be set up
- An agency to be provide marketing assistance and intelligence for small industries
- A Board for revival of sick small scale units on the lines of the Board for Industrial and Financial Reconstruction
- Certain areas of industrial production to be reserved for the small scale sector; entry of large industry and multinationals not to be permitted
- Differential rates of interest for small scale sector as well as extra tax benefits and credit facilities.

This is combined with pleas for the relaxation of licensing for the sugar industry, simplifying the procedure for setting up of new units in the large scale sector, disinvestments from public sector enterprises and sale of their equity to the public (but one presumes not foreign public). Having taken a pro-privatization stance on public sector units in its section on the industrial sector, when it comes to exit policy in the subsequent section on Full Employment and Industrial Relations the BJP is very close to the Left parties:

Factories may be closed down only with a golden handshake and that too only when sickness is terminally manifested and so decided by the appropriate authority. (BJP 1992c, p. 25; contrast this with statements on sick units on p. 22)

CONCLUSION

The BJP is an Opposition party and as such it follows the normal practice of such parties to be strong on promises and short on costing of the delivery of such promises. It promises full employment, price stability, poverty removal, the uplift and levelling up of each individual and section of society etc. It is wedded to modernization, liberalization, industrialization but in a self-reliant India way. It would like to lower internal and foreign debt, restrict the inflow of foreign (but not NRI) capital, protect agricultural subsidies, cut income taxes, etc.

There are questions to be asked. Is this a coherent strategy? Is it feasible given India's indebtedness? Will it actually solve the problem it sets out to tackle? Before answering these questions, let me add once more that party political documents are by their nature designed not to be intellectually coherent or internally consistent. They are propaganda documents. They are also not infallible guides to what the party would do if by chance it were to be elected to office. These things are true of all political parties, not just the BJP. Thus, relaying on political programmes and pamphlets is a somewhat treacherous exercise.

With those caveats, let me say that the BJP has no realistic idea of what a Swadeshi policy may imply in terms of a fiscal burden if India's internal and foreign debts were to be paid back. The party seems to understand internal debt better than the foreign debt problem. But even its policies of cutting internal debt are inconsistent with its reluctance to cut subsidies or increase taxes. It doesn't see the connection between the inflow of foreign capital and India's ability to pay back foreign debt. It does not face up to the fact that restricting the influx of foreign capital will increase the burden of debt repayment. An export surplus will have to be created over and above the amount necessary to cover imports. A budget surplus may help in this process though the connection is not one to one. It would be realistic to predict that when and if the BJP was to come to power, it would not be able to restrict the inflow of foreign capital since the budgetary consequences of this choice would be severe. (It was the unacceptability of cuts in domestic consumption designed to payback foreign debt that finally brought the Polish communist system down.) Nor would it be desirable for the flow of foreign to be so restricted.

But there is also the clear indication that the BJP has adopted the standard Government of India rhetoric on intervention and dirigisme as its own preferred model. Now, it can be argued that India's problems arise precisely because suitable though the Nehru–Mahalanobis model was for the 1950s and 1960s, it was not abandoned in the late 1970s in favour of an open economy approach. This was the choice made by the Asian tigers. Even if the Nehru–Mahalanobis model had been appropriate in the late 1970s, it is definitely outdated by the 1990s, as much due to globalization as due to an increasing sophistication of the Indian economy. The partial abandonment of the Nehru–Mahalanobis model in the 1980s led to the influx of foreign borrowing and a rise in the growth rate of GDP from 3.5 per cent to 5.5 per cent. It was, however, due to only a partial rather than a total abandonment that the debt crisis hit the Indian economy in the 1990s. Other developing economies, especially the Asian tigers—China, Indonesia, Malaysia, Thailand—have all abandoned protectionist, dirigiste economic policy. It leads neither to growth nor to economic justice. The BJP clearly has not appreciated this fact. (See Desai 1993 and chapter 15 for a critique of Indian economic policy.)

The BJP emerges from this examination as a conservative, interventionist party, high on populist rhetoric but unable to form a coherent strategy or indeed to see its undesirability. But then, in that it is probably not much different from Left parties of India.

REFERENCES

Pamphlets by the Bharatiya Janata Party:

(1991a), 'Towards Ram Rajya: Mid-Term Poll to Lok Sabha: Our Communities', May.

(1991b), 'National Executive Meeting in Thiruvananthapuram (Kerala): Report', September.

(1992a), 'National Executive Meeting in Bhopal (Madhya Pradesh): Report', August.

(1992b), 'Towards a Debt Free India'.

(1992c),'Humanistic Approach to Economic Development (A Swadeshi Alternative): Economic Policy Statement, 1992: Our Commitment to Antyodaya'.

Desai, Meghnad (1993), *Capitalism, Socialism and the Indian Economy*, Bombay: EXIM Bank. See also Chapter 15.

Gandhi, M.K. (1908), *Hind Swaraj*.

Jayaraman, T. (1993), *Science and Secularism*, Madras: Tamil Nadu Science Forum/Frontline.

Upadhyaya, Deen Dayal (1965), *Integral Humanism*, New Delhi: BJP.

5

India
End of the First Republic?

Forty-seven years ago on 26 January 1950, India became a sovereign democratic Republic. The Constituent Assembly elected on a limited franchise in 1946 had framed the Constitution of India, one of the longest documents of its kind. It was a Constitution which embodied the salient contents of the Government of India Act, 1935—in itself one of the longest pieces of legislation deliberated upon by the British Parliament—but also added innovative elements: universal adult franchise, a chapter on Fundamental Rights, and another on Directive Principles of State Policy. The Constitution gave India a federal structure albeit with a strong centralist bias. Unlike some other federations (Australia for instance), individual units of the Federation (states, Union territories) have no prior and autonomous existence. Their boundaries can be altered by legislation passed in the Union legislature with a simple majority. There have been many such changes and they continue to be proposed. There are, at any time, existent controversies surrounding the demands of some group or another that they be given a separate state. (Uttarkhand and Jharkhand come to mind as currently ongoing controversies. The mountain people in Darjeeling under the leadership of Ghaisingh are also active.)

Sometimes such demands have put intolerable strains on the Indian polity as in the case of Khalistan; other contentious cases raise the issue of whether the territories in question are a part of the Union at all—areas in the North East (Nagaland) and Kashmir are examples of this. That said, the major achievement of the last 50 years since independence has been the preservation of territorial integrity of India in a period during which many of the decolonized countries have been unable to do so. India has avoided a damaging civil war and managed to contain local dissidence, albeit at the cost of some formidable deployment of violence by the government.

Another and equally significant achievement has been the maintenance of

Caparo Lecture; Hull, 3 October 1997, Gresham Lecture; 10 November 1997. A version was published by *The Times Higher Education Supplement*, 21 November 1997.

parliamentary democracy built on universal adult franchise. Today, after the end of the Cold War, there seems to be a universal celebration of democracy, but it was not ever thus, not even in the so-called 'Free World'. In choosing to have a parliamentary democracy based on universal adult franchise, India became one of the pioneers of parliamentary democracy. France granted women franchise only in 1945. India became a democracy and has been one since about the same time as Germany and Italy, and longer than Spain, Portugal, and Greece. It is one of the older democracies in the modern world. It is also one of the toughest and most complex.

Despite these twin successes—preservation of territorial integrity and the practice of parliamentary democracy—there are considerable strains that the polity is under. I shall omit an important source of this strain and that is the inability of India to grow economically, sufficiently fast so as to relieve mass poverty. I have written extensively on this and do not wish to repeat it here beyond the broad cliché that the economic and the political are intertwined. Here, I wish to concentrate on the political.

The strains are visible in many ways:

(i)   Increased political volatility: Elections are more frequent now than before and governments change much more often. In the first 25 years of the Republic, there were five General Elections; in the next 22 years, there have been six. In the first 25 years, there were three prime ministers; in the next 21 years, nine (plus one who straddles both periods).

(ii)   Increased political fragmentation: The Indian Constitution was patterned on the Westminster model with an idealistic two-party system in mind. Though there have always been several parties, parliamentary success has been the reward of only a small number. In the last two decades, regional parties as well as parties based on caste affiliations have multiplied. One indication of this is the present United Front government, which is a coalition of 13 parties, none of which can claim to be an all-India party.

The Westminster Constitution, with a First Past the Post (FPP) electoral system does have the bane of disproportionality. It also gives the majority party nearly absolute powers. In India, one party dominance during the first four decades benefited from this disproportionality. During the first 20 years or so, this arbitrary power was not grotesquely misused. During the 1970s, Mrs Gandhi did misuse it and suffered defeat in 1977. However, upon return to power in 1980s, she resumed her practices.

Since 1989, when Congress dominance ended, there has not been a single-party majority government. Government formation in such a situation is not easily guided by the Westminster conventions. Indeed, India now has a Westminster Constitution, but Italian style politics where the head of State begins to play an active part in the formation of a majority coalition. There is much scope for learning as well as for quarrel here.

I should, however, note that increased fragmentation has brought the Indian electoral outcome closer to proportional representation although it is still conducted on a FPP basis. Measuring disproportionality by the sum of the absolute differences in percentage of votes polled and percentage of seats in the Lok Sabha, I find that the disproportionality drops from 8.44 per cent to 2.19 per cent in 1996. Though there are fluctuations along the way (a dip in 1967 and 1977, and an upsurge in 1984), the trend is clearly downward (Table 5.1).

(iii) Increased federal tensions: The Indian Constitution deliberately builds in a powerful Centre and weak states. This was also the case in the Government of India Act 1935. The leaders of independent India feared a Balkanization of the country more than anything else and the partition of India at the very outset confirmed their fears. Thus the Centre is given powers of unparalleled extent in a federal Constitution. Not only can the states be dismembered by boundary changes unilaterally and without their formal legislative consent by the Central Parliament, but the popularly elected government of state can be removed and President's Rule can be imposed by the Central government. Since the president acts strictly on the advice of the prime minister, there is a scope here for party political interference into the state by the Centre.

The use of President's Rule has also become more frequent in the second half of the life of the Republic than it was in the first half. Recently, in Uttar Pradesh, this has led to considerable tension when it was felt that the Central government was imposing President's Rule, even after fresh elections only to keep the BJP out of power. Similar sentiments have been expressed in Gujarat.

The states have reacted 'endogenously' as it were, by proliferating state

TABLE 5.1
Indian General Elections Lok Sabha Results
Discrepancy between Votes and Seats (average)

Year	Total no of seats	Discrepancy between votes and seats (average)
1953–7	489	8.439322
1957–62	494	9.100405
1962–7	494	7.092981
1967–71	520	3.02735
1971–7	518	4.850734
1977–9	542	3.75087
1980–4	529	6.183743
1984–9	515	7.601726
1989–91	510	3.140392
1991–6	506	4.552783
1996–	543	2.188195

[1] All figures are official, cited in Christophe Jaffrelot (1997), *The Hindu Nationalist Movement and Indian Politics 1925 to 1990s*, London: Hurst.

level parties which win seats in the Lok Sabha. In a virtual proportional representation system which requires majority commanding coalitions, this has given these parties—with their slivers of seats—a great deal of leverage. But having no national focus, these parties are also notoriously liable to shift loyalties and render governments unstable.

These strains have meant that political, as well as daily life in India is becoming volatile, violent, and precarious. Tensions between religious communities—Hindus and Muslims, Hindus and Sikhs, Hindus and neo-Buddhists (Dalits)—as well as within the Hindu population between upper and lower castes are on the increase and often take violent forms of communal riots between Hindus and Muslims, which were infrequent in the 1950s (60 per year on average for 1954–9) and claimed few casualties (25 per annum) but by 1987–92 had increased to 1000 riots per annum with casualties also at 1000 per annum. The social movements—Dalit, women, tribals, backward castes—have also frequently come in conflict with the police as well as members of the elite who can also be quite violent.[2] There are also complaints about the sinister nexus between politics and crime as well as of 'black' money. Politicians are portrayed in films, which is the popular medium, invariably as wicked and corrupt.

These strains are well known. The political volatility and fragmentation as well as the tensions in the federation can be seen dialectically. On the one hand, they are a decline from the stable days of the Nehru decade when parliamentary democracy functioned along the laid down Constitutional grooves. They can also be seen positively as evidence of democracy becoming more inclusive with the leadership no longer monopolized by the upper caste, wealthy, or university educated elite. There is an explosion of political democratic activity in India. People may dislike politicians but they have faith in politics.

Yet there is evidence that people are beginning to question whether these trends will render the Indian state dysfunctional. Even discounting the particular difficulties of the present fragile coalition in power, the inaction and instability at the Centre has been worrisome. Thus the former Speaker of the Lok Sabha, Mr Shivraj Patil, wrote recently:

The Union Scenario was stable and promising. But, now, it also has become very fragile and disturbing. If the state governments, district taluka and local governments do not work, the Union Government can help in the matter, if not fully, at least partially. However, if the Union Government does not work, there is no provision in the Constitution which can provide a solution to cope up with the situation correctly and effectively. As the situation at the Union level has become more dismal and likely to be still more dismal in the years to come, it is causing real concern to all those who can realise what it is not to have a working and stable national government.[3]

In his paper, Patil goes on to explore various constitutional changes that could alleviate the situation. Taking a coalition government to be the norm in the future

---

[2] See Gail Omvedt (1993), *Reinventing the Revolution: New Social Movements and the Socialist Tradition in India*, New York: M.E. Sharpe.

[3] Shivraj Patil (1997), 'Accountability, Stability and Democracy', Theme paper for the seminar on Coalition Governance in India, Rajiv Gandhi Foundation, 3 September.

rather than an exception, he explores large changes, such as adapting the French Fifth Republic Presidency as well as smaller changes such as rules for no-confidence motions which at present require a simple majority of those present. He also explores shifting to a proportional representation system. •

Of course, one answer to such a search for solutions is to say that there is no problem. As soon as a single party majority government comes back (as Mr Kesri deludes himself and Mr Vajpayee hopes), no change is necessary. But, I wish to go beyond the issue of coalition governments versus majority party ones. I want to argue that the Golden Jubilee of India's independence this year and the forthcoming Golden Jubilee of the Indian Republic in the year 2000 provide an opportunity to think more fundamentally about the issue of the governance of India.

The Constitution of India was framed between 1946 and 1949 by a Constituent Assembly elected on a restricted (though for the time the widest yet) franchise. The founding fathers (alas, all men) were laden with the Government of India Act 1935, as well as a fear of the Balkanization of India if the Constitution was not quickly drafted. They preferred a strong Centre and weak provinces. They thought that politics in India would be like British politics, a model of liberal democracy for them. Some of the leaders had revolutionary aims and others feared change. They made a Constitution which at once provided an iron frame to hold India together but is also suffocating the processes of growth, which they did not anticipate. Ambedkar did warn of the tension between the assumptions of liberal democracy (equality before the law, fundamental rights) and the society for which it was meant. Luckily for India, the contradictions have played themselves out despite growing violence within the constitutional framework of a democratic system.

But the democratic system itself has grown to be much more pluralistic, much more participative than either the Founding Fathers could have hoped or relative to comparative trends, say, in Western liberal democracies. For an electorate of about 550 million people and a turnout of 60–5 per cent, with scores of parties at the local, state, and national levels, with growing though by no means proportionate numbers of women, Dalit, and tribal candidates, India represents a unique democracy. But the Constitution has been built on a suspicion of action at the periphery or the bottom and treats it as something destabilizing, something to be nipped. This is a replay of the colonial mentality of the Government of India Act 1935. The innovative chapters on Fundamental Rights and the Directive Principles of State Policy are, on the other hand, based on an egalitarian democratic logic which has been allowed to flower superbly in a series of actual rights and liberties by the judiciary over the last 50 years.

The Constitution is also paradoxically very easy to amend, unilaterally by the Union legislature. This weapon of easy amendment has been used frequently by elected governments either to cancel a judicial decision which it did not like or to abridge some right which came in its way. The Constitution has been amended over 70 times. In the early 1970s, the Supreme Court of India had to state explicitly that there was a 'core' to the Constitution—the secular, democratic character of India—which was not amendable. But even in the matters of secularism, the ultimate crisis of the Indian secular state—the demolition of Babri

Masjid—demonstrated that political practice determines the content of secularism more than adjudication.[4] So, keeping democracy and secularism intact, can we change the Constitution? Of course, countries do not change constitutions in peaceful times; a major crisis—defeat in war, revolution, decolonization—is needed to make countries change constitutions. There is no likelihood of any such major event in India. All the same, schemes of constitutional change must be discussed. India's First Republic, already 47 years old, is becoming problematic. A solution must be found. The changes that I would like to see are as follows:

(i)   All states of the Union to be original members of the Federation and any change in their boundaries to be made subject to their legislative consent. This will of course also affect the ability of the Centre to impose President's Rule. The conditions for doing so will be more stringent. The states can also, *inter alia*, be given greater sources of revenue and be made fiscally responsible for servicing their debts.

(ii) The Constitution to be amended only by the consent of a majority of all states and the Union. [The majority can be defined in the same manner as is currently used for election of the President or in the way the US constitution does.]

(iii) Proportional representation for elections to the Lok Sabha with a relatively low threshold, say 2.5 per cent (this will allow regional parties to have legitimate representation). By this calculation in the 1996 elections, four parties (or party groups) holding 24 seats would have been barred. Recall that the disproportionality coefficient was already very low at 2.18 in 1996.

These three amendments are the only ones necessary, in my view, to overcome the major defects. A Westminster Constitution gives the party in power enormous and arbitrary powers to run the country. In India, these powers are exponentially larger because of the asymmetric situation of the Centre *vis-à-vis* the state as well as the ease of amending the Constitution. If politics is to be more democratic and more participative, this asymmetry has to be reversed. The first proposal above restricts the power of the Centre to alter the state's boundaries and to dismiss a state's elected government. There is no doubt that there is much bad government and even more bad politicians at the state level. But a system must recognize rules which are independent of personalities. Duly elected governments cannot and should not be removed. The set of reasons currently used smacks of the old powers of paramountcy under which the Viceroy could remove the ruler of a native state. The citizens of India have a vibrant political life at the state level where very often their primary identity lies. Indeed, states in India are enormous enough to constitute nations and India is, in this sense, a multinational polity. After 50 years, the fears of Balkanization can be laid to rest. State autonomy will be a positive thing. (There is already a de facto increase in the power of some states which are prospering under the New Economic Policy.)

The second major amendment will make it difficult for the Union government to amend the Constitution with ease. These powers have often been used

---

[4] I am grateful to Upendra Baxi for this insight. Professor Baxi is Professor of Law, University of Warwick. He has been Vice Chancellor of the University of Delhi and South Gujarat.

arbitrarily and populist ways have been utilized by governments, in part to encroach upon the neutral space which should be occupied by the judiciary, the civil service, and the police. Indeed, the Army is the only institution which has not been interfered with by the politicians. It is the arbitrary power of an elected majority government at the Centre to abridge constitutional rights which is at the core of the debate about secularism and communalism.[5]

The third amendment is a simple change in electoral rule. It recognizes de jure what has already happened de facto. It will make single party majority governments difficult, if not impossible. But given how single party majority governments have often behaved in the past or are likely to behave if they come to power (here again the fears of a BJP government come to mind), a coalition government would be more democratic and less arbitrary. It is less likely to encroach upon the neutral space of the judiciary, the civil service, and the police.

The proposals if adopted will mean the end of the First Republic and the de facto inauguration of the Second Republic. As Republics go, 47 years is a long age. Of the five French Republics, only one—the Third—managed a longer life. The Weimar Republic was short-lived as was the Third Reich. The Franco regime did not enjoy this length of life, nor did the Republic inaugurated in Austria after the collapse of the Hapsburgs. If India can manage a smooth transition from the First to the Second Republic, it will have registered another landmark in world history.

[5] M. Desai, *Communalism, Secularism and the Dilemma of Indian Nationhood,* chapter 23.

6

Why is India a Low Inflation Country?

INTRODUCTION

A lot of Prof. Vakil's work had to do with monetary economics, and especially the problem of inflation in the Indian economy. His writings are replete with warnings about how planning and deficit financing would lead to inflation. To warn about inflation and to monitor the fiscal and monetary policies which might lead to inflation was a lifelong passion for him. It may seem surprising, therefore, that the title of this paper characterizes India as a low inflation country. I need to define my terms more precisely. A recent book by Daniel Heyman and Axel Leijonhufvud titled *High Inflation*[1] defines three categories of inflation—moderate, high, and hyper. Moderate inflation is a situation where you can speak in terms of annual rates of inflation. High inflation is when *annual* rates get into double or triple digits. Hyper inflation is when you speak in terms of *monthly* rates of inflation. If you look at the data for Latin America, say, between 1981 and 1995 provided in the book, there are very few years for very few countries in which inflation was in single digits at an annual rate. Inflation was in either double or more often triple digits at annual rate or often monthly rates at double digits. Indeed in Brazil during the late 1980s, there was a debate as to whether a monthly inflation rate of less than 30 per cent could even be labelled as hyper inflation rather than merely high inflation!

India has not had that experience. There are very few years in which India has had double digit annual inflation rates. There are only three episodes in which there were two successive years of double digit inflation rates. As Ian Little and Vijay Joshi say in their World Bank study on India:

Nachane D. and M. J. M. Rao (eds), *Macroeconomic Challenges and Development Issues*, Bombay: Himalaya Publishing House, 1997, pp. 31–8.

This paper is based on my C.N. Vakil Memorial Lecture delivered at the University of Bombay on 13 July 1995. I am grateful to the Department of Economics and its Chairman Dr Nachane for inviting me and for providing a transcript of the Lecture. I have made some revisions to the original lecture.

[1] Daniel Heyman and Axel Leijonhufvud (1995), *High Inflation*, Oxford University Press.

Apart from occasional bubbles, India has been a relatively low inflation country during the whole period since Independence. India experienced a severe inflation and a major famine during the Second World War.

Indeed one could supplement these remarks by noting that India had two periods of severe inflation. The Wholesale Price Index (WPI) tripled between 1890 and 1920 and again between 1939 and 1946. These two periods have had a profound effect on the Indian mass psychology about inflation, as I shall argue below. But even during the Second World War, between 1940 and 1942, the inflation rate was 40 per cent—not quite hyper but still high inflation. In 1943, the year of the Bengal Famine, the inflation rate was 100 per cent.

India being a by and large low inflation country since independence is still something which needs an explanation. What is it about the Indian experience that results in a low rate, i.e. a single digit annual rate of inflation with a small number of years of a double digit rate and more rarely two consecutive years of double digit inflation? India is a democracy and that is not thought to be conducive to low inflation. Indeed, the manner in which the political economy of Indian democracy has been analyzed by authors such as Pranab Bardhan and Sukhamoy Chakravarty, Ian Little and Vijay Joshi suggests that India's democracy works by having no dominant class and a constant process of accommodation and compromise. Competing groups are bought out by subsidies. Politicians are not particularly known for economic rationality or fiscal responsibility. Indeed, if one reads the analysis of the political economy of Latin American inflation, many of the structural characteristics of Latin America are shared by India. Why then the low inflation?

One argument concerns what is called *hysteresis*. The very memory of high inflation during the early decades of this century and during the 1940s, made India's policy makers, politicians, and citizens inflation averse. This was especially because the high rate of inflation in the early decades arrived after decades of low or falling prices. Indeed, the second half of the nineteenth century combined expanding agricultural output and exports with falling prices of agriculture and manufactures. Although the evidence is not incontrovertible, the second of half of the nineteenth century was a period of economic growth for India. Goldsmith has put together many of the partial estimates for income growth during the period 1860–1900 and also collated the major estimates available for 1900–50. It is clear from these that there was positive growth during the last 40 years of the nineteenth century, from around 80 in 1860 (1913 = 100) to a real per capita income of 89 in 1900, though the peak value was 97 in 1885 and even in 1898 it was 94. Over the next 40 years we have 1946 values ranging from 109 (Sivasubromanian) to 93 (Maddison), though in 1929 it did reach 115 (Heston) or even 116 (Sivasubromanian).[2]

The point of this diversion is to say that Indians had no reason to associate inflation with positive economic growth as became fashionable in Keynesian macroeconomic thinking. Clearly there were fluctuations around the trend but the second half of the nineteenth century brought growth and low prices while the twentieth

[2] All the details from R.W. Goldsmith (1983), *The Financial Development of India 1860–1977*, Yale University Press.

century brought relative stagnation and episodes of inflation. Thus, inflation aversion was caused by the hysteresis effect of memories of high inflation episodes and the positive association of low inflation with growth.

In their comprehensive book on India's macroeconomic experience in the years since Nehru's death, Little and Joshi point out another factor. This is the character of the Civil Service. They point out that the Civil Service did not index its own salaries till the 1980s. Thus, if there was inflation, it had to bear the consequences like everyone else. In a society where the elite is cushioned against inflation, there is no real drive to control it. Thus, India's budgets were usually in surplus on the revenue account for the first three decades after independence. Goldsmith shows the public sector as a net saver for every year between 1947 and 1977.[3] The public sector did borrow on capital account but not on revenue account.

The fourth factor is the response of the public to inflation and the political pressure it exerts on the government of the day to reduce inflation. This is story of fluctuations rather than trends. Little and Joshi tell this story well. Whenever the inflation rate goes into double digits, two things happen. If it is an election year, the party in power suffers badly and in some cases may even lose power. The 1967 election was an instance when the Congress party lost a lot of seats but not power. In 1966–7, the inflation rate was 14 per cent and in 1967–8 it was 11.5 per cent. These two years envelop the election year. The Congress party lost control of many states for the first time in 1967. When Mrs Gandhi called an election in 1971, there had been two years of inflation at around 5 per cent. But soon after prices began to rise faster. Partly due to the oil crisis, the inflation rate was 20 per cent, and 25 per cent respectively in 1973–4 and 1974–5. That was the time when Jayaprakash Narayan took to the streets. In Gujarat, the Nav Nirman Morcha-led protests occurred and the final outcome of that series of protests after some time was the declaration of Emergency. In 1979 again, the inflation rate was 17 per cent. The Janata coalition lost the election since inflation was still 10 per cent in 1980. Through the 1980s inflation remained low but in 1990–1 it was in double digits and the government lost the election.

So there are three elements—long memory of a severe episode, non-association of inflation with growth, and the endogenous political reaction of citizens to high inflation in punishing the party in power. These three elements are sufficient in my view to form the outlines of a model. But let me now explore a more economic explanation. What about inflation and money supply? Figure 6.1 plots growth rates of money supply M1 and M3 against the Wholesale Price Index (WPI). I do not intend to do econometric modelling but instead make some suggestive remarks. First, that the WPI is much more volatile than either of the money supply series. Note especially the sharp reversals of high inflation episodes in the 1960s and early 1970s. While the inflation rate turns down, there is either no turning down in money growth or a very mild one. This is not, as I remarked above, a full formal answer but the control of inflation, especially its reversal from high points, seems to involve

[3] Ibid., p. 160, Table 3.14.

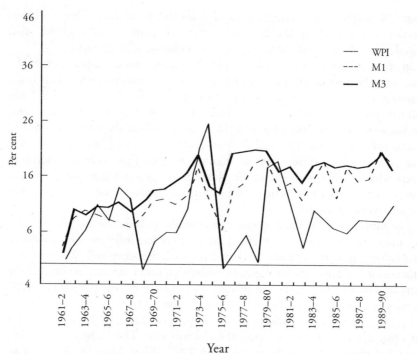

Fig. 6.1: 1961–91: Annual % Change in WPI, M1, and M3

more than monetary control. Balakrishnan in his econometric study of inflation comes to the conclusion that the monetary explanation does not add anything to the other explanations of inflation and indeed, he takes the view that money supply may be endogenous.

What about fiscal deficits, which was the main concern of Prof. Vakil? In

Table 6.1

India: Cenral and State Government Deficit 1960–1 to 1989–90
(percentage of GDP at market prices)

	1960–1 to 1964–5	1965–6 to 1969–70	1970–1 to 1974–5	1975–6 to 1979–80	1980–1 to 1984–5	1985–6 to 1989–90
Fiscal deficit	5.7	5.5	4.7	5.4	8.0	10.0
Domestic Borrowing	3.4	3.0	2.7	3.6	5.6	7.3
External borrowing	1.9	1.8	0.7	0.9	0.7	0.7
'Budgetary deficit'	0.4	0.8	1.2	0.9	1.7	2.0
Primary fiscal deficit	5.3	5.2	4.2	4.7	6.8	7.5

Source: Vijay Joshi and J.M.D. Little (1994), *India: Macroeconomics and Political Economy, 1964–1991,* Washington, D.C.: The World Bank.

Table 6.1, we have the data on government deficits under various definitions for the period 1960–1 to 1989–90. Deficits either taken as *fiscal deficits* or as *budgetary deficits* or as *primary fiscal deficits* show a similar pattern. They are relatively higher in the 1980s than in the 1960s or 1970s. But recall that through the 1980s we do not have a single period of high double digit inflation or of accelerating inflation. This is again a crude test but prima facie it would seem that the deficits or the way they were financed do not explain the broad pattern of Indian inflation. Balakrishnan's study does not contradict my conclusions.

What I think is the explanation by the structural role of foodgrain supply and prices. This is not novel by any means but it is worth following through. Demand for food grains is steady and rises with income. The supply of food grains fluctuates with varying harvests. Extreme shortfalls of output cause large rises in food grain prices and these have echo or multiplier effects which may even induce serial correlation in the WPI series. This is the explanation that Balakrishnan as well as Little and Joshi arrive at. Output fluctuations can be attributed more or less to rainfall, i.e. an exogenous variable. The trend in output is due to technical change—fertilizer inputs being a proxy. Then if output falls short due to rainfall failure, the price of food grains rises. This in turn causes budgetary deficits to rise. This then can have further effects on the WPI. The non-food economy is driven by the food economy, which is driven by rainfall.

In a world like this, control of inflation is a function of buffer stock policy or imports as means of smoothening the supply of food grains whatever the output series may do. So the failure to control inflation at certain times such as election years can be traced to buffer stock policy. Were there adequate buffer stocks available at the time is the question we need to ask for inflationary episodes. Remember that PL480 imports were cut off by President Johnson in the mid 1960s thus exacerbating the effects of two successive harvest failures. The 1973–5 period is one where we could not ignore oil prices. But once adequate supplies had been built up thanks to the Green Revolution, inflation control was easy. Of course timing was crucial. Often governments continued to be optimistic about the prospects of good harvests and moved stocks later than desirable. Once protests started, however, the politicians responded by releasing the stocks.

Thus, the basic model is a simple one of the link from rainfall via harvest fluctuations to price variability. With perfect foresight, one can write down the optimal rate of release of foodgrains. But of course there is uncertainty and there are recognition lags and implementation lags. One would need monthly prices to model this intra-year variability. But the general story is of a virtuous cycle in which people do not like inflation because they suffer from it. They punish politicians whom they hold responsible for inflation. Politicians thus know that the simple way to avoid inflation is to release stocks. The only uncertainty is then of timing. But except for rare events like two successive harvest failures (1960s) or oil shock (1970s), inflation has been contained by this endogenous political/policy response to an exogenously caused inflation.

MEASUREMENT ERRORS AND BLACK MONEY

I now want to take up some other aspects of inflation. First, one may ask whether inflation is not *understated* by the WPI in as much as it may miss out some items. Asset prices, especially housing rents and prices in urban areas, are anecdotally much more inflation prone than we see in the WPI data. Of course, house rents and prices are location specific and difficult to put in a national index but their mismeasure may explain some of the low inflation. I also wonder if there is not a deviation between recorded prices and actually paid prices. There may also be non inclusion of certain commodities which may be, a burden on consumers but may not appear at all or with a misleadingly low weight. A simple example is onions whose high prices have had some massive political fall-out at election times. Sugar was another volatile commodity from a politician's point of view as we found out in 1995. Thus, there is a broad question here about the contents of the WPI or even the Consumer Price Index (CPI).

The next issue is black money. There is no doubt that a lot of black money exists and that it is not all hoarded but circulates throughout the economy. As it circulates, some of it may leak into white money but often there is a complete circuit of black money which does not surface. Thus, commodities bought with black money will command a higher price than the same commodity bought with white money. Commodities are often available only for black money in which case their (high) prices will not affect the WPI. Thus, if we were to construct a black commodities' price index it may tell us a different story than the WPI tells us. The lack of fit between the money supply figures and inflation could also be due to the absorption of a part of the newly created money into the black economy, thereby removed from making any impact on the WPI.

Now the working people and the urban middle classes do not have much access to black money. Thus, to a large extent the black money and its inflationary impact will have a shadowy existence for them. The rich have black as well as white money and what they buy does not and need not appear in the CPI. But occasionally, there will be commodities which everyone buys and those with resources can hoard. In such cases, black money will impact indirectly on the welfare of the poor and middle class people. Otherwise, black money buys smuggled imports and luxuries and in a sense cushions the official inflation figure. This said, I think we need to model the circuit of black money properly as well as the interaction of the black and white economies and where one impinges on the other.

WILL INDIA STAY A LOW INFLATION ECONOMY?

The story so far is a virtuous, indeed a happy one. It is much happier than what Prof. Vakil thought it would be like. But can it stay that way? There are two grounds for worry. With liberalization and increasing openness, India has to be a low inflation economy to be able to compete with other low inflation economies. Inflation or fears about its recurrence may also cause an outflow of portfolio capital and put extra pressure on the exchange rate, thus adding to inflationary pressures. In this respect, the budgetary situation is much worse in the 1990s than it was when Prof. Vakil was writing in the 1950s and 1960s. The deficit also does not seem to be under control and the interest on domestic debt absorbs nearly half the total revenue. Politics is much more populist and the civil service has lost a lot of its old ethos of public service.

Liberalization, if vigorously pursued, will make the economy more competitive, faster growing, and consequently less inflation prone. On the other hand, the volatility of portfolio capital in the face of fiscal indiscipline will add to inflationary pressures. Thus, fiscal discipline will move centre stage in the 1990s as Prof. Vakil always thought it should. That is reason enough to keep on reading his writings and recalling his message.

7

Does India Need New Politics?

INTRODUCTION

This is an apt moment for giving a lecture on new politics for India. We are celebrating this month the fiftieth anniversary of the completion of the drafting of the Constitution of India, and the fiftieth anniversary of the Republic is only two months away. After a decade of unstable politics, there is now a government in power which has sufficient parliamentary strength to be able to last, bar accidents, the full five years in power. It is a coalition of the BJP and many small caste and regional parties though some carry ideological labels. On the eve of a new century and a new millennium (though both in, my view start on 1 January 2001) I want to ask whether the time has come for India to reconsider the nature of its politics.[1]

The reasons for this reconsideration are three-fold in my view. India has made an outstanding success of being a democracy. Indeed, I think no theory of democracy should be seriously entertained which does not explain the success of Indian democracy.[2] Yet India has disappointed the hopes raised when it gained independence. India has slipped in the league of industrial countries from the seventh place it had in 1947 (in volume terms) to somewhere below twenty. Half the children are malnourished and despite some progress, 35 per cent of the population is still classified as poor. India's Human Development Index (HDI) ranking is very low and so is its Gender Development Index (GDI). India is on the other hand, a nuclear power in all but name and can deploy missiles. Despite high aspirations, India's international standing in Asia and in the United Nations (UN) is not high. When they speak of Asia, people round the world exclude South Asia. In March 1947, Pandit Nehru was able to host an Asian Relations Conference since India was obviously the leader in Asia.

Indian Council for Research on International Economic Relations and The Maharaja Sayjirao University of Baroda, November 1999.

[1] This lecture is dedicated to I. G. Patel for being a constant example to us all. As this is a controversial lecture, I have made it clear in many places that these are my views rather than take an anonymous 'objective' tone.

[2] A large literature has been surveyed in Leipjhart (1994).

The reasons for this underperformance in some aspects and outstanding achievements in others are I think three-fold. First is that Indians are, confused about their national identity. The question posed by the colonizers, 'Is India a nation and if so why?', is still one which raises a lot of controversy. I shall argue that it is the confusion about our identity which has been one of the root causes of the uneven performance. The second aspect is related to the first. India has never had a clear response to modernity. The current contradictory response to globalization to the world at large and to rationality and secularization arise, in my opinion, from this lack of clarity about modernity. The connection of these two reasons with politics is that India now has arrived at a point where it can be much bolder and clearer about these two issues but to do that also requires adopting a new style politics. Luckily the results of the recent election create the opportunities for implementing a new politics.

NATIONHOOD

Ever since British domination and the rise of nationalism in response to that domination, a question has haunted Indians. Are they a nation and if so why? The British argued that India was a collection of many races (using the word race in the sense of nation or a people) and religions but not a single nation. The response of Indian nationalists over the hundred years preceding independence can be starkly put into three categories.[3]

1. A secular liberal democratic India defined by territory that comprised India. This strand started as loyal Imperial subjects fighting against 'Un-British' policies in India under Naoroji and Gokhale. With Gandhi and Nehru it became a much more assertive theory of Indian citizenship independent of religion or region. Partition dealt a blow to this theory in as much as the India it was proposed for was not the India that became independent. But Nehru quickly redefined Indian nationhood in terms of secularism, non-alignment, and economic development (socialist pattern). The Nehruvian vision held India together up to the early 1960s. The war with China, the two famines, and the two wars with Pakistan placed a great strain on it. Mrs Gandhi departed from it in practice though the rhetoric of secularist India was maintained. It is this model that has lost out in the 1990s.

2. A Hindu majority oriented view of India's nationhood. This model was revived by Tilak and linked up the dream of Hindu *patpadshahi* that the Maratha Empire cherished. In time the monarchical idea was dropped but the notion that India was a Hindu nation with other minority religions was put forward by many groups throughout the 50 years before independence. The decay of the Nehruvian model has strengthened the Hindutva model. The rise of the BJP from two seats to 180 in the course of the 1990s is a testimony to the popularity of that idea. (There had been before independence through the second half of the nineteenth century a parallel Muslim idea of a revived Delhi Sultanate but this too had matured into a secularized demand for a Pakistan by 1940.)

[3] I have dealt with this in greater detail in my article in Leifer (ed.), *Asian Nationalism*, Routledge (See Chapter 23).

Both these visions shared a common ideal—a strong centralized state. The nationhood was a single seamless one albeit with unity in diversity. All Indians were Indians first and anything else afterwards. Jinnah also shared that view for an independent undivided India—a unitary state with a single idea of nationhood.

3. The third theory of nationhood has a long and chequered history which has been almost forgotten thanks to the Congress view of Indian struggle for independence which has been dominant in the history books. This view was articulated at the First Round Table Conference in London in 1930. It was here that India was represented not by a single party [as Congress insisted] but by a wide conglomeration of regional leaders, caste and religious leaders, Maharajas of native states, and women leaders. This was the way the British saw India but it was also the Indian reality. Nationality was local—religion based or region based at the first level and all-India at the second level. The second all-India level had to be created; it could not be presumed.

After two more Round Table Conferences and a White Paper, a joint committee of both Houses of Parliament (including representatives from India) and The Government of India Bill 1935—the longest piece of legislation ever passed by Westminster, this view of India was enacted. India was to be a Federation but a loose one with a lot of provincial autonomy. Hindus, Muslims, Christians, Sikhs were recognized as separate entities. The Untouchables would have been too but for Gandhi's Yeravada fast.

In this view, India had to have a weak centre and strong states. India was a multinational community in which a single identity had to be forged in an evolutionary way, recognizing minority rights and building a consensus from disparate elements.

Nation Building on the Nehruvian Model

When independence was won, it was the Gandhi–Nehru vision of nationhood that dominated. A single seamless nationhood was presumed in which Indians were neither Hindus nor Muslims, neither North nor South Indians. There was unity in diversity but no attempt at autonomy was to be tolerated. This vision had its own contradictions especially in the asymmetric treatment of Hindus and Muslims. These contradictions came to the fore in the 1980s in the Khalistan battle, on the question of Muslim women's rights (Shah Bano case), and the Ramjanmabhoomi temple issue when Congress played both sides of the religious divide.

But even before that in the 1970s another contradiction of the Nehruvian model had arisen. In the Navanirman Andolan that Jayaprakash Narayan (JP) led and the people's movement that started before the Emergency and continued after 1977, a new politics was emerging which embodied the third nationhood model. Lokayan was a grass-roots movement of tribals and Dalits and Backward Caste groups, locally based and struggling against the Nehru–Gandhi state which had turned from being a friend of the poor to its enemy. The centralized state and its elitist development model had left these groups out. They had to self organize outside the Congress system to defend themselves. The Janata party was one concrete though unstable manifestation of this trend. The basic reason for this alienation of the masses from the state was, however, in the second of the three contradictions to which I now turn.

THE CHALLENGE OF MODERNITY

When he wrote his first book *Hind Swaraj* in 1909, Mohandas Gandhi was reacting to his recent trip to London where he had met Savarkar and Shyamji Krishnavarma. They had a nationalist programme for making India a strong independent military power. Savarkar's hero was Mazzini, the Italian freedom fighter. A modern India was to be technologically up-to-date and powerful. It was against this rather than Western industrialization that Gandhi put forward his philosophy which rejected modernity, root and branch, as far as India was concerned.[4] We know from his subsequent writings that Gandhi did modify his opposition to machinery but did insist on his rejection of a modern Western model for the independent Indian state.

It is proper to say, in my view, that the modern Indian state set up by Nehru as its major architect followed the Savarkar and not the Gandhi model. India was meant to be a strong centralized powerful military state. Nehru chose the Mahalanobis strategy because it gave the promise of an early build up of national production capacity for defence equipment. Self-sufficiency in military production was Nehru's hope as he told Marie Seton.[5] But this production had to be in the public sector. Modernity was acceptable to Nehru not in its Western capitalist form but in a modified socialist form. In many sectors, small scale production was perpetuated, thus ruining the chances of a world class textile industry to grow and compete. There was an ambivalence about modernity in the economic sphere which in my view cost India in its economic growth.[6]

THE CONSEQUENCES OF AMBIVALENCE

This ambivalence about modernity haunts India to this day, for example in its attitude towards globalization. India has been a trading nation throughout its history. It was one of the earliest nations to take to modern industrialization albeit not to the extent that the nationalist movement desired. There was, by 1947, a world class textile industry which was practically a century old. Since 1851 India had one of the major railroads in the world. But India was seen not as a putative capitalist country that could do better independently (say, as Japan did) but as a victim which

---

[4] See the excellent introduction to his new edition of *Hind Swaraj* by Anthony Pareil; Pareil (1997).

[5] Seton (1965), 'Thinking of the development of defence production as a means of expanding India's public sector, Nehru said, "You cannot develop an isolated industry without a general background of industrial development." Nehru's immediate objective was to build up heavy industry to ensure self reliance in general economic development. The remark was made in Lok Sabha in January 1957', p. 238.

[6] I have argued this in Desai (1998, 1999a). See also Chapters 14 and 18.

was deindustrialized by the Imperial power whose policies had to be reversed. Thus, foreign capital was replaced by domestic capital in banking and commerce and manufacturing in the early years after independence. Self-sufficiency in investment funding became a major objective of planning until it was abandoned in 1980 by Mrs Gandhi.

The ambivalence about modernity has given India not only an economy that failed for many years to be a 'tiger' and has thus fallen back relatively to other Asian countries. It has also fomented a mood which is simultaneously aware of India's failings but reluctant to learn from other nations' example, simultaneously a victim and eager to take on the world at the slightest hint of a slur or mere neglect on part of others. Indians crave to be taken notice of but when that happens they are quick to see some insult to their culture or history. (As trivially in the recent episode of the TV adventure serial 'Princess Xena' where reference to Lord Krishna was resented, though zillions of worse uses of the same name are made by Bollywood. What right had foreigners to do what Indians did routinely?) There is a desire for Western level riches and a pretence at renunciation when the growth forecasts fail to match up to hopes. India does not know whether it wants to be top of the league in the world or reject the world and go into a cocoon.[7]

EROSION OF PUBLIC SPACE

The centralized state created in the Nehru days became more arbitrary in the Gandhi period. The Westminster model of parliamentary democracy suits the Nehruvian vision of autonomous citizens. But it is also majoritarian in two senses. A majority can override all minorities and this was at the root of Jinnah's fears. But also a Prime Minister commanding sufficient majority in the lower house can ride roughshod over all opposition as Mrs Thatcher proved. What is more, under the first-past-the-post system the party that gets a majority of seats need not typically get a majority of votes. The discrepancy is quite wide so that 40 per cent of the popular vote gets 75 per cent plus of seats. This benefited Congress immensely. The continual Congress rule except for 1977–9 allowed the prime minister not only to amend the Constitution at the slightest pretext, but it also gave Mrs Gandhi power to suborn the judiciary, the police, and the bureaucracy. Such separation of powers as there was, was abridged by the Executive. People could not get redress for their grievances except by a clientilist relation to the Congress. Thus it was that Lokayan had to take to agitation to defend the interests of the poor people.

The arbitrariness of the Executive was not a Congress monopoly but a structural feature of one-party majority rule in the Westmintser model. In the United Kingdom there have been calls for a change in electoral methods from first-past-the-post to proportional representation. In India, the process was political rather than institutional. The ten years between Rajiv Gandhi's failure to obtain majority in 1989 to the BJP/NDA coalition's victory with about 300 seats have seen an endogenous solution to the majoritarianist fault in the Westminster system as used in

[7] See Desai (1999a). Also in Chapter 18.

India. Thus the first move was to destroy the ability of Congress to come to power on its own. This was the anti-Congress move of V.P. Singh and others in which the CPM and BJP joined. Then came the years of the anti-BJP coalition with the United Front/National Front governments of Deve Gowda and Gujral. The 1998 election did not settle the issue. It was only in 1999 that the issue had been settled.

New Politics

The way I will characterize the new dispensation in Indian politics is that no single one of the three theories of nationhood can command majority by itself to rule in comfort. A coalition of two of the three is needed. A Congress–BJP coalition which I advocated for some time would have continued a centralized monistic nation–state unmindful of minorities except those that came through as clients. A BJP/NDA coalition combines two rival theories of nationhood. One is centralist and the other confederationist/decentralist. The NDA element will guard the rights of regions and caste groups and religious minorities because that is where its support comes from. The fears about secularism (rhetorical in light of the actual, as against the pretended, record of Congress through the 1980s) can be assuaged by the tension between the two partners. Of course it is not inconceivable that a Congress coalition with regional and caste parties could have come to power had the Congress not played its cards so badly. What is more, that could yet be in the future. The point is that no single strand of nationhood commands absolute majority on its own. (I include the Left parties within Congress here as they share the same theory of nationhood.)

Many people were unhappy during the 1990s about the loss of stability, i.e. Congress hegemony. But the confusions of the 1990s have to be seen as creative. They saw the assertion of the grass roots, in their own right and not as clients of the Congress, of their legitimate demands. Sometimes these demands were made in a seemingly irrational fashion. Thus, Kanshi Ram of the Bahujan Samaj Party (BSP) has openly said that he does not like stability because 'his people'—the Dalits—lost out in the days of stability and upper caste hegemony. The BSP behaved quite selfishly when in power in Uttar Pradesh (UP). But this is one democratic way for the excluded to assert themselves. The proliferation of regional, religious, and caste parties is thus to be welcomed as a sign of an assertive democracy in India. The elitist assumptions of Congress hegemony needed to be challenged because whatever the good intentions of Nehru and even to an extent Mrs Gandhi, they could not presume to represent people's needs. People had to express it themselves through their own agents. The fashioning of a winning coalition has taken all of ten years but I believe it has done good to Indian democracy.

The tension between the two strands of the BJP/NDA coalition about modernity is not so straightforward. The Nehru assumption implicitly was that the Centre was modernizing and as you went down to the lower levels, backwardness persisted. India had to be modernized from the top. Fifty years on and with globalization, the pattern is more complex. Thus, Andhra Chief Minister, Chandra Babu Naidu, is the ideal modernizer/globalizer and many states are far ahead in the economic reform race than the Centre is. The acceptance of IT technology when much else was resented as Western import is by itself revealing. The younger generation is not hung up about modernity as much as their elders are. There is no fear of competition in the newer service industries that exists in the older manufacturing industries.

The globalizer/anti-globalizer divide is not the Left/Right divide nor the secular/Hindutva one. The CPM and Rashtriya Swayamsevak Sangh (RSS) are anti-globalizers. Parts of BJP and Congress are globalizers and the NDA is similarly divided. But through the 1990s the reforms have gone on albeit at a sluggish pace and often by stealth. Now the parliamentary arithmetic is much more permissive and signs are that the globalizers are going to push the boat out quickly. The insurance bill has already gone through Lok Sabha. Fiscal discipline is promised. Much can be achieved if the pace keeps up. The prime minister's speech to the Economic Summit on 5 December 1999 confirmed this new climate.

The support for globalization will come if the growth rate says up in the 7–8 per cent range. The promise of globalization is the promise of modernity—to make India a powerful, prosperous nation. The NDA groups gain from growth as they are the poorer people. The losers from reform are the Congress created vested interests: public sector employees and managers, large private sector industries established in the planning period who are protected by tariffs and subsidies. The newer younger entrepreneurs never had the subsidies and they know they have to compete to survive. As of now, their support is scattered across parties but they are willing to lobby whoever is in power. They know political interference is expensive. They are not willing to defend the old privileges even under the name of swadeshi or socialism.

But these two dimensions of tension—centralizers versus decentralizers and globalizers versus anti globalizers—will continue in the new century. I expect it to be healthy rather than not, because of the lack of one to one correspondence between the two. If all centralizers were globalizers and vice versa, there would be trouble. As it is, these lines are much more complex and cut across. There is every expectation that the government will stay in power for the full term and this by itself will help. This is stability but without the hegemony of a single group. This is plurality in diversity, not a forced unity.

CONCLUSION

India adopted a Western style democracy but favoured a left variant of economic policy at independence. In the 50 years since, the problems created by a majoritarian form of democracy with elite domination have been endogenously resolved. There remains a tension about the federalist/confederalist tendencies as about the victim/defiant conqueror psyches. But I expect that if India goes ahead boldly with economic reforms and as a higher growth rate follows, some of these tensions will wither away. India will fashion a pluralist multi-layered ideology of nationhood. When other federations such as the USSR and Yugoslavia have fallen apart and Indonesia is facing separatist demands from Aceh, it is remarkable that India may have found a solution to its thousand mutinies endogenously.

REFERENCES

Desai, M. (1998), 'Development Perspectives: Was there an Alternative to Mahalanobis', in Little, I.M.D. and Isher Judge Ahluwalia, *India's Economic Reforms and Development: Essays for Manmohan Singh*, Delhi: Oxford University Press, pp. 40–8. See also Chapter 14.

Desai, M. (1999a), 'What Should be India's Economic Priorities in a Globalising World', Lecture delivered at the Indian Council for Research on International on Economic Relations and The Associated Chambers of Commerce and Industry of India, New Delhi, 6 January. See also Chapter 18.

Desai, M. (1999b), 'PRB: An Appreciation of Brahmananda', Foreword in A. Vasudevan, D.M. Nachane, and A.V. Karnik (eds), *Fifty Years of Development Economics: From Planning to Liberalisation*, Bombay: Himalaya Publishing House.

Desai, M. (2000), 'Communalism, Secularism and the Dilemma of Indian Statehood', in M. Leifer (ed.), *Asian Nationalism*, London: Routledge.

Seton, Marie (1967), *Panditji: A Portrait of Jawaharlal Nehru*, London: Denis Dobson.

Pareil, A. (ed.), (1997), *Hind Swaraj*, Cambridge: Cambridge University Press.

8

Death, Democracy, and Decline

The millennium really started on 1 January 2001, whatever people may say about Y2K. The first year of the twenty-first century and of the third millennium has been quite traumatic for India. The persuasive image I have is of death—of Phoolan Devi, of Madhavrao Scindia, and earlier of Kumaramangalam and Rajesh Pilot. There is perpetual killing in Bihar's caste war and in Kashmir's version of religious wars. Then there was a killer earthquake in Bhuj and its surroundings, troubles as ever in Assam and Nagaland. There are criminal reprisals in Bollywood, and bandits on the loose in the Karnataka forests with abducted movie stars.

But the political system also suffered a stroke with Tehelka. The BJP/NDA coalition has not been the healthy, capable creature it was after the traumatic events of February. There has been a paralysis of will, a drift into decline, a sad resignation. When you think that just five years ago, there were fears that a BJP led government would be an unwelcome adventure into doing India over in the colours of Hindurva, that a secular democratic country would be plunged into fascism, one wonders now what all the fuss was about. There is a lot of sound and fury in the rhetoric of the on again, off again defence minister and the posturing of the home minister about Kashmir but little action.

And then the aftermath of September 11 has been a cruel joke for India. India is the world's most populous democracy, with a rule of law, a critical civil society, and a political elite conscious of its transgressions of human rights when it cannot avoid them. It has been hoping that one day its newly won friend, the USA, will see the truth about Pakistan and declare it a terrorist state. It has been through a Lahore bus ride, a Kargil surprise, and a failure at Agra. But it never thought that, irony of all ironies, in a 'war against terrorism' its arch enemy Pakistan would re-emerge as a darling of the global coalition, be forgiven for all past sins—economic and political—and be rewarded with a billion dollars and a seat at the top table.

The cynicism of realpolitik is such that the lack of democracy, or of fiscal discipline, or even the addiction to terrorism were no obstacles to Pakistan's

India Britannica Book of the Year, pp. viii–xvi, Hindu/Britannica Annual 2002.

glorification. Not only is virtue not its own reward but it is a positive drawback as far as India has been concerned. The Afghanistan war looks like proceeding to a rapid end as I write. Kabul has just fallen and may be by Christmas, the Talibans would be gone. But in the shape of any future Afghan government, the country that holds almost all the veto power is Pakistan.

The record is not any happier on the economic front. After 54 years of independence, India is not much better off than Pakistan. Indeed, until about 1998, the growth record of Pakistan's Gross Domestic Product (GDP) was better than India's. Pakistan that started with less than 5 per cent of industrial capacity of British India has not done any worse than India. True, India had the shiny Five Year Plans and the Mahalanobis model, many articulate and radical economists, and admiring foreign academics. But at the end of the longish run of 50 years, it is difficult to tell the difference. Pakistan's per capita income matches India's, its poverty statistics are better, and only in the Human Development Index does India rank higher than Pakistan, but just. Nuclear capability is not much help with it comes to human development.

In any case, both India and Pakistan are in the foothills of the Human Development Index. Be it in infant malnutrition, maternal mortality, female illiteracy, or access to clean water, there is not much to choose. Compared to the rest of Asia, South Asia has fallen relatively behind since 1947. Then, Nehru could convene an Asian Relations Conference and the world looked up to India/South Asia. Today Asia means South East and Eastern Asia, east of India. South Asia is rather like sub-Saharan Africa, an embarrassment to its friends. How did it happen? Where, when, and how did India lose its promise?

Few could have anticipated on that glorious midnight when India kept its 'Tryst with Destiny' that 50 plus years on, India would not be an economic giant. In 1945, India (undivided) was the seventh largest industrial country in terms of the total volume of industrial output. It was poor in per capita terms but it was well endowed with human resources compared to other ex-colonies. It had the largest pool of native industrialist and merchant entrepreneurs and a modern factory experience stretching back 90 years. It had a world-class textile industry built up by the nationalist capitalists of Ahmedabad and Bombay (now Mumbai). There was mass illiteracy but enough higher education among the elite to be able to run a national civil service as well as an army.

More than that, India had a moral and political standing unmatched in what came to be known later as the Third World. It was a model for colonial struggles in Asia, Africa, and the Caribbean. It was a founding member of the United Nations and a key player in redefining the Commonwealth for a post imperial age. It pioneered non-alignment and played a leading role in the United Nations (UN) in decolonization. India played a crucial role in the peace settlement in the Korean War and in the Indo-China war.

In another mirror, India was thought to be a prime candidate for a communist takeover. In hind-sight, ten years after the collapse of the Soviet Union this sounds fanciful. But there was a heated debate on the Left as to whether India could become communist in a single step or whether it would need to go through a two-phase transition in which the first step would be a bourgeois democratic revolution and then when the material conditions were ripe, a workers' revolution. Stalin took the former view that encouraged the struggle in Telengana in the years after independence. Only after his death did the doctrine change to a gradual transition.

In either case, India had a bourgeois democratic government. Yet the development has been so slow, so halted that one hesitates to call it a revolution. India's story in one sense is that of a failure of the Indian bourgeoisie to transform the social and economic conditions radically enough to make a difference. Forget a communist revolution, India has not even had a capitalist transformation. The colonial period, especially the four decades of the twentieth century, arguably saw a more radical change in the India economy as far as industrialization was concerned than the five decades since 1947. India's neighbours—Malaysia, Indonesia, Thailand, to say nothing about China—have surged ahead in capitalist development, China included in this (despite its communist governments), leaving India in the backwater. The failure of the Indian bourgeoisie is criminal.

The reasons for this failure are not at all complex, as I argue below. The real obstacle is an acknowledgement of that failure. When confronted with examples of South Korea or China or Malaysia, the Indian intellectual turns defensive/ aggressive. Every other country has an excuse for its success. China has an authoritarian government as did Korea in many periods of its recent history. Malaysia is a bit more difficult since it is a democracy as well as a multiracial, multireligious society. But then it is small relative to India. India is too large, too democratic, too tolerant or whatever, to succeed.

The one aspect on which India has been uniquely successful is as a democracy. The Founding Fathers were bold in gambling on universal adult franchise in a country where illiteracy was rife. But in granting the vote to everyone, there was a modernizing choice. India's successful democracy is indeed one major reason why it has contained the usual problems caused by poverty and discrimination. This is not to say that it is a problem but it has shaped and in my view distorted the solution to India's problems.

At the outset, India had to face the problems of social backwardness as well as economic underdevelopment. The economic underdevelopment was easy to measure and could be blamed on foreign rule. But the social structure was a different issue. The problems of caste and untouchability, of infanticide and widow remarriage, of *sati* and polygamy were ever present. In their early reforming zeal, the British had tried to modernize Indian society but had been frightened off by 1857. After that, reforms were left to the voluntary reform movements. But there was a constant debate in both Hindu and the Muslim communities between the modernizers and the traditionalists. The nationalist movement was ambivalent about this issue. Mahatma Gandhi, for instance, admitted the evils of untouchability but not of caste and he eschewed the radicalism of Ambedkar or Naicker. Thus Congress as the dominant ruling party remained uncertain as to the need for social reform. Nehru tried to reform Hindu family law but in this he was frustrated by Rajendra Prasad, C. Rajagopalachari, and G.B. Pant. Independent India did not tackle social backwardness at all.

As time passed, the practice of democracy forced not just the acknowledgement of caste and religious divisions but their active exploitation for electoral purposes.

Thus these forces became entrenched. Modernization of society was increasingly rejected in favour of assertive Indianness—Hindutva for Hindus and traditional Muslim social practices (Shah Bano's case is an example). These are reflected in the stories of Hindi films. The social reforming films of V. Shantaram or Bimal Roy of the 1940s and 1950s are replaced by the cosy acceptance of the *Hum Aapke Hai Kaun* genre.

Abdication of social modernization was over compensated by economic radicalism. Fire-breathing socialist radicals (safe in their upper-caste homes and marriages) wanted to reject capitalism and usher in socialism. Even the Congress managed for 40 years to espouse a 'Socialist pattern of society' with emasculation of privately owned modern industries (especially textiles), state ownership in new industries and the creation of permit–licence capitalism. What was a vigorous native entrepreneurial class was infantilized to become dependent on tariffs, quotas, and interest subsidies, ever supplicating for bigger handouts. India slipped from its high position of number seven in terms of industrial output. Its share of foreign trade fell steadily. For the planners, this was a desirable outcome. It was called self-sufficiency.

Industrialization in India was slow, costly, and lopsided. It was slow because it was limited by the domestic market, whether in consumption or investment goods, the latter being determined by the public sector. Since India failed to export it missed the enormous market that existed. It was not a question of State versus the market, or planning versus *laissez faire*. All the Asian tigers used the State as an instrument of economic growth but they made their industries export oriented. When Indians point to the protectionism of Korea or Taiwan, they forget that these countries used those devices as temporary measures to foster globally competitive industries. India only succeeded in keeping its infant industries infant.

More serious was the slow take-up of labour in the organized sector. Indian planners deliberately and proudly chose capital-intensive sectors to concentrate their resources in. This meant a very slow growth of employment. This employment was privileged by high wages and protective legislation. Thus employment in the organized sector stagnated. There was a throwaway line in the Second Five Year Plan to the effect that employment and the supply of consumer goods would be looked after by small-scale industries. What in effect happened was that rural and urban unemployment increased. Only a vast informal sector could supply jobs at low and insecure wages.

Indeed, a caste system was created in the economic sphere. At the top was employment in government bureaucracy—above that there could be none. Then there was the public sector with guaranteed lifetime employment, inflation indexed wages, and no need to demonstrate efficiency. Then came the organized private sector. Below them were the *shudras* of the informal sector, the hewers of wood and drawers of water, the colonials within an independent ex-colony. The rural landless were then the outcastes, beyond the pale, beyond recognition.

It is difficult to date the beginning of the decline. You could pick 1958 when the Second Five Year Plan had to be cut down to size because the import bill was enormous, or soon after when the problem of food scarcity was reported upon by the Ford Foundation, as well as the Asoka Mehta Inquiry. By 1961, it was already acknowledged that the growth in income over the previous ten years had not tackled poverty and in 1962 the India–China border incident brought Nehru's magic to an end.

The 1960s saw the end of optimism with two famines, two wars, and the death of two prime ministers. The Third Five Year Plan failed to deliver as much as it promised and the Fourth Five Year Plan was postponed in favour of a series of annual plans. For a brief period, the Westernized elite leadership in Congress was replaced by rough-hewn, local leaders such as Kamaraj Nadar and Lal Bahadur Shastri. But in 1969, Indira Gandhi struck back and regained the hegemony of the Westernized elite. She plumped for a further dose of economic radicalism—nationalization of banks, a deepening of statist planning, even a temporary nationalization of food grain trade. The devaluation of the rupee was seen as a humiliation to be avenged. In industrial policies, India lurched much more towards the Soviet model.

There was one welcome change and that was in agriculture. The rural leadership had forced attention to the under-investment in agriculture and forced the abandonment of cooperative farming (Charan Singh). Luckily for India, foreign technological innovation in the form of high yield variety of seeds combined with generous incentives to farmers brought forth a Green Revolution. Agriculture was by and large a private sector in which the government played an active role through input price subsidies and output price guarantee. The Green Revolution brought to the Indian countryside a belated capitalist transformation. Henceforth India's food problem had a private sector solution.

But industry stagnated, as did urban employment. The lack of urban growth led to unrest that was countered by political repression during the Emergency. There was further radicalization of the economic policy with forced sterilization and expansion of the public sector. There was an intensification of grassroots struggle with the Naxalites, the Railway workers' strike, and the growth of political movements among the tribals and Dalits (Lokayan). There was neither growth nor equity of a kind that could satisfy the demands of the poor.

The Indian State did, however register some military triumphs. The wars of 1965 and 1971 brought joy to Indian nationalism. A nuclear device was tested though not immediately developed. There was to be a Satellite programme. It was during the 1970s that the fruits of the Mahalanobis strategy began to emerge in India's capacity for weapons production. The Indian bourgeoisie could not deliver economic growth but it could manage to produce military might.

The combination of social conservatism and economic radicalism continued apace. Mrs Gandhi abandoned secularism to play the religious card, first helping the Hindus and later the Muslims. She herself took increasingly to going to temples, priests and *swamis*. The economy did not, however, improve. There was a realization that Nehruvian self-sufficiency would not generate the growth to keep the growth of poverty at bay. In 1980, upon her return to power, Mrs Gandhi abandoned the ideal of self-sufficiency and took a large loan from the International Monetary Fund (IMF).

And yet, the economic malaise continued. The 1980s saw an upturn in the growth rate, from the 'Hindu' rate of 3.5 per cent per annum to 5 per cent. But the growth was growth in inputs, not in productivity. The government, public and private sector continued to absorb labour while the organized industrial sector stagnated. It became clear that the route for advancement lay through securing jobs in the public sector. This required the political clout of an organized caste/regional/religious party rather than skill or merit.

This is when social conservatism, economic stagnation, and political democracy produced the lethal combination with which India is still plagued today. The lower (Other Backward) castes learnt the trick of using the ballot box to capture economic rent in political power. The State absorbed the surplus generated elsewhere in the system (by a dynamic agricultural sector and the informal economy). Thus access to State power gave any group with electoral clout a share of the State's expenditure. Suddenly budgets turned from surplus into deficits, public sector jobs mushroomed, parliamentarians became privileged creatures, cabinets expanded in size to accommodate multiple sectional interests, and loan *melas* mushroomed to bribe the electorate.

The 1980s witnessed growth without restructuring or increasing efficiency. The economy remained inward oriented and could not pay back the money borrowed from abroad. The IMF loan was swapped for private commercial borrowing from foreign banks and then again from non-resident Indians (NRIs) to service the earlier borrowing. The economy became a bonanza for political rent seeking and the private sector remained protected and infantilized.

Along the way, the malaise of the system led to a steep rise in violence. The Punjab exploded in the Khalistan agitations and suffered excessive coercion from both the government and the Khalistanis through the 1980s. Kashmir began to deteriorate in terms of law and order and in 1989 entered its long downward phase. There was violence in Assam, backlash from the Sri Lankan Tamil Tigers in the south and local intimidation from Shiv Sena in Maharashtra. These violence claimed the life of two prime ministers.

The end of the 1980s saw the splintering of the Congress party as one after another faction defected. The persistence of social backwardness, the strengthening of caste and religion facilitated the resurgence of Jan Sangh/BJP. The Congress party failed to project a viable, vibrant notion of Indian nationhood. The secular socialist democratic ideal was bankrupt after two decades of 'Gandhian' leadership. The time was ripe for Hindutva to offer an alternative vision—a non-secular, muscular nationalism that merged the neighbouring enemy Pakistan with a locally created enemy—the Indian Muslims or all non-Hindu minorities.

Parallel with the end of the Congress hegemony and the splintering of the party political structure came the nemesis of the permit–licence economy created by the Congress. By late 1991, it became clear that the Indian economy was bankrupt. By early 1992, there were humiliating trips abroad begging for foreign credit.

In a way the humiliation of near bankruptcy in 1991 was good. It was a triple bypass for a patient who had become grotesquely unhealthy but was in denial about his life style. India had clung to a mistaken economic policy when the rest of the world had abandoned it. There were clever economists of course who could twist and turn every piece of evidence and justify the past. Indeed those who had criticized Rajiv Gandhi or even Indira Gandhi as too liberal (!) were now claiming that India had already made all the reforms necessary and that this latest bout of reform was one too far. But Indira and Rajiv had borrowed money from abroad. They had abandoned the shibboleth of self-sufficiency. Yet they had not restructured the economy. They had not sought efficiency nor had they turned the economy in an export-oriented direction. There was no restructuring of the economy.

Plus ça Change

In the triad of social conservatism, economic radicalism, and political electoralism, the crisis of 1991 weakened at least the economic radicalism pillar. India seemed to be ready to swallow the bitter pill required to cure the pains of past indulgence. In the last ten years, the growth rate of GDP has gone up. If it was 3.5 per cent during the days of socialist self-sufficiency, it rose to 5 per cent during the profligate borrowing days of the Gandhis, and 6 to 7 per cent after 1991. There was a recognition that a more market-oriented way was the key to rapid growth and that India could catch up with its rivals in Asia, especially China, if it cared.

There was a distinct spurt in reforms for two years after 1991. Finance Minister Manmohan Singh was able to make his colleagues in the cabinet behave. Bur after the elections to some State Assemblies in late 1993, in which the economic reform was not an issue, the backsliding began. Suddenly Narasimha Rao was talking about the middle path at Davos and the signs were clear that India would not be a bold reforming country. Worse was to follow. After the 1996 elections, no single party won over 200 seats in the Lok Sabha and the single party dominance days of Congress were over. The BJP emerged as the alternative but two years were spent preventing it from forming a government and then another election challenging its right to rule. It was not until 1999 that one could say the issue of who governs was settled. The BJP emerged with less than 200 seats but with sufficient support to be guaranteed five years in power.

Political democracy, once the best achievement of the Indian bourgeoisie, was now turning into competitive populism. The social backwardness factor had led to a fragmentation of the party structure. The pursuit of politics for group advancement continued. The Other Backward Castes (OBCs), the Dalits, the regional parties all learned to play the game at the Centre and in the provinces. The budget was not an instrument of public policy but a *kamadhenu* for plundering for private gains. As coalitions had to be formed, every party whether large or small could enter its claims—for ministries, for perks, for MPs and MLAs—another way of lining their pockets. Despite the clear and admitted need to control the budget deficit at the Centre and in the states, the deficit has eluded control.

There have been perverse responses deliberately to sabotage reform. The Left parties when in power under two prime ministers—Gujral and Deve Gowda—did not abandon reform but did not advance it either. When they left they awarded the most damaging pay settlement for government employees—the

Brahmins of the 'working class'. It was a rare instance of employers outbidding Unions who, as could be expected, were outbidding the Pay Commission. This has landed the Centre and the state governments with an impossible fiscal task. The upper caste radicals of India's Left perpetuated the economic caste system. The costs of all this profligacy falls not on the rich but on the poor since the bulk of taxation is indirect or it results in inflation that falls disproportionately on the poor.

The ten years of reform have been slow and halting in their progress. India's entrepreneurs far from welcoming these reforms have been clinging to the nanny State even more desperately. What was once a class able to compete globally is now afraid of foreign competition. It wants reforms but no liberalization, at least no competition. They want release from the permit–licence *raj* but not the tariff–quota *raj*. The infantilization of Indian industry has been a deep process. There are some small businesses and some dynamic enterprises in recent years in Information Technology (IT) sector mainly that are exceptions to this rule but the bulk of Indian industry is not ready for the world.

In this it is happily supported by the political world, Left and Right. Too many vested interests have been created in political parties, in universities research centers, and in the media in favour of the ancient regime. The rhetoric is fiery—anti-imperialism, anti-Westernization, mawkishly pro poor but at all times anti reform, pro budget deficits, pro middle class subsidies. Politics also costs a lot of money so there has been a close tie-up with crime. Laws are passed but not enforced. This creates a market for high priced illegal products. Political parties have often been accused of getting their cut in theses proceeds and using gangs to deliver violent attacks on their rivals. Go to any capital city in any state and people will tell you about which party backs which gang.

Political structures are thus complementing social backwardness to frustrate reform and restructuring. The rents to be earned by privatizing are huge, especially if there are foreign buyers. The rhetoric has to be anti privatization as a tactic for eliciting a larger rent. A normally corrupt regime has apparently become mega corrupt. But even then the insiders cannot seem to agree on how to divide the spoils. Hence, every privatization is held up until all the diverse claims are met. The intellectuals are ready to justify each delay since delay is a vindication of the old regime and the detractors of the reform are insulated from paying its costs.

This is why despite well-known solutions to India's economic problems there is still not the breakthrough to double-digit growth. Even the growth rate of 7 per cent achieved briefly during the mid-1990s has been hard to sustain. Finance ministers despite their own commitment to reform—Manmohan Singh, Chidambaram, and Yashwant Sinha—have been unable to win over their cabinet colleagues on any sustained basis. A spurt occurs now and then and is dissipated within two years at most. The patient had his triple bypass but is now feeling well again and ignoring the physician's advice. Old habits cannot be given up. There are more important things than health—indulgence in the good things of life, for example. Another heart attack may induce another temporary regime of good behaviour but the patient is not into good health. Indeed, on good days he questions the very notion the physician advances of what constitutes good health.

After all, Western medicine is only one way of thinking about health; in his indulgence, he will seek other ways—perhaps Vedic medicine—to tell him that overindulgence cannot harm him.

WHAT IS TO BE DONE?

Politics has become the problem rather than a solution. But at the same time it is the only context within which a solution has to be found. India's vibrant democracy requires that any solution to its problems cannot be sought outside the political system—no knight in shining armour, no military general as in other polities. The party political system may be bankrupt but electoral politics has not lost its legitimacy. Voters may replace one party by another but they like the electoral system. This makes the solution doubly difficult. The solution has to be political. But the political structures defy reform or reconstruction.

While the Congress was the sole power for 40 of 42 years, the solution lay in reform of its party structures, to make it more democratic or more accountable. But eventually the Congress proved un-reformable. It has grasped the dynastic option much too firmly to be able to offer hope. The BJP gave a lot of hope when it emerged as the largest single party. It was to provide an alternative to Congress—less corrupt and more idealistic although some of the ideals were not to everyone's taste.

But the BJP has disappointed the voters even faster than Congress did. It has lacked decisiveness and since 'tehelka', has been exposed along with some of its partners as corrupt. Even the Rashtriya Swayamsevak Sangh (RSS) has been tarnished with that brush. It has been paralysed much of this year and has failed to pursue reform vigorously. Its leadership is like that of the entire party political structure—geriatric. There may be younger second rank leaders who may yet surprise us but for the moment there is little hope.

Nor can the 'Left Alternative' be taken seriously. Its rule was indecisive except in the matter of pay award mentioned earlier. If the BJP gave India the bomb and did it no favours, the Left gave it an unsustainable public sector pay structure. Both are expensive follies in pursuit of partisan delusions.

India deserves better. It has a good civil society with articulate, idealistic people dedicated to public welfare in a way few other countries in Asia or Africa have. This civil society has been active in the defence of civil liberties and against gender discrimination. The Dalit movement has generated a great deal of energetic politics outside the party political structures. There is after all an older tradition when India was under colonial rule of seeking social reform through non-governmental action. Independence and the idea of an active state have eroded that tradition. But it is the one hope that the tradition can be revived. The spirit of Servants of Indian Society needs to be reinvented.

Citizen groups will have to undertake the agitation of cleansing of political parties—all political parties. Voter groups should be formed monitoring parties' behaviour—their democratic credentials, their record of fulfilling promises that they made while in opposition, their record in choosing criminals while in office as their legislators—and compile a register of corrupt cases. These things should be available on an open website so that voters can see for themselves what each party's record is like. This will not be easy. Non-partisan organizations tend to be infiltrated or taken over if they are successful or threatening. But only a strict non-partisan basis will be the guarantee of success.

Groups like these exist in America (Voters' League for Reform) and were crucial to cleaning up politics. Independent and fearless media are also an important additional ingredient. But eventually India's citizens have to fashion the democracy they deserve. What may help in this instance is that slowly but surely a private sector will grow up which will not be dependent on government patronage. Party politics is resisting this as much as it can but the slippage has started. If independent businesses can support such activities by non-partisan groups to reform the politics then a symbiotic process of regeneration of politics can begin. The hope of India lies not in its politicians but in its citizens. They have to take their own future in hand and order its shape.

9

Democracy and Development
India 1947–2002

It gives me a particular pleasure to be giving the Narayanan Oration at the Australian National University (ANU). President Narayanan is a perfect example of how despite numerous obstacles merit will shine through. His life exemplifies the progress India has made, warts and all, over the entire twentieth century but especially since independence. The names of Harold Laski and Jawaharlal Nehru play a major part in his early story. On a personal note, he has also showed me immense kindness but perhaps more because I teach at his alma mater than for anything personal to me.

It is also a great pleasure to come back to the ANU where I twice spent a term teaching in 1980 and 1984 and where I claim many friends. Australia has taken a great interest in South Asia as the centers here and in other Australian universities testify.

INDIA SINCE 1991

It is 11 years since India had the economic shock of its life and had to rethink its economic policy and rearrange its economic institutions. It was nearly ten years ago that I had the opportunity to welcome the drastic change and wish that it would be more rather than less drastic, not a popular position among my economist friends in India at that time (Desai 1993 and Chapter 15). This is thus a good opportunity to see how far India has got in its response to the shock of near bankruptcy in early 1991.

But a lot more has also happened to India in its political life since 1991. Indeed it is hard to say whether it is the political or the economic map that has changed more in the last ten or more years. In various articles written over these years I have also tried to chart the political dynamics of the 1990s. While there was always implicitly a political background to my economic comments and an economic background to

K.R. Narayanan Oration, Australia South Asia Research Centre (ASARC) Research School of Pacific & Asian Studies, The Australian National University, Canberra, 5 December 2002.

my political comments, I would like to take this opportunity of the Narayanan Oration to try a synthesis.

The separate strands which need to be synthesized are as follows:

- In its first phase lasting just over three decades (1947–80), India's economic policy was driven by a model of national self-sufficiency. It was built around, indeed pioneered, an import-substitution industrialization (ISI) strategy. It also chose (and this is separate strictly from ISI) a capital intensive programme hoping that matters of employment creation, consumer goods supply, especially foodgrains, would take care of themselves. Political developments in the mid and late 1950s forced a situation in which the Planning authorities had to reverse the neglect of agriculture. The Green Revolution which occurred by accident in the 1960s corrected the earlier urban biases of the Second and Third Five Year Plans but the poor performance of the manufacturing sector—in terms of inefficiency, excess capacity, and low quality—persisted in both the private and public organized sectors. The growth rate was low relative both to early aspirations (Bombay Plan for instance) and to the rates achieved by other countries. This was the so-called Hindu Rate of Growth: 3.5 per cent per annum and 1.3 per cent per capita.

- Over this period 1947–80, India's political life exhibited a lot of stability and a solid, indeed unique achievement among post-colonial polities in creating and sustaining a vibrant political democracy. Single Party Dominance nurtured this democratic life except during the infamous Emergency which was brief and was reversed by that very democratic process it tried to subvert. The dominant vision of nationalism was built around secularism, non-alignment, and socialism. There was, however, beginning to be an assertion of the various regional, caste, and religious—by and large 'subaltern' forces—in the federal polity. Indeed the Janata government of 1977–9 reflected this.

- During the 1980s, there was a decade of restoration of Single Party Dominance but a relaxation of the imperative of economic self-sufficiency. There was borrowing from abroad—from the International Monetary Fund (IMF), from foreign commercial banks, and then from non-resident Indians (NRIs). But the economic institutions of permit–licence raj did not change and there was no relaxation of domestic economic policy parallel with foreign borrowing. The growth rate went up to 5.5 per cent per annum and 3.5 per cent per capita.

- The decade of the 1980s stored up much trouble for political life later on. Secularism was compromised into a parallel populism with accommodation of the orthodoxies of the two major religions as Rajiv Gandhi's decisions on the Shah Bano case and the shilanyas at Ayodhya showed. The subaltern elements continued to grow powerful at regional levels.

- The 1990s ruptured the old model in two ways. Economic dirigisme—often mislabelled socialism—became untenable as India could not repay its commercial borrowings without drastic reform. At the same time, the end of Congress dominance unleashed forces—implementation of the recommendations of the Mandal Commission with all it meant about valorization of caste distinctions, rise of the Hindutva Parivar, Dalit militancy—which ended for the decade and more any hope of a single party government. In a strange combination, the arrival of globalization saw India modernize and liberalize on the economic front but become less secular and more ethnically divided than before politically. Modernity in India thus took a different path from what its champions in the early days after independence had charted for it. It is not a secular socialist democratic India but a liberal, increasingly Hindu nationalist democratic India that is shaping its own future.

- On the economic front, the reform forced upon India by the trauma of 1991 has proved irreversible and effective. Despite much hesitation, the reform process has persisted and raised the growth rate nearer to 6.5 per cent per annum for GDP and 4.5 per cent per capita. The liberalization process has been slow relative to that in the Eastern European countries but it has been consensual. Even as politicians compete in populist rhetoric about protecting the jobs and the poor, it is clear that no possible combination of parties exists which upon gaining power would or even could reverse the liberalization process.

- There is one solid continuity despite the change in party dominance and in economic philosophy over the last 55 years. This is the nationalist programme of a militarily strong India. Even as India preached peace and non-alignment in the 1950s it built up its military production capacity, especially its atomic and nuclear research. Whether Congress or Bharatiya Janata Party (BJP), whether Nehru, Indira, and Rajiv Gandhi or Vajpayee, the determination to make India militarily strong has been common. There is no peace party in India. Indeed, it can be seen now that the ISI strategy and the insistence on self-sufficiency arose from a defence policy that meant India to be a powerful regional power. The election of President Narayanan's successor has crowned that policy with official recognition.

It is this cluster of trends that I wish to explore. The decline of secularism and socialism, the rise of liberalism and religiosity, the persistence of nationalism as a force even as its nature has changed. Democracy has been the universal solvent in his process. In order to appreciate the importance of Indian democracy, it is necessary to go back to the early history of independent India.

THE REVOLUTION OF 1946–9:
THE CONSTITUENT ASSEMBLY IN ACTION

The decision to adopt universal adult franchise with a Westminster style parliamentary system was a revolutionary decision of the Constituent Assembly. It was not inevitable nor was it a conservative decision. Given the experience of almost every other post-colonial country with constitutional change, it is a miracle that the Constituent Assembly (the Assembly hereafter), elected as it was on a restricted franchise, got it so right. But this choice, revolutionary as it is, profoundly constricted and shaped the subsequent trends.

The Assembly rejected the Gandhian option—a decentralized village republic with local autonomy and indirect democracy with an obviously weak Centre. A strong Centre was basic to Indian nationalism as its one great fear was, indeed is, of India breaking up into many nations. In the wake of Partition, a weak Centre was not going to be chosen whatever the Father of the Nation may say. The Assembly also firmly ruled out any role for the feudal order—the hundreds of native princes, for whom a role was envisaged in the 1935 Government of India Act. Unlike Malaysia, India did not give these princes even a ceremonial role. In copying the Westminster system, it replaced the Crown by an elected President with similar powers. It also rejected a single party polity which must have been tempting as it was for many African and Asian countries under the spurious rationalization that multi-party democracy was a Western luxury that a poor country could ill afford. The Communist alternative was also rejected. Private property, including foreign property, was not disturbed but could be subject to state takeover with compensation. Land was not confiscated or nationalized but land reform was made feasible.

The democracy that was chosen was radical in other ways as well. There was to be no recognition of any ethnic, religious, or caste basis of citizenship. There were to be no separate electorates, no religious qualification for holding office, nor a literacy test. Women were given the right to vote on the same terms as men when even in the developed countries, for example, France, women's suffrage had only recently (i.e 1945) been granted. But by the same token there were no guarantees of minority rights qua minority; no consociational arrangement in a formal sense whereby a minority had veto rights over drastic abridgements of its rights by the majority vote. Minorities, like majorities were treated qua Westminster as collections of individuals rather than ethnic blocks and therefore were to be looked after as part of the democratic process by legislative or by executive actions. Thus, despite its being elected from a small and restricted franchise which could have made it conservative, the Assembly chose an individualist atomistic model of democracy for India rather than one grounded in caste, religion, and language identities. Secularism was the implicit guarantee that a religious minority had nothing to fear from majority rule. Religion was not to be a subject which could be legislated about.[1]

It will be my contention that this bold revolutionary choice was crucial in shaping subsequent choices and indeed in making some of these subsequent choices less bold than they could have been. In making the Constitution ethnicity-blind and religion-blind, the Founding Fathers were rejecting the trauma which had led to the partition and hoping to avoid further fragmentation. But they were also denying reality, not only of the country at large but even of their own personal identities. Indians were individuals of course like anyone else but they also lived, in a vital sense their ethnic, religious, regional, linguistic identities. These identities were not to be left behind when they entered the political arena. Nor were these identities an invention of the colonial masters or a badge of poverty or underdevelopment ready to disappear at the first whiff of economic progress as Nehru in his more passionate moments thought.

Indian democracy was shaped by these ignored identities as they asserted

[1] Lijphart has argued that India's polity is de facto consociational. I have my doubts (Lijphart 1996).

themselves in the daily course of electoral politics. At the elite level, their own orthodox upbringing, their upper caste loyalties if they were Hindus, their relatively prosperous state meant that the choices taken were their choices. But they were also the progeny of Macaulay and had absorbed Western ideas of progress and equality, of liberty and the greatest good of the greatest number. They may have lived much as their fathers did at home but they thought and spoke the Englishman's language.

SOCIAL CONSERVATISM AND ECONOMIC RADICALISM

Two crucial choices were made early in the years after independence. One was to be socially conservative and not use the State apparatus to abolish the caste system with its inegalitarian logic of hierarchy and status. Primary education and adult literacy were state subjects and thus left to stagnate in those conservative states in the Hindi heartland where literacy, especially female and Dalit literacy, were seen to be threats to the social order. Although untouchability was made illegal in the Constitution, the attendant evils of caste were left undisturbed. Muslim society was even more delicately handled. As far as Hindu society was concerned an attempt was made mainly at Nehru's behest to codify and systematize the Hindu Family Law, though he met with resistance in his desire to modernize it from the then President Dr Rajendra Prasad. But Muslim Law was out of bounds even for Nehru. Thus political independence and the revolutionary decision to adopt democracy did not result in any state-led political programme of social reform. Indian society was allowed to reform itself in a *laissez-faire* way.

In the economic sphere, on the other hand, radicalism was the order of the day. India had, by 1947, one of the oldest modern industries in the Third World (though it was not so called till later). It had the largest group of native modern capitalist entrepreneurs, the largest jute industry, a cotton textile industry which was globally competitive, and was the seventh largest industrial country in terms of volume of industrial output. But the perception of the nationalist movement was that India had been deindustrialized by British rule and that industrialization was the first priority. Free trade and foreign capital imports were to be shunned. India would become a self-sufficient industrialized country by relying on planning led by the State.

This was not particularly surprising both in terms of the thinking of the Congress as moulded by Nehru and the climate of the times. Free market ideology was on the retreat and many thought that capitalism too was on its way out. India had been much taken by the Soviet example and indeed even by the German example of planning in a mixed economy. What was not necessary, however, to this strategy was to neglect if not punish the industries already established, especially the cotton textile industry and shifting resources to machine building. There was rampant export pessimism, unjustified as subsequent investigations showed (see articles in Ahluwalia and Little (1997) by Bhagwati, Desai and Sen). The strategy failed to take advantage of India's early start in modern industry and reinvented many of the things which were there but were tarred with foreign brush.

Thus India created a dependent entrepreneurial class in place of one that had survived foreign rule, depressed modern consumer goods industries and fostered small-scale ones which were capital wasting and inefficient, built at an enormous expense a basic goods sector with a long lead time before it could bring better consumer goods to the people and failed to generate industrial employment. The public sector, mainly in services, became the biggest provider of employment in the modern sector. Jointly the private and public organized industrial sector became a stagnant and highly privileged pool of a limited number of employees. Together the public services and the organized industrial sector employed 15 per cent of the labour force. This was called socialism (Desai 1993 and Chapter 15).

The strategy was wasteful of scarce capital and quite perverse in its determined neglect of the rules of efficient allocation. It is one thing not to get prices right but quite another to deliberately get them wrong. Restrictions on interest rates, multiple exchange rates, subsidies to inefficient industries, taxation on movement of agricultural commodities which constituted a tax on agriculture, perks to labour in the organized sector and de facto taxation of the informal sector by a lack of subsidies etc.—all this was done by an elite fully economically educated but determined to flout the rules of Western economics.

The results were predictable—slow growth of output and employment and persistence of poverty and inequality through the first phase of 30 years. With slow growth of jobs in the private sector, government jobs at all levels became much sought after and the democratic electoral system was harnessed to provide patronage. The first task of government became provision of jobs through the public fisc and then the sale of permits and licenses.

TRIANGULATION INDIAN STYLE

Thus we get a unique triangular interaction. Economic radicalism leads to slow growth biased towards elite jobs. Social conservatism strengthens caste, regional, and religious loyalties. Political democracy allows the mobilization of these loyalties in an electoral competition to capture governments at state and then at central levels. This capture then translates into jobs for the newly included. Yet the economic surplus does not expand by this route. So the system crashed in the 1970s under the weight of its own demands. A way out had to be found. It was the economic radicalism which began to be abandoned because that was the only way surplus could be enhanced. This is the way the model unfolded itself.

The interaction of social conservatism and economic radicalism in the context of political democracy produced a most interesting mutation. To get the fruits of patronage, non elite groups had to get organized and they did this through their caste and regional identities. Linguistic states had to be created during the 1950s in response to popular pressure from the local capitalists as well as local middle classes who wanted public jobs and public contracts. Next came, in the 1960s, the pressure from the rural areas to divert resources to agriculture. This happily bore fruits in the form of Green Revolution with input subsidies as well as price guarantees for outputs. But even then the discontent due to slow growth continued. This broke into a flood of protest from tribal, Dalit and lower caste groups in the 1970s, and were brought together under the Lokayan banner. This was what unhinged Indira Gandhi and led to the Emergency. Groups previously downtrodden were finding their voices and using the unreformed social structures of caste and religion to make their claims on the surplus. But the surplus was not expanding due to the elitist policies being followed.[2]

THE ESCAPE FROM TRIANGULATION

The Janata government was the transition between the first and the second phase. By itself ineffective, it mirrored the subaltern groups which had come to stake their claim to power. But Janata had no organizing vision to unite these groups as the elite vision of Nehruvian nationalism had. What Mrs Gandhi learned from her defeat was that the new India could not be run on old elite lines. She reinvented the Nehruvian vision, keeping the rhetoric of socialism and secularism but changing the content.

The two major changes were that in the economics sphere she abandoned self-sufficiency as a goal but retained dirigisme (socialism). Foreign loans were taken but the economy not restructured. On the political side, she used both Hindu and Muslim imagery to garner Hindu vote banks, and of course Muslim ones too. The foreign loans and some liberalization on import account led to higher growth. The Green Revolution was also now routinely yielding good harvests so food imports were no longer an item on the balance of trade. Of course, not all the regional and linguistic loyalties could be bought off. The demand for Khalistan was a demand that went too far and Indira Gandhi gave her life in her determination to combat that.

What was happening on the ideological front was less obvious but no less important than that. Indian nationalism had suffered a body blow with the Partition. The India that Nehru had 'discovered' during his final prison term was not the India that he came to be the leader of. He gave a new vision to the nation—of a non-aligned, secular modern, even socialist India. But the war with China shattered the non-alignment. Pragmatic consideration forced Indira Gandhi to replace secularism by parallel and simultaneous flattery of Hindu and Muslim religiosity. Socialism hung by a slim thread of dirigisme but one reinforced by foreign loans. Elsewhere, Asian countries were marching ahead economically; China had abandoned Maoism in favour of Deng's pragmatism. Even Pakistan was not inferior to India in terms of income levels or industrial performance.

What was going to be India's vision of nationhood if the modernist Nehruvian vision with its secularism, socialism, and non-alignment was no longer adequate? There were two rival models on offer. One was the religious Hindutva model which had been shunned aside in favour of the Congress one early in the independence movement which now began to be revived by the Jan Sangh/BJP. The other model—less articulated—was the one which came to the forth in the first Round

---

[2] For a most thoughtful account of the lower orders' entry into politics, see Jaffrelot (2002).

Table Conference in 1929. This was the India of regions, languages, and religious and ethnic identities. This was how the British saw India but the Congress rejected this vision in favour of a 'unity in diversity' vision. But this vision; somewhat subaltern, was what would have ruled India had the Cabinet Mission's plan been accepted. India would have remained united, unpartitioned but would have been a confederation. With provincial autonomy for big states like Punjab and Bengal and Sind, local nationalisms would have flourished.[3]

In the years since 1947, it was this vision which strengthened itself as linguistic and caste parties became electorally successful. It is these forces which have become the challenge to the Hindutva vision. Under the leadership of Mulayam Singh Yadav or Laloo Prasad Yadav or Karunanidhi/Jayalalitha or Chandrababu Naidu this confederate vision is also secular and can align either with the Left or the Centre Right (Congress). As the Congress hegemony fell apart at the end of the 1980s, this vision became a pillar of Indian politics.

The decisive change did not come with Rajiv Gandhi but after his defeat. He confirmed the abandonment of social reform by capitulating on the rights of Muslim women in the Shah Bano case and yielded to Hindu pressure on *shilanyas* for the potential Ramajanmabhumi temple on the site of the Babri mosque. It was electoral cynicism but it did not pay. But what a decade of growth at 5.5 per cent did was to create opportunities in the private sector which the old elite could exploit. It began to disengage from public sector jobs. There were better perks in the private sector. This created room for meeting the next explosion in subaltern demands which V.P. Singh tried to accommodate by undertaking to implement the Mandal Commission recommendations.

THE CRISIS OF 1991 AND THE NEW DISPENSATION

The uplift in the economic growth rate during the 1980s had been bought with foreign borrowings but without restructuring the economy. The economy's autarkic orientation continued and this meant that insufficient export income was generated to pay back the foreign debt. Had the borrowing been invested in exportables and India been given an open economy orientation, then repayment would have been easier. Had the capital come as equity rather than debt, the repayment would have not been a problem. But borrowings were made in debt form to retain political control over resources and this proved to be fatal. The economy crashed as it became unable to service its debt.

The political system crashed at the same time in as much as neither V.P. Singh nor Chandrashekhar could sustain a majority. The Budget for 1991 had to be postponed and central bankers had to scurry around raising money to pay back debt. The election of 1991 did not settle the issue though Congress (without Rajiv Gandhi) came back to power without a majority. A break away from the old model was now urgent in the economic sphere. Of the three sides of the triangle—social, political, and economic, it was the economic which was the easiest to change quickly. But the change, rapid as it was, soon became mired into a reluctant transformation.

[3] For a fuller discussion, see Desai (2000). See Chapter 23.

The two other dimensions constrained the speed and thoroughness of the abandonment of the old dirigiste model in favour of economic liberalism.

Through the 1990s and into the twenty-first century, coalition governments persisted. In its first 42 years after independence, India had six prime ministers of whom three had ruled for 38 years. In the next 13 years there have been six more prime ministers. Political continuity in the sense of one-party dominance has now gone. Economic self-sufficiency as an ideal has also been abandoned. The contending visions of nationhood have resulted in a marked rise in political and communal violence. There are caste wars in Bihar, Hindu–Muslim violence in 1992–3 and again in Gujarat in 2002 with smaller episodes in between. There is violence against Dalits and Christians from those who prefer a Hindu India.

At the same time India has remained a democracy in a most resilient fashion. For someone who grew up when the world was worried about 'after Nehru, who?', the question today seems absurd. Coalition governments have carried on Westminster politics in a most Indian fashion. Politics is more consensual, less elitist, but at the same time more corrupt and self-serving. Democracy is too deeply entrenched now to imagine any other form of governance in India, which, by the same token, makes it very difficult to imagine any drastic change in the second pillar of social conservatism. Thus, castes are valourized as are regional and religious divisions. They are cards to play in the electoral game. Political power is the solvent which brings gains of patronage to communities which have little chance in the liberal market order for economic gain. Of course, by resorting to political patronage, these 'backward' castes and Scheduled Castes dig themselves deeper into the mire of dependency. This strengthens the appeal of conservatism. The fact that some caste leaders spout secular or socialist slogans does not make them modern in any sense.

Thus, the burden of keeping the show on the road, of plastering the differences together falls on the economic dimension. Economic reform over the last ten years has been slow, hesitant but consensual. The strategy of implementing reform through the democratic process has meant that unlike in Eastern Europe there has been no shock therapy, no convulsion. The reformers of today were the dirigistes of yesterday. There is continuity. Thus the growth rate has gone up only modestly (relative to East Asian countries) to between six and six and a half percentage points. There has been a slow trickle of foreign direct investment (FDI) and India's export performance remains modest. The rate of privatization has been slow for a long time though it has perked up in the last year or so. Infrastructure development is urgent as is the need for restructuring of public sector infrastructure provision if FDI is to be attracted. The budget deficits of the Centre and the states together are too large and represent a waste of savings.

But then the deficits are the price of the twin pillars of social conservatism and political democracy. Coalition politics and the patronage politics of social factions combine to make government expenditure a variable outside political control. Despite the misgiving international financial institutions (IFIs) and credit rating agencies, Indian finance ministers carry on with the deficits as they are, knowing fully well that any effective curbing of government spending would end any coalition. The same is the case with corruption and the crime–politics nexus. The quality of public life has gone lower as India's democracy has become more inclusive. The costs of this democracy now constitute a non-negligible burden on India's growth rate. If even half of the deficit now running at 10 per cent of GDP is avoidable, we are speaking of around 2 per cent per annum in GDP growth rate.

THE PROSPECT

In one sense India is super stable and very resilient against drastic reform, social or economic. The strength of India's democracy vouches for its super stability. The revolutionary choice of the Constituent Assembly in 1946–9 has had counter-revolutionary consequences, much as it happened in nineteenth century France following the French Revolution. The country is immune to radical change. If there is a danger anywhere it comes from the overarching ideology of nationalism. Let me spell this out.

There are as I said above three competing visions of Indian nationhood (Desai 2000 and Chapter 23). The Nehru vision of secularism, socialism, and non-alignment is now moribund, if not dead. The BJP Hindutva vision is in ascendance. It is non-secular, non-socialist though uncomfortable with foreign capital. The third alternative is the confederate nationalist one which is deeply embedded in caste, language, and religion. It is secularist and dirigiste, if not socialist. (The Left parties—CPI, CPM—are a small presence in Lok Sabha and perhaps disproportionately large in India's political and intellectual life. They can be clubbed together with either the Congress or with the third cluster of confederationist parties.)

At present, the Congress is secularist but against economic liberalization. This is partly because it is in opposition and partly because the older vested interests in the socialist model are housed in the Congress. The rhetoric is all about the poor and anti-Western multinationals. The BJP and its parivar is split on economics. The Rashtriya Swayamsevak Sangh (RSS) is anti foreign capital and anti reform, But the parliamentary wing of the BJP is led by people who have made their peace with economic reform. This is again because they are in office and not in opposition. But the old Jan Sangh was always derided as a party of shopkeepers and merchants. It has anti-dirigiste instincts. Of course being in electoral competition, the financing of patronage makes every party love the public sector. The third cluster is anti-capitalist in most of its rhetoric.

The dilemma facing India is that it can have a secular but anti-reform coalition or a non-secular but economically liberal coalition. The latter variant is in power now but it may lose the next election to a combination of Congress and a number of smaller parties. Only a grand coalition of the type German politics has seen, one between Congress and BJP may overcome this dilemma. I have been long an advocate of such a coalition which everyone considers quite utopian.

Such a coalition would become a reality only for one reason. If India is to be a militarily powerful force in Asia comparable to China then it does need to accelerate its economic growth, while the obsession with Pakistan lasts, China is not clearly perceived as a challenge. But sooner or later Indian nationalists of whatever cluster will realize that China is the only serious competitor for India—a rival not an enemy. To catch up with China could yet become a nationalist ambition. To achieve that, India will have to set aside its fear of economic change and its parochial concerns with religious divisions.

REFERENCES

Ahluwalia, Isher and Ian Little (1998), *India's Economic Reforms and Development: Essays for Manmohan Singh*, Oxford: Oxford University Press.

Ayres, Alyssa and Philip Oldenburg (2002), *India Briefing: Quickening the Pace of Change*, Armonk, NY: M.E. Sharpe.

Desai, Meghnad (1993), *Capitalism, Socialism and the Indian Economy*, EXIM Bank Lecture, Mumbai: EXIM Bank. See also Chapter 15.

—— (1995), 'Economic Reform: Stalled by Politics?', in Philip Oldenburg, *India Briefing 1995*, Armonk, NY: M.E. Sharpe. See also Chapter 16.

—— (1996), 'India's Triple Bypass: Economic Liberalism, the BJP and the 1996 Elections', *Asian Studies Review*, Vol. 19, No. 3. See also Chapter 17.

—— (1998), 'Development Perspectives: Was There an Alternative to Mahalanobis?', in Isher Ahluwalia and Ian Little, *India's Economic Reforms and Development: Essays for Manmohan Singh*, Oxford: Oxford University Press. See also Chapter 14.

—— (2000), 'Communalism, Secularism and the Dilemma of Indian Nationhood', in Michael Leifer, *Asian Nationalism*, London: Routledge. See also Chapter 23.

—— (2002), 'Death, Development and Democracy in India 2002', Delhi: Encyclopaedia Britannica Hindu.

Jaffrelot, Christophe (2002), 'The Subordinate Caste Revolution', in Alyssa Ayres and Philip Oldenburg, *India Briefing: Quickening the Pace of Change*, Armonk, NY: M.E. Sharpe.

Leifer, Michael (2000), *Asian Nationalism*, London: Routledge.

Lijphart, A. (1996), 'The Puzzle of Indian Democracy: A Consociational Interpretation', *The American Political Science Review*, Vol. 90, No. 2, pp. 258–68, June.

Oldenburg, Philip (1995), *India Briefing 1995*, Armonk, NY: M.E. Sharpe

PLANNING

10

Planning by Numbers

It is a peculiar result of the institutional and intellectual nature of planning in India that any time more is known about the future course of the economy than about the present or the past. In the heyday of the Planning Commission, and especially the Perspective Planning Division, each shortfall in the achievement for the current targets was rewarded with a rosier perspective plan for the next 25 years. In a sense, sophisticated though such exercises were, they were jugglery with numbers. When the Third Five Year Plan, with a target of a 6 per cent growth rate, failed to achieve even 2 per cent in its first three years, targets and projections for future growth rates were immediately revised upwards so that the predictions about doubling total income and per capita income by specified dates could be met.

The reasons behind such exercises were no doubt partly political. Any shortfall in planning programmes was liable to expose the very idea of planning to political attacks. Ritual exercises had to be carried out to restore the fragile faith in planning to political attacks. In one of those curious dichotomies that arose in the early Cold War days and which still plague Indian politics, planning, even rose-tinted numerical exercises which were taken to be planning, was 'left wing' and socialist. To attack planning shortfalls or the Planning Commission was 'right wing'. Another equally important reason is intellectual. The Perspective Plans (and drafts of Five Year Plans) were formulated using that best available techniques. Final demand projections were made using econometrics and translated into output targets using input-output tables of respectable size, and so on. But every shortfall in achievements brought forth a technocratic improvement in plan formulation rather than an inquiry about implementation. If plans failed it was thought to be because of the lack of disaggregation in input–output tables, so a larger matrix was clearly needed. Or a proper objective function maximizing discounted consumption over time using dynamic programming techniques was substituted. The idea that these plans bore slender relation to real decision-making even at the Central Government level, and that they bore very little relevance (or resemblance) to the real economy, was never entertained within the

Source: India Survey 1972.

Planning Commission. Thus, as far as the Fourth Five Year Plan was concerned, everybody has been at pains to emphasize that it exists, although no complete formulation was available beforehand. But equally emphatically, the new style Planning Commission has moved on to discuss the next Five Year Plan, since they control the future much more than they do at present.

At no point could anyone, Indian or foreign, seriously claim that economic expertise was lacking in the Planning Commission. On the contrary, many sophisticated planning techniques were pioneered by Indian planners. Professor Mahalanobis blazed the trail by writing down for the first time an operational two-sector and four-sector growth model for the economy. While it was discovered later that the Russian economist Girgori Alexandrovic Feldman had done similar work in the 1920s, it must be said that at this time academic economics had certainly not gone anywhere near formulating such problems adequately. The Mahalanobis model was a distinct advance on the then fashionable Harrod–Domar model. For the formulation of the Third Five Year Plan; on the one hand the MIT Centre for International Studies had set up several joint projects with American and Indian economists (which bore fruit as two collections edited by Rosenstein-Rodan), and on the other many economists from Europe with 'left' inclinations visited the Indian Statistical Institute (ISI) in Delhi and Calcutta to help with planning. To cite a few names, Oscar Lange, Ragnar Frisch, Michael Kalecki, Thomas Balogh, John Kenneth Galbraith, Alan Manne, R. Eckaus, L. Lefeber, Paul Narcyz Rosenstein-Rodan, W.B. Reddaway, I.M.D. Little, and Charles Bettelheim (and there have been many others) have been associated with their equally talented Indian counterparts in the planning process.

If, therefore, after 20 years of planning, anywhere between 40 and 60 per cent of the population live below subsistence level (an estimate made by Dandekar and Rath in 1971),[1] and if unemployment, both rural and urban, has reached massive proportions, the blame cannot be laid on lack of technical expertise in planning. If the plans have failed to transform the Indian economy, failed to alleviate the miserable poverty of the majority of the population, exacerbated the unemployment situation, it cannot be because the model did not have 'enough equations' or had wrong values for its 'parameters'.

Of course, the planners only plan; they do not have any say in implementation. They can always blame politics and the politicians for messing things up. But in evaluating past performance and making future plans, surely the planner must give some recognition to this problem, instead of relying repeatedly on the rhetoric of participation, sacrifice, effort, and idealism. There is indeed no institutional set-up to ensure implementation. There are considerable rewards to continuing the make-believe game of 'new numbers for old' all in the pursuance of 'socialism' or the eradication of poverty. All the time, the failure to transform the economy becomes more glaring.

This is perhaps an unfair preface to attach to a review of Dr Gupta's book on planning.[2] It is a version of his Ph.D. thesis at Manchester, but it is emphasized

---

[1] V.M. Dandekar and N. Rath, 'Poverty in India'.
[2] S.P. Gupta, 'Planning Models in India with Projections to 1975', Praeger Special Study, Pall Mall Press, 1972.

that Dr Gupta has a practical background in the Planning Commission. In fact, his approach to planning reflects very faithfully the syndrome I have been describing above. Technically, it is an interesting exercise, though not entirely novel. It is a 22-sector model formulated both for a ten-year perspective plan and for the year-to-year transition. It has sub-models for exports, private consumption, public consumption, manpower, and so on. This part is done competently and some of the details may be of interest to a specialist on Indian planning models. One could make narrow technical criticisms of the approach on some of the empirical work, but that would miss the point. However, some general observations are in order.

Dr Gupta starts with an introduction and a survey of existing models. The latter part of his book consists of his own formulation and its empirical computation. In the introduction, Dr Gupta admits that his model ignores both prices and financial variables. But this does not worry him; he says: 'However, the above limitations (i.e. neglect of pricing and financial problems) may not be very serious, because if a bottleneck has not occasion to appear in a well-planned economy, and if all price changes are well anticipated beforehand (i.e. endogenous) then the quantity layouts in the plan are likely to be price neutral. Also if the financial sector of the market is under the strict control of the planning authority, the neglect of this sector may reduce the coverage of the plan but need not disturb the basic structure of the model' (p. 6). It is one thing to ignore certain problems in a pedagogic exercise. But from asserting that in a well-planned economy and with strict control on the part of the planning authority these problems may not affect a *theoretical model* it is then a short step to convincing yourself that in the Indian economy they do not matter. Between 1963–4 and 1968–9, price levels nearly doubled in India, and even after bank nationalization nothing like strict control exists over the financial sector, and this in any case has never been in the hands of the planning authority. The economy is notoriously not well-planned.

The Third Five Year Plan formulation as described by Dr Gupta throws some light on the sort of thinking which goes into the planning models. 'At an early stage in the work of the Third Plan, a sustained rate of growth of 5 per cent per annum was visualized. Given the assumed population growth rate of 1.2 per cent, this implied an increase in *per capita* income of a little less than 4 per cent per annum. However, as it was anticipated by the planners that over the next 15 years the population would be likely to increase at more than 2 per cent per annum, the development of the economy over the next 15 years should be conceived in terms of a revised cumulative rate of growth of approximately 6 per cent per annum' (p. 27). From one kind of wishful thinking, the Planning Commission leapt to another when it emphasized that all this was planned 'in the context of a severe domestic restraint, an intensive savings drive, a high level of exports, full utilization of resources and manpower and a considerable improvement in technology'. This is said of an economy which was and has been absurdly wasteful, has high levels of conspicuous consumption due to large money incomes generated as a result of many of the distortions of planning, where the government lacks the will and the capacity to impose a severe domestic restraint, and where manpower is not in any sense fully utilized.

In the Fourth Plan, the model was much more explicit, and, in the words of Dr Gupta, 'conforms satisfactorily to the standard programming concepts'. While constraints were important, in a rapidly growing economy they diminish in importance. As the Draft Fourth Plan said 'Constraints which loom large in the immediate present, tend to diminish or even disappear given timely decision and prompt action' (quoted by Dr Gupta on p. 32). (Needless to say, it took three years before the Fourth Plan was even officially launched.) The planners refused to lower the sights of the Perspective Plan (the 6 per cent growth rate cited above) except in the light of 'minimum changes', one of them being a reduction in inequalities in income. It turned out that to ensure a per capita income of Rs 35 a month in 1975 was desirable (Dr Gupta does not say in what year's prices: if it was at 1960–1 prices, these were totally out of date by 1966); but the best that could be done was to raise the third poorest 10 per cent above this level. But this proved too much even for a numbers exercise, so the standard was lowered to Rs 25 per month and the required growth rate was duly raised to 7 per cent. Everybody was happy thereafter, but the fact remains that even with the high food output from the Green Revolution, the economy has yet to grow at 7 per cent, and has at no previous time grown by 7 per cent for one year or for two years running. It was only an ivory tower exercise to satisfy the numerical requirements of a totally unrealistic exercise by technocrats.

Dr Gupta is convinced that these exercises need to be computed with a more elaborate mathematical model. He finds, in a final exercise, that his model calculations conform closely to those of the Fourth Plan. I hope his book has a better fate than the Fourth Plan suffered.

11

Indian Planning

Techniques, Perspective, and Context

I

Introduction and Overview

There are many aspects that make the Indian planning experience a unique one, not only among the less developed countries (LDCs) but anywhere in the world. Much will be said in its praise and even more to detract from it at this conference. For my part, I would argue the following four basic propositions:

(a) In no democratic polity has there been such a continuous experience of planning stretching over 40 years; among Socialist countries, the USSR obviously has a longer experience of planning but, that apart, not even China can match the Indian longevity.

(b) That planning has coincided with, and may even be the cause of, the raising of the long-term growth rate of Indian Gross Domestic Product (GDP) from under 1 per cent per annum or below in the period 1900–40 to 3½ per cent in the period 1950–86.

(c) If the recorded growth rate is even then regarded as inadequate (and I, for one, do so regard it), the fault cannot be laid at the door of the techniques used in planning; indeed, Indian planning in many ways pioneered many of the methods now regarded as routine, and it had the benefit of some of the finest economic minds, Indian and international, in its formation.

(d) If one were to seek the causes of the failure of the economy to experience rapid growth, it is not to the problems of implementation that one should look, but at the theoretical preconceptions within which planning operated. I shall argue that the pre-independence analysis of the root cause of India's

Paper read at SOAS Conference on State and Development Planning in India, Centre for South Asian Studies, April 1989.

underdevelopment was partial and flawed. It emphasized the Imperial seizure of the economic surplus (the drain) rather than analyzing the size of the economic surplus. It underplayed the issues of production and presumed that upon transfer of power and halt of drain, a correct allocation of the surplus to the appropriate sectors would solve the problem of Indian industrialization. In particular, in agriculture, the pre-independence critique emphasized the exploitative relations which took away the surplus from the cultivator in the form of rent or tax but never examined the issue of adequacy of the size of output or of surplus.

It was the neglect of production conditions in agriculture—the presumption that output was adequate but maldistributed—that proved the primary obstacle. The problem of agricultural productivity was finally solved in the 1960s by accident (exogenously) and *hors du plan*, as it were. A larger issue was the adequacy of overall surplus, both in the form of domestic savings and foreign exchange. Again, the Indian analysis was that there was, in principle, no shortage of surplus, the problem was to extract it in case of domestic savings by taxation or to control its allocation as in the case of foreign exchange. Within the first decade of planning, it was shown that these presumptions were too facile. The answer has been to blame feeble governments, international pressures, or domestic malpractices. But it was the inadequacy of surplus which compromised the Mahalanobis perspective plan. It was only after the agricultural question had been tackled, not by institutional reform but by an exogenous technocratic shock (the Green Revolution), that the resource constraint was relaxed. Planning can take no credit for this.

(e) At the end of the 1980s the economy is in a position where the presumptions of the 1940s have some validity. *In principle*, there is no lack of surplus, either in the form of food, domestic savings, or foreign exchange. So, in principle, planning could now transform the economy and take it on to a much higher growth path. In the meantime, however, the degree of control the planning authority could exercise (much less would like to exercise) has diminished much below what it was at the outset of planning. This diminution is not accidental; it is endogenous. The manner in which the agrarian productivity problem was tackled strengthened the rural capitalist forces and, along with them, the urban capitalists also gained. The fact that international agencies delivered the initial technology of the agrarian transformation allowed them a platform to play a much bigger role in India's economy than was envisaged in the original blueprints. In as much as these agencies were from the capitalist rather than the Communist camp, this compromised the Nehruvian socialist programme, to say nothing of the more radical variants of socialism.

(f) At the end of 40 years of planning, India has grown but moderately. The future of planning as a bureaucratic device for allocation of public funds is assured. The Indian polity may choose an interventionist or a liberal stance as its economic policy. But either way, it will be a capitalist economy that planning will function in. The notion that planning would be an instrument for a socialist transformation of the Indian polity must be abandoned, pro tem.

II

Planning in India has been quite a unique experience. In no other parliamentary democracy in the developed, much less the less developed world, has there been a sustained experiment with economic planning officially sponsored for 40 years plus. Planning is also a bipartisan programme in as much as during the brief Janata interlude of 1977–9, there was a reformulation but no abandonment of planning. Indeed, India's commitment to planning should be dated from 1938 when the then President of the Indian National Congress, Subhash Bose, appointed the National Planning Committee under the chairmanship of Jawaharlal Nehru and the secretaryship to K.T. Shah. The Committee reported over the years until 1945. The interim government had a Planning Advisory Board which reported in December 1946. Upon independence, the Congress set up in November 1947 the Constitution and Economic Programme Committee which reported on 25 January 1948, recommending the setting up of a Planning Commission. This was done in 1950.

It was not only the Congress that was keen on planning. As is well known, the industrialists issued their Bombay Plan and there was also a People's Plan. Planning, however vaguely understood, seemed to be the panacea to the problems of an independent India. In the event, the economic performance in the 40 years since independence has been better than the 40 years before, but not by much. During 1900–40 it would be generous to peg the growth rate of GDP at 1 per cent per annum; between 1951 and 1986, I estimate a compound growth rate of 3.5 per cent per annum. This growth rate is remarkably stable (the semi-log trend explains 99 per cent of the variance) but it is hardly dramatic. China on one side achieves a higher growth rate despite instability. South Korea and the Asian 'tigers' have shown that spectacular rates of industrial and economic growth are possible, Brazil, in 30 years, up to 1986, achieved 8 per cent growth rate in its real GDP. One could multiply the examples. Neither India's geographical size nor its population can explain away its moderate growth performance.

It is not possible in this paper to answer the larger question as to the costs of the mediocre growth performance. Even a relatively narrower question, 'Was planning the problem or was it despite the planning that the economic performance was what it turned out to be?', is quite difficult to answer. What I will try to do in this paper is to assess a related issue. The *technique* of Indian planning was perhaps its best feature: it would be impossible to fault it. Indeed, the sophisticated economic thinking which went into Indian planning was almost always in advance of the available academic economic thinking. But planning tried to embody in technical terms a certain vision, a model of the causes and cure of India's backwardness. It is in this *context* in which planning was undertaken which is, in my view, the major obstacle. Once undertaken to embody in a technical framework the received version of the answer to India's problems, there were further obstacles in the way in which planning operated. It is necessary to separate the *a priori theoretical context* of Indian planning from the *ex post operational context*. More is known about the latter and so I shall deal with it only briefly. Much of my emphasis is on the former.

Before I get into the context of planning, it is appropriate to see how innovative the planning technique was. In the 1930s when the National Planning Committee commenced its deliberations, there was no economic theory of development in the mainstream academic economics. *The General Theory*[1] had just appeared and was still winning over adherents in the Anglo-Saxon countries. There had not yet been that rediscovery of classical economics as a theory of economic growth that was to occur in the 1950s. Only in the socialist literature was there any effort to comprehend growth as a continuous process resulting from accumulation and/or technical progress. The Marxist framework was the only literature available for discussing underdevelopment and growth. Planning had become a popular nostrum after the First World War and much was written about various planning schemes. There was some knowledge of Russian planning and various socialist writers such as G.D.H. Cole were formulating schemes.

It is difficult to say without much further research how much of all this influenced the Indian planners. Nehru was certainly aware of Russian planning and enthusiastic about it. Fabian writings—of Webbs on Russia, for example—must have been read. Nothing, however, prepares one for the major effort by the Congress in planning. When independence came, the academic economic scene had not advanced much. Harrod had written on economic growth but his *Towards a Dynamic Economics* appeared only in 1949. There was no theory of underdevelopment apart from Rosenstein-Rodan's article on South Eastern Europe. Even Arthur Lewis' celebrated paper appears only in 1954, by which date the main lines of the Mahalanobis model were laid down.

The plan frame of Mahalanobis, which must have been formulated in the late 1940s or very early 1950s, is thus a totally original Indian contribution to the theory of economic planning and growth. Mahalanobis confesses that he had not heard of the Harrod–Domar model but, as we know now, no one had rediscovered the Felidman model at the time when Mahalanobis published his essay 'An Approach of Operational Research ...'. The origins of the model in Marx's Scheme for Extended Reproduction (SER) are traceable, but only after some academic exegesis. After all, the SER is not about a planned economy, although it has been found useful in that context. In as much as Mahalanobis arrived independently at this way of posing the problem of development, he must be regarded as India's first and most original economist.

It is even more remarkable in the face of these details that the Indian independence movement had an economic analysis of underdevelopment. Indeed, it had at least two major analyses. There was the Gandhian model, whose purest version was in Hind Swaraj (1909). It was based on a deurbanized, deindustrialized economy consisting of small, largely self-contained rural settlements with property held collectively or, if privately administered, as if it were in common interest. It was a Christian—anarchist model—Kropotkin (Peter Kropotkin

[1] John Maynard Keynes (1936), *The General Theory of Employment, Interest and Money*, London: Macmillan.

was a Russian Prince and a leader of the anarchist movement in the nineteenth century) without factories. I have not yet seen any thorough examination as to whether this model hangs together analytically, i.e. does it have a consistent logic? It does face the twin problems of rising population and growing wants which threaten the stationary equilibrium it aspires to. Gandhi's answer to both these problems was abstinence. In practical terms, it was never on except on a small, experimental basis like previous (and, no doubt, future) utopian experiments. It had, however, been a weapon in the independence struggle and spawned an immense home-spinning, handweaving, cottage industry lobby. The logic of this strategy was labour-intensive, low productivity activity for job creation. By implication these jobs would be low wage jobs as well.

The alternative model was one of industrialization—one that was favoured history of the previous 140 years. It was the path of modernization, of factory production, of energy and capital intensive industrialization. Its earliest prophet was Friedrich List, though the infant industry argument also came in handy. From its inception, the Congress party was anti-free trade, pro-tariff. It was interventionist in fiscal and monetary policy, as for example in the case of the Sterling–Rupee exchange rate. After 1930, when Nehru became the principal economic spokesman, this vision was of a self-sufficient, though not autarkic, industrial economy, complete with a capital goods as well as a consumer goods sector. It did not preclude foreign trade but it did not see trade as 'an engine of growth'.

As of 1945, this was not even very controversial. Planning was the universal panacea as evidenced by the Bombay Plan of the industrialists and the People's Plan of the Left. The controversy was about the extent of social ownership of existing industries and of new ones. Gandhian economics, having abandoned its utopian anarchic vision for all practical purposes, was an apologia for the nationalist industrialists who wanted growth but not at the expense of private accumulation. It was fearful of foreign, especially British, capital and so was not comprador. It needed a strong state to offer it tariff protection and help to buy out British capital. It did not want to be nationalized itself.[2]

Despite the two strategies—Gandhian and Nehruvian, for short, and the rival approaches within the Nehruvian strategy, public versus private ownership—there was a common analysis of India's poverty underlying them. The notion was that India was not backward or less developed but that it was deindustrialized. Thus, it was once as developed an economy as any other but the two centuries of foreign rule underdeveloped it. Foreign rule deliberately destroyed the sophisticated textile and silk exporting sectors and then flooded the country with cheap machine made cloth. By its stranglehold over the state revenues and its private mercantilist practices, foreign rule robbed the country. There was a large and continuous *transfer* of surplus from India to Britain. Dadabhai Naoroji, who pioneered this analysis, has perhaps the clearest expression of this view.

It is the exhaustion caused by the drain that disables us from building our railroads etc. from our own means. If we did not suffer the exhaustion we do, and even then if we found it to our benefit to borrow from England, the case would be one of a healthy natural business and the

[2] M. Kidron (1965), *Foreign Investment in India.*

interest then remitted would have nothing to be deplored in it as in the case of other countries ...' (Naoroj 1901/1969, p. 31)

The chief cause of India's poverty, misery, and all material evils is the exhaustion of its previous wealth, the continuously increasing exhausting and weakening drain from its annual production by the very excessive expenditure on the European portion of all its services, and the burden of a large amount a year to be paid to *foreign* countries for interest on the public debt, which is chiefly caused by the British rule.

The obvious remedy is to allow India to keep that it produces and to help it as much as it lies in the power of the British nation to reduce her burden of the interest or public debt; with a reasonable provision for the means absolutely necessary for the maintenance of the British rule. And for such means Britain must pay its proper share for its own interests. (Naoroji 1901/1969, p. 131).

The expression of loyalist sentiments notwithstanding, it is clear that in Dadabhai Naoroji's view it was not the size of the surplus that was the problem but who obtained it. If India could keep its surplus, it could build its own railroads, i.e. develop and modernize. But Dadabhai at the same time, had demonstrated extensively in the essay from which I am quoting how low the production level was and how it could not pay reasonable subsistence expenditure to the mass of the population.

There is a dualism here that should be noted. One could be saying that India was, in principle, a country with sufficient surplus to develop autonomously if only the surplus was not drained away. In this case, the question of development reduces to removing the foreign claimant of the surplus and handing it back to the natives (suspending the Indian class structure issues for the time being)—an issue of distribution, not of production. On the other hand, productivity could be so low that the total surplus was small. The fact that, in addition, this small surplus was robbed caused further problems. But removal of the foreign claimant, *of itself*, would not remove the root cause of underdevelopment—the small size of surplus.

These two possibilities are exclusive but not exhaustive. One could argue that foreign rule started by removing the large surplus that it found upon arrival and then proceeded to so alter the activities that low surpluses resulted from the continual drain. A liberal would then argue that in doing so, imperialism would hurt itself: the drain would slow to a trickle as the surplus shrank. A Marxist could say that such is the unintended consequence of imperialism and it increases the degree of repression necessary to go on extracting an ever higher share of surplus from a shrinking total.

As the years progressed, these issues were conflated but, by and large, the view was that there was enough surplus if only the drain could be stopped. Romesh Chandra Dutt's favourable account of zamindari in contrast to ryotwari has been noted for its anomaly in the light of subsequent views on these two tenurial systems. (See Gadgil's introduction to the reprint: R.C. Dutt). But the interesting point here is that as of the end of the nineteenth century, a shrewd and observant economist did not see Indian agriculture as not producing enough. The problem was what the cultivator or the owner was allowed to keep and what was taxed away. Thus, India's rural poverty was not due to low absolute productivity but was due to high taxation—once again, a problem of distribution, not of production. (Within zamindari, the surplus extraction by the zamindar is a problem much more emphasized since. Gadgil hints that this is what Dutt also argued in his book on the Bengal peasantry. I have no quarrel with it. The issue remains that the Bengal peasant had no problems of low productivity, only of low retained income.)

If one considers that India was deindustrialized by the introduction of machine-made fabrics, then Gandhi's remedy is one possibility. This is to say that abolition of machinery would restore those industries destroyed by the British. The superior productivity of the machinery by replacing labour becomes the problem, not the solution. Gandhi saw poverty as being a result of this surplus labour previously engaged in handloom and hand-spinning being thrown into agriculture: Give them back their occupation and then there would be enough to go around as long as you curbed your appetite; in agriculture there may be problems of indebtedness etc. but not of low productivity.

Throughout the *Discovery of India*, Nehru comes back again and again to an analysis of India's underdevelopment (chapter 6, sections 10, 14, 16; chapter 7, sections 2; 3, 4, 3, 9, 12.; chapter 8, sections 6, 7, 8; chapter 10, sections 6, 7, 8). Nehru's analysis is complex and in a much wider historical and geographical context. Thus, he begins by contrasting attitudes to science and technology of Abul Fazl with that of his Western contemporaries. But eventually Nehru also comes around to the view that India's 'could have been autonomous', that development was thwarted by foreign rule.

When the British came to India, though technologically somewhat backward, she was still among the advanced commercial nations of the world. Technical changes would undoubtedly have come and changed India as they had changed some Western countries. But her *normal* development was arrested by the British power. Industrial growth was checked and as a consequence social growth was also arrested. (Nehru 1945/1948, p. 429; emphases added.)

The problem then is 'this arrested growth and the prevention by British authorities of normal adjustments taking place' Nehru 1945/1948. Nehru is aware that a cultural and social modernization has to take place as well as economic modernization. But in the ultimate analysis, for Nehru as for the others mentioned above, the problem of development is one of redeploying the surplus rather than of facing up to its sheer size. This is why slightly later in the same chapter he says, 'India is not a poor country. She is abundantly supplied with everything that makes a country rich, and yet her people are very poor . ... Nothing can be clearer than the fact that India has the resources as well as the intelligence, skill and capacity to advance rapidly' (Nehru 1945/ 1948, p. 445).

Given the fact that the surplus was there, the tasks of allocation and redeployment were still formidable. In the long section on the National Planning Committee in chapter 8, Nehru lays down the general perspective of the Nehru–Mahalanobis plan. There is a ten-year period for the plan. 'The objective for the country as a whole was the attainment, as far as possible, of national sufficiency.' But Nehru also lists certain aims and 'objective tests' of planning. It may be worth recalling how much he thought they could achieve by planning. Indeed, these aims and 'objective tests' would make a good check on the achievements of planning 40 years after.

The 'aim was declared to be to ensure an adequate standard of living for the masses, in other words, to get rid of the appalling poverty of the people. The irreducible minimum, in terms of money, had been estimated by economists at figures varying from Rs 15 to Rs 25 per capita per month. (These are all pre-war figures) … . An approximate estimate of the average annual income per capita was Rs 65 … . The average income of the villager was estimated to be far less, probably about Rs 30 per capita per annum … . We calculated that a really progressive standard of living would necessitate the increase of the national wealth by 500 to 600 per cent. That was, however, too big a jump for us, and we aimed at a 200 to 300 per cent increase within ten years.

We fixed a ten-year period for the Plan, with control figures for different periods and different sectors of economic life. Certain objective tests were suggested:

(1) The improvement or nutrition—a balanced diet having a calorific value of 2,400 to 2,800 units for an adult worker.
(2) Improvement in clothing from the then consumption of about 15 yards to at least 30 yards per capita per annum.
(3) Housing standards to reach at least 100 sq feet per capita.

Further, certain indices of progress had to be kept in mind:

(i) Increase in agricultural production
(ii) Increase in industrial production
(iii) Diminution of unemployment
(iv) Increase in per capita income
(v) Liquidation of illiteracy
(vi) Increase in public utility services
(vii) Provisions of medical aid on the basis of one unit for 1,000 population
(viii) Increase in average expectation of life. (Nehru 1945/1948, p. 333.)

It would be easy to hold up this list as a proof of how much things have been scaled down. Nehru thought a growth in total income of 200 to 300 per cent over ten years was a moderate goal. At pre-1940 prices, he fixed Rs 15 a month per capita as adequate. In 1960, under his own leadership, an official committee was to fix Rs 15 at 1960 prices as adequate and even by that standard, poverty has not been overcome. It would then be possible to find culprits either in government or out of it for failure of nerve etc. After all, for even more moderate goals set out in the perspective plan in the 1950s, the achievements have not been matching.

The point I wish, to make, however, is a different one. I do not wish to question that there was a drain of wealth from India to Britain, nor that there was deindustrialization. While some destruction of handicrafts took place in the second half of the eighteenth century as a result of physical coercion, the real destruction happened as a result of cheap machine-made imports. However, this deindustrialization was not specific to India but occurred in all countries to which Britain exported, whether they were colonies or not. The weavers of Silesia were revolting in the 1840s when Marx came to analyse the problem and the reason was that after a lag of some 50 years, mechanization in weaving had caught up with mechanization in spinning. The handloom weavers had gained from the spinning revolution, since their raw material was now cheaper and they were much in demand. But by the 1840s, their labour was devalued. The dye makers of Toulouse were destroyed by the imports of indigo from India. It was capitalism and not imperialism that deindustrialized India, as it deindustrialized Germany, France, Russia, etc. When these countries came to industrialize they had the advantage of a national government but they had to face up to the problem of accumulation and raising productivity.

The signal failure of Indian analysis was its neglect of the problem of low productivity. This is especially true of the analysis of agricultural production, which after all was the basis of the economy. Tenurial conditions, rates of revenue settlement, indebtedness, and usurious interest rates are all mentioned as causes of the peasants' poverty. The answer seems simple. Remove the conditions which transfer surplus from the producer, invest the ownership of land in the hands of the direct cultivator, and you have tackled the problem of agrarian poverty. The only mention of production conditions occurs in the emphasis on fragmentation of land and the small size of holdings. This is what led the Congress to advocate co-operativization in agriculture. The idea was that increasing the size of the cultivated unit would increase productivity.

In the event, the land reform made co-operativization more difficult to achieve than otherwise. Through the 1950s, Nehru steadily lost ground on this plank. The studies by the Farm Management Committee undermined the notion that the large farm was more productive than the small farm. Charan Singh was able to defeat Nehru on the co-operatives issue by the end of the decade. In the meantime, it had become clear that 'land to the tiller' left out the landless labourer, already a problem by the 1950s, though ignored in the pre-independence literature. Though small farms may have been productive, the problem of food shortage had become urgent by the late 1950s. The Ford Foundation study team, the Asoka Mehta Committee, and the American aid givers were all clamouring for something to be done about agriculture.

By this time, the Second Five Year Plan had run into problems of resources. The Sterling balances accumulated during the war had been spent and there was a shortage of foreign exchange. The drain was either not reversed or was never large enough to meet the needs of accumulation. Domestic savings were not adequate to cover the resource needs of planning. Professor Nicholas Kaldor's taxation schemes were only half-heartedly taken up. Deficit financing was the main weapon for mobilizing surplus by way of former savings. Agricultural surplus was not adequate to prevent the inflation in farm prices. Within ten years of its inception, planning had run into the problem that there was not enough surplus to finance even the moderate goals of the Mahalanobis Plan, to say nothing of Nehru's dreams of the 1940s.

Why was Indian agricultural productivity low? This question was not posed with the same clarity as that of the *relative* performance of large and small farms. At a highly abstract level, I would put first the neglect of agricultural growth as a prerequisite of industrialization in the then prevalent theories of growth. The English Industrial Revolution followed after nearly a hundred years of an agricultural revolution. This was little appreciated in the then accepted analysis. Marx for one emphasizes the property rights issues of primitive accumulation and Maurice Dobb follows him in this. But the transformation of agriculture in the late seventeenth and early eighteenth centuries is not a major part of Marx's analysis of accumulation. Nor does it figure prominently in later discussions of the agrarian question. It is the American path and the German path that Karl Kautsky and Vladimir Ilyich Ulyanov-Lenin think are the main ones for capitalist development in agriculture. Agricultural productivity growth was taken for granted; agrarian relations were the main focus of interest.

But in the specific Indian context, there is a major problem in discussing this issue. As stated earlier, R.C. Dutt was confident that the problem of agriculture was the division of the surplus, not its size. Was he grossly misinformed or had something changed between 1901 and 1947? I want to argue that through much of the nineteenth century, India was a land-abundant, labour-scarce country. This is, of course, a relative statement. But the picture of India as a land-scarce and surplus-labour country is more appropriate to 1947 than to 1900. One does not have to be a Malthusian to admit that if population goes up from around 200 million to 360 million in 50 years, a process of agricultural involution is bound to take place in the absence of rapid industrial growth that can absorb such a phenomenal growth. In this phase, the zamindari province was much worse at adapting to population growth and agricultural involution was a much more immiserizing process where zamindars were ever present. Thus, a reasonably prosperous Bengal of R.C. Dutt's days was the famine starved land of the 1940s. Paul Greenaugh's account of this period in Bengal's history makes it clear that while British policy exacerbated the famine, the immiserizing process had begun somewhat earlier (Greenaugh 1984).

By contrast, ryotwari areas were able to manage better as population grew. Some of these areas had the good fortune to experience industrial growth in consumer goods industries while Bengal was tied to an exporting industry in the inter-war years of Depression. But even in agriculture, by the 1900s the ryotwari system no longer faced the rising revenue demands that Dutt had complained of and the lack of feudal landlords moderated the immiserizing process. This is, however, speculation on my part. Something surely must have happened in the period since Dutt wrote to give ryotwari a much better image than zamindari in the Indian economic literature.

If there was a large surplus in the days when Naoroji and Dutt wrote, a surplus which was drained away, by the time Nehru wrote, this surplus must have shrunk. Output per worker and per acre must have fallen all over the country, though not in the same proportion, of course. Areas of new settlement in the Punjab were obviously performing better than Bengal or Bihar. The ryotwari areas of western India benefited from industrial growth in the Bombay presidency. Poverty increased in South India where such growth was lacking.

The change in the production conditions is clear in retrospect but it could easily have been missed by contemporaries. It does not deny the drain theory but it makes it the less important element of any analysis of underdevelopment. Unprepared for this constraint, the Congress could be ambitious in its planning goals. The second half of the 1950s saw simultaneously the launch of an ambitious industrialization programme and its rapid compromise. Technically innovative, the Mahalanobis Plan was dealing with assumptions that were no longer valid, and thus had to be pruned.

During the 1960s the battleground shifted to agricultural growth. To begin with, the policy was the Stolypin one of betting on success. It was only after the two severe famines of 1965–6 and 1966–7 that the structural constraint in agricultural productivity was realized. Analysts began to ask the question which the earlier generations had not posed: could the low productivity be a result of exploitative agrarian relations of a semi-feudal or feudal kind (Bhaduri, Desai, Rudolph and Rudra 1984)

But at that very moment, as it were, an exogenous shock in the form of technical progress in agriculture occurred via the Green Revolution. In the 1970s, capitalism took over as the dominant mode in the Indian countryside. In many regions, agriculture became a profitable, net surplus generating activity. In these regions, the social relations of production were transformed with the growth of hired labour. The rural area became the repository of surplus in India once again since the nineteenth century. This is somewhat of a simplification but, in substance, correct. The Green Revolution, and the context of owner-cultivation in which it made its impact, brought capitalism irreversibly to the Indian countryside. Once there, it could only strengthen the urban capitalist forces.

This transformation occurred outside the Mahalanobis perspective. The Planning Commission did play its part as it happened but it did not initiate this change. Its focus was principally on industrial transformation. The bigger structural change in the Indian economy came independently of planning, outside its framework. What is more, this change undermined the presumption that planning would be an instrument for bringing socialism to the country.

Through the 1980s it has become clear that in terms of domestic savings ratios, of stocks of food grains, and the moderate size of foreign indebtedness, India has now arrived at a stage where the preconditions for rapid growth are now in place. But planning has lost the driving seat it once had and can no longer shape the economy. It will play a moderate role in the process but the driving force will come from the capitalist social relations in the Indian economy. Nothing that Rajiv Gandhi may do in response to short-run election-eering will detract from this.

12

Is there Life after Mahalanobis?
The Political Economy of India's
New Economic Policy 1992

INTRODUCTION

Economic growth both in its normative theoretical and its operational policy aspects was a lifelong concern of Sukhamoy Chakravarty. The last 20 years of his life were occupied with the guiding of the Indian economy from the very top level. Those who had known him before 1970 could not have predicted that the retiring, scholarly Sukhamoy would become a busy economic confidante of prime ministers. But if he did do so, it was surely because of his conviction in the basic correctness of the Nehru–Mahalanobis path for the nurturing of a just developing economy. But as we face the reality today, it is the Nehru–Mahalanobis path that is under the threat of abandonment. The (yet another) New Economic Policy, is a firm rejection of many of the elements of that strategy. In this essay, I wish to analyse the reactions for the rejection of the Nehru–Mahalanobis path and see if the strategy currently under implementation offers a feasible alternative. To anticipate my conclusion, I argue that the Nehru–Mahalanobis path became untraversable partly due to its own inherent inconsistency and even more due to the changes in the nature of capitalism and the debacle of Leninist socialism.

I shall take it that the essentials of the Nehru–Mahalanobis path are agreed upon (Chakravarty 1987). Starting as early as 1938 and the establishment of the National Planning Committee of the Indian National Congress by Subhash Bose as its then President under the secretaryship of Nehru, the main lines of the strategy for the development of the Indian economy were well laid and almost universally agreed to. The need was for industrialization with eventual self-sufficiency, though not autarky, as the goal. The State was to play the pivotal role both in planning and via the

The Indian Economic Review (Special Issue in Memory of Sukhamoy Chakravarty), Delhi School of Economics, 1992, pp. 155–6.

This is somewhat revised version of a paper given at the Political Economy of Development seminar of the School of Oriental and African Studies in October 1991. I am grateful to members of that seminar for their comment.

ownership and control of the commanding heights of the economy. There was to be a regulation of the unbridled play of market forces and there was to be equity in the distribution of income. Land reform was essential to raise productivity in agriculture as well as for economic justice. The fragmentation of land which hindered the use of machinery was to be overcome by a cooperative pooling of land plots voluntarily by the tenant, cultivators who were to become owners, thanks to the land reform (Nehru 1946).

While much spadework was done by the National Planning Committee on this strategy, it was not until Mahalanobis wrote his now famous paper on the operational approach to Indian planning that a coherent strategy could be said to have been formulated. The adoption of the Mahalanobis plan gave a firm long-run perspective to the strategy, mobilized the enthusiasm of the younger economists of Sukhamoy's generation, and gave flesh to Nehru's concept of socialism. As a modern version of the Marxian Scheme of Expanded Reproduction and a two or four sector extension of the Harrod–Domar model, the Mahalanobis model was an innovation in economic theory, notwithstanding the later discovery of Feldman's work (Mahalanobis 1955).

It is then no exaggeration to say that the general lines of the development of the Indian economy between 1956 and 1991 were laid down by the Mahalanobis scheme. Except for the brief sojourn of the 1977 Janata government, the main lines of the Nehru–Mahalanobis strategy have never been challenged. There have been debates about the size of the plan, about the sectoral composition of investment as between agriculture and industry or as between public and private sectors but growth through planning and the public sector has been the basic scheme of things even whet there was a cry for liberalization in the early 1980s, the role of the public sector was not challenged.

The atmosphere of crisis since 1989 and the complete abandonment of the main tenets of the Nehru–Mahalanobis strategy with deregulation of the private sector, opening up of the economy to foreign trade and especially to foreign capital, the urgency of seeking stopgap aid to prevent debt default—a sign itself of the failure of state control over the economy, the impending privatization of the public sector, the freeing of the interest rate and the exchange rate come as a surprise reversal to many. It seems as if the change is externally imposed by the International Monetary Fund (IMF), or due to a lack of political will or merely a parliamentary majority. But it can be argued, as I shall, that the collapse of the Nehru–Mahalanobis strategy is systemic and has its roots in the structure of Indian political economy.

PROMISE AND PERFORMANCE

As such, the performance of the Indian economy has not been abysmal. For the 40 years 1951–90, the average growth rate of Net National Product (NNP) has been 3.6 per cent and there is very little deviation around the trend line. There are episodes of faster growth during 1956 to 1964 and again in the mid-1980s, but apart from that, the remarkable thing about the Indian growth performance is its stability. The evidence of any marked acceleration of growth due to the liberalization of the 1980s is not very strong but it is there. Compared to its growth rate through the first half of the twentieth century—barely 1 per cent, this is a remarkable jump, specially since it has been sustained for 40 years.

There has, however, been much dissatisfaction with the growth performance of the Indian economy both on the Left and the Right. The Left has contrasted the growth of the recent years with the actual rates of the heydays of the Nehru–Mahalanobis strategy (1956–64). There has been a Kaleckian argument that the existing distribution of income constrains the ability to reap the economies of scale in industrial production since the market is limited due to poverty and inequality. A drastic redistribution of assets, hardly likely to be politically feasible, can be advocated by this analysis. The Right has criticized the planning for bureaucratic control and for the protectionist logic it adopts; the remedy is to adopt a market-oriented, open economy export-led growth of the kind that the Asian tigers have achieved (Lal 1989; Bhagwati and Desai 1970).

In his Radhakrishnan Lectures, Sukhamoy addressed these issues. To summarize his position starkly, one could say that these criticisms whose partial truth he acknowledged did not convince him enough to abandon his belief that the Nehru–Mahalanobis strategy was basically correct (Chakravarty 1987a; 1987b, see especially Chapter 19).

In what follows, I should like to advance a somewhat different explanation for the collapse of the Nehru–Mahalanobis strategy.

SURPLUS EXTRACTION VERSUS SURPLUS CREATION: TWO MODELS OF ANALYSIS

The operation of any economy within the capitalist mode, be the economy developed or not, colonial or not, can be analysed in terms of the production and disposal of surplus. One way of modelling the social relations of production is to say that one class extracts the surplus from another without contributing to its production. Thus the theory of the drain and of the recent analysis of underdevelopment by Gunder Frank and others can be said to argue that the core extracts and transfers away from the periphery surplus that already exists in the periphery. This is the extractive mode in which the key element is force or unequal exchange which allows this transfer to take place. Given this analysis once the power of the core is challenged and successfully removed, the surplus is at the disposal of the periphery to plough into its growth. National independence is the crucial event; once the surplus is there, the crucial question is its disposal. Thus an allocation towards basic industries to set the economy onto its self-sufficient growth path is one choice as against letting the consumer have hold of the surplus and letting the market determine the growth path. If the surplus is already there, the policy need is of mobilizing the surplus in the hands of the state so that it can be used in growth enhancing ways and prevent its dissipation in non-productive or productive but low priority areas. The issue, in short, is not of shortage of savings but of allocating investment in appropriate sectors.

An alternative model is to argue that underdevelopment arises from a shortage of surplus—due to backward technology, pre-capitalist relations of production, structural barriers, etc. The surplus is not there but has to be created and then channelled into further growth-enhancing areas. This analysis would recommend raising productivity either by transforming the relations of production or by importing technology and capital, i.e. external agents of change to raise surplus. The former is the radical socialist path; the latter is the capitalist path. (Primitive accumulation extracts surplus from the pre-capitalist sector and lets the capitalist channel it so as to raise surplus permanently.)

The Indian analysis of the roots of backwardness on the eve of independence was that in agriculture the primary reason for the impoverishment of the peasantry was the high rents extracted by the landlords on top of any land revenue collected by the government. If then landlords and intermediaries were removed, the surplus would flow back to the peasantry and it should prosper. There was another strand to this analysis and that was that the cultivating unit was small and fragmented. Thus, land pooling via cooperatives was necessary to raise productivity. This was, however, less urgent than land reform.

Thus agricultural surplus was not thought to be a binding constraint in the immediate analysis. If one were to add to this the drain to the British, this would constitute investible surplus. The sterling balances accumulated during the war already constituted one tangible source of investible funds. But in general the task at hand was to concentrate on the investment pattern rather than on the surplus constraint. It was in this spirit that the Mahalanobis plan framework was conceived. There is no worry in that framework about agricultural surplus; indeed the 1954–5 harvest was so good that one could be forgiven for thinking that agriculture was not a problem.

Another source for the neglect of the savings constraint could be the Keynesian influence via the Harrod–Domar models. Investment in this theory created its own savings via income creation. Given the capital-output ratio and the investment to income ratio, growth could be analysed and planned for. Indeed we could fix the desired growth rate and work backwards. An alternative variant of the no-saving constraint popular at this time was the Lewis model of surplus labour. In this model, the agricultural surplus takes the form of surplus labour which can be mobilized to produce non-agricultural products and thereby ensure growth.

In the light of this analysis, the problem of resource mobilization was that the government had to get hold of this surplus in its hands via taxation or deficit finance. It was for this reason that Nicholas Kaldor had been invited to suggests tax reforms which he did, proposing expenditure tax and wealth tax (Kaldor 1955).

Within two years of its launch, the Second Five Year Plan ran into a resource crisis. The Plan had to be pruned; there was a shortage of foreign exchange. In the same year, the fear rose that food prices may rise. First, the Ford Foundation and then the Ashok Mehta Comittee worried about the problem of the availability of marketable surplus. The Indian 'Scissors Crisis' loomed.

There were contingent reasons for each of these events. Thus, the import policy was far too loose and foreign exchange allocation had not been planned consistently. It was thought at that time that T.T. Krishnamachari, the then finance minister, was no friend of planning. With the urgent need of foreign aid, itself a signal of the lack of surplus, American pressures were beginning to be felt and hence perhaps the Ford Foundation report. But it could not be denied that before the 1950s were over, the insufficiency of surplus in foreign exchange and in food had been demonstrated. A fundamental assumption of the Mahalanobis plan and indeed of Indian nationalist analysis of backwardness had been exposed as unwarranted.

At the same time almost, i.e. in 1959, the other plank in the Congress analysis of agricultural backwardness was smashed. As the land reform of the late 1940s and early 1950s had given, albeit with many imperfections, land to the tenant cultivator, the policy of a co-operative pooling was defeated by Charan Singh at the All India Congress Committee (AICC) meeting that year. Agriculture from now on was going to be mainly the owner–cultivator leasing in or out, but not pooling. Already by that time the Farm Management Committee's researches had sown doubt on the notion that large farms were more productive than small farms. Thus, the argument for pooling was neither technically valid nor politically feasible.

The Nehru–Mahalanobis strategy had misplaced the crucial problem of the Indian economy; it neglected the creation of surplus while concentrating on its extraction and mobilization. The problem of surplus creation was to dog the Indian planners through the 1960s and when its solution came, it did so externally, without any effort from the planners. Worse, it came from the capitalist West, not from the socialist East.

To be fair to the policy-makers, some of them had seen the problem. Thus, the Chinese Communist policy of creating co-operatives and then communes in agriculture could be seen as concentrating on raising surplus by raising productivity. There was an opinion in the mid 1950s which advocated the adoption of the Chinese model, identified with, R.K. Patil of the Indian Civil Service (ICS). The Chinese tackled their backwardness by first removing the low productivity constraint in agriculture and hence when they suffered the loss of their foreign aid in 1959 as a result of the Sino-Soviet dispute they suffered only a temporary setback (exacerbated by the Great Leap Forward which caused a major famine).

In Indian planning debates, the agricultural lobby was always identified with the Right; the Left was for industrialization and for priority allocation to industry. The shift towards more agricultural investment in the Third Five Year Plan was seen as a mild setback for the Mahalanobis plan. But the push for more agricultural investment came also from a new force in Indian politics, namely the newly prominent rural politicians from the provinces who were replacing the urban Westernized lawyer types who had been prominent during the immediate post-independence days. Kamraj Nadar was the paradigmatic example of this type. It was his protégé, C. Subramanian, who as agriculture minister thought up the Intensive Agricultural Development Plans (IADP) and High Yield Variety (HYV) programmes. In the mid-1960s, the Agricultural Price Commission was established. Farmers had to have guaranteed output prices and subsidized input prices. The state had thus to put money in a sector with universal private ownership where it had no control over production. The agricultural strategy of the 1960s was the complete reverse of the industrial strategy of the Nehru–Mahalanobis path.

The Third Five Year Plan faltered in its growth performance in its first two years. It ended with two successive harvest shortfalls, a series of annual plan and the de-emphasis of industry under Prime Minister Lal Bahadur Shastri. By the end of the 1960s, the Green Revolution had already arrived, by the grace of the Rockefeller Foundation. The problem of agricultural productivity in India was about to be solved within the capitalist framework. The Left wrote much in those days denying the extent of the Green Revolution as well as predicting its dire consequences on the rural class relations. Some in hope rather than expectation said the Green Revolution will turn red. (See chapter 2 and Desai 1975 for a more positive assessment of the Green Revolution.)

It could easily have been the case that by the end of the 1960s, the Nehru–Mahalanobis strategy would have been abandoned. Annual plans with shift of emphasis towards agriculture and consumer industry relying much on foreign aid could have become the norm. By the mid 1960s, the rupee had to be devalued under severe pressure from the Western donors and the rural politicians dominated the syndicate.

Sukhamoy entered the official world of Indian planning in 1971. By then, however, a number of factors, some contingent and some structural, had revived the fortunes of the Mahalanobis strategy. Mrs Gandhi succeeded Shastri in early 1967 and had consolidated her rule by 1971. Her triumph in the Bangladesh war, the pro-Soviet move in Indian foreign policy to avenge the humiliation of US bullying at the worst of the times in the mid 1960s when Lyndon Johnson drove a hard bargain for the PL480 shipments, gave the Left the strength it needed to capture once again the levers of economic policy.

But from 1971 onwards, there was little innovation in Indian planning. Compared to the heady days of the 1950s and 1960s when many international star economists came to work with the Planning Commission and a whole new generation of bright Indian economists worked with them, the 1970s represented a routinization of the planning exercise. Some excitement was provided in the debate on the Fifth Five Year Plan when the key issues were distributional. As Sukhamoy's own discussion of the Fifth Five Year Plan framework and its final shape shows, despite much desire to reduce poverty by rapid planned growth there was recognition that growth was going to be moderate and inequality to persist. The plans continued on the tram lines set out by the Mahalanobis strategy and the Perspective Planning division. After that, plan followed plan with less and less evidence that the government was in control of the economy. Also as 1970s progressed, it became clear that the public sector was not a net saver on its revenue account but a borrower on revenue and on capital account. The 'fiscal crisis of the state' had arrived in India (Bardhan 1985). What was the reason?

THE RISE OF THE AGRARIAN BOURGEOISIE: THE BULLOCK CAPITALIST COMETH

The Mahalanobis strategy was a growth maximizing one and not meant to raise employment. But as growth proceeded, the Indian state was conscious of the equity issue; the Mahalanobis Committee had been appointed in 1960 to examine the distribution question. There was a growing disquiet that the fruits of growth were being inequitably shared. There was suddenly a great interest in measuring the extent of poverty. Mrs Gandhi turned this concern into a democratic compulsion in the 1971 election. Poverty relief became an expenditure item for the central budget. But the sector where surplus was growing fastest—the agriculture sector—was immune from taxation and indeed it was a net receiver of subsidies on input and output sides. The prospering Kisan had emerged as a political power base. As diverse analysts have recognized, India had for the first time in her history an agrarian bourgeoisie (Vanaik 1990) or bullock capitalists (as the Rudolphs 1988 have labelled them). Unlike the industrial bourgeoisie, the agrarian ones can mobilize in numbers and affect electoral outcomes. They kept their surplus and spent it as they liked outside the plan frame.

Planning was thus passive and supportive of a private sector in agriculture, and interventionist and active in the organized industrial sector; beyond lay the unorganized private sector whose unregulated growth was uneven. Since food prices remained high despite higher production, the poorer sections had relatively less to spend on clothing and other necessities. The textile industry was the first to go to the wall, and it was rescued at the public sector's expense. Budgetary problems mounted as the ability of the state to tax continued to be limited, and the compulsions of a progressive policy could not be fought off. The Emergency was one way out of this dilemma that eventually failed. Planning could not radically restructure the policy priorities nor could the political system change the fiscal powers of the state. The Constitution could be amended many times in other respects, but not repeal the tax-free status of agriculture.

Thus the 1970s settled down to a much slower growth rate than in the 1956–64 years. While agricultural growth was enough to eliminate the need for food imports, and thus the foreign exchange constraint was somewhat relieved, the budget constraint remained, with all it meant for inflation, labour unrest, etc. Now the problem was not so much of surplus but of its mobilization by the public sector. The Janata government of 1977 was solidly based on the kisan, as their leader Charan Singh was powerful; the industrial bourgeoisie had their representative in Morarji Desai. But it was not enough to be in power; the new alliance had no solution to the problem of mobilization of surplus.

LIBERALIZATION AS THE ESCAPE ROUTE

On the return to power of Mrs Gandhi in early 1980, the Nehru–Mahalanobis strategy came back into its own. The Sixth Five Year Plan (1980–5) tried to achieve a relatively high growth rate with a positive redistributive stance. Early in the Plan, loans were taken from the IMF to accommodate the second bout of higher oil prices. There was also much debate about the need to liberalize the economy. This was partly due to the changed climate of economic debate the world over which saw a resurgence of liberal market philosophy.

This first experiment with substantial IMF borrowing proved quite harmless. India did not take up the last tranche of her entitlement from the IMF and the debt servicing ratio as a proportion of export earning was only 11.6 per cent by 1983–4 and was expected to rise to about 12 per cent by the end of the plan (Chakravarty 1987a, p. 82). At this stage there seems to have been a shift in the strategy. A new, younger, and less experienced prime minister took over in 1984 and was re-elected with a convincing majority in 1985. The policy of liberalization was now adopted with much greater enthusiasm. There was large-scale borrowing and much of it was at commercial rates of interest which were at a historically high level.

There also seems to have been a sudden loss of control on the part of the Planning Commission at this juncture. That is the kindest interpretation one can put on the fact that within, four years, India had levels of foreign debt not previously seen and by early 1991 it faced the prospect of debt default. Money that was borrowed financed arms purchase, production of luxury consumer durables with foreign collaboration, and infrastructural projects which were to prove not very productive. The exporting capacity of the economy was not raised while imports did increase. The policy was one of liberalization without any structural reform of the economy, of large scale foreign borrowing without any control over its final disposal. India could have had its equivalent of the Green Revolution for its industrial sector if the money had been judiciously used, but this was not to be.

India at the end of the 1980s presented a paradox. There was no shortage of savings in the economy but this was private savings. The public sector was a net dissaver. What is more, the planning authorities had no clear strategy for redirecting the savings into the area where they could enhance exports or raise the long-run productive potential of the economy. The money was used to finance middle class consumption demands and to shore up inefficient industries. Much as in Poland during the 1980s, money had been borrowed and frittered away. Liberalization without reform thus proved to be no solution to the economy's problems. It is a counterfactual hypothesis but it is possible to conjecture that the economy could have responded to the extra resources if reform had accompanied liberalization. Just as the superiority of large farms had been challenged empirically and politically. In the 1950s, the superiority of the organized public or even private sector enterprise needed to be challenged, for structural reform to be implemented. But while the Kisans had numbers and the leadership of Charan Singh on their side, the industrial bourgeoisie had neither.

THE NEW ECONOMIC POLICY ARRIVES

Thus it is the new economic policy that is upon us. After a valiant effort for nearly 40 years of creating a dynamic mixed economy, India is on the brink of reintegrating itself fully into the world capitalist system; it never had quit that system but only been semi-detached from it. Now there is no second way or third way left to traverse. The other ideal presented by the Soviet Union has ignominiously collapsed. Despite the forewarnings of Baran and Gunder Frank, capitalist development has been shown to be possible in the Third World by South Korea as well as other countries of South East Asia. (Sukhamoy dealt with this experience in his Suzy Paine Lecture. Chakravarty 1987; see also Desai 1987 and 1991 for an analysis of the collapse of socialism.)

Given the abundance of private savings, the crucial constraint on the economy is of turning this saving into export surplus; this would imply redirecting production away from domestic heavy goods or loss-making consumption goods industry into export-oriented industries. In aggregate terms, consumption need not be curtailed but only be restructured. Savings have thus to be redirected to investments which are more export-oriented. In principle, this can be done within the original Nehru–Mahalanobis framework; the Planning Commission can decide to restructure the public sector away from its present activities and onto new ones. It would in any case involve shutting down certain activities which are absorbing resources and opening new ones. Again, in principle, the Planning Commission can decide to end subsidies to the farmers both for inputs and for output, thus reducing the budget deficit. Such a determined plan would bring about the transition without sacrificing the Nehru–Mahalanobis strategy; it requires the public sector to be firmly in command and appreciating the need for an export-oriented reallocation of investment implement it.

SOME SIMPLE POLITICAL ECONOMY OF THE NEW ECONOMIC POLICY

This is not likely to happen. Despite the abundance of savings and the shortage of debt servicing capacity, the solution will involve further inflow of foreign private capital on top of temporary IMF loans. It will involve privatization of the public sector. It is most likely as well that the subsidies which will be cut will be those which will most hurt the poor. The reasons for this are in the class composition of India. The agrarian bourgeoisie are not going to lose their subsidies without a fight and they have, demonstrated that they have political clout. Indeed as the fertilizer subsidy episode showed in the 1991 monsoon session of the Lok Sabha, they have all-party support for their privileges. The industrial bourgeoisie have much to gain from the perestroika but they have no mass political support behind them. Workers in the public as well as the private organized sector will resist the perestroika as they will suffer immediate unemployment even if in the longer run employment could increase. It is uncertain, however, whether they constitute a powerful enough element in Indian polity to stem the tide for privatization. One advantage of privatization for the government is budgetary; it will help reduce the debt if they can get a good price for the public assets. The efficiency gains of privatization are debatable.

As long as the largest surplus generating sector—agriculture—is immune to taxation, the budgetary problem will always be resolved by a tax on the urban and rural poor. The gains from privatization will ease the budgetary problems but throw the burden of adjustment on the workers in the organized sector; the latter are not the urban poor, but better off in the present regime. The rural agricultural labourer will align with the farmers and preserve the job creating resources in the countryside. The rather large urban and rural petty bourgeoisie will shift its alliance as between the farmers or the industrial bourgeoisie as the economic climate changes; they would be anti-inflation and anti-unionized urban workers.

I admit the simplifications in the above analysis but would argue that it does tell us about the prospect for the new economic policy. To the extent that the balances of class forces is not clearly on the urban or the rural bourgeoisie side (though the latter do command larger numbers), the Indian economy will waste some of its surplus and continue to borrow from abroad or suffer a loss of income via continued devaluation etc. If savings cannot be redirected away from existing uses to better ones, if loss making industries not originally part of the Nehru–Mahalanobis strategy (e.g. textiles) cannot be hived off from the public sector, also if the budget cannot be brought into revenue account surplus as used to be the case in the 1950s, then foreign borrowing on private and public account will be the norm.

There is a possible, but in my view not very likely, coalition of class forces that can escape this dilemma. If the urban workers and bourgeoisie could have a social contract to restructure but at minimal loss of jobs and if they can impose taxation on the agrarian bourgeoisie, if merely by canceling their subsidies and collecting the debts they have incurred from state lending agencies, then the public budget can be relieved without anti-poor moves. This would be India's equivalent of the Anti-Corn Law battle. Such a social contract can preserve by and large the domestic ownership of the economy and be selective about foreign capital. But this would require a high level of political leadership; at the present conjuncture in India it is unlikely that such leadership to fashion such a class coalition can be forthcoming.

CONCLUSION

This chapter has argued that the Nehru–Mahalanobis strategy misconstrued the nature of the root cause of backwardness, as that of mobilizing the surplus rather than of creating it. By its neglect of the forces of production in agriculture, it failed to remove the resource constraint. When agricultural surplus did emerge as a result of the Green Revolution, this meant the creation of a private sector in the economy which was politically powerful enough to keep its surplus to itself. The budgetary problem of the Indian economy is, therefore, such that it cannot tax its prosperous part. To overcome this, it borrowed from abroad but failed to tackle the problem of surplus creation in the industrial sector. The new economic policy is thus forced upon India by its own political configuration. The only way Nehru–Mahalanobis strategy can be saved is for the urban industrial sector to wage a corn law struggle to extract the surplus from the rural sector. This seems at present to be politically unlikely. India will thus be progressively integrated into the world capitalist economy, thus ending the 40 years of the Nehru–Mahalanobis strategy.

References

Bardhan, P.K. (1985), *The Political Economy of Development in India*, Oxford: Oxford University Press.

Bhagwati, J. and P. Desai (1970), *India: Planning for Industrialization: Industrialization and Trade Policies since 1951*, London: Oxford University Press.

Chakravarty, S. (1987a), *Development Planning: The Indian Experience*, Oxford: Oxford University Press.

—— (1987B), 'Marxist Economics and Contemporary Developing Economies', *Cambridge Journal of Economics*, Vol. 11, No. 1, pp. 3–22.

Desai, M. (1975), 'India: Emerging Contradictions of Slow Capitalist Development; in R. Blackburn (ed.), *Explosion in the Subcontinent*, London: Penguin. See also chapter 2.

—— (1987), 'Comments on Sukhamoy Chakravarty: Marxist Economics and Contemporary Developing Economies', *Cambridge Journal of Economics*, Vol. 11, No. 2, pp. 179–81.

—— (1991), 'Is Socialism Dead?', *Contention*.

Kaldor, N. (1955), *Indian Tax Reform*, New Delhi: Planning Commission, Government of India.

Lal, D. (1988), *The Hindu Equilibrium*, Oxford: Oxford University Press.

Mahalanobis, P.C. (1955), The Approach of Operational Research to Planning in India', *Sankhya*, Vol. 16, pp. 3–61.

—— (1962), *Report of the Committee on the Minimum Level of Living*, reprinted in P.K. Bardhan and T.N. Srinivasan (ed.), *Poverty and Income Distribution*, Calcutta: Statistical Publications.

Nehru, Jawaharlal (1946), *The Discovery of India*, London: Bodley Head.

—— (1961), *The Discovery of India*, Bombay: Asia Publishing House.

Rudolph, L. and S. Rudolph (1987), *In Pursuit of Lakshmi: The Political Economy of Indian State*, Chicago: University of Chicago Press.

Vanaik, A. (1990), *The Painful Transition*, London: Verso Publishers.

13

Planning in a New Perspective

INTRODUCTION

It is a great honour and privilege to be invited to give the Sukhamoy Chakravarty Memorial Lecture. I thank Professor Panchamukhi and Dr Kadekodi who invited me and I am happy to see that our friend Dr Manmohan Singh has found the time to chair the proceedings.

I came to know Sukhamoy rather late—in 1970 when I was visiting the Delhi School of Economics. I had, of course, been aware of his work, but being an applied economist—a number cruncher—I regarded theorists as inhabiting a rarer atmosphere. Sukhamoy encouraged me to dabble in theory when he introduced me to Goodwin's article 'A Growth Cycle' (Goodwin 1967). I spoke to him several times during my stay. He was also immensely helpful and concerned that my elderly mother living with us then should receive proper medical attention. I can never repay that debt. Subsequently we met on many occasions, usually when he came to the UK. I was a discussant of his Suzy Paine Memorial Lecture (Chakravarty 1991; Desai 1991) and was present for his David Glass Memorial Lecture at the London School of Economics (LSE)

Sukhamoy was many things. He was, of course, a first rate economic theorist but he used his theoretical concerns for what he called operational ends. Planning for development was the single thread running through his work. His first book *The Logic of Investment Planning* is stamped with that unique combination of rigour and concern. He was invited to join in the planning process in an active way and the last quarter century of his life was devoted to this active role which he combined with that of the widely read and deep thinking academic. I am sure I am not alone in thinking that Sukhamoy sacrificed many more years he could have had as an academic in answering the call of duty as he saw it.

'Sukhamoy Chakravarty Memorial Lecture', Delhi School of Economics, New Delhi, 1997.

I am grateful to the Institute of Economic Growth and its Director, Professor Pravin Visaria, for extending me hospitality and helpful support while preparing this Lecture. Discussions with K. Krishnamurty and Isher Ahluwalia were also of great value. I am of course solely responsible for the views expressed.

PLANNING IN THEORY AND PRACTICE

But in some sense, planning of the kind that Sukhamoy was concerned to advance did not outlive him. In his Radhakrishnan Memorial Lecture, he already takes on a defence of planning against the then deviations into market oriented policies both at home and abroad. He was conscious of the challenge to the Soviet model from Gorbachev as much as from the economic race that the Soviet Union was losing (Chakravarty 1987). In his Suzy Paine Memorial Lecture, he tried to come to terms with the rapid growth of East Asian economies within a capitalist mode contrary to the pessimistic projections of Paul Baran and Andre Gunder Frank in the 1950s and 1960s. He was able to defend his corner there as in the Radhakrishnan lectures. His was a fertile flexible mind (Baran 1957; Frank 1964).

I wish to argue, however, that planning of the sort Sukhamoy spent much of his time since 1971 on, and indeed contributed many innovations to its theory and practice in the Fifth and Sixth Five Year Plans, has no future in the late 1990s. Although in shape and size, the approach to the Ninth Five Year Plan looks very much like all the previous ones, the context in which it will operate is so different and likely to remain so that a fundamental and radical rethinking of planning is called for. My argument is not so much about replacing Plan with Market. That is a Punch and Judy show which no serious economist should waste any time with. I want to say that the economy for which plan methodology was built up by Mahalanobis, Pitamber Pant, and Sukhamoy Chakravarty as well as many others do not exist any more. Even before the advent of economic liberalization in India and the world there was always a distention between the Indian plan and the Indian economy. The plan was built around a constant Gross Domestic Product (GDP) target growth rate from which public investment allocations were derived. The economy showed year to year variations in the GDP growth rate. Typically the two growth rates diverged even on a quinquennial average basis (see Table 13.1). India's was not a planned economy; it was an economy for which a plan had been made. How much the actual outcome was a function of the plan and how much due to forces unforeseen in the plan or indeed beyond its reach even if foreseen is a complex question. The planning was never effective enough to determine the course of the economy. It loomed large enough in official thinking and intellectual discourse to attract a lot of blame for the underperformance of the economy. In the first 25 years, 1950 to 1975, the real per capita income grew by 37 per cent, which is barely 1 per cent per annum. It took 40 years for real per capita income to be doubled (by 1992). In comparative terms, India went from a leader to a laggard in Asia (see Table 13.2 for per capita income growth).

But even if it had been successful by 1975, there would have been ample reasons to justify changing its central objective of self-sufficiency. Other countries in Asia and Latin America switched to export orientation and openness. While we were all sceptical at first, the sheer pace of growth of Taiwan and South Korea was benumbing. When China shifted its strategy from a Maoist to a Bukharinist (or Dengist) one it was apparent that something was

TABLE 13.1

Planned and Actual Growth Rates of GDP in Real Terms

	Target	Actual
First Plan (1951–6)	2.1	3.61
Second Plan (1956–61)	4.5	4.27
Third Plan (1961–6)	5.6	2.84
Fourth Plan (1969–74)	5.7	3.80
Fifth Plan (1974–9)	4.4	4.80
Sixth Plan (1980–5)	5.2	5.66
Seventh Plan (1985–90)	5.0	6.01
Eighth Plan (1992–7)	5.6	6.08

Notes: (1) The growth targets for the First, Second, and Third Plans were set with respect to National Income. In the Fourth Plan, it was Net Domestic Product. In all Plans after that, the GDP has been used. (2) The Eigth Plan Actual is based on the Quick Estimates for 1995–6 and the Advance Estimates for 1996–7. These are subject to change.

TABLE 13.2

Per Capita Income Growth (in 1980–1 Prices)

Years	%
1950–6	14
1956–66	5
1966–76	16
1976–86	20
1986–96	49
1951–76	37
1976–96	79

astir in the objective material conditions of the global economy that straddled the Left/Right, State/Market divide.

A BRIEF HISTORY OF CAPITALISM

What was this? Let me briefly take an excursion into history to sharpen the contrast I wish to bring out. The capitalism that erupted in the eighteenth century and flowered in the nineteenth century—the mode of production so stunningly described by Marx and Engels in *The Communist Manifesto*—was global in nature with relatively free movement of labour and capital. The state played a very peripheral role in regulating the economy. Mr Gladstone no more than Dr Marx thought the state could run the economy. There was the Gold Standard to act as a discipline against fiscal profligacy and even Britain did not escape its rigour. It only designed a very efficient central banking policy to cushion the adverse effects of sudden outflows and inflows.

This world ended in 1914. The Great War gave birth to state planning. In Germany, Walter Rathenau convinced the Kaiser government that the German war effort had to be centrally planned so as to economize in the raw materials Germany had to import. This 'war socialism', as it was called in Germany, fascinated Larin whose articles came to Lenin's attention. Lenin dubbed it State Capitalism and in 1921 hitched the then fragile Soviet economy to this notion of planning but elsewhere the inter-war period disrupted the nineteenth century pattern. Trade and capital movements became fragmented, interrupted, and regulated. No one knew how to deal with capitalism in one country. It was during the worst crisis of capitalism that Keynes came up with a solution. The state had to regulate the volume of investment in the economy to keep up the level of effective demand.

The Keynesian theory spawned growth theory in post-war period. In developing countries especially in India, Soviet planning and Keynesian growth theory met in harmony. Even in developed countries, the state managed economies to deliver full employment and growth.

But the Keynesian solution relied on restrictions on the movement of capital. Through the late 1960s and early 1970s, capitalism in one country ran into the inflation barrier. This was actually a crisis of profitability caused by worker militancy as well as the strains borne by America's hegemonic ambitions in Vietnam and elsewhere. The system broke down when Bretton Woods was abandoned. Through the 1970s despite stagflation and fiscal crisis, a liberalization of capital movements took place. Deregulating capital movements was the Anglo-Saxon answer to the crises of profitability of capitalism. It worked. In the meantime, the Soviet Union and Eastern European economies ran into growth stagnation. Their crisis of surplus creation did not find an endogenous solution.

The short twentieth century 1914 to 1989—as Eric Hobsbawm has called it—was a serious challenge to the nineteenth century mode of capitalism. It was challenged by Leninism, Fascism, and Social Democracy. By the end, capitalism had emerged triumphant in its international, global mode. This was against all expectations, especially of those born like Sukhamoy in the inter-war period.

In returning to the nineteenth century pattern, capitalism has also gone up in spiral fashion with new innovations in information technology, transport, and communication, in financial products and services. It has forever set aside the notion that public ownership could be more efficient than private ownership in the sphere of marketable products and services. Against the doubts and protests of social democrats, democratic socialists, Leninists, and neo Fascists, privatization and liberalization have transformed the growth potential of economics. It has also in the process accelerated growth in the South East and East Asia.

How has it done this? Innovation, deregulation, liberalization, and competition have been the process whereby profitability has been restored after its crisis in the 1970s. Profits come from enhanced efficiency, from raising the relative surplus value rather than from monopoly power and extortion or raising the absolute surplus value. It was the failure of the Soviet system to be able to shift from the absolute to the relative surplus value that defeated it in the economic race.

PLANNING FOR AN OPEN ECONOMY

In this context, planning designed for an insulated national economy, with low intensity of trade and meager flow of external resources is not appropriate. There are gains to be made from an international division of labour as other developing countries have shown—China most spectacularly.

Planning for the post-twentieth century, for the new millennium has to come to terms with these new material conditions. It is a world in which trade and capital flows are strong currents. The economy has to be seen no longer as a car going down some turnpike but rather as a ship which has to negotiate these strong currents. If the sailor (the Helmsman ?) can take advantage of the currents and winds, the ship will get speedily to its destination. The trick is to swim with the currents. If the ship's helmsman sets his goal disregarding these currents and heads straight for the post, he will end up adrift.

India began to change hesitantly in the 1980s to adapt to these changes. India did not go as far as China but the doctrine of self-sufficiency, i.e. no net inflow of foreign aid, a major plank of the Fifth Five Year Plan, was abandoned. India began to borrow, first from the IMF and then from commercial and non-resident Indian (NRI) sources. But this borrowing did not lead to any change in the plan strategy of growth via public investment. The borrowing was on debt account rather than via equity. This process suffered a setback in 1991 when India ran into a foreign resources constraint. After that, a liberalization pro-gramme was launched. There has been a small trickle of foreign direct investment and of foreign portfolio investment. There has been deregulation though not much privatization and a growing relaxation of foreign exchange controls. This set of changes has increased the growth rate markedly.

In the Seventh and Eighth Plan, the GDP growth rate averaged 6 per cent, the highest quinquennial average ever. Real per capita income increased by 49 per cent over the decade 1986–96, the highest decadal growth rate recorded. India has thus demonstrably gained from opening out, though other factors like continuous good weather has also played a role. Despite this there is still a debate as to how to confront the challenge of openness. My own response is positive.

How to plan in this new perspective? The answer happily enough is in Sukhamoy's own work. At the core of *The Logic of Investment Planning* is chapter 6, 'The Model in an Open Economy'. Here Sukhamoy set up a multi-sectoral model with exports and imports which obeyed both the balance of trade constraint and the investment savings constraint. He assumed no capital flows in this model but as I shall describe later briefly, he did study the determinants of international capital movements (Chakravarty 1959).

The model is of a standard type with an accelerator type investment function and to begin with, exports and imports are not explained by any price differences. This model has $(2n^2 + 6n + 2)$ unknowns and $(2n^2 + 5n + 3)$

equations. Thus there are $(n - 1)$ degrees of freedom. As Sukhamoy says, you can close the model either by allocating $(n - 1)$ sectoral investments, or sectoral outputs or indeed exports. Once you choose one of these, the rest of the model is determined.

If exports were to be chosen, how should one do this? Sukhamoy sets up three simple models in which one can construct indices of comparative advantage by comparing domestic costs and foreign prices. He advocates that 'the country should specialize in the production of that group of commodities for which the rank (of comparative advantage) is the highest and the other commodities should be imported' (p. 109).

In a final extension of this open economy model, Sukhamoy introduces prices. This is in the penultimate chapter 9. Here, however, he finds that he has only one degree of freedom left. The planning model of an open economy with prices is of course the Walrasian General Equilibrium model albeit in its linearized Cassel–Leontief version.

The one degree of freedom he had, he said, could be used either to fix the accounting price of capital or if you like, the savings rate. This would mean either choosing the level of resources raised or the productivity of capital.

I would like to argue that nearly 40 years after it was finally put forward, Sukhamoy's model bears serious consideration. It is an open economy model with prices. It makes the strategic importance of choices clear. In the earlier model, as I said above, the choice was between fixing sectoral output growth rates or investment rates or net exports. The planning methodology has so far been to fix output growth rates. The planners however typically work with a model in which both the balance of trade constraint and the resource constraint have not always been strictly binding, *ex post* being much worse than *ex ante*. The models have treated the private sector and the government budget as passive variables reacting to whether the plan lays down. The results have been seen in the deviation of actual results from those in the Plan.

EXTENDING THE MODEL

Sukhamoy's model needs to be revised and extended. I suggest the following extensions in light of the changed context:

(a) Introduction of behavioural rules rather than a priori-constant coefficients. This is most important in private investment equations. Available macroeconometric models provide a very good starting point. Private investment is neither passive nor accommodating. It also is adversely affected by uncovered resource gaps on government accounts. This has been so even in the 1980s.

(b) Capital movements were ignored by Sukhamoy. He did carry out another study while at Rotterdam in which he modelled international capital movements as reacting to differences in profit rates, in available social infrastructure, and increasing return to scale. He even tried some econometrics. But the data availability was poor then, to say nothing of the restricted nature of capital movements. Now of course international capital movements either as portfolio or as direct fixed investment are much larger. India needs to attract large flows, especially for infrastructure. But across all activities and all sectors, capital inflows will be needed. These have to be taken into account. Soon ofcourse, Indian companies will also become capital exporters (Chakravarty 1960).

(c) Macroeconometric models show that the impact of public investment on output growth is at best 50 per cent on output and 50 per cent on inflation. But this effect has been eroding over the years. By 1989, results showed that public investment had a positive output effect only if it caused no budget deficit and no money creation. This result needs to be taken on board by the planners.

(d) Such results as we have also shown that public investment is more productive in infrastructure and agriculture than in industry or services. In the latter, I now think private investment should be left entirely alone to do the job using foreign equity investment where it can attract it.

(e) A much more urgent task is to raise investment levels in primary education, health, clean water, environmental protection, and research.

(f) The criteria for selection of export that Sukhamoy described in terms of foreign price/domestic cost ratio will need to be recalculated taking into account the effective rates of protection. Recent calculations by Ashok Gulati have shown how much the negative tariff on agriculture was hidden while there was positive tariff for industries. The time path of effective rate of protection will have to be downwards.

CONCLUSION

What then is the shape of planning in this new context? Planners have to be able to use best predictions on factors beyond their control—exogenous variables. They have to incorporate behavioural relations in the variables which they will control only imperfectly. Thus, private investment or consumer behaviour will have to be treated as if they were endogenous variables in the econometric sense. In the field of public investment, there is a further need to look at its volume, sectoral composition, and deployment, not in *a priori* fashion but in an interactive way with the private economy. At the same time, the resource constraint on government budget will have to be integrated with public and private investment. Just as public investment is modelled on a quinquennial basis, the government budget will also need a quinquennial profile.

Planning will thus become interactive and predictive in an econometric way. It will be strategic rather than pervasive. It will not start with a given growth rate. The growth rate that will emerge from the interactive predictive quinquennial exercise will set a feasible bound. It will require further iterative and counterfactual work with the available models to explore whether a higher growth path is achievable and if so, what constraints need to be removed.

In his Radhakrishnan Lectures, Sukhamoy described the conclusions of his work for the Fifth Five Year Plan as follows:

The main message of the (Fifth Five Year Plan) model was quite clear, however, despite all limitation. It showed that if the growth rate of around 5 to 6 per cent per annum was about the maximum one could have, it was impossible to bring about a significant reduction in poverty, howsoever defined, without attacking the problem directly. A higher growth rate was likely to be self defeating unless it was rendered possible by large scale transfer of external resources. (p. 36).

It is possible now to go for that higher growth rate since external resources are available. The problem of poverty can then be attacked on both fronts—via a higher growth rate and via well directed redistributive policies.

References

Baran, P.A. (1960), *The Political Economy of Growth*, New York: Monthly Review Press.

Chakravarty, S. (1959), *The Logic of Investment Planning*, Amsterdam: North Holland Publishing Company.

—— (1960), 'A Structural Study of International Capital Movements', the Netherlands Economic Institute, Divisions of Balanced Internatonal Growth, December, Rotterdam.

—— (1969), *Capital and Development Planning*, Cambridge, MA: MIT Press.

—— (1987), *Development Planning: The Indian Experience*, Oxford: Clarendon Press.

Desai, M. (1989), 'Marxian Economics and Contemporary Developing Economies': Comment on S. Chakravarty, *Cambridge Journal of Economics*, June.

Feinstein, C. (1967), *Capitalism, Socialism and Economic Development: Essays in Honour of Maurice Dobb*, Cambridge: Cambridge University Press.

Frank, A.G. (1964), *Capitalism and Underdevelopment*, New York: Monthly Review Press.

Goodwin, R.M. (1967), 'A Growth Cycle', in C. Feinstein.

14

Development Perspectives
Was there an Alternative to Mahalanobis?

INTRODUCTION

Without any doubt, Manmohan Singh's finest and most durable contribution was as the architect and the implementer of the New Economic Policy of 1991, which marked a major and irreversible shift from political/administrative to a market based ethos in Indian economic policymaking. By the wave of a magic wand, as it were, the planners of the previous week became the liberalizers on Monday morning. Unlike Poland, Czechoslovakia, and Russia, where reforms brought a complete change of personnel—Balcerowicz, Klaus, and Gaidar for instance—Indian economic policy was turned around by an insider. Not all the insiders agreed about this change by any means. Differences were there and persist, but, Manmohan was not an outsider like Balcerowicz bent on destroying the old system. It was all done in a very Indian fashion, by compromise and consensus rather than conflict and confrontation.

In this essay in his honour, I want to focus on an alternative model of development that was on offer but was not adopted. From the time of the famous blueprint by Mahalanobis submitted to Nehru as a framework for planning, Indian economic theory and policy have been directed away from the market. The academic backbone for this revolution was provided by Calcutta. The Indian Statistical Institute (ISI), Presidency College, the University of Calcutta, and later the Delhi School of Economics were the recruiting fields for the economists who shaped the framework that Manmohan began to dismantle/transform in 1991. There was, however, an alternative model of growth that was presented as such by the Bombay economists C. N. Vakil and P. R. Brahmanand. It is thus an alternative that I wish to examine.

I. M. D. Little and Isher Judge Ahluwalia (eds), *India's Economic Reforms and Development: Essays for Manmohan Singh*, (Oxford) 1998, pp. 40–8.

I am grateful to Joanne Hay of the London School of Economics for help in obtaining the sources used for this contribution. I continue to use the older name Bombay rather than Mumbai because that was the name then, 1998.

The Mahalanobis Model

The Mahalanobis model is well known. It focused on the need to achieve self-sufficiency in the production of capital goods as the first priority with a view to enhancing the output of consumer goods at a later stage. In the original paper, Mahalanobis presented a two sector and a four sector model with technical coefficients and a growth path. Questions of resource availability, inflation, and employment were neglected. There was some revision in this by the time the Mahalanobis framework became the Second Five Year Plan. The added element was a role accorded to cottage and village industries that were expected to resolve the dual problem of providing employment and consumer goods.

Criticisms of the Mahalanobis model and the Draft Plan frame, for example by the panel of economists convened by the Planning Commission, were rejected. The framework set Indian economic planning on its set path for the next 35 years. This was despite the fact that soon after its launch, the Plan ran into a resource constraint and had to be pruned in 1958. Inflation, especially of food grain prices, hit the economy in the late 1950s. The Plan's neglect of agriculture (inherited from the Mahalanobis model) became a major problem and remained so through the 1960s. Only the happy accident of the Green Revolution, a combination of Western technology, plus generous price incentives to India's largest private sector (agriculture), removed the foodgrains constraint in the 1970s.

But the policy of priority for the machine goods sector (Dept I in Marxist economics terminology), of restrictions on production by the mechanized consumer goods industries, of self-sufficiency and no imports of foreign equity capital remained. In the 1980s, there was a policy of foreign borrowing but on debt rather than equity account. The money so borrowed did not yield high enough returns to be able to make the debt servicing affordable. The economy hit the rocks in 1991.

Through the 35 years, from 1956–91, employment growth has remained sluggish and output growth, despite the pick-up in the 1980s, has been low by international standards. Low output and employment growth have led to a persistence of poverty in India while countries such as Indonesia and Malaysia, to say nothing of the Asian Tigers, have done better. Could India have done better?

The Bombay Alternative

Right from the outset, the two Bombay economists C. N. Vakil and P. R. Brahmanand criticized the Second Plan and offered an alternative. Their model was not as elegant and rigorous as the Mahalanobis one. Their book, *Planning for an Expanding Economy: Accumulation, Employment and Technical Progress in Underdeveloped Countries* (*PFE* hereafter), offered an account of the recent developments in the Indian economy (Part I), a detailed examination of the projections and assumptions of the second Plan (Part II), and the alternative (Part III).

The book purported to base its alternative on a different theoretical basis more suited to the conditions of an underdeveloped economy. The more general theoretical critique is not my concern here though it may have detracted from the book's immediate message. There was also no attempt made to present a set of targets or sectoral investment allocations. The emphasis was on putting together an alternative vision of how the Indian economy worked and how it could be made to grow faster.

The basic idea was that the Indian economy was characterized by disguised unemployment that was different in character from that in classical or Keynesian theories which was more suited for developed countries. The disguised unemployed had to be maintained even though at a fraction of the real wage of the productive worker. This feeding of the disguised unemployed represented a pool of saving. The task was to transfer these disguised unemployed to more productive work in the investment sector.

Ideas of surplus labour had suddenly come into vogue in the early 1950s. Nurkse had written his book on this topic in 1953 and Lewis' classic article was published in 1954. The Bombay authors quote Nurkse but do not cite Lewis. Lewis's model however, assumed that in moving surplus labour from agriculture to industry, there would be no problem of wage goods as in some sense these migrants will carry their 'lunch packets' with them (Nurkse 1953; Lewis 1954).

The Bombay model starts by assuming that while productive workers get paid a wage, w, the disguised unemployed get only a fraction, say, λw, $0 < \lambda < 1$. The surplus in the wage goods sector (food producing agriculture) is thus effectively reduced by the number of the disguised unemployed times λw. But if these people are to be redeployed to other activities and be productively employed, the missing fraction $(1 - \lambda)$ of the wage has to be found. For each unit of wage good produced, the number of disguised unemployed who are transferable is obviously $(1 - \lambda)^{-1}$.

If we allow for higher consumption on the farms, this multiplier has to be modified. It is not obvious of course that consumption will rise if the farms were organized on capitalist lines and the employed workers were already receiving their marginal product. (This is the implicit assumption in the Table, 'The Impact of Disguised Unemployment on PFE', p. 205). If the farms are organized according to Chayanov principles, there will be no difference between the consumption of the productive workers and the disguised unemployed. But assume that the wage of stay-on-farm workers goes up by a proportion μ of the prevailing wage, and that c is their marginal propensity to consume, then the multiplier is:

$$M = [(1 - \lambda) + \mu c]^{-1}$$

Clearly, it is the difference $(\lambda - \mu c)$ which is crucial to the size of the multiplier (a similar formula is given in PFE, p. 263, but assuming $\mu = \lambda$).

The authors were not hopeful of extra wage goods output. They rely instead on a forced savings argument. This has echoes of the debate in the Soviet Union in the 1920s concerning Preobrazhensky's[1] ideas. The authors do not estimate the likely size of forced savings, but they deploy the wage goods multiplier further in the argument by saying that if projects are chosen with a high output–investment

---

[1] Evegenü Preobrazhensky, *New Economics*.

ratio as well as a low ratio of wage costs to output, rapid accumulation can be achieved. They call the combination of the output-investment ratio and the profit-output ratio, the investment net revenue ratio. Call this r. Then:

If we multiply the investment net revenue ratio by the value of the consumption multiplier, we get the value of the *accumulation coefficient*. Accumulation increases at the rate given by the value of the *accumulation coefficient*. If the investment net revenue ratio is 10 per cent, and the value of the consumption multiplier is 2, accumulation will grow at the rate of 20 per cent, (PFE, p. 242).

The idea here is that the labour released from agriculture will be engaged in simple investment schemes where, without additional need for equipment, employment will turn into output. The analysis is not transparent here. A 'marginal capital-labour ratio' (dk/dl) equal to unity is needed somewhere in the argument to link up the wage goods/consumption multiplier that translates investment into profits. If we assume, in the Cambridge fashion, that all profits are invested we get:

$$\Delta K = (\pi/Y)\ (Y/I)\ (dK/dL)\ M\Delta s$$

Here Δs is the forced savings. $M = (= dL/dQ)$ is the multiplier. The first term on the right hand side is the profit-output ratio and the second the output-investment ratio, together forming the investment-net revenue ratio. Thus $M\Delta s$ number of workers released from agriculture at the unit marginal capital-labour ratio translates into investment I, which then works up to π. Of course (dK/dL), is not so much 'marginal capital-labour ratio' as the productivity of labour in terms of capital goods that constitute investment. Each worker fully fed constitutes equivalently one unit of investment.

Details apart, the basic idea of *PFE* is that unemployment in India was not due to shortage of capital, in the form of machine goods, but due to the shortage of wage goods. If low capital intensity, high yield projects were to be selected, employment, output, and accumulation could be expanded from the bottom-up as it were. Full employment was not impossible.

SOME POLITICAL ECONOMY

The contrast between the two approaches could not be greater. The Mahalanobis framework draft had neglected employment and the issue of inflation arising from shortages of consumer goods. It was, after all, a version of the Feldman model with priority for Dept I. As against this, the Vakil-Brahmanand plan was the equivalent of the Bukharin NEP (New Economic Policy) strategy.[2] To counter criticism from all quarters, the second Five Year Plan document deviated from the Mahalanobis framework, but only by sweeping the problem under the carpet. It was said that the cottage and village industry sectors would be responsible for supplying the non-agricultural wage goods. Since these were labour intensive, i.e. low productivity, by a miracle the problem of employment was also thereby

---

[2] For a simple analytical presentation of the Feldman model with Dept I priority and the Bukharin alternative with Dept II priority, see Desai (1979), ch. 3.

solved. This assertion does not bear serious examination and subsequent development showed its hollowness (Desai 1992, also Chapter 10).

The mid-1950s were heady days when Nehru persuaded the Congress party to accept the 'Socialist Pattern of Society' as its aim. There was also the growing friendship with the Soviet Union. Things Soviet were in fashion. In any battle between a machine goods oriented Feldman-Stalin Plan against a consumer goods oriented Bukharin Plan, victory was guaranteed for the former. Bombay lost. The opposition between Bombay and Calcutta was not so much Plan versus Market but about an employment versus an accumulation strategy .The Second Plan wanted rapid industrialization via the machine sector to achieve self-sufficient growth as soon as possible. Alternative strategies were suspect because they envisaged an open economy, dependent on indefinite imports of capital goods.

A COUNTERFACTUAL QUESTION

Their model was not as fully worked as that of Mahalanobis. But once having demonstrated that surplus labour could be mobilized as an investible resource by providing it with additional wage goods, the Bombay authors had done their work. It would have been possible, given the will, for the Planning Commission to have utilized this insight. It would have meant investing more in agriculture to increase the supply of foodgrains rather than rely on forced savings. It would have meant redeploying surplus labour in rural infrastructural schemes and some small agro-industrial enterprises. In the industrial sector, it would have meant expanding the manufactured consumer goods sector but with an eye on exports as well as for home consumption. It would have meant postponing or giving low priority to the machine goods industry.

Could India have tried the Vakil-Brahmananda path? This is an interesting counter-factual question of Indian economic history. It meant opting for employment and output growth but also a continued reliance on imports of capital goods.

A possible constraint could have been foreign exchange, but this would hardly have been peculiar to this strategy. The Second Five Year Plan ran into this constraint by 1958. Sterling balances were exhausted and foreign aid became necessary. Could the same have happened to the Bombay strategy? Perhaps not, and that for the following reasons. On the one hand, the capital goods to be imported were for consumer goods' industries, postponing the build-up of these industries. This capital would have been quicker yielding than was the case in the Mahalanobis model. On the other hand, there were export possibilities open in the Bombay strategy. This would have relaxed the foreign exchange constraint. Highly capital intensive, excess capacity creating investment would certainly have been avoided and, indeed, India could have received foreign investments. Thus, output and employment growth could have been faster than was actually the case.

All this is conjecture. In the 1950s, India wanted self-sufficiency, no foreign investments, and rapid industrialization. It was steel mills rather than textile factories that were taken to be the proud symbols of growth. It was the urban intelligentsia who had these visions, and they were in power. They not only rejected *laissez faire* which in any event had little support in India, but also dismissed all alternative development paths as not being socialist enough. (I recall how, in the debate about the size of the Third Five Year Plan during the late 1950s, we thought of anyone advocating a higher share for agriculture as more or less right-wing, an agent of the US, etc. Naive perhaps, but very much the fashion of the day.)

CONCLUSION

The price of self-sufficiency was paid for in terms of relatively low growth of per capita income and of employment. In the 1950s, perhaps this policy choice could be attributed to prevailing economic theory and the ideology of Left nationalism. But India had another opportunity during the 1970s when many countries switched from an import-substitution to an export-promotion strategy. But even then India refused to switch. More foreign borrowing was pursued in the 1980s, but without a change in the economic structure and incentives. This policy led to the foreign debt crisis of 1991 since the foreign exchange had been borrowed as debt rather than equity and was frittered away in low yield projects (Desai 1993). Thus, after having avoided the strategy in the 1950s, or even in the 1970s when the Asian Tigers began exploring export-oriented growth, India has finally come face to face with the alternative strategy. This time the result will be growth of output and employment, and the improvement of living standards and reduction of poverty rather than self-sufficiency in Dept I. It is to Manmohan Singh's credit that India has a second chance.

REFERENCES

Desai, M. (1979), *Marxian Economics*, Oxford: Blackwell.

—— (1992), 'Is there Life after Mahalanobis? The Political Economy or India's New Economic Policy', *The Indian Economic Review*, Special Number in Memory of Sukhamoy Chakravarty, pp. 155–64. See also Chapter 12.

—— (1993), 'Capitalism, Socialism and India's Economic Development, EXIM Bank Lecture. See also Chapter 15.

Lewis, W. A. (1954), 'Economic Development with Unlimited Supplies of Labour', *Manchester School*, Vol. 2, May, pp. 139–91.

Nurkse, R. (1953), *Problems of Capital Formation in Underdeveloped Countries*, Oxford: Blackwell.

Preobrazhensky, E. (1996), *The New Economics*, (Oxford; Clarendon Press).

Vakil, C. N. and P. R. Brahmanand (1956), *Planning for an Expanding Economy*, Bombay: Vora & Co.

Liberalization and Reform

15

Capitalism, Socialism, and the Indian Economy

I am greatly honoured to be asked to give the 1993 EXIM Bank lecture. A major question India faces is that of structural adjustment in the light of the near default situation in January 1991; the subsequent attempts to borrow short run and medium run foreign exchange; and the consequent economic reforms. There is in some quarters great enthusiasm for these changes. It is said that at last the Indian 'tiger' will be unchained, free of bureaucratic hindrances, to achieve high growth rates. Others fear that this is but the revival of imperialist domination that India experienced during the 150 years of colonial rule and that India's socialist project will be undermined.

I wish to put the questions before us quite starkly:

- Is capitalism desirable for India, inevitable though it may be?
- Is socialism, especially of the Indian variety, worth salvaging, difficult though such a task may be?
- Who will benefit, who will lose?
  If the present reform is halted or reversed, what are the alternatives?

I shall answer these questions but only after setting the broader context within which they must be viewed.

CAPITALISM VERSUS SOCIALISM

The twentieth century can be seen as a battleground between capitalism and socialism. Through much of this century, socialism has been the dominant creed of intellectuals, writers, and politicians. The Bolshevik Revolution of October 1917; the Great Depression suffered by the capitalist world to which the Soviet Union stood in contrast with its rapid growth; the transformation of

Eighth Exim Bank Commencement Day Annual Lecture, delivered at the State Bank of India, Bombay, published by EXIM Bank, Bombay, 1993.

laissez-faire capitalism into a mixed economy during the New Deal and the post-1945 Keynes–Beveridge welfare capitalism; the socialist revolutions in China, Yugoslavia, Cuba, and Vietnam; the spreading of the Soviet model albeit forcibly to Poland, Hungary, Czechoslovakia, and other Eastern European countries; the triumph of the Soviet Union in space technology; and the credible challenge Khruschev posed about socialism burying capitalism—these events occupied the middle 50 years of the twentieth century from 1917 to about 1967. Countries which became independent after 1945, with India in the vanguard of decolonization revolution, adopted socialism, whatever they have meant by it, as their guiding philosophy. Among the social scientists of the West there was a distinct anti-capitalist bias, if not a preference for socialist ideas.

There was at the same time much pessimism about the future of capitalism. The Marxists of course pronounced the imminent demise of capitalism; but even anti-Marxists such as Schumpeter and Rostow were not confident of its future, Socialism was either going to take over or at best there was to be a convergence between capitalism and socialism.

The economic strategies of many developing countries, especially India, evolved during this period when it was argued that rapid economic growth was impossible, taking a capitalist path. Paul Baran's influential book *The Political Economy of Growth* codified this argument for many. Indian planners decided on a strategy in which the public sector was going to be in a vanguard role, where basic capital goods industries were going to be built up before consumer goods or exports and with a strongly protectionist bias. Indian resistance to the capitalist path was based on the twin grounds of reluctance to be sucked back into the imperial relation we had just come out of and the relative inefficiency of the capitalist road in achieving high growth rates.

This pessimism about the prospect for capitalism and a belief in the superiority of socialist planning (with varying degrees of central control) were nearly universal in the 1950s and 1960s. The spectacular success of the Asian tigers in achieving rapid economic growth within capitalism began to throw doubt on the Baran thesis as early as the mid-1970s. But that was also a time of trouble for advanced capitalism with stagflation and political unrest. This trend hid the fact that the Socialist camp was also suffering from economic stagnation.

It was during the 1980s that the balance began to tilt against socialism and in favour of capitalism. Once again, to begin with, right-wing propaganda and monetarism seemed to be doomed to failure causing a massive recession in 1980–1. But by the end of the decade several things seemed to be established. It was possible for a backward country to reach the advanced capitalist stage as Japan showed. It was possible for backward Asian countries to compete seriously in world markets for manufacturing industries as the example of South Korea showed and which is now being emulated by Malaysia, Indonesia, and Thailand. China decisively broke away from Leninist/Maoist economics in its agricultural policy as far back as 1978 and achieved spectacular growth rates. China continued its conversion by opening up to foreign capital though still retaining public ownership in industry.

But the biggest blow for socialism was the collapse of the socialist Eastern

Europe and the Soviet Union. At the root of the political demand for democracy was the failure of socialist planning to generate sufficient economic surplus to meet the needs of its people, and though the transition to a market order is proving extremely painful, there is no sign of any revival of faith in central planning. Capitalism in the meantime has emerged triumphant. Seventy-five years after Lenin wrote his celebrated attack on it and 50 years after Schumpeter pronounced his pessimism, capitalism emerges as technologically dynamic and capable of offering the poorer majority the one way out (Schumpeter 1942; Lenin 1916).

Why has capitalism survived to confound its critics? Why has socialism lost so completely? Since I have answered the latter question in my 1990 Ahmedabad Lecture, let me concentrate on the first question on this occasion (Desai 1991).

In examining the causes for the success of capitalism, I should remind the audience that a dynamic successful capitalism does not generate harmony, nor does it rule out periodic crises or poverty and unemployment. Capitalism succeeds by innovations—the acts of creative destruction—whose aim is to restore profitability. Capitalism will continue as long as it displays this ability to generate innovations and to reproduce itself by guaranteeing profitability.

How has capitalism done this? One has to confront here the Marxist view that profits under capitalism represent exploitation of the workers. While Marx and Engels in the *Communist Manifesto* celebrated the tremendous achievements of capitalism in developing productive forces, there was always an expectation that this process would end either as a result of its own contradictions or due to the heightened nature of the class struggle. Later Marxists/ Leninists especially were even more pessimistic about capitalism and justified its continued existence on the grounds that imperialism expanded the bases for exploitation. The notion then was that it was monopoly capitalism peculiar to the stage of imperialism, the so-called higher stage, that prolonged the life of capitalism.

Is the present continued survival of capitalism a sign of heightened exploitation, of continuing resurgent imperialism? I would argue that this would be true if there was no technological dynamism to capitalism. Innovations raise labour productivity and restore profitability by enhancing the relative rate of surplus value rather than its absolute rate. The worker in the advanced capitalist countries is exploited, but only in a relative, abstract sense. Yes, there is a larger pool of unemployment in the European Community (EC) countries. Yes, we have had recession in the last two years. But these are normal ways in which capitalism reproduces itself.

An important way in which capitalism reproduces itself and which modifies, though not eliminate, the salience of the imperialism argument is that the centre of gravity of capitalism shifts continuously. During the nineteenth century it was Britain. There was an uncertain hiatus during the inter-war period. In the post-war period, the first 30 years saw a American hegemony. There has again been a hiatus since the mid-1970s. Since the collapse of the Bretton Woods system in 1971 and the stagflation caused by the quadrupling of oil prices in 1973 and the defeat of the US in Vietnam in 1975, there has been uncertainty as to where the centre of gravity of capitalism is. Now Germany and Japan vie for the role. With the US in a net debtor position, it must be clear that the future, for the next two or three decades, belongs to the Asia–Pacific region. This is where the rapidly growing capitalist countries are. There is no monopoly of leadership in capitalism. There is constant competition even in the world of the so-called monopoly capitalism.

Innovation displaces leading firms and devalues whole industries. It shifts the centre of gravity of capitalism. Thus, while capitalism remains an unequal system, it changes constantly. It is for this reason that Asian countries such as Japan, South Korea, Taiwan, Malaysia, Indonesia, and Thailand are emerging as the dynamic motors of capitalism.

What about inequality? Does capitalism not increase poverty? Doesn't the socialist policy that India has adopted better guarantee an egalitarian growth than a capitalist alternative?

Socialism and the Indian Economy

In what sense is India's economic policy socialist? What is the substance behind the designation of India as a sovereign democratic *socialist* republic. I need hardly remind this audience that the word 'Socialist' was added during the 1970s and was not originally there in the Preamble to the Constitution.

Socialism is about equality if it is about anything. Public ownership of the means of production, central economic planning, or even an extensive set of controls on the private sector are a means to an end. The promise of socialism is to utilize the productive potential available in modern technology so as to achieve a rapid enough rate of development which will eradicate poverty. This is because socialists, especially democratic socialists, prefer to achieve redistribution through growth rather than by confiscation.

The public sector is a major part of the Indian economy without doubt, contributing 27 per cent of the total Gross Domestic Product (GDP) in 1989–90, three times its level in 1960–1. In the organized sector, the State is the largest employer. The salaries in the public sector grew at a rate of 6.3 per cent in real terms per annum between 1950 and 1990, or twice the growth rate of GDP. Those that the State employs enjoy a variety of welfare state benefits besides guaranteed tenure in employment and some indexing of income against inflation, The average salary of public sector employees is 3.4 times the national average. It is no surprise that the subsidy absorbed by the public sector is estimated at about 20 per cent in the late 1980s compared to 3 per cent in 1970–1 (Dandekar 1992, Table 9). In 1981, the year for which we have figures on total labour force, employment in the organized sector was 23 million, of which the public sector was two-thirds at 15 million. This was, however, less than 10 per cent of the total labour force of 245 million.

We have now had 40 plus years of planning. Of course, Indian planning has not been like Soviet planning; it is more a framework for public investment and an indicative exercise for private sector. The Planning Commission looks after the macroeconomic financial balance anticipating the revenue gaps.

Thus, India has the trappings of socialism—public ownership and plan-ning—but what about the achievements? It can be convincingly argued that our economic growth rate is too low compared to countries in similar circum-stances who don't claim to be socialist.

As is well known, India's growth rate of GDP has been 3.71 per cent per annum over the 40 years of planning, 1950–1 to 1989–90. There was a distinct spurt in the growth rate during the 1980s from around the 3.5 per cent average of 1950–80 to 5.2 per cent during 1980–9. In per capita terms, this meant a growth rate of 1.37 per cent in the 30 years up to 1980 and 3.09 per cent during the 1980s or 1.5 per cent overall. This growth rate is lower than that of all developing countries as a group. I won't even mention the Asian tigers who achieved double India's growth rates.

Let me put this in another perspective. When India became independent it was the tenth largest industrial country as measured by the value of industrial output with a share of 1.2 per cent of total world industry. After 45 years of independence and 40 years of planning, India now ranks twenty-fifth, its share only 0.7 per cent. In 1947, Japan was roughly at the same level of per capita income as India. Some or much of this was the effect of wartime destruction. But starting from roughly similar situations, Japan has outstripped not only India, but now is in its own right the first Asian economic giant (Patel 1986). Korea's manufacturing output was one quarter ($2.35 billion) to India's ($10.23 billion) in 1970. By 1981, it was two-thirds ($10.58 to $16.19 billion). By 1990, Korean output had trebled while India's had only doubled and that of Korea was 96 per cent of India's level.

Now I don't wish to argue that India's growth record is an inevitable or inexorable consequence of its socialist policies. What is needed is a more historically nuanced approach. It is worth stating that there was every reason for the initial adoption of the Nehru–Mahalanobis strategy. The period of 1955–65 was one of high growth of income and of industrial output. Discounting the two years of famine in 1965 and 1966, it was the following period spanning the Fourth and Fifth Five Year Plans which set in the industrial stagnation

The industrial stagnation of the 1970s is puzzling. By this time, the Green Revolution had removed the constraint of food output which was severe during the 1960s. The 1970s was the crucial decade in which developing countries as a group raised their industrial growth rates. This was also the crucial decade in which many countries switched from an import substitution policy, in the 1950s and 1960s to an export oriented policy. India missed this opportunity to rethink the original strategy. The Nehru–Mahalanobis framework was frozen. The rhetoric of socialism and removal of poverty which characterized that decade (except briefly during the Janata regime of 1977–9) led to a continua-tion of the protectionist policies of the earlier decades. In laying the founda-tions of the industrial sector these policies were appropriate. But as the global conditions changed, India should have fashioned a new strategy.

During the 1980s there was a distinct shift of policy towards more openness or liberalization. A large loan was taken from the IMF and borrowing contin-ued, not from concessional sources but from commercial sources during the

Rajiv Gandhi regime. There was an acceleration in the growth rate without a doubt from 3.5 per cent to 5.2 per cent and the per capita growth rate more than doubled from 1.3 per cent to 3.1 per cent. There was much greater willingness to import not only goods but also capital. But this acceleration (*uskorenie* as the Soviet slogan had it) came without restructuring *perestroika*. The basic pattern of the economy as to its relative division between public and private remained, the public sector if anything increasing its share from 20 per cent in GDP to 27 per cent over the 1980s. India's commercial debt rose from $2 billion in 1980 to $21.4 billion in 1989. Total external debt was $7.9 billion in 1975 and rose by more than double to $20.6 billion by 1980. Its growth accelerated to $58.5 billion by 1989 and $70.1 billion by 1991.

This acceleration of the growth by means of foreign borrowing may on the one hand be said to give out contradictory signals. Thus while there was growth, its price was too high: why then are we back in the same strategy of borrowing more? There is a superficial truth to this association of borrowing with trouble, to say nothing of the loss of autonomy, but I wish to argue that it is simplistic. Borrowing is not the nub of the problem, be it domestically or from abroad. It is the form in which it is done and the use to which the money is put that are the important issues. Equity is better than debt since in the former the risks of failure are shared as are the fruits of success. Debt, though it seems to retain control in the hands of the borrower, puts a greater burden. Thus foreign direct or indirect equity investment is dollar for dollar better for the borrower than debt. But also the use of the borrowing to enhance export capacity would be a better justification than to increase the output of consumer durables for the middle classes. It is a reflection on the feebleness of India's planning machinery and personnel that a crisis of this immense magnitude was allowed to be built up without either a proper control on the direction of investment at an early stage or a warning at a stage well before catastrophe hit.

Let me take the two criticisms in turn.

Use of Borrowed Money: While it is difficult to trace the final use to which the money was put, a glance at the statistics of industrial output shows where the growth came from. Thus comparing 1990–1 to 1980–1, the fastest growing industrial sector was electrical machinery [5.62 times]. Miscellaneous products rose 3.2 times and the only other product line which more than doubled was chemical and chemical products. Thus, growth was mainly in electrical apparatus and appliances—television, refrigerators, etc. Durable goods rose by 3.4 times while non-durable goods rose by 1.6 times.

The borrowing financed a trade deficit at the rate of around $6.7 billion through the 1980s. The fastest growing category in the import bill was 'others' in manufacturing which one has to suspect are consumer goods. Thus, while capital goods imports doubled from $2.3 billion to $4.2 billion, 'others' rose from $1.4 billion to $5.3 billion, only to be outdone by 'gems' classified as intermediate/primary which rose from $0.5 billion to $1.8 billion. The share of these two categories in total imports rose from 1/8 to 1/3.

Source of Borrowed Money: As is well known, the source of money changed from official and concessional loans to commercial and non-concessional loans.

While official creditors were owed $36 billion in 1990–1 compared to $18 billion in 1983–4, private creditors were owed $25 billion in 1990–1 compared to $4.5 billion in 1983–4. Of these, the non-resident Indian (NRI) deposits represented nearly half by 1990–1.

The most liberal interpretation of the 1991 catastrophe is that it was a classic liquidity squeeze. India had been borrowing knowingly at a high interest rate from commercial sources in the hope that eventually some of the higher growth having satisfied the middle class appetites for TVs will spill over into manufacturing exports. When the commercial bank loans seemed to falter, a switch was made to NRI borrowing. But the succession of two weak governments, the decline in remittances from the Gulf in late 1990, and the increase in petroleum price at the same time put India in a liquidity squeeze and the reserves ran down. From a level of around $3 billion in March 1990–91, net reserves were at $0.219 billion in March 1991. They were negative during June and September 1991 and became positive only in December.

But this liberal interpretation still leaves many questions unanswered. Was this a deliberate strategy to fritter money away on consumer durables in the hope of some eventual 'trickle across' to exports? Was there any time perspective to this debt strategy; any notion of a perspective plan? Was liberalization tried merely as a sop to the middle classes, the citizens of Bel India as it was fashionable to call them during the halcyon days of Rajiv Gandhi's premiership, or was it a genuine strategy of importing new technology to restructure the economy?

A reluctant conclusion has to be drawn that by the 1980s, the Nehru–Mahalanobis strategy had become a meaningless *mantra*, chanted but without understanding or effectiveness. Other political economists, Pranab Bardhan and Sukhamoy Chakravarty, have analysed the class compromise which led to the fiscal crisis of the Indian state during the 1970s as the claims of the rich farmers and the industrialists and the organized sector workers, both public and private mounted (Bardhan 1984, Chakravarty 1987). In the 1980s the polity seems to have added one more vociferous claimant—the middle class consumer, albeit only another *swarup* of the three classes mentioned plus the enriching bourgeoises of the upper section of the unorganized private sector and the lumpenbourgeoisie living off black money. The State seemed to have bought them all off by borrowing from abroad. To the claims of the subsidies for the farmers costing Rs 181 billion or 12 per cent of agricultural output and 4 per cent of GDP in 1990–1 (Halden 1992), for the administrative and industrial public sector of Rs 18 billion in 1989–90[1] were added the demands of the consuming middle classes to have subsidized (i.e., buy now, pay later) imports.

Whatever this state of the world is, it is not socialism by any description. In choosing a strategy for slow growth, and growth was slow even after liberalization and in pandering to every powerful interest group as if the State were a

[1] I am unable to get the figures for later years. Bardhan cites a study by Mundle and Rao which calculates the subsidy to be 15 per cent of GDP in 1987–8, (Bardhan [1992], Mundle and Rao [1991]).

Kamadhenu, the cost was passed on to the poor. The anti-poverty programme claims much less money than what I would call the pro-poverty programme of profligate waste of public resources. In a public finance system where indirect taxes yield six times as much as direct taxes, every rupee of public sector loss, every rupee of fertilizer subsidy is a tax on the poor. Adding up the total employment in the public sector and even allowing for a generous multiplier for family size, the Indian variant of socialism does not cater for more than 10 per cent of the population.[2] This 10 per cent socialism, as I may label it, is getting rather expensive at nearly 6 per cent of GDP subsidy to non-departmental non-financial public sector enterprises calculated by Dandekar (1992) at 20 per cent of its output which in turn is 27 per cent of GDP for 1988–9. Add to this the subsidy to the farmers and in the tariffs and quotas and subsidized interest loans to the industrialists, and India wastes as much as say 15 per cent of its GDP.

The consequence is the failure to make even a dent on the poverty of the masses. It was shown in the World Development Report of 1990 how much more progress Indonesia had made relative to India in reducing poverty. As Minhas, et al. (1991) have shown, the number of poor are 361 million or 46 per cent of the population. This is, it is true, less in percentage terms than the level of 56 per cent in 1970–1 though in absolute terms there are 50 million extra poor. The World Bank's own internal estimates soon to be released show that the number of poor is nearer to 450 million or 49 per cent of the population if we take the higher poverty line of $31.23 in 1985 prices and purchasing power parity. But even this is less than good grounds for congratulation. The National Planning Committee of the Congress party set up by Subhash Bose under the leadership of Pandit Nehru had fixed the poverty level at Rs 15 per person per month in 1938–9 prices. This was the same level in current rupee terms chosen by the Mahalanobis committee in 1960–1. The prices had probably doubled by then, if not trebled. The goals set out by Nehru in *The Discovery of India* for planning by independent India are far from being achieved. In terms of the target level set out in that account, it would be hard to deny that two-thirds, if not three-quarters, of the population may be poor.

It is not only that India has 'retrogressed' in terms of its rank as an industrial power since independence: it is not only that the poor have been, if not abandoned, certainly betrayed; but an even bigger indictment is in the field of social policy. It is a scandal that illiteracy is still so widespread after 45 years of independence. The adult literacy rate in India is 44 per cent compared to 60 per cent in all developing countries and 72 per cent in China. Life expectancy is lower at 59 years as compared to 63 years and 70 years respectively for all underdeveloped countries and China. The school enrolment rate is lower at 66 and the under-five mortality is higher 145 as compared to school enrolment rate of 70 and 83 and under-five mortality rate of 116 and 43 for all underdeveloped countries and China respectively.

Countries similar in population size (China) or with a colonial past (Indonesia) or democracies (Malaysia) have achieved much better outcomes in social

[2] Taking 1988/89 estimates of 18 million public sector employees and multiplying by 4 we get 72 million, which is less than 9 per cent.

and economic well being of their poorest peoples. Their growth rates of GDP have been higher though they have not shunned foreign capital (China) or claimed socialism as their programme (Indonesia). If India is to get out of the rut it has to re-examine its ten per cent socialism

THE PRESENT CHALLENGE

At the present India faces a challenge. It is not that there is no alternative to following the capitalist path dictated by the World Bank/IMF. We have to ask ourselves whether it is credible that India can achieve the socialist ideal of the Nehru–Mahalanobis generation; whether there is any political agency with the courage to abandon the pandering of the top 10–15 per cent and mobilize the support of the bottom 60 per cent; whether there is anyone with the political courage to set about restructuring industry and agriculture so that it produces surplus for the betterment of the poor rather than gobble up subsidies; whether there is anyone to launch a social revolution in literacy and better health. Autonomy, national self-sufficiency, and even public ownership by themselves can only be means to betterment of the people. If they represent self-indulgence by a fraction of 10 to 15 per cent no matter how genuine their concern for the poor; the bottom line is still poverty and injustice.

It is in this context that I argue for a rapid integration of the Indian economy into capitalism. It is not a transition from socialism to capitalism, but merely one from hobbled and underdeveloped state capitalism to integration with the global economy. Other countries which have so integrated such as Korea, Taiwan, and even China, I would say, have achieved spectacular growth and poverty reduction. Capitalism in the meantime has emerged as the dynamic force no one anticipated. Within capitalism there are possibilities of pursuing pro-poor policies, for giving the state an active role in the economy as Korea shows, for generating rapid industrial growth, and exporting to markets of the rich countries as many South East and East Asian countries are showing even now. The market is a harsh discipline, as severe on the established rich as on the poor. In any case India's poor have always lived in a market economy, they have not had the benefits of socialism, they cannot afford to be employed in loss-making enterprises, or be subsidized for their water, electricity, fertilizers, and get cheap loans which they can afford not to pay back.

If, however, the present economic reforms are blocked by a combination of the political strength of the subsidized classes and the political parties which pander to them, what India will have saved is not a socialist economy. Not implementing the reforms is a choice available if India is intending to renege on its debts and face a long period of no foreign loans. But if there is no foreign inflow, how will India pay for all the imports to which its middle classes are addicted? There is no Soviet Union to help, nor any prospect that a programme of austerity could be implemented. Not reforming and reneging on the debt will mean that the subsidized classes will take up even more resources than before, battening down on the poor. Even if someone were to promise austerity to advance national autonomy s/he would be hardly credible. At the height of his power, Pandit Nehru was unable to impose a progressive wealth tax or expenditure tax. What chance is there now that such a programme will be implemented?

Not reforming, but still paying the debt back is another alternative. This would at best be a repeat of the 1980s, with no reduction in debt burden, rising debt service charges (due to loss of credibility), and accelerating devaluation of the rupee. This would be a Latin American style hyper-inflationary economy, a fertile seedbed for populist fascism as in the case of Peron in Argentina.

It is possible to be tough if the political will is there about cutting the subsidies to the rich and protecting the anti-poverty programme. I do not believe, indeed I know, that the World Bank will not stand in the way of such a programme. It is possible to redefine the role of the State in a more dynamic strategic framework, as Korea, Japan, Germany, and other countries are doing. Public ownership is necessary only in certain crucial selected sectors and public subsidy to credit almost never so when lending to enterprises which should be profit-making, be they farms or factories. It is possible to set a target of reduction of illiteracy by half in ten years if there is the will. Neither capitalism nor imperialism nor the World Bank will stand in the way.

It is possible for India to achieve high growth, less poverty, better health, and literacy. The transition will be painful, not least for those who will lose the cushion of guaranteed employment or may have to pay for the fertilizers they use or the electricity they burn. But the longer the delay, those at the bottom who have suffered for 50 years and more will go on suffering. As Lenin said long ago in another but similar context about Russia and the dreams of an instant leap to socialism, India's problem is not so much capitalism but that it is stuck with a backward version of capitalism. Calling it socialism is not the answer.

REFERENCES

Baran, P. (1957), *The Political of Economy Growth*, New York: Marzani and Munsell.

Bardhan, P. (1984), *The Political Economy of Development in India*, Oxford: Oxford University Press.

—— (1992), 'A Political Economy Perspective on Development', in B. Jalan (ed.), *The Indian Economy: Problems and Prospects*, Delhi: Viking.

Chakravarty, S. (1987), *Development Planning: The Indian Experience*, Delhi: Oxford University Press.

Dandekar, V.M. (1992), 'Forty Years After Independence', in B. Jalan (ed.), *The Indian Economy: Problems and Prospects*, Delhi: Viking.

Desai, M. (1991), 'Is Socialism Dead? V.S. Desai Memorial Lecture', 15 December 1990, at the H.L. College of Commerce, Ahmedabad, published in *Contention*, Indiana University Press, 1991.

Haldea, G. (1992), 'Indian Economy in the 1980s: A State of Drift', London School of Economics, unpublished.

Jalan, B. (ed.) (1992), *The Indian Economy: Problems and Prospects*, Delhi: Viking.

Lenin, V.I. (1916/1970), 'Imperialism, The Higher Stage of Capitalism', in *Selected Works, Vol. I*, Moscow: Progress Publishers.

Minhas, B., L.R. Jain and S. Tendulkar (1991), 'Declining Incidence of Poverty in the 1980s—Evidence versus Artefacts', *Economic and Political Weekly*, Vol. 26, Nos 27–8.

Mundle, S. and M.G.R. Rao (1991), 'The Volume and Composition of Government Subsidies in India, 1987–88', *Economic and Political Weekly*, Vol. 26, No. 18.

Patel, S.J. (1986), 'India's Regression in the World Economy', in S. Gulati and M. Shroff (eds), *Essays on Economic Progress and Welfare*.

Schumpeter, J.A. (1942), *Capitalism, Socialism and Democracy*.

16

Economic Reform

Stalled by Politics?

The Indian economic reform programme was launched in mid-1991, following the General Election in which the Congress emerged as the largest single party, though not with an absolute majority. Following the death of Rajiv Gandhi in May 1991, in the midst of the election campaign, P.V. Narasimha Rao was elected leader of the Congress party, and he duly became prime minister in June 1991. He chose as his finance minister Dr Manmohan Singh, who had previously been deputy chairman of the Planning Commission and governor of the Reserve Bank of India.

The need for reform was urgent. In January 1991, when foreign exchange reserves fell to a very low level and India's credit rating was downgraded, the country had been surprised and somewhat humiliated by the sudden prospect of defaulting on its international debt.[1] India at that time had foreign exchange reserves covering only two weeks' worth of imports, so a loan had to be raised in a hurry against the gold reserves of the Reserve Bank of India. The minority government of Chandra Shekhar, which had come into power only a few months previously, failed to do much to address this emergency. It was even unable to present the budget for 1991–2 (the Indian fiscal year runs from the first of April to the end of March) at its usual time in February, because the Congress party, which supported the minority government but was facing a particularly difficult election in the state of Tamil Nadu, did not wish to take responsibility for the higher taxes that had to be imposed, The presentation of the budget was, therefore, postponed, and in its place, a simple revenue statement was issued. Thus, even at a time of severe economic crisis, short-term and partisan political considerations had obstructed economic reform.

P. Oldenburg (ed.), *India Briefing: Staying the Course*, M.E. Sharpe, New York and London, 1995, pp. 79–95.

[1] See Deena Khatkhate (1992), 'India on an Economic Reform Trajectory', in Leonard A. Gordon and Philip Oldenburg (eds) (1992), *India Briefing, 1992*, Boulder, Colo: Westview, pp. 49–52.

The economic reforms subsequently launched by the Congress government surprised the world by their boldness. It seemed that the government was willing at last to jettison all the policies of the Nehru era. It took steps to abandon the dogma about self-sufficiency and fear of foreign capital; to cut tariffs and expose the economy to foreign competition; to end the special privileges enjoyed by big business by way of interest subsidies and favourable licenses to import and to expand capacity; to unleash the energy of small and medium-sized firms; and to contemplate the shutting down of loss-making public sector enterprises. All in all, this was a radical turnaround.

The surprise was that unlike the reforms in Eastern Europe, this radical change was not being initiated by a new party or even by new personnel. The same cadre that had been the guardian of the old order emerged as the champion of the new; the same ministers and officials who had defended the policies of protection and state guidance were now advocating and implementing liberalization programmes. Was this a genuine conversion or electoral window dressing? Will politics, unreformed and unrepentant of its role in causing the economic crisis, win again and stall the reforms before they have drastically changed the Indian economy?

Reforms: A Brief History

Reform was forced on India as much by the country's external debt position as by the liquidity squeeze caused by the Gulf war, which increased the oil bill and reduced the remittance payments of non-resident Indians, since large numbers of Indians were working in Iraq and had to flee from Kuwait. Moreover, as significant as the external debt, there was also a mounting internal debt. Although domestic savings had risen substantially between 1961 and 1990, from 12 per cent of Gross Domestic Product (GDP) to 24 per cent, the government had begun to eat into this source of funds since the mid-1970s when it began to be a net borrower on both the revenue (consumption) and capital (investment) accounts. The deficit on the revenue account mounted steadily through the years. Interest payments on the internal debt now amounted to one-fifth of the central budget. Something had to be done to tackle both external and internal debt.

During the first two years of reform there was progress on both fronts. Since then, foreign capital has flowed back, both in terms of portfolio capital and as direct investment. The budget deficit has come down. The foreign-exchange reserve position has dramatically improved since January 1991, to the point where $20 billion sits in the Reserve Bank's coffers and threatens to push up the rupee *vis-à-vis* hard currencies. Structural changes have been undertaken, in radical rejection of the Nehru–Mahalanobis strategy of developing India as a by and large closed capitalist economy with a leading public sector.[2] Tariffs are being cut; quotas are being converted into tariffs; restrictions on the expansion of private sector industries are being relaxed. Foreign capital is now being welcomed into a longer and longer list of activities—power, telecommunications, and oil

[2] For the Nehru–Mahalanobis strategy, see Meghnad Desai (1992), 'Is There Life After Mahalanobis? The Political Economy of India's New Economic Policy', *Indian Economic Review, Special Issue in Memory of Sukhamoy Chakravarty*, Vol. 27, pp. 155–64

exploration. Foreign collaboration with Indian private capital is also proceeding apace.

The 1992–3 budget had been bold in freeing the rupee from restrictions on the trade account, and the budget deficit was being cut along the lines laid down in the memorandum of understanding with the International Monetary Fund (IMF), reducing it from just over 8 per cent of GDP in 1990–1 to a projected 4.7 per cent of GDP in the budget of 1993–4. This radical budget, which liberalized the economy further, was an antidote to the fears raised by the Ayodhya events—the riots and turmoil in the wake of the destruction of the Babri mosque by militant Hindu nationalists in December 1992—that the Indian political system might not stand the strain of communal violence.[3] The liberalization of the rupee gave the signal that the reforms would not only continue but could accelerate.

Growth was, however, sluggish, and did not attain even the 5.5 per cent per annum rate reached in the 1980s. Another problem came from the considerable fear among the employees of public sector enterprises that they would lose their jobs as soon as an exit policy was in place, removing the restrictions that had made it all but impossible for management to fire workers in response to changed business conditions. During 1993 their fears were echoed by some of the leaders of the Bombay Club, an informal group from some of the largest Indian business houses, who met privately to coordinate their complaints about the liberalization process.[4] They articulated complaints about foreign capital being favoured and voiced the need for a level playing field to protect Indian capital.

Prime Minister Rao has never been a bold man. While he backed his finance minister to the hilt, he failed to generate any enthusiasm for reform. There was no platform in the party or in the country for drumming up popular support for the reforms. At the Davos Conference in February 1994, Rao articulated a cautious philosophy. He said that the collapse of communism did not necessarily mean the total acceptance of a market economy, and that India had been saved from 'political submission and economic dependence' because it had followed a 'middle path' between the two.[5]

Much of the rest of 1993 was quiescent on the reform front. The reason for this was obvious. The government was facing mid-term elections in some of the larger states in North India—Uttar Pradesh, Madhya Pradesh, and Rajasthan—and in Delhi and Himachal Pradesh. Electoral considerations can never be ignored in a democracy, and in the Indian federal polity elections come often. Since 1972 elections to state assemblies have tended not to coincide with the national general elections, particularly since the 1980s. Each set of elections compels caution at the national level as well as at state levels, as the party in power hopes to improve its fortunes. The Ayodhya events had put Congress on the defensive *vis-à-vis* the Bharatiya Janata Party (BJP), which had captured power in Uttar Pradesh and Madhya Pradesh in the previous round of state elections. So the Congress decided

---

[3] See Ashutosh Varshney, 'Battling the Past, Forging a Future? Ayodhya and Beyond', in Philip Oldenburg (ed.), 1993), *India Briefing, 1993*, Boulder, Colo.: Westview.

[4] The formal existence of the Bombay Club, which is also referred to as the Bombay Group, is difficult to confirm.

[5] See the report in the *Times of India* (Bombay), 2 February 1994.

that pushing reform too far, too fast might cost it valuable seats in the 1993 elections.

As it happened, the BJP's onward march was checked during those elections: although it won handsomely in Delhi and retained power in Rajasthan, it lost power (but not vote share) in Uttar Pradesh and Madhya Pradesh. Although the economic reform was not an issue in those elections, the pace of reform did not resume during 1994. The 1994–5 budget was a cautious one: the finance minister did not even attempt to cut the deficit and gave a signal thereby that the political resistance to cutting subsidies to farmers and to public enterprises was gaining ground.

Not only was the budget deficit not cut, it was stabilized at a relatively high level of 6 per cent, despite the fact that the deficit for 1993–4 had actually turned out to be 7.3 per cent as against the projected 4.7 per cent. There were rumours that the rupee might be liberalized further, allowing for convertibility on the capital account—restricted convertibility on the current account had already been introduced—but nothing was done in the budget about it.

Since early 1994 the reforms have been confined to areas outside the scrutiny of Parliament. Thus the government gave a formal assurance to the Reserve Bank that it would be restrained in its short-term borrowing and not finance its deficit by selling short-term Treasury bills (which banks could then use to expand their loans). In effect, this meant printing money, an indication that in order to finance its expenditure, the government was not willing either to increase taxation or to borrow with interest from the public. There was also a deregulation of the money markets and interest rates. Both these moves were accomplished by bilateral negotiations between the Ministry of Finance and the Reserve Bank, requiring no parliamentary discussions.

But, apart from these technical moves, reforms were put on hold. In November 1994, there was yet another round of state elections, this time largely in South India—Andhra Pradesh (the prime minister's home state), Karnataka, and Goa, along with Sikkim in the north. Congress lost power in Andhra Pradesh, and decisively so, coming in third behind Telugu Desam and the Communists. In Karnataka too, the Congress lost, and the Janata came to power again, with the BJP pushing Congress into third place. It was not at all clear whether the reforms were at fault, but many commentators claimed that the poor felt they had been neglected in recent years and that the reforms were benefiting only the middle classes. Whatever the truth of the matter, with the Congress having lost in three of the four major states that went to the polls in February and March 1995, the prime minister was unlikely to push reforms further at the present juncture.

As has often happened before—in the 1950s, 1960s, and 1980s—questions arise as to whether India can politically sustain radical economic policy, or whether politics will mould economics in its own conservative shape. Has reform had its day until the next crisis?

In its 44 years of planned economic development, India has repeatedly experienced short bursts of radical action on the economic front, which were then checked or reversed by political considerations. The first such episode was the launching in 1955 of the bold framework for the Second Five Year Plan by

P.C. Mahalanobis, then an unofficial but very powerful adviser to the prime minister. The Mahalanobis framework was not only a plan for eventual self-sufficient development of the Indian economy, but it was also a decisive move away from a *laissez-faire* strategy for Indian industrialization, as well as from the Gandhian strategy of decentralized, village-level, agriculture-oriented development. It asked for a big resource commitment by way of voluntary savings as well as taxation. Taxes on income, expenditure, and wealth were proposed; imports were to be curtailed, especially for consumer goods. This was the boldest move yet toward a socialist pattern of society, a goal that had been approved by the Congress party at Nehru's behest at the Awadi All-India Congress Committee meeting in 1954.

By 1958 there was a foreign exchange crisis, and the plan had to be pruned. It turned out that imports had been inadequately controlled, perhaps wilfully so, by the then finance minister, T.T. Krishnamachari, no friend of Nehruvian socialism. Taxation could not be increased because of resistance, within the Congress as well as from the rich and the middle classes, so the government had to borrow from abroad or get foreign aid. In addition, food shortage was imminent, dictating a resource transfer to agriculture, hitherto a low priority item in the Mahalanobis plan. And so the plan was pruned (the Planning Commission lowered the targets, protecting projects in iron and steel, power, railways, and the like, but cutting allocations to social services, among other things);[6] US aid was welcomed; and the need to keep food prices low was recognized.

The next such episode, though in the reverse direction from the leftward thrust of the 1950s, was in the mid-1960s. The Third Five Year Plan had continued the Nehru–Mahalanobis strategy of industrialization, but the outcome of the first two years was disappointing. The China–India war in 1962 further undermined Nehru's reputation and brought on the added burden of increased defence expenditure. After Nehru's death in 1964, there was an attempt by the new prime minister, Lal Bahadur Shastri, to change the emphasis and direct the plans more toward agriculture. There followed two bad harvests, reinforcing the need for agricultural development. The Fourth Five Year Plan, scheduled to start in 1965–6, was postponed; indeed, a four-year 'plan holiday' was declared. At the same time, the first 'miracle seeds' that made the Green Revolution possible were introduced. This turnaround from industry to agriculture, from rapid growth of capital goods to slow but consolidated growth in food output, constituted an alternative path of development for India, much more Gandhian and conservative, much less dirigiste and socialist. Even after the sudden death of Shastri in January 1966, his successor, Indira Gandhi, continued on this path. Her government devalued the rupee, as a gesture toward market-friendly policies, though not without extreme pressure from the United States.

This market-friendly, agriculture-oriented policy was reversed within three years. By 1969, Mrs Gandhi had decided to break with this pattern and go for another bout of nationalization, this time of commercial banks, and she reverted to the autarkic Mahalanobis strategy. Apart from a much more comfortable

---

[6] See Francine Frankel (1978), *India's Political Economy, 1947–1977: The Gradual Revolution*, Princeton, N.J.: Princeton University Press, pp. 147–9.

position in foodgrain supply, what had caused the reversal from the 'rightist' to the 'leftist' policy was the exigencies of domestic politics. Mrs Gandhi had been elevated to power by the right-wing Congress 'syndicate', a group of powerful regional bosses who thought they could manipulate her. Her bid for independence was couched in political terms as a change in policy and, with support from the two Communist parties [Communist Party of India (CPI) and Communist Party of India-Marxist (CPI(M))] she was able to carry it through. With the nationalization of the 14 largest banks and Indira Gandhi's backing of the rival presidential candidate against the Syndicate's nominee, the Congress party was split and India began the period of personalized politics.

This radical lurch lasted until 1974. Not only banks but insurance companies were nationalized. There was even an attempt at nationalizing wholesale trade in foodgrains, which backfired and had to be abandoned. The limits to this policy were again political, though this time the pressures were due to widespread unrest caused by inflationary pressures. Consumer agitation, an impending strike by railworkers, and a threat to Mrs Gandhi's position and power, triggered by a court decision that would have barred her from elective office, brought about the Emergency, in which, among other things, opposition leaders were jailed, press censorship imposed, and a series of constitutional amendments passed that curbed the power of the judiciary *vis-à-vis* Parliament. During the Emergency, despite the rhetoric, policy became less left-oriented

With the Janata Party's defeat of Mrs Gandhi in the general election of 1977, there was again a reversal in policy, though more in words than in implementation. The protectionist regime continued, as did the suspicion of foreign capital, symbolized by the steps that forced the departure of IBM and Coca-Cola. But as in the mid-1960s the emphasis was on rural development, on Gandhian principles, and on reserving a significant amount of manufacturing for the small-scale sector. Again, something akin to a plan holiday occurred, with reduced activity on the part of the government as a way to boost private investment. The Janata experiment fell apart in battles over policies and position between groups and parties as diverse as the Hindu nationalist Jan Sangh, former Socialist Party leaders, and peasant farmer leaders. General elections in the beginning of 1980 brought Mrs Gandhi back, with her slogan 'a government that works'.

The next episode of radical policy-making came under Rajiv Gandhi, who succeeded his mother after her assassination in October 1984. Mrs Gandhi had already moved toward borrowing from the IMF to relieve resource constraints due to the impact of the second 'oil shock'—itself a major departure for a Nehruvian. To be sure, the last installment of that record-sized approved loan was not taken, mainly because of left-wing political opposition, both within the Congress and without, to US-influenced international financial institutions. But Rajiv Gandhi accelerated both the borrowing and the opening up of the economy, instituting a policy of import liberalization and industry deregulation. The exchange rate was actively manipulated to depreciate the rupee and thereby encourage exports. Incentives were given to exporters: half of export profits were deductible for income tax purposes—for example, the interest rate on export trade was reduced from 12 per cent to 9 per cent, and duty-free input of capital goods was allowed in selected export industries. This policy did not touch the public sector, nor was the public sector given priority for new industrial products and processes. Rajiv's was a policy of accelerating growth by borrowing, but without any drastic restructuring of the economy.

Again by 1988, the policy had run aground. Political problems caused by unrest in Punjab, as well as allegations that bribes given by the Swedish defence manufacturer Bofors had been accepted at the highest level, led to a loss of confidence in the government, which produced the election result of late 1989, Rajiv Gandhi lost, inaugurating the period of minority party governments.

CONTINUITY AND CHANGE

Thus, one way of characterizing the Indian economic scene is as a series of experiments in changing policy, with each experiment halted on account of political exigencies. Usually the pressures are democratic—consumer agitation, as in 1974, or electoral considerations, as in 1977, 1980, and 1989. This view of the Indian polity as subject to frequently reversed lurches of policy is not the usual one.[7] Bardhan, Chakravarty, and others have argued that the Indian economy has been stalemated by a delicate balance of class forces. They have put this explanation forward to model the 30 years of low but persistent growth: at about 3.5 per cent per annum from 1950 to 1980, this was the so-called Hindu rate of growth ('so-called' only because the technical term for such a long-term growth rate is the 'secular' rate of growth and the contrast between 'secular' and 'Hindu' has a unique Indian flavour suggesting a long-term increase, but at a rate barely above stagnation). The argument is that the prosperous farmers, the big industrialists, and the urban unionized workers, along with the urban middle classes, each constitute a powerful force, but none so powerful as to dominate the others. In order to maintain the social balance, each has to accommodate the demands of the other. The farmers want subsidized inputs and high output prices; big business wants tariff protection, interest subsidies, and low income taxes; and the urban middle classes want job security and inflation-proof salaries. Together this leads to a wastage of resources and a low rate of accumulation and growth. If any one class could dominate, then a clear and bold accumulation policy, albeit in the interests of that class, would emerge.[8]

This explanation is partial in many respects. It was first advanced to explain the low growth of the Indian economy between 1950 and 1980 when, as mentioned above, GDP grew at an average rate of 3.5 per cent (1.25 per cent per capita). The 1980s witnessed an acceleration in this average to around 5.5 per cent (3.5 per cent in per capita terms). Thus both the stagnation and the acceleration need

[7] In a recently published book, Little and Joshi similarly periodize 1964–91. See I.M.D. Little and Vijay Joshi (1994), *India: Macroeconomics and Political Economy, 1964–1991*, Washington, D.C.: World Bank.

[8] Pranab Bardhan (1984), *The Political Economy of Development in India*, Oxford: Basil Blackwell and Sukhmoy Chakravarty (1987), *Development Planning: The Indian Experience*, Oxford: Clarendon Press; see also a different approach in Jagdish Bhagwati (1993), *India in Transition*, Oxford: Clarendon Press, and Deepak Lal (1988), *The Hindu Equilibrium*, Oxford: Clarendon Press.

explaining. But even in the earlier period the growth rate was characterized by volatile fluctuations around a steady trend. Take, for example, the 20 years between 1961 and 1980, when the GDP growth rate per annum averaged 3.5 per cent, but ranged from 3.7 per cent in 1965–6 to 9.0 per cent in 1975–6. Since 1980 the average has been higher, at 5.5 per cent, but the range has been from 10.4 per cent in 1988–9 to nearly zero in 1991–2.

Thus a pattern of short-run dash and reversal is a better way of characterizing the growth rate than 'slow and steady'. While the Latin American economies have been notorious for their hyperinflation and the East European economies in transition have experienced the same disease,[9] India has had a remarkable record in never having experienced sustained inflation at double-digit levels, measured annually. Only in three, widely separated periods (1967–8, 1973–5, and 1980–1) has it reached that level for any length of time, and only in nine years out of the last 35. However, inflation was a crucial issue in 1974—when measures to control it may have contributed to the challenge to Indira Gandhi—and in the 1980 election, where the price rise in onions was used as a symbol of inflation.

The political economy of India has to be rethought to explain both the low but volatile income growth, with occasional spurts due to radical policy change, and the absence of runaway inflation. It can be argued that a class analysis, though not wrong, is only a partial answer. What strikes the observer of the democratic political sphere—the arena of parliamentary elections and government formation and rule—is not a stable stalemate of class formations but a kaleidoscopic shift of alliances and groupings based on caste (*jati*), region, language, and religion. As we have seen, the 1970s witnessed a breakdown of the monolithic Congress party, which split into personalized factions. The merger of disparate parties to form the Janata in 1977 was quickly followed by their dissolution.

Since 1967, again with the exception of the Emergency, there has also been a shifting pattern of one- or multi-party rule at the state level. Purely regional parties dominate today in Tamil Nadu (Dravida Munnetra Kazhagam and All-India Anna Dravida Munnetra Kazhagam), Andhra Pradesh (Telugu Desam), Punjab (Akali Dal), and West Bengal (the CPI(M) is, despite everything, a Bengal party). Often, the party at the Centre (usually the Congress) is not in power in a majority of the states, a situation rarely encountered before 1967. Except for the Indira/Rajiv Gandhi governments of 1980–9, national governments have not been able to rely on one party for support. Mrs Gandhi relied heavily on Communist support in the 1967–77 period, and every other government has been forced to act similarly.

There is, however, a high level of competence in the country's civil service and technical personnel. Thus any government that fears inflation, and the consequent unpopularity, has at its disposal an effective set of officials who know how to reverse inflation; indeed, every government minority, coalition or otherwise, that has had to deal with this problem has, by and large, done so successfully. In addition to fiscal tightening, this has usually required importing food grains or other essential commodities, or releasing food grains from available stocks. There

[9] Michael Bruno (1993), *Crisis, Stabilisation and Economic Reform*, Oxford: Oxford University Press.

has been occasional delay, as in the sugar scam of 1994 when, whether because of bureaucratic and political incompetence and infighting, or something even less savory, the central government overestimated domestic sugar production and consequently was forced to enter the international market when prices had increased substantially. This led finally to the resignation of Food and Civil Supplies Minister Kalpanath Rai. But overall, especially when a short period of double digit inflation has led to unrest, the system has responded quickly.

It has been much more difficult to pursue growth-enhancing policies consistently, because in an inflationary situation, those who gain are a small minority: traders, hoarders, and speculators, for example. Growth requires resource mobilization, continued sacrifice of consumption in order to increase investment, and differential rewards. Growth raises distributional issues that divide the polity in different ways depending on the policy pursued. Thus, while the Green Revolution helped all farmers, those who grew wheat benefited more than those who grew other crops, and larger farmers benefited more than small farmers, especially when they had access to cheap water and power. Policies of retrenching the public sector to let the private sector expand, or deregulating interest rates so as to level the playing field between large and small business, benefit some factions and hurt others. A reduced public sector hurts trade unions linked to political parties, for example.[10] Interest rates that are allowed to fall to market levels make loans to many small businesses less attractive,

It is difficult, therefore, to build up a sustained coalition for reform. For a time the gainers support and the losers oppose, and a large proportion of the population stands in the middle waiting for the fruits of reform. But if the process falters or is seen to benefit particular groups persistently, then democratic opposition mounts. The coalitions that form the fragile majority are broken up. This process may start at the state level or at the national level, and change at one level feeds into the other. Thus the Congress party's electoral defeats of late 1994 and early 1995 at the state level will have an impact on the government at the centre, even though its own majority is formally not at risk. And there is already a factional split developing in the Congress party, with the expulsion of Arjun Singh and the fall of the Kerala government headed by Prime Minister Rao's ally Karunakaran in March 1995.

The fragility of the ruling coalition at the state and at the national level is heightened by the first-past-the-post electoral system, in which the winner takes all even when he or she does not command an absolute majority of the votes cast. This leads to small swings in the overall share of the votes translating into large swings in the number of seats won or lost. The system puts a premium on broad, all-encompassing coalitions representing every shade of opinion or every known vote bank, But by the same token, since their components have nothing but the desire to win office as a cement, these coalitions fall apart at the first whiff of likely defeat.

This is of course not an iron law. In the 1950s and 1960s, the Congress was a single broad-based party that represented such a coalition, but a well-disciplined

[10] See E.A. Ramaswamy (1995), 'Organized Labor and Economic Reform' in Philip Oldenburg (ed.), *India Briefing: Staying the Course*, New York: M.E. Sharpe, pp. 97–128.

one, The Congress leadership—the so-called High Command—gave orders to those levels below, who in turn fed back grass-roots reactions to policy changes. The presence of a nationally recognized, charismatic leader, Jawaharlal Nehru, also helped. Since 1969, when Indira Gandhi split the Congress party, not only had the discipline gone but so had the feedback mechanism. All that remains is the high-handedness of the High Command, which often dismisses provincial Congress chief ministers and party leaders only to settle personal scores.

Indian democracy can thus be seen as a continuous process of coalition formation, whatever the formal party labels of the people in power. This coalition formation is the result not only of the fragmentation of the once hegemonic Congress party, but also of the articulation of interest groups that are able to manipulate the electoral system by shifting large quantities of votes from one party to another in return for favours. Log-rolling and pork-barrelling, well-known phenomena in American politics, are constantly at play in India. Loan *melas* (literally, 'fairs'), where generous and not-to-be-repaid loans are given out by the touring ministers, are one example of pork-barrelling. Large budget deficits run by individual states eager to spend money but not to tax their citizens, and a similar indulgence at the central level only writ large, are elements in the same shifting equilibrium.

THE PROBLEM TODAY

Brief periods of implementing necessary but politically distasteful economic measures and exercising fiscal restraint have been quickly reversed; the recent course of reform is no exception. The initial budgets under the reform regime did succeed in cutting the deficit, from 8.25 per cent of GDP for 1989–90 and 1990–1 to 5.8 per cent in 1991–2, and just 5 per cent for 1992–3. For 1993–4, a lower budget deficit of around 4.7 per cent was envisaged, but, as had often been seen in the pre-reform days, as a consequence of the failure to reduce certain subsidies, among other things, it actually increased to 7.3 per cent. The remarkable feature of the 1994–5 budget is that even the attempt to bring the deficit down was abandoned. By forecasting a deficit of 6.5 per cent the finance minister signalled that there was no longer a sense of urgency in the government of India about economic reform.

True, to a limited extent the higher deficit of 1993–4 and the high deficit that came to pass in 1994–5 are due to the sluggishness of the economy. With import duties having been cut, and with the necessary upsurge in imports having failed to materialize, the revenue outcome was disappointing. But the prime culprit was the overrun in expenditure. Despite the higher-than-planned 1993–4 deficit, the finance minister still increased planned expenditure above previous projections. In 1993–4, expenditure was Rs 12,549 crores higher (about 9 per cent) than the projected Rs 131,323 crores, while revenue was Rs 8117 crores (or about 9.5 per cent) less than the projected Rs 84,867 crores. The expenditure overrun consisted of items like Rs 900 crores extra for fertilizer subsidies as well as Rs 632 crores to states for providing concessions to farmers on decontrolled fertilizers, Rs 856 crores were given to states to cover their open deficits, and Rs 2320 crores extra were given for defence. All these items, though individually minor, are signs of business as usual having resumed in the Indian polity.

It was no surprise also that for 1994–5 the non-plan expenditure was to be raised from Rs 97,846 crores to Rs 105,117 crores, while the plan expenditure was to be Rs 70,141 crores. (The category 'non-plan expenditure' corresponds to current consumption, and plan expenditure is capital/developmental expenditure, i.e. planned investment in particular projects—a new railway line, for example—or in a sector of the economy.) The pattern of non-plan expenditure exceeding plan expenditure, outturn exceeding estimates, and rising interest payments has come back as before.

It is not because of its inflationary impact that the size of the deficit is important. It was quite correct for the finance minister to say that the stocks of foodgrains, at 32 million tons by mid-1994, are an adequate guard against inflation. But what he did not say is that in such a case there was no call to offer the farmers higher procurement prices. It is not sound economics to subsidize food production when adequate buffer stocks exist. It is, however, a symptom of the ambivalence of Indian political circles about the reforms. Apart from the prime minister and the finance minister, no one else in the Cabinet has come out enthusiastically for the reform. No popular political platform in support of reform has been established. This has allowed opposition parties to build up an anti-reform coalition. The BJP has joined this coalition, despite its earlier image as a pro-business party. The BJP rhetoric is now economic nationalist, and repeats many of the things the Left used to say and still does: that foreign companies should not be allowed free rein to produce goods Indian companies make; that economic decision making has shifted to Washington (they made a great fuss over the alleged transmission of the budget to the IMF before it was presented to Parliament); and so on.

The BJP and the Left claim, not without some justification, that the reforms have only helped the rich. But it is more accurate to say that the reform has cleared a space in which business can grow and the middle classes will benefit, and that the reforms have not gone sufficiently deep in removing older vested interests—of the subsidized farmers, the loss-making public enterprises, and the interest-subsidized industries—in order to create room for redistribution to the poor.

The enemies of the reforms are those who did well out of the old subsidy/ protection/licence/permit raj. Politicians and bureaucrats were able to extend their patronage (by ensuring that industries hired far more workers than needed, for example) and often extracted large bribes from business executives, either to fight elections or to line their own pockets. While their rhetoric is pro-poor, in actual practice the politicians and bureaucrats delivered slow growth in income and slower alleviation of poverty than in, for example, Indonesia, Malaysia, or even Pakistan.

The defeat of the Congress party in the recent state elections can be traced in part to sophisticated voting behaviour by the Muslims and the lower castes, who no longer gravitate naturally to the Congress. Rao's compromises and delays on the Ayodhya temple problem and his reluctance to challenge the BJP on secularism may be as potent reasons as the reforms for Congress losses. But it is easier for the opposition to try to convince voters that India's sovereignty is under threat because the reforms are imposed from the outside. It will be very tempting for the Congress to soft-pedal reform.

THE ANTI-REFORM PLATFORM

The reforms have been attacked on several fronts: first, exit policy, changed laws that permit the closure of factories and other company units, including those in the public sector, at the complete discretion of the owners; second 'entry policy', the conditions under which foreign capital, including non-resident Indian capital, can buy into Indian firms; and third, the GATT treaty and liberalization of the trade regime. On each of these issues the government seems to have preferred to play down reform and introduce it almost by stealth, certainly without fanfare, and the popular stake in the success of the reforms has not been canvassed.

Exit Policy

The main resistance to an exit policy comes, of course, from trade unions supported by Left parties. The celebration for the third anniversary, of Narasimha Rao's accession to power was spoiled by a nationwide strike on 14 July 1994, in which all trade union federations except the Congress-affiliated one joined. Although the 2.3 million workers who honoured the strike represent a small minority of workers, or even of industrial workers, the political impact was considerable.

The government has failed to make clear to the public that losses in the public sector create high deficits, which in turn require high taxes and high interest rates.[11] It has not exposed the contribution to this problem that comes from the relatively privileged position of public sector workers, whose earnings have risen faster than per capita GDP over the last 25 years. In 1992–3, 104 of 237 state-owned units recorded losses amounting to Rs 40 billion. Of the remaining 133 units, many have low returns, while few have been highly successful.

The cautious approach to privatization has been to issue equity in the successful public sector units first. Thus, on the eve of the 1994–5 budget, it was announced that seven major state-owned enterprises would sell part of their equity. These were the Steel Authority of India Ltd., Hindustan Petroleum, Bharat Heavy Electricals Ltd., Hindustan Machine Tools Ltd., Bharat Petroleum, Hindustan Zinc Ltd., and Bharat Earth Movers Ltd. This partial equity sell-off, mainly to domestic buyers, was expected to raise Rs 35 billion (Rs 49.5 billion had been raised up to March 1995). There has also been a move to allow Videsh Sanchar Nigam Ltd. to raise capital abroad, and although the initial bid to raise $1 billion of global depository receipts, via Euroissue, had to be withdrawn, this will be accomplished sooner rather than later.[12]

[11] Meghnad Desai (1993), 'Capitalism, Socialism and the Indian Economy', Exim Bank Lecture, Bombay, January. See Chapter 15.

[12] Global depository receipts allow foreign investors to buy equity in India by proxy: an agent of a bank buys equity in India and puts the certificates in a safe deposit box in India. The receipt of deposit is traded in European and American markets.

But it is not enough to divest shares of profitable companies. The exit policy has been sluggish in shedding failed enterprises. Ironically, many of the loss-making industries in the public sector, such as the textile mills, do not fulfil any of the criteria of the original industrial policy strategy laid down in 1956. They are consumer-goods-producing, non-basic industries that were taken into the public sector as a way of nationalizing private sector losses, and they have continued to make losses. The National Renewal Fund, which was set up to cushion job losses, had spent Rs 78.62 billion by October 1993 on 60,000 workers.[13] Only 59 companies have been referred to the Board for Industrial and Financial Reconstruction to evaluate their solvency. Given the size of the workforce that could be let go without harming production, and the number of companies in deep financial trouble, these are very small steps.

The government's dilemma is clear. While it can partially or wholly privatize the profitable companies, loss-making companies cannot be privatized, since no one will buy equity in a negative net worth company. They have to be either shut down or kept open just to provide jobs. The latter 'solution' is epitomized, in the extreme, by the Hindustan Fertilizer plant at Haldia, which employs 1550 workers but has no production whatsoever! Indeed, the plant has produced nothing since 1986 when it was commissioned. As the *Financial Times* reported, 'There is a canteen, a personnel department, and an accounts department. There are promotions, job changes, pay rises, audits, and in-house trade unions. Engineers, electricians, plumbers and painters maintain the equipment with a care that is almost surreal.'[14]

It is doubtful that there will be any rapid move on exit policy. Since the National Renewal Fund is spending roughly Rs 1.3 million per redundant worker, the budgetary burden itself will be heavy. The recent election results will make exit policy even more problematical. Like China, India may live with an inefficient public sector for a long time.

Entry Policy

There has been much greater progress in throwing the economy open to foreign investment, though even here there are considerable doubts about loss of sovereignty, unfair competition from abroad, and the like. Thus the state telephone monopoly has been ended and private foreign capital has been invited to compete. Foreign companies have been allowed to enter the field of oil and gas exploration. The industry ministry announced on 6 June 1994, that it had cleared 7.3 new foreign investment proposals worth Rs 10 billion ($322.5 million). These ranged from food processing to textiles and agro-products, software, banking, information processing, medical instrumentation, and more. Foreign equity participation even up to 51 per cent will be allowed in high-priority sectors, and 100 per cent foreign-owned units will be allowed elsewhere.

This move toward opening out the economy did not meet with total enthusiasm on the part of the large industrialists, the organized private sector. Having

---

[13] Ministry of Finance, Government of India, *Economic Survey, 1994–1995*.
[14] Stefan Wagstyl, *Financial Times* (London), 6 June 1994.

lived for so many years behind the shelter of tariffs, subsidized interest rates, and valuable licenses, Indian big business finds the prospect of competition unnerving. The complaint was that these foreigners, including non-resident Indians, have special advantages inasmuch as they can borrow abroad at cheaper rates and have better deals regarding capacity expansion than the local business people. Yet, as 1994 progressed and direct foreign investment flowed in, many of the same business leaders were able to enter into collaborative arrangements with foreign companies. Business was, by the end of 1994, much happier with the reforms.

The opposition parties continued to be ambivalent, however. The BJP moved during the year to a much more accommodating position on foreign capital, criticizing only the kinds of product lines in which foreigners were entering. The Rashtriya Swayamsevak Sangh, the core 'cultural' organization of the Hindu nationalist 'family', is much more uncompromising about allowing in foreign capital. The election reverses of the Congress party, and the BJP's gains in Karnataka, Gujarat, and especially Maharashtra, may yet revive the nationalist fervor.

The indicators of business performance, despite misgivings on the part of business, look bullish. The Centre for Monitoring the Indian Economy (CMIE) reported in July 1994 that for a sample of 1200 companies, net profits for 1993–4 were 83 per cent higher than in the previous fiscal year. This is partly a result of changes in company law interpretations that permitted a lower provision for depreciation than previously, but is also due to lower interest rates. Tax incidence fell from 33 per cent in 1991–2 and 27 per cent in 1992–3 to 16 per cent in 1993–4. Sales growth in real terms also doubled between 1992–3 and 1993–4. But despite a fall in the interest rates, the ratio of interest to sales has grown over the last three years. The organized private sector is one interest group that stands to gain from accelerated reforms via lower interest rates as well as lower taxes.

GATT

Nowhere did economic nationalism show up more virulently and somewhat absurdly than in the Indian agitation against the Dunkel draft of the General Agreement on Tariffs and Trade (GATT). All sorts or unfounded fears were raised in the public mind about the likely effect of the GATT treaty on India. For example, the provision for patenting biotechnology innovations was alleged to mean that if they refused to pay royalties, Indians would be barred from planting neem trees, which scientists have shown to have important medicinal qualities (as Indian villagers have long believed). The campaign was a well-financed one based on the fears of industries such as pharmaceuticals that the new law on intellectual property would restrict their present evasion of the spirit of patent law (Indian law now protects processes but not ultimate product; one can thus legally 'reverse engineer' an imported product and develop a different method of making it). The government for a long time did little to counter some of the more absurd fears. Its attempt to forge a unified line for the G77 ('Group of 77' countries—now many more—that represent the South, or industrializing countries, in international debates and organizations) during the Uruguay Round negotiations had borne no fruit. This was because the initial impetus behind the Uruguay Round came from the industrializing countries themselves, as is clear from the Uruguayan origin of the conference. There is as much fear in the industrialized countries of competition from the cheap labour of the South as there is fear in India of the old adage that 'free trade equals neoimperialism'.

It is some indication of the isolation of Indian politicians of all parties that there was a serious demand to 'cancel the pact', or a fond hope that at the last minute the world would stop and modify the GATT treaty to suit India's demands: No one had pointed out that not signing the GATT treaty would lose India its Most Favored Nation status around the world and damage exports severely. While China is impatient to join GATT, India thought it could choose to leave it.[15] No one in the government was honest enough or bold enough to counter some of the wild propaganda. As in other areas of economic policy, reform is seen as a technical matter, to be defended only by the finance minister and his civil servants. All the other ministers and leading politicians are waiting to see if the reforms will succeed or falter, and keeping their powder dry for either eventuality. Now, with the defeat of Congress governments and some major leaders such as Sharad Pawar in state elections, some politicians may openly jump onto the anti-reform bandwagon.

The Prospect

In the short run, the Congress cannot disown the economic reforms. It has few other achievements to its credit. But, as was indicated by the prime minister in his first major speech on economic reform since the election reverses in late 1994 and early 1995, there will be a slowdown in opening the economy. The entry policy will be tightened and the exit policy will be put on hold. The budget for 1995–6 presented in mid-March 1995 confirmed this. The outcome for the budget deficit for 1994–5 was above the projected 6.5 per cent, but only slightly. For the coming year, there will be no attempt to bring it down much below 6 per cent, and the outcome may yet end up at 6.5 per cent. A gesture was made to increase rural employment, but no attempt was made to cut fertilizer subsidies or accelerate the exit of loss-making public sector units. While the budget did not go so far as giving a subsidy for rice for the poor, the message is that populism will be pursued.

There are systemic reasons for this, as I have argued above. A sustained reform package would require a government at the Centre with a substantial majority. This government would have to have its party in power in a large number of states. It would help if it were led by a nationally recognizable prime minister rather than one who has a fragile regional base. Such a leader might be able to build a pro-reform coalition from all the factions that stand to gain from the reforms: small and big business; employees in the unorganized sector; rural and urban poor, who would benefit if the burden of taxation and the benefits of subsidies were more equitably distributed; and consumers, who will enjoy lower

---

[15] For some popular fears, see Hardev S. Sanotra (1994), 'Anti-GATT Movement Spreading Waves of Confusion', *India Today*, 15 May. Even this excellent periodical did not deal with the GATT until the date of signing the treaty.

prices as the tariffs come down among others. Rajiv Gandhi created such a coalition briefly in the mid-1980s, as did Indira Gandhi for a different sort of platform in the early 1970s. But both these leaders also discovered that it is not enough to have the rhetoric for reform: there has to be effective delivery of change while, at the same time, careful watch is kept on any adverse turn in the economy that might exacerbate the negative effects. This means controlling inflation above all, securing steady food supplies, and taking swift action against unanticipated shocks like the recent outbreak of plague.

Such a powerful governing coalition seems highly unlikely, even in the long run. It is improbable that the number of political parties will decrease, or that the parties will become more disciplined or ideological. The best prospect would be for a revived Congress party that could fold back into itself some of the smaller fractions that have wandered off into the many Janata parties existing today. Such a Congress might even be able to reform the electoral rules to ensure proportional representation and greater stability in the political system. Economic policy requires a medium-term perspective to be effective. As of now, the political system cannot guarantee such a perspective. It is too dominated by electoral pressures and, given its current fragile state, elections occur far too often and cause far too many reversals of policy. An unreformed political system is an obstacle to fundamental and irreversible economic reform.

References

Bardhan, Pranab (1984), *The Political Economy of Development in India*, Oxford: Basil Blackwell.

Bhagwati, Jagdish (1993), *India in Transition*, Oxford: Clarendon Press.

Chakravarty, Sukhamoy (1987), *Development Planning: The Indian Experience*, Oxford: Clarendon Press.

Desai, Meghnad (1992), 'Is There Life After Mahalanobis? The Political Economy of India's New Economic Policy', *Indian Economic Review, Special Issue in Memory of Sukhamoy Chakravarty*, Vol. 27, pp. 155–64. See also Chapter 12.

Lal, Deepak (1988), *The Hindu Equilibrium*, Oxford: Clarendon Press.

Little, I.M.D., Vijay Joshi (1994), *India: Macroeconomics and Political Economy, 1964–1991*, Washington, D.C.: World Bank.

17

India's Triple Bypass

Economic Liberalization, the BJP, and the 1996 Elections

I have been asked to deal with three things: what has happened to economic reform in India since 1991, where does the Bharatiya Janata Party stand on liberalization, and what do the economic policies look like in the lead-up to the April 1996 elections.

The major thrust of liberal economic reform in India has now spent itself and while the reforms are irreversible the analogy is that of a bullock cart stuck in the mud: it is irreversible but that does not help very much: it is not going anywhere. It is not going anywhere because, as a lot of us have said, there are clearly tremendous democratic pressures in India. India is a federal polity with regular elections—and we are going to have national elections very soon. In the current pre-election climate, I see no political party, and no faction within any political party, which will take a positive view on liberalization. I think this is unfortunate. I think it is wrong. But that is my view. A consensus view has emerged in India that, yes, a lot of reform has happened, the economy has liberalized, and it is not likely to go back to the pre-1991 or the pre-1980 Indian economy (people forget that a lot of reforms happened in the 1980s and of course, there was another set of reforms in the 1990s). I do not think there is any danger of going back to the 1970s but by the same token there is going to be a great difficulty in pushing forward reforms in the one or two major areas in which they have not fully realized themselves.

The reason is that, in popular perception, the reforms by and large have not helped the poor. They have not generated extra jobs and they have basically benefited only a very small minority. Therefore, it is the task of a political party which wants to win political elections to say reforms are all right, but we must modify them, we must moderate them, we must qualify them and look after this other dimension. It is significant that in the national Cabinet, except

'Heretical Views of Modern India,' *Asian Studies Review*, Vol. 19, No. 3, April 1996.

for Dr Manmohan Singh (finance minister) and now Commerce Minister Mr Chidambaram, there is no minister who is positively for economic reform and willing to argue its case up and down the country .

The case for reform, a case which I argued back in 1993,[1] is that fast and radical integration a globalizing economy is India's best imaginable anti-poverty programme. Everything India did before 1991 failed to alleviate poverty. It is not true that before the economic liberalization, India was a socialist heaven. Indeed, in all the statistics one can think of, such as literacy and life expectancy, India was behind the average of all developing economies and therefore, despite its claim to be a democratic socialist republic, it was not actually doing very well compared to capitalist countries like Indonesia and Malaysia in terms of its anti-poverty programme or the health or well-being of its people. So I think that nobody has been able to say that all that rhetoric is convincing.

The reform process has been slower than one would like to see partly because old vested interests have been very hard to contain. So all those subsidies continue and all those old burdens on the fiscal budget continue and state chief ministers are not stopped from getting into fiscal adventurism of the most gross nature (such as giving away rice at Rs 2 per kilo). I do not care if they do it provided they raise enough taxation to pay for it. The point of saying that the deficits are bad is not to say that deficits are inflationary—I am not saying that—but by and large the burden of taxation in India falls on the poor. And to the extent that government expenditure is not retrenched, the poor go on paying the extra burden of taxation. Taxation in India is not progressive. Taxation is not progressive almost anywhere in the world but if you examine it carefully in India it certainly is not.

The reform process has indeed helped the economy, much more than the sceptics said it would. Nevertheless, although exports are growing very rapidly, the overall economic growth rate is stuck at 5 per cent, or perhaps it was 6 per cent in 1995 as the government claims. But by and large, India has not been taken even into a high, single-digit growth rate of 8 or 9 per cent, let alone Chinese-type growth rates of 11 or 12 per cent. And because India is a democracy, one has to understand that this in some sense is a choice which the people have made. And that if people make that choice, one has got to respect it. I expect that between now and six months after the elections of 1996 are over, there will not be any great dramatic gesture in terms of reform. A lot of small technical things which can escape the scrutiny of the Lok Sabha will go on. Technical reforms which the Finance Ministry, the Reserve Bank of India, or various other bodies like the stock exchanges can put through, will go through, and a lot of those things are going through. The reforms which have already been implemented have generated a dynamic in terms of what business is doing. This will go on and will create further opportunities in India. But the analogy I would give is that of a person who has followed a very unhealthy lifestyle in terms of eating, drinking, and smoking and has a triple bypass. For the first six months or so he does what the doctor tells him. You know that India had a triple bypass in 1991 and the doctor came and said you

[1] M. Desai (1993), *Capitalism, Socialism and the Indian Economy*, Bombay: Exim Bank. See also Chapter 15.

must do such and such. Of course, the doctor said that not because the doctor happens to be evil but because it is in the best interests of the patient. But after a while the patient thinks 'ah ... who is the doctor? What does he know? I am all right!' And the patient goes back to the old habits. This is basically what is now happening. Now from the Indian point of view, it looks as if it is all the fault of the International Monetary Fund (IMF) that we had to liberalize—as if it was no fault of our own at all, and it is somebody else's fault that the country practically became bankrupt.

But I think none of this is new. You can study previous episodes of radical economic policy-making in India. I have recently published a paper in *India Briefing* in which I analyse this history.[2] You go through the last 30 or so years and see that each radical experiment has had a life of about three to three-and-a-half or four years before it loses momentum. You can look at the Nehru–Mahalanobis experiment of the Second Five Year Plan in 1955, then the Green Revolution, on to what happened to Mrs Gandhi's *'garibi hatao'*,[3] followed by the Janata government's experiment, and so on. This happens to radical policy reform because eventually, if you cannot create a sufficient coalition of interests which sees itself benefiting from economic reform (I mean a numerically large coalition of interests), then a combination of old interests which have been hurt by the reform, plus those people who are not benefiting, and those whose hopes have been dashed, will eventually stop the reform. So what we will see in the forthcoming elections is that nobody will actually come out strongly against economic liberalization as such. Liberalization has joined ice-cream and motherhood as something everybody has to swear by. But everyone will qualify economic liberalization in two respects: exit policy and entry policy.

The exit policy, by which we mean the reform of public sector enterprises, is necessary. Whilst there are some profitable public enterprises, there is an unacceptably large number which are loss making. But the public sector work force is the protected sector of the Indian working class. It represents about 8 per cent of the labour force, enjoys special favours, and is especially well organized. I do not think there exists a political party in India which will touch it this side of the election and perhaps not the other side of the election. But what am I saying—after all, I am standing here in Melbourne and all the local newspapers are full of battles between the Australian Congress of Trade Unions (ACTU) and CRA. Who am I to talk about the justice of trade union claims in Australia? China has a very similar sort of problem even without trade unions. China has also carried for a long time, despite its rapid economic growth, a large state sector which is considerably less efficient than its village and town enterprises or its private sector. Thus I think it is unlikely that a dynamic exit policy will be pursued by any government that is likely to emerge after the next election.

Let me briefly indulge in an election forecast. Needless to say, a lot of other people will have other forecasts. I do not expect any single party to emerge with a

[2] M. Desai (1995), 'Economic Reform: Stalled by Politics?', in Philip Oldenburgh (ed.), *India Briefing: Staying the Course*, New York: The Asia Society and M.E. Sharpe, pp. 75–95. See also Chapter 16.

[3] *Garibi hatao*—'poverty out' or abolish poverty.

majority sufficient to form a government in the next election. I do not think anyone will disagree on that. What the people will have differences on will be the identity of the largest single party. I will stick my neck out and say it is going to be the BJP. And I would say that despite what has happened in Gujarat recently, which considerably tarnished the BJP's reputation as a clean party, the BJP has about 120 seats now and it will possibly get between 180 and 200 seats. Some people say this is madness. And we have been taking bets ever since I arrived in Melbourne. I am going to be inundated with bottles of champagne, I can tell you. Congress will be the next largest party—I imagine it will be between 140 and 160 seats, and then there will be a variety of other parties. It is conceivable that the BJP will form the next government in India if it can put together a coalition with lots of small regional parties. Its tactic in Uttar Pradesh of supporting the Bahujan Samaj Party (BSP), a backward caste party which is normally anti-BJP, is a sign that at least the most sober part of the BJP (which is not always necessarily in control) wants to project itself as a minority-friendly, certainly not a minority-hostile, political party. I believe that no political party can come to power in India without having some sort of pro-minority stand. There are far too many minorities—it is worthwhile for groups to define themselves as minorities in Indian democratic politics, and people have to come to terms with the backward castes, Dalits, Muslims, and regional influences. Therefore, I think that the BJP has been trying to give signals, not entirely with the full approval of its membership because there are differences amongst them, but the BJP certainly has been downplaying the Hindu part of its image since earlier events. It may not be possible for them to find sufficient strength to form a government, but I believe that they will do so in 1996.

There is another possibility: that the Congress will form the next government with the National Left Front (hereafter NLF) coalition of parties. Such a coalition will have to take a much cooler view of liberalization because the NLF parties are not very pro-liberalization. Certainly on the exit policy, nothing will happen.

Regarding the entry of foreign capital, much has already happened—there has been a lot of legislation which is not going to be reversed. India is by and large a very law-abiding country and if people want to change something they have to get a new law passed, so I do not think that they are going to do anything suddenly. The Enron case, in which the newly elected BJP-Shiv Sena government in Maharashtra tried to cancel the power contract, was shocking to a lot of people not because the stance was right or wrong but because it was done in such an arbitrary and extralegal way. This was shocking. Now you can see the Enron case unravelling itself and the Maharashtra government finally finding out that there are financial penalties for this sort of indulgence. And so now they are renegotiating the Enron deal. Apparently nobody had told them that commercial agreements are binding.

A Congress–NLF coalition will definitely be cool on exit policy, and it will be unenthusiastic but not obstructionist on entry policy. Much will depend on who stays on as finance minister. If Manmohan Singh stays, we may have some guarantee that sanity will continue. Otherwise, I cannot give any such guarantee. If the BJP forms a government, there is likely to be a modification of the entry policy. Those of you who have been following the BJP's policy will know that it has been all over the place since liberalization started. Historically it was a very anti-dirigiste party. It was against this 'permit-licence raj'. It argued the case for the private sector. But the BJP is not a free market party. While it is against planning, it is always complaining about how pure capitalism is no good; but pure socialism is no good either, and they want something in the middle, whatever that is.

More important than that, since liberalization started, the BJP has moved itself into the arena vacated by the Congress. By and large, it stands for an autonomous, self-sufficient, foreign-capital-free development of the Indian economy. It is what I would call the Nehru–Mahalanobis model. The fact that this model has planning and restrictions is conveniently forgotten by the BJP. But that is what they now say they want—liberalization but with an Indian image. Yes, we will globalize but not at any cost; we will continue to have an Indian stamp. If you look at the BJP's various statements it is quite clear that they have not actually thought through very carefully the possible consequences of following a self-sufficient path in terms of taxation and other sacrifices, I do not think it is a feasible path. And I do not think that the BJP realizes what is going on. But I believe that when in power they will more or less do what has been done so far, with one important caveat. For a long time they have been backtracking on the foreign capital issue except for the matter of foreign capital in consumer goods industries. The BJP takes the view that we only want foreign capital in high technology areas, and in areas where we 'need' foreign capital. They say we do not need foreign capital in the consumer goods industries. This is taking us back to the Janata Dal government of 1978–9 when, if you remember, we had problems with Coca-Cola. This is an interesting variant of the Gandhian small and local industries stream of right-wing economic nationalism in India in which there is not so much interventionism in a planning sense but very much a protectionist position against foreign capital.

Now two things have happened which gives credence to this idea. One is, of course, the agitation against Kentucky Fried Chicken (KFC) in Bangalore. This was very much on a *swadeshi*[4] platform. The same forces which opposed the Cargill Seeds office also have put obstacles in the way of KFC. In Delhi, the local government is BJP-run, and when KFC opened recently, they had their licence revoked on health-grounds. I do not want to go into the merits of whether KFC is actually worth eating or not—I have never eaten KFC, so I do not know. The argument that there are health hazards in KFC, if it were true, should be systemically applied to non-foreign consumer goods being sold. If all the kitchens in all Delhi restaurants were examined (and not all the *tandoors* are always empty either) one would not find that KFC was the most unhealthy product available. But because it is foreign, it will be opposed. This is the reality. You cannot get on your high horse and say, how can they do this? If these are the perceptions, nothing can be done.[5] Nobody from the Central Cabinet has got up and said how dare you do this—they did not say anything about Enron, and they did not say

---

[4] *Swadeshi*, literally 'of one's own nation', was originally based on an anti-British tactic by Tilak, and then later by Gandhi, to boycott British imports and encourage Indian products.

[5] In the event, the Delhi magistrates ruled the action against KFC as illegal.

anything about KFC. For the stake of obtaining a small partisan advantage the Rao government is substantially compromising India's ability to obtain foreign capital in the future.

What will happen is that the BJP will try to discourage the entry of foreign capital in the consumer goods industries—they cannot actually stop it because the legal situation is what it is. What I hope will not happen, and I can give no guarantee that it will not happen, is that they will not actually try to throw someone out. Even what has been done in Delhi is clearly not an action that a party aspiring to national office should lightly undertake. But then the BJP has a problem in that the national high command cannot always control its state units, and so this has been allowed to happen. When Mr Advani[6] was recently in London he tried to say that the BJP was absolutely in favour of foreign capital, and how dare you say anything else. By and large, he is trying to project a pro-foreign capital image. I think there are problems within his own party. There are people who actually do have very strong feelings against foreign capital and the Indian Left is not likely to differ from the BJP on that question.

And so the pro-liberalization enclave is surrounded on all sides. What I think will happen, because legal changes have already occurred, is that there will be no change in the law but that the climate may change. I am not speaking on behalf of the Government of India so I do not have to be upbeat on this. I am merely making an analysis, and my analysis is that to the extent that the BJP can keep the Rashtriya Swayamsevak Sangh[7] under control and under the Swadeshi banner, they will be able to have just a change of climate but not a change of policy. But clearly there is going to be a modification of the terms under which foreign capital will be admitted.

This is extremely bad news. I do not think there is a great nationalist path that India can follow which will benefit the people more than the path of globalization. If it were possible, they had 40 years to do it and they failed to do so. Therefore, I do not see that the nationalist path will suddenly become the solution. But even in India's large-scale private-sector boardrooms there is not yet a complete willingness for liberalization—and why should there be? Who likes competition? Who does not enjoy protection, high tariffs, and subsidized industries such as the large private sector has been enjoying? There are very few, positive, pro-globalization forces which are pushing India forward.

I do not see much further happening except for one, perhaps technically very important change—the complete liberalization of the rupee on capital account something I have been urging for some time. I think that the Reserve Bank of India dipped its toe into the water and the rupee slipped down, and I think the rupee will go down a little further. It will not be like the peso crisis but it will go

---

[6] Lal Krishna Advani was the leader of the BJP in the Lok Sabha and thus leader of the Opposition. In January 1996, he resigned from leadership of BJP in the Lok Sabha while facing corruption charges.

[7] Rashtriya Swayamsevak Sangh (National Volunteer Corps) is a paramilitary pro-Hindu movement started before independence by the leaders of the Hindu Mahasabha. A member of the RSS, Nathuram Vinayak Godse was convicted for the assassination of Gandhi. The RSS has flourished in the last 25 years and is a fellow traveller of the BJP .

down in the next year, and it will be some time before the liberalization of the rupee on capital account happens. But it will be necessary. It will happen if the Congress is part of the next government, but it will not happen if the BJP is part of the next government.

18

What Should India's Economic Priorities be in a Globalizing World

It is a great honour to give this lecture organized jointly by the Indian Council for Research on International Economic Relations (ICRIER) and the Associated Chambers of Commerce and Industry of India (ASSOCHAM) at the beginning of this new year. This is also a topic in which the two powerful interest groups—academic researchers and industrial entrepreneurs—should be actively engaged in debating policy, promoting alternatives, and pushing implementation. Let me first define globalization as it is often argued by its detractors that it is a vague and woolly notion. It has also been demonized to such an extent that one can be forgiven for thinking that before the advent of globalization (whenever that was supposed to be) everything was alright and the world was an equitable place with no poverty and no business cycles. I shall then argue about India's endowments, its attitudes, and its opportunities in face of globalization.

What is Globalization?

The characteristics of globalization are now well known. They are:

(i)   deregulated capital markets with the possibility of speedy transfer of capital;
(ii) communications and information technology which makes possible 'action at a distance in real time' which can be very short;
(iii) active forex markets with supporting financial markets with new products [e.g. derivatives, options] which allows speculators to take positions in any currency around the world where there are potential profit opportunities;
(iv) greater geographical spread and increased mobility of fixed, i.e. direct, investment;
(v)   rapid and linked reactions as between different financial markets which

Indian Council for Research on International Economic Relations and The Associated Chambers of Commers and Industry of India, 6 January 1999.

work round the world round the clock, as well as between financial markets and forex markets;

(vi) the emergence of a global media linked with a global communication network;

(vii) the fashioning of a global consumer culture and a global music/film/TV culture benefiting from all the above, especially (ii)and (vi)

(viii) increased but as yet imperfect and legally impeded mobility of labour;

(ix) greater awareness, though, as yet, not very effective redress of human rights violations, ecological disasters, famines, and refugee problems, benefiting from (ii) and (vi)

(x) speeding up of technological change leading to increased concentration of capital via mergers and takeovers but at the same time increased competition between the surviving large companies.

I do not wish to argue that globalization is a natural phenomenon in the sense of an earthquake or typhoon. But even natural phenomena can be studied and mapped and forecast. We can take steps to minimize their effects so even if I did regard globalization as a natural phenomenon, it does not imply that we are helpless in its face. Globalization is, however, a supra-national or global force to which all countries—North and South, rich and poor—have to adjust. It is a result of action by millions of investors and traders and many large global corporations and governments and international institutions and non-governmental organizations (NGOs) and workers and farmers and refugees and migrants etc. Globalization or what is sometimes called the Market is just all of us acting in our own interests and responding to opportunities and adjusting to constraints. Globalization is us. It is not some mysterious Other.

The big debate about globalization has been about the power of governments, the state if you like, to counter the effects of globalization. There is much controversy here as between the views that the state is helpless against outside forces and that if only we had the will the state could do anything whatsoever, like it used to be able to [or thought it was able to] do. All governments find that their capacity to shape their economies are limited in the late twentieth century. This is difficult for many to recognize and they refuse to admit the validity of the limits. This is because throughout much of the twentieth century we have been accustomed to the idea of the State—the territorial state—as capable of running the economy. This idea is totally absent on the Left or on the Right in the nineteenth century. Neither Marx nor Gladstone thought the government could or should run the economy.

It is only during the First World War and after that the idea of the state running the economy became popular. Keynes then gave us the tools for running the economy not only in wartime but also on an on-going basis in peacetime for the advanced capitalist economies. But this was conditional on strict control over capital movements. So while trade was liberalized during the 1950s and 1960s, capital movements were regulated. It was only when, in the 1970s after the oil shock and the long continuous full employment, inflation became an insoluble problem for Keynesian policy-makers that capital immobility was abandoned. This was really a crisis of profitability but it put pressures to liberalize capital movements and this was done by USA, Germany, and UK during the 1970s. After that it was difficult to pursue Keynesian policies.

For developing countries independence meant an opportunity to launch development plans. Given the high prestige of the USSR in the post-war period many—India especially—followed the autarkic policies of Soviet style planning with minimal reliance on trade, import substitution, and protection to public and private sectors. With hardly any exceptions this model proved to be a recipe for slow growth. Countries which went on to an export growth path grew faster. Many developing countries got caught in the global financial nexus during the 1970s when they borrowed petro-dollars and failed to repay. India came late on to this problem, yet the end result was the same. It borrowed abroad but failed to reorient its economy in an export oriented way and got caught in 1991 in a debt crisis.

Although India started on the path of economic reform in June 1991, there is still a great deal of reluctance to pursue that path in an enthusiastic way. The case for India to liberalize has to be argued again and again. India's political leaders have given the impression that economic reform has happened because someone (the International Monetary Fund) has told us so, or because it is fashionable, or because we wish to attract foreign investment to build up reserves, etc. There has been no positive platform built up for reforms nor a pro-reform coalition among the people. This is not because reform is not in people's interest; indeed, it is and more so than a continuation of the old policies which consigned India to be a laggard in Asia for the first 40 years after independence. The case for India's economic integration into the global economy has to be argued positively and boldly and I hope to do so in this lecture.

Inheritance

The Indian independence struggle got caught in a xenophobic dislike of foreign trade and foreign capital as marks of India's loss of freedom. But in the history of India, it has always been a trading nation from times immemorial. The ancient Indian economy was well integrated with its trading partners in Europe–Greece, Rome, and the Arab countries, as well as East Africa and South East Asia. There was overland trade with Russia and China and typically India enjoyed a balance of trade surplus which drained its trading partners of gold. India has never been totally self-sufficient and does not need to be. The export pessimism which became fashionable in the late 1950s and 1960s had a fragile support in actual data and much more in dogma.

In fact, India was, among the colonized countries, the one with the largest industrial sector. It had a native entrepreneurial class which had started modern manufacturing in the mid-nineteenth century and by 1947 had built up a world class textile industry. In terms of volume of industrial output, India was the seventh largest industrial country on the eve of independence. It had a trained industrial workforce in the larger cities, a good infrastructure of rail, roads, and ports and a higher education establishment which though small was of high quality. India was well poised for rapid industrial development.

ENDOWMENTS

India is well endowed for competing in global markets. First and foremost, it has a large pool of educated personnel. It is true that the overall literacy rate is low and should be increased, but as far as higher education is concerned India has built on its earlier foundations. Thus while many bad universities have proliferated and politics has ruined much higher education, there has been a growth of the Indian Institute of Management (IIMs) and the Indian Institute of Technology (IITs) which have maintained a high quality.

India has also a system of laws and courts which though slow and cumbersome guarantees due process. Thus the attempt some years ago to shut down Kentucky Fried Chicken (KFC) in Delhi was soon put right by recourse to the courts. There is a financial system, one of the oldest Stock Exchanges in the world, and a habit of trading in sophisticated instruments. Here again, reform is needed but it is also in hand. Banking is also an old established industry and there are formal as well as informal linkages in financial markets.

ATTITUDES

India's biggest problem with globalization is one of attitude. Despite the good endowments and the sound inheritance of being an open trading economy through much of its history, Indian policymakers have never been enthusiastic about globalization. This comes from a variety of sources. As a fledgling independent country, India identified all foreign capital and trade with imperial dependence. Thus independence meant autonomy as well as autarchy. This tendency was deepened after the resources crisis of the Second Five Year Plan in 1958 when an anti trade philosophy began to take hold. A slight relaxation in the early years of Mrs Gandhi's prime ministership, when India devalued and relaxed controls, was soon reversed because of US hostility to India which led to the World Bank reneging on the post devaluation package which India had been promised. From then on till the early 1980s, it was the Soviet model which had the appeal to India's planners. India did not liberalize when many other Asian countries—Sri Lanka, for instance—did.

Opening out the economy to foreign borrowing on official account in the 1980s was the beginning of an admission that self–reliance was not a successful strategy, that the Indian economy was trapped in a low growth equilibrium [3.5 per cent total and 1.3 per cent per capita income growth per annum during 1950–79]. But while capital imports accelerated growth [upto 5 per cent] there was no restructuring of the economy and no reorientation towards exports. Thus when the foreign exchange crisis hit India in 1991, the planners were, as if, caught unawares. An economy which had successfully raised its rate of growth from 3.5 to 5.5 per cent was caught in a debt trap. There was much resentment that a stabilization programme was forced on India.

The radical change of economic policy inaugurated by Manmohan Singh in 1991 was seen to be an emergency package. Without any change in personnel, the planners of yesteryear became the liberalizers of tomorrow, but there was no searching analysis of the causes of the crisis nor any internalization of the need for a drastic restructuring of the economy. The lack of change in personnel also meant that old vested interests which had done well out of the old dirigiste regime, and who never admitted that the old model had failed, were still in commanding positions waiting for their time to restore the old status quo. Thus India became a reluctant liberalizer. A strong anti-capitalist, anti-profit ideology permeates the elite including, unfortunately, the business elite. A lifetime of living off tariffs and subsidized interest rates has inured the Big Business classes against the virtues of competition. The establishment of the Bombay Club soon after 1991 shows this. India's socialists (virtually everyone in politics) as well as its capitalists are hostile to liberalization.

Yet it is quite clear that India must liberalize. This is for several reasons. First because it is in India's long term interests. The old Nehruvian strategy had lost usefulness by about 1970. India should have switched to an export oriented path having established an industrial base and solved its agricultural surplus problem thanks to the Green Revolution (itself a combination of foreign technology and Indian private sector, i.e., farmers' responsiveness). This is what the countries of East Asia and South East Asia did. They used the state to transform their economies to be globally competitive. Korea whose per capita income was the same as India's in 1960 went on to achieve an income level 25 times that of India by following that path (and the recent crisis will hardly dent that advantage). Liberalization is the only way left for India to gear its economy up to a high growth path at 7 to 8 per cent per annum.

Secondly, although it is argued that liberalization leads to inequitable outcomes, there is little evidence for this. It is true that any restructuring will have losers and gainers, in India's case the losers are those who have benefited enormously from the old structures and who have contributed to the low performance of the economy. They enjoy subsidies of various sorts—tariffs for big business, water/electricity/fertilizer subsidies for farmers, guaranteed jobs at indexed and rising salaries for government employees, comforts of non–competitive behaviour for bankers, and the corrupt gains from the business–politics tie up for the politicians. These forces resist change. But the change will help reduce poverty at an accelerated pace if higher growth is achieved. India's past record in poverty reduction shows this. There was no reduction of poverty in the years upto 1980 but rapid progress afterwards thanks to the acceleration of growth. Although growth alone need not necessarily lead to poverty reduction, it is a necessary condition. What is more the pattern of growth in the old regime was hostile to poverty reduction.

This is because resources went into industrial growth which was capital intensive and low employment generating. The average tariff protection for industry was 45 per cent with subsidized capital inputs. Agriculture was on the other hand subjected to a 22 per cent tax which held back rural development. Since poverty is in rural areas, the sectoral pattern of growth in the first six Five Year Plans was anti–poor despite the rhetoric.

Thus it was the old model which was a hindrance to poverty reduction. Its insistence on import-substitution industrialization without regard to price or profit considerations meant inefficient allocation of resources and slow growth as well as stagnant employment. When the insistence of an exclusive reliance on domestic resources was dropped, growth picked up and poverty began to go down. But there was yet a need for restructuring as well as for foreign investment, it is this phase that is now being reluctantly undertaken.

India has adopted a victim mentality when it really needs to adopt a winner mentality. It appears that its policy makers think as if the entire outside world has nothing better to do than to conspire against India. But in fact, its slow growth has marginalized India to the extent that a country which was in 1947 the leader of Asia, is now thought to be no part of the dynamic Asian experience. The approach to GATT negotiations exaggerated the harm that could be done to India by signing the Dunkel draft. But no one explained the advantages of the Most Favoured Nation (MFN) status which could only be had by being in the GATT process, that India, like many other developing but industrialized countries, had a lot to gain from access to developed country markets and that withdrawing from GATT was never ever an option. But the Rao government did nothing to counter populist rhetoric until one fine day it went ahead and signed the Treaty. Thus an opportunity to argue the advantages of freer trade was lost. India has a lot to gain from being a dynamic export economy. Our record in software shows that we can do it.

The same is true of foreign direct investment (FDI). One of the cardial errors of the 1980s was that India borrowed from abroad in the form of loans and debt rather than equity. This meant that the risk of failure was borne by India while with equity investment it would have been borne by the lender. India has also wasted a lot of resources chasing the chimera of national technology as in the Sam Pitroda affair. The smart thing is to let FDI bring in the latest technology and combine it with India's skilled labour pool to export. This is the lesson of Bangalore; borrow the hardware and inject the software. It is no longer possible today to borrow the money and buy the technology off the shelf. Technology comes embodied in the FDI along with the latest management techniques. It is better to import and adapt and benefit that way than insist on having local technology which may fuel national pride but is a waste of resources.

India has indeed gone about foreign capital the wrong way around. Portfolio capital has been imported and now forms the bulk of the $30 billion reserves. But this is short term capital while what is more stable and growth enhancing is FDI. So India has put obstacles in the path of beneficial FDI and welcomed the volatile short–term capital. China has done much better in this respect and got a large inflow of FDI. It is India's reluctance to adopt liberalization in wholehearted way which prevents FDI from coming to India.

This is not to say that there are no problems with liberalization. But the correct comparison is not with some ideal world in which liberalization is combined with equity but the alternative India has been pursuing which yielded neither growth nor equity. There are attempts nowadays to portray all problems as arising out of globalization as if India was a paradise before 1991 or 1981. The truth is that poverty has come down faster since 1981 and growth has accelerated since 1991, with 7 per cent plus growth being registered for the first time in Indian economic history since records began. The difficulty is to sustain the growth and if that has not been possible the reason is not too much, but too little liberalization.

Indian resistance to liberalization has deep roots not only in the ideology of anti-imperialism (which after 50 years can hardly be more than nostalgia) but also by material interests. But these are elite interests not those of the poor. At the forefront are the organized sector industrialists who have benefited from tariffs and subsidies. It is clear that they fear opening out of the economy because they fear competition. They speak of a level playing field as a prerequisite before liberalization. But they have enjoyed tariffs, subsidized low interest loans, and quotas. Even the small and medium enterprises (SMEs), who should really be competitive, have been given reservation quotas for exports. India has a lot to gain by unleashing competition and cutting tariffs down. This will make Indian products competitive unlike now. When the Multi Fibre Agreement comes to an end, India could be in the forefront using its long run lead in textiles at every level but only if they are competitive.

This is not an issue of the state against the market. South Korea was able via state aid to build up a competitive car industry while India fostered an uncompetitive technologically stagnant one. It is not that India has to give up state intervention because of ideological reasons. It is because state intervention in India is of a low quality and merely an excuse for rent seeking that India has to give up state intervention. After all in a country blessed with an active native entrepreneurship as of 1947, how has India managed to lose that edge and failed to build up truly global competitive industries? The blame must be laid at the door of the economic strategy chosen in the 1950s and the bad implementation of the strategy.

The modern need is of a state that can swim with the tide and take advantage of globalization. Rather than govern the market, the need is to benefit from the market. Defying the market is no longer the answer but learning to play the market for what it is worth is the real need of the hour. It is not *laissez faire* since there is need for competition as well as regulation. What must be junked is state ownership as it has proven to be wasteful and growth retarding and shift over to state regulation of privatized industries or services. Surplus needs to be generated by the industrial sector whereas now it is surplus absorbing. India needs to abandon anti–profit policies and ideologies and take up the challenge of building productive profitable industries. This lesson has been learned in agriculture during the Green Revolution. It has also been learned in many service industries such as software and privatized tourist industry.

The siren sounds of protectionism come from two angles. First are the people who will never admit that the Nehru model failed to work especially after 1975 and would like to get back to old style planning. They dress up their demands with complaints about the inequities of globalization. But as I have already said above, the first 25 years of Nehruvian planning did not lower poverty, nor did they lead to greater equality of income or wealth. Top-down elitist planning which retards employment growth cannot tackle poverty; nor does it make industries competitive.

The other strand is much more short term and that is caused by the recession which has plagued the Indian economy since 1996. The roots of this recession are, however, domestic, not foreign. It was the insistence of the Rao government facing an election that the Reserve Bank of India (RBI) squeezed out demand to bring the headline figures on inflation down. This was overdone and while inflation came down (Congress, however, lost the election!) but the industrial sector received a nasty shock from which it has not as yet recovered. Frequent changes of government have not helped nor have irresponsible fiscal policies. But protectionism is not the answer to the recession. The answer is a drastic retrenchment of budget deficit which will ensure an easier monetary policy. Tight fiscal policy allows the pursuit of an easier monetary policy.

The logic of the global economy as well as India's interests dictate that India become proactive in its liberalization policies. There is a big market out there and India has all the advantages to be able to expand its exports. If the developed countries are resorting to non–tariff barriers (NTBs), it is because they are afraid of competition from countries like India. If India is to fight this tide of NTBs, it can only do so by adopting an active open economy trade stance. After 50 years of industrialization, India surely cannot insist on eternal infant status.

But a bold open stance will also help at the next Ministerial meeting of the World Trade Organization (WTO) later this year. India should take the lead in denying the developed world any grounds of expanding NTBs under dubious grounds of labour or environmental conditions. It should take the lead in insisting on an open global economy in which cost-effective labour-intensive exports will have unhindered access. If India tries to hide behind some protectionist covers, it will strengthen the developed countries' ability to arm themselves with super non-tariff weapons. Then there will be no hiding place.

Conclusion

India must liberalize—not because it has no choice—because it is the best choice. India must liberalize because that way alone can it become a rich and prosperous nation, that way alone is there any hope of conquering poverty. Globalization requires a well-educated healthy population. Education and health, long neglected under the old regime [though it called itself socialist] will get their proper place in the new order of things. The state will stop wasting resources, owning old unprofitable industries, subsidizing an aristocracy of workers, and put the money saved thereby in education and health of the poor people. India must globalize because it is the path of human development as well as material prosperity.

19

Has Liberalization Worked in India? Mumbai, 2002

I feel greatly honoured being invited to give the R.S. Bhatt Memorial Lecture. I met him several times mainly in connection with the London School of Economics (LSE) to which he was deeply attached. He was one of its most distinguished alumni as he was one of that pioneer band of economists who laid the institutional foundations for the economy of independent India. As an LSE graduate he must have been in something of a quandary in engaging himself in the development of a structure which defied some of the lessons he had learnt at the LSE.

The LSE may have a left-wing reputation worldwide but its Economics Department was deeply committed to market oriented policies. Lionel [Lord] Robbins, Friedrich Hayek, Arnold Plant, and Theodore Gregory—all of whom were among his teachers—were responsible for developing a paradigm in which the market was champion. The LSE paradigm has outlived the alternative paradigm associated with Cambridge of market failure which needed state intervention. But in the heady days of the first decade after independence, market failure and planning were the norm. The banking and financial sector escaped the close attention of the planning fraternity but finance was at all times subordinate to the real economy. Finance was supposed to be generated by the state and provided at subsidized rates to industries. Private savings were to be harnessed via the financial institutions to feed the demands of planned industrial development. What private savings could not do was to be supplemented by deficit financing.

There was of course a longer tradition of market oriented development in India. Regions, especially western India had witnessed commercial and industrial development over centuries. Much of this development had taken place without state encouragement. The textile mills of Bombay and Ahmedabad as much as the pioneering developments of the Tata industries had been achieved by harnessing private finance privately. Bombay had a stock exchange and a commodity exchange and a sophisticated financial system both in the modern and indigenous

R. S. Bhatt Memorial Lecture, Mumbai 2001.

forms. There has been a long tradition of trade and finance in India going back to millennia before Christ. India has been an open trading economy for all of its history, trading with Greece and Rome as well as Africa and China with credit networks that spread out from South India towards South East Asia and from Gujarat to the Gulf and beyond.

The decision to discard the institutional structure inherited from colonial times—the managing agency system for example—was taken more on nationalist rather than rational grounds. The rejection of the market was driven by the historically false idea that the market and capitalism were foreign Western imports. India had after all taken to British law and legal system like a duck to water and lawyers were in the vanguard of the independence movement. It had mastered military technology and produced some outstanding military officers who had fought bravely in the two wars. How come we could adopt Western law and Constitution, Western arms and technology, but not Western economic practices of capitalism?

Of course, planning was also Western economics. It had originated in Germany during the First World War and then practised by the Third Reich during the 1930s as a way of rearming Germany and providing full employment. German planning was in the context of a mixed economy. Soviet planning of course totally rejected any private property. In adopting planning, Indians thought they were copying Soviet planning but it is the German and Italian experience in the inter-war period which is more relevant.

Planning is effective when there is a single objective which overrides all other goals. There is not and cannot be any trade-off. This is why planning was adopted in Germany during the First World War. It is also ideal for a closed economy which was Germany's situation during 1914–18 due to the blockade. But India did not just have one objective for its development path. It wanted industrialization to build a strong basic industry core to ensure some capacity for defence production. It also wanted to tackle poverty and unemployment. It had to feed its population and modernize the countryside.

But above all, India was not a closed economy nor was it a backward undeveloped economy. It had modern industry, modern finance, and modern education. All inadequate for the population at hand but it did not have to start from scratch. It had the largest jute industry in the world, one of the three or four largest textile industries, and one of the longest railroad network. In choosing to portray India as de-industrialized, rural, and depressed, the national elite—politicians, academics, and businessmen—threw away a lot of advantage. India's native entrepreneurial class—the largest of any ex-colony—lost an opportunity to grow on its own strength when it aligned itself with the dirigiste development plan. The important thing about India was not that it had 600,000 villages but that millions already lived in cities some of which had modern industry of several decades standing.

One can discern that the financial and banking sector, especially its parts based in Bombay, ran a subversive market oriented alternative to planning. Compared to Delhi or Calcutta, Bombay was more market friendly and finance was safe from nationalization on a large scale. There was the State Bank and then in the mid-1950s the Mundhra affair and LIC. But by and large in finance, new institutions such as State Finance Corporation and India Investment Centre in which R.S. Bhatt played a large part, or ICICI, another unique Bombay institution, were created rather than old ones nationalized until Mrs Gandhi's spasm in 1969. It was another innovative move to set up the Unit Trust of India (UTI) since that connected the small savers to the stock market rather than the post office.

India could have adapted its planning to be more open economy oriented or more market friendly any time after the 1950s. In my view, the sudden death of Lal Bahadur Shastri was a great tragedy because he could have made a move in that direction. He was firmly rooted in the Indian soil and knew the capabilities of the ordinary Indian in economic affairs. The Plan holiday after the Third Five Year Plan, the devaluation of the rupee, and the massive commitment towards the Green Revolution in the second half of the 1960s show his lingering influence. If Lyndon Johnson had not foolishly antagonized India and forced the World Bank to renege on its promised aid after devaluation, India could have yet done a Korea. Mrs Gandhi could have been the first liberalizer.

Politics delayed liberalization for a decade. In 1980, on her return to power, Mrs Gandhi began partial liberalization. She broke the silly rule that India had to finance its development solely from its own resources. Foreign borrowing was accepted but as yet only as debt, not as equity. The economy was injected with extra resources but its restructuring to make it export oriented was delayed. But the fears of the Left about IMF borrowing were not realized. India stepped up its growth rate beyond the Hindu rate of 3.5 to 5.0 per cent, and trebled the per capita growth rate. Poverty began to come down, thanks to the higher growth rate and the increased demand for agricultural labour and cheaper food, thanks to the Green Revolution.

It took another shock in 1991 to get India fully on the path of economic reform. By then, China and the Asian tigers and even the four South East Asian baby tigers had shown that growth could be much faster, poverty much lower, and income much higher if only the country followed market friendly policies. India, which was the seventh largest industrial country in 1947, had lost its place because it had foolishly believed the myths about deindustrialization. Since 1991, the path of reform has been adhered to, across governments of every political hue, by parties hostile to reforms when in opposition but realistic when in office. It has not been thrown off course by international 'bullying' as happened in the late 1960s. Thus, the sanctions following Pokhran did not lead to an autarkic spasm. Reluctantly, slowly but surely, there has been a consensus built up in India that the reform process is irreversible.

Reform is still a contentious issue. India is not an enthusiastic reformer. Our intellectual elite of a certain vintage—people of my age and most of their students—are still stuck in the Leninist model of planning. Any and every excuse is used to show that liberalization does not work or that it is unfair. All the losers from the reforms—the employees of the public sector undertakings (PSUs) with their job security and indexed wages and salaries; the farmers who receive subsidies on output and input prices; the government bureaucracy with its gravy trains, the politicos who strive to secure their rent seeking mandates have vested interests and they can block the gainers—the silent majority, the landless who pay high indirect taxes, the informal sector employees with their precarious jobs and no wage indexation. After ten years of reform, the prospect of a dynamic market oriented economy in India is still in balance. It is time, therefore, to strike a balance and assert that reforms have been good.

First, let us note what has not happened. India has not been caught in a foreign debt trap as many warned. There is no domination of foreign capital that would take away India's sovereignty. Any country that manages to explore a nuclear device in defiance of world opinion (though I do not think that was the right thing to do) cannot be in thrall to anyone. India's foreign exchange reserve position is sound, its trade deficit is moderate. If anything, India could use more foreign direct investment (FDI) than it has received so far. If anything, PSUs have been divested too slowly. Labour laws have not been reformed and so the employment generation in the organized sector is still abysmal. The latest budget has promised reform but the government has been thrown off course due to the 'Tehelka' incident so it is hard to predict whether Yashwant Sinha will succeed in his intentions.

But the ten years since the shock of 1991 have been good. Let us note the achievements:

1. GDP growth rate has nearly doubled since the heady days of Nehruvian socialism. The growth rate went up from the Hindu rate of growth of 3.7 per cent during 1951–81 to 5.6 per cent during 1982–90 and in the 1990s, apart from the low growth rate of 0.8 per cent in 1991–2 has never been below 5.0 per cent and was as high as 7.8 per cent.

2. In constant dollar terms, i.e., discounting for inflation and depreciation, India's Gross Domestic Product (GDP) doubled over 20 years between 1960 and 1980 [$79.6 billion to $159.1 billion] but doubled again in 14 years between 1980 and 1994 [$336.9 billion] and was $435 billion, nearly three times, by 1998.

3. The 1990s was the first decade when one could say that there was a deep structural change in the economy. This was firstly in the sense that the dependence on agriculture was reduced. Ten years are too short to have a regression but there were two years of a bad harvest and the overall GDP growth rate held up. These years were 1996–7 when agriculture grew at 0.2 (–2.5 old series) per cent while income grew at 7.6 per cent and 1997–8 when the numbers were respectively –1.0 per cent and 5.0 per cent.

4. Poverty has come down. Through much of the first 30 years, 1950 to 1980, poverty (measured as head count) hardly moved. In 1977, it was still 51.3 per cent. It was 36 per cent in 1993 and the higher of the two most recent estimates (by the two methods of recall used by the National Sample Survey (NSS)) is 26 per cent (the lower is 23 per cent but let me not claim that). So the deceleration of poverty has been faster in the last 20 years than in any similar period before. Indeed, the drop from 36 per cent in 1993 to 26 per cent in 2000—a ten percentage point drop—is also astonishingly rapid. There are massive inter-state variations within this downward trend. Punjab and Haryana have poverty below 10 per cent—almost at the Chinese level.

The pockets of high poverty, Orissa, Bihar, Madhya Pradesh, and Assam—all above 30 per cent or even West Bengal, UP, and Maharashtra all above 20 per cent contrast with the eight states which are below 20 per cent. The answer to poverty reduction is thus as much in local governance and policy effectiveness as structural problems. Poverty can be eliminated in India in our life time. What is needed is growth but employment oriented growth rather than capital intensive growth of the Mahalanobis type.[1]

But it is not all a bright picture:

5.   There still remain obstacles to rapid growth and equity. But these are the remnants of the old model rather than liberalization and reform. Thus, subsidies which go to the well-off farmers or PSUs are at a conservative estimate of 1.4 per cent of GDP and thus remain at more than twice the level of health expenditure and at 40 per cent total government expenditure, disturbingly high proportion of the budget deficit. The government spends much too much on things it does inefficiently and in aid of a regressive fiscal outcome and much too little for health and education and clean water. Subsidies to food grains and for water and electricity are far too large for comfort. As I have often said before, India's spending on the anti-poverty programme is a fraction of its spending on enhancing poverty by misallocation of resources.

6.   India has hardly begun to liberalize. Its record on FDI is sad when compared to that of China. Far too much capital has come in the portfolio variant and while that is welcome, it is FDI which is needed India has barely cleared the decks as far as reform is concerned. The longer it delays reforms, the less likely it is to get the real benefits of liberalization. The contrast with Malaysia or Korea or China is stark. FDI flows are six times what they were in 1991 but still less than 1 per cent of GDP.

7.   Politics remains a major bottleneck. While India should be proud of its democracy, there can be no doubt that its quality has deteriorated over the last 50 years. Politics is corrupt and costly. It is slow and cumbersome in its capacity for initiating change. In terms of leadership, the first decade after independence or even the second decade cannot be matched. Neither Nehru nor Shastri has found a worthy successor. The inability to tackle the deficit is symptomatic of this. The Indian state remains reluctant to tax progressively and is too pusillanimous to stand up to special interests. At the state level, things are if anything worse. Legislators are costly in terms of their perks and privileges. Relative to per capita income, Indian politics is much more expensive than British politics. Its ties with crime are fed by the inefficient dirigisme of the past 40 years and if not corrected soon it could destroy democracy.

8.   Despite the machinery of the Planning Commission (or perhaps because it

[1] Such numbers as I can lay my hands on tell me that income distribution may be improving. The ratio of the income share of the top 20 per cent to the bottom 20 per cent has gone down from 8 + (49.4/5.9) in 1975 to less than 5 (41.4/8.8) in 1990. I find these numbers hard to believe. As in many other growth contexts, I believe poverty may have gone down but inequality may have increased.

is such a useless organization), Indian development policy lacks any long-run strategy. Thus there has been stagnation in the manufacturing industry since the late 1970s. The share of manufacturing in GDP is stuck at 16 to 17 per cent. This is probably a reflection of the inefficiencies of the organized sector, both public and private, which is characterized by loss making and, in some cases, negative value added.

And yet:

9.   By contrast agriculture is the success story of the last 50 years. Its growth rate has been sustained and even accelerated. Yields grew at three times in the 1980s and later relative to that in the 1950s. This is the triumph of the small unorganized private sector. There are lessons to be learnt here for industrial growth which have not been learnt yet. These lessons go back to what I was saying at the outset about the ability of Indians to handle economic change in the private sector which was stifled for 50 years in the industrial sector.

The Indian economy has suffered from myths and misconceptions. It used to be one of the most successful examples of capitalism in the colonial context. It was a modern economy with all the bases for a successful industrialization building on its high rank in the 1940s. The rejection of market based policies pursued, no doubt sincerely, for national reasons stymied and stagnated the economy for 30 years until 1980. Slowly and reluctantly, there has been a resumption of history, the glorious history of India as a trading and manufacturing nation able to compete on a world scale as it proved with the cotton textile industry in the days before independence.

Liberalization has up to now been a positive thing. Not as much as one would like has been done. But the task is to argue boldly and with conviction that India was always a market oriented successful economy when free or when slaved, with or without state aid. It has now to resume that path.

NATION AND IDENTITY

20

Birth and Death of Nation-states

Speculations about Germany and India

My aim in this chapter is to exploit the distance between the notions of nation and nation-state, in order to say something about the life cycle of nation-states. Nations have no precise chronology of birth and death, no life cycle. Indeed one feature of nationhood is the need for the champions of a nation to argue that the nation in question has very early origins and also that all assertions of its death are exaggerated—the nation will rise again, etc. States by contrast can and do have a finite life cycle—upstart, dissident states which end up at the losing end of civil wars—the Confederacy, Katanga, Biafra are examples of finitely lived states. But I am more concerned in particular with states which claim to be nation-states but where the nationhood of the state is at issue and in turn determines the shape of its life cycle.

This happens in my view when the nation and the state which purports to embody the nation don't coincide. Although nations are said to be timeless entities, nationalists have taken the view that statehood is necessary for the continued life of the nation. But when statehood arrives—when the nation-state is born—it often incorporates either a fraction of the nation or it contains more than one nation. Given the ambiguity of nationhood, statehood and nation-statehood, it is often the case that both these alternatives—multinationality and partinationality—can be used to characterize the state. When this happens, the life cycle of the state is affected, if not foreshortened.

My examples to illustrate this contention are Germany and India. In each case, I shall argue that the process of constituting a nation-state involved a choice among several alternatives, some more inclusive than others. A variety of historical, ideological, and personality forces conspired in each case for the nation-state to be constituted around the exclusive rather than the inclusive option. In the case of

M. Mann, F. Halliday and J. Hobson (eds), *Rise and Decline of the Nation State*, Oxford: Blackwell, 1990.

The author would like to thank Gary Llewellyn of the London School of Economics and Geography Department Drawing Office for drawing the maps which appear in this chapter.

Germany, the Reich embodied a particular variant of the alternatives available: the *Kleindeutsch* solution. The Reich had a finite life of 75 years. The Indian case is parallel. In constituting an independent nation-state, there was a partition with two states—India and Pakistan. In the 41 years since idependence, Pakistan has again fragmented into two: Pakistan and Bangladesh. India has had to deal severely with subnational movements, the most recent of which—Khalistan—had been quite bloody. There are noises of Baluch or Sind nationalism within Pakistan.

Argument by analogy is a procedure which raises many problems. Obviously there are many ways in which Germany and India differ. In comparing two cases across centuries and continents, one expects this. I shall later dwell on the differences which are crucial to my argument. But well before we get into problems posed by analogy, there is a prior problem. The case of Germany is an *ex post* one. Here the nation is already dead. But even then it is difficult to establish a causal link between the choices made at the moment of the formation of nation-state and its eventual death. Other hypotheses concerning the death of the Reich have been advanced. There is a lively and still unsettled debate between those who see a continuity in German history from Bismarck (if not before) to Hitler, and those who argue that the Third Reich represents a structural break. I have no hope of being able to add to that debate but in as much as this chapter relates to it, the argument here locates a structural break in the 1860s *prior* to the formation of the Reich but does not necessarily take a view on the continuity/structural break post-1871.

It is at this stage, granting that I am able to establish a causal connection, that the argument by analogy faces its real-obstacle. While for Germany we are talking of birth and death of the nation-state as facts of the past, for India we are talking about a prospective, possible event. This is of course liable to invite the most hostile reaction especially in India where the talk of break-up of India is attributed to be a bloodsport practised by the imperialists. In partial mitigation of this, I wish to point out that India not only split in 1947 but that one of the two constituent states, Pakistan, split again in 1971. Pakistan thus represents an analogy closer to the ground of the German case since the nation-state of Pakistan as of 1947 had a life of 23½ years. Pakistan is also closer to India culturally and historically, hence, although the German analogy may not be directly transferable to India, mediated through the experience of Pakistan, the argument becomes slightly stronger. But that having been said, the bulk of my discussion about India will also rely on events which took place before 1947, i.e. which are facts although their interpretation still raises many differences.

AMBIGUITIES

To begin with, even the names Germany and India are ambiguous. As a cultural notion, Germany comprised a larger area than what we now call Germany. In 1801, 1848, or even up to 1865, the word Germany comprised Austria, Prussia, and what came to be called The Third Germany: the many smaller states add principalities which were vassals of the Holy Roman Empire and got reconstituted in the course of the Napoleonic War and especially by the Congress of Vienna.

The Confederation, as it was called, with its Diet in Frankfurt was the most comprehensive territorial expression of Germany but it was not a nation-state. But in the 1860s, Germany meant the Confederation. It was only after 1871 that it meant Germany as we understand it today.

India is a similarly ambiguous word. Like Germany we come across India as a cultural expression in ancient times. But the Government of India (GOI) Act of 1935, one of the longest pieces of legislation debated by the British Parliament to date was meant to apply to British India and the 660 native states. The GOI Act 1935 was a result of seven years of discussion following the Simon Commission Report, three Round Table Conferences in London, parliamentary debates, and the visit of a joint party delegation from Westminster to India. Throughout this debate the discussion concerned the self-governance of India as defined in these larger terms. This continued to be the case up to April 1947 although by then proposals for two separate states had been put forward. When independence came in August 1947, two nation-states were set up. Calling the larger of the two successor states India meant a lot to the Congress party and to Nehru, its leader. This meant that India continued from British India and Pakistan was a breakaway state. For Jinnah, this was a distortion of facts. He thought of India as comprising Pakistan and Hindustan, a Muslim and a Hindu nation each embodied in a nation-state. In its constitution, the country is called 'India that is Bharat', thus coming half-way between India and Hindustan. When Pakistan split in 1971, the larger successor state called itself Pakistan and the dissident state called itself Bangladesh. Thus, India of 1935 was different from India of 1956, and Pakistan of 1950 differed from Pakistan of 1975. Germany of 1850 was not Germany of 1875.

There is a higher order ambiguity about nationality which, though somewhat obscure, merits attention. Although nationalism arose in the nineteenth century as a reaction to the French Revolution and in the periphery as a reaction to the experience of imperial domination, the territorial limits of nations have been as much a product of the external—imperial domination as anything else. Napoleon had more to do with giving a German nation territorial extent than anyone else, by his dismantling of the Holy Roman Empire. It was this defeat in the first wave of Napoleonic wars that began the crystallization process of German nationalism. If Napoleon had won at Waterloo, it is a moot question whether European nationalism would have taken the shape it did.

In the case of India, there is a similar ambiguity. Between AD 1500 and 1800, various European maritime countries competed with each other in the Arabian Sea and the Indian Ocean for a monopoly of trade. What they faced was a multiplicity of kingdoms. The Indo-Gangetic plain—Hindustan narrowly de-fined—had been ruled by one or other dynasty ruling from Delhi, first Afghan, followed by the Mughals in the mid-sixteenth century. Southern India was often beyond the reach of the Delhi Sultanate and was an open, seafaring economy in contrast to the landlocked subcontinental economy of northern India. If there was a unifying notion combining these various areas, it was that of a Hindu society. Hinduism, however, was not a unifying creed, certainly not in its six-teenth-century form before it reformed in reaction to the Western challenge. The notion, therefore, that foreigners ruled over India, or that the British conquered India, is a nineteenth-century reconstruction of a much more chaotic process. The Portuguese, the Dutch, the Danes, the French, and the English at various times between AD 1500 and 1800 occupied bits of territory of what we now call India. If they had all stayed, the geography of India could have been very much like that of Africa today with several constituent 'nations'. The English marginalized the Portuguese and the French. With the Dutch and the Danes having quit earlier on, by the middle of the nineteenth century the English had succeeded the Moghuls and even extended into the South much more than any previous kingdom. This allowed the Indian nationalists to reconstruct their national past in territorial rather than religious terms alone. It was, therefore, only then that one could speak of the 'Aryan invasion of India' or of the 'Battle of Plassey' in 1757 marking the beginning of the British conquest of India when both these were regional events, one in the Punjab and the other in Bengal.

Thus it is impossible to avoid some ambiguity in using national labels. It is the essence of nationalism to repudiate the notion advanced above that the nation did not exist prior to its conquest. But if we can avoid teleology, we have to admit that as of, say, 1750, alternative counterfactual scenarios were plausible which could have given us different territorial and political arrangements than those which became Germany and India by 1900.

In order, therefore, to keep ambiguity to the minimum and even at the risk of seeming pretentious, I shall call Germany before 1871 Germania, and India before 1947 Indica.

TWO TENTATIVE PROPOSITIONS AND A COROLLARY

The ambiguity in the terminology of nation-states is not an accident but constitutes the essence of the problem. Nations can be defined vaguely. The sense of 'an imagined community' is constituted by some common cultural bond—language, religion, a common historical experience—but need not involve a precisely defined territory. A nation-state, on the other hand, has to have defined boundaries. It is a legal not a sentimental entity. But nations are often much larger than the state which purports to embody them: the Jewish nation is not coextensive with Israel as a nation-state. The Palestinian nation, when it acquires a nation-state, may well be in a similar situation. In the case of both Germania and Indica, two interrelated propositions can be advanced as true:

1. The process of forming a state to embody the nation was subjected to compulsions which argued for a powerful (in military–economic sense) nation-state even at the cost of leaving some of the nation outside its boundaries, i.e. a fragmented nation-state was formed.
2. The fragmented nation-state having been formed, it sought to reconstitute nationhood in terms of its boundaries; i.e. the nation was redefined in the narrower territorial terms, with the excluded portion of the erstwhile nation being redefined as non-national in the new, narrower sense of nationhood.

I shall advance evidence for these two propositions in the subsequent sections. But before I do that, let me advance a corollary of the above two propositions which is not a question of fact but of an arguable speculative nature.

3. That the attempt to reconstitute nationhood as under (2) above becomes problematic precisely because the basis on which the ur-nation was defined is no longer appropriate. The new fragmented nation-state ends up giving territory a much more prominent place in defining nationhood than previously, and assigns uncertain status to cultural factors such as language or religion. Territorial integrity and its defence become nationalist ideology.

Germania to Germany

The Holy Roman Empire was dissolved as a result of the Napoleonic wars in 1806. Prussia's defeat goaded it into a series of reforms to make it a model of rational bureaucratic absolutism. In 1815 at the Congress of Vienna, the German Confederation was set up with Austria as the senior member and Prussia as the junior member and 36 (much fewer than in 1806) smaller states comprising Third Germany. The Confederation, with its Federal Diet in Frankfurt, was a loose association of independent princely states, its *raison d'être* being the preservation of the balance of power in Central Europe.

Starting in late eighteenth century but intensified by the French Revolution as well as the Wars of Liberation from French rule, German nationalism grew among the conscious middle classes. *Kulturstaat* as an ideal was a popular, liberal, if not entirely democratic, nation. It saw the 'unity (of Germany) via common spirit founded upon the equality of all human beings and growing out of the development of human liberty'.[1] But the liberal *Kulturstaat* movement had no clout. It operated in a monarchical and imperial context within the Confederation and internationally in the context of a balance of power. Without the acquiescence of the larger and smaller princes, a German nation-state could not be realized.

The Confederation was not a nation-state but a conclave of princedoms, many small, some medium-sized such as Bavaria and Prussia, and of course Austria. It was supposed to be guided by Austria as the major power but Prussia, especially after 1848, wanted a bigger say in running it. The Federal Diet was an assembly of ambassadors from the princely states meeting in Frankfurt. The Confederation could not, however, act as a unit; it could not, for example, sign international treaties. As such, liberal nationalism saw the Confederation as the machinery of reform to obtain a strong German nation-state.

But the liberals operated not in a parliamentary constitutional climate but in monarchical absolutism of various degrees. A constitutional monarchy represented the limit of their radical imagination. Thus, when the princely order was temporarily undermined in 1848, the Federal Assembly (elected on a limited franchise but elected nonetheless) could only invite the Prussian king to take the crown of all Germany, i.e. the Confederation. The Habsburg empire had been eclipsed by the uprising in Vienna, and Prussia was always more to the liberals

---

[1] Darmstaedter (1948), *Bismarck*, London: Methuen, p. 330

liking than reactionary Austria. But the liberals realized their limitation when Frederick William IV of Prussia rejected their offer. In his view, such an assembly had no authority to cancel the crowns of princes and choose one among them. 'If the thousand year crown of the German nation, which for forty two years has been in abeyance is to be awarded once again, it is *I* and those such as I who will award it.[2] He also rejected the offer of the crown of Germany without Austria when it was offer by the same Assembly in April 1849.

The 1848–9 episode established several things. A liberal democratic movement did not have the power to bring about a German nation-state. It needed the willing support of at least one major monarch. But the monarchs together were jealous of their legitimacy and suspicious of the revolution, i.e. anything which might overthrow legitimate rulers. Thus, for someone like Frederick William IV, a voluntary agreement of the princes was the only way to bring about a German kingdom.

But the Assembly also articulated the two alternatives for a German state *Grossdeutsch,* i.e. the Confederation, or *Kleindeutsch,* the Confederation minus Austria. It is around these two alternatives that subsequent debate centred. The *Kleindeutsch* alternative had a firm basis in reality in as much as the *Zollverein*— the customs union of the kingdoms in the Confederation excluding Austria— already existed. Austria tried under its new Chancellor Schwarzenberg in the early 1850s to bully its way into the *Zollverein*. Austria wanted a tariff agreement for the whole of Central Europe, i.e. the Confederation as a prelude to a *Grossdeutsch* run by Austria. But Prussia prevented this and the *Zollverein* stayed within *Kleindeutsch*. On Schwarzenberg's death, the issue fell by the wayside.

In the late 1850s, the liberals formed the *nationalverein,* a lobby for the *Kleindeutsch* programme. They were in office in Prussia between 1859 and 1862. For the liberals, a programme of nationalism was also a programme for parliamentarism. They asked Prussia to take the lead in encouraging the growth of a constitutional monarchy at home and pushing the electoral principle in the federal Diet. They also pushed the *Zollverein* as the mechanism for integration. But the Prussian Regent who later succeeded to his brother's throne was reluctant to toe the parliamentary line. By September 1862, he had appointed Bismarck as his Minister President and the liberals, while in parliamentary majority, were out of office. It looked like the death of the *Kleindeutsch* idea.

Austria, on the other hand, was dead against the *Kleindeutsch*. It sponsored the *Reformverein* which would promote the *Grossdeutsch* alternatives but Austria's commitment to the electoral principle was suspect. It preferred an indirectly elected assembly for the federal parliament. In 1862, Austria put such a proposal forward in Frankfurt. A federal parliament was to be made up of delegates from the parliaments of individual states. The new federation was to be administered jointly by a committee of five princes of which Austria, Prussia, and Bavaria would be permanent members. This was discussed at a Congress of Princes of the Confederation in August 1863. The King of Prussia refused to attend and, on the urging of Bismarck, proceeded to scuttle this plan for a stronger version of the

[2] L. Gall (1986), *Bismarck the White Revolutionary*, vol. 1, 1815–1871, London: Allen & Unwin, p. 63.

confederation. As a diversionary card, Prussia proposed a directly elected federal parliament. There was, however, a problem. Not only were many suspicious of Bismarck's parilamentarist credentials but there was a regional divide as well. In the South, there was a greater preference for the *Grossdeutsch* solution. There was a religious affinity in catholic Bavaria and Austria while Prussia was a protestant stronghold.

Thus, as of 1863 several possibilities were open for Germania:

1. A gradual strengthening of the Confederation run jointly by a conservative alliance between Austria and Prussia. Prussia, however, wanted parity with Austria and did not wish decisions regarding defence and foreign policy to be subject to majority vote in the Confederation.

2. A Confederation dominated and run by Austria. This was the Schwarzenberg plan tried in 1849–50 and revised in a milder form by Austria in 1862. This was the principle of majority decision in the Confederation but by a chamber of princes. Such a confederation would have evolved towards a stronger state if the *Zollverein* could have been extended to Austria. This would have created a Central European Free Trade Area covering all of Germania.

    Bismarck was against both these alternatives as he feared the weakening of Prussia within such a Confederation. His alternative plans were as in (3) and (4) below.

3. A Prussian led Germany comprising Germania excluding Austria. This was the liberal *Nationalverein* formulation but the liberals wanted it through a move towards parliamentarism among all the princely states. Bismarck preferred Prussia to absorb *Kleindeutsch* under its domination.

4. A minimal plan proposed by Bismarck to the Austrians was of Prussia dominating a protestant North German Confederation, restricting the *Zollverein* to this region, thus excluding the catholic states of South Germany and especially Bavaria. This could have led to a division of Germania into North and South along protestant/catholic lines. With Austria leading the South and Prussia the North. (See Map 20.1 for the various alternatives mentioned.)

Of these four alternatives, only (1) and (2) preserved Germania intact. They were both *Grossdeutch* solutions. But apart from the Schwarzenberg variant of (2) which was no longer feasible in 1862, they both meant a weak or a gradually strengthening nation-state. For the liberals, both solutions also denied or at least restricted the principle of nationalism, i.e. democracy, and were conservative monarchical condominium arrangements. Bismarck wrecked (2) by advancing the principle of adult franchise for the election to federal parliament which he knew Austria would not accept. He proposed (1) as his maximal plan and (4) as his minimal plan.

As it happened, the *Zollverein* proved too strong a binding force for the South German states of Bavaria and Wurttemburg to break off and form a *Kerndeutsch* union with Austria. After the renewal of the *Zollverein* treaty in 1865, the German national question was decided by the war in two phases. In 1866, the war between

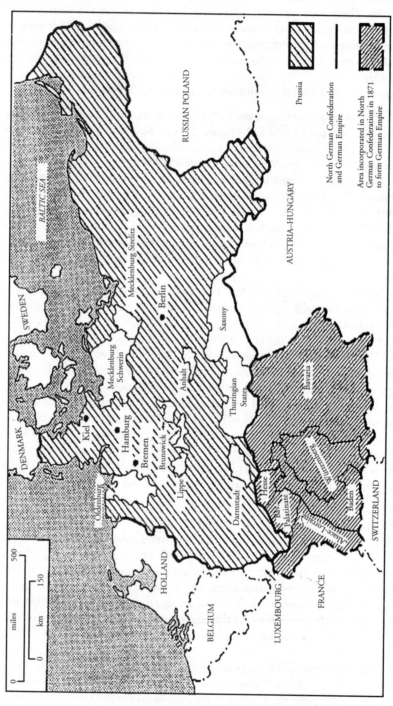

Map 20.1: Germany Before and After the Reich

Source: Agatha Ramm (1967), *Germany 1789–1919*, London: Methuen.

Austria and Prussia (a civil war in a sense) quickly decided the issue in favour of Prussia. Bismarck got a North German Confederation with a directly elected federal parliament. This was the pattern of the Reich which was established after the Franco-Prussian War of 1870–1. By this time, the South German members of the *Zollverein* joined as well. The Reich was created in 1871.

The German nationalist movement got its *Kleindeutsch,* but it came as a revolution from above. Instead of being created out of a popular unity as a *Kulturstaat* it was created by war as a *Kriegstaat.* It was not so much a *Kleindeutsch* (Lesser Germany) as *Grosspreussisch* (Greater Prussia). Bismarck was quite conscious that it was the national idea by itself that was integrative:

Its cachet and its power had come to consist much more in the fact that it had a unifying effect that spanned all political division and all decisions of class and interest and that even spanned denominational barriers... . The national idea together with all the hopes and expectations that depended on it, changed after 1866 from being a distinctly oppositional ideology, as it had been up until 1848–9, to being an integrative ideology.[3]

But in achieving national integration of a fragment of Germania, and especially doing it in a revolutionary abrupt way via two wars, the nature of nationalism had to be changed. It was no longer a cultural union of all German-speaking people. Even the *Kleindeutsch* union had not evolved by sinking its differences and defining a German identity. The Reich was militaristic and illiberal; its creation compelled it to create a national ideology in terms of territory and power.

Given that the *Reich* had come into being as the product of military and power related manoeuverings, rather than through the democratic process, it had from the very outset, never been sufficiently integrated politically. This particular type of deficit created a perpetual search for some kind of compensation ... or fear of a relapse into weakness and impotence, categories such as 'unity, solidarity and adaptability' were valued more highly than others such as 'freedom, tolerance and a plurality of opinion'.[4]

I am aware that there is an arguable link here. A *Grossdeutch* solution along the lines proposed by Austria in 1862–3 with a Central European Free Trade Area and initially indirectly elected but ultimately directly elected is not just a counterfactual hypothesis. It was one of the three or four real alternatives. It had the cultural logic and the history of a Holy Roman Empire on its side. Such a state would not have been a federation with a centralizing logic but could have integrated as a result of economic forces (as the European Community seems to be doing). *Ex post* it has been argued by many that the logic of economic growth favoured the *Zollverein* and integrating Austria would have been economically damaging. I cannot at the present evaluate this argument since it would require a close examination of the economic structures of the regions at that time. It has also been argued that in some sense history was not on Austria's side but on Prussia's side but that need not prejudge the outcome as of 1865. As August Bebel speculated.

If Austria had won (i.e. in 1866), its government would in all probability have attempted to rule Germany by reaction. In so doing, it would have aroused the hostility of not only the entire

[3] Gall, *Bismarck,* p. 331.
[4] R, Von Thadden (1987), *Prussia: The History of a Last State,* Cambridge: Cambridge University Press, p. 62.

Prussian population, but also the majority of Germans and a good number of Austrians. If ever a revolution had fair prospects of success, it was against Austria and at that particular time. The result would have been the democratic union of the *Reich*, something which Prussia's victory made impossible.[5]

Thus Prussia's victory in 1866 led to the less inclusive alternative of *Kleindeutsch* being chosen. The desire for a strong state had a lot to do with the connivances of the liberals in this. The liberals were convinced, Bismarck's biographer tells us, that the chief reason for their failure in 1848 'had in fact been neglect of the power question ... To the detriment of its own cause it had pursued more "ideal politik" and not, ... "real politik".'[6] The power question for the nationalists had to do with military strength of the nation-state. As Bismarck articulated it, for them 'the upsurge in national feeling, part of the whole trend of the time, is pushing us, as is the demand *for protection against attacks from abroad,* towards the objective of closer German unification, at least in the fields of defence and material interests'.[7] But once such a feeling is articulated, the wish can become father to the thought. Thus the only 'attack from abroad' that led the Confederation to a national integration was from Austria. To justify the strong but fragmented nation-state, a part of the erstwhile nation had to become the enemy. Later when it had served its purpose, the threat could shift and come from others—catholics at home (*kultukampf*), the social democrats.

When the Imperial Reich ended, the habit of searching for the enemy, for 'attacks from abroad' did not cease. The Weimar Republic was haunted by the 'stab in the back' idea. A nation-state built on war and militarism had lost a war and thus a new logic had to be defined for the nationhood. A defeat in war could not be a unifying theme but betrayal at home and the humiliation of the Versailles Treaty did become surrogate unifying themes. In the Anschluss, the Confederation was realized as a nation-state in a perverse, degenerate way.

As Rathenau once put it, 'Compare the Holy Roman Empire and the German Reich: what do you have left? Prussia. Remove Prussia from Germany and what do you have left? The Confederation of the Rhine. An extended version of Austria. A clerical republic'.[8] After the Second World War, we are back to this. A Prussia without Poland and its borders as of before 1815, a confederation of the Rhine and Austria. Maybe the counterfactuals in German history have yet time to realize themselves.

FROM INDICA TO SOUTH ASIA

Indian nationalism grew up in an imperial context and in some ways, like German nationalism, it was not up to people alone to achieve a nation-state. A major part of the answer lay in Westminster and its Viceregal agent in Delhi. The certainty that Indica would be part of the British Empire as a self-governing dominion for the next 30 or 40 years was accepted as late as the 1930s by various Indian leaders

---

[5] Quoted in Von Thadden, *Prussia*, p. 63.
[6] Gall, *Bismarck*, p. 204.
[7] Ibid., p. 117 (my emphasis).
[8] Rathenau (1919), *Der Neue Staat*, Berlin, p. 24.

including Nehru and Jinnah. There had been promises of increasing but strictly supervised self-government in 1909 (Morley–Minto) and 1919 (Montagu–Chelmsford). Under Gandhi, the Indian National Congress had abandoned the moderate constitutional path and launched a non-cooperation movement in 1921. Gandhi had deep religious convictions and used the religious idiom to mobilize a much larger movement than the Congress had been able to hitherto. He harnessed the Muslims by championing the Caliphate's survival against the threat of its abolition by the Allied Powers after 1918. Thus was born the Hindu-Muslim unity under the banner of the Congress strategy for independence. Gandhi had envisaged independence within the year of launching non-coopera-tion. Despite the tremendous mass response, he abruptly called off the movement when a police station was burned down in Chaurichaura. The movement col-lapsed among bitter recriminations.

This was the high point of a mass disobedience movement as a way of winning power. Gandhi had succeeded by shrewdly combining religious symbolism in an ecumenical way in launching an all-Indica movement. The odds against doing so were formidable. Indica was then administratively divided into British India (five-sixths of the population) and 660 'native' princely states (one-sixth). Never before in its long history, had a single 'ruler' controlled directly as much as five-sixths of the population and had 'paramountcy' over the rest. The alien power was a formidable one, not just in being militarily well equipped to control the popula-tion but also ideologically in offering in its domestic politics much that was admired by the nationalists. In addition to the administrative divisions, there were other divisions. A very small number of 'Europeans' and a slightly larger but still small number of Anglo-Indians claimed privileged status of belonging to the ruling caste. Beyond this were the Indians, the majority (over 75 per cent) Hindus, the largest minority Muslims plus Christians, Parsees, Jains, Sikhs, etc. There were several languages, although English was the lingua franca of politics. The population in 1921 was around 300 million, the overwhelming majority of whom were illiterate, rural, and poor.

The Indian National Congress had begun in 1886 but until the turn of the century had been a loyal organization of urban, Westernized professionals. It took a popular turn in the agitation against the partition of Bengal into West and East roughly along the lines of Hindu and Muslim majority areas. In East Bengal, Muslims were the bulk of the peasantry and Hindus were sub-infeudating rent collectors and absentee landlords. In the event, the agitation was successful and the partition of Bengal was undone after five years. The First World War had further radicalized the situation. In return for Indica's war contribution, a further instalment of self-government was promised whereby at provincial level there would be some ministers chosen from the elected element. There were legislatures elected on a limited franchise in British Indian provinces and at the Centre but no popular element in the Viceroy's Council at the Centre.

In disrupting the path of a slow growth of constitutional rule, Gandhi articulated a radical demand for self-government (*swaraj*). In mobilizing a large mass to disobey the established order, he profoundly altered political conscious-ness but in failing to deliver the promised independence, he exposed the limits of the popular path. From here on, Indian nationalists had to deploy the mass movement in combination with negotiation in committee rooms.

The major parties to the negotiations were:

(i)   The British government operating within its own party and parliamentary context;
(ii)   The Indian government although formally subordinate, still a powerful voice being close to the ground;
(iii) The Indian native states;
(iv)   Indian political parties—constitutional ones such as the Liberal Party and popular ones such as Indian National Congress and All India Muslim League.

The Muslim League was not a mass party as the Congress was. It was as the Congress used to be in the first 20 years of its life, a loyalist organization which purported to represent Muslim interests. Muslims were not only the largest religious minority; they also had special problems of economic and social deprivation. The last rulers in North India had been Muslims before the British came and they had spawned a landed aristocracy of Muslims in North India. There were also professional Muslims who served as functionaries as did Hindus. With the introduction of Western liberal education, Hindus adapted much quicker than Muslims to the new opportunities. By the end of the nineteenth century, Hindus were predominant in professional, commercial and industrial spheres. Muslims did not take to the new opportunities until special efforts were made by their leaders such as Syed Ahmad Khan. Muslim society had feudal lords and poor peasants and artisans; the middle class was sorely lacking. A small articulate Muslim middle class began to grow only during the twentieth century. The leadership of the Muslim League was shared between the feudal elements and the middle class. But middle class Muslims belonged to both the Congress as well as the Muslim League till the late 1930s.

A major plank of the Muslim League's programme was protection of its minority population and what we would today call positive discrimination in favour of Muslims—reservation of jobs etc. The League also demanded separate electorates for Muslims. This demand was known to be potentially divisive in the nationalist movement. At various stages, there were 'pacts' emphasizing the need for Hindu–Muslim unity and safeguards were promised. Jinnah, who was later to be credited with the creation of Pakistan, was in the early decades called an ambassador of Hindu–Muslim unity, being a member both of the Congress and the Muslim League.

The difficult problem was one of combining electoral politics with protection of minority interests. The Congress was committed to a demand for total independence with a popularly elected constituent assembly to frame the constitution of the independent state. The British government was offering limited autonomy with a quasi-popular element in administration elected on a limited franchise and with differentiated representation for minorities. For the Congress there was at stake the principle of equality of all citizens. The Congress wanted universal adult franchise with minority rights to be discussed by the constituent assembly. The British government took the view, partly as a way of delaying radical change, that it could not hand over power without certain guarantees. A small but noisy minority of the Conservative Party in Parliament led by Churchill was against any concessions.

With universal adult franchise and first-past-the-post elections, Muslims feared that they would be swamped by Hindus who were better educated and more likely to grab the economic perks which the state was now handing out. They wanted special seats reserved for Muslims. In most provinces of British India, Muslims were in minority ranging from as small as 8 per cent in Madras to 33 per cent in Assam and Delhi. In the heartland of Indica, United Provinces (now Uttar Pradesh)—Indica's Prussia so to speak, out of a population of 55 million in 1941, 15 per cent were Muslim. In two states, Bengal and Punjab, the Muslims had a bare majority of 55 per cent and 51 per cent respectively. In the states of Sind and North West Frontier Province they had an overwhelming majority of 72 per cent and 91 per cent. (These areas are marked in Map 17.2, which is taken from a pre-Partition publication.) A major stage was reached in the negotiations when, after the appointment of a Commission (1928), and three Round Table Conferences (1930, 1931, 1932), a bill was passed in the British Parliament. This was the Government of India Act 1935. It provided for popularly elected ministries at the provincial level in British India, for reserved seats for Muslims (as well as some other minorities), and for some elements of popular ministry at the Centre. It also proposed in eventual federation for India if a sufficient number of native states acceded. There was to be a Council of States (Upper Chamber) and a Federal Assembly (Lower Chamber). In these, the native states had respectively 40 per cent and 33 ½ per cent of the seats despite a much smaller proportion of the population. The Federation was to come into effect if the number of states acceding was sufficient to occupy half of the seats in the Council of States and represent half the total population of the states.

The Constitution was heavily weighted against the popular nationalist element. The federation would be compromised by the large weight for the native states and the fact that in the provincial assemblies only 657 seats out of 1585 were open, the remainder being reserved for some minority or other. Muslims had 482 seats out of 1585, about 30 per cent as compared to their population of 25 per cent.

Not enough native states joined in (or were cajoled to join in) by the time war broke out in September 1939 when the context changed. But while the federal part never became a reality, the British India part did. Despite severe misgivings, the nationalists decided to try the scheme by taking part in the election. Elections were held in 1937. These were the first elections to be held in Indica with the promise of office for the winning party although the franchise was limited. The seats reserved for Muslims were a major matter of contention. Although Congress purported to represent all sections of the population, it contested very few Muslim seats. Overall it emerged as the largest single party contesting 1161 (out of 1585) seats, and winning 716 (26 Muslim) seats. It had outright majority in six provinces: United Provinces, Bihar, Orissa, Central Provinces, Madras, and Bombay. In Punjab and Bengal a local coalition party won a majority by

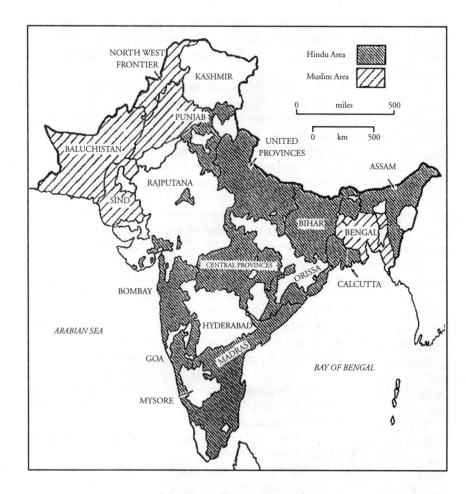

Map 20.2: Pre-Partition India

Source: Rajendra Prasad (1946), *India Divided*, Bombay: Hind Kitabs.

combining the various religious communities, although in both, the Chief Minister was a Muslim. The Muslim League won 109 out of 482 seats reserved for Muslims. However, it claimed to have contested only 226 seats.[9]

The composition of its leadership was such that the League could not be seen as a democratic party. It was shocked to find that seats reserved for Muslims did not guarantee office for the Muslim League. The League had no majority in any province in 1937, not even in Muslim majority provinces. The League's strength was in those provinces where Muslims were in a minority—Uttar Pradesh (27 out of 64 Muslim seats) and Bombay (20 out of 29)—but also where there was a professional Muslim middle class. The numerical majority of the Muslim population, however, lay elsewhere. The League was also shocked that Congress refused

[9] *The Encyclopaedia of Asian History*, The Asia Society, New York: 1988.

to form coalition cabinets with the League. The Congress did not need to; it also refused to countenance the League as anything but a collection of British Government toadies.[10]

Just as the German national question was transformed between 1863 and 1871, the Indian situation was also completely transformed in the ten years between 1937 and 1947. Here again it was a war that caused it, though the war was not started by one of the parties as an instrument to solve the question. On the declaration of war in Europe, the Viceroy in India also announced India's adherence on the British side. Since he did this without consulting any of the elected representatives at the Centre or in the provinces, the Congress ministries resigned in protest. The Congress took the view that while it was keen to fight for democracy on the Allied side, it was a mockery to do so without popular participation in the war effort. Retrospectively many have argued that this was a tactical blunder. The Congress lost power and initiative in the subsequent developments. The Muslim League was able to form government in some provinces and collaborate with the government in the hour of its need. The Congress launched a popular Quit India agitation in August 1942 but this was put down and its leadership jailed for the remainder of the war.

By the time the war ended many things had changed. Britain had been weakened despite winning the war and its hegemonic position had passed to the USA. The latter had been goading its ally through the early 1940s to make a gesture towards Indian opinion. With the end of the war and the election of a Labour government, events were speeding up. The Labour Party had long maintained fraternal relations with the Indian National Congress and so the latter was confident of winning the argument.

But if in 1935 only weak federation was on the cards, now the argument had shifted. For one thing the Congress demand for a Constituent Assembly elected with universal adult franchise was the staring point. But on the other hand, the Muslim League had grown in the meantime. Jinnah had been able to transform it into a mass nation-wide party. It had some experience of office. It had also articulated a two-nation theory and formulated a demand for Pakistan.

Of all the various issues in Indian history, the late emergence and very quick crystallization of the demand for Pakistan came as a complete surprise at the time and led to a continuing controversy for ever afterwards.[11] It was a demand originally thought up by some Muslim students studying in Britain meeting in the Waldorf Hotel on the Aldwych. The Joint Parliamentary Committee on the Government of India Bill asked two leading Muslim politicians their view of this recently articulated demand for Pakistan. One of them, A. Yusuf Ali, said Pakistan was 'a student's scheme which no responsible people had put forward'. The other politician was Sir Mohammed Zafrullah Khan, later to be Pakistan's Foreign Minister said, 'we consider it chimerical and impracticable'.[12]

---

[10] Hamida Khusro, *Our Forgotten Commitment*, Dawn, 2 June 2003.

[11] C.H. Philips and M.D. Wainwright (eds), (1970), *The Partition of India: Policies and Perspective, 1935–1947*, London: Allen & Unwin.

[12] Quoted by B. Shiva Rao in Philips and Wainwright, *The Partition of India*, p. 416.

This was said in 1934. In 1940, at its Lahore Congress Session, the Muslim League adopted the Pakistan resolution. The idea was that the Muslim majority provinces in the north-west, i.e. Sind, North West Frontier Province (NWFP), and Punjab, and those in north-east Bengal plus, for good measure, Assam (34 per cent Muslim), would form independent states. But as yet there was only the vaguest notion of what such independence would entail. In 1940 and even till 1945, all discussions had proceeded on the assumption that the subjects of defence and foreign affairs would be co-ordinated with Westminster even after dominion status had been granted to Indica, as was the case with Australia, New Zealand, and Canada. So the Centre was to have these portfolios. Were these clusters of states to be independent nation-states, to be subfederations, or what?

The theory now put forward was that there were two nations in India–a Hindu nation, Hindustan, and a Muslim nation, Pakistan. But of course, the Muslim 'nation' was scattered all over Indica, and not only in the two clusters. At this stage it was not envisaged that there would be any population transfers. Indeed, it was said that the Hindu minority in Muslim majority provinces would act as hostage to ensure the safety of the Muslim minority in Hindu majority provinces. Thus there were two nations and two states, but each nation (i.e. population professing a religion) would be split in the two states.

Although in 1940 the Muslim League had articulated the demand for Pakistan, it was not a negotiating plank when negotiations resumed after the war. The League wanted to be acknowledged as the sole representative of all Muslims, with the right to nominate Muslims for reserved cabinet seats if there were to be any. It wanted some safeguard for Muslims and a large degree of autonomy for Muslim majority areas.

The Congress at first refused to recognize the League as the sole representative of the Muslims, or to contemplate partition. But a lot of things had happened since 1937 and particularly since the imprisonment of its leaders in 1942. Step by step they began to come to terms with the demand for Pakistan, which by 1944 could not be evaded. First was a proposal by Rajagopalachari for a plebiscite in the Muslim majority areas on the issue of partition. In case of partition there would still be a common purposes agreement on defence, communication, and commerce. Having got Congress to talk of Pakistan, Jinnah raised the ante by rejecting this proposal as one for a 'moth-eaten Pakistan'.

Jinnah's view was that Muslims were a nation with the right to self-determination, and hence in any plebiscite only Muslims should be allowed to vote on the issue of partition. Of course the Congress did not counter by saying that in that case all Muslims, of majority as well as minority provinces, should be allowed to vote. Jinnah wanted the plebiscite before Indica was free and not after as was being proposed. He also rejected the idea of a common agreement on joint subjects.

Congress continued to insist that while Congress and the League could have parity in any interim government, Congress could not be confined to choosing only Hindus. After all a Muslim, Maulana Azad, was the Congress President. The Muslim League may exclusively represent Muslims but Congress would represent everyone. Here was a clash of two different views.

In July 1945, Labour party came to power in Britain and the Indian situation began to change dramatically. In the 1946 elections, the changed position of the League became clear. In the Central Legislature, the Congress had a majority of 57 out of 162 but the League won all 30 Muslim seats. In the provinces, the League also won handsomely in Bengal and Sind but not a majority in Punjab or in NWFP. It did, however, win 439 out of 494 Muslim seats in the provinces. In the nine years since 1937, the League had moved up to fulfil its boast of being the sole representative of the Muslims. The question still was did that imply the separate sovereign nation-states cutting the two nations in two ways?

There was here a fundamental clash about the concept of nationhood. The Congress saw nationality as an attribute of all 'native born' Indians by virtue of their being in India and also implicitly by being ruled by a foreign country. Only independence would bequeath full nationality on Indians by giving them a nation-state to embody nationality. Congress defined national as meaning not communal, i.e. neither Hindu nor Muslim but Indian. There were other communal parties representing Hindus, Sikhs, and others, but the main contention was with the League. The League took the view that religion defined nationality .

In June 1946, the Cabinet Mission which had been negotiating for three months with the various Indian groups proposed a confederate solution. This would have made the provinces primary units free to write their own constitution. A second tier was provinces to form groups to see if they wished to have a regional, sub-federal grouping. Two such groups were the one in north-west and the other in the north-east. There was to be some freedom for individual provinces to leave a group if they saw fit but only after the Constitution had been written. There was to be a central legislature with reserved seats. The Centre was to have only a few subjects—defence, foreign affairs, communications. There was to be an interim cabinet at the Centre with representatives of the major groups. Between June 1946 when the proposal was made and about nine months later, the plan was abandoned. The precise details as to which party accepted and which didn't, the qualifications made, the mistake of angry statements and violent retaliation, are too complicated to dwell on here. Many, however, have felt then and since that such a Confederation was the best way to keep the country together. It was the 'Grossindische' solution.

The reasons why it broke down included a clash of views concerning the nature of the nation-state. When the Congress accepted the plan it did so with many reservations and caveats. The League accepted in toto to begin with but reserved its right to move towards Pakistan. The Congress view was that the Constituent Assembly which was to determine the Constitution must be sovereign and could not be made to submit to restriction; in short, the view was independence first, discus concessions later. The League view was independence only if the two-nation principle was conceded. The Congress had also over years formed the view that independent India would need a strong central authority to tackle the economic problems it faced. Thus one major reservation the Congress had concerned the list of subjects the Centre would control. It wanted planning, foreign trade, currency, and finance to be central responsibility. The League was reluctant to grant taxation as a central subject.

When the final parting came it was not until May–June 1947. By then the

Congress had worked in an interim government with the League and found its hands severely tied. It had always sought undisputed power for effective economic and social action. It agreed to a partition of Indica with two sovereign states only when it seemed the only way to have a strong state. The Constitution of India as framed by the Constituent Assembly made a strong quasi-federal arrangement with the Centre as paramount. The provinces and their boundaries were change-able at the Centre's behest. This was as the 1935 Act would have it. By 1947, the native states did not obstruct the arrangement. They were persuaded by the outgoing British to accede and most did so willingly. Only in the case of Kashmir did it lead to an armed conflict of a protracted nature.

Thus between 1935 and 1947, the Indian discussions centred on federal or quasi-federal arrangements to keep together the various communities and the native states. The 1935 Act was one such gross solution but the native states imposed an indirectness in the elective element. For their small proportions of the population, these states were treated indulgently by those elements in Britain which hoped to bolster reaction. At that time, much was made of the difficulty of getting the states to agree. The then Viceroy could not get half of them to agree within four years. In 1947, it took less than four months. The 1935 Act is rather like Austria's proposal of 1863 for reform of the Confederation. But the national-ists were committed to parliamentarism in Indica as in Germania.

The 1946 solution (leaving aside many which were advanced in between the two dates) foundered not on the native states question but on the issue of the nature of the nation-state. If the nation-state was to be independent and autono-mous as well as strong, it had to be free to make its own internal arrangements about minority rights. If the nation-state was to embody a nation defined on religious lines, then the internal arrangements would be made prior to the independence.

Despite the acceptance of Confederation, albeit temporarily and with reserva-tions, the conduct of the two sovereign states subsequently makes clear that they wanted strong centralized states. Pakistan went through the problem again in 1970 when the strong Centre fell foul of the desire for regional autonomy on the part of the Bengali Muslims. Having assumed that being Muslim was the only criterion of Pakistani nationhood, no care had been taken to accommodate other dimensions. Thus the federation broke again in 1971. It broke on the incompat-ibility of the electoral principle with the theory of nationality when East Paki-stanis had numerical majority in the Parliament, the hitherto majority West Pakistan decided to retain power by armed action. It took a civil war to settle issue.

So in the end, three nation-states emerged out of Indica—India, Pakistan, and Bangladesh. The inclusive solutions which would have kept a loose: confederation were rejected in favour of an exclusive but powerful solution. Even before the break-up of Pakistan in 1971, it was quite clear that both sovereign states had a problem of constructing a nationalism. Unlike Germania, Indica lacked a com-mon language. A history that could have been common to a single nation became contentious as soon as two nations were discerned side by side. Since the nation-state did not embody the entire nation, Pakistan had the additional problem of having to piece together its history. When did Pakistan's history as a nation begin?

In 1947? surely not. Did it begin with the founding of the Muslim League or did it begin with the first arrival of Muslims in India? Since the history of Muslim kingdoms from the tenth to the eighteenth century centres around Delhi and the Indo-Gangetic plain, was that history Pakistan's history?

But India's task has been no easier. History writing and teaching has not been treated as an academic matter anywhere but certainly not in India. History is one way of creating, and especially re-creating, the consciousness of nationhood but if the nature of nationhood is itself disputed so will be the content of the history. If one accepts the theory of the Muslim League that there were two nations in Indica—a Muslim nation and a Hindu nation—and that Pakistan represents a crystallization of the Muslim nation within Indica as a nation-state, then the partition left behind India (that is Bharat) as a Hindu nation. The history of such a nation must treat the entire period since the arrival of the Afghan kings in the eighth century as a long period of foreign rule against which various Hindu kings struggled. But the Congress, while accepting partition, denied the two-nation theory—Muslims are still a substantial minority in India because Pakistan did not embody the Muslim nation within Indica if such there ever was. Pakistan was only the accidental creation of contiguous Muslim majority provinces in the north-west and the north-east of Indica. Muslims were scattered all over Indica and were 24 per cent of its population in 1941. Even after the partition, enough remained behind for India to be one of the three or four largest Muslim population states in the world. Thus, the Muslim nation if there was a separate identifiable one within Indica was split into Pakistan, its fragmented national state, and those remaining behind. India maintains that it is a secular democratic republic and as such, religion has no official status in its Constitution. In practice, the official version of Indian history emphasizes Hindu–Muslim tolerance, praises kings of the past who enjoined tolerance, and is mildly embarrassed about fanatical Hindu leaders who fought Muslims as enemy. Needless to say, the official version of Indian history is only one version and it is contested from a Hindu India angle, among other rival interpretations.

In suppressing religion as a dimension along which Indian nationhood could be defined, the Congress ideologues (Nehru in particular) left open the question as to what does define Indian nationhood. A common history is a dubious resting place for an effort to define nationhood. As I said briefly above, history at the Indica level is a disputed terrain. There are also many regional differences, with the heroes of one region being villains of another. Much of Maratha history, which Hindu nationalists want to claim as a glorious last fight against Muslim domination, becomes an episode best forgotten in the regions that received Maratha Army depredations. The south of the country resents northern domination in the culture of history writing as well as in other dimensions and so on.

Denied history and religion as uniting forces, the construction of Indian nationhood has become a problem. The official ecumenical—secular version of India's past and present is contested. There is no common language—as a basic element in any grid defining nationhood. The split of East from West Pakistan hinged on language as well as other issues. The Bengali-speaking Muslims have shown by their struggle that it is the language–religion combination that most satisfactorily defines nationhood on the subcontinent if not elsewhere. Thus as India's leading sociologist, T.N. Madan, has observed, the Bengali Muslims behaved as Muslims in 1947 in joining Pakistan and as Bengalis in 1971 in liberating themselves from Pakistan. They did not, however, join their West Bengal brethren in founding an independent Bengal nation. It is precisely the combination of language and religion that constitutes nationhood in Bangladesh.

But if that is so, India is either a fragment nation-state of the one ecumenical—secular nation that was embedded in Indica and for which the nationalist movement fought. Or it is a conglomerate of many nations defined on language or language–religion grounds. It is in this latter sense a multinational entity with national consciousnesses defined along a matrix of the main religions of Hinduism, Islam, Sikhism, (plus Christianity, Zoroastrianism, Buddhism) and the 16 languages officially listed in the Constitution. This is not fanciful. The demand for Khalistan at the present is an attempt of a part of the Punjabi-speaking state to distinguish itself from the rest. Punjabi-speaking Sikhs wish for a separate state of their own from Punjabi-speaking Hindus. Once Pakistan had happened, religion could not be ignored as a factor in defining nationhood. Once Bangladesh had happened, religion by itself is shown to be not enough to define nationhood. If Khalistan is not realized, one reason, though by no means a major one, will be that unlike East Pakistan which was distant from West Pakistan, while Punjab is contiguous with Indian territory. Territoriality will remain the residual reason for defining nationhood at the Indian level. Thus, again it is the fragmented nation-state that in its turn has the need to construct a nationhood to suit its territory.

Conclusion

Despite its length, this paper must be considered preliminary and somewhat short on details. In one sense, the parallel between Germany and India seems slight. The German national question was solved by sovereign German princes without any formal pressure from outside. The formal proceedings of Frankfurt were the shadow and the cabinet manoueverings were the substance. It was a swift war in 1866 that settled the issue in favour of *Kleindeutsch* and against *Grossdeuttschi*. In the Indian case, the context was colonial but the negotiations were the real theatre. The issue was discussed again and again in a legalistic atmosphere as much due to the nature of British Parliament as due to the circumstance that most of the leading negotiators (Jinnah, Gandhi, Nehru, Patel) were lawyers. It was not a swift war but a rising climate of communal violence from August 1946 onwards that forced the pace as did the determination of the Labour Government to give up India. But here again, the issue was settled against the inclusive solution.

The formal similarity is thus the *Gross-Klein* dichotomy and the rejection of the *Gross* alternative. But beyond that, there is the unsustainability of the solution. In Pakistan's case, within 25 years there was a break-up. In Germany's case, there were three constitutions within 75 years and then a break-up.

The real structural similarity is about the relationship between nation and nation-state. The nationalist movement in both cases had liberal parliamentary connotations. But the nationalist movement also was ambivalent about whether it wished to realize the cultural nation or was willing to settle for what would prove effective and powerful. The German liberals suffered the same dilemma as the Indian National Congress. Ultimately they preferred a strong state to the nation they championed. But the strong state in turn compelled them to redefine the nation.

There is a further similarity in the rapidity with which the situation changed. In Germany's case, the 1860s was the crucial decade; for India, the 1940s. There is perhaps a further parallel to explore between Bismarck and Jinnah, in their combative style. Each started virtually no popular base but read the changing circumstances shrewdly—let the opponents make the running and all the mistakes—and made rapid gains which no one gave them credit for. But that needs to be argued elsewhere.

21

Towards a Syncretic Vision of India

While in India soon after the Babri Masjid demolition last year, I was struck by the demoralization and confusion among the 'secularists' who until then had been complacent. The destruction of the Masjid brought out in them a wrong response. Many rushed to profess their knowledge of and sympathy with religion, dusting off their Vivekanands, re-reading their Kabir, and being quite unhinged under the onslaught of *Hindutva*.

The mistake is to think of the *Hindutva* concept as a religious challenge. The point is not about religion in my view and whether one is secular (*dharma nirapeksha*) or ecumenical (*sarvadharma samabhava*) is beside the point. Religion has been part of India's private and public life; it has been manipulated by political leaders from Tilak onwards. It will be a rare Indian leader who will refrain from doing so. Indeed, the only political leader who had no religiosity was Nehru. The problem of secularism is tied with Nehru, not so much his personality but as a vision of what it meant to be Indian.

That India was not a nation had been for a long time the British critique. As a cultural concept, there has of course been *Indica* since Greek times, with Hindu/ Sindhu current in the Arabian world as an expression for India. Whether India was a nation or merely a collection of regions was the question the nationalists had to answer. India is not unique of course in this. Germania was an expression long before Germany became a nation-state in 1870.

MORE THAN BHARAT

The India that Nehru discovered was of course not the India that is Bharat of the Constitution. That India, call it *Indica* to keep pre-partition India separate from post-partition India, never became a nation-state. So what we told the British about why we were a nation and what that nation comprised never materialized. Indeed our national anthem speaks off an India that is more than Bharat. *Indica* was partitioned twice during the last 46 years; first into India and Pakistan and then into India, Pakistan, and Bangladesh. By 1971, *Indica* had taken the shape that the Cabinet Mission plan wanted to give it, albeit as part of a confederate *Indica*.

But if India was not the one that Nehru had pledged to liberate at the Lahore Congress in 1930, what was the nation that had emerged? The foreign power which unified us had gone; parts had been lopped off. Religion had been the cause of the partition though Congress denied the two-nation theory. But if religion was not the defining essence of India, what was it? We had no common language despite the efforts of Hindi *pracharaks* to make us learn one. History is a divisive force as we well know. Why then was India a nation? Unlike Eire, there is nothing in the Constitution nor has there been in the political life to pledge a reversal of partition.

Nehru's implicit answer was to build up a national consciousness around secularism, non-alignment and planned economic development. These three elements were to define India's uniqueness. Unity in diversity was demonstrated at home by bringing together tribal dancers and different state troupers at the Republic Day parade. All India Radio and the Films Division constantly reminded us about the diversity in India and also the unity. A nationalist syncretic history of India was constructed by Kevalan Madhav Pannikar and others under Nehru's guidance.

By the time of his death, the Nehru vision had fallen apart. The trauma of 1962 was luckily quickly reversed by the triumph of 1965 in the war against Pakistan. India was a nation by virtue of its ability to defend its territory. Indeed, India is defined by its territory. Lacking language or religion or history as a unifying characteristic, territoriality is the sole consensual ground on which India's nationhood is defined.

Had Lal Bahadur Shastri lived, we may have seen a new attempt, more *desi,* less internationalist, to define Indian-ness or Bharatiyata. Indira Gandhi carried on as if the Nehru vision had not dented at all; secularism, socialism, and non-alignment were the continuing themes. But, in her private life there was much more religion and politically she was not above manipulating religion. Territoriality and military strength were the de facto themes of nationhood as the Bangladesh liberation showed.

22

Constructing Nationality in a Multinational Democracy
The Case of India

INTRODUCTION

The Gujarati poet Khabardar expressed the notion of nationality succinctly when he wrote early in this century, 'Wherever there dwells a Gujarati, there is forever Gujarat.' As a sentiment, this must have been echoed in many other languages. Rupert Brooke spoke of himself when dead and buried as making his grave a corner which will be forever England. Nation is thus territoriality, but an internalized one that you can carry with yourself forever. This is because Gujarat/England are cultural expressions defined by a language (Gujarati/English) and a history, which is shared by the 'nation'.

But history can divide as well as unite, especially when the territory is a disputed one or at least a shared one. The Ulstermen are forever insisting that it is their history which unites them with the mainland and not with the Republic to which their land is contiguous. History and religion drive a wedge and make the construction of nationality a problematical one. In this paper, I wish to trace the varying influences of language, religion, history, and territory in defining nationality. In particular, I shall deal with India which, in my view, is a classic multinational polity determined to assert a single nationality. Although 'unity in diversity' is a motto as well as a cliche of Indian politics, there are still problems, in my opinion, in constructing an organic rather than an administrative unity. But India has also chosen the path of constitutional liberal democracy to affect that organic unity. Thus the contradictions of nationalism intersect with those of liberalism in a post-colonial democracy. Add to these problems that of achieving economic development and you have almost a unique case. Much is to be gained, however, by not treating India as a unique case but to put it in a comparative perspective.

R. Michener (ed.), *Nationality, Patriotism and Nationalism in Liberal Democratic Societies*, St. Paul, Minnesota: PWPA, 1993, pp. 225–41.

LIBERALISM AND NATIONALISM

Liberalism in its eighteenth century origins is a universalist, rationalist creed. It disdains to speak of excluding categories such as nationality. Although Adam Smith called his book *The Wealth of Nations*, he meant the wealth of all nations. Economics which is indelibly stamped with liberal rationalism has the greatest difficulty in coming to terms with nationalism. The pursuit of nationalist economic aims is, for the economist, a snare and a delusion, a fraud perpetrated by one section of the population on the majority, a tax on consumers (a category less exclusive than nationals), and a deviation from the universal and undoubted benefits of Free Trade. From Smith through Marx to Hobson (and even more so in the recent neoclassical resurgence), nations do not and should not exist. All human race is one or will be so in the long run, and it is the benefit of all and not some that economics is concerned with.

Nationalism came to oppose this classical universalist discourse of economic theory in the field of international trade. Friedrich List, in challenging the doctrine of free trade, first questioned the universality of the classical economic doctrine by labelling it–'English'. (British may have been better given the Scottish origins of political economy.) He accepted the principle of *laissez-faire* in internal trade, within that is the *Zollverein* a protonation. In this, he was following the Physiocrats, who also viewed *laissez-faire* as an intra-country policy. As far as international trade was concerned, List, like the French and later the Americans, was for protective tariffs as a way of promoting economic growth. Thus, though politically German nationalism was a reaction against French (Napoleonic) imperialism, in its economics, it was adopting a French (Colbertist) stand against English free trade imperialism.

MARX ON INDIA AND BRITISH IMPERIALISM

Friedrich List pioneered the economics of nationalism. To the liberals as to Marx at this juncture in the nineteenth century 'capitalism in one country' was anathema. It is a defensive strategy bound to cost dearly in the long run, if not immediately. Marx took the view that capitalism was bound to spread allover the world by its sheer technological superiority and its social relations which were systemically rational for the mode of production. By emphasizing accumulation to the exclusion of all other considerations, capitalism hastened the removal of pre-capitalist fetishes such as tribal loyalties, religious superstition, and feudal sentimentality. Capitalism has its own contradictions which grow as it develops but at all times it is superior to that which it replaces. It was for this reason that Marx was dismissive of the German economists of his day as they dreamed, like many nationalists since, of a unique German path. De Te Fabula Narratur, Marx, like Engels, is an anti-nationalist writer. Later in the days of the Third International when the anti-imperialist struggle led the Leninists to emphasize nationalism as opposed to imperialism (the highest stage of capitalism), some of the writings of Marx and Engels on the 'colonies' were an embarrassment. Marx's writings on India are a mixture of praise for the English in the task of destruction that they had performed but critical for their having not gone far enough. He was at this time reporting on the debate in the Parliament about the renewal of the charter of the East India Company (1853). By 1857, when there was an anti-British uprising, the East India Company's regime came to an end. After 1857, the British did even less by way of destroying the old, pre-capitalist social structure. Although Marx did not return to publishing any writing about India after the 1850s, his earlier critique of the British failure to affect a root and branch social transformation became even more valid. Social reform was from now on left to the private voluntary efforts of the 'natives' and a pretty botched-up job it turned out to be, leaving independent India with a huge unfinished task. It could even be argued that after 1857 the British, far from destroying the old order, were busy shoring it up. The consequences for Indian nationalism were going to be fatal.

ORIGINS OF INDIAN NATIONALISM

The incomplete but positive part of the British reform of Indian society had, however, created a Western educated elite in the provincial capitals of Calcutta, Bombay, and Madras. This elite spoke beside their 'native' tongue English and became conscious of a common identity as no previous generation was. The aspirations of 1857 were to re-establish the Mughal empire or to replace it by a Delhi based Hindu kingship (Hindu *Patapadshahi*). Both of these were, by and large, North Indian constructs. Despite the strenuous efforts of nationalist historians, it would be difficult to show that any India-wide ideal inspired the uprising. It was the 'babus' of the 1870s and 1880s who brought a new rhetoric and a new consciousness to the fore. (Bengal having had a Western inspired renaissance some decades earlier developed a Bengali consciousness in advance of the other regions of India. It would take me too far away from the theme of the present paper to deal with this differential start properly.)

The argument for Indian nationalism was at its outset framed in terms of economics. These new Indians were thoroughly schooled in English liberalism, but they also saw the contradiction between liberalism and imperialism. The avowed universalism of the Free Trade doctrine conflicted with the narrow pursuit of the interests of the Lancashire textile industry and the racist bias of imperialism in the distribution of the benefits of the Raj. Liberalism is deliberately blind to the inequalities among people; each of us is a rational individual capable of the pursuit of private gain. Marx had seen through this, but for his own reasons, retained much of the apparatus of classical liberal economic theory, seeking instead to subvert it from within by marrying it with the theory of the class struggle. Imperialism, however, added a dimension of inequality not along the lines of economic property relations but along those of racial (national) identity. A rich Indian industrialist, merchant, or professional was inferior to the English-man, be he ever so humble in his status *vis-à-vis* other Englishmen.(English racism was compounded by the attitude of the English upper classes being no better toward their own proletariat, nor to the underclass they had exported to the antipodes. The colour of the Indian skin was an additional, not the differential, element in the English attitude. The reaction of the Indian, and to some extent the Australian, was along nationalist lines.)

The pioneering generation of Indian nationalist thus concentrated on the 'unBritish' nature of the policy followed in India. When revenue considerations made it necessary to put a tax on imports of British cotton textiles, Manchester demanded and obtained a countervailing excise duty on the fledgling Indian cotton textile industry. This fuelled Indian nationalism and a demand for fiscal autonomy became a major plank of the early Indian National Congress, a demand that was conceded as early as 1907. The language of Indian nationalism in those days was almost exclusively economic tariffs, the Sterling/Rupee exchange rate, the immiserizing, effects of the British rule, etc. Its perspective was India-wide, although the policies it advocated to speed up capitalist development would have benefited some regions more than others; and, in representing an elite educated in the provincial capitals, it underrepresented the Interior.

RELIGION, HISTORY, AND LANGUAGE IN INDIAN NATIONALISM

It was, however, an elite movement with very shallow roots in the *moffusil*. It reflected the twin processes of administrative unification and early capitalist development over a vast territory that only rarely in the past had been ruled by a single power or from a single Centre. Apart from these 'imported' cementing factors, the forces that defined a nation were as unifying as they were divisive. If the presence of a foreign ruler was to unite the locals in a struggle to overthrow him (as, for example, argued by Bnankim Chatterji in his nationalist novel *Anand Math*, published In the late nineteenth century), then it was easy to identify the Muslim minority as a hangover from the earlier 'foreign' rulers. Indeed, *Anand Math* had to disguise the enemy as being Muslim in order to avoid censorship. But given that reading of Indian history, foreign rule went back to the seventh century. In addition to this, if one talked of an Aryan 'invasion' of India, there was little basis for a local nationalism. Hindu nationalism was left to argue that the Aryans were natives, but all who came subsequently were foreigners. Religion then became a unifying argument for some but immediately it divided as it has ever since.

Even within religion, however, all was not well. Lacking a church or an ecclesiastical structure, Hinduism was not then, nor is it now a single seamless whole. The late nineteenth century saw a number of efforts to reform Hinduism–Arya Samaj, (somewhat earlier) Brahmo Samaj, the Ramakrishna movement, Swaminarayan, etc. The mainstream religion had multiple fractures between the Shaivates and the Vaishnavites, the mother worshippers and beneath them all subsisted a religion of the ordinary people which was an amalgam of animism and local gods, Muslim pirs, etc. The Hinduism written up today in the learned books as timeless is as much a by-product of the nationalist reformism as anything else. (A historical account of Hinduism is badly needed.) History, by the same token, was not a unifying force. A nationalist history of sorts was written. It praised the periods in which India had a strong central ruler, of whatever religion, and deplored the tendency toward internecine quarrels which let in the European invader. This historiography marginalized much of South India, which had a different history but that complaint was muted till just before independence. Later, the south Indian experience was to become a rallying point for the Dravidian nationalist movement which did take the view that the Aryans were foreign invaders. But even within the North (the classic Hindustan), history was divided. The brave Maratha attempt to fight the Mughal rule, successful as it was, could be said to have weakened the 'nation' against European assault, and in any way was unwelcome in areas like Bengal which suffered from their depredations. Contemporary Hindu nationalism is stuck with the glorification of Maratha history as the last episode of nearly pan-Indian Hindu rule. There was, of course, no single language in the country. English was the language of early nationalism and continues in its Indianized way to be the language of formal politics. An attempt was made by Gandhi to popularize Hindi as a national language; indeed, the Constitution said that ten years after its promulgation, Hindi will be the national language, but the North-South divide as well as the fragility of the Hindi language forced the dilution of that rule. India continues uneasily bilingual at the federal level and trilingual at the state level. India of course did not have the 'luxury' that the USA had of being able to ask all other languages but English to take a subordinate status as a condition of citizenship, nor did it have the equivalent of the Great Russian State which while constitutionally recognizing all languages could proceed to subordinate them to Russian. Nor do the Hindi-speaking people constitute an overwhelming majority as the Han people do in China.

TERRITORIALITY: THE UNIFYING FACTOR

Lacking the unifying bases of religion, language, or history, Indian nationalism in the early twentieth century had at least a territorial basis. The term 'all-India' looms large in many descriptions. As of, say, 1914, it meant all that now comprises India, Pakistan, and Bangladesh; what then comprised British India and scores of 'native' states. In the course of winning independence by means of a broad based, and for all practical purposes, non-violent movement, this slender thread of territoriality was lost. To appeal to the broad masses, Gandhi quite shrewdly used the idioms of religion, an ecumenical combination of his version of simplified (dare I say Christianized) Hinduism, with a single text, the *Bhagavad Gita*, and a set of common prayers, and an Islam that soon discovered itself to be obscurantist when defending the Caliphate against the British plans to abolish it, only to find the Ata Turk doing the same. But once the genie of religion had been let loose, it could not be put back into the bottle. Jinnah and the Muslim League defined nationality along religious lines. The Congress, taking the territorialist line, had to construct in opposition to this a theory of nationality that transcended religion, the divisions of history, and the lack of common language. It did not have such a theory. In vain it tried to claim that it had popular support across all religious communities; a claim that was true until 1939, but frittered away by 1946. Its argument that the Muslim League was an agent of the imperialist power carried less weight when in the run-up to independence it, as much as the League, was relying on British goodwill for a smooth transfer of power. Indeed, the Congress needed an extra helping of goodwill because it wanted to paint itself as the legitimate heir to the Empire, continuing as India, with the Muslim League being the breakaway splinter. Jinnah could and did complain that Nehru and the Congress were the inside favourites and he was the rebel.

Partition and After

The full story of the partition of India is a complex and much disputed one. For our present purpose, it is enough to look at the problem it created for the construction of Indian nationality. The Congress denied, as it had to, that it had agreed to the division of the country along religious lines. It refused to accept the two-nation theory. Apart from anything else, the two nations by the religion criterion did not constitute in any neat fashion two territorial nations. The majority of Muslims in pre-partition India lived in Hindu majority provinces, while the Muslim majority provinces of the north-west were sparsely populated. Two populous provinces, Punjab and Bengal had a razor-thin Muslim majority. The partition created two-nation states and three territories—two for Pakistan and one for India. To that extent, the Congress could pride itself on having preserved the territory, lopped off at the sides but with the torso intact. But if religion did not define Indian nationality, what did?

In the course of the independence movement, the Congress had allowed the creation of provincial offices along linguistic rather than the existing administrative lines. Thus, immediately upon independence, it faced a demand for redrawing the state boundaries along linguistic lines. The divisive force of a common history was much in evidence as claims were made to slices of neighboring territories on the basis of the hoary past. The newly independent government saw this as a danger to be avoided. It had a problem on its hands of absorbing the 'native' states which had been cajoled and bullied into giving up their sovereignty and signing up with the new heirs of the Empire. Partition was a traumatic shock, but even before that, the Indian independence movement was committed to the theory that only a strong central rule could guarantee the unity of India. It is obvious that if one were to define nationality in a purely territorial way, this is indeed a tautology. Indian nationalism has always held that the unity is much more than administrative but in political practice, in dealing with the dissident movements in the north-east or in Punjab, it has stuck to the centralist imperative. The Indian Constitution, federal though it is, recognizes only all-India as an autonomous and indivisible entity. The individual states are creatures of all-India as represented by the Central government, that is, the party which has majority in the Lok Sabha.

This constitutional structure has provided the context in which the construction of Indian nationality has had to take place. It is at best a negative or restrictive context. It prevents, if necessary by the full use of the force of the State, any attempt at breakaway. It is this aspect that has been under intensive display in the battle in the Punjab against the demand for a Sikh nation of Khalistan. It was also displayed against the Nagaland guerrilla movement and in Kashmir. At the same time, one could argue that the interplay of a democratic polity with a centralist Constitution has exacerbated the tendency to use the local nationality card as a bargaining ploy. It only requires a separatist movement to find enough support in the Central Parliament to leverage a small faction of the ruling parliamentary party into a full-scale demand for statehood. After initial resistance to the demand for linguistic states, it was the fast unto death of a Telugu-speaking activist in support of a demand for a separate state that forced the Central government to concede Andhra Pradesh and then all the linguistic states.

But language by itself did not prove a sufficiently disruptive force as had been feared. A quarter century later, it was the combination of religion and language that sparked the most threatening separatist movement in Punjab. Pakistan had already by then split into two, demonstrating that for the East Pakistanis, a common religion was not sufficient to constitute nationality; nor was a common language by itself enough. In breaking away from Pakistan but not joining West Bengal to form a Bengali nation, the Bangladeshis demonstrated the power of the combination of religion and language plus of course concentration in a single territory in making a nation. Even then, they needed a bloody civil war and the intervention of a superior military power to win. The Khalistan movement has neither the majority support (so far), nor the open help of a superior military power. It does, however, have a plausible basis for defining nationality.

CONSTRUCTING NATIONALITY

If the Constitution provides the negative context, what is the positive context for the construction of Indian nationality? To begin with, no nation can admit that it needs to construct nationality. It has to assert as a fact that it is and always has been a nation. Granting that, one can discern in post-independent Indian policy a number of strands which go toward a positive effort to build a nation. The role that Nehru, as a conscious intellectual, played in this is hard to separate from overall policy. This is because in the first 15 years after independence, Nehru was all pervasive. He was a modernizer as well as an internationalist while being a fervent nationalist. The modernist in him was committed to a nationalism built on secular, not just ecumenical lines. Science and economic progress to him were as important binding forces as tradition and history. Nehru directed his efforts at building a set of cultural institutions and transforming existing ones into vehicles for nationality construction. All-India Radio was harnessed to be a cultural force both in its national news broadcasts, taking priority over local news, and more controversially, in fostering an education in the heritage of Indian classical music in defiance of popular taste for film music. National academies were formed, conveniently called Akademies, for music and drama, fine arts, and literature. The idea was to break down the parochialism of regional art forms, to introduce North India to the beauty of South Indian music and dance and vice versa. The Films Division of India, a branch of the official Ministry of Information and Broadcasting through its weekly newsreels and occasional documentaries reached the vast cinema-going public, consciously slanting the news toward unifying themes. The Republic Day celebrations always showed the dancers from the remote parts of the country, integrating them into the popular mind as part of India. I do not believe this vast effort has yet been properly studied but its educative effect on one who grew up looking at them is undeniable.

The idea was to make people aware of the extent of India, its diversity, its strangeness in parts, its age, and its timelessness, all arguments which had been deployed by the articulate nationalist movement but now had to be conveyed to much larger numbers. It was all the more important in a country where the lives of most people revolved around strictly local events. India was then made up of a series of local agrarian economies, with only a thin overarch of railroads and industry. It was as important to build up a national economy as a single integrated structure as it was to build up national polity. The planning effort launched by independent India has to be understood, therefore, both in an economic context of raising incomes as well as of knitting an economy together from its various local strands.

From the beginning of the modern independence movement in the late nineteenth century, the industrialization of India had always been a central part of the agenda. Once the Congress had come to power in the first widespread elections of pre-independent India in a majority of provinces, Subhash Bose as the Congress President convened the National Planning Committee, in which Nehru was to play a prominent part. This Committee laid the foundation of the economic programme that was embodied in the post-independence planning. Self-sufficiency was a keynote of this plan, not just for economic reasons but also for the nationalist sentiment which regarded all imports from the West as marks of imperial dependence. India stayed within the international capitalist nexus and hence the drive for self-sufficiency never became one for autarky. But the giant steel plants and the massive hydroelectric dams were as much to foster national pride as to build up the economy. The Mahalanobis plan was to build up machine making capacity by redirecting imports to capital goods only. At this juncture, this capacity for manufacturing the heavy industry products was not meant to be available for military purposes.

Nehru had another plank in his policy which was meant both to give an internationalist perspective to independent India and to boost national pride. This was the distinctive foreign policy India had in the teeth of fierce opposition from the Cold War powers. Through the 1950s, India played a prominent part in the Non-Aligned Movement (Bandung), in the cease-fire negotiations in Korea and Indo-China, and in supporting the anti-imperialist struggle in Africa. Prominent world figures visited India—Khrushchev, Bulganin, Ho Chi Minh, Chou En Lai, Tito, Eisenhower—and the effect was not lost on the citizens.

This strategy of gradual nation-building by acting along the triple fronts of cultural integration, economic planning, and foreign policy could indeed have worked for all we know had it been given sufficient time. It remains, however, a counterfactual because the early 1960s saw the Nehruvian strategy fall apart. The border clash with China undermined all the assumptions on which Nehru had built his policy. The defence of these remote and strange sounding tracts of land, inherited from the imperial power, was not undertaken with total enthusiasm by the prime minister or his defence minister (Krishna Menon) till they were finally pushed into it by public clamour. The military outcome was humiliating for the Indian Army. It was ill-prepared and ill-equipped. In the panic that briefly ensued, there was a mad rush to buy or borrow armaments from the USA in total abandonment of the previous posture. The manner of the Chinese withdrawal, sudden and unilateral as it was, was even more humiliating to the Indian nation. Until 1962, the main worry of the federal government had been of break-up of India from within, a replay of the trauma of partition. After 1962, territorial integrity from external attack moved up the agenda. The Army now became a much more prominent part of the nation's psychology and has since been able to command a substantial amount of resources.

After 1962, territoriality became the first if not the sole plank of the new nationality. In 1965, the successful battle with the old enemy Pakistan restored national pride. I recall witnessing the transformation of the then Prime Minister Lal Bahadur Shastri from a diminutive figure of fun to a national hero in the brief few weeks of that summer. Never as well known or as charismatic as Nehru, he delivered what his predecessor could not—a clear military victory. The 'jawan', the ordinary soldier, was now a hero; a sure mark of this was the proliferation of films with soldiers as the hero. The year 1965 could be said to be the arrival of India at the solution of its nationality problem. Those remote scraps of territory in the Himalayas had brought home to the citizens the vastness of their country as nothing else had. They now seemed to care about all the territory of the country. The humiliation of 1962 was reversed so quickly that one could again believe that had the politicians not neglected the Army, it would never have lost. This feeling was strengthened by the Bangladesh war in which India's well timed intervention dismembered the old enemy. Since then, in relation with the Himalayan kingdoms of Sikkim, Bhutan, and Nepal, India has behaved as the true their of the British Raj. Lately, it has extended its subcontinental policing role to Sri Lanka and briefly the Maldives. Internally, the Army has been deployed in every situation where there is a threat of dissension; indeed, faced with local dissent, only the Army is a nationally trusted institution. The local police has long since been found to be inadequate and suspect. The prominence of the Army in the construction of national unity has been helped by the strictly constitutional stance adopted by the Army. The democratic way has been more threatened by the civilian politicians (as in the Emergency as well as suspension of democratic life in some states under President's rule) than by the armed forces. Indeed as politics and politicians lose their glow, the Army remains the one respected institution.

CONCLUSION

The problem of constructing nationality in a country with multiple languages, many religions, and a divisive history is a serious one. The Partition, once agreed to, fractured the idea that an ecumenical citizenship could be a basis of Indian nationality. The local linguistic culture is, in any case, more real and even Hindu society is regionally differentiated. The only unifying theme remains territoriality-—the sense of inhabiting a common land mass. Luckily for India, this became a positive cementing theme as the result of a national humiliation and its quick reversal. Tensions, however, remain. Whatever its virtues, territoriality has limited emotional hold except in times of invasion. There remains a strong current which would like to construct nationality on the lines of Hindu religion. The fundamentalist revivals in Islam and in Sikhism, close at home have fuelled this current further. It is a militant, populist demand. It does not as yet command a majority. Against it stands the old Nehruvian vision of an ecumenical if not a secular state, where the successful modernization would eventually weaken the hold of divisive religion. This older vision is yet needed, but it has to increase the rate of its spread to be able to withstand the opposition of Hindu militancy. The economic growth in the last 40 years, moderate though its pace is, has created a nationally mobile modern middle class; these 200 million people have weak regional and religious loyalties and a lot of stake in a continuing modernizing economy. These are Nehru's children; they may yet realize his vision of Indian nationality, though one should never take such things for granted.

23

Communalism, Secularism, and the Dilemma of Indian Nationhood

INTRODUCTION

'Communalism' is a word that has special connotations with regard to events in South Asia. The term was used in both India and Ceylon (as it then was) in colonial times. Community/communitarian are words with a good image in British life, but community/communalism have a particular imperial connotation of how the British saw communities as forces for damage in the Indian empire. Communalism signifies riots—between Hindus and Muslims in India, and Buddhists and Christians in Sri Lanka—which are always called 'communal' riots. Riots between Sikhs and Hindus or upper-caste Hindus and the Dalits are not called communal riots. In this sense, then, communalism is any ideology, attitude, or behaviour that is likely to incite or lead to a Hindu–Muslim riot.[1] (It is interesting to note that in the UK the 'troubles' in Ulster are called sectarian, and the bloody war in the former Yugoslavia led to the term 'ethnic cleansing'. These are similar phenomena, but each deserves its own treatment.)

In the year preceding independence/partition on 15 August 1947, India experienced a continuous stream of Hindu–Muslim riots across the country. It was a civil war in a not very civil society. The war climaxed in the partition of Indica into India and Pakistan.[2] The partition, an event which was unforeseen as late as the end of 1946, was hastily decided upon within weeks of the arrival of Mountbatten as the last British Viceroy in March 1947. In the aftermath of

M. Leifer (ed.), *Asian Nationalism*, Routledge, 2000.

I am grateful to the following for their helpful comments with regard to this chapter: Philip Oldenburg, Yunas Samad, Katharine Adeney, as well as members of the Asian Nationalism seminar and its Chairman, Professor Michael Leifer.

[1] I shall concentrate on the Indian subcontinent in this chapter, although Sri Lanka offers an interesting parallel. For Sri Lanka, see Jayawardene (1986).

[2] At the risk of appearing pretentious, I shall use the term 'Indica' for India before the partition and India for after the partition. British India, of course, refers to pre-1947. I have used this term before in Desai (1990). See also Chapter 20.

partition and the flood of fleeing families—Hindus, Muslims, and Sikhs who managed to cross alive the recently drawn borders—there followed even more riots. Nehru was appalled at these events (see Gopal 1979, chapter 1), and so too was Gandhi, who eventually died trying to stop Hindu–Muslim violence. Communal riots and the forces that may eventuate in them—communalism—have been for ever the nightmare of the Indian polity.

Since independence/partition, India has managed a miracle. It has chosen parliamentary democracy, universal adult franchise, a multi-party system, and a free press. Over a period of approximately 50 years, the number of voters has trebled to around 600 million. India's position as a multilingual, multi-religious, multi-ethnic polity is unique. Apart from the 14 languages listed in its Constitution, there are a further 700 languages spoken throughout the country, not including many dialects. The majority of the 950 million people are Hindu, although that term covers a wide variety of beliefs.[3] There are 110 million Muslims, making India the third largest country after Indonesia and Pakistan in terms of Muslim population. In addition, there are Sikhs, Christians, Jews, Zoroastrians, Buddhists, Jain, as well as many tribal religions.

The partition of Indica was a sudden, traumatic event. No one in the early 1930s took seriously the talk by some Cambridge students about Pakistan as a separate nation for the Muslims.[4] However, by 1940 this idea had become the official policy of the Muslim League. Even so, it is not obvious that Mohammad Ali Jinnah, the leader of the Muslim League, envisaged a separate nation-state. He argued that there were two nations in Indica. But the question is: were there two nation-states? The majority of Muslims in 1940 lived in provinces where they were in a minority. The Muslim-majority provinces were, relatively speaking, sparsely populated. In only two provinces—Punjab and Bengal—was there a large Muslim population in a state of precarious majority. These provinces were divided in the partition and were the scenes of bloody massacres.

In contrast to Pakistan which was set up as an Islamic republic, India chose to be a non-religious, non-theocratic democratic republic.[5] The Indian state's neutrality with regard to religion was partly a rejection or, and a reaction to, the two-nations theory which had led in the view of the Congress party to the partition. The Congress party had been the principal negotiator of Indica's independence (although it was ultimately pipped at the post by the Muslim League), and it had taken the view that all of Indica represented a single nation and a single people, though professing different religions and speaking different languages. However,

[3] Hinduism is a portmanteau word for the variety of sects and paths which constitute the religion of the majority people. It is somewhat peculiar that there is no name for this religion in any of the original languages. Hindu is a Persian word but religion is not adequate to describe the Sanatan Dharma. There is no single book, no single prophet or martyr or founder, no single or even a fixed hierarchy of gods. There is no Church and no parallel to clergy or ulema. I shall return to this below.

[4] Chaudhury Rehmat Ali (who was a Cambridge student) and Khwaja Abdur Rahim (a civil servant) are credited with this name. A recent account of the origins of Pakistan as a concept is in Ahmed (1998). The poet Iqbal had spoken of Pakistan at a private meeting as early as 1930.

[5] Pakistan's founder, Mohammad Ali Jinnah, had a broad ecumenical view of Pakistan which he spoke of in a speech given on 14 August 1947. That speech was subsequently suppressed as it contradicted the more Islamist view of his successors.

the British denied the label of nation to Indica as vehemently as the Congress asserted it.

Another reason for the State's stance on religion was the Congress party's claim that it was the direct successor, rather than a joint inheritor along with Pakistan, of British power, and the fact that the outgoing colonial state was secular (that the Mother country was one where the monarch was also the Head of the Church or England was of little consequence).[6] This had been the case since the East India Company which was the *bete noire* of Christian missionaries. The Christian Church in any of its many sectarian forms was not allowed undue importance in India under British rule. At the same time, of course, both Hindus and Muslims complained that the British favoured one group over the other. It was therefore logical that an independent India would choose to be secular in her Constitution. However, this was not stated officially in the original Constitution, which declared India a 'sovereign democratic republic'. In 1976, while the 'democratic' bit was under some strain, the then prime minister Mrs Indira Gandhi added the words 'secular socialist' to the Constitution. Since then, if anything, the secularism of the Indian union has been more in question than ever.

Secularism, as an ideology, was propagated by Nehru as the cement to hold together the newly independent India and to act as a counter to the communal riots and the communalism of the Hindu Mahasabha and the Rashtriya Swayam Sevak Sangh (RSS) movements. Nehru was a modernist and an atheist who tried to inculcate secularist habits of thought and behaviour into India's public political life. By contrast, most of Nehru's Congress colleagues were religious and held orthodox social views. This meant that Nehru had to fight a constant battle with his own party members—Patel, Pant, Prasad, Tandon, Kripalani—in the first decade after 1947 to assert secularism as a positive philosophy and as a code of behaviour in public life.

For a period of about 25 years following independence, communalism was held hack and communal riots were infrequent, isolated events quickly put down by the Indian state. Indeed, during the 1950s and 1960s other fissures—especially linguistic divisions, as well as the possible alienation of the South—were much more feared as possible causes of the Balkanization of India. The reorganization of the states along linguistic lines and the agitation in the South opposing the recognition of Hindi as the sole national language caused more street violence than did communal riots. The unrest in the Telangana region in the immediate aftermath of independence and in the Naxalbari region from the mid-1960s to the present day were also 'secular' challenges faced by the Indian state.

The concern about Balkanization was not misplaced. After all, Pakistan which was created as a mono-religious nation split between West and East Pakistan, creating Bangladesh in 1971. This showed that the spectre of multinationality haunted both the countries into which Indica was partitioned. In Pakistan's case, the nationality of the East Pakistanis was defined by a different language, as well as the homogeneous territory which they occupied at some distance from West

---

[6] Lord Curzon when Viceroy, in an argument with the Bishop of Calcutta (Weldon) who wanted to proselytize, said: 'The policy of the government was not to interfere with the religious views of the inhabitants of the sub-continent' (Churchill 1964, p. 325).

Pakistan. Religion, language, and territory have proved to be a potent combination, threatening the stability of both India and Pakistan.

The Khalistan movement in Punjab and the riots in Assam during the 1970s and 1980s, plus the continual problem in Kashmir, have all taken their toll in terms of violence against the Indian state and individuals. Further, in the northeast, the Mizo and the Naga nationalisms have resulted in constant state surveillance and the suppression of disorder, showing that the Indian state is capable of deploying formidable force when its existence is even slightly at risk. Pakistan, too, has experienced nationality problems, with the Baluchis, Pakhtoons, Sindhis, and Mohajirs. But while Pakistan's nationality problems are based on language and territory, India has to cope with religion as the sole divisive element within its society. This is why communalism can be considered a peculiarly Indian problem. (That said, there are of course the Shi'a/Sunni divisions within the Muslim religion, and the persecution of minor Muslim sects such as the Ahmadiyas in Pakistan.)

Communalism, however, is not confined to particular regions or states within India: although more virulent in the north than in the south, it is the central problem of the Indian polity as a whole. This is because what is communalism to some is an alternative basis for defining India's nationhood—*Hindutva*—to others, the latter view expressed by the Bharatiya Janata Party (BJP). Since 1990, the BJP has gained increasing public support: in 1992, it was the principal opposition party in Parliament; in the 1996 election, it was the largest single party; and in 1998, after forming a majority coalition with various parties, it came to power. Interestingly, as the party's appeal has broadened, it has soft-pedalled over the issue of *Hindutva*, especially after the demolition of the Babri Masjid on 6 December 1992 by large mobs of Hindu communalists.

Since 1989, India has not had a single party majority in power—and often not even a coalition in a majority. Between 1947 and 1989, India saw six prime ministers come and go, and the same number again between 1989 and 2000. The Congress party has in the meantime lost support across the country: it has split at least twice and shows little sign of winning office. The Congress was meant to be the guardian of secularism, a role it fulfilled in the first 30 years of its rule, i.e. 1947–77. However, in the 1980s, although still officially adhering to the principle of secularism, it began to adopt a more compromising attitude towards the communalists. On the issue of secularism, the Congress party has always relied on the support of left-wing parties—including the Communist Party India (CPI), the Communist Party Marxist (CPM), and some socialist parties. In the past, the Left and the Congress party seldom questioned the meaning of secularism. If anything, it meant simply not siding with the Hindu communalists who had been part of the sorry episodes of violence at the time of independence/partition; it meant being against a party which under one name or another—Hindu Mahasabha, Jan Sangh, BJP—represented the Hindu communalist alternative.

As a footnote to the glorious *temps perdu*, I should mention that for the Indian Left, religion and caste were seen as a diversion from the main issue: that of the class struggle. The heated debate that took place on the Left were mainly about the strategy which would take India from the bourgeois revolution to a socialist one. The issues of caste and religion were generally considered irrelevant—USSR–China divide mattered more than the communal question. The Left is still a formidable presence in Indian politics, and it has taken up the issue of secularism much more seriously since the 1992 Babri Masjid incident (and as the prospect of a socialist revolution has dimmed).

The urgency of the political challenge raised by the prospect of the BJP coming to power, as well as the shock of the Babri Masjid incident, has led to much writing on the subject of communalism in India.[7] Although this literature is important, any discussion of communalism and secularism must take, in my opinion, a broader view. For example, there is the centrality of Gandhi, the relative economic failure of Nehru's strategy which led to stagnation in employment and output growth (and its eventual abandonment in 1991), the worldwide resurgence religion in politics, the prospering diaspora and the phenomenon of globalization and its instant communication technology. The aim of this chapter is to weave these themes into a wider critique of secularism and communalism in India.

The Background to Communalism

There is no one appropriate point at which to start a discussion of the history of communalism. Religious clashes are not unknown in India, and Hindu-Muslim riots have some record in pre-colonial times. But communalism is a special kind of ideological problem since it is about nationality as sought to be defined in terms of *religious identity*. Thus, neither Shi'a–Sunni riots nor Hindu–Sikh riots have attracted the same attention as have Hindu–Muslim clashes, and this is because of the way in which nationality was defined under British colonial rule. (One exception is the anti-Sikh riots in Delhi in 1984, following Indira Gandhi's assassination. But Khalistan was mixed up with this event in a very vital way. This does not, of course, excuse the shocking delay in bringing the culprits to justice.)

The question we must ask is: was Indica a nation? The British rulers always denied that it was. This was based on the fact that, since before the arrival of the Westerners in Indica in 1498, there had not been a single government across the country. Indeed, while the idea of Indica was well known as a cultural entity, its boundaries were never clear. Did they extend beyond the Khyber Pass into what was later Afghanistan, where Kanishka and later Mughal kings ruled? How far in the East did they extend—as far as Burma? And what was the line in the Himalayas where Indica stopped and Tibet began? These issues were the cause of a lot of conflict later on, but they were up in the air in the early part of the nineteenth century, by which time the East India Company had acquired territory in more than one region of Indica.

No single king had ruled over this territory, even vaguely defined. We can perhaps look to the 100 year period from around the middle of Akbar's reign in

---

[7] For example, Achin Vanaik's *The Furies of Indian Communalisms* (1997), and Mushirul Hasan's *Legacy of a Divided Nation* (1997) about India's Muslims. For work on the formation of communalism in the north, see Pandey (1990); for an account of the pre-history of Pakistan see Samad (1995).

approximately 1580 to the ebbing away of Aurangzeb's strength in approximately 1680, as the one point when there was a single powerful government which ruled over much of what later came to be occupied jointly by India and Pakistan. Thus, *administratively*, India's boundaries were defined by the British Raj some time in the late nineteenth century, after Sind had been captured and Afghanistan proved difficult to conquer.

But if Indica could be defined territorially without colonial help, could it be defined culturally—as an imagined community? This is where the battlefield was pitched in colonial times, mainly by Indians who had received a Western-style education. Through the Bengal renaissance of the first half of the nineteenth century to western Indian reform movements of the latter half of that same century, the three seaports—Calcutta, Bombay, and Madras, by and large all colonial cities—became the centres where a national consciousness was forged. This consciousness had to be forged in reaction to the criticisms of the ruling power, using the tools of the British but deployed in a different way. Thus, the professed liberalism and parliamentary constitutionalism as well as the much-vaunted tradition of a free press of the imperial country were all harnessed by the subjects of British India to build up an ideology of nationhood.

In the first phase of establishing a sense of nationhood, Muslims played a very minor role. This was because the British had singled them out as the hostile people in the early nineteenth century and blamed them for the events of 1857. In addition, the Muslim community did not take to Western education with the same alacrity as did Hindus and Parsees. The reformist debates were very much Hindu-centred if they related to social and religious life or Hindu- and Parsee-centred when concerned with civic matters in Bombay. It was not until the late nineteenth century that the Muslims, under the leadership of Saiyad Ahmad Khan, embraced Western education. It is of some significance that Saiyad's appeal had to be made in terms of the nation-wide Muslim community, and opposition to him was from orthodox Muslim quarters. For Hindus, Western education came at different paces in different provinces, and different communities took to it at varying speeds. Brahmins and upper castes were the first groups to benefit, but they could not prevent other (lower) castes from gaining access to education as successfully as they had done in the past, thus ending their monopoly on education.

National consciousness in Indica, as against the sense of Hindu or Muslim identity and the need to reform society, has its roots in the final quarter of the nineteenth century. It is necessary to retell this familiar tale because national consciousness was defined very much in the context of a likely concession by the rulers, of the granting of some legislative presence to the native community. With their knowledge of the British parliamentary system, the native elite was rightly excited by this prospect. Here it is important to point out the differentiation on the side of the colonial rulers as well, as political events at that time in Britain were very relevant to the changing fortunes of constitutional reform in British India, with the nationalist movement experiencing waves of reform or repression depending on who was in power. The imperialists may have divided and ruled, but they were divided at home as well, and some of their divisions were not just for show. Thus, the Liberal ascendancy under Gladstone—while it lasted—did better for Indica compared to when Salisbury and the Tories were in power. It was for a good reason, then, that the early Indian nationalists were Liberals.

Thus it was with the debates around the Ilbert Bill in 1883 that the first organized nationalist agitations began and the Congress party was formed. However, it was Viceroy Curzon, a Tory, who gave the best fillip to the nationalist movement by partitioning Bengal. The partition inflamed nationalist sentiments, but it also exposed the fissures within the nationalist movement and within Indica itself. The Congress party was split between the moderates and the extremists. Divisions appeared between the Hindu landlords and Bhadralok of Bengal and their tenant Muslim peasants who lived in East Bengal. The Nawabs of Dacca led the upper and middle-class Muslims of Bengal who were the principal beneficiaries of the partition. The Western liberal rhetoric employed by the Congress party was challenged by a Hindu rhetoric in Bengal by Bankim Chandra, in Punjab by Lala Lajpat Rai, and in Maharashtra by Tilak. There was thus already emerging a diversity in the construction of Indian nationhood.

Varieties of Indian Nationhood

What was the notion of nationhood in, say, 1900? I would argue that it was constructed around the liberal concept of loyal subjects aspiring to be granted some self-rule, for example the right of Indians to take part in the Civil Service. This developed into an economic argument in favour of protectionism following the placing of duties on cotton yarn, imposed at Manchester's request, on Indian cotton mills, and the disquiet about the exchange rate for the rupee. But apart from that, we can see by referring to the works of Dadabhai Naoroji or R.C. Dutt (Naoroji 1901; Dutt 1908) that the case against the British was economic rather than political. Independence, or even some sort of autonomy was not on the cards. Nor for that matter was the situation all that different in the white parts of the British Empire, as the war in South Africa or the land agitation in Ireland were demonstrating.

Apart from this theory of the Westernized Indian elite about loyal subjects demanding the end of 'un-British' behaviour from the rulers, were there any other theories of nationhood? I believe there was the same theory naturalized, but with two variants. Thus people were loyal subjects, but not of the British Empire; rather, they looked to a bygone one of their own which had to be revived. Two theories had been mooted in 1857, but had lost out. Nonetheless, they simmered. One was the revival of the Hindu *Pata Padshahi* that the Maratha Empire had aspired to and even briefly enjoyed before its loss at Panipat in 1761. This remained a shining ideal for the Maharashtrians and many others. (The strength of Marathi-speaking thinkers in the later construction of *Hindutva* is not unrelated to this ideal.) The Maratha's was the most recent of the Hindu kingdoms that tried to establish an all-Indica hegemony (for another example, one would need to go back a thousand years). The second and alternative movement was the revival of the Mughal Empire, which was not formally dissolved until 1857 and constituted a rallying point for some groups at that time. Indeed, it was this experience and the bitterness surrounding 1857 that made the British suspicious of the Muslims right up until the end of the nineteenth century. There was also a Bengali version of Hindu nationalism which appealed to some hoary past when Hindus ruled. Bankim Chandra's *Anand Math* belongs to this vision, though attempts have been made subsequently to secularize him. This strain of Bengali–Hindu nationalism waned during the 1930s and 1940s. The Punjabi variant was based on the *Arya Samajist* movement, which remained powerful throughout the 1920s before fading away.

Thus, there were three subjecthoods on offer in 1900: the British Empire, the Maratha Empire, and the Mughal Empire. Of these, only the British version was modern, though colonial, and only it had the force of progress behind it—something which Gandhi recognized during his time spent in South Africa. Gandhi believed that subjecthood of the British Empire, especially given the Proclamation of the Queen in 1858, was a very good deal. The Proclamation had promised equal treatment of all British subjects regardless of race or religion, and Gandhi tried to leverage that promise in his fight with the powers in South Africa. He joined loyally on the British side, albeit in the medical corps, in the Boer War, the Zulu War, and the First World War, precisely because of his belief in these principles of equality for all. Although Gandhi's attitude may appear shocking in the context of contemporary notions of racism and imperialism, we have to remember the historical context in which he was fighting for justice.

The Morely–Minto Reforms and the Muslim League

The 1909 Morley–Minto reforms offered the next step in this progressive British subjecthood, recognizing the need for constitutional reform in British India. However, faced with the prospect of granting universal franchise, the British had to decide on what basis. One should recall that adult franchise had not yet been granted in Britain—women and poor people were excluded from the right to vote. As well, Britain saw itself as a Protestant nation: Catholic emancipation had been achieved in 1829, but Oxbridge colleges restricted fellowships to practising Anglicans late into the nineteenth century, and Jews were discriminated against in society (even though Disraeli had been the leader of the Conservative Party). Little surprise then, that Indica was primarily seen in religious terms—as a patchwork of religious communities—and that the notion of a liberal democracy with individual voters was alien. In British India, the Muslims were on the whole poorer than the Hindus, and numerically in a minority at whatever level the property qualifications for the franchise could be pitched.

The Morle–Minto decision to have separate electorates for Muslims is believed by many to have sown the seeds of the subsequent partition. Fenner Brockway, for example, has described the issue of separate electorates as 'a small cloud on the horizon, an anticipation of a later fatal division' (1971, p. 82). I believe this view is too teleological, however. The Congress was Hindu dominated, who else could it be dominated by? Of course, there were prominent Parsees, Anglo-Indians, and Muslims—Jinnah, for instance—in the Congress. But the Bengal partition movement had played on Hindu symbols and disregarded the interests of the East Bengal Muslim peasantry. Congress extremists were led by Tilak who mobilized people by using Hindu symbolism. From 1909, the movement was split between loyal British Empire subjects petitioning for more rights and a nationalist movement which evoked the Maratha Empire and Hindu symbolism.

It is a staple of Indian historiography that once the Muslim League was established, the pro-Muslim bias of the Raj became transparent, as seen in the Morley–Minto decision to establish separate electorates for Hindus and Muslims. However, it was not long before the Muslims were complaining about the ending of Bengal partition in 1911 and the lack of official support for making Aligarh—which was intended to bring Western education to Muslims—a full-scale university (Nanda 1989). Thus hindsight, especially of Indian nationalist historiography, can be misleading. Britain was neither consistently pro nor consistently anti Hindu or Muslim. This was partly because there was no single British view on the matter; and even if there had been one, the British genius is not in tight conceptualization but in a commonsense muddling through. Thus, the British view on nationalities in Indica was at best fuzzy.

The powers at Westminster, including even the Liberal Party, saw Indica as made up of different religious and social groups. In this regard, India was not unique within the British Empire, Ireland, the major headache for the Liberals, was also divided along religious lines, and South Africa, too, had two Christian Churches. So it was not entirely scheming and far-sighted of the British to concede to the demand by the Aga Khan and the Muslim League for separate Muslim electorates. Mushirul Hasan (1997) dates the formation of Muslim national consciousness from this point in history. I would argue that the prospect of electoral representation also sharpened Hindu national identity. Questions such as whether the untouchables were Hindus took on a new importance since numbers were about to become a vital source of political strength. The 1911 Census went into much greater detail about the 'caste system' and received petitions from many Jatis about upgrading their Varna status. Indeed, casteism could be said to be a product of the ballot box. Once group identification was used as a marker for franchise, then group solidarity became a political asset.

The result was that both groups, Hindus and Muslims, began to crystallize their nationalities much more strongly once the possibility of even limited representation had been presented to British India. From 1909 onwards, despite the Nehru Report which in 1928 ruled out communal electorates in an independent India, Congress also operated on the system that was on offer, for example in the 1922 elections in which the Swarajists took part and, later, in the 1937 elections. The Congress may have been ecumenical but it did not, and could not challenge the theory of political membership on offer. This is why the 1916 Lucknow Pact makes so much sense. It was by combining across the separate electorates that Jinnah was trying to forge a vision of a united India. Jinnah hailed the Lucknow Pact as 'the birth of United India' (Brockway 1971, p. 87).

The Lucknow Pact was perhaps the climax of old-style nationalist politics in India, with its exclusive reliance on subjecthoods. The Great War transformed the nature of nationalism across the world. There was rampant inflation for the first time in India on a sustained long-term basis after falling prices during much of the nineteenth century. India had begun to enjoy some freedom on tariffs and the Industrial Commission of 1916 had pointed out the potential for limited guided industrialization. But just as the demands of economic nationalism were about to be accommodated, the emphasis shifted to political nationalism.

Gandhi and the New Indian Nationalism

The entire map of the Indian struggle for self-rule changed after the Jalianwala Bagh incident of 13 April 1919. Gandhi had returned to India and begun his own style of politics in Champaran, Ahmedabad, and Kheda. But the Rowlatt Act and the firing on unarmed crowds at Jalianwala Bagh shattered for ever the illusion that 'unBritish' behaviour was exceptional. Gandhi, who had up to this point been loyal to the British Empire, concluded that this was an evil with which he could not co-operate. Subjecthood was no longer an adequate ideal. Despite the official reprimand that General Dyer received, the militant wing of the Congress did not believe the British could be trusted.

Thus despite the Montagu–Chelmsford reforms of 1917 and the inclusion of an Indian—Sir Satyendra Sinha (later to become Lord Sinha)—into the Imperial War Cabinet, constitutionalism was put on the defensive and the constitutional wing of the Congress lost its dominance. But in fashioning the weapon of mass mobilization, Gandhi also deployed the religious card. Hinduism guided his life and he therefore assumed that religion guided everyone's life. The choice of Khilafat—the movement to re-establish the Caliph as head of the Muslims—as an issue on which to recruit Muslims into the non-cooperation movement was perhaps even more significant than the sectional electorates set up by the Morley–Minto reforms. It recognized the Muslims as a separate estate to be recruited into the independence struggle not on *national* issues but on *religious* ones. Gandhi thus legitimized the vote-bank that the Morley–Minto reforms had created. After this there was no question of an Indian nationhood: there was always a Muslim agenda and a Sikh agenda and, by default, the all-India agenda that remained was a Hindu agenda.

Gandhi's sudden and idiosyncratic suspension of the non-cooperation movement after the violence in the village of Chauri Chaura in 1922 bitterly disappointed the Muslims (Khaliquzzaman 1961). Of course, Atatürk had already devalued the Khilafat demand as being contrary to modernity for the Muslims of Turkey. He had opted for Turkey to be a secular state while Gandhi was encouraging the mullahs to consolidate their stranglehold on Muslims. Modernists such as Abul Kalam Azad were treated on par with the more orthodox Ali brothers. Disappointed with Gandhi and the Congress after Chauri Chaura, the Muslims began to think that an alliance with the Congress was a risky option (Khaliquzaman 1961; Nanda 1989; Samad 1995).

It would seem that neither Gandhi nor the Congress appreciated the deep wounds that the suspension of the non-cooperation movement inflicted on the Muslim community. Accounts of the formation of Pakistan highlight the Khilafat episode and the cavalier way in which Gandhi abandoned the movement as crucial breaking points for the Muslims, who had just ventured for the first time *en masse* to throw in their lot with the wider nationalist movement. There was never again a Hindu–Muslim joint platform; there were Congress Muslims and Muslim League Muslims, but no single, broad movement (Samad 1995).

After 1921 the Congress began to presume that it was the sole all-Indian nationalist movement. While its leadership remained overwhelmingly Hindu—and upper-caste Hindu at that—it began to project a nationalism based not on subjecthood but on citizenship. While the Sawarajists who took part in the 1922 dyarchy elections still adhered to the loyal subjecthood idea, albeit with stiffer demands, the Congress for the first time during the 1920s espoused a nationhood based on the possibility of dominion status. This was later changed to a demand for independence after the Lahore Congress in 1930, where Jawaharlal Nehru was president. The 1928 Nehru Report that had preceded the Lahore Congress, and which had been the response of the Congress to the Simon Commission Report of 1929, ruled out any Muslim electorates. Jinnah tried desperately through the 1920s to propose various *modi vivendi* going beyond the Morley–Minto reforms which would trade separate Muslim electorates for some protected rights for Muslims, but the Congress did not agree to any of the suggestions (Nanda 1989; Samad 1995).

The sidelining of the Congress after the Simon Commission Report and the Round Table conference (at which a federal solution for British India and the native states began to be formulated) resulted in Gandhi launching the Dandi Satyagraha (or Dandi March). This led to the Gandhi–Irwin pact; the first time that His Imperial Majesty's Viceroy had signed a document on equal terms with a private subject. However, it only managed to get the Congress to the second Round Table conference, and even then Ramsay MacDonald stuck with a separate electorate scheme. Thus the Congress gained little from the Dandi March.

Significantly, however, Gandhi's fast in Yeravada prison on the issue of separate electorates for the untouchables reinforced his religious view of politics. His insistence that the untouchables should be counted as Hindu rather than be given separate electorates vindicated the Morley–Minto view of religious nationalities. Had Gandhi not objected to the Award, these arrangements could have been seen as *minority protection*—mixture of religion and deprived status—rather than as *religious separation*. Indeed, additional separate electorates could have been encouraged, diluting the religious principle and emphasizing the secular one of minority rights. By his protest to remove the small amount of protection won for the untouchables by Ambedkar at the Round Table conference, Gandhi cemented the religious principle in politics. Although this was consistent with his worldview, it was a fatal step for Indian independence. Ambedkar never forgave Gandhi for helping to take away from the untouchables a small amount of hard-won political clout. The failure in post-independent India to raise the status of the untouchables—as evidenced by their dissatisfaction, first in neo-Buddhist conversions and later in the Dalit movement—shows that the Congress and Gandhi were unable to resist the religious principle. And in so doing, they deprived the downtrodden the power of self-emancipation through the political process.[8]

[8] The recent election of K.R. Narayanan as President does not significantly change this conclusion, just as the election of Muslims to positions of power has been no guarantee of the protection of Muslim rights.

A Federal India?

By the beginning of the 1930s, theories of subjecthood had taken a back seat. While there were loyalists still willing to take part in various elections to provincial councils, dominion status had been put on the table by Irwin. Neither a revived Muslim kingdom nor a Hindu one was attracting any support. The proposed models of nationhood were based around the size and structure of franchise, the power of the provinces versus Delhi, and native states versus Delhi. The Government of India Act 1935 was the culmination of a long process that had begun with the Simon Commission (itself a review of the workings of the Montagu–Chelmsford reforms), the Round Table conferences and the various parliamentary commissions that followed, and the debating and enacting of the longest piece of legislation to be seen at that time in Westminster.

From the point of view of British politics, the Act was a remarkable piece of all-party co-operation. The Simon Commission had been appointed by F.E. Smith (Lord Birkenhead) during the 1924–9 government. The Commission's report had come during a Labour government (1929–31), and Wedgewood Benn conspired with Irwin and Baldwin to set it aside and to hold the Round Table conference. (It was this as much as his dislike for Baldwin that made Churchill resign from the Shadow Cabinet and join the backbenches as a stalwart on India). The British government kept up the pace after 1931. Except for Churchill and his 50 supporters, there was no opposition to the passage of the Act. Thus, by 1935 some form of eventual self-government for Indica was a fixture of British politics.[9]

In terms of subjecthood, the 1927–35 process moved the debate about Indica's future towards the possibility of dominion status akin to such countries as New Zealand and Australia. The date at which such status was to be given was not made clear but, the Congress party apart, the participants in the Round Table conference saw the Montagu–Chelmsford promises delivered in the 1927–35 process. The people of Indica were to be absorbed within a single federation—native states and British India—as subjects of the Crown, capable of self government. The concept of a single nationhood was not defined in this proposal. That was the rival model put forward by the Nehru-led wing of the Congress which forced the pace to adopt the Lahore Resolution asking for full independence in 1930.

There were three rival models of nationhood. First, the Congress vision was of an independent Indica with the Congress representing the nation of undifferentiated Indians (at least as far as Nehru was concerned) who in their private lives could remain Hindus, Muslims, Sikhs, etc. The second was Gandhi's model which was not as secular as Nehru's vision but was equally inclusive of all people of Indica. Gandhi had formed his model during his time in South Africa where he

---

[9] Two caveats need noting. Churchill deserves a detailed treatment of his own. Surprisingly, given his demonic status in India, no major work has been done on Churchill and India. I hope to write an essay on this topic as a companion to this chapter. Also, the Labour Party suffered a severe defeat in 1931 and was not a major force. And even after 1935 it was still politically weak. It was only its inclusion in the War Cabinet after Churchill became prime minister that allowed it a say in negotiations over India. Even then, Cripps and Attlee were not as one on India during the War (for background history on this, see Gilbert 1976; French 1977).

had organized the immigrant Indian community to fight for its rights as a single undifferentiated group contrasted to the whites and the blacks. The third model was a 'federalist' one that emerged out of the 1927–35 process. This was based on a view of Indica as a multinational polity. Provinces were, in this view, nations with their own language (usually) and history. Punjab, Bengal, Sind were already such single-language provinces. The native states, at least the larger ones—Hyderabad, Mysore, Gwalior—had pretensions to autonomy. By emphasizing the local nationality, the federalists did not deny an Indian super-identity: one could be Bengali *and* Indian or Punjabi *and* Indian.

Again, it is necessary to avoid hindsight. In 1935, proposals for Pakistan were dismissed as nonsense by sober Muslim leaders like Zafrullah Khan. And Jinnah refused to push them on the subject. What was on offer was a large extension of democracy at the provincial level and some arrangement—in the event, never implemented—to bring British India and the native states into a federation. This was the Act which shaped the contours of the partition of Indica. Elections in 1937 and 1946 were conducted on this basis. Its treatment of minorities—untouchables and tribals—has become part of the Constitution of India via its Schedules, hence Scheduled Castes and Tribes. Its division of powers between the Centre and the provinces has survived the test of time in the Indian Constitution. It was a map for the eventual dominion status for Indica; it could have been the blueprint for an undivided Indica.

War and the Coming of Partition

An undivided Indica was not the eventual outcome, however. I would argue that there are at least two reasons for this. The first was, of course, the outbreak of the Second World War and the revival of Churchill's career. But the second and more contentious reason was the behaviour of the Congress in power between 1931 and 1939 and, further, its decision to resign and go into exile/prison for five years from 1939 to 1944.

Churchill had spent the 1930s in exile on the Tory backbenches. His quarrel with Baldwin had started over the issue of India and the treatment of the Simon Commission's report by the two front benches. By the end of the decade, he had begun to campaign for the need to arm against the threat of a hostile Germany. The leadership of the Conservative Party was against him on both issues—India and armament. The outbreak of war in September 1939 returned Churchill to the Cabinet as First Lord of the Admiralty, the same position he had held in the previous war. He began immediately to make his views felt on India but was restrained by Chamberlain and his Secretary of State for India, Zetland. Churchill's main concern when he eventually became prime minister was winning the war. Nevertheless, he continued to have his say on India, and appointed Leo Amery as his Secretary of State for India. Churchill understood the importance of retaining India at the heart of the British Empire. His father, Lord Randolph Churchill, had been Secretary of State for India, and Churchill himself had been stationed there. Nevertheless, his knowledge of India was sparse and peculiar, and he hated Indians, especially educated, middle-class ones. Churchill's accession to power transformed the Indian negotiations.

The decision by the Congress to contest the elections at the provincial level to implement part of the 1935 Act led to, and coincided with, the emergence of Nehru as the undisputed leader of the Congress after Gandhi. Nehru headed the electoral wing of the Congress while Patel, as Chairman of the Congress Parliamentary Board, undertook the organizational role. Nehru's theories about citizenship and democracy were far more radical than Gandhi's. A liberal democrat who advocated a left-wing economic programme, Nehru was also an atheist who believed religion had no role to play in India's political life. He viewed voters as atomistic individual citizens whose religious, caste, or regional affiliations were a sign of backwardness which would melt away once economic progress was achieved. In his writing, he frequently attributes communalism to lack of employment. His was a simple majoritarian view of democratic politics without any religious distraction. He also had a fairly well formulated (though not Comintern) view of class: backwardness and poverty were due to economic forces and religion/caste/regionality were part of the superstructure that needed to be removed from politics. Nehru's views formed the classic formulation of secularism in post-independent India.

Nehru was always unhappy with Gandhi's religiosity, and some of this anger can be seen in his autobiography (Nehru 1936). He made peace with Gandhi following that outburst, but a sense of unease remained between the two until the end. Nehru's anti-communalism was anti-religious *in toto* as opposed to Gandhi's ecumenical view. Nehru's conduct as the leader of the electoral wing of the Congress was crucial for the elections of 1937 and what the party did after that. But before turning to the elections, we need to look at the background to the 1935 Act which led to them.

The long process of negotiations about India's future status, which started with the appointment of the Simon Commission in 1927 and ended with the passage of the Government of India Act in 1935, was carried out without the full participation of the Congress. Congress joined only in one of the three Round Table conferences, sending Gandhi as their sole delegate. He chose to speak last and took the stance that Congress was the *only* party with which the government should negotiate. But the Round Table conference process had brought together a variety of political interests—princes of native states, representative delegations of provincial governments, leaders of Muslims, Sikhs, Hindus, and untouchables. It was during the first Round Table conference that the Maharaja of Bikaner had proposed a federal arrangement for the future government of India. What he meant by 'federation' was a confederation, with considerable local autonomy for native states and provinces. The representatives of Punjab and Bengal agreed with this demand for autonomy. Congress, and indeed Jinnah, also preferred a strong Centre and weak provinces. The Congress believed that a weak Centre would Balkanize India. Jinnah consented, but wanted solid guarantees for the largest single minority. However, his problem was that Muslim politicians preferred provincial autonomy—in Punjab, Bengal, and Sind—and they did not want to come under a single Muslim League umbrella (Samad 1995; Jalal 1985).

The Muslim League did not have much success in the 1937 elections. Despite his best efforts, Jinnah could not persuade Muslim candidates to fight under the aegis of the Muslim League Parliamentary Board. But Congress, too, had very few Muslim members and those who were Congress Muslims (for example, Ansari and Azad) were told to fight not as Muslims but as Congressmen. By contrast, the orthodox Hindus in the Congress—Jayakar, Rajendra Prasad, Gobind Vallabh Pant—were not limited in the same way. As the majority community, they did not have to fight as Hindus, but merely had to strengthen the anti-modernist forces that Gandhi represented and which frustrated Nehru (Nehru 1936).

Although the Congress party won seven out of eleven provinces and the Muslim League managed to form a coalition government in only one province—Bengal—neither party represented the Muslims. Hence the drive to recruit Muslims to the Congress that Nehru encouraged in Uttar Pradesh (UP). This was after negotiations between the Congress and the Muslim League for power sharing in UP had broken down. Nehru did not want to encourage the League; indeed, he thought all sectarian parties—Muslim League or Hindu Mahasabha—should be driven out of politics. Needless to say, Nehru's views were in a minority. Many Congress leaders sympathized with the Hindu Mahasabha, whose leader, Pandit Madan Mohan Malaviya, held a higher place than Jinnah in the affections of the Congress, although both men represented sectarian parties.

The Congress drive to recruit Muslims was not fully successful in its aim but it did finally end any hope of an accommodation with the Muslim League, either at the UP level or at the national level. Jinnah realized that he could not succeed in his plans to negotiate a trade-off with the Congress in return for giving up separate Muslim seats. After 1937, Jinnah became more inclined to accept the Pakistan proposal which hitherto he and other secular Muslim leaders such as Zafarullah Khan had dismissed. He too had to recruit more Muslims to the banner of the Muslim League to prove his credibility.

Jinnah's hand was strengthened by the outbreak of the war. The behaviour of the Congress party at the time was presumptuous, parochial, and, ultimately, counterproductive. Linlithgow, the Viceroy and Governor-General, was a Tory, and Zetland, the Secretary of State for India, was no friend of the Congress. Together they discouraged the native states from fulfilling the 1935 Act's provisions which would have brought about a Central Legislature, no matter how reactionary in its composition. But when war broke out, there was no directly elected majority on the Central Legislature and no elected representation on the Viceroy's Council. That was the constitutional position in which the Congress had connived, by taking part in the 1937 election.

The presumption of the Congress party to act as the sole representative of the people of India was rather far-fetched, even considering its victory in seven out of 11 states. Six of the seven states were in what is now India (with the exception of the North-West Frontier Province). But while the Congress controlled a majority of the seats in the general electorate, it did not represent Muslims, nor had it won over the untouchables and anti-Brahmin forces in the South. Ramaswamy Naicker, the Periyar, was willing to share an anti-Congress platform with the Muslim League. Ambedkar was also very suspicious of a Congress government in any eventual post-British India (Ambedkar 1940).

The declaration of war by Britain committed the British Empire as a whole.

There had been no consultation with Australia, Canada, or New Zealand over the matter, so although India may have commanded special attention, the Congress could not claim primacy. The high point of the Gandhi–Irwin pact was past. Labour was no longer in power, and Linlithgow was far less liberal than Irwin. But more than that, the Congress party failed to understand the seriousness of the war for Britain. The resignations of provincial Congress governments over the lack of consultation over entry into the war were precipitate. But as a bargaining ploy, it failed. In Britain, parliamentary elections due by 1940 were suspended. The British were not about to take the Congress party seriously on this issue, especially once Churchill was prime minister.

The episode of the 1937 governments, especially Congress's drive for Muslim recruitment and, most important, the declaration of war and the resignation of the Congress governments, gave credence to a third and rival theory of nationality—Jinnah's theory of dual nationality. The paradox is that Jinnah was an atheist and a modernist in the same mould as Nehru. He also had a unitary—as opposed to a federalist—view of how independent Indica should constitute itself. The view of Jalal (1985) and others that Jinnah used Pakistan as a bargaining ploy for securing the rights of the Muslim minority in post-independent Indica is convincing. But the important thing is that apart from the Hindu Mahasabha, a religious view of nationhood had been avoided by *all* parties. The League represented Muslims as a constituency not as a separate nation. Muslims, of course, were asserted to be a nation but they shared neither a common language (unlike Punjabis, Bengalis, Sindhis, for example) nor a common territory. Nor for that matter did the Hindus or Christians. (The Sikhs were the only community that had a religion, a language, and a territory which they could call their own. Before 1947, this was in separate pockets in West Punjab in the canal zone and in East Punjab. After the partition, the Sikhs were concentrated in Indian Punjab. This was to cause a lot of trouble 40 years later with Khalistan.)

Thus, by 1940, three models of nationhood were being advanced. First, the Congress model was of all Indians, undifferentiated by religion, region, or language, forming one nation; cultural diversity was acknowledged and the Congress gave linguistic regions a recognition that supplemented the provincial boundaries of British India. This was a unitarian, centralist model ever worried about Balkanization. Second, the federal model made region (province/nation-state) the primary basis for defining nationhood with the overarching India as a supra-nation. The Centre would have a small number of portfolios but would remain powerful, and the provinces would have many portfolios and a lot of autonomy. Finally, the Pakistan model argued for two nations in Indica—Hindus and Muslims. In 1940, its territorial ambitions were not well articulated and indeed over the next seven years were variable.

A good way to illustrate the three models is to take the example of someone from Bengal. To the Congress, he was an Indian who belonged to the Bengal province; to the federalists, he was a Bengali whose province would federate to India; and to the Muslim League, he was a citizen of a Muslim-majority province which was part of Pakistan. To begin with, the Muslim League was not concerned about differences of religion since it wanted all of Bengal, Hindus and Muslims.

Pakistan, as an exclusively Muslim nation-state, was not to emerge in public until after 1946. Before 1946, the idea was that the Hindu minority in the future Pakistan would be a hostage for the Muslim minority in Hindu-majority provinces.

An illustrative account of the issues at stake at this time is given in Ambedkar's book on Pakistan, *Pakistan or the Partition of India* (1940). Relying on his reading of the formation of new nation-states after the First World War, Ambedkar raised the question about the transfer of populations. He was quite clear that no one on either side of the Pakistan debate had any idea what the demand for a separate state really involved. As of 1940, the demand for a Muslim nation was an alternative federal model with groupings of Muslim majority provinces. However, the list of such provinces was not precise.

I want to leave the story of the partition to another essay. But suffice to say that between 1940 and 1945, Congress lost a considerable amount of time, influence and bargaining power *vis-à-vis* the British and Jinnah. Burdened by the war, Britain appreciated any help it could get, whether from Jinnah or the communists. It became irritated by Gandhi and the Congress, mainly due to Gandhi's stand on non-violence and on an independent India's attitude in the event of Japanese invasion. This gave Churchill a propaganda weapon to represent Gandhi to the Americans as a collaborator of the Japanese. The high command of the Congress party was forced to distance itself from Gandhi for a time during 1940–1, only to go running back to him when even without Gandhi the British would not negotiate on anywhere near the terms laid down by the Congress. The entry of the US into the war put pressure on Churchill, but he was able to fend this off by sending Stafford Cripps on a mission in 1942 with an offer for post-war settlement, which he then sabotaged.[10] Frustrated by the failure of the quiet, principled, and individual protest that he had led, Gandhi turned again, after the failure of the Cripps Mission, to his old tactics of mass mobilization, leading the Quit India campaign. He hoped that this show of power would bring the Viceroy to the negotiating table. But what had worked with Dandi and Irwin did not work with Quit India and Linlithgow. The government made a pre-emptive arrest of the Congress leadership. The unguided and spontaneous struggle that broke out after 8 August 1942 was brutally handled by the government. Subversion in the middle of a war, especially a war that had come to India's borders, was not tolerated. Thus Gandhi's Quit India gamble failed. Of course, this is not the view taken by Indian nationalist historiography.

Luckily for the Congress, the Allies won the war and, more important, the Labour Party won the 1945 General Election.[11] The Viceroy Field Marshal

[10] For a pro-Indian account of the American–British negotiations on India, see Venkataraman and Srivastava (1983).

[11] Again, teleology has to be avoided. In retrospect, Labour's 1945 victory looks obvious and independence/partition follows in 1947. But the Labour Party is also often accused of being no different to the Tories. However, Indian independence was a manifesto promise of the Labour Party in the run-up to the 1945 election. Had the Conservatives won, Winston Churchill would have been prime minister. No matter how exhausted Britain might have been after the war, Churchill would not have been so quick to negotiate towards independence as Attlee was. After all, France and Holland despite their wartime experiences resisted (for a time) independence movements in Vietnam and Indonesia. Had Churchill come to power, the native states would not have been forced to integrate

Wavell who replaced Linlithgow was as suspicious as his predecessor had been of Gandhi, but he realized the urgent need for talks between the two sides: However, the long and complex negotiations about India's independence—which had in some sense gone on since the Gandhi–Irwin Pact, if not earlier with the Round Table conferences—came to a sudden and unexpected end within less than two years of Labour coming to power. Within that time, a scheme for a compromise between the three models of nationhood—the federal model, the Muslim League model and the Congress model—was put forward by the 1946 Cabinet Mission, but the eventual agreement reached did not stick. Jinnah's resort to mass mobilization on 16 August 1946, declaring it a 'black day', was to inaugurate a year-long bloody communal war.

There were no further negotiations after August 1946 with British parliamentary parties. By March 1947, and following the experience of the interim government, partition had become unavoidable. Despite the denials of the Congress, Jinnah's theory of nationality had won—at least as far as Pakistan was concerned. Even after 12 June 1947, when it had agreed to the partition, the Congress denied that this was the case, insisting instead that its own theory of nationhood had won. The federal model ostensibly lost out. The native states were bundled into one of the two post-partition states. Here again, the status of the native states in independent India/Pakistan was not decided until July 1947. Had Mountbatten stuck to the Attlee timetable of independence by June 1948, this problem might have been contained. As it was, all but three complied. Two out of the three states—Junagadh and Hyderabad—were dealt firmly by India under the newly inherited doctrine of paramountcy. Only one—Kashmir—on the border of both India and Pakistan, and large enough to have dreamed of autonomy, dithered over which country to sign up with. In the event, efforts by Pakistan to force the Maharaja's hand by launching an agitation (a tactic the Congress successfully tried in Junagadh, though with unarmed civilians led by Shamaldas Gandhi) faltered, resulting in Kashmir's accession to India. The problem that festers to this day in this area is a vivid illustration of the irreconcilable theories on which the partition of India occurred.

GANDHI AND THE PARTITION

The Congress agreed to the partition while at the same time denying the two-nations theory. The contradiction in this position is irresolvable and is one aspect at the heart of the problem of communalism. But Gandhi's attitude in the three years following his release from prison was equally inconsistent. He refused Jinnah's demand to acknowledge Pakistan but opened negotiations with him in 1944, based on a formula of the province of Rajagopalachari which accommodated the two-nations theory. At various times during the talks, Gandhi offered peculiar solutions—such as proposing the handing of all power to the Muslim League to save Indica as a single entity.

---

into an Indian Union at the very least. The final shape of India would have been quite different, and partition might have been avoided.

Considering that he had negotiated one to one with Jinnah (and had conferred upon him the title of 'Qaid-e-Azam'), it is difficult to understand Gandhi's shock at the partition and the communal riots. Indeed, Gandhi never understood or accepted the riotous behaviour of the mobs, either in 1921, in 1942, or in 1946–7. Seeking to find an answer for the eruption in violence, he blamed imperfections in his own character and thought that only his personal suffering would atone for the violence (Parekh 1989). But neither his suffering nor his pilgrimage through Bengal and Bihar during the civil war made a difference. The killings continued, albeit less in the east than in the west, and partition went ahead.

Gandhi's theory of nationhood was, of course, not the same as Nehru's, but like Nehru's it was inclusive. He regarded religion as the prime identifier of an individual, and his politics were guided by his own religious beliefs which were a form of Christianized-Hinduism (Parekh 1989). As such, he was a religious nationalist; but he was also ecumenical which meant he did not understand communalism. For Gandhi, the Indian nation consisted of the main religious communities—Hindus, Muslims, Sikhs—living side by side. This view stemmed directly from his experiences in South Africa where he had seen Gujarati Hindus and Gujarati Muslims living in peace. And it was this ideal vision that he projected on to Indica.

Gandhi's denial of Jinnah's theory of nationality thus appeared strained but was perhaps very subtle and impractical. His belief in the primacy of religion but the denial of it in politics as a basis for defining nationality are not irreconcilable views; however, it is easier to establish this position in principle than it is in practice. It is also an obstacle if you want to base a secular state on the liberal-democratic principle that individuals are citizens in their public life and only Hindus or Muslims in their private life. Hence, the discomfort of Nehru with Gandhi. Gandhi used religion as a mobilizing factor in the independence movement. His entry into the Congress party alienated constitutional modernists such as Jinnah and C.R. Das, though he won over many others, especially Nehru and his supporters. In mixing up non-cooperation with Khilafat, Gandhi helped to mobilize Muslims on a Muslim issue, rather than on an Indian one. In abandoning non-cooperation unilaterally before the Khilafat issue was resolved, he alienated Muslims and never fully regained their confidence. His Yeravada fast on the issue of the separate electorate for untouchables showed his conservative Hindu electoral concerns. He did not contemplate a similar fast on the issue of Muslim electorates, though that could be due to the fact that it was a *fait accompli* from 1909. Gandhi may have helped to win India's independence, but he arguably also bequeathed it partition and its associated problems.

Thus, at its birth, India was not the nation that the Congress party wanted, one which corresponded to its theory of nationhood—an undivided Indica—nor was Pakistan what Jinnah wanted. Punjab had lost its battle to stay united and autonomous as had Bengal. But unlike China and its view of Taiwan, India did not treat Pakistan as a breakaway 'province' which needed to be brought under control. If the partition was legitimate, then what was needed was a new model of Indian nationhood. Why was India, as opposed to Indica, a nation? Was it not a large fragment of Indica and hence an incomplete nation? Or was it the coming together of many regional nationalities based on language and territory, but not religion?

CONSTRUCTING INDIAN NATIONHOOD

In 1947, an independent India emerged out of Indica, which was divided into three parts and two nation-states. However, the year-long civil war and the increasingly fanatical behaviour of the Muslim League led to an unanticipated outcome. Rather than becoming a nation-state with a Muslim majority, Pakistan, with a few exceptions, became a totally Muslim state. This was due to a late and large-scale transfer of population caused by decentralized but severe violence in the border areas. Sind, Punjab, and Bengal were the main sites of population transfer. The outgoing colonial power lost all control of the partitioned territories (French 1997). This left the independent nation-states with a huge problem of resettlement as well as the more serious problem of reconciliation. In the 50 years since independence, the fragments of Indica have been at war with each other three times, dividing from two nation-states into three (East Pakistan gained independence in 1971 to become Bangladesh). Today, India and Pakistan are engaged in a constant state of military confrontation in the northern region around Kashmir and Punjab. To add to the tension, both countries have nuclear weapons.

Ironically, the political situation that emerged in 1971—three separate political units—was foreseen in the proposals of the 1946 Cabinet Mission. In first accepting then rejecting these proposals, the politicians of pre-independence wasted 25 years in futile conflicts. This 'international' context cannot be ignored when looking at the problem of communalism in India. But the appropriate way of examining the communalism issue is to see it as a problem of constructing a theory of nationhood for India. All the writings before independence argued that Indica *was* a nation against the British denial. Events after independence in part vindicated the British argument, and even blaming them for the trouble was only a partial answer. The question that remained was: is India a nation or a part-nation, that is an incomplete nation (as in the case of China and its claim over Hong Kong, Macao, and Taiwan)? Was the history of Indica also the history of India? Pakistan, of course, had a more serious problem when it came to writing its history. For example, should the Indus Valley civilization found in the Mohanjo Daro be included as part of Pakistan's history, or did the country's history begin with the invasion of Mahmud of Gaznavi, or did it date from the establishment of the Muslim League? (Desai 1993; see also Chapter 22)

Ultimately, it was Nehru who recognized the need for the construction of a form of Indian nationhood. Before partition, he had argued in his book *The Discovery of India* (Nehru 1946) that Indica was a nation. Following partition, he was faced with a new challenge of establishing India's nationhood. During his 17 years in power, Nehru set about using available institutions and creating new ones which contributed to this construction of nationhood. His vision had to counter both the two-nations theory by emphasizing secularism of the new nation-state and the multinational theory of the federalists by creating a sense of 'unity in diversity'. I have dealt with the latter point elsewhere (Desai 1993), so I shall concentrate on the former: the construction of a secular state.

Secularism was badly dented by the partition. The right-wing Congress leadership was Hindu and took a religious view of nationhood. This manifested itself in several ways against the Muslims. Doubts were cast over the loyalty of the Muslims who remained in India, and whether they were entitled to enjoy equal rights with the Hindu-majority community. For Patel, Prasad, Kripalani, and Pant, the two-nations theory was the cause of partition. They did not agree with it nor of course did the Hindu Mahasabha which wanted an undivided India. But once partition was agreed they held that it had to be implemented in India as well. There were discussions immediately after independence that advocated the merging of the Hindu Mahasabha and the RSS into the Congress party (Jaffrelot 1997), and had it not been for Gandhi's assassination, this would have come to fruition.

Nehru used Gandhi's name and his ecumenical vision of Indian nationhood to counter the pro-Hindu vision of the Congress right. However, he encountered strong opposition from many of his Congress colleagues over the issue of the treatment of Muslims—their right to stay in India, to leave India, and/or to return to India at a later date. Nehru had Azad, Kidwai, and the Congress Socialists on his side, but little else.

Nehru's Struggle against the Hindu Revivalists

Between 1947 and 1951, Nehru battled against the pro-Hindu faction. They managed to defeat him at first by electing Tandon to the Congress presidency. But once Patel passed away in December 1950, Nehru had Tandon thrown out. This was a tough battle, and Nehru had to summon up all his reserves in the Congress high command to win. But by 1951, Nehru was in total command of the Congress. This resulted in Kripalani leaving to found the Kisan Mazdoor Praja Party, and the successful containment of Pant and Prasad (Jaffrelot 1997; Gopal 1979). But Nehru was not entirely victorious. During 1947–51, he accepted a shoddy compromise over the issue of Babri Masjid. Pant and Patel had made only half-hearted gestures to prevent the installation of the idols of Ram in the periphery of the Masjid, and Nehru did not insist on their removal—a decision which would come back to haunt India in 1992.

Even with Nehru in control of the Congress, the battle over secularism was not over. This continued in a number of ways, three of which are worth highlighting:

(i) The Sanskritization of Hindi and the downgrading of Hindustani and Urdu was one area in which organized forces worked against secularism. (Indeed, the only thing that saved India from Sanskritized Hindi was the Hindi film industry.)

(ii) The forces of Hindu revivalism had financial support from Hindu merchants and industrialists. The rebuilding of the Somanath temple was initiated by K.M. Munshi whose Bharatiya Vidya Bhavan became a leading movement in Hindu revivalism.

(iii) A major battle was fought over the question of India's history. Nehru mobilized academics and intellectuals on the side of constructing a secularist and ecumenical history. In this respect, Pannikar's *Survey of Indian History* was seen as an important text. Support came from the Left, around the CPI, as well as from the various Socialist Party formations and from left-wing historians who held hegemonic positions in universities. A rival project was commissioned by the Bharatiya Vidya Bhavan, but this multi-volume history failed to attain the national standing of the secular vision. The secularists found a much more engaging enemy in 'neo-imperialist' history (as they called it) which emerged from Cambridge University in the UK and, increasingly, from US functionalist accounts.

In the 1980s and 1990s, Indian history was once again an issue for debate with Romila Thapar taking up cudgels on behalf of a secularist history. It is a mark of the success of the Nehru programme as secularist historiography that the Hindu version of history did not seriously challenge it for nearly 40 years.

Secularism in Practice

Due to partition and the Congress party's confused attitude over the two-nations theory—which involved an ideological/rhetorical rejection of the theory but a pragmatic/operational acceptance of it—policy aimed at Hindus and Muslims developed along different lines. Nehru pleaded with his colleagues and the country at large to treat the Muslims in India with greater and asymmetric tolerance as compared to the majority Hindu community. To aid in this, the reform of Hindu family law became part of Nehru's modernizing agenda, and he pursued this through the attempt to codify Hindu law. The Hindu Code Bill had a stormy passage, with President Rajendra Prasad unhappy with its progress. In the end, Nehru was forced to compromise by breaking up the large *portmanteau* Bill into several separate legislations. There was no parallel attempt to codify and/ or modernize Muslim law. Indeed, as with the Shah Bano case in the 1980s, the Congress always took a reactionary stance on the reform of Muslim law.

Secularism, then, meant state neutrality towards religion but not symmetry when it came to the interrelationship between religion and social practice between the majority and the minority communities. This could have been justified in terms of protection of minority rights. However, although positive discrimination was constitutionally possible with respect to Scheduled Castes and Scheduled Tribes, Muslims were not classified as a 'Scheduled' minority. Thus there was no attempt to give them special constitutional protection.

Despite these caveats while Nehru was prime minister, especially during 1951–64, a secular state flourished in India. Nehru's construction of nationhood involved making India 'special': this meant non-alignment, rapid economic development with a strong public sector role and planning (the socialist pattern of society), and the establishment of a secular democracy. Republic Day festivals were used to demonstrate the diversity of India's many cultures, but also the underlying unity which joined them. The Ministry of Information and Broadcasting utilized its control of All India Radio and Films Division to disseminate a positive image of the Indian nation. The weekly *Film News Reel* was shown in cinemas across the country and All India Radio promoted classical Indian music and broadcast the news in local languages and in English. In addition, the various academies encouraged the teaching of syncretic Indian culture (for a further discussion on this, see Chapter 20, also in Desai 1993).

The result was a very low incidence of communal riots during this period (see Fig. 23.1). Although there was a sharp upsurge in rioting in 1964, India experienced a period of relative stability—except for the 500-plus riots that took place in 1969 and again in 1970—which lasted through the 1970s. The average number of riots in the 1970s was around 220 per year. But in 1979 this figure rose to 304, the highest since 1971. In the mid-1980s, the average number of riots per year was 700, and in the early 1990s it was 1000. The freak rise in communal riots in 1964 coincided eerily with the death of Nehru, the one person who embodied the secularist ideal. And, although the numbers dropped after 1964, they never returned to the low levels of 1954–63. Thus we can hypothesize that the increase in riots was in part due to the collapse of Nehru's programme of reform; or perhaps it was Nehru's personality and commanding reputation that managed to keep the number down.

Nehru's reputation was severely dented towards the end of his life due to the India–China border war. In the confusion that prevailed in Delhi after the first setback on the borders, there was an unseemly rush by India into the arms of the Western powers for military help. India regained its nerve when the Chinese unilaterally withdrew and declared a ceasefire, but India's policy of non-alignment, as well as its pride in the Indian Army, was seriously harmed by this incident. On the economic front, the early 1960s saw a severe fall in the rate of growth in income—well below the set targets outlined in the government's Third Five Year Plan. Although the economy showed some signs of recovery after 1962, it failed to meet the targets on time. This was followed by two severe droughts in 1965 and 1966. Economic plans based on Nehruvian lines were sufficiently discredited for the new prime minister—Lal Bahadur Shastri—to declare the suspension of the Fourth Five Year Plan, and shift to annual plans. Neither the dent to the national pride in the Indian Army nor the check to Nehruvian economic plans lasted long, however. India won the war with Pakistan in 1965, thus restoring the Army's prestige. However, the war also revealed the first signs of a fundamental change in post-Nehru India. Throughout the three-month war, Muslims in India had been regarded with suspicion and many of their leaders incarcerated. Although Prime Minister Shastri was not on the right wing of the Congress, nor was he a Hindu revivalist, the loss of neutrality between Hindus and Muslims signalled to both communities that the Nehru era of secularism was over.[12]

Indira Gandhi and the Crisis of Secularism

The effects of slow economic growth and the two famines were felt in the decision to devalue the rupee taken by the new prime minister, Indira Gandhi, in 1966. However, the promised relief from Western donors as a reward for devaluing the

[12] I am grateful to M.J. Akbar for reminding me of this crucial episode.

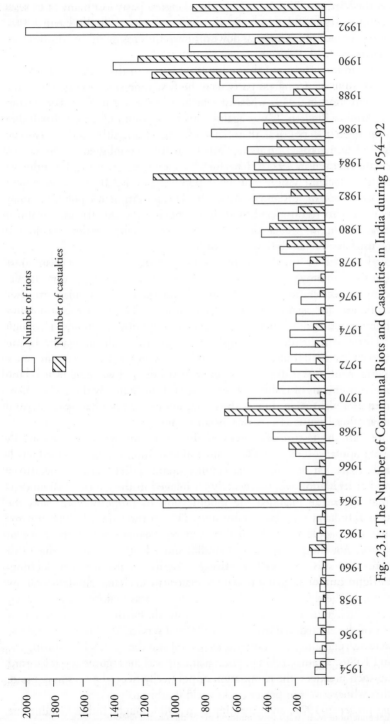

Fig. 23.1: The Number of Communal Riots and Casualties in India during 1954–92

Source: Jaffrelot, C. (1996), *The Hindu Nationalist Movement and Indian Politics: 1925 to the 1990s*, London: Hurst and Company, p. 553.

255

rupee did not materialize, mainly because the US wanted to punish India for its stance on the Vietnam War. As a result, the Congress party lost many of its seats in the 1967 election and was lucky to survive in power at the Centre. One contributing factor to the Congress downturn was the erosion of the Muslim vote following the war with Pakistan.

Indira Gandhi nationalized the commercial banks in the summer of 1969, a move which split the Congress party. For the first time since the defeat of the Telangana rebellion in 1949, a Maoist rebellion broke out in West Bengal and spread to Andhra Pradesh. It was against this background of unrest that Indira Gandhi changed the political rhetoric: under her leadership, India's sense of nationhood became based on its territorial integrity, established by the war to liberate East Pakistan in 1971. Henceforth, armed strength was given pride of place, Nehru's socialist vision took on a populist hue led by the government slogan, 'Garibi Hatao' ('Remove Poverty'). The government's policy of non-alignment was also reconsidered, with India moving towards friendly relations with the Soviet Union. Secularism, the third plank of Nehru's vision, was for the first time used as a blatant bid for the Muslim vote.

Throughout the 1970s, the rhetoric of poverty removal and socialism grew louder but the economy's growth rate failed to improve to any significant degree. This led to an acceleration of social conflict, but these were 'secular' struggles against inflation and against government repression. The tight economic and social situation resulted in a battle between various groups over funds. This took a political form, with linguistic, regional, and casteist forces all taking part. By the end of the 1970s the 'Hindu rate of growth'—a low 3.5 per cent per annum— looked permanent. It was during this period that Lokayan was established—the grass-roots movements of Dalits and tribals against the State. By the 1970s, then, the illusion of a Nehruvian state as the champion of the poor had gone, despite India's now official status as a secular socialist state.

A more alarming feature of Indira Gandhi's leadership was her government's doctrine of popular sovereignty. The Constitution of India can be amended much more easily than that of many other countries, and Indira Gandhi amended it whenever her legislation was successfully challenged in the courts. Two amendments that she made included the modification of property rights and the declaration of India as a secular socialist state. This attitude towards the Constitution—that the people through their elected representatives had the right to amend it—is not unique to Indira Gandhi; indeed, it was part of the Left's programme that also embraced secularism. But it is a majoritarian doctrine. Minority rights cannot be guaranteed if the majority can change fundamental law at its whim. In the debates before independence, it was majoritarianism, albeit defined along religious lines, that had haunted Jinnah. Further moves in favour of the power of the elected majority against the civil service, the judiciary, and the police were also encouraged at both the state level and the central level during the 1970s and 1980s. Again, while a popular mandate was the argument put forward to defend such practices, the elimination of politically neutral places in the state meant that whoever was in power could wield it arbitrarily.

Losing power in 1977, and regaining it in 1980, taught Indira Gandhi one thing: it was not enough to be populist. Her success depended on the majority community—the Hindus. The populist doctrine enunciated by her was practised by the Janata government as well. But to reclaim power, she had to make a passionate bid for the Hindu vote. Henceforth, she saw all religious groups as separate vote-banks to be placated depending on their size and degree of support.

During the Gandhi family period of rule, 1980–9, the strains of Indian nationhood became clearer. In the early 1980s, the Sikhs suffered a similar situation to that of the Muslims in 1965, experiencing suspicion and discrimination because of India's battle against the Khalistan movement. Kashmir and the North-East became more troublesome and violent, and many 'secular' struggles—involving the Dalits, the tribals, and women—continued. The civil war in Sri Lanka washed on to India's shores and claimed the life of Rajiv Gandhi.

The Decline of Secularism and the Rise of the Bharatiya Janata Party

After 1989 and the defeat of the Congress party, India experienced a decade of coalition governments. The 1990s was the decade in which the BJP strengthened its power base. The Nehru version of nationhood had long ago become hollow, and the end of the Cold War had made India's policy of non-alignment redundant. The advent of globalization and India's own economic crisis in 1991 meant that Nehruvian planning was considered a handicap to progress. In addition, secularism had been compromised and weakened by the two Gandhis throughout the 1980s.

It was within this context that the BJP was able to offer *Hindutva* as an alternative positive theory of Indian nationhood. Tracing the argument back to Savarkar against Gandhi in the early part of the twentieth century, the BJP merely codified the hidden agenda of the right wing of the Congress party and the actual practice of Lal Bahadur Shastri and the two Gandhis which favoured the Hindus and, marginalized the Muslims. In the next three elections (1989, 1991, and 1996), the BJP increased its representation in the Lok Sabha, becoming the largest single party in office. The prospect of a BJP government was finally realized in March 1998. The increasing strength of the BJP is not merely electoral. The party, along with the RSS and the Vishwa Hindu Parishad (VHP), has been waging a *Kulturkampf* against the theory of secularism, as well as its contradictory practice. The evasions of the Congress about the two-nation theory, the neutral but asymmetric treatment of Hindu and Muslim communities, the blatant playing opportunistically and erratically—of both the Hindu card and the Muslim card by the Congress under the two Gandhis, all served to strengthen the BJP. Against this threadbare secularism, asserted rather than understood or argued, the BJP and its intellectuals posed the view that India is a nation because it is a Hindu country with a Hindu religious majority and a Hindu society, that is all but encompassing even of the minorities. The BJP constructed a monist but popular version of Hinduism around the figure of Ram and, in a parody of the Mahatma, tried to mobilize the Indian masses around religious symbols. The possibility of bricklaying for a temple on the site of the Babri Mosque in Ayodhya was the BJP equivalent of the Dandi Salt Satyagraha—a highly inflammatory gesture.

In the event, the destruction of the Babri Masjid in 1992 initiated the first serious discussion of the meaning of secularism in India. The BJP had overplayed its hand, though even then its Lok Sabha representation increased in 1996 but fell short of a majority. Temporarily at least, the BJP was thwarted from power. An alternative coalition built around the divisive but democratic forces of caste, region, and religious politics came to power. This coalition harked back to the vision expressed in the Round Table conferences of India, of a multinational polity with nationality defined along the lines of region, language, and religion. But neither the vision nor the coalition government was sustainable. It lost power in 1997 and new elections were held in early 1998 which brought a coalition led by the BJP to office. In another election, in September 1999, the BJP was re-elected along with its coalition partners to a majority in the Lok Sabha.

Nationhoods on Offer

At the dawn of the twenty-first century, then, there are several competing theories of Indian nationhood. The first is a vision of Indian nationhood based on an inclusive but single nationality that Nehru tried to articulate. This vision has been badly tarnished but is still capable of a fresh reformulation.[13] The leading alternative is a notion of India as a Hindu nation with ostensible and formal guarantees for the Muslims. This puts forward the idea of India as a state built around the religious beliefs of the majority. The practice of previous 'secular' governments regarding legalities and constitutional guarantees renders any promises of minority rights fragile and incredible.

The third vision has come about through the grass-roots struggle of the 1970s against the failure of the Nehruvian economic programme to deliver growth or equity. Backward castes, Dalits, Muslims, and women—overlapping groups often at odds with one another but united by their exclusion from the privileged elite which has enjoyed power and patronage—have formed a loose and shifting coalition of national and regional parties. Although they do not offer a coherent theory of nationhood, inasmuch as these coalitions have arisen from the vigorous practice of electoral democratic politics, they embody a realistic practice of Indian nationhood. It is a multinational vision of nationhood—in which region, language, social status are combined (along with an anti-religious streak among the Dalits), and one which offers the Muslims a haven. It is not a secular vision as such, but it is anti-elitist and anti-centralist, and it is trying precariously to hold the tide against the BJP and its pro-Hindu stance.

One of the main arguments in Indian political life since the Babri Masjid incident concerns secularism versus the BJP. In their narrow anti-BJP focus, the secularists display much the same asymmetry as was shown in the past towards the Hindus and the Muslims. Inasmuch as the proponents are left-oriented, they adopt the Nehruvian theory of nationhood along with the economic programme as well. But the decline and drift in the Congress has weakened the secularists. Its arguments against the BJP's theory of *Hindutva* are based on a rejection of religion as the basis for defining nationhood; as well, they object to the BJP's monistic

[13] Vanaik (1997) is one such attempt. Hasan (1997) argues for a modernist, secular programme for Muslims.

version of Hinduism, preferring instead a pluralist and heterogeneous version (see Vanaik 1997).

The BJP has always nominally denied that it is an exclusively Hindu party. Its Parivar (literally meaning 'family', and comprising of parallel political formations such as the RSS, Vishwa Hindu Parishad, Bajrang Dal, Rashtriya Jagaran Morcha, etc.) is another matter. The Babri Masjid episode was an embarrassment for the BJP because its nationalist colours were exposed as exclusively Hindu and aggressively anti-Muslim. As a party, the BJP has sought to use Hindu religious symbolism to mobilize the masses almost in a parody of Gandhi, but without his ecumenism.

The intellectual arguments against the BJP's version of Hinduism are, in my opinion, less potent than the Ambedkarite root and branch antagonism to Hinduism displayed by the Dalits. Added to this has been the practical political mobilization around the Mandal Commission, which recommended the reservation of government jobs for lower castes and untouchables. Ideologically, it exposes Hinduism not as a seamless whole, as some upper-caste intellectuals have tried to demonstrate since Raja Ram Mohan Roy, but as a kaleidoscope mosaic of little traditions and multiple sects. Politically, it has shown that while Hindu religious symbols may have helped Gandhi mobilize people (though even here after Khilafat, the Muslim support for the Congress party diminished), in post colonial democratic India it is the fissurers in Hindu society which shape party politics at the regional, local, and national levels. There is no single Hindu vote-bank.

Yet a BJP-led coalition with regional and caste parties came to power in 1998. In October 1999, a coalition of the BJP with a large collection of regional and 'backward class' parties won the election with a convincing majority. I believe that this reaffirmation of the winning formula vindicates my argument in this chapter. The coalition shows that to construct a majority in government in India today, one has to encompass at least two of the three nationhoods on offer. In the 1999 elections, the Congress party, under Sonia Gandhi, tried to win a majority and lost. This means that the BJP is now the new ruling party. The question this poses is, why is there fear concerning the BJP and its rise to power? The answer, in my view, has to do not with communalism but with constitutionalism.

Communalism or Constitutionalism

The issue of the constitution is now the central difficulty facing the secularist programme. There is a serious prospect that a majoritarian government in India may be openly non-secular. Since in practice, if not in theory, an elected government can abridge the authority of the civil service and the police as it likes, the fragility of minority rights is all too clear. The Left is used to thinking that it will be perennially in the majority in government. If the balance of power in India were to shift to the Right (and as of 2000, this had not yet been the case), then the Left would wake up to the value of the old-fashioned virtues of a neutral civil service and a constitution beyond the reach of easy manipulation by a government.[14] I would argue that there is a need to look at the fragility of the present

---

[14] This happened to the British Left when Margaret Thatcher was prime minister. This led to

constitutional arrangements in India, which in turn implies a reconsideration of the nature and purpose of secularism; that is, its instrumentality in terms of minority rights rather than its ideology *vis-à-vis* religion.[15] Nehruvian secularism has also been asymmetrically more anti-Hindu religiosity and obscurantism, more anti-BJP (and the Sangh Parivar) than against all religious obscurantism. Thus, the modernist, secular forces in the Muslim community have not had much support from the Nehruvian secular forces. I would maintain that secularism needs to be a philosophy of secularization and modernization for *all* religious communities (Hasan 1997; Vanaik 1997).

Secularism within the Indian political context has also been an elite philosophy that has been fiercely defended by the leadership of certain left-oriented parties, though it has not had mass support. Until the end of the 1970s, one could have said that the large support for the Congress party was a sign of support for secularism. But during the 1980s, this ceased to be the case. As the Congress party played the Hindu card and the Muslim card simultaneously, it was obvious that the Muslims were thought of as a special vote-bank, as they had been in 1909 with the Morley–Minto reforms. The Congress party now pays slightly greater lip-service to secularism because it wishes to recapture the Muslim vote which it lost in the 1996 elections, but it is difficult to take its profession seriously.

The connection of secularism with the dirigisme of the Nehruvian economic policy is, in my view, also unfortunate. Achin Vanaik (1997) argues passionately, but wrongly in my opinion, that liberal economic reform will strengthen the forces of Hindu fundamentalism and that a return to socialist economic policy is the only guarantee for secularism. I believe it is the economic stagnation, wastage, and corruption of the old policies, as seen clearly in the 1980s, that have discredited secularism (see Chapter 16 and Desai 1995). India's economic failure was compounded by a failure to act decisively on literacy, health, and social projects such as clean water. It also gave the state, and of course whichever party controlled the government, enormous and arbitrary powers. The case for secularism has, therefore, to be argued independently of the dirigiste economics which have become part of the problem facing India today.

Finally, secularism must be separated from majoritarianism. No matter who is in power, certain fundamental rights must be guaranteed—by the police, the judiciary, and the civil service. Thus, secularism must be part and parcel of a civil libertarian philosophy, in which civil society plays a vigilant role. Civil rights should not depend on who is in power. As a consequence of these considerations, a movement to restore the neutrality of the civil service, the judiciary and the police, in short to restore the rule of law, is imperative. Institutions that were inherited from the British and strengthened in the 1950s, and new institutions created in the 1950s and 1960s to implement a rule of law, have eroded alarmingly over the past three decades. Secularism must be dissociated from government and indeed from religion. What is required is the expansion of a neutral, government-free space in civil society. It is not just a question of Hindu–Muslim riots or of the

formations such as Charter 88 advocating electoral reform to avoid a repetition of what Lord Hailsham labelled 'an elective dictatorship'.

[15] See Chapter 5. Also in Desai (1997).

validity of a Hindu fundamentalist reading of Indian history as against Islamic fundamentalism and its defensiveness of its family law. The caste Hindu–Dalit riots, the Hindu–Sikh riots, the Shi'a–Sunni riots, and the many violent attacks on women in all the social orders by the orthodox patriarchy, are all signs that the rule of law has broken down in India. Religious beliefs are a private matter. Naturally, there are times when religion will spill over into politics (and this has been the case since the days of Tilak and Gandhi). But a space needs to be created and expanded which is outside the domain of the government in office, which gives hope that the many and excellent fundamental rights guaranteed by the Indian Constitution are actually enjoyed by all citizens, no matter what their religion, sex, or caste or which region they are from.

Conclusion

The decision by Morley and Minto to create separate electorates crystallized nationalism in India around electoral politics. As two further episodes of franchise expansion and relatively greater self-government occurred in 1917 and 1935, the contention of various groups within Indica to have a formal representation became insistent. In contrast to this was the vision of a single nation defined either in terms of a harmonious collection of religious communities (as espoused by Gandhi) or as a liberal-democratic community of citizens who in their public life were neutral, or at least unmindful of their own and others' religion (as advocated by Nehru). Fears of the rights of a minority in the face of a majoritarian interpretation of democracy led to the articulation of a two-nations theory (by Jinnah). In the hurried and messy negotiations for India's independence between 1944 and 1947, the two-nations theory won and secured the partition of India. All the various parties to the negotiation connived in this state of affairs and were responsible for partition.

Partition created a challenge of defining a nationhood for India. Nehru consciously, and for a while successfully, accomplished this based on a vision of a secular, non-aligned country engaged in planned economic development. However, this model has in recent years come under considerable strain. Since 1975 a number of social and political movements have contested the hegemonic vision of the Congress, causing the party under the weight of electoral pressure to abandon Nehru's secular vision for India. Communalism in this sense is just one of many opposition movements. Its danger lies in the fact that the subversion of a neutral political space by the Congress following a majoritarian logic exposed India to the possibility of a non-secular party coming to power and oppressing the Muslim minority. With the BJP's victory in the 1998 and 1999 elections, this possibility became a reality, although the BJP-led coalition did not disavow secularism which is enshrined in the Constitution. India needs to restore the neutral space from majoritarian political predations as a guarantee of human rights for all minorities. The partners of the BJP in the present coalition (created in the 1999 election) represent the grass-roots and anti-elite elements of society. Perhaps they can ensure the establishment of a neutral political space. India's future will be hopeful if they do so.

REFERENCES

Ahmed, Khaled (1998), 'Karakalpakistan', *HIMAL*, Vol. 11, No. 2, February.

Ambedkar, B. R. (1940) 2nd edn 1945), *Pakistan or the Partition of India*, Bombay: Thacker and Co.

Brockway, F. (1973), *The Colonial Revolution*, London: Hart-Davis McGibbon.

Charmley, J. (1993), *Churchill: The End of Glory: A Political Biography*, London: Hodder and Stoughton.

Churchill, R. (1964), *Churchill, Volume 1*, London: Heineman.

Desai, M. (1990), 'Birth and Death of Nation States: Speculations about Germany and India', in M. Mann, F. Halliday and J. Hobson (eds), *Rise and Decline of the Nation-State*, Oxford: Blackwell. See also Chapter 20.

—— (1993), 'Constructing Nationality in a Multinational Democracy: The Case of India', in R. Michener (ed.), *Economics, Culture and Education*, St Paul Minnesota: Professors for World Peace Academy, pp. 225–41. See also Chapter 22.

—— (1995), 'Economic Reform: Stalled by Politics' in P. Oldenburg, *India Briefing*, New York/London: M.E. Sharpe, pp. 75–95. See also Chapter 16.

—— (1997), 'India: End of the First Republic?', *Times Higher Educational Supplement*, November 1997. See also Chapter 5.

Dutt, R.C. (1908), *The Economic History of India Under Early British Rule*, London: K. Paul, Trench, Trubner and Co. Ltd.

French, P. (1997), *Liberty or Death?: India's Journey to Independence and Division*, London: HarperCollins.

Gilbert, M. (1976), *Churchill. Volume 5: 1922–1939*, London: Heinemann.

Gopal, S. (1975), *Jawaharlal Nehru: A Biography. Volume 1: 1889–1947*, London: Jonathan Cape.

—— (1979), *Jawaharlal Nehru: A Biography. Volume 2: 1947–1956*, London: Jonathan Cape.

—— (1985), *Jawaharlal Nehru: A Biography. Volume 3: 1956–1964*, London: Jonathan Cape.

Hasan, M. (1997), *Legacy of a Divided Nation; India's Muslims Since Independence*, London: Hurst and Co.

Jaffrelot, C. (1997), *The Hindu Nationalist Movement and Indian Politics, 1925 to 1990s*, London: Hurst and Co.

Jalal, A. (1985), *The Sole Spokesman: Jinnah, the Muslim League and the Demand for Pakistan*, Cambridge: Cambridge University Press.

Jayawardene, K. (1986), *Ethnic and Class Conflicts in Sri Lanka: Some Aspects of Sinhala Buddhist Consciousness Over the Past 100 Years*, Colombo: Centre for Social Analysis.

Khaliquzaman, C. (1961), *Pathway to Pakistan*, Lahore: Longmans.

Naoroji, D. (1901), *Poverty and UnBritish Rule in India*, London: S. Sonnenschein.

Nanda, B.R. (1989), *Gandhi: Pan-Islamism, Imperialism and Nationalism in India*, Bombay: Oxford University Press.

Nehru, J. (1936), *Autobiography*, London: Bodley Head.

—— (1946), *The Discovery of India*, London: Bodley Head.

Pandey, G. (1990), *The Construction of Communalism in North India*, New Delhi: Oxford University Press.

Parekh, B. (1989), *Colonialism, Tradition and Reform: An Analysis of Gandhi's Political Discourse*, New Delhi: Sage.

Samad, Y. (1995), *A Nation in Turmoil: Nationalism and Ethnicity in Pakistan, 1937*–1958, New Delhi: Sage.

Vanaik, A. (1997), *The Furies of Indian Communalism: Religion, Modernity and Secularisation*, London: Versa.

Venkataraman, M.S. and B.S. Srivastava (1983), *Roosevelt, Gandhi, Churchill: America and the Last Phase of India's Freedom Struggle*, London: Sangam Book.

24

Gujarat and its Bhasmita

The renowned Gujarati author and politician K.M. Munshi wrote a classic novel, *Gujarat No Nath*.[1] In the novel, there is an episode of Muslim houses being set on fire in Khambhat, the fief of the villainous Uda Mehta. Kaak, the hero, rescues a Muslim called Khatib. Munshi adds that Kaak insists on calling him Khatip, exercising the age-old privilege of the powerful to distort the names of the downtrodden. Khatib is produced at the court of Raja Siddharaja at a crucial moment and Uda Mehta's atrocities are exposed. Having served his purpose, Khatib disappears from the narrative. It is the perennial fate of the weak to be a pawn in the power struggle of the elite.

I doubt if anyone would write such a story today. Surely for present day Gujaratis, Uda Mehta is a hero for burning Muslim houses and Kaak a secularist villain. Even Munshi who became a leader of Hindu revivalism, started the Bharatiya Vidya Bhavan, sponsored a Hindu nationalist multi-volume history of India, and helped rebuild the Somnath temple would not have endorsed Kaak's conduct were he around today. Yet he wrote, *I Follow the Mahatma*. The other political hero of Gujarat, Sardar Patel, despite his staunch role in the independence movement, has now been appropriated by the Bharatiya Janata Party (BJP) and projected as a hardline alternative on Pakistan and Kashmir to the soft secularist Nehru. Yet I doubt that Sardar Patel, though on the right wing of the Congress, was in any sense a Hindu fundamentalist. Yet that is the way he is celebrated today. Is Gandhi himself being disowned now for his tolerance?

Gujarat has redefined itself from a peace-loving tolerant place full of civility into an aggressive assertive Hindu domain. This has been the result of a steady and assiduous *Kulturkampf* fought by the Jan Sangh/BJP through the 1980s and the 1990s. On my periodic visits to India during those days, I found good, gentle, middle class Gujaratis, prosperous, not poor, steadily turning anti-Muslim. One of my great nieces shocked me when she said, apropos of Dilip Kumar, 'He is a

Seminar, No. 513, pp. 56–7, May 2002.

There is of course no such word as *bhasmita*, but *bhasma* is ashes and *asmita* is self-image. The connection should then be obvious.

[1] Kanaiyalal Maneklal Munshi (1921), *Gujarat No Nath*, Ahmedabad: Granthalaya.

Muslim; he should not get any film roles'. I had never ever thought of Dilip Kumar as anything but Dilip Kumar and while everyone knew he was Yusuf Khan, no one thought of him as other than an Indian till the poison began to spread in the 1980s.

There is a parallel story of the rise of Muslim fundamentalism. After the oil crisis of 1973, the suddenly enriched Saudi Arabia strove to reverse all the modernizing tendencies in Islam and wound the clock back to medieval Wahabbism. The Iranian Revolution that followed in 1979 added fuel to the fire. The moral collapse of the Government of India over Salman Rushdie's *Satanic Verses* showed that secularism had come to mean equal licence for both fundamentalisms. Afghanistan with its Taliban revolution did not help matters either. Its anti-Americanism was the fig leaf for masking fundamentalism, which was both anti-women and anti-modernity.

But even before all that, Ahmedabad had riots in 1969 and as Ashutosh Varshney argues in his new book, *Ethnic Conflict and Civic Life*, it is one of the most riot-prone cities in India. Along with Vadodara, it accounts for 80 per cent of the deaths from communal riots in the state. While other states have endemic communalism, Gujarat suffers from episodic or discontinuous communalism. Riots are occasional but when they occur they are extremely vicious. But even so we have to ask, why does Gujarat display this behaviour pattern?

Ashutosh Varshney traces the erosion of civic institutions such as political parties, trade unions, and business associations in Gujarat as the proximate cause. The Congress declined relative to the BJP, the textile industry also declined, and so did the unions. Thus, civic networks where Hindus and Muslims worked together became weak. I would add to this analysis a few more elements. Democracy, which we much celebrate, has not been good for communal relations. This is because competitive politics has crystallized communities by treating them as vote banks.

Thus Muslims are a vote bank and as a matter of practice religious leaders become the gatekeepers of that vote bank. Among Hindus, different castes are vote banks—Patidars as against Kshatriyas, Dalits against the other Backward Castes, and so on. Thus, far from democracy making India free of caste and communal divisions, as the people of Nehru's generation hoped, all these divisions have been valorized by competitive electoral politics. Far from becoming a republic of citizens, India has become an archipelago of communities.

Alongside we have experienced a relatively slow economic growth rate, an overwhelming weight of the public sector for jobs and patronage, and the deliberate growth of crime by the maintenance of state interventions such as prohibition and import controls or tariffs. Crime depends on politics and feeds on it. Politics needs criminals for money and muscle. If you want a job or a contract, you have to show your community/vote bank identity and you have to channel your demand through political agents who look after your community. There is no neutral public space left where citizens *qua* citizens can have redress for their grievances or satisfy their demand for publicly provided goods and services. The army and the judiciary are the only two institutions that have not been thoroughly politicized.

Yet this again is an all-India story, Gujarat remains an exception in its sudden bursts of extreme violence. Again one can only speculate. In the civility for which Gujaratis were known, religion, especially Vaishnavism and Jainism, played a large part. Gujarat could be said to have had its bourgeois revolution sometime in the early twentieth century. The business classes became dominant socially relative to Brahmins or Patidars. These business classes were Jain or Vaishnava and were largely mild, non-coercive, albeit exploitative, capitalists. Yet that was before independence. Subsequent to the formation of the Gujarat state, politicians emerged as an elite group competing with businessmen and indeed more powerful than them, thanks to 'socialist' economic policies. So the importance of this class has diminished. Other groups have emerged—Patidars first and then other caste groups.

But over the years Gujarat has also prospered faster than many other Indian states. In the last 10 or 15 years, a lot of accumulation has taken place, by bursting through regulations and breaking laws. Defiance of rules and laws has marked this new prosperity. At the same time religion has increasingly become more of a consumable good which has to be flaunted with expensive rituals than a code for civic behaviour, Readings of the *Bhagvad Gita* or the *Ramayana* have become festivals of conspicuous consumption. Instead of Vaishnavite pacifism we have Bajrang aggression.

Thus Gujaratis have turned from being meek and mild and proverbially passive to being macho and aggressive. This was indeed how K.M. Munshi fantasized Gujarat to be. That bit about Khatib may have been there to bolster his image as a Gandhian. It is now best forgotten.

SOUTH ASIA

25

South Asia

Economic Stagnation and Economic Change

INTRODUCTION

South Asia for the purposes of this chapter is defined as Bangladesh, India, and Pakistan, the three nations that were once a single entity before 1947. Thus, it excludes Sri Lanka, Nepal, Bhutan, and Myanmar. In previous papers, I have labelled the region *Indica,* comprising British India and the native states. Indica was twice partitioned in the last 50 odd years, first in 1947 into India and Pakistan, and then in 1971 Pakistan was partitioned into Pakistan and Bangladesh (Chapter 17 and Desai 1990).

In 1941, the Census put the population of Indica at 400 million. Today the population is three times as much—India 913 million, Pakistan 133 million, and Bangladesh 116 million (all 1994 figures from Human Development Report 1997). By comparison, Sri Lanka has 18 million, Nepal 21 million, and Bhutan 1.7 million. Thus, Indica is the second most populous region in the world after China, but has the largest concentration of Muslim population in the world, as well as of course, of Hindu population.

Over the 50 years since independence [25 years for Bangladesh] the region has *retrogressed* rather than progressed. Thus, its relative position in terms of income was higher in 1947 than it is today. Thus in a United Nations (UN) study of national incomes in 1949, of the 70 countries cited, India's rank was 55, and Pakistan 57, while China's rank was 69, Indonesia 67, and South Korea was 68. In the ranking of income, the real GDP per capita (PPP$) in 1997, out of 175 countries, India is 143 and Pakistan 120, while Bangladesh is 144. China by comparison is 111, South Korea 37, and Indonesia 92 [*Human Development Report* 1997]. The region also has the largest concentration of poor people in the world. Using head count (though Indica's economists have enriched the world by

Paper read at World Bank Conference on South Asian Economies, Colombo, 1997.

offering many sophisticated measures of poverty) and income as a measure, the proportions in poverty were India (35), Pakistan (34), and Bangladesh (48). Around 500 million people are poor in the region and they represent 40 per cent of the world's poor. Despite a general political rhetoric in favour of equity and social justice, the nations of Indica have failed to achieve either and hence there can be no excuse that low growth was traded off for equity. In human development terms, the region is the most backward in Asia and its performance is comparable with that of sub-Saharan Africa (Haq 1997).

Thus Indica is a region of relatively slow growth of Gross Domestic Product (GDP), as well as GDP per capita. Average annual growth rate of GDP per capita (US$) for 1960–94 for the countries in the region were 2.0 per cent for India, 3.0 per cent for Pakistan, and 0.9 per cent for Bangladesh. It is not a tiger; at best perhaps a flat footed elephant which is in danger of missing the train as other countries catch up with the pace of globalization. There has been, however, during the last ten years a change in perceptions and attitudes, which, if sustained, may yet accelerate the growth of income and decline of poverty in the economy.

The paradox of the historical record is that, as of 1947 Indica was the seventh largest industrial economy (in terms of volume of output) and had an experience of national and not just foreign entrepreneurship which went back 90 years. Tariff protection had been granted at the turn of the century by the ruling colonial power and both the World Wars saw a speeding up of industrial growth. There remained severe regional imbalances as well as lopsidedness in the sectoral composition of industrial output. The economies were predominantly agricultural and had suffered low growth if not stagnation of per capita income, especially due to nil or low growth of agricultural output during the twentieth century. (These statements are somewhat vague because the debate on Indian national income statistics is quite unsettled; see Heston 1984 and Morris 1984.)

In the following sections, I will attempt to describe the record as well as explain this paradox on a comparative basis—how did Indica, a leader in Asia in 1947, become a laggard. While there is a large literature on India and a respectable amount on the other two countries, there is little that is on a comparative basis for the region as a whole. Thus I take individual country studies as a background, and concentrate on the issues and trends which are common. The explanation I shall offer is largely endogenous and economic, and downplays external or indigenous influences. This is somewhat in contrast to the notion that it was the experience of colonialism and the subsequent domination by imperialism/monopoly capitalism that stunted India's growth possibilities. This explanation, deriving from the works of Baran and Gunder Frank, was quite influential in Indian discussions (Baran 1957; Gunder-Frank 1967; Pattanaik 1975). Nor will I blame the stagnation on religious or cultural values as has also been done.

In the following, all references to Indica are either to the pre-1947 India or to the whole region after that date. References to Pakistan are to both wings till 1971 and only to the (West) Pakistan after 1971. Bangladesh is of course post-1971. References to India are to post-1947 India.

INITIAL ENDOWMENTS

The partition which occurred simultaneously with the independence of India and Pakistan meant that what was once an integrated economy, albeit with many local regional economies, was sundered into two countries and three regions. This had two consequences. First was the extra economic burden of settling refugees who moved from one part of Indica to another—around 7,000,000 each side. Second was the cessation of trade between these two countries, which led to attempts within each to replace the benefits of trade by domestic substitution. Thus the jute factories of West Bengal in India could no longer rely on the supply of raw jute from East Pakistan, and hence land was diverted to raw jute production in India and jute factories had to be built in Pakistan—a double misallocation of resources. Similarly trade in raw cotton between India and West Pakistan was also disrupted with parallel effects.

The exact cost of this partition induced adjustment has never been, to my knowledge, estimated. Today it is forgotten that these three nations were once one region. Bangladesh suffered a similar cost again when it became independent, but in its case the physical distance from West Pakistan meant that, there was a weak division of labour between the two regions in any case. In rough terms, two to three years after independence should be considered to have been affected by these shocks.

Of the two nations in 1947, India was bigger and better endowed in terms of manufacturing industry, infrastructure and skilled manpower, as well as entrepreneurs. Pakistan was relatively better endowed in terms of agriculture and irrigation facilities with a relatively favourable land–labour ratio overall, but markedly so in West Pakistan (see Bhatia 1990 for data). Both countries were ideologically wedded to import-substitution industrialization as the strategy for development. In Pakistan's case, there was no indigenous industry to speak of and new enterprise had to be started from scratch. In India's case, there was an industrial structure, much of it rather simple and at the consumer goods end, but there was a vibrant machine textile industry which had export potential. However, the perception of the leaders at the time of independence was that India was in need of sustained industrialization as a key to solving the problems of poverty. The state was to play an important part in this development and planning of a rudimentary sort had been started by the Indian National Congress's National Planning Committee even before independence.

Of course, the countries were predominantly agricultural and the bulk of the population, as well as the workforce, was in the rural areas. The peasantry was poor and burdened by rent and tax claims which came from the intermediaries as well as the state. Since the rural population had been mobilized in the independence struggle by the Congress, promises had been made of remission of land revenue demands as well as of land reform. The landlords faced a loss of lands and many Muslim landlords joined the Muslim League. The League was thus against land reforms and did not pursue land reforms in Pakistan after independence. The problem of low productivity of land was, as we shall see below, accorded lower priority than land reform.

Pakistan had not only no industry or industrial entrepreneurs to speak of, but even in terms of civil service it was dealt a less strong suit than India was. Merchants, large landlords, a few top civil servants, army officers, and the leadership of the Muslim League comprised the small elite that Pakistan had to begin with. In India, by contrast, there was a large civil service and academic elite as well as industrialists, landlords, and merchants. The political life was also livelier because of the Congress's democratic culture and the number of smaller opposition parties it had spawned.

While both elites were committed to growth and to industrialization, what they had perhaps not anticipated was that partition would impose such large transition costs. In addition, the two countries fought a war in 1948—on the issue of Kashmir—and have been in a state of semi-hot, semi-cold war with each other ever since. This has led to some diversion of resources to military technology and personnel which could well have been used elsewhere. The maintenance of territorial integrity has been perhaps a bigger priority than economic growth and for all countries in the region. While Pakistan failed in this attempt and was divided again, India has devoted large resources to internal integrity. These costs were not anticipated at the time of independence.

THE RECORD

Against this background, we can begin to look at the strategy adopted for development and its consequences. It could be thought that given the relatively better industrial endowments India had, especially its textile industry, an export oriented strategy based on an expansion of textile industry could be tried. There was a demand by the industrialists in the Bombay Plan for rapid growth via industrialization using India's existing strength. There was a demand by the Gandhians to concentrate on low technology, labour absorbing cottage industries, and rural development, and by some nationalist economists associated with Congress, for concentration on employment growth via agricultural development (and Chapter 14). This demand would have relied on export growth of India's traditional export, including textiles, and would have been a bottom-up approach.

Despite these proposals, the decision was taken to launch an industrialization programme from 1956 onwards, which not only adopted import-substitution industrialization but was biased towards building a capital goods sector while discouraging the expansion of the modern consumer goods sector. This was the Mahalanobis strategy as outlined in the Second and subsequent Five Year Plans. The discouragement of the modern textile industry was politically expedient and not a necessary part of the strategy. Export pessimism was rampant and the notion of expanding the internationally competitive textile sector was never, as far as I know, entertained. (Recently several authors have revisited these issues in the festschrift presented to Manmohan Singh. See articles by Sen 1998 and Bhagwati 1998.) Although Planning in Pakistan started a bit later and was not as articulated as Indian planning till the 1960s, the overall policy in Pakistan was the same (Haq 1963).

Import-substitution industrialization was also accompanied by a distrust of price oriented policies, especially in the international sphere. This was partly the climate in economics worldwide in the 1950s, but it was also reinforced by the adverse international forces that began to affect the region. Pakistan, for example, refused to devalue the rupee when sterling was devalued in 1949 for what can only be called perverse nationalist reasons, but had to devalue by 1955. India devalued in 1949 along with UK as it were by instinct and long practice, but reluctantly and under duress in 1966. Though this was warranted by the data at hand this episode strengthened the hands of those who wanted autarkic policies. The preferred model was of an inward looking—self-sufficient, if you like—growth pattern led by the public sector as in India or at least largely assisted by the state as in Pakistan. After its independence, Bangladesh also followed the same pattern, though more on Indian than Pakistani lines to begin with under the Mujib regime, but later with greater private sector participation. But whatever the mix of public and private sector, the growth strategy was not market oriented nor planned in the Soviet sense. It is best described as state bureaucratic capitalism.

If industry was import-substitution industrialization led, agriculture was, to begin with, neglected. It was thought in India that the principal problem in agriculture was not productivity but redistribution through land reform. Land to the tenant/cultivator was the general pattern of land reform with local variations in the various states of India. To the extent that productivity was seen as a problem, it was blamed on the small size of the cultivating unit due to fragmentation and subinfeudation. The Congress Agrarian Reforms Committee had recommended a resort to co-operative farming in which independent tenant cultivators would pool their land and thus augment the size of the cultivating unit. Once land reforms had happened, however, the cultivators were reluctant to pool their land. Research by the Farm Management Committee in the mid 1950s showed that small farms were just as productive as large farms (sparking off a long debate in *Economic Weekly* and *Economic and Political Weekly* among economists). The leader of small farmers in the Congress party, Charan Singh, defeated Nehru's attempts to adopt co-operative farming as official policy. Thus India was stuck with independent tenant cultivators, many of them with small sized farms. The agricultural problem had to be solved on the technological rather than social side. East Pakistan had a highly egalitarian land ownership in any case due to the Tebhaga movement which had preceded partition. Most land owners were Hindus and lived in West Bengal anyway while the peasants were Muslims. Thus partition facilitated land reform of a radical sort. In West Pakistan, land was, and remains, highly unequally distributed. Half the cultivated area in West Pakistan was in holdings of more than 500 acres owned by the top 1 per cent of owners. At the bottom, 65 per cent of cultivators had farms of less than 5 acres. While in East Pakistan only 6 per cent were tenants, in West Pakistan 35 per cent were tenants (Bhatia, 1990).

Each country, especially India, ran against the constraint of inadequate food supplies by the mid 1950s. This took the form of inflationary pressures and/or reliance on food aid (under PL480) from the USA. It was the fortuitous occurrence of the Green Revolution in the 1960s, first in wheat and then in rice, that relieved the region of the food problem. The availability of foodgrains—a major problem in the mid 1950s to mid 1960s period—was eased by the 1970s. India is now a food surplus country as is Pakistan. Despite its poverty, Bangladesh was never a food importing country, except in years of famine.

The relatively slow rate of growth has meant that the economies of this region have failed to generate sufficient employment to absorb the growing population. Population growth has been given much more prominence in other treatments of the region's economic problems. But even without sounding neo-Malthusian, the population growth rate of this region is on the high side compared to other developing countries, though it is slowing down.[1] Within the region, Pakistan has the highest growth rate of population—3 per cent per annum on average for 1960–93, Bangladesh 2.5 per cent, and India 2.3 per cent over the same period.

These high growth rates lead to a growth of landlessness in rural areas and open unemployment in the urban areas. Industrial policies which were biased towards capital-intensive techniques in the larger plants did not help either, though there is a large informal/unorganized sector which absorbs labour. The Green Revolution also increased the demand for labour by facilitating double cropping etc. However, low labour absorption remains a problem.[2]

But while it has been a slow growth area, Indica has also been a relatively low inflation area, relative that is, to Latin America (See Chapter 6 and Desai 1997). It has no experience of hyperinflation or even of sustained double-digit annual inflation rates. In this, India has done the best with Pakistan second and Bangladesh some way behind. All of them have had balance of payments problems—shortage of domestic savings in other words. India has consciously tried to eliminate dependence on development assistance and raised its domestic savings rate to respectable levels of 25 per cent. Pakistan has relied much more on foreign flows and often lurched in and out of balance of payments crises. India of course ran into its most serious foreign exchange crisis in 1991 when it had to liberalize. In the case of Bangladesh, there has been an almost permanent reliance on foreign flows to cover the budget deficit, as well as to fill the saving-investment gap.

Thus, the region as a whole undersaves relative to its investment as well as, in the case of Bangladesh, consumption needs and also relatively to other Asian countries. Its slow growth rate can also be attributed to policies which lead to allocation inefficiencies and/or making the wrong dynamic choices by way of investment priorities. Thus one has to look in the aggregate at the total of domestic savings (high in India, lower in Pakistan, and lowest in Bangladesh) plus foreign flows (highest in Pakistan, followed by Bangladesh, then India), relative to the incremental capital-output ratio (as a short hand for investment efficiency) to explain growth performance in the region.

The entire region has not only been a slow growth area but it has also been shown to have followed unsustainable policies. Foreign resource barriers have been hit, growth policies initially followed shown to be inefficient and myopic,

[1] South Asia's share of world population rose from 19 per cent in 1960 to 22 per cent in 1993. See Table 1.1 and Figure 1.1 in Haq (1997).

[2] Early evaluations of the Green Revolution were rather pessimistic. See, however, Chapter 6 Desai (1975) for a robust counterview.

and human development issues have been neglected. The future is, however, better since there is a recognition across the region of the strictures expressed in the previous sentence. Thus a forward looking assessment will be different from a backward looking one. [There is a extensive literature on this. See Joshi and Little (1994) on India, Khan (1992) on Pakistan, and Hossain (1996) on Bangladesh.]

In the next section, the proximate causes of low growth performance are explored in greater detail and some attention will be paid to each country separately, though the comparative perspective is more illuminating.

REASONS BEHIND THE RECORD

It is best to divide the account into two periods; 1947 to 1971 when Pakistan split again, and 1971 to 1997 for the three countries. As we examine the record, the similarities of experience are much more striking than the differences. Across the region, similar policies were followed—planning, protectionism, overvalued exchange rates, neglect of human capital, profligacy in public budgeting, dependence on foreign aid—and of course the results were similar—low growth rates and persistent poverty with crisis conditions due to foreign exchange reserves constraints being hit.

The nationalist movement in Indica was convinced that rapid industrialization was the key to development and eradication of poverty (Gandhi had somewhat different views but his followers were unable to influence policies in India and had no standing in Pakistan). It was also agreed that the state would play an active role. A general assumption/explanation about the poverty of the region was the theory of the drain. This argued that Indica was poor because surplus was drained away to Britain as part of an elaborate system of home purchases, exchange rate manipulation to favour sterling, and other policies to keep the region underindustrialized.[3] Upon independence the drain would stop and the surplus would be invested at home.

This account implied that the crucial barrier to development was the diversion of surplus which would be removed by independence. There was thus no shortage of resources as such, only their misdirection. When Bangladesh was formed, the critique by East Pakistan intellectuals of the relative backwardness of their region had exactly the same themes (see Blackburn 1975). In agriculture as well, the poverty of the peasantry was traced to the tenurial structures and the drain of surplus away by landlords and intermediaries. Here again, land reform, i.e. changing the ownership of the surplus, was thought to be the key to growth. Thus at the outset, the thinking on growth was dominated by issues of sectoral allocation of resources assumed to be available, rather than the issue of raising resources. Thus low productivity per acre and per worker in agriculture was not immediately seen to be the problem regardless of tenure, but allocation of surplus was.

When it came to industry, the analysis said that the Imperial power had subjected Indica to Free Trade policies which were more in the interest of the metropolis than of the colony. The independence movement since its inception

[3] Nehru's *Discovery of India* offers a representative and, given its author, an influential account.

had demanded tariffs as basic to its strategy for Indian independence. Independence when it came in 1947 meant the freedom to impose tariffs for the protection of home industries. There was, in the 1950s, terms of trade pessimism (Prebisch–Singer hypothesis), as well as export pessimism (see Sen 1998 for a review of the export pessimism debate in India). India (and Pakistan similarly), was planning to build up an industrialized economy by using protection in the form of tariffs, quotas etc.

These policies on the industrial side solidified by the late 1950s. During the First Five Year Plan, it seemed that India would follow a policy continuing the previous trends and concentrate on the production of food grains and consumer goods. India also gave a much more prominent role to the state and to basic machine-made goods industries in the Second Five Year Plan (1956–61) than it had before. Planning in Pakistan began with the Colombo Plan—a Commonwealth effort for the period 1950–7 and First Five Year Plan was for 1955–60 but was not approved till 1958. It was only after Ayub Khan's installation as President that planning took off.

The first decade of development, say 1950 to 1960, was thus very much based on these assumptions. The sterling balances which had been accumulated during the War years were to provide a cushion to the region, for a while. But by the end of 1950s, there were problems. Both countries had started on a course of Planning Commission led development, India more determinedly than Pakistan. India also had a better start than Pakistan. Both countries had an exceptional harvest in 1953–4 with Pakistan registering a 10 per cent growth rate of GDP and India 6 per cent. But the first half of the 1950s was better for India than for Pakistan which had a weak political system and took some time to overcome its initial lack of endowments.

India dates its real planning from the mid 1950s and the Second Five Year Plan onwards. This ambitious plan based on the Mahalanobis model committed India to a capital goods investment strategy. The investment rate was stepped up and was mainly devoted to industry and infrastructure, on the assumption that the agriculture situation was alright.

It was in the second half of the 1950s that food shortages and inflationary problems were encountered by both countries. Foreign exchange constraints began to bite. Pakistan ran out of its sterling balances in 1954 and devalued its rupee in 1955 from 3.3 rupees to the dollar to 4.7 rupees. India ran out of sterling balances in 1957 and had to prune the ambitious Second Plan. The Indian GDP growth rate in 1957–8 was negative due to this shock. (Perhaps India should have devalued as well?). But, miraculously as it were, the Cold War helped to generate a larger flow of foreign aid than anyone had hoped in the early 1950s. From the late 1950s onwards, the region became a large recipient of US and other aid. If India had a negative GDP growth rate in 1957–8, Pakistan had a growth rate down to 0.88 per cent in 1958–9. These shocks made the growth policies much more dependent on foreign resources when they should have sparked better resource mobilization policies at home, (Thus, India was unable to implement the tax reforms suggested by Kaldor, which were meant to enhance the tax take from direct taxes. The failure was political rather than administrative). In this sense, the

(Cold War inspired) foreign aid let the countries of the region off the task of domestic resource mobilization and could be said to have (with hindsight) been harmful in the long run. The other favourable 'external shock' which helped the region was the Green Revolution.

The 1960s began with a hope that given resources from abroad, the food constraint on growth could be removed and growth could be sustained. Pakistan had a good decade of growth under Ayub Khan's Presidency (1958–69)—the growth rate of GDP averaged around 6 per cent. India on the other hand, saw two famine years 1965–6 and 1966–7, wars with China (1962) and Pakistan (1965), and the death of two prime ministers—Nehru and Shastri. Growth was volatile in the 1960s but by the end of the decade the foundations of the Green Revolution had been laid.

By the end of the 1960s thus there had been one good decade and one indifferent one for India and Pakistan, though in different order. India went off to a good start in the 1950s and stalled in the 1960s with Pakistan exactly the reverse. But, during this decade India and Pakistan fought a war in 1965 in which India showed it had superior military power. However, if the 1965 war was a draw, it was in 1971—after unrest in East Pakistan—that India managed to dismember Pakistan and help in the Bangladesh liberation war. The defeat of the Pakistan army and the secession of East Pakistan were traumatic events for Pakistan.

Now We are Three—1971–90

The circumstances of its birth were not immediately conducive to rapid growth in Bangladesh. Inflation, food shortages, floods, and finally famine were the main events in the first five years of its existence. Inflation rates were 49.0 per cent in 1973, 54.8 per cent in 1974, and 21.9 per cent in 1975—some of the highest rates ever seen in the subcontinent; 1974 saw floods, and 1974 and 1975 were also famine years (Sen 1981). Its initial endowments were even worse than those of Pakistan at the moment of birth. Bangladesh was less industrialized than even West Pakistan was in 1947 and over the years things had not improved much. It was, on the other hand, much more unfavourably endowed relative to its western part in land-labour ratio.

Bangladesh also carried the burden that whatever the growth performance of Pakistan as a whole, it was West which was favoured rather than the East. This is confirmed by such data as are available.

To the extent that the regional growth rates for West and East Pakistan can be separately estimated, the growth record of East Pakistan/Bangladesh is worse compared to its western counterpart, West Pakistan. Thus the GDP and per capita GDP growth rates are given in Table 25.1.

Since the 1960s decade was of rapid growth for both wings of Pakistan, one can say that the independence struggle and its aftermath cost Bangladesh a decade of low, if not negative growth. In this respect, the post-partition transition costs were lower for Pakistan and India than they were for Bangladesh.

In this sense, there is a parallel between Pakistan in 1947 and Bangladesh in 1972. When each was born, there were doubts about its economic viability—

TABLE 25.1

GDP Growth Rates in East and West Pakistan

	East Pakistan		West Pakistan	
	GDP(%)	GDP per capita (%)	GDP(%)	GDP per capita (%)
1950–5	1.7	–0.5	3.9	1.5
1955–60	1.7	–0.6	3.2	0.9
1960–5	5.2	2.6	7.2	4.4

Source: Papanek (1967).

For later periods, the data are as in Table 25.2:

Table 25.2

GDP Growth Rates, 1965–90

	Bangladesh	Pakistan	India
1965–80	1.7	5.2	3.6
1980–90	4.3	6.3	5.3

Source: Hossain (1996) citing *World Development Report* 1992.

poorly endowed, cut off from its economic surroundings and from a rational division of labour, and suffering shortage of skilled personnel as well as manufacturing capital. Pakistan, whatever its other problems, can be said to have shown that the initial conditions did not matter, though there are costs in the beginning.

The 1970s were a period of uneven development for this region. The oil shocks on the one hand caused severe inflation. India had a rare episode of two consecutive years of double digit inflation while Pakistan had four years—1973–4 to 1976–7—of double digit inflation. India experienced low GDP growth in 1971–2 (0.90 per cent), 1972–3 (0.30 per cent) as well as 1974–5 (1.60 per cent) and 1976–7 (1.30 per cent). Pakistan, by comparison, had only one year of growth rate blow 2 per cent in 1970–1, but 1971–2 and 1976–7 were below 3 per cent growth rate years. Given that Pakistan has grown at around 1 percentage point more than India in per capita terms over the period, this counts as a low growth rate for her. Thus the 1970s were low growth and high inflation years for India and Pakistan.

In neither country did the oil shock and the resultant troubles lead to any rethinking of the growth strategy. The 1970s was the decade when many developing countries moved away from an import-substitution industrialization policy to an export oriented one. Indica proved an exception. Pakistan had to devalue its rupee drastically in May 1972 by 56.8 per cent. India had devalued its rupee in 1966 and did not need to devalue during the 1970s. One gain from the oil shock was the subsequent rise in remittances sent by the workers from the region who had gone to the Gulf region. Thus unskilled and semi-skilled labour became a substantial export item for the region. In 1972–3, remittance were equal to 20 per cent of the value of commodity exports for Pakistan but by 1977–8 this had risen to 90 per cent, as they were again in 1985–6. Pakistan needed standby agreements with the International Monetary Fund (IMF) in every year from 1972 to 1975 and again in 1977–8. A three-year Extended Fund Facility was negotiated in 1980 for three years.

India also opened out to IMF aid in 1980. The second oil shock was a severe one for India and 1979–80 saw 4.9 per cent GDP growth. A loan was negotiated by the incoming government of Mrs Gandhi which proved controversial at the time and was not fully taken up. For India and for Mrs Gandhi, this seeking of foreign aid meant a major reversal of policy. In the 1980s, India began to import foreign capital—official, commercial, and private loans were negotiated. India in a sense adopted what has always been Pakistan's growth strategy—growth with foreign resources. Through the 1980s, although the planning model did not change much, India relieved its resource constraint by foreign borrowing and achieved a substantial step-up in the growth rate of GDP. Thus, while between 1950 to 1980 the growth rate had been at the 'Hindu' rate of 3.5 per cent, in the 1980s it went up to 5.5 per cent.

The 1980s also turned out to be good for Pakistan and for Bangladesh. Under Zia Ul-Haq's presidency [1977–88], Pakistan resumed its pattern of rapid growth with rising foreign resources, GDP growth averaging 6.5 per cent during these 12 years. But the international capital markets were moving from official aid to soft loans and later to commercial ones. Pakistan, like India, got caught in the foreign debt problem during the 1980s.

Bangladesh also had its decade of growth, albeit at 4.3 per cent during the 1980s. Agricultural output as measured in GDP terms grew at 2.8 per cent during 1973–85 and 2.6 per cent during 1980–90. This compares to the growth rate in India (3.1 per cent) and Pakistan (4.3 per cent) in 1990. It is in manufacturing that Bangladesh had a relatively low growth rate. Thus for 1980–90 it averaged 2.8 per cent while India chalked up 7.1 per cent and Pakistan 7.7 per cent. But services grew faster in Bangladesh with 5.8 per cent—twice as fast as manufacturing—while in India with 6.7 per cent and Pakistan with 6.9 per cent services grew less rapidly than manufacturing.

There was, however, a change in the international context which made the strategy of undersaving and reliance on foreign resources adopted by this region unfeasible. Concessional lending was difficult to obtain for India and Pakistan and they were encouraged to resort to commercial borrowing. At the same time, their preferred import-substitutional industrialization model of tariff led domestic industrial development went out of fashion as the export oriented model demonstrated spectacular success in East Asia. The question became not so much of planning as such, but the strategy of industrialization to be adopted. External financial constraints were imposed on Pakistan via the IMF in the 1980s; India escaped the strictures for a while only to run into the ground in 1991.

In 1982, Pakistan removed the rupee–dollar peg imposed at its previous 1972 devaluation and the rupee was allowed a managed float. India did not devalue till 1991, when it did so in three quick steps [hop, skip, and jump, as it was codenamed by the Finance Ministry and the Reserve Bank of India]. India also now has a managed float. Thus to some extent, one of the distortions of the old policy—overvalued exchange rates—may be on its way out. The float is, however, still managed and no country in the region has attained full convertibility status for its currency. India has managed trade convertibility and is on the way to introducing capital convertibility in the next two or three years.

Summing Up the First 40 Years

Thus the first 40 years roughly speaking after independence (20 for Bangladesh) saw similar, if not parallel, developments in the countries of the region. While there were significant differences in their political developments, in economic terms the course was similar: planned development, whether labelled socialist or not, tariff and quota protected industrial development with excess capital intensity, low employment generation and low efficiency of investment, heavy reliance on internal borrowing by way of deficit finance from a captive banking sector, overvalued exchange rates, depreciated too late in each instance, excessive reliance on foreign resources, low GDP growth rate, low investment in human development, and little progress on the inequality front.

It is only in agricultural growth that the Green Revolution solved the urgent problem of the region. Despite many fears to the contrary, even as late as the early 1970s, Indica can now feed itself. That this is true of about a billion and a quarter people is a considerable achievement in global food availability terms. There is a lot of poverty and indeed malnutrition and starvation, but not due to a shortage of food. The misallocation of resources continues yet, despite as it were, pushing out the production possibility frontier in agriculture. Thus, as Ashok Gulati has convincingly shown, agriculture has had to pay a negative tariff of around 23 per cent while industry has enjoyed a tariff of 45 per cent. As a consequence of this and also due to its political clout, the farming interest has been able to extract input subsidies for water, electricity, and fertilizers which are distortionary (Gulati 1998).

There has also been a degree of structural transformation as indicated by the changing sectoral composition of output and workforce, from agriculture to manufacturing and infrastructure. The region, as many other developing countries, always had a large proportion of labour force in services. This large proportion has remained, though within that constancy there has been a movement from traditional service sectors to modern service sectors, such as the financial services and tourism, etc. (Hossain 1996, Table 10.4, p. 37). At the same time the slow pace of growth has meant slow transformation. Thus, in Korea and Indonesia the share of output in agriculture (all in percentages) fell from 38 and 51 in 1965 to 9 and 22 in 1990. In India, for example, it fell from 44 to 31, for Pakistan 40 to 26, and for Bangladesh 53 to 38.

But while industrial growth occurred over this period, one cannot say that it was in any way efficient. An industrial structure was constructed and capital goods which could not be made before can now be made in the region–steel, machine tools, heavy electricals etc., as well as consumer durables–cars, scooters, washing machines. But while (for India at least), the Green Revolution was a fruitful combination of government incentives and private sector response to reap the benefits of an imported technology, in industry there was a reluctance either to import foreign technology, say via foreign direct investment, or to rely on price incentives and private sector response. The private sector, which obtained all the tariff protection became a mirror image of the public sector—inefficient, non–competitive, reliant on public subsidies, forever infant. Industry is, for India and for the region as a whole, a surplus absorbing rather than a surplus producing sector, at least as far as the organized public and private sector industrial establishments are concerned. This has worsened the resource crisis.

The twin burdens of internal and external debt have, therefore, been high for the countries of this region. These are signs of malinvestment and undersaving. It is not so much that Indica is poor, though that is true, but compared to similarly placed countries it fails to raise sufficient resources through taxation. The tax-GDP ratio in the countries of this region is below the average for developing countries, the tendency to resort to deficit finance addictive, and there has been a constant reliance on foreign resources. The resource gap is in the region of 3 per cent of GDP for Pakistan; larger at 6 per cent for Bangladesh, and somewhat smaller for India at 2 per cent (Human Development Report 1997, Table 25). The external debt-GDP ratio was 34 per cent for India, 57 per cent for Pakistan, and 63 per cent for Bangladesh (all figures for 1994; Human Development Report 1997; World Development Report 1997 figures, Table 17 are somewhat different but broadly in agreement). The debt-service ratio was 27 per cent, 35 per cent, and 16 per cent respectively.

As far as internal debt is concerned, the estimates are more difficult to come by. Each country has a captive banking system which is obliged to hold government paper. Thus, it is easy to finance deficits. For India, some estimates have put the internal debt–GDP ratio at 100 per cent (Amaresh Bagchi). Bangladesh has run a budget deficit every year since independence at an average of 7 per cent GDP. Indian budget discipline was good in the 1950s and 1960s with the revenue budget in surplus. During the 1970s and since, this track record has been reversed with the revenue as well as the capital budget in deficit. Pakistan has been very much the same as its neighbours in this respect. Khan (1992) estimates the deficit between 1972 and 1988 as and 7 per cent of GNP. In 1994, the gap between public expenditure and public revenue as a percentage of GDP for the three countries was 7 per cent for India and 11 per cent for Pakistan [Human Development Report 1997; Bangladesh is not given in source].

The taxation is not only light but it is inequitable. The bulk of the revenue comes from indirect taxes with no offsetting redistribute corrective from the pattern of expenditure. Subsidies have been estimated in India to be as high as 15 per cent of GDP but go mainly to the producers in agriculture and, indirectly via them, to producers of farm inputs such as fertilizers.

Some Political Economy

It is clear as to what happened and in terms of a simple growth accounting we can also see the proximate causes. But why do societies undersave and what makes them persist in policies which generate low growth?. This is a question of political economy. In the region, there has been a considerable amount of writing about India on the causes of stagnation, many explanations have been put forward:

(i)   A Kaleckian explanation of low demand for essential goods due to unequal income distribution combined with monopoly power of industrialists leading to excess capacity, hence low growth;

(ii)   An elite comprising of industrial bourgeoisie, big landlords /bullock capitalists, and urban organized workers–each of whom can neutralize the power of the others which in turn leads to a stalemate at the state level and no clarity in accumulation policy–this leads to undersaving and waste of resources;

(iii) International forces of imperialism, by bequeathing a lopsided economy and subsequently preventing India from pursuing radical policies of surplus mobilization and industrial independence via the state and by harnessing the Indian bourgeoisie in a comprador fashion, force a low growth outcome;

(iv)   Rent seeking by industrialists connived in by urban public sector workers and politicians who pursue policies of tariffs and quotas, which lead to an expansion of bureaucracy at the cost and accumulation;

(v)   Values, especially in Hindu culture, which discourage material pursuits and accumulation; which sanction irrational practices such as caste divisions, which in turn hinder a sensible division of labour and resist modernization.

These are thumbnail sketches of explanations which have filled many books by prominent Indian economists. In the comparative perspective, it may be useful to 'test' some of these explanations against the experience of the other two countries. Except for the argument about cultural values of Hinduism, the other four explanations apply with some variations to all the countries in this region. One reason for such a possibility is that not only had all the countries a common colonial legacy but they seem to have followed rather similar policies with similar outcomes. The differences among the countries within this region are, therefore, interesting as a way of differentiating among the explanations .

Income and wealth inequality are similar in the three countries but, given the inequality of land ownership in Pakistan being the highest in the region, it would make sense to say that in Pakistan inequality was perhaps the highest in the region. Also, given the hothouse growth of the industrial structure, the concentration of industrial assets is also much greater in Pakistan compared to India. India was able to modify industrial concentration by creating a large public sector as well as pursuing anti-monopoly practices. This income and wealth inequality seems to have led to undersaving. I offer this as a tentative result—*the higher the inequality of income and wealth and the larger the concentration of industrial capital in private hands, the lower will the domestic savings be.* This conflicts with the old Keynesian growth models in which inequality was good for savings but agrees with the new political economy.

A strong and wealthy elite is also able to pass on the costs of slow growth onto poorer sections of the community. This is independent of the formal degree of democracy in the country. Thus, direct taxation contributes less than indirect taxation and accumulation is financed by deficit financing rather than mobilizing domestic resources. This requires a minimal theory of the state and what it does. But whether old or new political economy is taken as one's standpoint, it is obvious that an elite will control the levers of the state and use it to its own advantage. If the elite is small and not at conflict within itself, then this control will be strong and the passing on of costs to the majority effective. If the elite is divided, as is said to be the case in India, then the control is contested and the passing on of costs less effective. The state is less of an elite capture and less capable of cornering the gains exclusively for the elite.

In this respect, the Pakistan and India cases fit this simple analysis. The case of Bangladesh is not so simple. There is less by way of inequality in land ownership relative to Pakistan. There is concentration of industrial capital, again as in Pakistan, because of the way in which the industrial structure was created. But though the data are lacking, one gets the impression that small and medium enterprises are more important in this economy than in the other two. The undersaving in Bangladesh is partly due to this concentration but also partly due to its low level of income. However, in explaining undersaving, the India and Pakistan cases fit the 'inequality plus tightness of elite leads to undersaving' thesis.

The growth of bureaucracy and the wasteful state can be traced to the size of the urban educated class and the demands for job creation as (small) rent seeking. In this matter, Bangladesh is nearer to India and Pakistan is somewhat apart. The state in the former two has been more dirigiste and more job creating than in Pakistan (Army apart). The democratic pressures are also stronger in this respect in India and Bangladesh. Thus the larger rent seekers—industrialists demanding tariff protection—have to share it with the bureaucracy in the democratic states while in Pakistan they have a tighter control of rents which do not need to be shared with a large public sector. (Although Bangladesh has not always been a parliamentary democracy in the strict sense of the term, the nature of its birth has meant that Zia and Ershad were subject to considerable populist pressure from urban educated classes).

In all the three countries, there was never an independent powerful financial oligarchy. The banking system is a creature of the state even when in private hands and thus the financing of public debt is not impeded by the financial community insisting on rules of prudence. In the East Asian model, the banking system is used to siphon funds from high saving households who are paid low interest rates, to industrialists who invest in export oriented industries. This Japanese–Korean model works until the savers can access global markets for their funds and then there is a banking crisis, as there is at present in Japan and Korea. But in India, the banks divert 'depositors' money into government paper as much as into industrial and commercial loans. The situation of these banks is, therefore, even more precarious. They are holding liabilities of what are financially profligate, though not yet technically bankrupt, states.

The international dimension has paradoxically bailed out this region and kept it in the bad habits it is accustomed to. In the context of a neocolonial paradigm this may seem like a very subtle plot to keep the economies stagnant by bankrolling their inefficient policies. More likely, the compulsions—real or perceived—of the

Cold War made this region a priority for the Big Powers. While the USA championed Pakistan, it did also give a lot of money to India. The USSR championed India more than it did Pakistan but mainly for defence equipment, a costly addiction in the region. But above all, by funding deficits, providing food grains when needed, and selling arms indiscriminately, the international powers kept the region from facing up to the need for resource mobilization. It is a moot point as to whether in the absence of such aid, resources would have been mobilized by the local elites or they would have been destabilized by constant threats of popular revolts. As it was, the bailout was successful in keeping the elites in power.

There has, even then, been a lot of violence in the public elite of these countries which cannot be ignored in any political economy discourse. Pakistan has had one prime minister assassinated and one hanged, and one president died under dubious circumstances. India has had two prime ministers assassinated while Bangladesh also has had two heads of state assassinated. The entire region has also had many subnational revolts—Baluchistan, Khalistan, Assam, Nagaland, and the perpetual problem of Kashmir which cuts across the partition of Indica, as well as the problems its successor states have had in coping with religious, linguistic, and regional forces. The break-up of Pakistan in 1971–2 was the classic instance of this inability. Other revolts have been 'secular'—the Mohajirs in Karachi, Telangana in 1948 and again in the 1970s and since, Naxalbari in West Bengal in the 1960s and 1970s, the endemic violence in Bihar. There is also an intimate connection between crime, black money, and politics which is a mirror image of the bureaucratic rent seeking polity which the region has tolerated.

Regional diversity was inherited at independence and to some extent there was bound to be a conflict between the confederate nature of the polity and the attempt at independence to impose strongly centralist federal constitutions. There was, after all, a collection of strong regional economies with weak interlinkages across regions. Indica was perhaps the most advanced among the colonial economies but at the same time, being largely agricultural the local economies were primary. Creating national economies and national markets in agricultural and industrial products has been done in a political context— planning as well as some pork-barrelling and imposing of *de facto* regional tariffs. The elite has often had regional loyalties which dominated national ones— Punjabis in Pakistan, for instance. The uneven development of the regions at independence and the overlay of policies, partly to correct these biases and partly to create national markets, have had contradictory effects. Thus, the southern states of India have been given priority in industrialization, a laudable aim but one that has costs which are resentfully shared across the country.

Bangladesh is a single region economy by and large. But India as well as Pakistan have severe regional imbalances. Thus, the north Indian heartland—the BIMARU (Bihar, Madhya Pradesh, Rajasthan, Uttar Pradesh) states—where the bulk of the population lives has been left behind by other states in the growth race. Pakistan has had the perpetual problem of domination of Punjab in the national economy. The Punjab-Sind rivalry leaves Baluchistan and the North West Frontier Province behind. Slow growth has exacerbated these regional tensions; they are in one sense an indication of the failure to create a truly national economy.[4]

RECENT DEVELOPMENTS

Indica hit the buffers almost simultaneously in the late 1980s/early 1990s. In Pakistan, the event was the death of Zia ul Haq in 1988; in India, the defeat of the Congress in 1989 elections; In Bangladesh, the end of the Ershad regime and the beginning of democracy. The Cold War ended and with it the easy availability of foreign funds at low or no cost. The forces of liberalization and globalization devalorized the growth strategy followed in Indica and made it costly to depend on foreign resources. The old model became unsustainable. In each of the three countries, attempts were made, perhaps more rhetorical than real, to ditch the old regime and start a new one. But unlike in Eastern Europe, the personnel in charge of the change have been the same as those that were there before. Thus there has been no root and branch rejection of the old model as a Balcerowicz or a Klaus did. The change is gradual, reluctant, forced by external compulsions rather than adopted by internal conviction. Some of the changes is formal though not without real consequences. Thus the reliance on foreign resources continues but with a switch to foreign direct private investment rather than concessional governmental funds. The required fiscal and exchange rate discipline has not been fully adopted. Tariff cutting has been reluctant and tardy, and public sector rationalization or privatization adopted only for budgetary rather than efficiency reasons. Deficits are being brought down, at least in India, but the pace is slow.

There is, however, the realization that economic reform is irreversible, that sooner or later the industries of these countries will have to become competitive and that there is a very narrow time window within which adjustments will have to be made. India has enjoyed some years of 7 per cent growth GDP but since 1996 the economy has slowed down to 5.5 per cent in 1997 (early estimate). The latest election does not appear (at the time of writing in early March) to have produced a decisive outcome. Any new government will be a fragile coalition and subject to populist pressures. This will make decisive economic policy making difficult though not impossible as the experience of the 1996–8 United Front government showed. It is unlikely that the new coalition can last out five years and hence uncertainty will persist.

Pakistan went through a transitory period when a caretaker technocratic government tried to run its affairs, but in early 1997 the Muslim League emerged with a decisive majority. Bold economic policies were promised, but since April 1997 things seem to have run into the ground. The Pakistan rupee is fragile and IMF conditions are not being met. Bangladesh has also settled the issue of government and Shaikh Hasina's government could stay for a while. But the final two years of the Begum Zia government, faced with near paralysis due to the opposition party's non-cooperation bodes ill for stability. Bangladesh has liberalized its economy and made tremendous efforts to increase exports.

---

[4] I highlighted these issues in Desai (1970) but they are still relevant. See Dreze and Sen (1997) for some recent regional studies in India about the imbalances.

The 1990s saw a convergence in the growth rates GDP across the three countries—4.6 per cent for Pakistan and India for 1990–5, and 4.1 per cent for Bangladesh (*World Development Report* 1997). This was because growth in India and Bangladesh improved while growth in Pakistan faltered during the 1990s. In the last two years since 1995, India has had slower growth.

CONCLUSIONS

Has Indica turned the corner and will it become a medium pace growth country or will it decelerate back to its old habits?

It would be tempting to say that growth at around 6–7 per cent per annum of GDP and around 4 per cent per capita is highly likely. The World Bank in its *Global Economic Prospects and the Developing Countries 1997* publication takes an optimistic view, projecting per capita growth rate at 4 per cent. But if my earlier political economy analysis has any validity, one has to ask what has changed in the underlying structural forces to warrant such a conclusion. The global context has no doubt changed and foreign direct investment (FDI) is available if the conditions are right. It is also quite clear to Indica's elite that it is falling behind in the global race though even here much complacency remains (which will no doubt be fed by the Asian economic crisis).

But while there are always reactions to crises in the region's policies, the reactions are not sustained. The appetite for radical change is sated in three to four years and business as usual resumes.[5] The single minded pursuit of growth seen in East Asia or South East Asia is absent in Indica. Within three years of the shock of 1991, India had gone back to the rhetoric of the middle way and no rapid change. Within a year of its election, Pakistan's new government seems to be faltering on the economic front. There is no political harmony between government and opposition in Bangladesh.

Thus, there is little by way of genuine structural change in Indica. There may yet be an acceleration of growth purely due to external circumstances —flow of FDI, crisis of internal or foreign debt leading to fiscal tightening on a sustained basis, a willingness to jettison the unprofitable in the public sector, opening out of the economies to external competition thanks to the World Trade Organization (WTO). But that is the only hope.

REFERENCES

Ahluwalia, I. and I. M. D. Little (eds) (1998), *India's Economic Reforms and Development*, Delhi: Oxford University Press.

Baran, P. (1957), *The Political Economy of Growth*, New York: Monthly Review Press.

Bhagwati, J. (1998), 'The Design of Indian Development', in I. Ahluwalia and I. M. D. Little (eds), *India's Economic Reforms and Development*, Delhi: Oxford University Press, pp. 23–39.

[5] I have analysed India's trajectory in these terms; see Desai (1995). But for a similar view, see also Joshi and Little (1994).

Bhatia, B. M. (1990), *Pakistan's Economic Development*, Lahore: Vanguard.

Blackburn, R. (ed.) (1975), *Explosion in a Subcontinent*, Harmondsworth: Penguin.

Desai, M. (1970), 'The Vortex in India', *New Left Review*, Vol. 70.

—— (1975), 'India: Emerging Contradictions of Slow Capitalist Development', in. R. Blackburn (ed.), *Explosion in a Subcontinent*, Harmondsworth: Penguin, pp. 11-50. See also Chapter 2.

—— (1990), ' Birth and Death of Nation States: Speculations about Germany and India', in M. Mann, F. Halliday and J. Hobson (eds), *Rise and Decline of the Nation State*, Oxford; Blackwell, pp. 188–209. See also Chapter 20.

—— (1992), ' Is There Life After Mahalanobis? The Political Economy of India's New Economic Policy', *The Indian Economic Review*, Special Number in Memory of Sukhamoy Chakravarty, pp. 155–64. See also Chapter 12.

—— (1993a), *Capitalism, Socialism and India's Economic Development*, Bombay. EXIM Bank. See also Chapter 15.

—— (1993b), 'Constructing Nationality in a Multinational Democracy: The Case of India', in R. Michener (ed.), *Nationality, Patriotism and Nationalism in Liberal Democratic Societies*, St Paul Minnesota: PWPA, pp. 225–41. See also Chapter 22.

—— (1995), 'Economic Reform: Stalled by Politics?', in P. Oldenburg (ed.), *India Briefing*, New York & London: M. E. Sharpe, pp. 75–95. See also Chapter 16.

—— (1997), 'Why is India a Low inflation Country', C. N. Vakil Memorial Lecture, in D. Nachane and M. J. M. Rao (eds) (1997), *Macroeconomic Challenges and Development Issues*, Bombay: Himalaya Publishing House, pp. 31–8. See also Chapter 6.

—— (1998), 'Development Prespectives: Was There An Alternative to Mahalanobis', in I. Ahluwalia and I.M.D. Little (eds), *India's Economic Reforms and Development*, Delhi: Oxford University Press, pp. 40–7. See also Chapter 14.

Dreze, J. and A.K. Sen (1996), *Indian Development: Selected Regional Perspectives*, New Delhi: Oxford University Press.

Gulati, A. (1998), 'Indian Agriculture in an Open Economy: Will It Prosper?', in I. Ahulwalia and I.M.D. Little (eds), *India's Economic Reforms and Development*, Delhi: Oxford University Press, pp.122–46.

Gunder–Frank, A. (1997), *Capitaslism and Underdevelopment in Latin America*, New York: Monthly Review Press.

Haq, M. (1963), *The Strategy of Economic Planning*, Karachi: Oxford University Press.

—— (1997), *Human Development in South Asia*, Karachi: Oxford University Press.

Heston, A. (1984), 'National Income, in Dharma Kumar and M. Desai (eds), *The Cambridge Economic History of India*, Cambridge: Cambridge University Press, pp. 376–462.

Hossain, A. (1996), *Macroeconomic Issue and Policies: The Case of Bangladesh*, New Delhi: Sage.

James, W.E. and S. Roy (eds) (1992), *Foundations of Pakistan's Political Economy*, New Delhi: Sage.

Joshi, V. and I. M. D. Little (1994), *India: Macroeconomics and Political Economy 1964–1991*, Washington, DC and New Delhi: World Bank and Oxford University Press.

Khan, Mohsin (1992), 'Macroeconomic Balances', in W.E. James and S. Roy (eds), *Foundations of Pakistan's Political Economy*, New Delhi: Sage, pp. 145–76.

Kumar, Dharma with M. Desai (eds), *The Cambridge Economic History of India,* Cambridge: Cambridge University Press.

Morris M.D. (1984), 'The Growth of Large Scale Industry to 1947', in Dharma Kumar and M. Desai (eds), *The Cambridge Economic History of India*, Cambridge: Cambridge University Press, pp. 553–676

Papanek, G. (1967), *Pakistan's Development: Social Goals and Private Incentives*, Cambridge, MA: Harvard University Press.

Pattanaik, P. (1975), 'Imperialism and the Growth of Indian Capitalism', in R. Blackburn (ed.), *Explosion in a Subcontinent*, Harmondsworth: Penguin, pp. 51–78

Sen, A. K. (1981), *Poverty and Famines: An Essay on Entitlement and Deprivation*, Oxford: Clarendon Press.

—— (1988), 'Theory and Practice of Development', in I. Ahluwalia and I. M. D. Little (eds), *India's Economic Reforms and Development*, Delhi: Oxford University Press, pp. 73–84.

26

Economic Problems of South Asia

Thank you, Governor. It is difficult in an audience of such distinction to know what to say and what not to say, because there are many people here who have a lot of knowledge. What I want to say this afternoon is, first of all, that it is very important that we think of South Asia as a region—genuinely together—rather than a collection of countries. Dr Mahbub ul Haq—some of you knew him—a distinguished Pakistani economist and originator of the Human Development Report, just the year before he died, had tried to get together a South Asian Commission on the Asian Challenge for the 21st Century. His idea was that we ought to begin thinking about South Asia in a homogeneous way and I think it is very important to do that. What I want to do tonight is to think along that line.

In a way, the European Union, since the Second World War, has gone in a very interesting direction. Countries which were enemies of each other and fought relentless wars for over 100 years, at last have begun to think of themselves as a unity. Europe has come together first of all, purely as an economic area—increasing integration in terms of the single market and monetary union. There are also various plans for a political confederation though different countries, of course, in Europe have integrated at different speeds. My own country, the UK, as you know is not a member of the monetary union, but is a very enthusiastic member of the Single Market. South Asia has gone exactly the opposite way. In 1945, South Asia was a single market, practically a single currency area. In the last 55 years, South Asia has built barriers against the flow of goods and people. It has now divided into four separate countries with four currencies.

Due to restrictions against the movement of capital and labour, South Asia essentially lost what tremendous advantages it had as a single economy. Obviously the desire for independence was so strong in South Asia that when independence came, the countries of South Asia very much wanted to emphasize their separateness, rather than their similarity; so the Indian sub-continent which had road networks which spread from Dacca to Peshawar has now been split into three separate countries. It is very difficult now, if you are an Indian or a Pakistani

Central Bank of Sri Lanka, Centre for Banking Studies, 6 January 2000.

citizen, to cross over the border at Wagah; in fact, it has become practically impossible. It helps very much to have a foreign passport—then you can pass from one to another very easily. In essence, what the countries of South Asia have done for themselves during the first 50 years of independence is what could be called self-indulgence in growing up. I, as a father of three children, am familiar with how kids have to go through their own experiments to grow up. During the last 55 years the countries of South Asia have been very self-indulgent in their politics. We have also obviously corrupted politics. Politics meant almost deliberate miscalculations of economic costs of such self-indulgence; but I think and hope that the people of South Asia will now realize that the economic costs of self–indulgence are excessive. These costs cannot be nationalized away, they cannot be bribed away. Other countries don't owe South Asia anything. And whatever South Asians may think of themselves, they only have to go abroad and look at a newspaper to know that nobody has heard of South Asia. South Asia has become a backwater of the world.

South Asia has also suffered from the cost of very slow growth. It was a growth which was not sufficiently rapid to transform the economies; and despite their best efforts and sincerity, politicians were pursuing policies which were not employment generating or effective at poverty alleviation. So, although they may have avowed socialism in India, policies which were adopted from 1947 through to the 1980s were not really policies which could have rapidly developed the economy. The rest of Asia did much better. In 1960, South Korea had the same level of income as India and Pakistan, in 1995, its income level was 25 times that of India and Pakistan. It was not that South Korea was fantastically endowed with natural resources. It had been through war and partition. Koreans were told in 1960 that they would stay an agricultural country forever. Yet they grew and showed that it can be done. Economic success is possible in Asia.

South Asians abroad have shown that they can make a success in any country they go to. In most countries in the West, the South Asian groups which have settled there have succeeded against most adverse circumstances. Without complaining, they got on with their business and have emerged successfully. The UK is a prime example of this. It is now established that the Asian community, as we call it, is a successful business community. It is not that the South Asians lack skills; it is not that capitalism is some strange Western concept that we cannot grasp, it is not that a powerful force of monopoly capital is conspiring against South Asia—we are much too unimportant for the West to bother to conspire against us. It is none of that. Basically, the failure of South Asia is South Asian in origin. Politics has been at the heart of the problem. Well meaning, sincere, dedicated, and patriotic politicians have wrecked the economies that they won over from the colonial powers.

But I think there is hope at hand. Since 1977, there has been a growing realization of economic laws or rather economic compulsion. I think if it started with the change of economic policy in Sri Lanka steadily over the last 25 years, much ground has been cleared. Reforms have now spread to the other South Asian countries. Let me take the case of India, the largest South Asian economy. The most interesting thing which has happened in India over the 1990s is that

India has sorted out the most crucial of its political problems. This is the problem of constructing a coalition from disparate parties which would command the majority of seats in the Lok Sabha and command a majority in the country at large. Congress lost its capacity to form a majority and various unstable coalitions were tried through the 1990s. But they failed to command a majority for a simple reason. Let me explain.

I believe that in India there are three different theories of nationalism. One is the Congress theory of secular liberal nationhood. Then there is a Bharatiya Janata Party (BJP) version of Hindutva. Then there is a third version which I call the grass-root theory, of the regions, caste and, religious groups which are very locally rooted. They do not mind being Indian but they are also Telugu, Bengali, Punjabi, or whatever. They have a very strong sense of national identity but also want to be an untouchable party or a Buddhist party or a Telugu party.

The latest elections in India showed that it needs at least two out of the three alternatives to form a coalition to command a majority. No single notion of India would work, nor did it work. The United Left did not command a majority. The BJP did not command a majority. It had to have a broad coalition with people whose views were almost diametrically opposed to its own. What we now have in India after 10 years of instability is a viable coalition, because it is not based on one single theory of nationhood.

At the same time there is another problem, and that is one of economic reforms. No Indian government was willing to accept in public the necessity of economic reform, but they were convinced in private that reform was necessary, especially after the traumatic shock of 1991. Governments liked and needed reforms—Left governments and Right governments, but they did not want to go out on the hustings and say so. The new Indian government has quickly and publicly grasped the agenda of economic reforms. They have privatized insurance, they have increased diesel prices and have stood up to the blackmail of diesel users. They have gone ahead with foreign exchange reforms. So it seems that if you can settle the politics of a country, economic reform will begin to yield fruit.

I could go across to other parts of South Asia. In Bangladesh, for example, for reasons I cannot understand, the politics are not rational. They always have strikes regardless of what party is in power, because whichever party is in power, the opposition party refuses to co-operate. Again we are going through another stalemate in the Bangladesh parliament, it happens every other year and economically it is extremely costly.

Now again, Bangladesh has grasped the need for economic reform; it has enterprising industrialists and very hard-working people with very successful innovations like the Grameen Bank. But again politics is a great obstacle though I am not saying it will always remain so. Pakistan has a similar problem inasmuch as its civilian democracy failed to provide good or stable government and behaved recklessly on the economic front. There were structural reasons for this.

First of all, Pakistan broke up in 1971 over a quarrel about the true nature of Pakistan nationhood. And the break-up has not really sorted out its problems because the process of democracy in Pakistan has been too shallow. The elite stayed in power no matter which party governed and the elite considered itself above the laws, especially economic laws. I hesitate to approve of the military dictatorship but if it can make Pakistanis pay income taxes then my vote is for it.

Politics is the problem in South Asia as a region. But after the first 50 years of self-indulgence, now is the time to employ the next 50 years in seeking ways in which South Asia can develop rapidly. We are independent, we are liberated, we are separated. Can we now arrange our affairs in such a way that we could exploit the common advantages which South Asia has as a region rather than fight one another?. There are fights within each country, there are fights between countries. The South Asian Association of Regional Co-operation (SAARC) is stagnant because India and Pakistan cannot agree on Kashmir. SAARC has become a non-starter, but bilateral pacts like the Indo-Sri Lanka Trade Pact, is a very good thing. I think there should be lots of bilateral pacts within SAARC: Sri Lanka–Bangladesh, India–Sri Lanka, Sri Lanka–Pakistan. Since India and Pakistan quarrel, multilaterism is a non-starter; bilateral pacts will have to provide the bridge.

It is very important to make South Asia a common market, like it used to be, with free movement of people which is even more important than the free entry of goods. There should be a free movement of people across South Asia so that locals and foreigners could move any time and anywhere they want to. We complain about multinationals. But multinationals can move across South Asia easily. Any domestic corporation cannot start business in other South Asian countries. So it happens to Indian companies that they find it difficult to do business in Pakistan or Bangladesh. This is a problem South Asians have created for themselves.

Next is the issue of currency convertibility which at present is handled via the Asian Clearing Union (ACU). It makes absolutely no sense to have four different currencies, not being freely convertible into each other. There are no rational grounds for maintaining non-convertibility among them. No currency crisis can be caused by all these currencies being made convertible against each other. They have similar purchasing power and have 'converged' in the sense used in the European Union (EU). They have all depreciated, some more than the others, against the dollar, over the last 25 years.

We could learn from the European experience and start treating the Asian Clearing Union as an embryo of an Asian Monetary Union (AMU). To begin with, you could issue the accounting currencies like ECU in which people could issue bonds and you could make all the currencies completely freely convertible into each other. It is a risk that South Asian countries should be willing to take for themselves. I would even say that perhaps a beginning can be made in the Indo–Sri Lanka trade pact. Start with that. Why should not those two currencies become convertible? Not immediately but in the near future. Other currencies can join later. If South Asia is to take advantage of itself it will have to think about a monetary union in a 50-year perspective. The trick is not to think of political union. I think political union is a very bad idea to start with. The European Union has succeeded because it did not start with a political union. It remains the biggest obstacle, especially in the UK about its attitude towards European Monitory Union (EMU).

No country wants to lose its independence. Quite right, no country should have to. However, there are lots of areas for co-operation; trade, transport, movement of goods, movement of people, and monetary union. The Asian Clearing Union which has completed about 25 years this year, should plan to arrive at an Asian Monetary Union in the next 50 years. Even in the European system, several ambitious early plans failed. There was to be a European monetary union in 1970s, but it did not happen until the late 1990s. So, even in fairly similar developed countries, the formation of a monetary union is not an easy job, but I think steadily one should think of things to do towards AMU. The currencies should be easily exchangeable against each other, and full convertibility should be established as the initial step. Fears will be expressed against such a step by governments. Arguments will be made about increased smuggling, but there is smuggling anyway. The unrecorded Indo-Pakistan trade is larger than the recorded one. We know this goes on. Any natural flow of goods which already is happening, in spite of restrictions, should be encouraged. Let it happen—there is no great danger of economic instability from intra South Asia trade.

There is nothing but advantages to gain from freer trade. South Asia, which is actually the most populous region in the world, larger than China when you put it together, has cured itself of most of the economic irrationalities as far as policy thinking goes. I think the logic of the South Asian Monetary Union, the logic of the South Asia common market will be obvious to politicians. It is more obvious to the population, especially the younger population. The younger population now knows that economic growth is through the market, and not through restrictions. That is the way growth happens. Our people know how to make use of market opportunities. If you don't believe me, I will take you where I have been for the last 2 weeks, on the beach at Hikkaduwa. The beach boys who are around, are fantastic entrepreneurs—they learn German, French, Italian and chat to tourists. They become tourist guides, swimming guides or anything, to make money. The energy with which these people operate is great. Let the people take hold of the normal economic opportunities. I know there will be a tremendous upsurge in growth. South Asia which has been growing very slowly, will grow faster. South Asia is capable of 7–8 per cent growth per annum. Over the next 25 years, it is very important that the South Asian economic policy makers, even before the political leaders, should begin to make room for the kind of policies which I have discussed. One thing, there is no going back to the old regimes.

What we call globalization is likely to continue despite what has happened in Seattle.[1] Due to expanding free trade and greater access to Western markets, especially after the Multi-Fibre Agreement comes to an end, tremendous opportunities will exist for South Asia, in textile and other markets. All these things are waiting for South Asia to take advantage of, because South Asia has shown in various industries that it can succeed globally. The economic problems of South Asia are much more about perceptions, of politics, problems of imagined wrongs or historical wrongs. For example, I was here in January 1999 when the Indo–Sri Lanka free trade agreement was being argued about. It was very clear that Sri Lankan traders were very afraid of Indian domination and so on. Indian industrialists behave exactly like that when it comes to the West entering into trade with

---

[1] The WTO had a ministerial meeting which broke up due to hordes of protections outside the venue of the meet.

India. Indians complain of Europeans and Americans over free trade. They fear they will not play by the rules. But this is exactly the way they behaved towards Sri Lanka. There is no logic in either of these complaints. The West is not going to eat up India, and India is not going to eat up Sri Lanka. Nor will Sri Lanka ruin India as a result of trade.

We have to realize that we have traded all along our history. I have a vision of South Asia as a single market where currencies are freely convertible, with free movement of goods, and where people are permitted to travel freely within the region. Together we can make a real impact on world trade, and can take a dynamic position in a global economy. It may be necessary in this respect to create institutions which will bypass obstacles. I think institutions which are relatively non-controversial, such as ACU can make a positive contribution. The Asian Clearing Union has been quietly working for these past 25 years. Obviously there are lots of problems—ACU can be improved. The fear of currency instability and fear of convertibility, I think are irrational. The recent Asian crisis has proved this—it only lasted for 18 months. The Mexican Peso crises lasted 16 months, not more than that. While that crisis was going on, everybody who did not like globalization was hoping that it would prove that liberalization would never work. Some people thought the great successful economies of Asia had gone down the drain, but they hadn't gone down the drain; they recovered very quickly because their fundamentals were right. As the late Dr Mahbub ul Haq said, 'Here is a man going in a bullock cart, he sees a car with a puncture, then he says "these cars never work, and bullock carts are much better".' It is not that the bullock carts are better than cars. The car, once the puncture is repaired, will very soon overtake the bullock cart. That is exactly what happened in the strong Asian economies. Capitalism has cycles in it—business cycles. If you are afraid of the cycle, you will never grow. Growth and cycles will always come together. There is no real growth when there are no cycles. Last year, South Korea's growth was 7 per cent. Mexico had a crisis in December 1994 and 1995 and was bad. However, by 1996 Mexico had recovered. The opportunity and volatility in international financial market work both ways. On the one hand, there may he a sudden withdrawal of funds, but as prices go down there will be an inflow of funds, because people are not stupid. If they can buy South Korean equity cheap, they will come back and buy. So, the Mexican crisis and the Asian crisis show to me that these problems are temporary. These cycles are short and sharp as against the cycles which were there before 1981. When the Mexican debt crisis happened in 1981–91, it took Mexico 9 years to recover. At that time, capital markets were not ready to move into Mexico quickly, because nobody had realized how to invest in Mexico. Now markets are knowledgeable, and money is willing to go into emerging markets. Obviously, you have to have a monetary policy which will guard against excess volatility, but it will not be done by denying convertibility. It will be done by having convertibility with supporting in situations. In that respect, it is very important that the Indian government act on the Tarapore Committee report, regardless of what happened in the Asian crisis. Once that kind of barrier is overcome, lots of other things can immediately follow, because if we remove the fear of globalization, then South Asia can really grow. South Asia's fear of foreign trade is recent. Foreign trade is not a recent thing in South Asia's history, because the region has always been a global trading area. Sri Lanka has been trading for the last 4000 years as has South India. Trade is not unknown to South Asia. Trade was once vital for South Asia. All that happened in colonial times was a change in the commodity composition of exports and imports, and that has changed again since 1947. But it has changed partly because it was forced into a change by an export pessimistic regime. In the middle of 1950, even Sri Lanka adopted an Indian type plan. It was very unsuitable for an open trading island economy such as Sri Lanka; howsoever suitable or not it was for a sub continental economy like India. It was based on export pessimism and a denial of the market. It was all very costly in terms of economic growth based on a misapprehension about markets.

Markets are not alien to South Asian culture. Now is the time to get over the teething problems of the newly found independence. having indulged in all sorts of political mischief, the time has come for South Asia to behave rationally. For this we need not wait for government action. We talk about non-governmental organizations (NGOs), but the best NGOs are shops and factories people in the business on the road. These NGOs actually generate economic prosperity. Governments do not generate economic prosperity, the best they can do is not to wreck it. The contrast between the self-employed people on the beach of Hikkaduwa and people employed in public offices in Colombo is fantastic. A lovely lot of NGOs are there in individual citizens who want, and are capable of grasping, economic opportunities! The task of South Asian governments over the next 50 years is to let the self-employed people get on with their entrepreneurial activities and not stand in the way.

ON THE QUESTION ON CORRUPTION

The civil society is an important force which made the countries of the Western society less corrupt. They were corrupt about 100 years ago. Governments became less corrupt because of certain critical actions of citizens and journalists. In South Asian society and in many Third World societies, what is lacking is the civil society of conscious—literate and politically active—people who are not dependent upon political patronage. It is where the civil society strengthens that corruption is combated and it is very important to have that. It is also important that politicians behave like ordinary citizens, for example ex-cabinet ministers of UK travel in buses, travel underground, they don't have any problems. Even the members of the House of Lords enjoy no privileges. The other day an ex-Chancellor of Exchequer, Kenneth Clark, had by mistake traveled on the underground beyond where his ticket was valid and he was fined. But he did not argue—he paid up. That culture of politicians behaving like ordinary citizens is lacking in South Asia. The *South Asian Human Development Report* which was launched in Colombo last September has a very good chapter on corruption and the whole problem of governance in South Asia. South Asian politicians, especially elected politicians, have set themselves up above the people, they persistently grab privileges, they behave as if they are above the law. Not only they, but even their relations behave as if they are above the law. The ministers and their relations should not be treated differently. Indian Members of Parliament (MPs) don't vacate the houses they occupy even after they lose elections. They don't pay rent, they think none of the laws should apply to them. After all, they are the lawmakers! No British or French or American parliamentarian is allowed to behave like that. This sort of culture does not come easily. In this respect, dismantling of government regulations about lots and lots of petty things would help immensely. In the UK, when privatization came, people thought that privatization would make things difficult. My party also opposed privatization. But we were wrong. If you have government controls, corruption results. I think dismantling of government regulation is very essential. Corruption eradication is citizens' business.

27

Defining a New Vision for South Asia

SOUTH ASIA: THE VISION

South Asia today stands at the cusp of several possibilities from which it may either thrive or perish. The last 50 years of inadequate economic performance can be either enhanced by a creative response to globalization, or South Asia can sink into an even poorer part of the global economy. Similarly, the past 50 years of division and conflict between the region's two largest countries—India and Pakistan—can lead to a destructive nuclear war, or the balance of terror can be transformed into a permanent détente and active co-operation in the fields of trade, culture, environmental protection, energy use, and free movement across the subcontinent.

Divisions along religious, regional, ethnic, caste, and linguistic lines which have led to many violent confrontations within and between the countries of South Asia can be understood positively as part of the plurality in diversity within an overarching South Asian identity, or they can continue to divide and destroy the region physically as well as morally. Fifty years from now, South Asia can—besides being the world's most populous region—also achieve a high level of human development by sustained efforts towards eliminating poverty and gender discrimination or it can retain the dubious distinction of being home to the largest proportion of the world's poor.

How we respond to these challenges, which part of the divide we fall into, is a matter of South Asia's choice. It requires a collective effort on the part of its thinkers, artists, politicians, business people, policy-makers, and active and concerned citizens. The choices we make today will affect the life chances of the children and the youth of today. Their views are as important as those of us who 'present at the creation' will not be there to live the future.

This chapter sets out the vision that we believe should guide our efforts if we are to be the most dynamic region in the twenty-first century; if we are to be the home to a rich efflorescence of art, culture and music, films, electronic media, literature, sporting achievement; if we are to be the innovators and the inventors

Khadija Haq (ed.), *The South Asian Challenge*, Pakistan: Oxford University Press, 2002, pp. 1–33.

that the world will look to for the next upsurge of the global economy; and if we are to be a healthy, happy people, at peace with each other and at peace with the world. This is not an impossible dream.

Three great development waves have swept over Asia in the last five decades. The first wave started in Japan in the 1940s and 1950s when Japan combined its cheap labour with education and technical skills and took over rapidly the global markets in the export of low and medium technology consumer goods.

Then came the second wave as the low income East Asian societies stepped into this growing void in the 1960s and 1970s following the same simple but brilliant model where low wages became a powerful engine of competition and growth as they were combined with an educated and skilled labour force and open economies.

The third wave emerged in China in the 1980s and 1990s and still continues unabated, based on simple human development models as followed by Japan and East Asian industrialising tigers in the past.

An intriguing question remains: will the fourth great wave of development touch the shores of South Asia? Can South Asia become the next economic frontier in the 21st century? Or, will it miss the opportunity once again, as it has so often done in the past?[1]

To do that, we have to answer three separate but related questions: What were we? What are we? Where could we be?

These questions ask us to confront our difficult and often divisive but also long and glorious history. South Asia has, after all, been the cradle of some of the great religions of the world, a pioneer in mathematics and advanced technology in the early millennia, a powerful stream of world literature, music, art, and philosophy, renowned across the world for its finest textiles and sought after for its spices so much so that for about a thousand years, Europe ran an adverse balance of trade vis-à-vis South Asia and poured its gold and silver into South Asian coffers. Arab historians of the eighth to the eleventh centuries confirm that India and China were the richest countries in the world. Angus Maddison, who is a leading expert on long-term economic trends, says that Asia, especially China and South Asia, were the richest regions in the world during the early eighteenth century. The World Bank has projected that by 2050 Asia's share of world income could be back at the level it was at the beginning of the nineteenth century. We have been there, and we can be there again.

WHAT WERE WE?

South Asia is one of the oldest settled regions in the world. The ruins of Mohenjo Daro and Harappa bear testimony to one of the earliest urban settlements anywhere in the world. These civilizations boast seven millennia of settled habitat and literate culture (though the language of Mohenjo Daro has not been deciphered yet). Scores of peoples came into the territory, now marked off as South Asia, over those seven millennia turning this region into a racial melting pot. Unlike the Han people of China, there is no dominant race or ethnic community here. Though there are gradations in skin pigmentation, there are no racial differences. Centuries of migration and movement within South Asia and inter-

[1] Mahbub ul Haq, *Dawn*, 27 April 1998.

marriages have made its peoples similar. The world has little difficulty in telling South Asians apart from the Chinese or the Japanese or the South East Asians, though it may have much difficulty in telling an Indian apart from a Pakistani or a Sri Lankan from a Bangladeshi.

Over these seven millennia, the region became home to some of the great religions of the world and it contributed more of its own. Among the great religions born in South Asia are Hinduism, Buddhism, Jainism, and Sikhism. Add to that the early arrival of the Jews, Syrian (Nestorian) Christians, Muslims, and Zoroastrians. By the fifteenth century, South Asia had become one of the first ecumenical regions in the world. When the second wave of Christians came in the form of traders and empire builders, it was not their religion which made much impact on the subcontinent; it was their secular material achievements.

Religion has been a cohesive factor within each religious community of South Asia but it has often divided people across different religions. In this, the history of South Asia is not all that different from that of Europe except that in Europe, especially after the Reformation, it was the divisions within Christianity that led to endless wars. Religious, military, or cultural battles have been endemic to the region. Their earliest portrayal can be found in the Vedas with the Aryans battling the native people of the Indus Valley. The battles between Buddhism and the Hindu religion of that era (–500 to +700 CE) lasted over a long period and ultimately led to the dominance of the (reformed) Hindu religion, and the migration of Buddhism to the peripheries of South Asia and beyond.

The next thousand years witnessed the arrival of Islam and the dialectic of conflict and accomodation between Hinduism and Islam until a syncretic culture evolved in North India which even today unites the music, art, and cuisine of Pakistan and northern India.

Muslims came to South India and Sri Lanka as traders, not as conquerors. They were following the well-trodden lanes of the Indian Ocean that Arab traders had been using since the first century AD. They settled in Malabar and Tamil Nadu as well as Sri Lanka, and their syncretic culture took a different shape in the South. The 500 years since the first arrival of Vasco da Gama put a much tougher secular challenge to all religions in the region. Much of the modern history of South Asia was shaped by that challenge—the challenge of modernity.

The shape of that challenge was, however, economic and military and congealed into imperialism. For much of the seven millennia before the eighteenth century, there had been no single political authority over South Asia. Kingdoms, even when they became empires, remained confined to more or less the north or the south of the subcontinent. South Asian society was unique in surviving and growing in a more or less stable fashion, without a strong political state. Dynasties waxed and waned but the society continued to evolve without any massive disruption, until the establishment of British hegemony in Sri Lanka and the Indian subcontinent.

The British were the last to come to South Asia, but they stayed to rule. The present configuration of South Asia into separate nation-states is thus a creation of imperialism. Indeed even the borders of the various nation-states of South Asia solidified under British rule. The separation of Afghanistan from what is now

Pakistan, the border marking off Tibet from India (the MacMahon line), the border between Myanmar (Burma) (also a former British colony) and the North East regions of India, are all legacies of imperialism. Remarkably, along each of those borders there have been international conflicts in the past 50 years.

Yet, it has to be said that if South Asia has a definite shape and is divided into only a small number of nation-states, it is due to imperial rule. One can only wonder what the region would look like if each of the four or five European powers had carved out for itself a chunk of South Asia, or if no European power had succeeded in establishing rule over any part of it.

Then it is not difficult to assert that just as Europe is constituted of many nation-states, so would have South Asia. After all there are linguistic differences in the region besides the ethnic and religious ones. These could have been solidified into separate nationhoods. Despite that speculation, what has exercised much thought, and not an inconsiderable amount of conflict, has been the partition of the Indian subcontinent into two nation states and subsequently, the further break-up of Pakistan into Pakistan and Bangladesh. Partition has had a lasting impact on the region, and its legacy is without doubt the biggest obstacle to cooperation within South Asia.

Our common imperial past has given us a common legal, administrative, and constitutional framework. Westminster style of parliamentary practice remains the ideal, if not the reality. The fact is that until 1947, there was a single economic area with a single currency across the subcontinent even when there were several jurisdictions besides the British. There was free labour migration within South Asia as shown by the presence of estate workers in Sri Lanka. There was an internal division of labour and a large volume of intra-regional trade. Raw cotton from Sindh and West Punjab went to the textile mills of Bombay, raw jute from East Bengal went to the jute mills of Calcutta. There was a single grain market linked by railroads which spanned the subcontinent. Western Europe has managed with tremendous efforts since the end of the Second World War to construct first the Coal and Steel Communities, Euratom for sharing atomic energy research, the European Economic Community, and now the European Union. It was the vision of Jean Monnet and Robert Schuman to construct a Europe which would never go to war again after a century of Franco-German enmity that made possible the realization of this Union. From the creation of the Coal and Steel Community to the Maastricht Treaty, it took 40 years.

But then Europe did not have the advantage that South Asia has of being a single market in the recent past, with a single currency, with rail and road links and an independence movement lasting 60 years in which many common aspirations were shared, a single albeit foreign language which became the lingua franca of the political classes and a common ideal of parliamentary democracy. Europe has to reconcile various legal traditions; South Asia does not have to do so. Europe has different parliamentary and constitutional traditions; South Asia has a single common legacy.

In some sense, then, South Asia has many advantages and few of the disadvantages that Europe had in 1945 when Jean Monnet had his vision. It is a polyglot society but with a single language dominant in political discourse. Though religion-based legal codes are available, a single Anglo-Saxon legal tradition operates in all parts of region. The experience of a single currency is not only recent but the movements of individual Rupees (note the significance of the common nomenclature) and the Taka have been so close that unlike Europe, an Economic and Monetary Union with a single currency should pose fewer problems. Our labour markets are flexible, not rigid; our developments are similar, unlike the extremes of Greece or Spain and Germany or Sweden in the European Union.

Of course, there are problems and obstacles in the path of co-operation in South Asia. The history of the South Asian Association for Regional Corporation (SAARC) shows that substantive as against formal cooperation is difficult. The problems are the result of the first moments of independence but also or much that has happened since. The problems are within each country as much as between countries. To appreciate the nature of this difficulty, once again, we have to confront our past.

The Greeks in their heyday traded with an entity they called Indica, in which they included Sri Lanka. The Arabs traded with the region in the eighth century, and later called it Al-Hind which for them stretched from Sindh to Indonesia. Such foreign traders defined the boundaries of India as a trading area, and also as a cultural entity. Yet when the British fought and took over the rump of the Mughal Empire, they saw not a single national political entity but a vast collection of separate kingdoms, many languages, at least three major religions—Hinduism, Islam, and Buddhism—and an area as large as Europe but more populous. They, in turn, posed a double challenge. First was the challenge of modernity—a materialist, rational, functionalist regime with a strong legal tradition of equality before the law which had, soon after the early conquests, been strengthened by the Industrial Revolution in England.

It was a challenge to a proud civilization to adapt its ways, especially its beliefs and social practices, or be converted to the victor's religion. Sri Lanka faced this challenge to a much lesser extent since it had taken to Christianity from early on, and Buddhism did not have the same encrustation of social practices as the subcontinental religions, Hinduism and Islam, had. Several movements of religious and social reform were launched during the nineteenth century to meet this challenge. Names such as Raja Rammohan Roy, Ishwarchandra Vidyasagar, Dayanand Saraswati, Vivekanand, and Sir Syed Ahmad Khan readily come to mind.

The other challenge was political, and this became explicit after the replacement of the East India Company by the British Crown as the ruler of the subcontinent. It was the assertion of the imperialists that no such political entity as India existed. There was no nation such as India. What there was had been given shape by the imperial adinistration. Thus, asserting that India was a nation prior to the arrival of, and independent of, British Rule and, indeed, that it was a single nation became the primary concern of the independence movement once it became active from the beginning of the twentieth century. The definition of India as a nation, the basis of its unity, apart from the administrative frame that the British had imposed, became the concern of nationalist thinkers. Sri Lanka did not have this problem. Its territorial compactness as an island made it an obvious nation, which, during its history had often though not always been ruled by a single ruler. And yet the problem of defining nationhood in Sri Lanka has surfaced with a greater intensity in recent years. Nepal and Bhutan were kingdoms throughout the modern period, and were under the British umbrella.

Nationalism, though not unknown in the nineteenth century is very much a twentieth century phenomenon. There are many ways of defining a nation. Each cataclysmic event of the twentieth century—the First World War, the October Revolution of 1917, the rise of Hitler and Nazi Germany, the Second World War, and finally the collapse of the Berlin Wall and the demise of the USSR has unleashed new waves of nationalistic upsurges and the formation of new nation-states. Since the Second World War and the establishment of the United Nations, the number of nation-states in the world has risen from 45 in 1945 to more than 190 by 1998. Thus, South Asia's nationalist struggle was in the vanguard of the movement to form new nations.

Nations are difficult to define. They are, according to Benedict Anderson, in his suggestive phrase, 'imagined communities'. They can be defined by language, by religion, by race, by territory, by a common shared history or any combination of these. A sense of community is often fostered by a sense of injustice at the hands of a foreign ruler or a predatory neighbour or even within a previously defined nation by interregional imbalances, as for example illustrated by the break-up of Pakistan in 1971.

The nationalists of the subcontinent did not have many choices on the basis of which to assert that India was a single nation. Of course, language was ruled out, although an attempt was made to make Hindi the national language. There were no racial differences within the subcontinent. The British differentiated among the Indians by classifying them as martial and non-martial races (the word race being used here in the sense of a nation), while the independence movement was keen to deny such distinctions).

There were two major, and some minor, religions. For the Indian National Congress, at least, religion could not be the basis for defining nationhood. What was left was history and territory as grounds for a theory of Indian nationhood. India was thus asserted to be a single nation because of shared history and a well-defined territory. There were problems with this theory because the territory had been given shape by the foreign rulers.

The region's history was common, but contentious and not fully shared. The presence of a foreign ruler had given it some semblance of unity, but the prospect of the imperialists departing and relinquishing the tight reins of power revealed substantial differences in the nationalist discourse.

There were two factors that made the differences sharper. Since the beginning of the East India Company's rule in Bengal, the development—both administrative and economic—of various provinces had been unequal, and the position of the native states subject to paramountcy of the British, anomalous. There were large provinces which could be considered countries on their own. By 1930, when serious discussions began at the Round Table conferences in London on constitutional reform in India, there were 300 million people living in the subcontinent. Much of this population lived in large provinces with a single dominant language, like Punjab and Bengal, while others were multilingual such as Bombay (where Gujarati, Marathi, Sindhi, and Kannada were spoken) and Madras (where Tamil and Telugu were spoken). There were still others, such as UP and Bihar, where variants of Hindi and Urdu were spoken.

The Reforms of 1919 had granted limited autonomy to the provinces with some portfolios being run by popularly elected legislators. In 1930, it was proposed that the degree of provincial autonomy be increased. At contention between the nationalist movements, especially the Congress and the British, was the degree of autonomy at the Centre. The issue was crystallized by the granting of Dominion Status leading to full independence. But the shape of the polity under either case became the centre of debate, and became inextricably bound with the question of nationhood.

The second aspect which gave the debate a particular shape was the commitment of the nationalist movements, particularly of the Congress, that independent India was going to be run on Westminster lines, where the Lower House, elected on a single territorial basis, may by a majority decide everything and anything. The Congress was also committed to a strong Centre. The Muslim League, though not a major force as of 1930 but still a substantial one, agreed with the strong Centre but had grave reservations about the majoritarian logic. Its spokesmen feared that Muslims as a collective entity would be swamped by Hindus, who formed the vast majority of the population.

The very first Round Table Conference (RTC) brought together a bewildering variety of interest groups from India to London to confer with a delegation of British MPs about the nature of constitutional reform. Dominion Status had been promised as the end goal of these deliberations. It was then that the idea of a loose confederation with substantial provincial and native state autonomy was first mooted. This proposal was backed by the leaders of Punjab and Bengal and the representatives of the native states. This proposal, in fact, saw the Indian subcontinent as a multinational polity with provinces, especially the single language ones, being nations within the larger entity. Congress, however, was not at the first RTC, though Gandhi did go to the second RTC.

The Government of India Act 1935, which resulted from these discussions, opted for a federal structure for British India, and a loose arrangement by which native states could join the federation. When a certain proportion of native states had joined, the full federation would come into effect. The Centre was powerful, but had very few functions in the 1935 proposals. The legislature had a strong Lower House but the Upper House with a substantial presence of native states had veto power. Provinces had many functions and the revenue to perform them. We revisit this old story because the 1935 Act was the last instrument for governance over the entire subcontinent. It combined a Centre with *few* functions but strong reserve powers and provincial autonomy to satisfy local nationalism. It was accepted by both the Congress and the Muslim League which contested the provincial elections under its aegis. Its federal part never came into effect because not enough native states had joined by the time the Second World War broke out. It is ironic that the native states, who had been active in proposing the federation at the first RTC, failed to grasp the opportunity to realize it when the time came. They might have retained their kingdoms for much longer than they eventually did.

In the subsequent eight years after 1939, the issues of Centre versus provinces, of majority versus minority, the question of the position of the native states in any federation of an independent subcontinent became unresolvable. Even as late as 1946, after the election or a Labour Government committed not just to dominion status but to independence, an effort was made by the Cabinet Mission to get agreement for a proposed confederation that would not only provide substantial autonomy for the provinces, but also the possibility or regional associations of provinces within the confederation, to reconcile the conflicting issues of Centre versus the native states and majority versus minority. But soon after both Congress and the Muslim League had agreed, the interpretations placed on it by the two parties conflicted, and the last chance for an undivided, independent Indian subcontinent was lost. From then on, there are bitter disagreements as to who was responsible, but it may take many more years for historians to settle the issue.

The two entities which were created from British India each took a monistic view of nationhood though on different bases. Each constructed a federation with a strong Centre with many functions, and made provinces creatures of the Centre whose boundaries could be redrawn at the behest of the Centre. Each has faced challenges of linguistic/religious subnationalisms, in Pakistan with the serious consequence of the breakaway of Bangladesh, and in India with the bloody though unsuccessful movement for Khalistan. The tensions continue as each tries to reconcile the diversity of languages, religions, and local histories within an overarching national framework. The construction of nationhood remains a contentious issue even now, especially for India with regard to the importance of religion in the definition of nationhood. Both India and Pakistan started as secular entities, but over the years (more in Pakistan than in India, but more recently in India as well) the arguments for a religion-based nationalism are increasing.

Sri Lanka, which did not have any of these problems and whose march to independence was paved by constitutional commissions proposed by the British, experienced a particularly virulent form of the majoritarian logic or the Westminster tradition, thwarting the minority community in its aspirations. Attempts were made in the decade following independence to define nationhood along the identity of the Sinhalese majority community. Declaring Sri Lanka to be a Sinhala nation rendered the position of the largest minority Tamil community precarious. In an ironic way, Jinnah's fears for a Muslim minority in a Hindu majority state with a British type majoritarian constitution were realized in Sri Lanka by the Tamil minority.

The Constitution inherited from the British could only be changed by majority vote in Parliament, and minority rights cannot be guaranteed independent of the majority's connivance in the Westminster tradition (the United Kingdom itself has been facing up to these problems recently in the devolution debates with reference to Scotland and Wales). But in the United Kingdom, the devolution has occurred within the majoritarian logic of Westminster Parliament. In Sri Lanka, however, from the mid-1950s onwards, several attempts were made to have bilateral talks outside the parliamentary framework to meet the minority community's concerns. But over time, the majoritarian logic became tighter and constitutional changes alienated the minority community. The result has been a continuing and very violent strife in the north and north-east parts of Sri Lanka even though renewed efforts at constitutional reform and reconciliation are going on simultaneously with the armed battles.

South Asia thus has had problems of defining nationhood—the second of the two challenges posed by the British. It has led to conflict within each of the three entities that gained independence in 1947–8. But the most serious conflict had to do with the anomalous position of the native states within any independent subcontinent. The reluctance of the native states to join the federation in 1935 was honoured. But by 1947, patience had run out and the last viceroy, Lord Mountbatten, soon after arriving in March 1947, proceeded to seek agreement of the two main parties in British India to a partition. This having been secured by June 1947, he then proceeded to instruct the native states to make no delay in choosing which of the two proposed entities they were going to join. Under the paramountcy which the Viceroy enjoyed, it was within his right to do so, but the individual rulers were still free to delay, if not refuse, to join. A question that remained unanswered at the time was: once the British had departed, who was to be the paramount power: the succeeding independent states of India and Pakistan, or was paramountcy to lapse?

It would be easy to say that such speculation is idle. But in the final push to sign up various native states, some were still not in the bag by the time of Independence in August 1947. Of these, all but one, are deeply embedded in the territory of India—Hyderabad, for instance. Whatever the technical issues about paramountcy, they were not sovereign. But the native state that was on the border of both the two new nation-states, and was a Muslim majority kingdom with a Hindu king fell athwart of all the contradictions of the 1947 settlement. Had Jammu and Kashmir been part of British India, chances were it would have been in Pakistan. But once the right of native princes to accede to whichever entity they liked was conceded, the religious majority principle was overridden by princely prerogative. In the event, much confusion followed and the Maharaja of Kashmir's accession came in the middle of a military emergency. India, which the Maharaja of Kashmir joined, took military action to save the kingdom. A ceasefire was agreed to after an appeal to the United Nations, which passed two Resolutions about settling the dispute and installed a military observer presence to patrol the Line of Control.

The Kashmir issue has remained unsettled till now. Each side, India and Pakistan, has firm but contrary positions on the question—does Kashmir belong to Pakistan by virtue of its Muslim majority or does it belong to India by virtue of the Hindu Maharaja's accession? But it is really a question about the nature of nationhood for each of the two contenders, whether nationhood is constituted by religion or by a common history and territory. Because of the fundamental question it raises about nationhood, there is no easy solution to the problem.

After two further wars in 1965 and 1971, there was a high-level meeting which led to the Shimla Accord of 1972. This agreement to settle the issue through bilateral negotiations stays on the books but no progress has been made beyond that. There the matter rested until two years ago.

Everything changed in May 1998 when India took the fateful decision to conduct nuclear tests on 11 May 1998 and Pakistan followed suit on 28 and 30 May 1998. It is not clear whether the seriousness of the escalation to a nuclear level of the arms race in the subcontinent has been appreciated by the, as yet, euphoric ruling classes of the two countries. Given the high level of damage over an extended period of time that may be inflicted by the detonation of a single nuclear device, even a small probability of accidental war, or war due to a chance misreading of the other's intentions is a frightening prospect. Of course, the number of devices in possession of India and Pakistan is small when compared to those in possession of the other five nuclear powers in the world.

There is no doubt that the behaviour of the previous five declared nuclear powers is hypocritical on this question. But that does not minimize the dangers to South Asia. In the case of India and Pakistan, the proximity of two potential nuclear weapon stales is alarmingly close, with the time required to reach the target in the other country's territory being counted in only a few minutes. The population likely to be affected is extremely large in number and very poor, and would be unable to withstand the rigours of post-nuclear attack complications in terms of radiation related diseases or even simple burns. The death toll could easily be in tens of millions of people, worse than a dozen Hiroshimas or Nagasakis.

The conflict that broke out in the Kargil area of the mountainous border of Kashmir in May 1999 did not escalate to a nuclear war. That is a good omen, but the resurgence of armed conflict between the two countries cannot be ruled out. Here perhaps it may be relevant to recall the European experience.

The three wars that France and Germany fought between 1870 and 1945 were very destructive, and two of them led to world wars. But these wars were fought with conventional weapons not nuclear ones (with the exception of the atom bombs dropped by the United States of America on the Japanese cities of Hiroshima and Nagasaki). It was to avoid the prospect of a fourth war between the European powers that Jean Monnet proposed the series of institutions starting with the Coal and Steel Community that has now led to the European Union.

These three wars were also about Alsace and Lorraine which changed hands each time the war ended. Today no one cares whether Alsace and Lorraine belong to France or to Germany, the border being irrelevant. Kashmir too may one day become irrelevant to the two countries, one hopes in the way Alsace and Lorraine are today. But for that there has to be a sustained effort at creating a large and prosperous trading area in South Asia where economic cooperation and integration in areas of energy, environment, transport, and communications will enhance the benefits of mutuality and take the pressure off the political leaders to fight over scraps of land. It depends on whether we can get from the present state of South Asia to a bright and prosperous future. The answer to that question takes us to the next one.

What Are We?

South Asia, at the end of the twentieth century, is the second most populous region in the world, and carries the burden of the largest concentration of the world's poor. It has one of the worst records in human development, with the shining exception of Sri Lanka. It has countries of very uneven size and population, from India with its population of 915 million to Bhutan with 2 million. The subcontinent dominates with the other three countries—Sri Lanka, Nepal, and Bhutan—having a combined population of 40 million people compared to the 1160 million of the other three. Largely poor, the region's countries have a per capita income ranging from a high for Sri Lanka of $802 to $217 for Nepal. All except Sri Lanka and the Maldives have Human Development Index (HDI) ranks of 128 and below out of a total of 180 countries.

South Asia is today a laggard in Asia though it was a leader in 1947, when Nehru hosted a meeting of the Asian nations in Delhi in January 1947. East Asia and South East Asia (despite the crisis of 1997) have moved far ahead. China is fast emerging as a world class economic power, having enjoyed double-digit growth rates of Gross Domestic Product (GDP) for two decades. By contrast, South Asian economies have found it difficult to sustain a six or seven per cent growth rate for any length of time. Savings rates are typically lower than in other parts of Asia, and the productivity of capital—a mark of efficiency with which scarce capital resources are used—is also very low. There has been an excessive reliance on official foreign aid flows or borrowings from the International Monetary Fund (IMF) and the World Bank to bridge the gap between domestic resources and investment needs.

And yet South Asia manages to be a highly militarized area and an area of violent confrontations both within and between countries. Sri Lanka was an exception to this rule till the end of the 1970s but now even that country has had to gear up to fight the internal insurgency of the Tamil Tigers. Military expenditure as a percentage of GDP has come down in the world from 4.3 per cent in 1985 to 3.2 per cent in 1994, while in South Asia it has gone up from 2.4 to 3.4 per cent over the same period, and recent developments in the nuclear arena are going to push these numbers further up. If India and Pakistan were to freeze their defence expenditure at the pre-nuclear level of 1996, it has been calculated that by 2010 there would be a 35 per cent peace dividend in terms of the cumulative savings. If, by any chance, the expenditure on defence could be cut by even 2 per cent per annum in real terms, the savings rise from 40 to 45 per cent (according to estimates from The Search for a Peace Dividend in South Asia, SACAC Secretariat, 2 April 1998).

Of course, military expenditure is as important for internal security reasons as it is for external security. In the past 50 years each of the newly independent states, including Nepal and Bhutan, has fought hard to maintain its territorial integrity. This has meant dealing with internal unrest as much as fighting international battles. India, Pakistan, and Bangladesh have had to deal with severe internal struggles to maintain their territorial integrity. India has faced 'secular/class' struggles in Telangana in the 1940s, Naxalbari in the 1960s, and similar left-wing struggles in Bihar and Andhra Pradesh continue today. It has also faced sub-nationalist struggles in Assam, Nagaland and Mizoram in the north-east, in Punjab with Khalistan, as well as in Kashmir since 1989. None of these has seriously threatened the integrity of India, but these tensions have posed a burden on the exchequer. Pakistan not only lost its eastern wing in 1971, but also has had to contend with problems in Baluchistan, in Karachi with the Mohajir Qaumi Movement (MQM), and in the North West Frontier Province (NWFP).

Sri Lanka has, of course, faced the greatest threat to her existence with the insurgency of the Liberation Tigers of Tamil Eelam (LTTE). This has meant not only an on-going civil war in the north and north-east of the Island but also terrorist attacks in Colombo and elsewhere. Sri Lanka has not only had to bear the burden of extra military spending but also suffered from the loss of foreign investment and tourism. As already mentioned above, many of these struggles are a mark of the difficulty of defining nationhood in South Asia. Each independent state has embarked on a quest of a monistic definition of nationhood, a single all encompassing national identity despite the multiple dimensions of language, religion, culture, and historical memories that they contain.

A South Asian has a multi-layered identity at his/her base, defined not only by culture and/or religion, but also by language and region. A Tamil speaking Muslim from Sri Lanka is different from one from Tamil Nadu, but may share the sentiment of being an Indian with a Gujarati-speaking Parsee from Bombay and a sentiment of being a Tamilian with his Sri Lankan counterpart. In 1947 when Bengal was divided, the Muslims of East Bengal asserted their Muslim identity and chose to join Pakistan, but in 1971 it was their Bengali identity which made them break away from their fellow Muslims of Pakistan. However, in doing so they did not join West Bengal and create a 'United (Red) Bengal' as some were predicting in 1971. They chose to be a separate nation defined by language (Bengali), religion (Muslim), and territory (East Bengal). Their sense of injustice against their previous fellow nationals gives them a common history to identify with. Bangladesh is an 'imagined community' perhaps the one region of South Asia where a monistic definition of a nation is the easiest to sustain.

A Culture of Violence and Instability

But even Bangladesh, in common with all the other newly independent countries of South Asia, has endured phases of violent politics. Across South Asia, many top political leaders have been killed in the past 50 years. Pakistan has had one prime minister assassinated, one executed, and a president killed in an air crash under mysterious circumstances. India has witnessed the murders of three Gandhis—the Mahatma, Prime Minister Indira Gandhi and her son, Prime Minister Rajiv Gandhi. Bangladesh's founder Mujibur Rahman, as well as one of his successors, Zia ur Rahman, were assassinated. In Sri Lanka, Prime Minister Solomon Bandaranaike, as well as President Ranasinghe Premadasa, were assassinated. In addition, Sri Lanka has also seen the murders of politicians who could have played positive roles in reconciling the two warring communities.

The violence in South Asian political life spreads far beyond just the top leadership, in fact, beyond political life—there is violence in our daily lives too. But the point of emphasizing the precariousness of our leaders' lives is that this gives the impression to the world at large that South Asia is an unstable region. The fact that the majority of these assassinations happened in democratic polities, where there were legitimate ways of removing these leaders, has not impressed the outside world. In the now increasingly fashionable cross-country indices of comparative political stability or freedom, South Asia scores low. This is partly due to the ignorance of the compilers of such indices, but also partly due to the high visibility of the assassinations at the top. Although Sri Lanka and India have maintained a democratic polity, each for 50 years and more, and the norm in the region is democracy rather than dictatorship, the world outside has failed to give due credit to the region for this achievement. India is of course the largest by far of the countries of South Asia, and its weight in various measures of the region's economy or polity is very large. More than 85 per cent of the population of the subcontinent live in India. Its signal achievements have been the preservation of its territorial integrity and the maintenance of a democratic polity for the 53 years of its independent existence. It is a strong centralist federation, with the Centre having the power to make or unmake provinces. The Centre has large revenue-raising powers, and despite constitutional arrangements for revenue sharing it retains vast reserve sources of revenue which it can selectively dole out to the provinces. This has led to frequent complaints that federalism is tainted by party politics of the worst kind. These complaints have been long-standing, and on occasions have been examined by commissions. In recent times, the Centre itself has lost the cohesion it had in the first 40 years of the federation, when a single party—the Congress—dominated Indian politics (the Congress party split in 1969, but the dominant faction kept its hegemony intact). While in the first 40 years, India had six prime ministers and eight general elections, in the last twelve years it has had six prime ministers and five general elections. Only one of the last six prime ministers enjoyed a full five years in office—Mr Rao from 1991 to 1996, though he too did not have a majority in the Lok Sabha. The remaining six years were divided between five prime ministers, each of whom was at the head of a multi-party coalition and only one of whom has commanded a slender majority.

Frequent changes of government, even when legitimately carried out within the rules of parliamentary democracy, portray political instability. But in India's case, the instability relates to the difficulty of building a hegemonic coalition across the country which can contain the diversity—regional, social, caste, and religious—of India. Since the decline of the hegemonic position of the Congress party, which used to contain these multiple factions within itself, there has been a rapid growth in regional (state) parties, caste parties [Other Backward Castes (OBC) and Dalit], religious fundamentalist parties [Bharatiya Janata Party (BJP)], as well as ideological parties of the Left.

The multi-layered identity of South Asia is nowhere else more visible than in the Indian Lok Sabha. Attempts to build a single nationhood around the Hindu religious identity are being made by the BJP, although the religious element was modified during its recent electoral campaigns. The significance of the nuclear tests for India was that the BJP could claim to have delivered the additional dimension of military power to the two older ones of territory and a common history. Of course, the BJP would rewrite the Indian history if it had the choice. The debate in India ranges around secularism which is about the nature of Indian history as well as the original foundations of Indian nationhood after partition.

But a weaker Centre is not all bad news since it gives the individual constituents of the federation more room for manoeuvre. Some of the states of India are larger than many members of the United Nations. They have also, over the past 50 years, developed sophisticated local economies. In the new climate of liberalization and globalization, individual chief ministers of various provinces have made forays abroad for foreign investment, though the authority for final approval stays with the Centre. This innovative effort has increased the ability of the states to pursue variants of the overall national strategy for growth. From a time when the Centre was totally dominant and the states were completely reliant on the goodwill of the Centre, and indeed were arguing for a 'new' federalism which would give the states more autonomy, we are now at a stage where the fears are that the more advanced states may march ahead, leaving the poorer states behind and exacerbating the regional economic and social inequalities.

There has been for a long time in South Asia a well-rehearsed argument that movements for religious or regional sub-nationalisms are in essence struggles for redressing income inequalities. If only economic opportunities were more evenly available, as stated by Nehru, the demand for Pakistan would lose its edge. This argument has been repeated at each juncture where a region or a caste group has asserted a desire for a separate political identity. This factor was cited as one reason for the breakup of Pakistan, and is no doubt one of the explanations for the origin of the Sinhala–Tamil divisions. Having your own state within a federation, or at the extreme having your own nation-state, is seen as one way of redressing the uneven distribution of resources and opportunities. This desire is often combined with the feeling that somehow the 'legitimate' share of the region/the social group/the nation is being siphoned off by the other region [s]. It is a local version of the 'drain theory' used against the British and again used with great effect during the break-up of Pakistan.

But such arguments are based upon at least two misperceptions. The drain theory assumes that the surplus is already there, but just not coming to the nation. As soon as the nation is independent the drain stops, the surplus comes to the nation, and all is well. The experience of India, Pakistan, as well as Sri Lanka in the decades after independence should convince anyone that the drain was not large enough to ease the problem of economic development. If there was any doubt, the economic history of Bangladesh since 1971 should remove it. The problem of South Asia, as that of any other developing country, ex-colony or not, is not that the surplus is available and only needs to be snatched back from the foreigner usurper but that the 'real task in development', is to create the surplus. This requires radical transformation of the institutions of land ownership, the creation of accessible credit markets, the transformation of the social conditions of feudalism, paternalism, and patriarchy, the elimination of illiteracy and improved health programmes, and the mobilization of resources which lie latent in the unequal distribution of income and wealth. China is, in this case, the appropriate case for South Asia to study. Rather than rely on any bonanza as a result of the Revolution, it set about transforming its institutions of land ownership. Despite the setbacks caused by adventurist policies in the 1950s and 1960s, the foundations laid down in the early years by way of radical transformation of the economic and social order enabled China to profit from liberalization when the time came.

The history of other Asian countries is similar. Japan and South Korea at different times in their histories transformed their rural institutions by pursuing radical land reforms, investing in education, and creating appropriate credit markets. Taiwan is another example of a successful transformation resulting from radical policies of land reform.

Thus, South Asia does not have to look to Western models for development; it has many successful ones within Asia. All the countries mentioned above have been free of sub-nationalist struggles (though Korea is still divided). It is not simply because they have more racially homogenous populations than South Asia. Homogeneity is often an endogenous variable; populations previously thought homogenous have often found murderous divisions within themselves. It is just that they have grasped the falsehood of the distributive path of development and pursued the more correct productivity enhancing one. In the process, they have not only transformed their economies, but have modernized their societies as well.

This social modernization also points to the fallacy of the other simplification in South Asia about the roots of divisiveness. In posing a crude economic explanation of the religious or regional or caste divisions, the intellectuals of South Asia have missed a glaring fact of their societies. The social backwardness of their societies—the persistence of caste divisions in India, the continuing burden of superstitions borne by an illiterate population, the low status of women of all ages, the proliferation of *sadhus, fakirs, priests, mullahs, gurus, swamis*, many of them of dubious moral and social quality, the perpetuation of a hierarchical order originally local, but enhanced by contact with the British, who are also given to hierarchical gradations—was obvious at the time of independence, but left untouched by the new nation-states. In India, if anything, the caste divisions have been strengthened by the electoral process and are now even more deeply entrenched. Religiosity of an exhibitionist consumer-durable-goods kind, has increased where the point seems not so much to worship but to display wealth and power.

Things are, if anything, worse in Pakistan, especially since the revival of a fundamentalist movement in Islam. Scholars in the subcontinent, like Maulana Azad, had been at the forefront of the modernist wave in Islam in the first half of this century. Muslim theological schools debated these issues in great detail. There was an intimate link between the debates in the subcontinent and those in the Middle East and Turkey. Much of this ferment led to the modernization of Muslim societies in Egypt, Iraq, Syria, and Turkey. However, since the 1970s there has been a reversal of this trend throughout the Middle East, North Africa, and Turkey. The oil-rich states of the Gulf, which escaped the modernizing forces in the early twentieth century, have emerged as the driving force in this revival of a fundamentalist interpretation. This is, of course, true not only with respect to Islam. India is witnessing a revival of Hindu fundamentalism.

Religious fundamentalism is not simply a religious reawakening but a political programme. It seeks political power, and promises to transform society by doctrinal purification. In a world troubled by violence and insecurity, family break-up and drug addiction, crime and pornography, it seems to offer a haven of peace and tranquility. But it is also setting its face against the forces of modernity which are, through technological and economic changes, inexorably providing better opportunities of social communication, geographical mobility, and economic empowerment. Indeed, even the fundamentalists use technological gadgets such as the Internet, but deny the values of scientific rationality. They stay flat earthists, creationists, and believers in miracles. They drive their cars, use their mobile telephones, and fly in jets, but hold on to the idea that statues can drink milk or that diseases are caused or cured by supernatural powers.

Sri Lanka had, for a long time, escaped the religious divisiveness of the larger countries of the region. But even before independence, there was already an established pattern of communal riots in which Buddhist monks led the charge against Christians or Muslims. After independence, a form of militant Buddhism (paradoxical though it may sound for a religion known for its non-violent creed), has become increasingly articulate. It has diminished the space for a secular culture in Sri Lankan society steadily since the mid-1950s. Its assertion of Sinhala Buddhist nationalism has been one of the causes of the alienation of the Tamil minority. It has also been responsible for political turmoil in the 1950s, when Bandaranaike was assassinated. Sri Lanka is now officially a Buddhist state but it is far from being a non-violent society.

South Asia presents a paradox. No other region, emerging from centuries of colonial rule had as much going for it as South Asia when it became independent. In the last 50 years South Asians have been major players in the social sciences— economics, sociology, anthropology—and in mathematics and statistics, in English literature, in music, art, films, dance, in philosophy and history. In all these areas, South Asia has produced giants who can hold their own in the world. There has been high-minded political leadership, at least in an earlier generation, which genuinely wanted to better the plight of their people, and who understood that political independence was meaningless without economic betterment of their people. There have been dedicated, talented civil servants, who have successfully wrestled with problems of bringing order amidst chaos in delivering necessities throughout the region. There have been people who have worked at the grassroots, innovated people-friendly delivery of goods or credit (the world-famous Grameen Bank). There are some world class companies, imaginative entrepreneurs, including among them millions of farmers who made the Green Revolution possible. Our people are not hide-bound. They have spread themselves all over the world and made a success of it, wherever they have gone.

And yet South Asia is a laggard in Asia and in the world. Is it that we have released the potential of some at the top social echelon, the Brahmins of all religions so to speak, but left the rest behind in their stupor? Is it that we always do better abroad than at home since something in our families and our societies holds us back at home? Is it that we have failed to save enough and invest enough in the things that enhance people's capabilities to improve their own lives? Have we perhaps spent too much of our energies fighting ourselves with each other and within each of us, so that opportunities have passed by? Have our leaders seen that their predecessors tried their best and yet failed to budge the mountain of woe, and thus given up the effort, pausing only to pursue their private ends? Are our problems severely greater to face than they would be if we had some sense of unity of purpose, some semblance of the spirit of co-operation? Should we recall and recover our commonalities rather than cultivate and nurture things that divide us?

Can we transform our history; turn enemies into friends, into a positive force to win the forthcoming battles of globalization? Can we agree to disagree and turn to the task of winning the battles of here and now; the material battles of overcoming poverty, ill-health, disease, gender discrimination, child abuse, and illiteracy? Why should we make and test nuclear bombs and intercontinental missiles, yet not provide clean water or a working sewage system, a decent urban transport system, telephones that work, an efficient postal system, adequate housing, or food that is not poisonous?

It is surely not the lack of talent, nor yet the reluctance to work hard. But the talented are at one end of our society and those who toil hard, at the other end. Our culture still demands that the educated person stops physical effort; it is a *sahib* culture. Even the egalitarian religions, Islam and Buddhism, have been domesticated into the love of hierarchy so that we not only have economic inequalities but social inequalities of birth reinforced by those of status. Even those of us who profess the secular religion of equality—socialism—persist in our daily lives with our caste and social labels. Muslims in India have acquired castes; while the communists stay Brahmins, if born as such.

We have to learn that being equal does not mean being the same, that being South Asian does not mean ceasing to be Pakistani or Indian or Nepalese or Sri Lankan, or yet again that being Indian does not prevent one from being Sikh or Bengali or Kannadiga. A Bengali could be a Hindu, a Muslim, or a Christian. We need to feel confident after 50 years of independence that we need not seek to impose on ourselves cast-iron shells of monistic nationhoods. We can relax and carry our multi-layered identities and loyalties with our nationhood. We have to seek, not unity in diversity, but plurality in diversity. We have to feel confident that we can be good South Asians as well as all the other things—national patriots, rooted regionalists, helpful city dwellers or rural people, loving family members, and autonomous creative individuals. This will enhance our chances of winning the battles of the coming century and will strengthen us to deal with obstacles that stand in our way. We need not lose our nationalities. We need to regain our supra-nationality as South Asians.

Where Could We Be?

We could be the South Asia Community, rather like the European Community. Not today, but maybe by 2020. It is important here to distinguish between a community and a union. A union involves some overall federal structure and pooling of sovereignty among the member countries. The European Community, on the other hand, is a single market entity where, within the borders of the Community, free movement of labour and capital is proposed. The Single European Act was passed in various legislatures in 1987, the Single Market directives were issued and the Market was inaugurated in 1992. Not all the 15 members passed all the legislation immediately, and there are miles to go before a full single market is realized. In 1991, the Maastricht Treaty created the European Union with common pillars of foreign policy, immigration policy, democracy and human rights, and finally economic and monetary union. The last mentioned, the European Monetary Union (EMU), is the project for a single currency and the European Central Bank, launched in 1999 is to be completed in 2002.

The South Asian Community should stay a community of independent sovereign states, which would become a single market. They need go no further. Having won nationhood after bitter and bloody struggles, it is unlikely that South Asians want to give up their nation-states and merge into some larger entity. The European Union has won very little popular support. It is seen as a creature of bureaucrats and top leaders. The South Asian Community should avoid the mistakes of the European Community. Thus, there should be no central bureaucracy on the lines of the European Commission which rules via directives and has low accountability. The European Union has been singularly unsuccessful in pursuing a joint foreign policy as the example of Bosnia has tragically shown. Thus, the South Asian Community should stay a free trade area, a single market which will maximize benefits of economic cooperation without incurring financial costs or political unpopularity.

That is where we could be. But of course we are not there yet. There are several signs that despite the low level of co-operation at the inter-governmental level, there is a lot of informal, even illegal co-operation across the borders. Official trade between India and Pakistan may be limited but smugglers do a roaring trade across the porous border. This trade is competitive, price-sensitive, and responsive to consumer needs. Sri Lanka is also an entrepôt in a triangular trade between India and Pakistan, though official estimates of this trade are lacking. The Gulf states are another such node of this triangular trade. If we go back to any time between the first and the fifteenth centuries, there was always a raging traffic between the Gulf countries as well as Egypt down the west coast of the Indian subcontinent, all the way to Sri Lanka. These old trading lanes had built-in advantages of favourable winds and low costs.

Borders are created by governments, and in world history, are essentially a recent twentieth-century phenomenon. Earlier, there was free movement of people across South Asia and even between Iran and the Indian subcontinent. Nowadays we have demarcated national boundaries and the 50 miles from Amritsar to Lahore are more difficult to traverse than the 1000 miles from Lahore to Karachi or from Amritsar to Madras (Chennai).

But that does not stop people from moving across boundaries and borders in search of better opportunities or to escape persecution. The flow of people across the borders of Bangladesh and India, and across the Palk Straits from Sri Lanka into Tamil Nadu and back, causes difficulties for the Sri Lankan government and can be said to have contributed to Rajiv Gandhi's death. But that does not render all such flows bad. Criminal activities can be eliminated by cross-border co-operation among the law enforcing agencies, while economic migration is almost always beneficial to the migrant and the country receiving him/her. What is more, the migrant then remits money back to his/her home. Thus migration is a win–win situation in economic terms, though in the context of nation-states with boundaries it becomes a problem. The United States has always had a half 'open door' policy and gained much from immigration, while much of Western Europe has lately set its face against it. Yet even the ex-imperial countries of Europe have gained from the migration of their former colonial peoples.

It would be easy to relax rules for movement across the region, and provide people with proper identification papers. Nationality should, however, not be a barrier for people; they should be allowed to work in any of the countries comprising South Asia. Of course each nation-state will complain that it will be flooded by immigrants from elsewhere but the simultaneity of the complaints themselves will show that the flow will be multidirectional, and each country will benefit from the process. After all, all we would be doing will be going back to the 1940s before the barriers came down.

We share a common ocean and our ecology is also common. Questions on preservation of fish stocks, for example, will require that South Asian countries devise a common strategy if Russian and Japanese fishing boats are not going to plunder them with their superior technology. Global warming and the prospect of climate change threaten the very existence of the islands of Maldives as well as parts of Bangladesh and Sri Lanka. South Asia needs a common bargaining strategy at the international level to defend its territory and its ecology.

We share our rivers which do not respect the national boundaries that we have drawn so recently. These rivers provide a vital source of living for our populations. Sharing of these rivers has so far been managed by bilateral negotiations, the Accord between India and Bangladesh in 1997 being the latest example. But sharing of waters sensibly is important between countries and within a country, as in the two parallel debates in India and Pakistan over the Kaveri River water sharing and the Kalabagh dam respectively.

A common South Asian musical culture is developing, thanks to cable television networks. Early in the 1950s, the Minister for Information and Broadcasting in India banned film music from the government-owned All India Radio on the ground that he wanted to encourage appreciation of classical music. However, the listeners turned to the Commercial Service of Radio Ceylon which was happy to cater to their needs. Soon, All India Radio saw the light and began to play film music once more. Now, despite the state ownership of television in every South Asian country, cable television and even private satellite dishes in India have made channels like MTV available for all of South Asia. There is thus already a single South Asian pop music/film music area, and even the music is an innovative fusion of all the strands of classical and folk music found throughout the region as anyone who has heard Asian rap music can testify. For the younger generation, this music spreads all across South Asia and even on to the immigrants living in the United States of America and Europe. The reputation of Nusrat Fateh Ali

Khan, for example, transcended all national boundaries within South Asia and indeed became global.

Thus an informal 'people's' SAARC is emerging unaided by any governmental effort. South Asia is already a single market for music and television. A large market of anywhere between 400 to 800 million people, depending on what you want to sell, is available not just for foreign multinationals but even for South Asian companies. Currently, this huge market is being exploited by MTV and STAR and BBC in the field of music, by Coca Cola and Pepsi in drinks, by Nike and Adidas in footwear. We are preventing ourselves from benefiting from our own markets because we fear we will destroy each other's industry, while all the time we are happy to let foreign companies sell in our markets without any such compunction. If we implement liberalization *vis-à-vis* the world, why not between ourselves? Why should we be a single market for others and not for ourselves?

CONCLUSION

A South Asian Community is a distant dream, but it could start with small steps. We could ease travel across South Asia, both by relaxing visa restrictions and making more flights available between our airports, and letting our trains and cars run across boundaries. We need not have a single currency, but we could make our currencies freely convertible into each other's currencies. Indeed, we could extend trade and capital convertibility within the region without any greater problems than our respective currencies have already faced. We allow our companies to raise capital abroad; why not in each other's stock markets?

We have a vibrant film industry that is shown around the world but there is little showing of each other's films at home. Why not have South Asian film festivals and collaborative productions? At present Indian (Bollywood) films are shown on cable television channels, but all the other film industries lose out. If an active collaborative strategy was followed, showing each others' films, then Pakistani, Bangladeshi, and Sri Lankan films would also get greater airing. We could share our art by having South Asian art festivals, share our great dancers, musicians, painters, and poets.

We were a people once without any common political authority. We then were enslaved by a foreign power and felt our common predicament. Then we became free and divided. We discovered our separate national identities. Now after 50 years we can explore the possibility that without giving up our national identities we can revive some of what we had when we were the same people—because we are yet the same people.

MEASURING THE ECONOMY

28

Demand for Cotton Textiles in
Nineteenth Century India

I

The question of the demand curve for cotton textiles in nineteenth century India has recently been brought up in the controversy surrounding Prof. Morris D. Morris's article.[1] In the article, he said, 'Manchester exported both yarn and cloth. While British cloth was competitive with Indian handloom production, machine made yarn seems to have strengthened the competitive position of the indigenous handloom sector despite the fall in cloth prices. The demand for cloth in India seems to have been fairly elastic. The fall in price led to a movement down the demand curve. In addition, there seems to have been a shift to the right of the demand curve for cotton cloth. Not only was there population growth; there was also changes in custom which increased the amount of cloth consumed *per capita*. Finally there seems to have been a shift away from inferior fabrics to cotton.'[2] And also '..., at worst, the vast expansion of British cloth exports to India skimmed off the expanding demand. The handloom weavers were at least no fewer in number and no worse off economically at the end of the period than at the beginning.'[3] These remarks have led Dr Bipan Chandra to say: 'But from what evidence are such sophisticated tools of modern economics, as demand elasticity and demand curve derived especially the notion of the latter's shift to the right? Not from any available statistics nor from any other type of evidence. There is hardly any material in economic literature to enable one to draw such an advanced curve and

The Indian Economic and Social History Review, December 1971.

I am grateful to Sourin Roy for his valuable help with nineteenth century source material. Mr M.N. Gupta of the Delhi School of Economics Computer Centre helped with the computations. Thanks are due to Dharma Kumar, Arjun Sengupta, and Pranab Bardhan for their suggestions.

[1] Morris D. Morris (1968), 'Towards a Reinterpretation of Nineteenth Century Indian Economic History', *Journal of Economic History*, December 1963 and reprinted in *Indian Economic and Social History Review*, Vol. V, No. 1, March.

[2] Morris, 'Towards a Reinterpretation of Nineteenth Century Indian Economic History', p. 9.

[3] Morris, 'Towards a Reinterpretation of Nineteenth Century Indian Economic History', p. 9.

point to its shifting. In fact, the curve is a fiction and words like "led and a shift" merely give it an illusion of firm existence.' [4]

The purpose of this paper is to look at the question of the elasticity of the demand curve for cotton textiles in the nineteenth century raised in the above questions. Prof. Morris's contention is that a demand curve for cotton textiles in India can be identified and that it is 'fairly elastic'. The fall in the price of British textiles led to their increased import into India. He also seems to assert that however, the consequent fall in handloom production, if any, was not very large since the increase in imports 'skimmed off the expanding demand' arising out of the rightward shift of the demand curve due to growth of population and change in tastes. Dr Bipan Chandra on the other hand raises doubts about whether one can identify the demand curve from available (or any other) information, let alone estimate its elasticity or its shift. Thus the debate centres round the identification of the demand curve and at a later stage the measurement of its elasticity.

It is not necessary at this point to go into the identification problem either in general or in the context of economic history.[5] The particular problem here is that we have data on imports of British cloth into India and their price. We observe that while price went down over the years of the nineteenth century the quantity imported went up. We have by comparison very little information on the domestic cloth industry (handloom) as to price, output or even the number of weavers in the nineteenth century. Can we from such information conclude anything about the demand curve for cloth in India? Assuming we can say something about the demand curve, the next stage is to see whether we can conclude anything about the course of the handloom industry and the welfare of the weavers in the nineteenth century since that is a related part of Prof. Morris' contention about the textile industry. We first take up the question of the demand curve.

Given the fact that at present we have data only on imports, we need to make two simplifying assumptions which will help us formulate the question precisely: (a) locally made (handloom) cloth and imported (machine-made) British cloth were perfect substitutes; (b) the supply curve of British cloth for India was perfectly elastic. These are both drastic assumptions and made only to circumvent the lack of data. To begin with, imported cloth may have differed in quality from domestic cloth. The coarser and plainer the cloth variety, the less likely is such a difference. In the later part of the nineteenth century, the Indian consumers may have had a marked preference for 'foreign' cloth thus making foreign cloth and domestic cloth imperfect substitutes. In the concluding section of this paper, I shall try to suggest ways in which this assumption can be relaxed. The second assumption can be defended on the grounds that India was only one of the many markets supplied by the British textile industry (the share of exports to India to total exports was 15 per cent for 1821–30 and 30 per cent for 1871–80). If this assumption is to be relaxed then we need to estimate the supply curve of British cloth for India.

[4] Bipan Chandra, 'Reinterpretation of Nineteenth Century Indian Economic History', *Indian Economic and Social History Review,* Vol. V, No. 1, p. 58, 2 March 1968.

[5] 'I have already discussed the problem in economic history in my 'Some Issues in Economic History', *Economic History Review',* April 1968, Vol. XXI, No. 1.

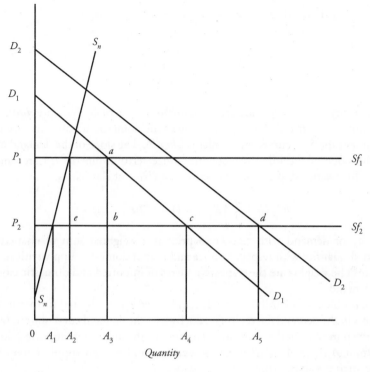

Fig 28.1

We begin the analysis by assuming no shift in the Indian demand curve and the domestic supply curve for cloth but a downward shift in the British supply curve. In Fig. 28.1, D_1D_1 is the Indian demand curve for cloth (both British and domestic). S_nS_n is the domestic supply curve. The British, supply curve shifts from $P_1P_1(Sf_1)$ to $P_2P_2(Sf_2)$. All the relationships are assumed linear at this stage, but this does not affect the analysis as we shall show. At price OP_1, the total quantity demanded (Q_1) is OA_3 of which OA_2 is domestically produced (h_1) and A_2A_3 is imported (f_1). When the price falls to OP_2 total quantity demanded (Q_2) goes up to OA_4—a net increase of A_3A_4—but the shares of domestic and imported cloth change. Domestic cloth (h_2) bought goes down from OA_2 to OA_1—a net reduction of A_1A_2—and imported cloth (f_2) now equals A_1A_4. Thus,

At price OP_1, Q_1 $(OA_3) = h_1$ $(AO_2) + f_1$ (A_2A_3);

At price OP_2, Q_2 $(OA_4) = h_2$ $(AO_1) + f_2$ (A_1A_4).

When talking about the elasticity of the demand curve, one is referring to the relative movement from OA_3 to OA_4 as a result of the relative fall in price from OP_1 to OP_2. Since we have assumed linear relationships, let us first express the problem in slopes and then in elasticities. The slope we wish to measure is bc/ab or A_3A_4/P_1P_3. But we have observations only on imports and therefore we can only observe the change in imported quantity from A_2A_3 to A_1A_4, and compare it with the change in price P_1P_2. Now,

$$\frac{A_1 A_4 - A_2 A_3}{P_1 P_2} = \frac{A_3 A_4 + A_1 A_2}{P_1 P_2} = \frac{A_3 A_4}{P_1 P_2} + \frac{A_1 A_2}{P_1 P_2}$$

$$\frac{df}{dP} = \frac{dQ}{dP} - \frac{dh}{dP} \ .$$

The quantity we want to measure is dQ/dP and we actually measure df/dP, thus overstating the demand slope by the slope of the domestic supply curve (dh/dP). The steeper the $S_n S_n$ curve, the smaller is (dh/dP). The slope of the demand curve and the slope of the imported quantity–price relationship (df/dP) are not the same. This relationship can also be written in terms of elasticities:

$$E_{Q,P} = \left(\frac{f}{Q}\right) E_{f,P} + (1 - f/Q) E_{h,P} \ .$$

Elasticity of demand with respect to price is a weighted sum of elasticity of imported quantity with respect to price and that of domestic supply with respect to price. The weights are the respective shares of imported and domestic cloth in total demand.

The problem of identifying the demand curve is complicated further if there are shifts in the demand curve. In Fig. 28.1 we let the demand curve shift to $D_2 D_2$. Here the pure shift of the demand curve is $A_4 A_5$, the increase in imported cloth is now from $A_2 A_3$ to $A_1 A_5$. If both the demand and foreign supply curves have shifted then the slope estimated is:

$$\frac{A_1 A_5 - A_2 A_3}{P_1 P_2} = \frac{A_3 A_4}{P_1 P_2} = \frac{A_1 A_2}{P_1 P_2} + \frac{A_4 A_5}{P_1 P_2}$$

On rearranging,
$$\frac{(df - dD)}{dP} = \frac{dQ}{dP}\bigg|_{D_1 D_1} - \frac{dh}{dP}$$

where dD is the pure shift of the demand curve.

The larger the shift of the demand curve, the more will a price–quantity slope of imports overstate the slope of the demand curve. Looking only at import price–quantity relationship (bd/ab) will lead to the conclusion of a very elastic demand curve. The true demand curve may even be inelastic but a large shift in it accompanied by a large shift in the supply curve may make the resulting price–quantity scatter elastic. Shifts in the domestic supply curve are easy to handle by analogy. A leftward shift will further complicate the problem. A rightward shift of the supply curve will alleviate the problem.

We can now look again at Prof. Morris' statement. His statement combines a fairly elastic demand curve (perhaps a constant elasticity demand curve) with a rightward shift of the same due to population growth and change in tastes. The rightward shift is difficult to separate until we have some reliable information on these shift factors. He also says that imports perhaps only skimmed off the expanding demand. This means that a shift in the demand curve to the right to $D_2 D_2$ should leave domestic cloth sales unchanged at OA_2. Thus we have along with a shift of the demand curve a shift of the domestic supply curve to the right until the new domestic supply curve passes through points a and e. This would leave domestic sales at $0A_2$, imports would go up from A_2A_3 to A_2A_5—A_3A_4 due to the supply shift and A_4A_5 due to demand shift. Thus, expanding demand A_3A_5 at P_1 or A_4A_5 at P_2 is skimmed off entirely by imports. This is the most precise interpretation one can put on Prof. Morris' statement quoted at the beginning of this article. Even if you do not have such precise movements, tendencies in these directions should be observable to validate his hypothesis. The difficulty is that once again we need information on the course of the handloom industry to measure the shift. Measurement of the elasticity of demand curve requires information about the state of the domestic cloth industry and the state of the economy besides the available information on import price and quantity.

We need, therefore, some additional evidence on the supply conditions in the domestic cloth industry. Two factors are mentioned by Prof. Morris and Dr Bipan Chandra in their articles quoted above which point towards a rightward shift of the supply curve. One is the import of cheap yarn and the other is a decline in the wages or the subsistence level of weavers. But the importance of these two factors can be gauged only from further evidence about their quantitative importance. Even if we have evidence on the number of handloom weavers throughout this period, we need additional evidence on the size of output. If (a) the number of weavers remained the same *or* (b) even increased but (c) if output per weaver was declining, then the supply curve may have shifted to the left (a and c) or moved to the right (b and c) or remained unchanged (also b and c).

In the next section, I would like to present some statistical evidence on the price–quantity relationship of imported cloth. While this is clearly not a measure of the elasticity of demand, it gives us more information than we now seem to have about the question. Also if the supply curve of imported cloth shifted much more than the demand curve, i.e. if in Fig. 28.1 ab is much larger than cd, then the observed points a, d, will lie across two demand curves. This will not give us the correct answer but a limiting value for the true elasticity. There are good reasons for hypothesizing that in the nineteenth century, whatever the course of income and population, the supply curve shift due to technological change in cotton textile manufacture must have caused a relatively larger shift than the demand shift. In the second half of the nineteenth century, the transport revolution caused a further downward shift in the supply curve of British cloth.

II

There are two sets of data on quantity and value of cloth imports for the nineteenth century which are easily accessible. MacGregor[6] gives figures on the quantity and value of British exports to all places east of the Cape of Good Hope (except China for 1814–32). In the category of cotton manufactures, he lists five items:

(a) Calicoes white or plain;

[6] For the complete reference, see Table 28.1

TABLE 28.1

Quantities and Values of Imports of British Cloth by Types (1814–32)

Year	Calicoes white		Calicoes printed, checked stained or dyed		Muslins white or plain		Muslins printed checked, stained, or dyed		Hosiery and smallware	Total	Imports of twist and yarn	
	Yds	£	Yds	£	Yds	£	Yds	£	£	£	lbs	£
(1)	(2)	(3)	(4)	(5)	(6)	(7)	(8)	(9)	(10)	(11)	(12)	(13)
1814	82,638	11,341	597,395	59,206	130,770	19,476	7205	894	18,563	109,480	–	–
1815	239,027	27,511	849,322	71,341	250,372	30,455	16,755	1619	11,484	142,410	–	–
1816	232,500	23,439	978,423	70,903	462,051	47,388	12,724	1484	17,390	160,534	–	–
1817	938,650	63,023	2,842,363	107,371	1,539,244	137,143	5713	959	29,314	422,814	–	–
1818.	2,971,234	161,765	4,317,798	391,535	2,343,067	211,908	5940	940	34,977	700,892	–	–
1819	1,877,196	106,530	3,712,551	233,533	1,536,864	112,870	1050	86	8249	461,268	–	–
1820	3,764,843	169,568	7,496,771	462,413	2,719,413	164,493	12,829	903	32,732	834,118	–	–
1821	5,353,693	234,211	9,682,316	569,403	4,069,639	254,392	33,058	2398	23,724	1,084,440	–	–
1822	5,661,908	246,236	9,023,394	496,318	6,050,931	363,096	5910	372	43,458	1,145,057	–	–
1823*	9,325,978	461,347	9,304,159	490,568	5,783,475	291,998	40,513	2450	32,987	1,128,468	–	–
1824	10,954,049	428,919	9,575,049	490,389	3,904,466	173,762	36,831	3398	17,009	1,113,477	105,350	13,041
1825	11,278,099	448,275	8,756,807	410,623	2,982,797	148,657	69,908	5244	24,072	1,036,871	235,360	35,345
1826	11,200,283	372,068	9,624,730	400,626	4,048,499	160,995	123,346	7150	33,298	994,019	918,507	100,804

(cont.)

Table 28.1 (cont.)

Year	Calicoes white or plain		Calicoes printed, checked stained or dyed		Muslins white or plain		Muslins printed checked, stained, or dyed		Hosiery and smallware	Total	Imports of twist and yarn	
	Yds	£	Yds	£	Yds	£	Yds	£	£	£	lbs	£
(1)	(2)	(3)	(4)	(5)	(6)	(7)	(8)	(9)	(10)	(11)	(12)	(13)
1827	19,160,430	647,072	14,237,190	506,619	8,134,854	317,602	37,664	2283	31,943	1,614,517	3,063,098	274,008
1828*	22,461,558	754,006	13,581,511	496,587	7,956,230	281,445	28,700	1096	46,348	1,621,560	4,558,293	Illegible
1829	26,218,516	746,912	11,107,429	427,211	6,675,415	239,885	108,314	3436	36,860	1,453,404	2,927,478	200,558
1830	37,563,187	1,009,163	15,439,893	536,111	5,917,069	185,940	166,971	7668	21,834	1,760,552	4,689,570	324,956
1831	28,649,977	728,706	13,972,119	471,688	6,369,975	179,638	597,473	22,578	19,810	1,419,995	6,541,853	483,762
1832	34,084,254	819,189	17,007,098	531,634	5,199,287	163,169	284,563	14,183	23,243	1,531,393	Before 1824, quantities were less than 100,000 lbs.	

Source: 'An Account of the Exports from Great Britain to all Places Eastward of Cape Good Hope (except China) distinguishing the Principal Articles and Whether Exported by East India Company or by Private Traders in each year from 1814 to 1832', in J. MacGregor (1848), *Commercial Tariffs and Regulations, Resources and Trade of the Several States of Europe and America together with The Commercial Treaties Between England and Foreign Countries*, Part Twenty Third—India, Ceylon and the Oriental Countries, London, pp. 148–54.

Note: The data for years marked with an asterisk should be used only after rechecking against the original, since they are likely to contain reading and copying errors. The italicized numbers are especially doubtful.

325

(b) Calicoes printed, checked, stained, or dyed;

(c) Muslins white or plain;

(d) Muslins printed, checked, stained, or dyed;

(e) Hosiery and smallware.

For items (a) to (d), we have data on value of exports as well as quantity in yards. The last item, which is minor, is only given in value terms. MacGregor also lists for 1833–9 British manufactures exported to the East India Company's territories and Ceylon. But in Table 28.1 for cotton manufactures only total quantity and value are available.[7]

For the second part of the nineteenth-century, the Statistical Abstract of British India gives data on the value of imports of cotton manufactures from 1849 onwards. Data on quantities are available from 1868 onwards. There is thus a gap for 1840–67.

The first problem is that for 1814–32 as well as for 1833–9, the data relate to an area larger than India. At a later stage, therefore, these need to be checked against imports into Madras, Bombay, and Calcutta. Secondly, for 1833–9 and 1868–1901, the value and quantity data are for all cotton manufactures, creating all the familiar index number problems. In the context of Fig. 28.1, we can no longer talk of the price or cloth but some sort of average value per unit of imports. Any observed movements in this variable need not always reflect movements of the supply curve. They may come about due to a change in composition of imports. We can check how serious this problem is by looking for the particular items as well as total imports for the period 1814–32.

Over the period 1814–32, the total quantity of British cloth exported to countries east of the Cape of Good Hope, except China, rose from 818,000 yds to 56,575,202 yds or nearly 70 times, whereas the total value of exports rose from £ 909,17 to £ 1,508,150 or about 16½ times. The average unit value of exports fell from £ 0.111 to £ 0.0267. So the unit value at the end of the period was one-quarter of that at the beginning.

This growth, though impressive, was uneven for different types of cloth. The quantity of white or plain calicoes increased 400 times over 19 years, their value only 70 times. The other three varieties grew less rapidly. Exports of printed calicoes rose nearly 30 times in quantity and nine times in value, of plain muslins 40 times in quantity and about eight and a half times in value. Exports of printed muslins were the most variable, showing extreme year to year fluctuations. For the last three years of the sample for example, the quantity exported was 166,971 yds, 597,473 yds, and 284,563 yds. This variability may indicate that the domestic cloth industry was perhaps in a stronger, more competitive position regarding this item than plainer stuff such as white calicoes. In the period 1814–32, for all exports as well as for the individual items, a sharp drop occurs in 1819 and 1831, while the years 1824–6 have stagnant or diminishing exports. White or plain calicoes show the least stagnation while all the others underwent a longer period

---

[7] These are the data I have been able to find easily. I will be grateful for further suggestions.

TABLE 28.2

Quantities and Value of Imports of British Cloth and Twist Yarn (1833–9)

Year	Cotton manufactures		Hosiery and smallware	Twist and yarn	
	Yds	£	£	lbs	£
(1)	(2)	(3)	(4)	(5)	(6)
1833	45,775,910	1,152,486	21,153	4,783,794	324,553
1834	38,972,059	943,504	15,717	4,207,653	315,583
1835	51,777,277	1,338,323	30,631	5,399,703	432,081
1836	74,280,596	1,972,216	47,596	6,592,310	561,878
1837	64,212,633	1,530,240	30,444	8,472,081	608,898
1838	80,085,122	1,781,294	24,181	10,710,136	640,205
1839	100,048,791	2,293,918	27,820	10,812,915	640,015

Source: 'British and Irish Produce and Manufactures Exported from the United Kingdom to East India Company's Territories and Ceylon', in J. MacGregor, See *Commercial Tariffs and Regulations*.

of stagnation—printed calicoes in 1821–6, plain muslins in 1822–6 and after 1829.

This pattern of cyclical growth continues for the years 1833-9 (see Table 28.2). Total exports to the East India Company's territories and Ceylon rose from 45,775,910 yds to 100,048,791 yds or by 120 per cent in seven years while the value rose from £ 1,152,486 to £ 2,293,918 or by 100 per cent. The unit value of exports fell from £ 0.0252 to £ 0.0229. There were cyclical declines in 1834 and 1837. For the period 1868–1901, the data relate to imports into India. Here the growth is much less spectacular and much more cyclical, compared to the earlier period. Imports doubled in quantity over the 34 years while the values of imports went up by between 60 to 75 per cent. The unit values of imports show a marked drop between the first half of the 1870s and the second half. Except for this drop, there is no clear downward trend in unit value as in the earlier period. This drop in unit value after 1875 comes about mainly due to the transport revolution and we can conjecture that by this time there were no longer any spectacular gains in the productivity of the textile industry in England but only in the transport industry.

The data for 1868–1901 fall into three distinct periods. The first period is 1868–75 when the unit value is around Re 0.15. A transition period 1876–9 follows when price declines to around Re 0.13 and the quantity imported also increases over this period. The third period is 1880–1901 when unit value fluctuates between Re 0.12 and Re 0.13 and quantities show a cyclical growth. The earlier period 1868–75 constitutes a counter-clockwise loop. The period 1880–1901 has alternate clockwise and counter-clockwise loops. This evidence of some sort of cyclical phenomenon will be looked at in the next section where we discuss some statistical results.

III

In this section, we shall describe the multiple regression results using the data for 1814–32 given in Table 28.1 and the data for 1868–1901 given in Table 28.3. Each regression equation takes the quantity of cloth imported as a function of its 'price'. Since we do not have any price measure, we take the unit value measure obtained by taking the ratio of the value of imports to quantity imported. For narrowly defined items like 'plain calicoes', the unit value measure is a reasonable approximation to price. When it comes to total cloth, we can no longer be so sure. In the absence of anything better, we use it.

Table 28.3
Quantity and Value of Imports of Cloth into India (1868–1901)

Year ending 31 March	Value: Imports of Cotton Goods (in Rupees lakhs)	Quantity: Imports of Cotton Goods (in Yds millions)	Total Govt. Revenues (Million Rs)
(1)	(2)	(3)	(4)
1868	1499.99	957.917	485.3
1869	1607.25	967.813	492.6
1870	1355.58	919.637	509.0
1871	1568.75	1096.242	514.1
1872	1505.88	1011.144	501.1
1873	1460.59	928.064	565.5
1874	1515.57	944.612	564.1
1875	1626.36	1039.036	580.1
1876	1645.02	1186.141	589.6
1877	1599.17	1186.419	586.5
1878	1732.22	1358.861	619.7
1879	1412.68	1127.732	651.9
1880	1691.55	1333.741	684.3
1881	2291.07	1778.507	742.0
1882	2077.21	1624.452	756.8
1883	2143.20	1642.800	702.7
1884	2164.24	1724.096	718.4
1885	2119.74	1734.098	706.9
1886	2111.05	1743.378	744.6
1887	2584.65	2155.713	773.4

(cont.)

Table 1.3 (cont.)

Year ending 31 March	Value: Imports of Cotton Goods (in Rupees lakhs)	Quantity: Imports of Cotton Goods (in Yds millions)	Total Govt. Revenues (Million Rs)
(1)	(2)	(3)	(4)
1888	2392.45	1839.118	787.6
1889	2776.45	2126.553	817.0
1890	2639.14	1997.233	850.8
1891	2724.20	2014.443	857.4
1892	2517.49	1882.884	891.4
1893	2294.20	1808.341	901.7
1894	2926.85	2129.705	905.6
1895	2982.24	2259.427	951.9
1896	2278.48	1717.507	981.3
1897	2642.43	1998.962	822.6
1898	2290.18	1861.849	842.1
1899	2467.81	2070.777	883.2
1900	2700.21	2194.087	892.1
1901	2734.61	2004.568	970.8

Source: Statistical Abstract of British India (various years).

For the period 1814–32, we estimated the quantity-unit value relationship for each of the four categories separately as well as for the total. The results in every case gave a high value for the elasticity estimate. The equations are as follows:

$$\log f_1 = 1.9195 - 3.5685 \log p_1 \quad \bar{R}^2 = 0.9622 \quad DW = 1.68$$
$$(0.2193) \quad (0.1619) \quad \bar{S} = 0.1495$$

$$\log f_2 = 3.8415 - 2.2745 \log p_2 \quad \bar{R}^2 = 0.5712 \quad DW = 1.04$$
$$(0.5673) \quad (0.4352) \quad \bar{S} = 0.2846$$

$$\log f_3 = 3.7445 - 2.1401 \log p_3 \quad \bar{R}^2 = 0.7609 \quad DW = 0.66$$
$$(0.3440) \quad (0.2707) \quad \bar{S} = 0.2449$$

$$\log f_4 = 1.8244 - 2.2973 \log p_4 \quad \bar{R}^2 = 0.4084 \quad DW = 1.31$$
$$(0.6881) \quad (0.5909) \quad \bar{S} = 0.5121$$

$$\log f = 4.9416 - 1.7736 \log p \quad \bar{R}^2 = 0.7152 \quad DW = 1.14$$
$$(0.3232) \quad (0.2516) \quad \bar{S} = 0.2930$$

Here f_1 is calicoes white or plain, f_2 printed calicoes, f_3 white or plain muslins, f_4 printed muslins, and f total of all four items. The variables p_1 to p_4 as well as p are their respective unit values. The figures in parentheses are standard errors of the coefficients, S is the standard error of estimate, $\bar{R}^2$ is the coefficient of determination adjusted for degrees of freedom, and DW is the Durbin–Watson statistic. We have chosen the double-log relationship since it yields elasticity estimates. These elasticities are all high. In the case of all five equations, the estimated elasticity is significantly above unity at the 5 per cent confidence level and except for f_4 also at the 10 per cent confidence level. The elasticity for plain or white calicoes is strikingly high—3.57. The elasticity for printed muslins is also high though with a high standard error and a low $\bar{R}^2$. This confirms what we saw above regarding the contrasting trend of quantities and values of these two items.

We need hardly add that these estimated elasticities are *not* to be confused with the elasticity of the demand curve. They are also not the elasticity of demand for imports. This is because we have failed to account for the possible shift of the demand curve. We have not done this because we do not have any satisfactory measure of income and/or population available, to say nothing of changes in tastes and preferences. What we have estimated is a quantity of imports-unit value elasticity, and no more.

The question of demand shift is important. We try to take account of it for the second period—1868–1901. Our variable representing factors which cause the demand curve to shift is highly unsatisfactory. The only justification for its inclusion is to indicate the dramatic change in the estimated elasticity brought about by its inclusion. The variable is total revenue of the Government of India (TR). TR is a surrogate for shift factors like population and income but has the added merit that there are published annual data for TR for this period. Once again, f is the total import of cloth and p is the unit value. The results for a double-log relationship are:

$$\log f = \begin{array}{cc} 3.5162 & - & 2.5733 \\ (0.0539) & & (0.4016) \end{array} \quad \log p,$$

$$\bar{R}^2 = 0.5346; \quad DW = 0.65; \quad \bar{S} = 0.0893;$$

$$\log f = \begin{array}{cc} 0.1409 & - & 0.8033 \\ (0.3465) & & (0.2713) \end{array} \quad \log p + \begin{array}{c} 1.1024 \log TR, \\ (0.1128) \end{array}$$

$$\bar{R}^2 = 0.8823; \quad DW = 1.87; \quad \bar{S} = 0.0449.$$

In both equations, all the coefficients are significant at the usual 5 per cent level of significance. The coefficient of $\log p$, our elasticity estimate, drops dramatically from 2.57 to 0.80. In the first equation, it is significantly higher than unity at the 1 per cent level significance. In the latter case it is not different from unity. Even given the highly unsatisfactory nature of the shift variable chosen, this does point out the importance of separating the shift of the demand curve from movement along the demand curve. The inclusion of the shift variable also reduces the auto-correlation as indicated by the DW statistic. Some of the clockwise and counter-clockwise loops we mentioned above may be due to the presence of a shift factor.

Can we conclude anything about the elasticity of the demand curve from the above numbers? Let us try and use our formulation in the section I. We had for the case of no shift in the demand curve and the domestic supply curve the following formula:

$$E_{Q,P} = \left(\frac{f}{Q}\right) E_{f,P} + (1 - f/Q) E_{h,P}$$

We have obtained an estimate of $E_{f,P}$: We now need some information *on f/Q* and $E_{h,p}$ to estimate $E_{Q,p}$.

For the earlier period 1814–32, we have tentative estimate of *f/Q* from Ellison. According to him, 'The consumption of cotton goods in India, according to the most recent official authorities, is about 2 ½ lb per head per annum. On this basis the shipments from Great Britain supplied only 3.9 per cent in 1831–35, but 35.3 per cent in 1856–60 and 58.4 per cent in 1880–81.'[8] Ellison arrives at these figures by assuming a population of 150 million for 1831–5, 182 million for 1856–60, and 240 million for 1880–1. Taking 2 ½ lbs per capita per annum as consumption, he gets a figure for total consumption. He estimates imports from Great Britain to be 14.35 million lbs, for 1831–5, 160.42 million lbs. for 1856–60, and 350 million lbs for 1880–1 to arrive at the per cent share or imports for these three periods. He does not cite any sources for his estimates. His population estimates for 1856–60 and 1880–1 are certainly on the low side.[9] For the assumption of 2 ½ lbs per capita per annum, we have no corroborative evidence.

Let us take a figure of 5 per cent as the share of imports for the earlier period. We then have the following relation:

$$E_{Q,P} = 0.05\,(1.77) + 0.95\,(E_{h,P}) = 0.0885 + 0.95\,(E_{h,P}).$$

In order for the elasticity of demand $E_{Q,P}$ substantially above one, we also need the domestic supply elasticity to be fairly high. A supply elasticity of unity will yield an estimated demand elasticity of 1.04 only. If the domestic supply curve is highly elastic, then the reduction in demand for home-produced cloth due to imports will be all the greater. To maintain its competitive position in terms of output and the number of people employed will require a massive rightward shift of the supply curve.

We do not have any hard evidence on the elasticity of the domestic supply curve. Morris himself thinks that the domestic supply curve was inelastic. He cites the evidence of early European travellers and English factory records. Given the primitive technology and low per-loom productivity his presumption is in favour of an inelastic supply curve.[10] Given our elasticity relationships above, low elasticity of supply would lead to a presumption in favour of low elasticity of demand.

[8] T. Ellison (1968), *The Cotton Trade of Great Britain,* 1866, reprinted by Frank Cass and Co., London, p. 63.

[9] Prof. M. Mukherjee in *National Income of India,* chapter 2, cites Kingsley Davis's estimate for 1856 as 175 million but he himself revises it to 227 million. For 1871, he accepts Davis's estimate of 255 million.

[10] Morris, 'Towards a Reinterpretation of Nineteenth Century Indian Economic History', p. 6, fn. 14. Also see T. Raychaudhuri's reply in the same issue, p. 85, fn. 11.

IV

Our relationship above, however, is based on the assumption of no shifts of the demand curve and the domestic supply curve. We have also assumed perfect substitutability of domestic and foreign cloth. We have already referred to the lack of data on factors causing shifts of the demand and supply curves. In the absence or such data, any discussion can only be highly speculative. But two points can be made on these speculative lines.

Demand Shift

Over a short period of 19 years during 1814–32, it would not seem very likely that income, population, and tastes would change very much. This observation should be qualified somewhat, however. Consumption of imported cloth must have been concentrated in the three Presidency areas. We should really talk only about population and income shifts in these three regions. Is there any presumption that they were changing rapidly in these years? Ellison's calculation is based on no shift of the per capita demand curve, but even if we allow for a 100 per cent growth of per capita cloth consumption from 1¼ lbs. In 1831–5 to 2½ lbs. in 1880–1, it will only raise the share of imports to less than 10 per cent. We are concerned here with the shift within the period 1814–32.

Supply Shift

The supply curve for domestic cloth may have shifted to the right for several reasons. Morris mentions two factors: more people specializing in full-time hand loom weaving analogous to an increase in the number of firms in the industry; availability of cheaper yarn from England. This would lead to a once-and-for-all drop in yarn cost for a weaver switching from domestic yarn to cheaper imported yarn and then to a steady decline in yarn cost as the price went down due to higher productivity in the English spinning industry. For the industry as a whole these two factors would be fused together since the adoption of cheaper yarn would be spaced out over time for different weavers. Let us assume that the introduction of competitive imported yarn also brings down the price of domestic yarn, due to a combination of the factors similar to those listed above. The third factor is the one pointed out by Professor Bipan Chandra—the decline in the subsistence level of the weavers. All these factors and many more could have caused a rightward shift of the supply curve. Any assessment of their relative importance can only be made with quantitative information which is not available. A theoretical discussion can, however, bring out the sort of magnitudes involved.

The price of cloth, domestic or foreign, is made up of labour cost, cost of yarn, and cost of capital and other material inputs. A change in price is made up of changes in the cost components appropriately weighted. For example, a change in the unit labour cost would be made up of a change in wage rates and a change in labour productivity. This would be weighted by the share of unit labour cost in price to give the appropriate change in price. It is better to put all this down formally.

Notation:

p	=	price of cloth;
pm	=	price of yarn, identical for foreign and domestic by assumption;
l	=	labour input;
k	=	capital and other material inputs;
m	=	yarn input;
q	=	output;
w	=	wage rate;
v	=	price of capital and other material inputs;
h and f	=	subscripts for domestic and foreign;
ulc	=	unit labour cost equal to $(l/q)w$;
umc	=	unit material cost equal to $(m/q)pm$;
ukc	=	unit capital cost equal to $(k/q)v$;

$$p_h = ulc_h + umc_h + ukc_h$$
$$= \left(\frac{1}{q}\right)_h w_h + \left(\frac{m}{q}\right)_h pm + \left(\frac{k}{q}\right)_h v_h$$
$$p_f = ulc_f + umc_f + ukc_f$$
$$= \left(\frac{1}{q}\right)_f w_f + \left(\frac{m}{q}\right)_f pm + \left(\frac{k}{q}\right)_f v_f.$$

The proportionate rate of change in these prices is then made up of the rates of change of input costs. We use the notation dp_h/p_h, dp/p_f, etc., for denoting the proportionate rate of change in these variables. With a little manipulation, we can express the rates of change of these two prices as follows:

$$(dp/p)_h = (ulc/p)_h (dulc/ulc)_h + (umc/p)_h (dumc/umc)_h + (ukc/p)_h (dukc/ukc)_h$$

Similarly for $(dp/p)_f$. This equation can also be written in percentage change terms as follows:

percentage change in cloth price
= share of unit labour cost in price x per cent change in unit labour cost
+ share of unit yarn cost in price x per cent change in unit yarn cost
+ share of unit capital cost in price x per cent change in unit capital cost.

We have information on changes in the price of imported cloth, the price of imported yarn, unit labour cost in England, and also some sketchy information on the shares of the different cost components in price from Ellison.[11] Bipan Chandra has already cited some of this evidence in his comment.[12] If domestic cloth retained its competitive position, and/or if we assume perfect substitutability, the per cent change in the two prices should be equal. Thus, $(dp/p)_h = (dp/p)_f$. We can substitute the value of $(dp/p)_f$ in the $(dp/p)_h$ equation and look at the

[11] Ellison, *The Cotton Trade of Great Britain*, pp. 57–70.
[12] Bipan Chandra, 'Reinterpretation of Nineteenth Century Indian Economic History', pp. 55–60.

implied change. Let us first assume that the share of cost of capital etc. in the price of domestic cloth was negligible and that there was no change in the unit capital cost. The shares of labour, yarn, and capital costs in English textile manufacturing are given as 35 per cent, 21 per cent, and 44 per cent respectively for 1829–21 and 1829–31 by Ellison.[13] One would hypothesize that while the share of yarn was no different, the share of labour must be 70 per cent or more, and the share of capital 10 per cent or less in India.

Between 1819–21 and 1829–31 the price of English cloth went down from 70.3d per lb to 40.6d per lb, a drop of 30d from an initial price of 70.3d (40 per cent) or from an average price of 55d (about 55 per cent). By our assumption, to maintain a competitive position, domestic cloth prices should have declined equally. Let us take the lower figure of a 40 per cent drop. Given the share of yarn cost equal to 20 per cent, the percentage change in unit yarn cost needs to be estimated. This is made up of two elements. One is the per cent change in the price of yarn, which for this period from Ellison's data, cited by Bipan Chandra, works out at roughly 50 per cent, (from 29.0d per lb in 1819–21 to 15.3d per lb in 1829–31). The second element is the per cent change in the ratio of yarn input to cloth output. Since there is no evidence of any dramatic change in technology, we can take this as negligible. We have, therefore, the following equation:

Per cent change in price of cloth = share of unit labour cost x per cent change in unit labour cost + share of yarn cost x per cent change in unit yarn cost.

40 per cent = 0.70 (per cent change in unit labour cost) + 0.20 (50 per cent).

To maintain a competitive position, the required per cent change in unit labour cost over 10 years from 1819–2l to 1829–31 for Indian handloom weavers can be worked out at:

$$\text{Per cent change in unit labour cost} = \frac{40 \text{ per cent} - 0.20 \,(50 \text{ per cent})}{0.70} = 43 \text{ per cent}.$$

Now per cent change in unit labour costs is also made up of two elements. One is the per cent change in money wages and the other the per cent change in labour productivity. Together they have to make up a 43 per cent drop over 10 years. In order for wages not to decline over the 10 years, productivity will have to rise by 43 per cent. Is this plausible?

These calculations are, of course, full of heroic assumptions. If we take a specific type of cloth which India imported rather than the general category, the conclusions will not change much. If we take plain or white calicoes and muslins, the price of these went down from 11.15d per yd. in 1821 to 6.09d per yd., which is a drop in the region of 35 to 40 per cent. It is not the particular price series we choose that matters but the enormous gap in our knowledge of the other factors concerned. As already mentioned, these discussions are only speculative. Much more information is needed on the regional pattern of demand and output, the quality composition of output, income, and population changes.

---

[13] Ellison, *The Cotton Trade of Great Britain*, p. 69.

V

One part of Morris's argument related to the need for applying tools of economic theory and quantitive techniques to the study of Indian economic history. We fully agree with this. We have tried to apply these tools to the problem of elasticity of the demand curve. We find, however, that these tools do not necessarily yield any strong conclusions. They point out the need for more historical data and cannot be a substitute for them.

One negative conclusion we reach is that it is difficult to say much about the elasticity of the demand curve for cotton cloth in India. Available data on quantities imported show a high elasticity with respect to their unit values. But the leap from this to the demand curve is fraught with problems. A dramatic shift outwards in the demand curve is enough to throw doubt on even the estimated elasticity between import quantities and unit values. While we cannot say much about shifts in the supply curve, it seems that we equally cannot infer much about the state of the domestic industry from *a priori* notions about the elasticity of the demand curve. In fact, the elasticity of the demand curve for imported cloth is a function of the elasticity of the domestic supply curve and nor the other way around.

If we are to relax some of the highly restrictive assumptions made at the beginning of this paper, our data requirements increase. But correspondingly, we get a better and more realistic picture of the interaction of British and Indian textile industries. While it is not our task here to sketch out a complete model, some suggestions can be made about future work:

(a)   To relax the hypothesis of perfect substitutability between foreign and domestic cloth, we need data on price and output of domestic hand loom cloth. This is clearly impossible in the near future. A beginning can be made by estimating handloom output by taking data on cotton output and converting it into yarn and cloth output, assuming some simple technical coefficients. Wherever data on imported yarn are available (as they are in MacGregor as well as in the statistical Abstract of British India), they can be added to the estimate of domestic yarn output to obtain an index of domestic hand loom cloth output. The relationship between cotton to yarn to handloom cloth is direct for the first half of the nineteenth century. For the second half, the Indian factory production of yarn and cloth has to be taken into account. Given an output index, we can introduce a domestic output as an additional variable in the import quantity equation to obtain some quantity cross elasticities between imported and domestic cloth.

(b)   The data on imports for the earlier period relate to a region larger than India. There are some data on cloth imported into the three principal ports. These may help us construct regional import data. These regional data can then be added up to give the national total or we may assume that these markets were separate and study the interaction of the foreign and domestic cloth industries in each region separately. This will require construction of regional cotton output and cloth output indices.

(c)   The British supply curve of cloth can be estimated from British data. This will make the import price a function of wage–productivity relationships in the British textile industry.

(d)   More data are needed on income and population trends nationally or at regional levels for this entire period. Some of our demand equations need to be recalculated with these variables.

These requirements are not impossible. They are necessary because we can formulate the problem of the Indian handloom industry only in a simultaneous equations model of British factory, Indian handloom, and Indian factory textile industries. In order to formulate the model properly, we must also relate it to the growth/stagnation of the economy as a whole. All this is agenda for further research.

29

Macro Econometric Models for India
A Survey

Macro econometric model building is now a well established part of economic research. Following the pioneering efforts of Tinbergen and Klein, models have been constructed for many countries for various time periods. These models have grown in size and in sophistication. For the US economy, several small annual and many large quarterly econometric models are available. The Brookings–SSRC model, the FRB–MIT model, the Wharton–EFU model, and the Department of Commerce–OBE model readily come to mind. For the UK economy, after an initial dearth of econometric models, the Klein–Ball–Hazelwood–Vandome quarterly model has now been followed by the London Business School model, the National Institute of Economic and Social Research model and the Southampton model, among others. Similar examples can be cited for Canada, Netherlands, Greece, Japan, Australia, Colombia, etc.[1]

The purpose of this chapter is to survey some of the models constructed for the Indian economy. Our coverage will be of the Tinbergen–Klein type of simultaneous

Sankhya: The Indian Journal of Statistics, Series B, vol. 35, Part 2, June 1973.

This paper forms a part of the Econometric Model Project for India headed by Professor Nagar. It was written during my stay at the Delhi School of Economics as a Visiting Fellow during 1970–1. I am grateful to Professor A.L. Nagar, Dr D.B. Gupta, and M.S. Ramanujam. I am especially thankful to Dr K. Krishnamurty, who first suggested that I write this Survey, for lending me his library of unpublished material and for his help and comments at various stages. The anonymous referees made many helpful comments which helped in revising the original draft.

[1] While it is not possible to list all models, a few examples can be given. For USA: (a) Duesenberry et al. (1963), *The Brookings Econometric Model of the United State*, Rand McNally, New York; (b) De Leeuw and Gramlich (1968), 'The FRB–MIT Model', *Federal Reserve Bulletin*, February. (c) Klein and Evans (1968), *The Wharton Econometric Forecasting Model*, University of Pennsylvania, Philadelphia, Pa. For UK: (a) Klein, Ball, Hazelwood and Vandome (1960), *An Econometric Model of the U.K. Economy*, OUP, Oxford, (b) Hilton and Heathfield (eds) (1970), *The Econometric Study of the U.K. Economy*, MacMillan, London, for an account of the NIESR, LBS, and Southampton models, For models of less developed countries: (a) Klein and Behrman (Brazil) in Eltis (ed.) (1970), Induction, Trade and Growth, *Essays in honour of Sir Roy Harrod*, OUP, Oxford, (b) Thorbecke (Columbia) (1968), *The Theory and Design of Economic Development*, edited by Adelman and Thorbecke, Johns Hopkins University Press, Baltimore, Maryland.

equation macro econometric models. Programming models of which there are quite a few for India, will not be dealt with here.[2] Nerlove[3] has surveyed many of the published models for the developed countries. Our survey is, however, confined mainly to unpublished works. Most, if not all of these are the results of Ph.D. dissertations but they are not all available in the forms of articles or books. An annotated list of the models being surveyed here is given in Appendix 29.1.

As will be apparent from the list in Appendix 29.1, there is substantial evidence of activity on the model building front. We have listed eight items only, one of which—Narasimham's model—was published before the 1960s. All the other models are of similar vintage. As a collection, their intellectual origins are also remarkably similar. Thus some of the items cited in Appendix 29.1 have been Ph.D. dissertations under the guidance of Tinbergen, Klein or their students. The rest of the items by these authors are along the lines of their Ph.D. dissertations. If models were to be classified like thoroughbreds, these are clearly from the Tinbergen–Klein stable.

These models are also constructed from data which overlap in time. Narasimham, Marwah, and Choudhry take their data from pre-independence as well as for post-independence years. Krishnamurty, Agarwala, Mammen and Krishnamurty–Choudhry confine themselves to the post-independence period of 1947 onwards. All the models use annual time series data. Use of annual time series data means a rather small size sample. All the models have been constructed with less than 30 observations. This lack of data availability has forced the authors to adopt certain simplifications. As we shall see later, they tend to use dummy variables often for overcoming this problem and they are also restricted from using simultaneous equation techniques like 3SLS, FIML. In all cases, estimation is by some single–equation technique, OLS, 2SLS, or LIML.

All the models cover the economy as a whole.[4] But within this general framework there are considerable differences. Thus, Choudhry and Narasimham specify their expenditure equations in nominal terms while Marwah, Krishnamurty, and Mammen specify them in real terms. Agarwala's system is built on different lines, though he too has an investment function and import demand function in real terms. While all the other systems are income–expenditure models with

[2] See for example Alan Manne and Ashok Rudra (1965), 'A Consistency Model of India's Fourth Plan', *Sankhya*, B. 27, 57–144.

[3] Marc Nerlove (1965), 'Two Models of the British Economy: Fragments of Critical Survey', *International Economic Review*, May .

[4] There are many sectoral models of the Indian economy we have ignored in this survey. For example, M. Dutta's study of Indian imports (University of Pennsylvania, 1962), M. Handa's study of imports of chemicals (Ph.D. dissertation, University of London, 1969), V.K. Sastry's study of corporate investment (Ph.D. dissertation, University of Pennsylvania, 1965), S. Chakravarti's model of inflation (Ph.D. dissertation, University of London, 1971), V. Pandit's inflation model (Ph.D. dissertation, University of Pennsylvania, 1971), Khusro and Siddarthan, 'Model of Banking', (Institute of Economic Growth, Delhi, 1971). Two macro models which have come to our attention since writing this survey are P.K. Pani (1971) 'Some Aspects of Macro Modelling of Indian Economy', University of Pennsylvania, and B.B. Bhattacharya (1971), 'The Role of Real and Monetary Factors in short Term Determination of Income in India', (Ph.D. dissertation, University of Delhi).

greater or less coverage of prices and money market, Agarwala's system is built on the lines of W.A. Lewis's two-sector growth model[5] with feedback from agriculture to industry. As such, for him price equations and expenditure equations are only a means of closing the model. Krishnamurty's model is specified entirely in real terms and there is no explanation for the price level in his model. On the other hand, Krishnamurty's model (also that of Krishnamurty–Choudhry) is unique in having an endogenous explanation of population growth. Mammen's thesis has the most explicit treatment of the monetary sector but all the other models except Narasimham's have equations of interest-rate structure and/or demand for money.

Anticipating some of the discussion later on, we should like to suggest that these various models should be seen as explorations in specification for the economic relationships valid for the Indian economy. The bulk of each study constitutes the OLS results derived by their authors and discussions of the conformity of the OLS results with prior expectations in terms of signs, R^2, etc. While estimation by 2SLS or LIML is attempted, the emphasis is not on estimation but on specification. This is evident in treatment of non-linearities. Since some equations are in money terms, some in real terms, non-linearities are present in these models. Also as in Agarwala, Mammen, and Krishnamurty's population equations, some equations are in log-linear form and others in actual value of variables. Ratios, percentages, products all appear in these models but are all treated as linear variables. The problems of autocorrelation in the errors are also, by and large, ignored.

Before concluding these introductory remarks, another aspect of these models should be pointed out. All the models are fairly large in size, not perhaps by Brookings–SSRC standards, but by standards of most existing models. They are on an average models of 20 equations or more. Krishnamurty's model has 21 equations, Marwah's 47 equations, Mammen's 24 equations, and Choudhry's final model has 22 equations. The smallness of sample size has not constrained these model builders though it has forced them into adopting single equation estimation techniques. The size as well as the presence of non-linearities has meant that the authors have not always been able to evaluate the reduced forms of their models. Except Choudhry, most authors have preferred to explore the dynamics of their estimated models by numerical solution and simulation rather than by explicit treatment of impact and dynamic multipliers.

A substantial hurdle in the task of model building for the Indian economy (as for most less developed countries) is that the model builder has to be also his own data producer. Often, data are unavailable, partially available, and scattered in different places in addition to being subject to frequent revisions and often being very unreliable. On items such as capital formation or employment, the model builder has to construct his own series from raw data. Continuous series have to be built up by patching up together two or three shorter series. Some variables have long continuous series while others may be available only since the early 1950s. In these circumstances, model builders have the choice of either reducing all equations to the common (shorter) time period or to have different equations

---

[5] W.A. Lewis, *Economic Developments with Unlimited Supplies of Labour*, Manchester School Manchester: University of Manchester, 1954.

estimated for different time periods in the model. In general, all the model builders have chosen the latter alternative.

As already mentioned above, many of these models were built as part of a Ph.D. dissertation. The influence of this circumstance on the model builders cannot be exaggerated. A Ph.D. student is denied the benefits of team work. He is often short of money and in a hurry to finish. Precedents in the literature weigh heavily and he has no time to break out in original directions. If a certain specification 'works' he may not have the patience or the time to improve it further in the light of newer developments in economic theory or estimation theory. He is very unlike other model builders who may be writing a monograph with the Ph.D. behind them. Many of the models for US, UK, or Japan fall outside the Ph.D. category.

Sometimes, the paucity and unreliability of time series data have been sought to be compensated by the use of cross-section data. Agarwala uses cross-section data from the Farm Management Survey for different states and the Census of Manufacturing Industry data to estimate cross-section production function as a check on returns-to-scale estimates. The evidence of a low and often negative coefficient of labour in the agricultural production function based on the cross-section Farm Management Survey determines his specification of the agricultural production function. Marwah has also used cross-section data for estimation of import demand functions in the extension of her original model. Available cross-section data such as National Sample Survey (NSS) data on consumer expenditure, Reserve Bank of India (RBI) data on investments, or state-wise data on many agricultural and industrial variables have not, however, been exploited by the authors. A thorough exploration of these data remains one of the primary tasks of any future attempts at model building in India.

These models together cover a long period (1920–65) and many far-reaching changes have taken place in the economic and political life of the country in that period. Can one say that the structure of the Indian economy was unchanged over the entire period? This question of structural change is crucial to model building. There is a clear break in the role of government in accumulation and growth, a much higher level of investment, and reshaping of foreign trade patterns in 1950s. One may say that the coming of independence (1947) or the beginning of planning (1951) represents a structural break. Political independence did change the context of government policy and potentially the government had a wide range of choices in shaping economic policy. The pre-independence period also requires an artificial splitting up of the data for Undivided India into data for Indian Union and Pakistan. For matters such as movement of food grains, export earnings, and industrial growth, any separation is meaningless. One may regard the year of independence as a watershed. The need for longer time series has led model builders to minimize the importance of this change and they have been able to construct related series for the earlier period. With the availability of about 20 and more observations now, we may be able to do away with the use of earlier data. An alternative may be to construct a model for undivided India for years up to 1947 and see whether a separate model for Indian Union for the earlier period can be meaningfully separated from the larger model.

There is a less clear possibility of structural change in the post-1947 phase. Thus, while plan strategies changed over years, the years after 1964–5 show the persisting crucial role of food grains output, capital inflow, and government investment activity even after (or perhaps because of) the strain of two famines. There is a limited scope for testing for structural change in the 1950s and 1960s. Cross-section data may also aid in checking for structural change over the sample period. Thus, it is expedient and perhaps not too far wrong to regard the period 1947–8 up to date as a homogeneous time period.

One problem which faces the model builder concerned with less developed countries is the choice of an appropriate theoretical framework. It is not just that one frequently encounters assertions to the effect that Western economic theory built on premises prevalent in developed countries is unsuitable to the underdeveloped dual economy. A controversy surrounds the applicability of the Keynesian models for underdeveloped countries.[6] With reference to Indian conditions, a substantial body of literature has grown up in this respect. Whatever the merits of the different views in the controversy, the model builder is under a special handicap because most of the available published or unpublished econometric models are built round a Keynesian theoretical framework. The income–expenditure relationship, e.g. the consumption function, investment function, and wage bill–profit division, are the important relationships in the model. More is known about the econometric specifications of these relationships than about those arising out of some non-Keynesian model such as Arthur Lewis' two-sector growth model with unlimited supplies of labour. National income statisticians too, adopt the income–expenditure framework in presenting their data. Among the available econometric models, few are growth-oriented. The choice of a Keynesian framework for model building seems, therefore, obvious and, given data availability, logical. The question remains, however, whether the Keynesian categories represent causally important variables in an economy where development is to be generated deliberately and where failure of accumulation effort may be the main obstacle to growth.

Of the eight models surveyed, only one—Agarwala's model—is built round an explicitly non-Keynesian framework. Agarwala has taken Arthur Lewis' model of development with unlimited supplies of labour as his framework. His disaggregation is according to industry–agriculture division. His main concern is with outputs of the two sectors and the link from agriculture to industry through surplus foodgrains supply to provide employment in industrial sector. Apart from investment and import functions, his model does not have any expenditure relationship. All the other models have been built with disaggregation primarily in terms of expenditure categories. They also have output equations and price relationships but as we shall see later, the causal mechanism is Keynesian in nature.

The major objection to the Keynesian approach for an underdeveloped economy is that while inadequacy of aggregate effective demand is the primary cause of

---

[6] See for example, V.K.R.V. Rao (1952), 'Investments Income and the Multiplier in an Underdeveloped Economy', *Indian Economic Review* and L.R. Klein (1965), 'What Kind of Macro Econometric Models for Developing Economies', *Indian Economic Journal*.

unemployment in the model, underdeveloped economies have structural unemployment due to lack of complementary inputs, e.g. capital. Obstacles to capital accumulation are only partly on the demand side but mainly the problem is one of mobilizing hidden surpluses to step up the rate of accumulation. There is no idle capacity which can be activated by deficit spending.

Realistic models of course have to be much more detailed than either of the simplistic alternatives outlined above. Thus, even the Lewis model does not spell out the role of Government as an agent for growth or the importance of capital inflow. Its picture of the agricultural sector is quite abstract and the intersectoral flows are rather sketchily outlined. Questions of money, prices, and sectoral demand–supply balances have to be figured out by the model builder. Whichever framework the model builder adopts there are large uncharted areas for him to pioneer. If he adopts a Keynesian framework he has some sort of map to guide him. Since the earlier discussions of applicability of the Keynesian model were carried out in non-empirical terms this collection of models could be studied to answer that question in a much more concrete fashion. This shall be one of the major themes in our survey of the results of those models, to which task we must now turn.

The eight models being surveyed are described in the annotated bibliography in Appendix 29.1. Appendix 29.2 provides a standard notation for the variables used in the various models. Appendix 29.3 lists all the equations of each of the eight models in the standard notation of Appendix 29.2. In our description of the results, we shall follow the numbering of equations in Appendix 29.3. As we have said in Appendix 29.3, only OLS results are listed unless they were unavailable. Our concern here is mainly with the specification of the equations and the causal structure of the models. We shall have only a few remarks regarding estimation problems.

We shall often have to divide our models into Keynesian and non-Keynesian categories. This is because Agarwala's model is in some respects different from all the other models. Narasimham's model is also dissimilar in some respects from the other six Keynesian models. But since it follows a Keynesian disaggregation of expenditure items, we shall club it together with the others. If our statements apply to both these groups, we shall explicitly say so. Otherwise, generalization will be made about one or the other group.

The first overriding impression while surveying these models is the great similarity in their structures. There are differences in the degree of disaggregation. Thus Mammen has a large explicit monetary sector, Marwah has sectoral and aggregate price relationships, while Krishnamurty alone has an endogenous population variable. In their specification of investment function, consumption function, demand for money, and structure of interest rates equations, these models are remarkable in similarity.

Thus, regarding consumption function, Narasimham (A29.3.8.6) and Choudhry A29.3.2.3a,b) specify their relationships in terms of nominal values while all the others do so in real terms. The choice of independent variables is, of course, similar. Choudhry and Marwah (A29.3.6.1 and A29.3.7.1) have liquid asssets in their functions—Marwah with a lag of two years and deflated by current price level. Krishnamurty (A29.3.3.l) and Mammen (A29.3.5.1) have ignored the liquidity variable. Krishnamurty has a distributional variable—the ratio of non-agricultural to agricultural income—with a positive coefficient. Narasimham has the most elaborate distributional breakdown between non-farm labour income, farm income net of tax, and profits of unincorporated business. In this respect, his consumption function is closest to the Klein–Goldberger specification and the Tinbergen specification.

The population variable has a rather uncertain role in these consumption functions. Thus, Choudhry obtains a negative and significant coefficient for the population variable in his consumption function (2.3a), while Marwah obtains a positive but non-significant coefficient. Krishnamurty's consumption function is specified in per capita terms but he gets a non-significant declining trend. For some of the single equation specifications in his Ph.D. thesis (not listed in Appendix 29.3 here) Krishnamurty also noticed a negative but non-significant coefficient for population. Krishnamurty and Choudhry specify private dispos-able income while Marwah and Mammen stick to some Net National Product (NNP) measure. In their attempts to specify distributional variable, especially as regards farm and non-farm income, some attempt has been made to adapt the consumption function to Indian conditions. It is unclear, however, which way one's *a priori* expectation is about the sign of such a distributional variable. We have to check cross-section evidence regarding any marked difference in the propensity to save of these two sectors in India. The role of inflation and of the growing resort to indirect taxation by the Government of India also needs to be evaluated in these functions. In this field, we have sample cross-section data available, although their reliability is sometimes questionable. The NSS data on household expenditure and the National Council of Applied Economic Research (NCAER) data on savings can be used in this respect.[7] The changing patterns of consumption, especially as between food grains and other items, need to be identified as does the rural–urban differential.

While we shall not carry out a comparative survey of each relationship, one would like to do a similar analysis for the investment function. All the eight models specify investment functions. Krishnamurty (eqns A29.3.2 to A29.3.4) specifies separate investment functions for machinery and equipment, construc-tion, and inventories (all private). Agarwala disaggregates private investment into agricultural and non-agricultural. Choudhry (eqns A29.3.2.4a, A29.3.2.5b, and A29.3.2.5c) specifies the total investment at first and then confines himself to private investment. Marwah follows up a total investment function A29.3.6.2) with total and government investment functions (eqns A29.3.7.2, A29.3.7.3, and A29.3.7.4). Mammen A29.3.5.2) and Narasimham A29.3.8.7) have private investment functions without any disaggregation. Both the accelerator and profit versions are tried. Krishnamurty, Mammen, and Narasimham have profit as an independent variable. Narasimham specifies corporate as well as non-corporate profits net of tax while the other two have only corporate profits. Agarwala

---

[7] National Sample Survey, Survey of Consumer's Expenditure (various rounds); National Council of Applied Economic Research (1965), *Savings in India*, Asia Publishing House.

specifies sectoral income net of taxes. Mawah tries output in both her specifications. Choudhry tries private disposable income as well as total income but finally plumps for profits.

In view of the crucial importance of imports of capital goods in making up investment expenditure, it is surprising that only Mammen and Marwah (in eqn. A29.3.7.2) specify import of machinery and equipment and inflow of capital as independent variables. In view of the extensive government controls on private investment in the 1950s and later, it is also surprising that only Agarwala specifies the total amount of capital issues licensed as an independent variable. In fact, all the investment functions are demand functions. In view of the government restrictions, the limited capacity of the domestic capital goods sector (as witnessed by frequent complaints of shortage of steel and cement) and the need for imports of capital goods constrained by foreign exchange availability, one would expect the investment function to be supply-constrained where the demand may be assumed to be quite high once the government has embarked the economy on an investment programme. While a number of other variables are specified such as capacity utilization in the economy, liquidity, and capital–output ratio, all these are demand factors. The outputs of producer goods industries plus imports may give a better idea of the relationship.

A related problem is the comparative neglect of government investment. As already mentioned above, only Marwah (eqn. A29.3.7.3) specifies a separate government investment function. But even there, the available prior information on the government investment programmes as specified in the plans is not used. Government investment remains exogenous for most of the models and the constraints—budgetary and real—on government investment are nowhere specified.

The quality of data is an acute problem in investment analysis. The stock adjustment types of hypotheses have not been tried by any of the authors because of the paucity of data. Capital stock data are scarce and only point estimates of capital stock are available. A time series of gross investment further classified by sectors and into private and government is available. Capital stock time series have to be constructed with some estimates of depreciation combined with the gross investment series. This has also an important bearing on the specification of the production function. Only Choudhry has used capital stock as a variable in the investment function. Agarwala uses capital stock as a variable in his production function as does Marwah. Krishnamurty has an ingenious device for deriving estimate of initial capital stock from his production function as we shall see later. He is, therefore, not plagued by non-availability of stock figures but he does not specify them in his investment function.

In general, this lack of data has meant that the lag specification of the investment function is very weak in all the models. Here again, the RBI data on corporate investment which are available in single year cross-sections continuously since the early 1950s can be of great help in understanding the dynamics as well as the impact of government regulatory measures and foreign exchange constraints. Lags due to delays in licensing procedures at various stages should also be examined. A combination of investment intentions as indicated by license applications and the various stages to fulfilment of investment plans on the lines of Jorgensen's study can be very useful in seeing the stage at which at procedural delays, against supply constraints, become binding.

We would like now to take up the nature of aggregate supply constraints in these models. We shall first see how the supply side is specified in the models and then see the causal interaction between the aggregate demand and aggregate supply. Supply constraints appear mainly as production function and price equations in these models, Thus, Narasimham's model specifies supply curves as price equations and so does Choudhry in his first model. The other models combine some production function with price equations. Agarwala has two production functions—one each for agricultural and non-agricultural income—and this division is present in the Krishnamurty–Choudhry models and in the later model of Marwah. Agarwala's (eqn. A29.3.1.1) agricultural production function is specified in terms of capital stock in agriculture and a measure of the effects of rainfall. The capital stock in agriculture includes government as well as private capital stock (Agarwala 1970, p. 79). Choudhry (eqn. A29.3.2.2b) includes rainfall and employment in agriculture as a constant proportion (0.71) of total employment. It is difficult to see the logic of this, especially since, as far as we can ascertain, Choudhry has used Narasimham's employment index and the latter defines it only as including railway and factory personnel. Choudhry finds the coefficient of agricultural employment negative and significant. His findings are similar to Agarwala's cross-section results. Krishnamurty (eqn. A29.3.3.5) has included gross cropped acreage and the per cent of area irrigated as his two independent variables. Both these variables are assumed to be exogenous in his model. In a later revision, the Krishnamurty–Choudhry model (eqn. A29.3.4.5 and A29.3.4.6) makes the irrigated acreage an endogenous variable, thus tying it to the rest of the model.

Industrial production functions are included by Choudhry, Krishnamurty, and Agarwala. Choudhry in his first model and Marwah in her second model have an aggregate production function. Marwah's second model (eqn. A29.3.7.5) relates real NNP to lagged capital stock multiplied by a utilization index, The utilization index in turn is a function of lagged values of income velocity of money, stock–output ratio of manufactured goods, and its utilization. The utilization index is thus a demand determined variable. Aggregate output in this model is then a function of pre-determined variables. In Choudhry's model 1, the production function is linear and the independent variables are current capital stock and employment, both of which have coefficients with t ratios below two. Agarwala (eqn. A29.3.1.4) has a constant returns to scale Cobb-Douglas production function for industrial output.

Krishnamurty (eqn. A29.3.3.6) has a linear production function in capital stock times utilization and employment. As we have mentioned before, Krishnamurty estimates initial capital stock as a parameter. His method can be illustrated as follows:

$$Y_{nagt} = a_0 + a_1 \left(\frac{K_{nagt} + K_{nagt-1}}{2} \right) U_{nagt} + a_2 N_{nagt} + e_t.$$

Now
$$K_{nagt} = K_0 + \sum_{\tau=1}^{t} I_{nag\tau}$$

So we write

$$Y_{nagt} = a_0 + a_1 \left(K_0 + \frac{\overset{t}{\Sigma} I_{nagt} + \overset{t}{\Sigma} I_{nagt-1}}{2} \right) U_{nagt} + a_2 N_{nagt} + e_t.$$

$$= a_0 + (a_1 K_0) U_{nagt} + a_1 \left(\frac{\overset{t}{\Sigma} I_{nagt} + \overset{t}{\Sigma} I_{nagt-1}}{2} \right) U_{nagt} + a_2 N_{nagt} + e_t.$$

K_0 can then be derived from the coefficient estimates of a_1 and of $a_1 K_0$. Mammen has no production function in his model, nor does Marwah in her first model.

We can now go on to consider the role of the supply constraint in each of these models. For this purpose, it is best to give a separate treatment to each model in some detail. We can begin with Mammen's model. As far as one can see, there is no supply constraint in his model. The expenditure equations for consumption, investment, and imports are all in real terms and they determine the real value of NNP except for the exogenous variables—government expenditure and exports—and the endogenous variable indirect taxes net of subsidies. The implicit price deflator is determined by agricultural prices (eqns A29.3.5.7 and A29.3.5.8 and also in a non-linear fashion in eqns A29.3.5.7, A29.3.5.8a, A29.3.5.8b, and A29.3.5.8c). The role of the implicit price deflator seems to be to bring about the adjustment between real and monetary values of G, F_e, and T_i, where T_i stands for indirect taxes. The role of the real NNP Identity (eqn. 5a) seems to be determined by Y_{nag}, given exogenous values of Y_{ag}. Then Y_{nag} determines the level of real profits. Thus, the role of price equation as an implicit supply equation is to determine the real value of minor items G, F_e, and T_i. It does not affect C, I, or F_m.

In Marwah's first model, we have only all aggregate price level equation in terms of change in the money value of NNP or in terms of the gap between actual and desired level of money stock. The desired level of money stock is decided by the rate of change of income velocity and of real output multiplied by initial money stock. The only role of the price level is once again to bridge the gap between the money and real value of the catch-all variable H which equals NNP less C and I. The price level in turn also influences sectoral prices but there is no feedback from sectoral price level.

In Krishnamurty's model, total real income is determined by the expenditure equations which all in real terms. The agricultural production function gives the value of agricultural output which as we have seen above is a function of predetermined variables alone. One of the two NNP identities (eqn. A29.3.3.17) along with the value of Y_{ag} gives Y_{nag}. The production function for Y_{nag} (eqn. A29.3.3.6) then only determines the demand for labour in the non-agricultural sector. Thus, Krishnamurty's model, like those of Mammen and Marwah, is a pure Keynesian model where aggregate real effective demand gives the value of NNP and that in turn determines the level of employment in non-agricultural sector. This combined with a real wage level which is determined by a trend gives the level of corporate profits.

In Choudhry's first model, the multiplier process determines the nominal value of national income. The aggregate production function gives the real value of output and the interaction of these two magnitudes determines the price level. However, the price level in its turn affects real output since it determines the real value of current investment which enters current capital stock which affects output. This pattern is continued in the other models. The only other effect of price level is on the components of aggregate demand via its influence on the demand for liquid assets. In Choudhry's model, supply constraints act on the income determination process through the price level. The price level plays an equilibrating role by affecting output as well as demand.

Supply equations are reflected in the price variable in Narasimham's model. Expenditure equations give the money value of national income. The only influence of price level on expenditure is through its influence on real wage rate and then via the wage bill upon the level of profits which influence C' (consumption), I' (investment). Price level is determined by import price, agricultural prices, and real wage rate. In combination with money level of national income, the price level gives us the real level of national income; the relative price of consumption to investment goods in turn gives the split of real output between C and I. The output levels of C and I in turn determine employment and the price level after a lag. The model is thus fully simultaneous.

Being a classical model, Agarwala's system underplays demand relationships. Agricultural output determines food surplus, which in turn gives the employment level in industry. Non-agricultural output is then given by combining employment with capital. The general price level is given by a quantity-theoretic framework. Agricultural prices determine cost of living and in turn money wage. Money wage influences the price of manufactured goods. This along with import prices gives the level of non-agricultural prices. Given the general price level, eqn. (A29.3.1.8) in turn determines agricultural price level. The role of the price equations then is to determine the sectoral terms of trade and the absolute price level. Demand relationships come in only through determining the level of investment demand, which in turn gives the sectoral capital stock levels. The system is closed by the sectoral capital stock levels giving the level of output.

This rather detailed survey of the role of supply constraints shows that in many of the models, supply is assumed to be infinitely elastic or there is no feedback from supply via price on demand. Demand forces determine income and the general price level in turn gives the real level of output. The causal pattern is, therefore, block recursive in Mammen, Krishnamurty, and Marwah. In Choudhry, Narasimham, and Agarwala, the causal pattern is more simultaneous although mediated by some lags. The interaction is not always contemporaneous but dynamically simultaneous.[8] Even in Choudhry's model impact of food prices and import prices is not brought out. Our sketchy survey of economic trends would

---

[8] The expression 'dynamically simultaneous' is used to denote interdependence through lagged values bf endogenous variables. Since the error terms of these equations may be vector autoregressive, lagged endogenous variables are not truly predetermined and simultaneity comes through lags. In the standard notation used for simultaneous equation models, we have $By_t + \Gamma_1 x_t + \Gamma_2 y_{t-1} = U_t$ where $U_t = RU_{t-1} + e_t$. Whereas B may be diagonal or triangular, Γ_2 may not be so and R may also be non-diagonal. Either Γ_2 or R would introduce dynamic simultaneity in the sense used above.

indicate that these are the main determinants of the price level. In Marwah's first model, the sectoral prices of foodgrains, manufactured goods, etc. are influenced by the general price level but do not in turn influence it. In the second model, there is a small feedback through foodgrain prices in the general price level equation. In an economy with quantitative restrictions on imports and output, and many price restrictions on investment goods items such as steel, the role of supply bottlenecks is crucial. We have already indicated this in our discussion of investment equations and we shall have more to say on this matter later on.

Given the increasing role of government in capital accumulation and growth in the 1950s and 1960s, it is also remarkable that the government sector in these model is so under specified. In most cases, government expenditure and government investment are exogenous. This is true of the models of Agarwala, Choudhry (models 2 and 3). Krishnamurty, and Mammen. Marwah's first model as well as Choudhry model make no distinction between private and government investment. Marwah's second model has separate equations for government and total investment but the independent variables are nearly identical; while there are tax equations in Krishnamurty–Choudhry (eqns A29.3.4.13, A29.3.4.14), Mammen (eqn. A29.3.5.5), and Marwah (eqn. A29.3.7.18), there is no identity connecting the capital and current expenditure of government and total receipts. This is especially important for the monetary sector since the method of financing the budgetary gap has monetary consequences. Mammen has a variable for total government securities held by banks and public in his model, but he fails to connect this with government expenditure and tax revenue on the real side of his model. This is also true of Agarwala, Marwah, and Choudhry who have a monetary sector in their models. This structure also applies to Krishnamurty–Choudhry but not to Krishnamurty since his model does not have a monetary supply variable.

The absence of a well-defined government sector then leads to weakness in the links between real and monetary sectors. This is also true of many of the models of the US, UK, and Japan. In fact, the FMP model in the US has as its main aim the exploration of this link.[9] Mammen who has made the most systematic attempt at inclusion of a monetary sector finds only a weak link through the effect of income velocity on price level. This is also the case in both of Marwah's models. Choudhry and Marwah explore the monetary link through the introduction of liquid assets in C and I equations. Krishnamurty introduces the effect of long-term interest rates on investment but this effect is weak. Except for Mammen's model, money supply is an exogenous variable for the models though often it is not clearly specified. The feedback from the real sector to the monetary sector is even weaker.

The above remarks on specification of the government sector and of money supply lead to a methodological observation. Many of the models have left unspecified certain implicit relations between the variables. This leads to an

[9] The FMP Model was formerly the FRB–MIT model of the US economy, cited in fn. 3 above. Now it is called FRB–MIT–PENN (FMP for short). It is described in many separate articles. For the latest position regarding this continuing enterprise, see C.R. Nelson (1972), 'The Prediction Performance of the FRB–MIT–PENN Model of the U.S. Economy', *American Economic Review*, December.

undercounting of the number of equations. The connection between the money supply and the government budget has been mentioned. There is clearly a set of identities missing in this respect. When including foreign exchange reserves or foreign aid, the balance of payments identity is not specified to show the interconnection between these variables. In Marwah's model, there are sectoral output equations but the identity linking these sectoral outputs with one another (e.g. X_{10} in eqn. A29.3.7.40 and X_5, X_8 in other equations) and with total output (e.g. the identity linking Y with the sum of Y_{ag}, X_8, X_5, X_2, etc. in both the models) is not made explicit. Choudhry and Krishnamurty–Chouahry use the expression for liquidity (currency plus demand deposit) but its relation with money supply is not made clear. These are clearly missing equations, which may also mean that there may be missing variables. These examples could be multiplied but the point we hope has been made clear.

If on the one hand then, these models have too few equations, in another sense the block recursive and block independent pattern implies there may be superfluous equations in them. We have already remarked that in Marwah's first model, the sectoral equations are a function of the aggregate variables but that there is no feedback. The sectoral equations can be safely excluded from the aggregate model. Krishnamurty's model is the only one with endogenous population variables but these variables have very little effect on the rest of the model. It is only through the specification of the consumption function (eqn. A29.3.3.1) that there is a link but even this is dropped in the revised equation (eqn. A29.3.3.1a). We have already remarked on the lack of many links between Mammen's real model and monetary model.

The exploratory nature of these efforts at model building is also evident in the sparing use of prior information. In specifying relationships or in testing hypotheses, little use is made of prior restrictions on parameters. Agarwala imposes constant returns to scale on his non-agricultural production function. Narasimham sets the marginal propensity to consume (mpc) out of wage income *a priori* equal to one. But apart from these isolated examples, in general, most parameters are left unrestricted. In choosing between alternate specifications, the null hypotheses are usually of parameters being equal to zero. In many instances, more interesting null hypotheses thrown up by the available theoretical framework are not explored. Thus in Agarwala's model, it is crucial that the elasticity of non-agricultural employment with respect to surplus food grains be equal to unity. It is also of interest to check the elasticity of money wage with respect to cost of living index. While such hypotheses could have been tested with available regression results, no attempt has been made to do so. In estimating the quantity-theoretic explanation of price level or the explanation through excess demand hypothesis, the implicit elasticity predictions are not tested by Marwah, Choudhry, Agarwala, or Mammen. While specifying the expenditure equations in money or real terms, no check is made for the presence of money illusion.

These remarks are not meant to detract from the value of these contributions. Far from it. These are pioneering efforts at exploring what is an uncharted and immensely complex economy. Unlike for other economic systems, the econometrician here cannot draw upon complementary quantitative work of, say, the National Bureau of Economic Research or of the US Department of Commerce. We need to look at this large collection of results and draw upon it as much as we can for further research. For this, we need to extract as much information from these results as possible. Our discussion has been structured to derive the information contained in these models—the structure of demand–supply interaction, the nature of implicit prior restrictions, the problem of missing implicit equations, etc. Any future effort at model building in India should be a team effort. Being a team effort, the coverage of such a model can also be much larger than any of these individual efforts. The sectoral disaggregation can be much finer and detailed specification of policy constraints can be introduced by pooling time series and cross-section information. A preliminary task for this should be to put these available models together and see how some of their parts can fit into the larger model and also what areas are left totally unexplored. In this sense, these models are complementary to each other and to the future effort at model blooding. The gaps that they have left unexplored can be a priority task of the team effort.[10]

Planning effort in India has been concerned on the theoretical side with building consistency models which fit into a framework of specified overall targets. Thus, given the perspective plan for the long run (say 25 years), the short run targets of national income growth rate, requisite aggregate investment, and other macro magnitudes have been specified. The detailed plan then works out a consistent dynamic input–output model for these targets. Actual performance has, however, frequently fallen short of these targets. The consistency plans need to be supplemented by some research on the actual growth rate achieved. This is the task of econometric model building. Taking previous experience as datum, technological, behavioural, and institutional relationships can be estimated that will help us identify the actual bottlenecks, constraints, lags, etc. which lead to actual growth rate achieved. The relation of actual to target growth rate can also be explored here to indicate the possibilities of future planning.

The above is not just an empty statement of intentions. In fact, the usefulness of these models can be illustrated by their predictive performance. Marwah, Krishnamurty, and Agarwala simulated their models for the period of the Third Five Year Plan. Marwah and Krishnamurty specifically take the Third Plan investment figures to see whether these are adequate to achieve the desired growth. Agarwala explores the requirements of 10 per cent per annum growth rate of non-agricultural output. *These exercises all successfully predict the shortfall in the Third Plan achievements.* Thus, Krishnamurty predicts a 16 per cent growth of national income over five years as contrasted to the target of 30 per cent. He does this by taking the Third Plan information and making some reasonable approximation. Even without taking into account the strain on resources due to higher defence expenditure, his model predicts a shortfall. Marwah also combines Little's estimates about the time pattern of investment and the Third Plan targets. Her

---

[10] Since this was first written in early 1971, the Indian Council of Social Science Research (ICSSR) agreed to support such a team project at Delhi School of Economics with the participation of Professors A. L. Nagar, K. Krishnamurty, N. Choudhry, and Drs K. L. Krishna, D. B. Gupta, and the present author.

model predicts a 20 per cent or 24 per cent rise in price level (depending on taking eqn. (A29.3.6.5) or (A29.3.6.5a)), a 14 per cent or 16 per cent rise in NNP, and 37 per cent or 44 per cent rise in money value of NNP. Thus, the shortfall in growth of real output and the increasing inflationary pressures during the Third Plan are correctly predicted by her model. Agarwala finds that for a 10 per cent growth in non-agricultural output, an increasing allocation of investment resources to agricultural sector is required. These are all just illustrative results but they indicate the value of an econometric model as an outside check on a planning exercise.

It may be argued that a successful prediction of the shortfall in the Third Plan by these models does not by itself validate their specifications since it may be a case of spurious correlation. This may indeed be so and we cannot without further rigorous tests of the restrictions do more than mention that many of these predictions were genuinely *ex ante* simulations. These simulations by projecting forward past trends with new values of exogenous variables may only indicate that each successive Plan requires lifting the economy onto a path higher than that predicted by previous experience. But it may be equally consistent with saying that the growth targets of the Third Plan were chosen with inadequate regard to past shortfalls. The econometric models being descriptive of these shortfalls estimate this lower bound of the potential growth of the economy. Planning must certainly result in better than such predictions. A successful prediction by econometric model builders can then be taken as an indicator of a flaw in plan design or implementation.

We do not, however, wish to set up any false rivalry between planning by use of consistency models or optimizing exercises and econometric model building. Econometric models are a useful device for short term forecasting. Their predictions would be very useful as an aid for the planners since they may lead to improvements in plan design or in its implementation. On the other hand, for medium and long-term policy-making and for affecting change in real magnitudes (as against describing past changes), planning is clearly the superior alternative.

One purpose of this survey has been pedagogic but we have also tried to keep in mind the guidelines indicated by these models for further research. Many interesting insights, theoretical as well as empirical, contained in these models have been left unexplored. Thus, this survey has not been exhaustive. These models merit further careful study and one may be permitted to end with the plea that many of the unpublished models surveyed here can be published with benefit for future workers in this fast growing field.

Appendix 29.1

In this chapter, the following models are surveyed:

(1) *Agarwala, Ramgopal:* An Econometric Model of India 1948–61, London: 'Frank Cass & Co. Ltd, 1970. Twenty-four equations model with sectoral division in agriculture and industry. Theoretical framework of W.A. Lewis model combined with explicit investment functions and a quantity-theoretic explanation of price behaviour. All equations estimated by OLS, some by TSLS and LIML Simulations over the sample period and also for the years 1960–1 to 1964–5. Based on a Ph.D. dissertation submitted to the Manchester University.

(2) *Choudhry, Nanda Kumar:* 'An Econometric Model of India 1930–1955', unpublished Ph.D. dissertation submitted to the University of Wisconsin, 1963. Income–expenditure models along the lines of the Klein–Goldberger model. Three successively larger models of 10 equations, 20 equations, and 22 equations. Expenditure equations specified in nominal terms. In addition to components of GNP, liquidity preference as well as price level are explained. The explanation of price level is in terms of excess demand. All equations estimated by OLS and also by LIML. Policy experiments are performed on the model.

(3) *Krishnamurty, K.:* 'An Econometric Model of India 1948–1961', Ph.D. dissertation submitted to the University of Pennsylvania, 1964, unpublished. Income–expenditure model along the lines of the Klein–Goldberger model. Twenty-one equations model with subsequent revisions of subsets of the equations set in the model. All equations in real terms estimated by OLS and TSLS. Population growth is made endogenous by estimating a subset of three equations for 1921–61. Production function for agricultural sector. Degree of capacity utilization features in the non-agricultural sector to determine employment level via production function. No explanation for price level; money market is represented by equations for short and long term rates of interest. Simulation for the period of the Third Five Year Plan 1961–2 to 1965–6.

(4) *Krishnamurty, K.* and *Choudhry, N. K.:* 'Towards a Post-War Econometric Model of India, Working Paper No. 6814 of the Institute for the Quantitative Analysis of Social and Economic Policy, University of Toronto, June, 1968, unpublished. Thirty-equations model estimated by OLS for the period 1948–61. It is an extension of the model described in (3) above with relationships from (2) above. Liquidity preference equations and tax equations are also added. Supply of demand deposits is made endogenous in the model. No simulations performed.

(5) *Mammen, Thampy:* 'An Econometric Study of the Money Market in India', Ph.D. dissertation submitted to the University of Pennsylvania, 1967, unpublished. Income–expenditure model combined with a model of the money market and price behaviour. A 12-equations 'real' model combined with a 12- equations 'money' model estimated by OLS and 2SLS Principal Components for 1948–9 to 1963–4. Expenditure equations specified in real terms. Price level explained alternatively by the exogenous price level in agricultural sector via wages and by a wage cost mark-up equation. Money market equations cover the three components of demand for money—short and long term interest rates, commercial banks' portfolio, and the level of excess reserves. Simulations are performed for 1964–5 to 1970–1.

(6) *Marwah, Kanta Kumari:* 'An Econometric Model of Price Behaviour in India', Ph.D. dissertation submitted to the University of Pennsylvania, 1964, unpublished. Income–expenditure model with endogenous explanation for price behaviour. Main lines of the model follow the Klein–Goldberger model. Two versions of price behaviour—one in terms of excess demand and the other in terms of quantity-theoretic explanation. Two models of seven and nine equations estimated by OLS and TSLS for 1939–60 with some equations re-specified for 1947–60. A sector model of price behaviour is appended explaining: (1) Prices of manufacturing goods (four equations in terms of wage-cost mark-up or one equation in terms of inventory–output ratio); (2) Price of semimanufactures (one in terms of inventory–output ratio); (3) Price of industrial raw materials (in terms of export and domestic demands); (4) Price of food grains (four equations for demand, domestic supply, imports, and price-explanations in terms of excess demand as measured by imports). The sectoral model is also estimated by OLS and TSLS. In the aggregate model, expenditure equations are specified in real terms. There is a liquidity preference equation as well as one equation for the long term rate of interest. Simulations were performed for the period of Third Five Year Plan.

(7) *Marwah, Kanta Kumari:* 'An Econometric Model of India', Carleton Economic Papers, 1969, Mimeo. Extension of the author's original model described in (6) above. A 47-equations model estimated by OLS and TSLS combining time series and cross-section data for 1939–65. The model of (6) is extended by explicit introduction of aggregate production function using capacity utilization variable, disaggregated imports equations for eight categories of imports, export equations, sectoral output equations linked to aggregate output, and sectoral price equations in terms of inventory–output ratio or average cost markup behaviour. No simulations performed but the forecasting performance of the model is tested and the benefits of devaluation are estimated by using the multipliers of the model.

(8) *Narasimham, N.V.A.:* A Short-Term Planning Model for India, Amsterdam: North-Holland Publishing Co., 1956. Income-expenditure model with price behaviour equations on the lines of Tinbergen's model for UK and USA Eighteen-equations model estimated by OLS with variables specified in terms of deviations from nine year moving average for 1923–8. Disaggregation in terms of consumption goods and investment goods: demand functions for consumption, investment, imports, and employment. Corresponding prices also explained (except for imports). Policy experiments carried out with the model.

Appendix 29.2

The equations in the different models are described in Appendix 29.3 after reduction to common notation in this appendix. Only OLS results are listed since the TSLS results are fairly close to the OLS results and also since many alternate specifications listed below have been estimated only by OLS.

Notation:

(1) C Private consumption expenditure

(2) I Investment expenditure including fixed capital as well as inventory investment

(3) I_p Private investment expenditure

(4) I_g Government investment expenditure

(5) I_{pme} Private investment in machinery and equipment

(6) I_{gme} Government investment in machinery and equipment

(7) I_{pb} Private investment in construction

(8) I_{pst} Private investment in inventories

(10) I_{gst} Government investment in inventories

(11) K Capital stock at end of period

(12) D Depreciation

(13) I_{grp} Government expenditure on repair and maintenance

(14) G Government expenditure

(15) Y_{ag} Income originating in agriculture

(16) Yn_{ag} Income originating outside agriculture

(17) Y National income or net national product

(18) π Index of industrial profits

(19) K_{ag} Capital stock at end of period in agriculture

(20) K_{nag} Capital stock at end of period in non-agricultural sector

(21) L Gross acreage sown

(22) L_t Gross acreage irrigated

(23) N_{nag} Non agricultural employment

(24) PDY Personal disposable income

(25) Y_{nag} Capacity level of non-agricultural income

(26) u_{nag} Utilisation of capacity in non-agricultural sector

(27) F_x Foreign exchange reserves at the beginning of period

(28) R_3 Rate of interest on three month treasury bills

(29) R_{12} Rate of interest paid by commercial banks on 12 month time deposits

(30) R_s Short term rate of interest (variously computed)

(31) R_L Long term rate of interest-yield on non-terminable 3 per cent paper

(32) R_B Bank rate

(33) C_g Government consumption expenditure

(34) R_{eM} Call money rate—Inter-bank loan rate

(35) Nonπ Non-profit incomes

(36) N_{ag} Agricultural employment

(37) N Total employment

(38) RF Index of rainfall (variously measured)

(39) Y_{LDC} Income of LDC (less developed countries)

(40) YDC Income of DC (developed countries)

(41) YW World income

(42) TRW World trade

(43) LQD Liquid assets—current liquidity (variously measured)

(44) MS Money supply (variously measured)

(45)	DD	Demand deposits
(46)	TD	Time deposits also called saving deposits
(47)	CR	Currency
(48)	BHS	Commercial banks' holdings of Government securities
(49)	PHS	Public holdings of Government securities
(50)	BAD	Commercial banks total credit
(51)	ER	Excess reserves
(52)	RR	Required reserves
(53)	G	Government expenditure (excluding Government investment)
(54)	W	Index of wage earnings (money wage rate)
(55)	F_{imp}	Private imports
(56)	F_{mg}	Government imports
(57)	F_m	Total imports
(58)	F_{m1}	Imports of food and beverages
(59)	F_{m2}	Imports of raw materials
(60)	F_{m3}	Imports of fuel
(61)	F_{m4}	Imports of chemicals
(62)	F_{m5}	Imports of manufactured goods
(63)	F_{m6}	Imports of machinery and equipment
(64)	F_{m7}	Other imports
(65)	F_{mm}	Total merchandise imports
(66)	F_{ms}	Total imports of services
(67)	F_{mk}	Capital goods imports (Agarwala)
(68)	F_{mc}	Consumer goods and raw material imports (Agarwala)
(69)	F_{mo}	Food and other imports (Agarwala)
(70)	F_{em}	Total merchandise exports
(71)	F_{es}	Total exports of services
(72)	F_e	Total exports
(73)	F_{eT}	Exports of tea
(74)	F_{ej}	Jute exports
(75)	F_{ex}	Textile exports
(76)	F_{eo}	Other exports
(77)	P	General price level—implicit deflator of Y
(78)	P_c	Cost of living index
(79)	P_{ag}	Agricultural Price Index—Implicit deflator of Y_{ag}
(80)	P_{nag}	Non-agricultural price index—implicit deflator of Y_{nag}
(81)	PF_e	Unit value of total exports
(82)	PF_m	Unit value of total imports
(83)	PF_{m1}	Unit value of F_{m1} (food and beverage imports)
(84)	PF_{m2}	Unit value of F_{m2} (raw materials imports)
(85)	PF_{m3}	Unit value of F_{m3} (fuel imports)
(86)	PF_{m4}	Unit value of F_{m4} (chemicals imports)

(87) PF_{m5} Unit value of F_{m5} (manufactured goods imports)

(88) PF_{m6} Unit value of F_{m6} (machinery and equipment imports)

(89) PF_{m7} Unit value of $\dot{F}_{m7}$ (other imports)

(90) P_1 Price of food grains

(91) P_2 Price of raw materials

(92) P_3 Price of fuel

(93) P_4 Price of chemicals

(94) P_5 Price of manufactured goods

(95) P_6 Price of machinery and equipment

(96) P_8 Price of semi-manufactures

(97) P_9 Price of industrial securities

(98) PW World prices

(99) P_{10} Wholesale price index

(100) X_{Ag} Index of agricultural output

(101) X_2 Index of raw materials output

(102) X_5 Index of manufactured goods output

(103) X_8 Index of semi-manufactures output

(104) X_{10} Index of industrial production

(105) ST_5 Stocks of manufactured goods

(106) ST_8 Stocks of semi-manufactured goods

(107) D_1 Demand for food grains

(108) X_1 Output of food grains

(109) θ Inverse of the income velocity of money

(110) PF_{eldc} Price of LDC exports

(111) F_{mldc} LDC imports from LDC

(112) F_{mdc} DC imports from LDC

(113) ΔFK Net inflow of foreign capital]

(114) FA Foreign aid

(115) POP Total population

(116) b Birth rate per 1000

(117) d Death rate per 1000

(118) T_y Yield of direct taxes

(119) T_c Yield of indirect taxes net of subsidies

(120) GW Government welfare expenditure

(121) t Trend variable

Notes:
(1) When variables are in current prices this will be indicated by a prime.
(2) There is some overlap in the variables defined above. This is unavoidable since different authors use different definitions/descriptions of the same variable. As far as possible, I have tried to locate cases where two variables are identically defined but labelled differently by two authors.
(3) Definitions of variables are not always explicitly provided by the authors. This is especially true when sectoral relations are involved. The same label *may* mean two different things. Thus in imports, Marwah (7) makes a distinction between manufactured goods and machinery-equipment while on

the production side, the division is between manufactures and semi-manufactures. One presumes the imports refer to finished *consumer* goods but this is not clear from the context. This ambiguity of definition recurs in other models as well. Short of rechecking the definition from data source for each item, the only alternative is to preserve the authors' labelling. This has been done. When the ambiguity of definition is conceptually important, this will be pointed out in the text.

(4) Each model has some dummy variables. These would be defined along with the numerical estimates in the appropriate places. This has also been done for some minor variables, variables which are sums or products of other variables etc.

(5) Most of the value magnitudes are in billions of rupees. Prices are in index numbers, base year varying in different models but usually 1938–9 or 1953–4. Production variables are in indices.

Appendix 29.3

In listing the equations, as much statistical information is given as is provided by the authors. No attempt has been made to reduce the statistics to a strictly comparable basis. Thus, some authors give R^2 while others give $\bar{R}^2$; some provide von-Neumann statistics, some DW statistic, while others give no such information. DW and von-Neumann statistics are provided if the authors list them even when they are inappropriate as in situations with lagged values of the dependent variable among the regressors (see Nerlove and Wallis (1966), *Econometrica*, January). Niceties of inference are dispensed within the knowledge that readers usually want to know only whether *t*-ratio is above two or below. We indicate a *t*-ratio of two and above (numerically) by ** and between one and two by *, with no asterisk for *t*-ratio if less than one. Where provided by the authors, *t*-ratios of constants are also given. As usual

R^2	Coefficient of determination
$\bar{R}^2$	R^2 adjusted for degrees of freedom
S	Standard error of estimate
DW	Durbin Watson Statistic
VN	von-Neumann Statistic.

Coefficients are rounded to two decimal places except where loss of information may have occurred.

1. *R. Agarwala*, 1920–1 to 1960–1

$$\log Y_{ag} = 2.91 + 0.65 \log K_{agt-\frac{1}{2}} - 0.0347 \log RF \qquad \bar{R}^2 = 0.72, \quad VN = 1.86 \qquad \text{(A29.3.1.1)}$$
$$\quad\;\; (**) \quad\; (**) \qquad\qquad\quad (*)$$

$$X1 = -3836.18 + 2.07\, Y_{ag} \qquad\qquad\qquad\qquad \bar{R}^2 = 0.95, \quad VN = 1.17 \qquad \text{(A29.3.1.2)}$$
$$\quad\;\; (**) \qquad\quad (**)$$

$$N_{nag} = 1803.04 + 0.33 X_1 + 1.18\, (F_{m1}-F_{e1}) \qquad \bar{R}^2 = 0.87, \quad VN = 2.37 \qquad \text{(A29.3.1.3)}$$
$$\quad\;\; (**) \qquad\;\; (**) \qquad (**)$$

$$\log Y_{nag} = -0.44 + 0.56 \log K_{nagt-\frac{1}{2}} + 0.44 \log N_{nag} \qquad \bar{R}^2 = 0.87, \quad VN = 0.71 \qquad \text{(A29.3.1.4)}$$
$$\quad\;\; (**) \qquad\;\; (**)$$

N.B. Constant returns to scale assumed.

$$Y = Y_{ag} + Y_{nag} \tag{A29.3.1.5}$$

$$MS' = -59.54 + 1.47 \ CR' + 1.40t \qquad \bar{R}^2 = 0.99, \quad VN = 0.21 \tag{A29.3.1.6}$$
$$(**) \qquad (**) \qquad\quad (*)$$

$$Y' = 115.36 + 1.15 \ MS' + 0.80 Y'_{-1} \qquad \bar{R}^2 = 0.99, \quad VN = 2.15 \tag{A29.3.1.7}$$
$$(*) \qquad (**) \qquad\quad (**)$$

N.B. $\quad Y' = P.Y \qquad MS' = P.MS$

$$P = P_{ag} \frac{Y_{ag}}{Y} + P_{nag} \frac{Y_{nag}}{Y} \tag{A29.3.1.8}$$

$$Pc = -20.71 + 0.38 \ P_{ag} + 0.84 \ P_{ct-1} \qquad \bar{R}^2 = 0.85, \quad VN = 1.71 \tag{A29.3.1.9}$$
$$(*) \qquad\quad (**) \qquad\quad (**)$$

$$P_{nag} = 73.19 + 0.27 \ P_5 \qquad\qquad\qquad \bar{R}^2 = 0.54, \quad VN = 0.82 \tag{A29.3.1.10}$$
$$(**) \quad (**)$$

$$P_5 = 3.11 + 25.26 \ \frac{W}{(\partial Y_{nag}/\partial L_{nag})} + 0.71 \ P_{5t-1} \qquad \bar{R}^2 = 0.74, \quad VN = 1.96 \tag{A29.3.1.11}$$
$$(*) \qquad\qquad\qquad\qquad (**)$$

N.B. $(\partial Y_{nag}/\partial L_{nag})$ was evaluated from (1.4) using sample vaues K_{nag} and L_{nag}.

$$P_6 = -3.08 + 0.79 \ P5 + 0.23 \ W \qquad\qquad \bar{R}^2 = 0.99, \quad VN = 2.14 \tag{A29.3.1.12}$$
$$(**) \qquad\qquad (**)$$

$$W = -0.83 + 0.32 \ Pc + 0.77 \ W_{t-1} \qquad\qquad \bar{R}^2 = 0.99, \quad VN = 1.81 \tag{A29.3.1.13}$$
$$(**) \qquad\quad (**)$$

$$I_{ag} = 159.71 + 0.05 \left(\frac{Y_{ag} - T_{ag}}{P_6} \right) - 300.36 \ \frac{P_{ag}}{P_6}, \qquad \bar{R}^2 = 0.76, \quad VN = 1.36 \tag{A29.3.1.14}$$
$$(**) \qquad\qquad\qquad\qquad (**)$$

$$I_{pnag} = \frac{G_c}{100} \left[-1219.72 + 0.36 \left(\frac{Y_{ag} - I_{nag}}{P_6} \right) - 20.92 \left(\frac{\Delta P_t}{P_{t-1}} \right).100 \right]$$
$$(**) \qquad\quad (**) \qquad\qquad\qquad (**)$$

$$\bar{R}^2 = 0.77, \quad VN = 2.85 \tag{A29.3.1.15}$$

N.B. G_c–Capital issue sanctioned by Govt.

$$PFe = -219.72 + 1.26 \ P + 1.98 \ PF_{cidc} \qquad \bar{R}^2 = 0.79, \quad VN = 2.09 \tag{A29.3.1.16}$$
$$(**) \qquad\quad (**) \qquad\quad (**)$$

$$F_e = 575.39 + 2.08 \ Y_w - 208.50 \ PF_e / PF_{cidc}; \qquad \bar{R}^2 = 0.35, \quad VN = 2.27 \tag{A29.3.1.17}$$
$$(**) \qquad\quad (**) \qquad\quad (*)$$

$$F_m = -F_e = \Delta FK \tag{A29.3.1.18}$$

$$F_{mk} = 59.96 + 0.28 \ I_{nag} \qquad\qquad\qquad \bar{R}^2 = 0.68, \quad VN = 1.75 \tag{A29.3.1.19}$$
$$(*) \qquad\quad (**)$$

Presumably $F_{mk} = F_{m4} + F_{m6}$

$$F_{mc} / Y_{nag} = 0.055 - 0.0023t \qquad\qquad \bar{R}^2 = 0.68, \quad VN = 2.50 \tag{A29.3.1.20}$$
$$(**) \qquad\quad (**)$$

Presumably $\quad F_{mc} = F_m2 + F_m5$

$$F_m = F_{mk} + F_{mo} + F_{mc} \tag{A29.3.1.21}$$

$$I_{gnag} = I_{nag} - I_{pnag} \tag{A29.3.1.22}$$

$$K_{agt - \frac{1}{2}} = (2K_{agt-1} + I_{ag})/2. = \frac{K_{nagt} + K_{nagt-1}}{2} \tag{A29.3.1.23}$$

$$K_{nagt - \frac{1}{2}} = (2K_{nagt-1} + I_{nag})/2 = \frac{K_{agt} + K_{agt - 1}}{2} \qquad \text{(A29.3.1.24)}$$

Notes:
(1) RF Percentage deviation of actual rainfall from normal rainfall, weighted average of different regions.
(2) Equation (A29.3.1.1) was estimated for 1920–1 to 1960–1.
(3) Equations (A29.3.1.6) and (A29.3.1.7) were estimated for 1901–2 to 1961–2.
(4) MS' is defined as currency plus demand deposits.
(5) ΔFK in (A29.3.1.8) includes errors and omissions, invisible as well as net inflow of foreign capital.

2. *N.K. Choudhry*: As already mentioned in Appendix 29.1, Choudhry has three models. These are indicated by letters *a, b, c.*

$$P_t = 343.05 + 4.39 \; Y'_t -13.03 Y_t \qquad\qquad \bar{R}^2 = 0.9651, \quad \bar{S} = 25.3 \qquad \text{(A29.3.2.1a)}$$
$$\quad\quad\quad (**) \quad\quad (**)$$

$$Y_t = 21.32 + 0.087 \; K_t + \; 0.031 N_t \qquad\qquad \bar{R}^2 = 0.6724, \quad \bar{S} = 1.51 \qquad \text{(A29.3.2.2a)}$$
$$\quad\quad\quad (**) \quad\quad (**)$$

$$C'_t = 13.41 + 0.92 \; (PDY)'_t + \; 0.074(LQD)'_t \quad\; - 0.14 \; POP_t \; + 0.024 \; C'_{t-1}$$
$$\quad\quad\quad (**) \quad\quad\quad\quad (*)$$
$$\bar{R}^2 = 0.99, \quad \bar{S} = 8.30 \qquad \text{(A29.3.2.3a)}$$

$$I'_t = -3.05 + 0.028 \; (PDY)'_t \; + 0.02 \; Y'_t - 1 + 0.14 \; R_{Lt-1} -0.13 \; (LQD)' + 0.098 \; K'_{t-1}$$
$$\quad\quad (*) \quad\quad\quad (*) \quad\quad\quad\quad (*) \quad\quad\quad\quad\quad\quad (**) \quad\quad\quad\quad (**)$$
$$\bar{R}^2 = 0.94, \quad \bar{S} = 0.58 \qquad \text{(A29.3.2.4}_a\text{)}$$

$$F'_{tmt} = -0.20 + 0.057 \; Y'_t - 0.012 \; (P-Pw) + 0.08 \; FX, \quad \bar{R}^2 = 0.82, \quad \bar{S} = 1.05 \qquad \text{(A29.3.2.5}_a\text{)}$$
$$\quad\quad\quad (**) \quad\quad\quad\quad (*)$$

$$(LQD)'_t = -0.028 + 0.16 \; Y'_t - 0.07 \; (\Delta P/P_{t-1}) -0.078 \; R_{Lt-1} + 0.048 P_9,$$
$$\quad\quad\quad\quad (**) \quad\quad (*) \quad\quad\quad\quad\quad\quad\quad (**)$$
$$\bar{R}^2 = 0.92, \quad \bar{S} = 2.28 \qquad \text{(A29.3.2.6a)}$$

$$F'_{et} = -1.27 + 0.07 \; Y'_w + 0.0016 \; (P - Pw) \qquad \bar{R}^2 = 0.87, \quad \bar{S} = 0.61 \qquad \text{(A29.3.2.7a)}$$
$$\quad\quad\quad (**) \quad\quad (**) \quad\quad\quad (**)$$

$$Y'_t = C'_t + I'_t + G'_t + F'_{et} - F'_{mt} - T_i \qquad\qquad\qquad \text{(A29.3.2.8a)}$$

$$(PDY)'_t = Y'_t + T'_{rt} - T'_{yt} - S_t^{b'} \qquad\qquad\qquad\qquad \text{(A29.3.2.9a)}$$

$$K^o_t - K^o_{t-1} = I'_t / P_t \qquad\qquad\qquad\qquad\qquad\qquad \text{(A29.3.2.10a)}$$

N.B. T_r is ransfer payments and S^b business saving in the second model, the following equations occur.

$$P_t - \text{Same as} \quad \text{(A29.3.2.1a)} \qquad\qquad\qquad\qquad\qquad \text{(A29.3.2.1b)}$$

$$Y_{Agt} = 18.96 - 0.016 \; N_{agt} - 0.29 \; RF_t \qquad R^2 =0.75, \bar{S} = 0.47, \; VN = 1.46 \qquad \text{(A29.3.2.2b)}$$
$$\quad\quad\quad (**) \quad\quad\quad (**) \quad\quad (**)$$

$$Y_{nag} = 7.76 + 0.08 \; K_t \; + 0.06 \; N_{nagt} + 0.11_t \qquad R^2 = 0.89, \bar{S} = 0.94, \; VN = 0.46 \qquad \text{(A29.3.2.3b)}$$
$$\quad\quad\quad (*)$$

$$C'_t = -0.94 + 0.88(PDY)'_t + 0.17 \; (LQD)'_t + 0.05 C_{ot}$$
$$\quad\quad (*) \quad\quad (**) \quad\quad\quad\quad (*) \quad\quad\quad\quad (*)$$
$$R^2 = 0.99, \quad \bar{S} = 1.20, \; VN = 1.02 \qquad \text{(A29.3.2.4b)}$$

N.B. C_o is highest previous consumption.

$I'_{pt} = 0.27 + 0.024 (PDY)'_t - 0.15 (LQD)'_{t-1} + 0.016 Y'_{t-1} - 0.16 R_{Lt-1} + 0.05 K_{t-1}$
$\quad\quad\;\; (**) \quad\quad\quad\; (**) \quad\quad\quad\quad (*) \quad\quad\quad\quad\quad (**)$

$$R^2 = 0.94, \; \bar{S} = 0.35, \; VN = 1.13. \quad\quad\quad\text{(A29.3.2.5b)}$$

$F'_m 1 = 16.99 + 0.004(FA)' - 1.16 Y_{agt} - 0.0015 \; SHIP \quad\quad\quad\text{(A29.3.2.6b)}$
$\quad\quad\quad\quad\quad (**)$

R^2 not given. Equation standardized on Y_{ag} by the computer programme. Standard errors of the coefficients of FA' and $SHIP$ also not given.

$SHIP$ — % decline in shipping due to war (1942–6) over 1937–9 average.

$F'_{mK} = 0.0074 + 0.053 (LQD)'_t - 0.0001 (FA)'_t - 0.0005 \; SHIP$
$\quad\quad\quad\quad (**)$

$$R^2 = 0.27, \quad \bar{S} = 0.20, \quad VN = 2.08. \quad\quad\quad\text{(A29.3.2.7b)}$$

F_{mk} is producer goods imports. In model 2, it includes machinery imports only.

$(F'_m - F'_{m1} - F'_{mk}) = 0.56 + 0.097 d'_t Y'_t - 0.026 (P - P_W)_t - 0.024 \; SHIP$
$\quad\quad\quad\quad\quad\quad\quad\quad\quad (**) \quad\quad\quad (**) \quad\quad\quad\quad (**)$

$$R^2 = 0.60, \quad \bar{S} = 1.20, \quad VN = 1.22. \quad\quad\quad\text{(A29.3.2.8b)}$$

N.B. α_r: Coefficient of liberality of imports assumed to vary between 0.25 and 1.00.

$(LQD)'_t = 0.70 + 0.16 Y'_t - 0.073 (\Delta P_t / P_{t-1}) - 0.91 R_{Lt-1} + 0.047 P_9$
$\quad\quad\quad\quad\quad (**) \quad\quad\quad (*) \quad\quad\quad\quad\quad (*) \quad\quad\quad\quad (**)$

$$R^2 = 0.92, \quad \bar{S} = 2.27, \quad VN = 0.60 \quad\quad\quad\text{(A29.3.2.9b)}$$

$(F_{e1})'_t = -0.42 + 0.011 Y'_{Wt} + 0.011 (PF_{eT})_t - 0.0045 t$
$\quad\quad\quad\;\; (**) \quad\;\; (**) \quad\quad\;\; (**)$

$$R^2 = 0.92, \quad \bar{S} = 0.10, \quad VN = 1.79. \quad\quad\quad\text{(A29.3.2.10b)}$$

$(F_{ej})'_t = -0.56 + 0.017 Y_{Wt} + 0.014 t$
$\quad\quad\quad\;\; (*) \quad\;\; (*)$

$$R^2 = 0.65, \quad S = 0.35, \quad VN = 1.89. \quad\quad\quad\text{(A29.3.2.11b)}$$

$(F_{eX})'_t = -0.33 + 0.0065 Y_{Wt} + 0.014 t$
$\quad\quad\quad\;\; (**) \quad\quad\;\; (*) \quad\quad\quad (*)$

$$R^2 = 0.71, \quad S = 0.16, \quad VN = 1.56. \quad\quad\quad\text{(A29.3.2.12b)}$$

$(F_{eo})'_t = -0.46 + 0.055 Y_{wt} + 0.026 (P - P_W) t - 0.097 t$
$\quad\quad\quad\;\; (**) \quad\quad (**) \quad\quad (**)$

$$R^2 = 0.64, \quad S = 0.43, \quad VN = 1.23. \quad\quad\quad\text{(A29.3.2.13b)}$$

$Y = Yag + Ynag \quad\quad\quad\text{(A29.3.2.14b)}$

Y'_t as in (A29.3.2.8a) $\quad\quad\quad\text{(A29.3.2.15b)}$

K'_t as in (A29.3.2.10a) $\quad\quad\quad\text{(A29.3.2.16b)}$

PDY as in (A29.3.2.9a) $\quad\quad\quad\text{(A29.3.2.17b)}$

$I_t = Ipt + Igt \quad\quad\quad\text{(A29.3.2.18b)}$

$F'_m = F'_{mk} + F'_{m1} + (F'_m F'_{mk} - F'_{m1}) \quad\quad\quad\text{(A29.3.2.19b)}$

$F'_e = F'_{eT} + F'_{ej} + F'_{eX} + F'_{e0} \quad\quad\quad\text{(A29.3.2.20b)}$

The only changes in model c were regarding equations for I'_{pt}, F'_{mk} and $(F'_m - F'_{mk} - F'_{m1})$, $(LQD)'_t$. An equation was added for Non π with a corresponding identity. Thus (A29.3.2.1b) to (A29.3.2.4b) unchanged.

$$I'_{pt} = -3.46 + 1.18 \frac{\pi'_t + \pi'_{t-1}}{2} - 0.0001\Delta P_t/P_{t-1} + 1.39 \frac{K_{t-1}}{Y_{t-1}} - 0.039 (LQD)'_{t-1},$$
$$\quad\;\; (**) \qquad\qquad\qquad\qquad\qquad\qquad (**) \qquad\; (*)$$
$$R^2 = 0.95, \quad \bar{S} = 0.30, \quad VN \text{ not given.} \qquad\qquad (A29.3.2.5c)$$

(A29.3.2.6b) as before

$$(F'_{mk} + F'_{m2}) = 0.12 + 0.14I'_t + 0.014 (FA)'_t - 0.0078 \; SHIP$$
$$\qquad\qquad\quad (*) \qquad (**) \qquad (**) \qquad\quad\; (**)$$
$$R^2 = 0.93, \quad S = 0.21, \quad VN = 1.94 \qquad\qquad (A29.3.2.7c)$$

$$(F'_m - F'_{m1} - F'_{mk} - F'_{m2}) = 0.61 + 0.067 \; \alpha_t Y'_t - 0.0093 \; (P - P_W)_t - 0.017 \; SHIP$$
$$\qquad\qquad\qquad\qquad\qquad (*) \qquad (**) \qquad\quad (*) \qquad (**)$$
$$R^2 = 0.73, \quad S = 0.77, \quad VN = 1.53 \qquad\qquad (A29.3.2.8c)$$

$$(LQD)'_t = -3.91 + 0.17 \; Y'_t - 0.058 \; (\Delta P_t/p_{t-1}) + 0.052 \; P_{9t}$$
$$\qquad\quad\; (**) \quad (**) \qquad\quad (*) \qquad\qquad\; (**)$$
$$R^2 = 0.92, \quad S = 2.27, \quad VN \text{ not given.} \qquad\qquad (A29.3.2.9c)$$

(A29.3.2.10b to A29.3.2.20b) as before.

$$\text{Non } \pi_t = -50.88 + 0.042 \; N_{ag} + 2.96 \; N_{nag} + 0.41\Delta P/P_{t-1}$$
$$\qquad\qquad\qquad\qquad\qquad (*) \qquad\qquad (*)$$
$$R^2 = 0.89, \quad \bar{S} = 12.1, \quad VN \text{ not given.} \qquad\qquad (A29.3.2.21c)$$

$$\pi'_t = Y'_t - \text{Non } \pi'_t \qquad\qquad\qquad\qquad\qquad (A29.3.2.22c)$$

3. *K. Krishnamurty:*

$$(C/POP)t = -17.54 + 0.81 \; (PDY/POP) + 0.54 \; Y_{ag}/Y_{nag} - 1.70t$$
$$\qquad\qquad\quad (**) \qquad\qquad\qquad\quad (*) \qquad\qquad (*)$$
$$\qquad\qquad\qquad\qquad\qquad\qquad\qquad R^2 = 0.85, \quad \bar{S} = 3.65 \qquad (A29.3.3.1)$$

$$I_{pme} = -2.15 + 0.10 \; U_{nagt-1} + 0.026\pi_{t-1} - 1.2a \; R_{Lt-1}$$
$$\qquad\qquad\quad (*) \qquad\qquad\qquad\qquad (*)$$
$$\qquad\qquad\qquad\qquad\qquad R^2 = 0.73, \quad \bar{S} = 0.47 \qquad (A29.3.3.2)$$

$$I_{pb} = -6.15 + 0.04(PDY)_t + 0.11 \; U_{nagt-1} \qquad R^2 = 0.92, \quad \bar{S} = 1.36 \qquad (A29.3.3.3)$$
$$\quad\; (*) \qquad\qquad (**)$$

$$\sum_{i=1}^{t} I_{pSti} = -30.18 + 0.38 \; (Y - I_{pSt} - I_{gSt})_t \qquad R^2 = 0.93, \quad \bar{S} = 1.36 \qquad (A29.3.3.4)$$

$$Y_{agt} = -63.71 + 0.16 \; L_t + 3.30(L_{t'/L\%})_t \qquad R^2 = 0.83, \quad \bar{S} = 1.94 \qquad (A29.3.3.5)$$

For 1948–59.

$$Y_{nagt} = 26.77 + 0.17 \frac{(K_t + K_{t-1})}{2} \; U_{nag} + 0.06N_{nagt} \qquad R^2 = 0.99, \quad \bar{S} = 0.57 \qquad (A29.3.3.6)$$
$$\qquad\qquad (**) \qquad\qquad\qquad\qquad\qquad (*)$$

$$Y_{nag} = \text{obtained by setting } U_{nag} = 1 \text{ and raising } N_{nag} \text{ by } I/U_{nag}. \qquad (A29.3.3.7)$$

$$D_{nagt} = 5.60 + 0.007 \frac{(K_t + K_{t-1})}{2} \; U_{nag} \qquad R^2 = 0.76, \quad \bar{S} = 0.18 \qquad (A29.3.3.8)$$
$$\qquad\qquad (**)$$

$$F_{mpt} = -21.03 + 0.18 \; PDY_t + 0.96FX \qquad R^2 = 0.70, \quad \bar{S} = 0.76 \qquad (A29.3.3.9)$$
$$\qquad\qquad\quad (**) \qquad\qquad (**)$$

For 1949 – 61.

$$R_{Lt} = 1.45 + 0.23 \; R_{St} + 0.48 \; R_{Lt-1} \qquad R^2 = 0.96, \quad \bar{S} = 0.08 \qquad (A29.3.3.10)$$
$$\qquad\quad (**) \qquad\qquad (**)$$

$$R_{st} = -1.34 - 0.04 \ (ER/RR)\% +1.39 \ R_{Bt} \qquad\qquad R^2 = 0.85, \quad \bar{S} = 0.63 \qquad (A29.3.3.11)$$
$$(**) \qquad\qquad\qquad (**)$$

$$\pi_t = -47.89 - 0.79W_t + 2.46 \ U_{nagt} \qquad\qquad R^2 = 0.74, \quad \bar{S} = 8.47 \qquad (A29.3.3.12)$$
$$(**) \qquad\qquad (**)$$

$$W_t = 100.90 + 2.93t \qquad\qquad\qquad\qquad R^2 = 0.56, \quad \bar{S} = 0.74 \qquad (A29.3.3.13)$$
$$(**)$$

$$\log b_t = 4.62 - 1.21 \log \frac{1}{4} \sum_{i=4}^{1} (Y/P_{op})_{t-i} - 0.022 \ \log t_1 - 0.07D_1$$
$$(**) \qquad\qquad\qquad\qquad\qquad (*) \qquad\qquad (**)$$
$$R^2 = 0.71, \quad \bar{S} = 0.02 \qquad (A29.3.3.14)$$

$$\log d_t = 6.05 - 1.79 \log \frac{1}{4} \sum_{i=4}^{1} (Y/Pop)_{t-i} \qquad\qquad\qquad\qquad (A29.3.3.15)$$
$$(**)$$

For 1902– 61.

$$- 0.10 \ GW_t - 0.04 \ \log t_1 - 0.18D_1 \qquad\qquad R^2 = 0.93, \quad \bar{S} = 0.03.$$
$$(**) \qquad\qquad (**) \qquad\quad (**)$$

t_1 is a trend variable starting in 1992. D_1 is a dummy variable taking on a value of 0 for for 1902–47 and 1 for 1948–61. G_W was deflated by P_{10} (Wholesale Prrice Index). G_W stand for government expenditure.

$$K_t - K_{t-1} = I_{Pmet} + I_{gmet} + I_{Pb} + I_{gb} + I_{grP} - D_{nag} = I_t \qquad\qquad (A29.3.3.16)$$

$$Y_{agt} + Y_{nagt} = Y \qquad\qquad (A29.3.3.17)$$

$$U_{nagt} = 100 \ \frac{Y_{nagt}}{Y_{nagt}} \qquad\qquad (A29.3.3.18)$$

$PDY = Y + NATDEB - TY.$ *NATDEB* is national debt interest
payments plus other small transfer items.   (A29.3.3.19)

$$POP_t = POP_{t-1} \ (1 + b - d) \qquad\qquad (A29.3.3.20)$$

$$Y = C + I_{pme} + I_{gme} + I_{pb} + I_{gb} + I_{DSt} + I_{gSt} + I_{grp} - D_{nag} + G + F_e - F_m - T_i \qquad (A29.3.3.21)$$

In Krishnamurty's model, π has been deflated by index of price of machinery and and equipment and earnings (w) by Wholesale Price Index, R_{st} is measured as an average of treasury bill rate and three month deposit rate of commercial banks.

Subsequent revisions were made in some of the equations above before carrying out simulation experiments.

In the *C/POP* equation, Y_{ag}/Y_{nag} and t were dropped. The equations was run in terms of total rather than per capita.

$$C = 17.15 + 0.75 \ PDY \qquad\qquad R^2 = 0.98. \qquad (A29.3.3.1a)$$
$$(**)$$

In the I_{pmet} equation (A29.3.3.2) above, π_{t-1} was dropped.

$$I_{pmet} = -3.64 + 0.16U_{nagt-1} - 1.75R_{Lt-1} \qquad R^2 = 0.68. \qquad (A29.3.3.2a)$$
$$(**) \qquad\qquad\qquad (**)$$

Equation (A29.3.3.4) for I_{PSt} was revised as

$$\sum_{i=1}^{t} I_{pSti} = -244.77 + 0.32(Y - I_{pSt} - I_{gSt})t + 0.17 \sum_{i=1}^{t-1} I_{pSti} \qquad R^2 = 0.93. \qquad (A29.3.3.4a)$$
$$(**)$$

Equation (A29.3.3.6) for Y_{nag} was revised as

$$N_{nag} = 12.90 + 2.15 \ Y_{nag} \qquad R^2 = 0.95. \qquad \text{(A29.3.3.6a)}$$
$$(**)$$

4. *Krishnamurty–Choudhry:* As mentioned in Appendix 29.1, this model combines many of the relationships of the Krishnamurty model with those of the Choudhry model, both described above. There are some additional equations and some variables are redefined. We have

$$(C/POP)_t = -17.54 + 0.81 \ (PDY/POP)_t + 0.54 \ \frac{Y_{nag}}{Y} - 1.70t$$
$$(**) \qquad\qquad (*) \qquad\qquad (*)$$
$$R^2 = 0.8504. \qquad \text{(A29.3.4.1)}$$

$$I_{pme} = -2.35 + 0.017 \ (PDY)_t + 9.93 \ U_{nagt-1} - 1.23R_L \quad \bar{R}^2 = 0.4257. \qquad \text{(A29.3.4.2)}$$

N.B. U_t in this model seems to be equal to U_t in the Krishnamurty model devided by 100.

$$I_{pb} = -5.63 + 0.04 \ PDY + 10.97 \ U_{nagt-1} \qquad \bar{R}^2 = 0.8981. \qquad \text{(A29.3.4.3)}$$
$$(*) \qquad\qquad (**)$$

$$\sum_{i=1}^{t} I_{pSt} - i = -25.78 + 0.33(Y - I_{PSt} - I_{gSt})_t + 0.11 \sum_{i=1}^{t-1} + I_{PSt-i} \quad \bar{R}^2 = 0.9045. \qquad \text{(A29.3.4.4)}$$
$$(*)$$

$$Y_{agt} = -56.72 + 0.50 \ L_t + 203.96 \ (L_i/L)_t \qquad \bar{R}^2 = 0.9016. \qquad \text{(A29.3.4.5)}$$
$$+ \qquad (**) \qquad (*)$$

$$L_{it} = 22.44 + 0.0162 \sum_{i=1}^{t-1} \ (I^f - D)_i \qquad \bar{R}^2 = 0.9209. \qquad \text{(A29.3.4.6)}$$
$$(**)$$

$$Y_{nagt} = 0.17 \ N_{nag} + 0.18 \left[95.8 + \frac{\sum_{i=1}^{t} (I^f - D)_i + \sum_{i=1}^{t-1} (I^f - D)_i}{2} \right] \times U_{nag}$$
$$(*)$$
$$\bar{R}^2 = 0.9580. \qquad \text{(A29.3.4.7)}$$

Y_{nagt} = Non-agricultural output at time t.

Y_{magt}^{+} = is output of Mining, Manufacturing, and Trade. It excludes from residual output that which we call $Y_{\overline{nag}}$

$$U_{nagt} = 0.26 + 0.0045 \ \frac{Y_t + Y_{t-1}}{2} + 0.030 \ (F_{mk} + F_{m2}) \qquad \bar{R}^2 = 0.9163 \qquad \text{(A29.34.8)}$$
$$(**) \qquad\qquad\qquad (**)$$

$$Y_{\overline{nagt}} = -26.18 + 111.49 \ POP \qquad \bar{R}^2 = 0.9916 \qquad \text{(A29.3.4.9)}$$
$$(**)$$

$$(F_{mk} + F_{m2})_t = -0.26 + 0.73 \ (I_{pme} + I_{gme} + I_{pb} + I_{gb})t + 0.11(FX - 1 + FA_t) \quad \bar{R}^2 = 0.7212.$$
$$(**)$$
$$\text{(A29.3.4.10)}$$

N.B. $FX - 1$ and FA are deflated by import Price Index.

$$(F_m - F_{mk} - F_{m2})_t = 2.70 + 0.0040PL480_t \qquad \bar{R}^2 = 0.5327. \qquad \text{(A29.3.4.11)}$$

$$D_t = 5.53 + 0.0074 \ [95.8 + \sum_{i=1}^{t-1} (If - D)_i] \ U_{nagt-1} \qquad \bar{R}^2 = 0.7417 \qquad \text{(A29.3.4.12)}$$
$$(**)$$

N.B. Here, as in the equation (A29.3.4.7), 95.8 is the estimate of initial capital stock K_0 derived from the estimated coefficients of equation (A29.3.4.7), for which see the text. The variable in brackets in equation (A29.3.4.12) is then K_{t-1}.

$$T_Y = -0.46 + 0.030Y \qquad \bar{R}^2 = 0.6773 \qquad \text{(A29.3.4.13)}$$
$$(**)$$

$$T_i = -10.28 + 0.16Y \qquad \bar{R}^2 = 0.9443 \qquad \text{(A29.3.4.14)}$$

$$\log b_t = 3.88 - 0.93 \log \frac{1}{4} \sum_{i=4}^{1} (Y/POP)_{t-i} - 0.043 \log t \qquad \bar{R}^2 = 0.4987 \qquad \text{(A29.3.4.15)}$$
$$(**)$$

$$\log d_t = 5.81 - 1.78 \log \frac{1}{4} \sum_{i=4}^{1} (Y/POP)_{t-i} - 0.040 \log G_W - 0.049 \log t$$
$$\text{(**)} \qquad\qquad\qquad\qquad \text{(*)} \qquad\qquad \text{(**)}$$

$$\bar{R}^2 = 0.88 \qquad \text{(A29.3.4.16)}$$

$$P_t = 153.91 - 2.11 \frac{Y_{agt}}{Y_{t-1}} + 0.5 + P_{t-1} \qquad\qquad \bar{R}^2 = 0.4104 \qquad \text{(A29.3.4.17)}$$
$$\text{(*)} \qquad\qquad \text{(**)}$$

$$R_{Lt} = 1.44 + 0.21\, R_{St} + 0.50 R_{Lt-1} \qquad\qquad \bar{R}^2 = 0.9382 \qquad \text{(A29.3.4.18)}$$
$$\text{(**)} \qquad\quad \text{(**)}$$

$$(DD_t + DD_{t-1})' / 2 = 3.05 + 0.91 R_S/RBt + 4.99\,(ER + RR) \qquad \bar{R}^2 = 0.7428 \qquad \text{(A29.3.4.19)}$$
$$\text{(*)} \qquad\qquad \text{(**)}$$

$$(DD + CR)'_t = -2.35 + 0.22\, Y - 0.11 RSt + 2.15\, P_t/PP_{t-1} \qquad \bar{R}^2 = 0.7608 \qquad \text{(A29.3.4.20)}$$
$$\text{(**)} \qquad\qquad\qquad \text{(not given)}$$

$$I^f - D = I_{pme} + I_{gme} + I_{pb} + I_{gb} + I_{grp} - D \qquad\qquad \text{(A29.3.4.21)}$$

$$Y = Y_{ag} + Y_{nag}^+ + Y_{nag}^- \qquad\qquad \text{(A29.3.4.22)}$$

$$I_{pSt} = \sum_{i=1}^{t} I_{pSti} - \sum_{i=1}^{t-1} I_{pSti} \qquad\qquad \text{(A29.3.4.23)}$$

$$C = (C/POP)\, POP \qquad\qquad \text{(A29.3.4.24)}$$

$$PDY = Y + NATDEB - T_Y. \qquad\qquad \text{(A29.3.4.25)}$$

NATDEB as in Krishnamurty's model is interest on national debt + transfer payments + net private donations from abroad–income from domestic product accruing to government.

$$Y = C + (I^f - D) + I_{PSt} + I_{gt} + F_e - F_m + G - T_i \qquad\qquad \text{(A29.3.4.26)}$$

$$F_m = F_{mk} + F_{m2} + (F_m - F_{mk} - F_{m2}) \qquad\qquad \text{(A29.3.4.27)}$$

$$POP_t = POP_{t-1}\, (I + b - d) \qquad\qquad \text{(A29.3.4.28)}$$

$$PY = Y' \qquad\qquad \text{(A29.3.4.29)}$$

$$L'_t + L'_{t-1} = DD' + PC' \qquad\qquad \text{(A29.3.4.30)}$$

5. *T. Mammen: Real Model*

$$C = 11.47 + 0.81 Y \qquad\qquad \bar{R}^2 = 0.99,\ \bar{S} = 1.2,\ DW = 1.31 \qquad \text{(A29.3.5.1)}$$

$$I_p = 1.18 + 1.12\, \pi + 0.64\, \Delta FK \qquad \bar{R}^2 = 07359,\ \bar{S} = 1.4,\ DW = 1.3 \qquad \text{(A29.3.5.2)}$$

N.B. FK was deflated by $PF_{m,\,\pi}$, C and I by P.

$$I_g = 0.4 + 0.09\,(Y^* - Y)_t + 0.48\, I_{gt-1} \qquad \bar{R}^2 = 0.91,\ \bar{S} = 0.73,\ DW = 1.3$$
$$\text{(**)} \qquad\qquad \text{(**)}$$

Y^* targeted income $Y_t = Y_0\,(1 + .05)^t$

$$F = 6.30 + 0.03 Y + 1.02 \Delta FK - 0.02 PF_m \qquad \bar{R}^2 = 0.95,\ \bar{S} = 0.49,\ DW = 1.6 \qquad \text{(A29.3.5.4)}$$
$$\text{*}$$

$$T'_i = -8.67 + 0.15\, Y' \qquad\qquad \bar{R}^2 = 0.98,\ \bar{S} = 0.57,\ DW = 2.1 \qquad \text{(A29.3.5.5)}$$

$$\pi_t = -2.03 + 0.06\, Y_{nag} + 0.68\pi_{t-1} \qquad \bar{R}^2 = 0.96,\ \bar{S} = 0.28,\ DW = 1.48 \qquad \text{(A29.3.5.6)}$$

$$P = 42.54 + 0.57\, P_{10} \qquad\qquad \bar{R}^2 = 0.91,\ \bar{S} = 2.21,\ DW = 1.78 \qquad \text{(A29.3.5.7)}$$

$$P_{10} = -0.66 + 1.01\, P_{ag} \qquad\qquad \bar{R}^2 = 0.96,\ \bar{S} = 2.48,\ DW = 0.89 \qquad \text{(A29.3.5.8)}$$

$$Y = Y_{ag} + Y_{nag} \qquad\qquad \text{(A29.3.5.9)}$$

$$Y = Y'/P. \qquad\qquad \text{(A29.3.5.10)}$$

$$Y' = C' + I'_p + I'_g + G'_{gg} - A'_g - T'_i \qquad\qquad \text{(A29.3.5.11)}$$

$$\Delta F_K = F_m + Z - F_e \tag{A29.3.5.12}$$

Z-Non cash inflow and retained earnings of branches and subsidiaries of foreign companies in India. Alternative equations for P_{10}.

$$P_{10} = 6.17 + 0.05\,W' + 0.80\ P_{ag} \qquad \bar{R}^2 = 0.99,\ \bar{S} = 1.12,\ DW = 1.95 \tag{A29.3.5.8a}$$
$$\phantom{P_{10} = 6.17 + }(**) \qquad\quad (**)$$

$$W = -117.36 + 0.41\ (Y'/N) \qquad \bar{R}^2 = 0.96,\ \bar{S} = 13.4,\ DW = 1.70 \tag{A29.3.5.8b}$$

$$N = 53.57 + 0.47\ Y \qquad \bar{R}^2 = 0.98,\ \bar{S} = 1.06,\ DW = 1.17 \tag{A29.3.5.8c}$$

Monetary Model

$$CR'_t = 4.28 + 0.077\ Y'_t - 3.36\ log\ R_{3t} + 0.68t$$
$$(**)\qquad\quad (**)\qquad\qquad (**)$$
$$\bar{R}^2 = 0.98,\ \bar{S} = 0.48,\ DW = 1.8 \tag{A29.3.5.13}$$

$$CR'_t = 3.42 + 0.084\ Y'_t - 3.60\ log\ R_{3t} + 0.74t - 0.81Z_{It}$$
$$(**)\qquad\quad (**)\qquad\qquad (**)\qquad (*)$$
$$\bar{R}^2 = 0.99,\ \bar{S} = 0.46,\ DW = 1.8 \tag{A29.3.5.13a}$$

Z_1: Dummy variable taking a value 1 from 1958–9 on for inter–bank agreement on ceiling on interest rates at 4 per cent on 3 months time deposits.

$$DD'_t = 0.96 + 0.099\ Y'_{nagt} - 0.51\ log\ R_{3t} \qquad \bar{R}^2 = 0.93,\ \bar{S} = 0.33, DW = 1.05 \tag{A29.3.5.14}$$
$$(**)\qquad\qquad (*)$$

$$TD'_t = -3.71 + 0.094\ Y'_t - 0.68\ R_{9t} + 0.81 R_{12t}$$
$$(**)\qquad\quad (**)\qquad (**)$$
$$\bar{R}^2 = 0.98,\ \bar{S} = 0.40,\ DW = 2.7 \tag{A29.3.5.15}$$

R_9 is return on industrial securities. It is presumably linked with P_a –price of industrial securities but the connection has not been defined by the author.

$$R_{9t} = 0.66 + 1.70 R_{Lt} - 0.55\pi'_t \qquad \bar{R}^2 = 0.63,\ \bar{S} = 0.37,\ DW = 1.5 \tag{A29.3.5.16}$$
$$\phantom{R_{9t} = 0.66}(**)\qquad (**)$$

$$R_{12t} = -1.57 + 0.73 R_{Lt} - 0.59\ R_{12t-1} \qquad \bar{R}^2 = 0.93,\ \bar{S} = 0.21,\ DW = 1.8 \tag{A29.3.5.17}$$
$$\phantom{R_{12t} = -1.57}(**)$$

$$R_{Lt} = 2.01 + 0.38R3 + 0.06\ (BHS + PHS) \qquad \bar{R}^2 = 0.95,\ \bar{S} = 0.105,\ DW = 1.00 \tag{A29.3.5.18}$$
$$\phantom{R_{Lt} = 2.01}(**)\qquad\quad (**)$$

$$(BHS/BAD)_t = 1.27 - 0.80\ R_3/R_{Lt} - 0.013(BHS + BAD)$$
$$(**)\qquad\qquad (**)\quad \bar{R}^2 = 0.91,\ \bar{S} = 0.067,\ DW = 1.8 \tag{A29.3.5.19}$$

$$BHS' + BAD' - (DD + TD)' = 0.9953\ (DD + TD)$$
$$(**)\qquad \bar{R}^2 = 0.99,\ \bar{S} = 0.44,\ DW = 1.85 \tag{A29.3.5.20}$$

$$ER/(DD + TD)' = 8.87 - 1.27\ RCM \qquad \bar{R}^2 = 0.89,\ \bar{S} = 0.54,\ DW = 1.9 \tag{A29.3.5.21}$$
$$(**)$$

$$RCM = -1.60 + 0.69\ R_3 + 0.63 R_B \qquad \bar{R}^2 = 0.91,\ \bar{S} = 0.35,\ DW = 1.26 \tag{A29.3.5.22}$$
$$(**)\qquad (**)$$

$$RR = 0.09 + 0.034\ (DD + TD)' \qquad \bar{R}^2 = 0.83,\ \bar{S} = 0.067,\ DW = 1.51 \tag{A29.3.5.23}$$
$$(**)$$

In linking the real and monetary models, the equation for P_{10} was revised.

$$P_{10} = -17.95 + 0.92 P_{ag} + 1.13\ \frac{(CR' + DD' + TD')}{Y'}\ \% \tag{A29.3.5.8b}$$
$$\phantom{P_{10} = -17.95 + }(**)$$

An explicit supply function of money was also added instead of treating the equations for ER and RR as arising from an implicit supply function. In the monetary model above, ER is treated as a measure of the discrepancy between demand and supply of $(DD + TD)$. Now they are assumed to be equal.

$$L' = DD' + TD'$$

$$B' = CR' + ER' + R'_R$$

$$L' = 4.92 + 0.82B' - 4.65 \left(\frac{CR'}{DD'}\right) + 5.55\,(TD/DD)$$
$$\quad\;\;\; (**) \qquad\;\; (**) \qquad\qquad\quad (**)$$

$$\bar{R}^2 = 0.99,\; \bar{S} = 0.24,\; DW = 0.58 \qquad\qquad \text{(A29.3.5.23a)}$$

6. K. Marwah:

$$C = 17.21 + 0.87\,Y + 0.23\,\frac{L'_{t-2}}{P} + 0.046POP \qquad\qquad \bar{R}^2 = 0.98 \qquad \text{(A29.3.6.1)}$$
$$\quad\;\; (**) \qquad\;(**) \qquad\qquad\qquad\qquad (*)$$

$$L = 14.69 + 0.57\left(\frac{Y_t + Y_{t-1}}{2}\right) + 4.78\,R_{Lt} \qquad\qquad \bar{R}^2 = 0.80 \qquad \text{(A29.3.6.2)}$$
$$\quad\;\; (**) \quad\;\; (*) \qquad\qquad\qquad\quad (**)$$

For 1947–60 subsample

$$I_t = 6.27 + 0.089\,Y_t + 0.74I_{t-1} \qquad\qquad\qquad\qquad \bar{R}^2 = 0.90 \qquad \text{(A29.3.6.2a)}$$
$$\quad\;\; (*) \qquad (*) \qquad\quad (**)$$

$$(MS)'_t = 3.13 + 0.17\,Yt + 0.83R_{Lt} + 0.073P_9 \qquad\qquad \bar{R}^2 = 0.95 \qquad \text{(A29.3.6.3)}$$
$$\qquad\qquad (**) \qquad\qquad\quad (**)$$

$$R_{Lt} = 0.89 + 0.10RS_t + 0.65\,R_{Lt-1} \qquad\qquad\qquad \bar{R}^2 = 0.87 \qquad \text{(A29.3.6.4)}$$
$$\qquad\;\; (**) \qquad (**)$$

$$P_t = 5.03 + 0.68\,\Delta Y't + 0.95\,P_{t-1} \qquad\qquad\qquad \bar{R}^2 = 0.98 \qquad \text{(A29.3.6.5)}$$
$$\qquad\;\; (**) \qquad\quad (**)$$

An alternate explanation for price level is in quantity–theoretic terms.

$$Pt = 20.57 + 0.53(\Delta MS' - \Delta\overline{MS}) + 0.83P_{t-1} \qquad\qquad \bar{R}^2 = 0.95 \qquad \text{(A29.3.6.5a)}$$
$$\qquad\qquad\qquad (*)$$

$$\theta = 0.053 + 0.45\,I/RL + 0.0012P_9 \qquad\qquad\qquad \bar{R}^2 = 0.798 \qquad \text{(A29.3.6.6a)}$$
$$\qquad\;\; (**) \qquad\qquad (**)$$

Connected with equation (A29.3.6.5) for P_t are two identities

$$Y' = PY \qquad\qquad\qquad\qquad\qquad\qquad\qquad\qquad \text{(A29.3.6.7a)}$$

$$Y' = C' + I' + H'. \qquad\qquad\qquad\qquad\qquad\qquad \text{(A29.3.6.8)}$$

Connected with equations (A29.3.6.5a) and (A29.3.6.6a) are the following identities.

$$Y' = PY \qquad\qquad\qquad\qquad\qquad\qquad\qquad\qquad \text{(A29.3.6.7a)}$$

$$Y' = C' + I' + M \qquad\qquad\qquad\qquad\qquad\qquad \text{(A29.3.6.8a)}$$

$$M = QPY \qquad\qquad\qquad\qquad\qquad\qquad\qquad \text{(A29.3.6.9a)}$$

$$\Delta MS' = MS_t - MS_{1953} \qquad\qquad\qquad\qquad\qquad \text{(A29.3.6.10a)}$$

$$\Delta MS' = \left(\frac{\Delta Y_t}{Y1953} + \frac{\Delta\theta_t}{\theta 1953}\right)MS'1953. \qquad\qquad \text{(A29.3.6.11a)}$$

Sectoral Model: Manufacturing price:

$$P_5 = 19.31 + 0.33\,\frac{WN_{nag}}{X_5} + 0.48\,PF_m \qquad\qquad \bar{R}^2 = 0.96 \qquad \text{(A29.3.6.12)}$$
$$\quad\;\; (**) \qquad\qquad\qquad\; (**)$$

$$X_5 = 45.84 + 0.51\, N_{nag} \qquad\qquad R^2 = 0.70 \qquad\qquad\text{(A29.3.6.13a)}$$
$$\text{(**)}\quad\text{(**)}$$

$$W = 4.44 + 0.16\Delta\, P_c + 0.17 \left(\frac{X_5\, P_5}{N_{nag}}\right) + 0.99 W_{t-1} \quad R^2 = 0.99 \qquad\qquad\text{(A29.3.6.14)}$$
$$\text{(**)}\quad\text{(*)}\qquad\qquad\qquad\qquad\quad\text{(**)}$$

$$P_c = 4.65 + 0.93P \qquad\qquad\qquad R^2 = 0.97 \qquad\qquad\text{(A29.3.6.15)}$$
$$\text{(*)}\quad\text{(**)}$$

Alternative equation for P_5.

$$P_{5t} = 75.86 + 0.15 \left(\frac{ST_5}{X_5}\right)_{t-1} + 0.56 P_{5t-1} \qquad R^2 = 0.84 \qquad\qquad\text{(A29.3.6.15a)}$$
$$\phantom{P_{5t} =}\text{(**)}\qquad\qquad\qquad\quad\text{(**)}$$

1947–60.

Semi Manufactures.

$$P_{8t} = 48.56 + 11.25 \left(\frac{ST_8}{X_8}\right)_{t-1} + 0.65\, P_{8t-1} \qquad R^2 = 0.79 \qquad\qquad\text{(A29.3.6.16)}$$
$$\phantom{P_{8t} =}\text{(**)}\qquad\qquad\qquad\text{(**)}$$

1947–60.

Industrial Raw Materials.

$$P_{2t} = 33.68 + 0.32 X_{10} + 47.16 \left(\frac{F_e}{X_2}\right)_{t-1} + 0.51\, P \qquad R^2 = 0.96 \qquad\qquad\text{(A29.3.6.17)}$$
$$\phantom{P_{2t} =}\text{(**)}\qquad\qquad\qquad\qquad\text{(**)}$$

1944–60.

Foodgrains Sector.

$$D_1 = 548.16 + 3.59\, Y_{t-1} + 2.16 POP \qquad\qquad R^2 = 0.93 \qquad\qquad\text{(A29.3.6.18)}$$

1944 –60.

$$X_1 = 21.79 + 6.07\, Y_{ag} + 0.40 P_{1t-1} - 45.97 Z \qquad R^2 = 0.98 \qquad\qquad\text{(A29.3.6.19)}$$
$$\text{(**)}\qquad\qquad\qquad\text{(**)}$$

$$P_1 + 32.87 + 0.41\, F_{m1} + 0.60\, P_{1t-1} - 7.93 Z_2 \qquad R^2 = 0.80 \qquad\qquad\text{(A29.3.6.20)}$$
$$\text{(*)}\qquad\text{(**)}\qquad\qquad\text{(*)}$$

$$D_1 = X_1 + F_{m1}. \qquad\qquad\qquad\text{(A29.3.6.21)}$$

7. K. Marwah:

This model is an adaptation and elaboration of the Marwah model described in(6) above. The major features are introduction of a disaggregated foreign sector and use of combined cross–section and time–series estimates.

$$C = -10.63 + 0.84\, Y + 0.27\, \frac{L'_{t-2}}{P} + 31.8\, POP,$$
$$\text{(**)}\qquad\text{(*)}$$
$$\bar{R}^2 = 0.96,\ \ \bar{S} = 3.16,\ DW = 1.42 \qquad\qquad\text{(A29.3.7.1)}$$

$$I = [-5.78 + 0.82\ Y + 0.76 I_{-1} - 2.05 Z_1]\ 1939{-}60$$
$$\text{(**)}\qquad\text{(**)}\qquad\text{(**)}\qquad 2\ SLS$$
$$\left[-0.135 + 0.063 Y + \frac{F_{m6}}{P}\right]\ 1961{-}5 \qquad\qquad\qquad\text{(A29.3.7.2)}$$
$$\text{(*)}\qquad\qquad\qquad OLS$$
$$\bar{R}^2 = 0.89,\ \ \bar{S} = 0.99,\ DW = 1.46$$

Z_1 is explained as followed as Marwah (7): Z_1 'Dummy variable taking value 1 for post-1960 and zero every where else, used to capture the effect of a change in the construction of the series.' Since two time periods 1939–60 and 1961–5 are separated any way in I equation, this may be a typing error. One presumes the text should say post 1950 years or just for the year 1950 years or just for the year

1960. The precise meaning to be attached to the R^2 figure when the two subsamples parameters one presumes are estimated by different methods in the different specifications is also not clear.

$$I_g = -11.35 + 0.125\,Y + 0.3I_{t-1} + 1.20Z_1 \qquad \bar{R}^2 = 0.94, \bar{S} = 0.76, \; DW = 121 \qquad \text{(A29.3.7.3)}$$
$$\quad\;\; (**) \qquad\quad (**)$$

2 SLS

$$Ip = I - I_g \tag{A29.3.7.4}$$

$$Y = 76.7 + 0.27\,(U).K_{-1} \qquad\qquad \bar{R}^2 = 0.91, \; DW = 1.23, \; \bar{S} = 4.94 \qquad \text{(A29.3.7.5)}$$

Foreign Trade.

$$F'_{mm}/PF_{mm}) = -3.61 + 0.04Y + 2.32F\,X_{t-1} + 6.7\,\frac{P}{PF_{mm}}$$
$$\qquad\qquad (**) \qquad (**) \qquad\qquad (**)$$

$$\bar{R}^2 = 0.97(TS)\; \bar{R}^2 = 0.94(CS) \qquad \text{(A29.3.7.6)}$$

Cross Section (CS) $\Big\}$ Combined
Time Series (TS)

$$(F'_{m1}/PF_{m1}) = -4.52 + 0.011\,Y + 0.0008\,\frac{Y}{POP} + 3.20P_1 + 1.29\,\frac{Y_{nag}}{Y_{ag}}$$
$$\qquad\qquad\quad (**) \qquad (*) \qquad\qquad (**) \qquad (**)$$

$$\begin{Bmatrix} CS \\ TS \end{Bmatrix} \quad \bar{R}^2 = 0.83(CS), \;\; \bar{R}^2 = 0.95(TS) \tag{A29.3.7.7}$$

$$(F'_{m2}/PF_{m2}) = 3.82 + 0.006\,Y + 0.34\,F_{Xt-1} - 0.14t$$
$$\qquad\qquad\quad (**) \qquad (*) \qquad\quad (**)$$

$$\bar{R}^2 = 0.72(CS), \bar{R}^2 = 0.98(TS) \qquad \text{(A29.3.7.8)}$$

CS – TS combined

$$(F'_{m3}/PF_{m3}) = -0.98 + 0.00015\,\frac{Y}{POP} + 1.42POP + 1.17\,\frac{P_3}{P} + 0.19Z_2 \qquad \text{(A29.3.7.9)}$$
$$\qquad\qquad\quad (**) \qquad\qquad\quad (**) \qquad (*) \qquad (**)$$

CS –TS combined $\qquad\qquad\qquad\qquad \bar{R}^2 = 0.86(CS), \;\; \bar{R}^2 = 0.76(TS)$

Z_2 : dummy variable with value 1 for border war with China

$$(F'_{m4}/PF_{m4}) = -0.62 + 0.0036Y + 1.14\,\frac{P_4}{PF_{m4(1+Di)}} \qquad \text{(A29.3.7.10)}$$
$$\qquad\qquad\quad (**) \qquad (**)$$

CS –TS combined $\qquad\qquad\qquad \bar{R}^2 = 0.76(CS), \;\; \bar{R}^2 = 0.97(TS)$

D_i = rate of import duties

$$(F'_{m5}/PF_{m5}) = 0.52 + 0.016Y + 0.00023\,Y/POP + 1.08\,\frac{P_5}{PF_{m5(1+Di)}}$$
$$\qquad\qquad\quad (**) \qquad (**) \tag{A29.3.7.11}$$

$$-1.11\,\frac{Y_{nag}}{Y_{ag}} \qquad \bar{R}^2 = 0.90(CS), \;\; \bar{R}^2 = 0.86(TS)$$
$$\;\; (**)$$

CS –TS combined

$$(F'_{m6}/PF_{m6}) = 2.78 + 0.016Y + 0.26FX_{-1} - 1.96\,\frac{P_6}{P} \qquad \text{(A29.3.7.12)}$$
$$\qquad\qquad\quad (**) \qquad (*) \qquad\quad (*)$$

CS – TS combined $\qquad\qquad\qquad \bar{R}^2 = 0.91(CS), \bar{R}^2 = 0.36(TS)$

$$F'_{mm} = F_{m1} + F'_{m2} + F'_{m3} + F'_{m4} + F'_{m5} + F'_{m6} + F'_{m7} \tag{A29.3.7.13}$$

$$(F'_{m1dc}/PF_{e1dc}) = 1.38 + 0.028Y_{1dc} \qquad \bar{R}^2 = 0.98, \; DW = 1.26, \bar{S} = 0.12 \qquad \text{(A29.3.7.14)}$$
$$\qquad\qquad\qquad\quad (**)$$

1952 – 64

$$(F'_{mdc} / PF_{e1dc}) = -5.44 + 0.027 \ Ydc \quad \bar{R}^2 = 0.99, DW = 1.56, \bar{S} = 0.40 \qquad \text{(A29.3.7.15)}$$

1952 – 64

$$(F'_e P / F_e) = -0.35 + 0.15 \ \frac{(F'_{m1dc} + F'_{mdc})}{PF_{e1dc}} + 2.99 \ \left(\frac{PF_{e1dc}}{P_{Fe}} \right) \qquad \text{(A29.3.7.16)}$$

1951– 65

$$\bar{R}^2 = 0.82, DW = 1.26, \bar{S} = 0.31$$

$$DF_e = 0.06Z_1 + 0.30P + 0.62 \ PF_{et-1} \quad \bar{R}^2 = 0.89, DW = 1.83, \bar{S} = 0.10 \qquad \text{(A29.3.7.17)}$$
2SLS

In all the foreign trade equations above, *FX* is defined as gold and foreign exchanfge reserves in billion of US dollars at the end of the year.

Price and Money Market etc.

$$T'_i = -5.85 + 0.12 \ Y' \qquad\qquad \bar{R}^2 = 0.97, \bar{S} = 0.78, \ DW = 0.95 \qquad \text{(A29.3.7.18)}$$
$$(**)$$

2SLS

1951– 65

$$\frac{CR' + DD' + \Delta TD'}{Y} = -0.19 + 0.24 \ \frac{1}{RL} + 0.0001 \ P_9 + 0.20t-1$$
$$(*) \qquad (**) \qquad (*)$$

2SLS

$$\bar{R}^2 = 0.75, DW = 1.76, \bar{S} = 0.03 \qquad \text{(A29.3.7.19)}$$

$$RL = 1.59 + 0.27 \ Rs + 0.26R_{Lt-1} \quad \bar{R}^2 = 0.94, DW = 1.38, \bar{S} = 0.13 \qquad \text{(A29.3.7.20)}$$
$$(**) \qquad (*)$$

1951 – 65

$$P = 0.13 + 0.00058 \ (\Delta MS' - \Delta MS') + 0.19PF_m + 0.72P_1 \qquad \text{(A29.3.7.21)}$$
$$(**) \qquad\qquad (**) \qquad (**)$$

2SLS

$$\bar{R}^2 = 0.99, \ \bar{S} = 0.03, DW = 1.57$$

$\Delta MS'$ and $\Delta MS'$ are defined as in   (A29.3.6.10a) and (A29.3.6.11a)

$$TD' / CR + DD' = -0.05 + 0.02 \ RL + 0.88 \ (TD' / CR' + DD')_{t-1} \qquad \text{(A29.3.7.22)}$$
$$(*) \qquad (**)$$
2SLS
$$\bar{R}^2 = 0.91, \ DW = 0.90, \bar{S} = 0.03$$

$$L' = CR' + DD' + TD' \qquad\qquad\qquad \text{(A29.3.7.23)}$$

$$U_t = 0.80 - 0.34L' / Y'_{t-1} - 0.05 \ \frac{ST_5}{X_{5t-1}} + 0.27U_{t-1} \qquad \text{(A29.3.7.24)}$$
$$(*) \qquad\qquad (*) \qquad$$

1947– 65

$$\bar{R}^2 = 0.41, \ DW = 1.93, \ \bar{S} = 0.043$$

Foodgrains Sector.

$$Y_{ag} = -16.20 + 0.63Y + 0.58 \ Y_{agt-1} \quad \bar{R}^2 = 0.93, \ DW = 2.53, \ \bar{S} = 5.76 \qquad \text{(A29.3.7.25)}$$
$$(**) \qquad (**)$$
2SLS

$$D_1 = -56.88 + 0.23 \ Y_{t-1} + 280.0POP - 9.65P_1 \quad \bar{R}^2 = 0.95, DW = 1.80, \bar{S} = 3.21 \quad \text{(A29.3.7.26)}$$
$$(*) \qquad\qquad (**) \qquad\quad (*)$$

$$X_1 = 1.83 + 0.60Y_{ag} - 0.49\,F_{mit-1} - 3.46Z_3 \qquad \bar{R}^2 = 0.98,\, DW = 1.44,\, \bar{S} = 1.61 \qquad \text{(A29.3.7.27)}$$
$$(^{**}) \qquad\qquad (^{*}) \qquad\quad (^{**})$$

1945 – 65.

Z_1: Dummy variable for shifts in food supply = 0 for 1939–43, 1 for 1944–8 and for 1953–65, 2 for 1949–52. Alternate equation for X_1.

$$X_1 = -5.27 + 0.70\,Y_{ag} - 0.95P_1 \qquad\qquad \bar{R}^2 = 0.98,\, DW = 1.47,\, \bar{S} = 11.90 \quad \text{(A29.3.7.27a)}$$
$$(^{**}) \qquad (^{**})$$

1944–65.

$$P_1 = 0.28 + 0.06F_{m1} + 0.62P_{1t-1} - 0.095Z_4 \qquad \bar{R}^2 = 0.90,\, DW = 1.96,\, \bar{S} = 0.08. \qquad \text{(A29.3.7.28)}$$
$$(^{**}) \qquad\quad (^{**}) \qquad\quad (^{*})$$

1944–65.

$$D_1 = X_1 + F_{m1} \qquad\qquad\qquad\qquad\qquad\qquad\qquad\qquad\qquad \text{(A29.3.7.29)}$$

Z_i: A dummy variable for years of World War II and other rationing yea, 0 everywhere else.

Manufactured Goods.

$$X_5 = -21.29 + 0.50Y + 0.75X_{5t-1} \qquad\qquad \bar{R}^2 = 0.97,\, DW = 1.94,\, \bar{S} = 4.13 \qquad \text{(A29.3.7.30)}$$
$$(^{**}) \qquad\quad (^{**})$$

$$N_{nag} = -1.79 + 0.22X_5 + 0.82N_{nagt-1} \qquad\qquad \bar{R}^2 = 0.98,\, \bar{S} = 3.31,\, DW = 2.72 \qquad \text{(A29.3.7.31)}$$
$$(^{**}) \qquad\quad (^{**})$$

1940–65.

$$P_5 = -0.20 + 0.27\left(\frac{WN_{nag}}{X_5}\right) + 0.34\,\frac{X_5}{X_5} + 0.33P_1 + 0.32PF_m + 0.08Z$$
$$(^{**}) \qquad\qquad (^{**}) \qquad\quad (^{**}) \quad (^{**}) \qquad (^{**})$$

$$\bar{R}^2 = 0.99,\, DW = 1.23,\, \bar{S} = 0.04 \qquad \text{(A29.3.7.32)}$$

$$W = 0.06 + 0.18\Delta\,P_c + 0.97W_{-1} \qquad\qquad \bar{R}^2 = 0.99,\, DW = 1.83,\, \bar{S} = 0.03 \qquad \text{(A29.3.7.33)}$$
$$(^{*}) \qquad\quad (^{**})$$

$$P_c = 0.03 + 0.55P_1 + 0.40P \qquad\qquad\qquad \bar{R}^2 = 0.99,\, DW = 0.96,\, \bar{S} = 0.04 \qquad \text{(A29.3.7.34)}$$
$$(^{**}) \qquad (^{**})$$

$$X_5/X_{5t-1} = -0.05 + 0.49\,L'/Y' - 0.127\,\frac{ST_5}{X_{5t-1}} + 0.99U$$

$$\bar{R}^2 = 0.69,\, DW = 1.66,\, \bar{S} = 0.04 \qquad \text{(A29.3.7.35)}$$

1947 – 61

$$ST_5/X_5 = 0.52 - 0.025\,H + 0.48\left(\frac{ST_5}{X_5}\right)_{t-1} \quad \bar{R}^2 = 0.45,\, DW = 1.62,\, \bar{S} = 0.16 \qquad \text{(A29.3.7.36)}$$
$$(^{*}) \qquad\quad (^{**})$$

1951–65

$$H = G + F_{es} - F_{ms} + \text{net foreign income.}$$

Semi–Manufactures.

$$X_8 = 29.06 - 0.43Y + 1.21X_{8t-1} \qquad\qquad \bar{R}^2 = 0.99,\, DW = 2.1,\, \bar{S} = 3.44 \qquad \text{(A29.3.7.37)}$$
$$(^{*}) \qquad (^{**})$$

1951– 65.

2SLS

Alternative equation for X_8.

$X_8 = -120.22 + 2.24Y$ $\bar{R}^2 = 0.93,\ DW = 1.06,\ \bar{S} = 7.38$ (A29.3.7.37a)
      (**)

1951– 65

2SLS

$P_8 = -0.004 + 0.064\,(ST_8/X_8)_{t-1}$ $\bar{R}^2 = 0.97,\ DW = 1.55,\ \bar{S} = 0.04$ (A29.3.7.38)
      (**)

1947–65

2SLS

Raw Materials.

$X_2 = -38.90 + 0.85Y + 0.60X_{2t-1}$ $\bar{R}^2 = 0.90,\ \bar{S} = 10.01,\ DW = 2.55$ (A29.3.7.39)
      (**)   (**)

$P_2 = -0.34 + 0.003\,X_{10} + 7.50\,\dfrac{F'_e}{X_8} + 0.63P$ $\bar{R}^2 = 0.98,\ \bar{S} = 0.005,\ DW = 1.8$ (A29.3.7.40)
  (**)   (**)   (**)

Other Prices.

$P_3 = 0.25 + 0.78P$ $\bar{R}^2 = 0.89,\ \bar{S} = 0.04,\ DW = \text{not given}$ (A29.3.7.41)
     (**)

$P_4 = 0.54 + 0.45\,P$ $\bar{R}^2 = 0.77,\ \bar{S} = 0.04,\ DW = \text{not given}$ (A29.3.7.42)
     (**)

$P_6 = 0.49 + 0.52P$ $\bar{R}^2 = 0.91,\ \bar{S} = 0.03,\ DW = \text{not given}$ (A29.3.7.43)

Identities.

$Y' = PY$ (A29.3.7.44)

$\theta = M / PY$ (A29.3.7.45)

$K_t = K_{t-1} + I'/P$ (A29.3.7.46)

$Y + Ti = C + I + F_{em} - F_{mm} + H$ where $H = G + F_{es} - F_{ms}$ + net foreign income

         (A29.3.7.47)

8. *N.V.A. Narasimham*: Narasimham's disaggregation is in terms of consumer goods output and investment goods output. The variables will be taken as identical to C and I as defined in Appendix II. Prices of consumer goods are labelled P_e and those of investment goods P_I.

$$Y = C + I \tag{A29.3.8.1}$$

$$P = 0.94P_c + 0.06P1 \tag{A29.3.8.2}$$

$$Y' = 1.65Y + 0.29P \tag{A29.3.8.3}$$

$$Y' = G + C_g + I_p + I_g + F_e - F_m - T_i \tag{A29.3.8.4}$$

$$\pi'' = Y' - WBG' - WBP' - Yag - \pi'CP \tag{A29.3.8.5}$$

Profits of unicorporated business, $\pi'CP$: profits of corporation, WBG: govt. wage bill, WBP private nonfarm wage bill.

$C' = (WBG + WBP) + 0.96\,(Y'_{ag} - T'_{ag}) + 0.85\,(\pi'^u - T_{\pi'u}) - 0.12$ $R = 0.99,\ VN = 0.54$
      (**)   (**)

         (A29.3.8.6)

$T_{\pi'u}$: Tax on Profits of unicorporated business. $T_{\pi cp'}$: Tax on Corporate Profits.

$I' = 0.0228(_{\pi'}u - T_{\pi''u})_{t-\frac{1}{2}} + 1.23\ (\pi\ CP' - T\pi\ CP')_{t-\frac{1}{2}} - 3.32\ -3.32\quad R = 0.93\ VN = 2.04$

(A29.3.8.7)

$F'_m = 0.11\ (Y' - T'_{ag} - T\pi'CP) + 4.32$ $\qquad R = 0.76\ VN = 1.23$ $\qquad$ (A29.3.8.8)
$ (**)$

$N_{nag} = 0.03C + 0.20\ I_{t-\frac{1}{2}} + 0.03$ $\qquad R = 0.81\ VN = 0.95$ $\qquad$ (A29.3.8.9)
$\phantom{N_{nag} =} (**) (**)$

$P_I = 0.16\ W_{t-\frac{1}{2}} + 0.35\ PF_{m6t-1} + 46.40\ I_{t-1} - 0.46$ $\qquad R = 0.71\ VN = 1.57$ $\qquad$ (A29.3.8.10)
(Not given) $ (**) (**)$

$P_c = 0.20\ W + 0.62C\,P_1 + 6.42C + 1.42$ $\qquad R = 0.87\ VN = 1.36$ $\qquad$ (A29.3.8.11)
(Not given) $(**) (**)$

$W = 3.23\ P_c + 0.84\ \dfrac{(N_{nag})}{POP} - 0.70t - 2.32$ $\qquad R = 0.87\ VN = 1.23$ $\qquad$ (A29.3.8.12)
$ (**) (**) \phantom{\dfrac{(N)}{POP}} (**)$

$P_1 = -17.90\ (Y_{ag} - F_{eag})_{t-\frac{1}{2}} + 2.72\ P_W + 4.18$ $\qquad R = 0.\ 91,\ VN = 1.23$ $\qquad$ (A29.3.8.13)
$ (*) \phantom{(Y_{ag} - F_{eag})_{t-\frac{1}{2}} +} (**)$

P_W is confined to price levels in countries importing from India. F_{eag} is exports of farm products. $(Y_{ag} - F_{eag})$ is therefore an indicator of availability of farm products.

$\pi'^u = 0.58(C + C_g) + 0.28$ $\qquad R = 0.95,\ VN = 1.64$ $\qquad$ (A29.3.8.14)
$ (**)$

$\pi'CP = 0.53(I_p + I_g) + 0.04$ $\qquad R = 0.92,\ VN = 1.78$ $\qquad$ (A29.3.8.15)
$ (**)$

$Y'_{ag} = 1{,}93\ Y_{ag} + 0.08P_{ag}$ $\qquad\qquad\qquad\qquad\qquad\qquad$ (A29.3.8.16)

$WBP' = 1.53\ N_{nag} + 0.01W$ $\qquad\qquad\qquad\qquad\qquad\qquad$ (A29.3.8.17)

$T'\pi = 0.022\ \pi'^u_t + 0.028\ \pi'_{t-1} + 0.064$ $\qquad R = 0.85,\ VN = 0.89$ $\qquad$ (A29.3.8.18)
$ (**) (**)$

30

Power and Agrarian Relations
Some Concepts and Measurements

I

This essay hopes to deal with one facet of the basic question concerning the interrelationship of political power and the agrarian economy. I shall address the question as much from the point of view of clarifying concepts and definitions, constructing operationally viable measures of these concepts (e.g. power), and outlining fairly simple dynamic models which may help to study this interrelationship of power and the agrarian economy.

The agrarian economy will be defined for the purpose of this essay as comprising landlords (zamindars), tenants, sharecroppers, and landless labourers. These four basic categories describe a variety of economic and social relationships around the two basic inputs of land and labour. There are other groups in the rural economy who may not be exclusively concerned with agriculture—moneylenders, for instance. These categories are, of course, abstractions. There is now a vast body of literature on South Asia which tells us about inter-regional as well as intra-regional variations in this classification—a rich pattern of differentiation in the agrarian economy due to natural and environmental factors, historical and institutional backgrounds, and more recent experience or commercialization, modernization, etc.[1] I am aware that this rich pattern implies that in any specific

M. Desai, S. Rudolph and A. Rudra (eds), *Agrarian Power and Agricultural Productivity in South Asia*, Berkeley, California: University of California Press, 1984.

This is a revised version of a paper which was presented in a first draft form to the South Asia Political Economy (SAPE) conference in November 1979, and some more drafts later to the SAPE Conference in December 1980. I am grateful to Hamza Alavi, Sukhamoy Chakravarty, David Ludden, Susanne and Lloyd Rudolph, Ashok Rudra, T.N. Srinivasan, and Myron Weiner for their comments on earlier drafts. The LSE–ICERD workshop in February 1980 on Economic Theory also heard a version of this paper and I am grateful to Ken Binmore and Tony Horsley for their encouraging comments. The usual caveat applies.

[1] The essays by Ludden, Herring, Rudolph and Rudolph, and Rudra in Meghnad Desai et al. (1984) illustrated various historical, regional, and local aspects of the agrarian economy. Reference

local agrarian situation, our categories will have to be modified or the model extended and revised. But for the time being, I intend to take this simple approach.

The economic activities of these people in the agrarian economy comprise production, consumption, exchange, and accumulation. These activities are carried out against a background of non-agricultural activity in the rest of the (local) economy and there are also traditional and kinship networks besides economic exchange relationships which form the set off social relationships. These production, consumption, exchange, and accumulation activities are not to be seen as static, once and for all outcomes. They allow the basic agrarian economy with its set of economic and social relationships to *reproduce* itself. Reproduction implies not only biological and physical survival but the renewal of the relationships such as landlord-sharecropper, landlord–landless labourer, etc. Reproduction means that from one production cycle to the next, the economy may change (output may grow, etc.) but its features retain a sufficient similarity to the earlier periods so as to not mark a sharp structural break.[2]

Against this general background, what does it mean to say, for example, that the landlord has power over the sharecropper? Can we make the notion of economic and/or political power more precise and perhaps amenable to operational use in fieldwork?

First, let me define power. Power is the ability to do things to others which you do not expect they can do unto you. In its economic and political meaning, power involves *access* to resources, *control* over certain instruments, and a *social relationship*. It involves *access* in the sense of outright ownership of resources with freedom to dispose of them as the owner wishes, or in so many cases access to institutions and agencies which may provide or withhold such resources. Resources may comprise land, water, credit, grain stocks, labour power, licences to sell certain inputs, etc. Access to resources in its turn provides a person with *control* over certain instruments whereby he can exert some control over other people's action. Control over the amount of land to lease out, over the wage to be paid, over the rate of interest to be charged, over the timing and amount of water input, etc. are examples. The instruments enable the owner to control the actions of others on the labour process, over the cropping pattern, over the rights to unionize, to strike, etc. But in the final analysis, power is a *social relationship* between people mediated by their unequal access to resources, and consequently unequal control

---

should be made to the work of André Béteille on Tanjore (as an early example of a study bringing together the ecological, historical, ad economic aspects for the local economy to study power). A comprehensive annotated bibliography of all the village studies in South Asia as well as elsewhere has been made by the Institute of Development Studies in its Village Studies Programme. See Claire Lambert (ed.); (1976), *Village Studies: Data Analysis and Bibliography*, Bowker/IDS.

[2] Though formal definitions may often obscure rather than clarify, let us formalize reproduction as a mapping from the set of variables X_t comparing economic and social relationships in period t to X_{t+1}. If a mapping exists, then the system reproduces itself. A more restrictive definition would be to say that if a function F exists taking X_t into X_{t+1}, then the system is reproducing itself, X can then be defined quite generally. Further restrictions on F are required to account for stability, steady state growth or disequilibrium, etc.

over instruments. Some forms of control involve all or nothing divisions of power—if one party has the power, the other does not; if the employer has the right to hire and fire, the employee does not. But other levers of power may modify the overall relationship which may involve several instruments. Thus, while the employer has the right to hire and fire, the employee may redress the balance by invoking the right to strike. This will modify the overall balance of power. Extraneous circumstances such as employment opportunities elsewhere or the possibility of substituting labour by machinery will again modify the balance of power. It will be helpful, therefore, to define power in a continuous scale between 0 and 1 whereby one can have either a complete dichotomy or a fluctuating share.[3]

So far I have not separated economic from political power though many of the examples have been economic. There is, however, a central difficulty about speaking of power in the economic context which must be squarely faced. The most frequently used paradigm in economics—neo-classical general equilibrium theory—has been able to provide explanations of economic phenomenon and predictions about likely outcomes of economic situations without any recourse to the concept of power. While institutionalist economists have demurred at this, by and large the challenge of general equilibrium theory must be faced if we are to demonstrate the necessity and usefulness of the concept of power. Various points can be made here.[4]

It frequently is the case in social sciences (and even in natural sciences on occasions) that two rival modes of explaining the same observable phenomenon coexist with no clear way of choosing between them. In the narrower context of econometrics, this is known as underidentification whereby rival structural models lead to the same observable outcomes. More generally, the rival models may take a dramatically opposite view of the way societies function. The general equilibrium model is well known to be an ahistorical, by and large static, equilibrium formulation of economic relationships where the units are individual economic agents. Its competitive version is the most fully worked out version and here all agents are price takers and no agent is quantity constrained on the demand or the soppy side. If a complete set of markets exists in each of which the price-taking–quantity non-constraint assumptions are satisfied, the competitive model can generate explanations of many observed outcomes. This world exists outside and independent of any political context, and power, economic or political, has no role to play in it.[5]

Even within the general equilibrium paradigm, there has been dissatisfaction with the stringent assumptions required to obtain the equilibrium result. A variety of market imperfections has been explored in recent years to accommodate more complex aspects of the economic reality. Thus, price rigidity, price distortion,

---

[3] My earlier formulations were in terms of an all or nothing, *zero/one* measure. It was only during the discussions at the SAPE conferences that I was persuaded to modify my view. I am especially grateful to Susanne and Lloyd Rudolph for pointing this out.

[4] Much of this discussion owes a lot to the lively and searching criticism of T.N. Srinivasan of an earlier draft. While I have not met his criticisms, I have made my own assumptions more explicit.

[5] See Sukhamoy Chakravarty's essay in Desai et al. (1984). He also shows that Marx having taken over a Ricardian classical model, power has no role in Marx's *economic* scheme of value relations.

quantity constraint, and lack of a complete set of markets in the face of uncertainty may all lead to outcomes different from the competitive one. But even here methodological individualism, exclusive concentration on economic relationships, and a preference for an ahistorical equilibrium characterization remain the features of this new development. This has been especially the case in recent research on the relationship of landlord to sharecropper where a large body of results has been generated explaining the observed share-cropping arrangements in terms of economic theory. This model has been extended to take in the problem that often there are interrelated transactions in more than one market between the landlord and tenant. Thus, landlord may double as moneylender dispensing (grain) credit and land lease simultaneously, his 'power' in one market reinforcing his 'power' in another.

The essence of this extended competitive model seems to be that while the notion of power conveys compulsion, all its results are derived assuming *voluntary* optimizing behaviour on the part of the agents. The observed outcome is still the same as we shall see below—sharecroppers taking up contracts affording them little more than the wage they would earn as wage labourers.[6]

An alternate formulation of the same observed outcome is in game-theoretic terms. This emphasizes the bargaining behaviour of landlords against sharecroppers and explicitly deals with strategies employed by each side. In the game-theoretic literature, the landlord–sharecropper arrangement is explained not so much by uncertainty or incompleteness of markets but by the presence of imperfect competition elements—asymmetry in size between participants for instance.[7]

I shall eschew the game-theoretic approach as well as the approach of general equilibrium theory. Again, while I shall be explaining the same observed outcome, my approach derives more from the Marxian political economy tradition.[8] It is partly a matter of taste but I also think that a political economy approach leaves one free to endogenize many more aspects of a situation than the general equilibrium approach. Thus it is not enough to assume that there is an infinitely elastic supply of labour/sharecroppers at a given wage. The task is to explain how it comes about that such is the situation. Without attention to the history of the region and of the distribution of landed property, it would be hard to do anything but to take the situation as given. This does not mean that our argument will not be analytical but that we hope it will be qualitatively different from that of the general equilibrium approach.

[6] The bibliography here is quite large. See, for a recent example, Braverman and Srinivasan (1979). They set up a model of individual utility maximizing behaviour in which the landlord faces an infinitely elastic supply of (sharecropping) tenants at a wage no better than what they would earn as labourers. The landlord has three instruments—plot size, output share, and the rate of interest on grain loans. Avoiding any reference to power, they prove the existence of a share-cropping equilibrium. There are indeed many parallels in my argument with theirs but our approaches differ. See also the references under Bell (1976) and Bardhan (1979) in the bibliography.

[7] For a game-theoretic treatment of the share-cropping problem, see Bell and Zusman (1976, 1977, 1979).

[8] I do not, however, make any formal use of the labour theory of value. Most of the argument below relies on a one-good model where the explicit approach of a labour theory is unnecessary.

Even within the approach of political economy, there are contending schools. A major argument concerns the characterization of the mode of production prevalent in South Asia. Some scholars believe that it is the semi-feudal character of the mode of production which explains exploitative relations in a backward agriculture.[9] Others contend that the mode of production in Indian agriculture is capitalist. My own view is that given the uneven regional development of different parts of South Asia, a product of ecological and historical forces, it is incorrect to put a single label on the entire subcontinent. The increasingly dominant tendency in Indian agriculture at least is capitalistic though the contrast between the modern capitalism of Punjab/Haryana as against the backward nature of Bihar/Bengal agriculture is obvious. Indian agriculture, as indeed the whole economy, is a social formation characterized by multiple, overlapping modes of production but the dominant mode is the capitalist one. This said, when it comes to analysing local situations, sufficient attention has to be paid to the historical background before adopting a single view.

Thus I take a political economy approach, emphasizing market relationships but making the historical background explicit. The notion of reproduction imposes explicit dynamic requirements upon our modelling strategy. Since I also wish to derive an operational measure and link it with political power, I have to go beyond a single economic unit. The purpose is very much a methodological one of forging concepts. In the political economy approach especially, empirical measurements have in my view gone ahead of the theoretical formulation. The theory of agrarian relations is still very derivative of the pre-revolutionary Russian debates between Lenin and the Narodniks, of the researches of Chayanov and Kautsky. There is much, therefore, which can be done to build explicit analytical models using the notion of surplus and the struggle for the share of surplus.

A simple way to characterize the model outlined in Section II below is to say that surplus is a measure of power. It is in terms of maximal and actual shares in the economic surplus of the various groups—landlords, tenants, sharecroppers, and labourers—that we define and measure power. I set up the model in terms of a single landlord *vis-à-vis* tenants, sharecroppers, and landless labourers. But in setting up the determinants of the share of surplus, there needs to be a dynamic link between one period and the next to highlight the reproduction process. Some simple measures of power in terms of 'distance' are derived in the single period and the dynamic contexts. These measures which relate to a single landlord are then aggregated over all landlords to derive a measure of the *power structure*. No attempt is made in this essay to implement the measure empirically but I do make some remarks toward the end as to the ways this can be done.

Thus the political economy approach is used here as an alternative to the general equilibrium or game-theoretic approaches. The emphasis will be on analytical, operational concepts and this inevitably means that the more qualitative,

[9] The semi-feudalism approach has been popularized by Bhaduri (1973, 1977). My own view that the mode of production in Indian agriculture is predominantly capitalist was presented in Desai (1970, 1975). I have benefited much from Ashok Rudra's comments on my earlier draft and his written work in this respect. See Bardhan and Rudra (1980a, 1980b) and Rudra's essay in Desai et al. (1984).

sociological–historical considerations which are usually given prominence in political economic writings will be ignored. My only defence in the face of that criticism is that it is in the analytical area that the political economy approach has been lacking. It also means that the approach can be compared with the usual paradigm.

II

In this section, I set up the basic model within which we can discuss some of the questions outlined above. The model is fairly abstract and only land and labour inputs will be discussed. There will be only one homogeneous output produced which will be called grain. I ignore here the problem of many outputs, relative prices of various crops, and the relation of acreage under different crops to price fluctuations.

Following the example of the Circuits of capital in Marx's *Capital* (Vol. 2), we set up an Exchange–Production–Exchange cycle. The Production cycle will be assumed to occupy two time periods—a slack season (period 1) when ploughing, weeding, planting operations take place, and a busy season (period 2) when harvesting takes place. The two periods need not be of equal length though nothing will hinge on their relative length. In the third period, no production takes place but contracts for the following production cycle are made in this period. This period also witnesses the division of output, payment of rent, repayment of loans. So schematically we have

Exchange	$\rightarrow$	Production	$\rightarrow$	Production	$\rightarrow$	Exchange	$\rightarrow$	Production
		slack		busy				slack
3		1		2		3		1

In the village economy, there are landowners, tenants, and sharecroppers as far as dealings in land are concerned. I recognize that often tenancy contracts are illegal or laws stipulate such tenurial conditions or rent, that share-cropping entirely displaces tenancy arrangements. It still helps to think of all these three arrangements at once. Thus there may be own cultivation of land or leasing-in and leasing-out of land at an agreed rent or a share-cropping contract specifying the share in output. We propose to begin with the case of one landowner, labelled zamindar, who cultivates some of his land and enters into tenancy and share-cropping contracts with others. The zamindar is thus endowed with land and implements as well as stocks of grain from previous harvests.

The tenant leases in land at an agreed rent, provides his own inputs, and has control over the disposal of his output net of rent. He may borrow from the landlord but this is not essential to the tenancy contract. The tenant will thus be assumed to be endowed with implements and some grain stocks to sustain production over the two periods until output appears.

The sharecropper will be assumed to enter into a share-cropping contract, but as is now usual in the literature, we shall introduce in a later part the assumption that he has to borrow some grain from the zamindar to sustain himself over the production cycle. The zamindar stipulates the interest rate on the grain loan. The degree of the sharecropper's dependence on the zamindar will be measured by the proportion of the loan to his consumption requirements over the production cycle. These consumption requirements will be labeled C_t for each period and are measured in grain units.

Apart from these three categories of dealers in land services, there are landless labourers. They work in agriculture during the production cycle at wage rates w_i for periods $i = 1$ and 2. In the exchange period, they work 'outside' agriculture at wage w_3. This outside wage is related to the overall economic conditions, e.g., in nearby urban area or in rural non-agricultural activity, etc. There is of course no full employment but I shall assume, for the sake of convenience, that enough wage income is generated to cover subsistence consumption. Also in this section, I shall assume that wages are paid in grain, even during period 3.

We take now the case of one zamindar with tenancy contracts, share-cropping contracts, and own cultivation/labour hiring contracts. The zamindar uses only hired labour but no household labour. The tenant will use household labour as well as hired labour. But the sharecropper will be assumed to use only household labour. All other inputs will be ignored for the time being. How does power impinge here?

In terms of our definition or power in the previous section, note that the different endowments of the different categories tell us about the *access* they have to resources. The zamindar has land and grain stocks, the tenant has grain stocks, and the sharecropper may have grain stocks but not sufficient to sustain himself over the production cycle. One index of relative power would be the ratio or grain stocks at the beginning of the production cycle to the required subsistence consumption over the cycle. Thus, if grain stocks are G_j for the jth category of agent $G_j / (C_1 + C_2)_j$ is a measure of the jth agent's power. Another element will be other opportunities available for earning subsistence (expected wage income in agriculture or outside agriculture in relation to subsistence requirements), as far as the tenant and sharecropper are concerned. For the landlord, a consideration is the availability of enough hired labour to be able to use all his land if no tenancy or share-cropping contracts can be made. But some of these things will depend on other elements in the village economy. So let us ignore them for the time being.

In terms of control, there are two main aspects in the production cycle—the commitment of labour input at various stages and the choice of cropping pattern. The zamindar has *no* control over the labour input of the tenant, *absolute* control over his own hired labour, and *variable* control over the sharecropper. We shall see later what determines the degree of control over the sharecropper's labour input. (It is not only labour input but the entire 'labour process' which is at issue here. But I prefer the label 'labour input'.) As far as control over cropping pattern is concerned, we delay any discussion till later since we have chosen a single crop economy here. But the graduation of low, variable, and absolute control will also apply in the case of crop choice.

Net output will be labeled Y and will be taken to be a function of land and labour inputs l_1, l_2 in each period. At this stage, we do not need to specify the production function specifically except to note that both l_1 and l_2 are needed to get output and that there is limmited substitutability between them.

As a first approximation, we can treat labour input in the two periods in terms of the total. Differentiation by season will matter when we wish to look at wage determination.

Let us suppose that the sharecropper contracts to give the landlord a portion α of the net output. His inputs are leased-in land L_s and his own labour l_s. To begin with, we can leave the question of borrowing for consumption over the production cycle open. Then, there are two ways of defining the outcome of the operation that the sharecropper undergoes. His 'income' can be measured at that maximum level of consumption C_s' which will leave his previous grain stocks intact. So if he has started the production cycle with stocks G_s then C_s' will leave $\Delta G_s = 0$. Thus

$$\Delta G_s = (1 - \alpha)\, Y_s\, (I_s,\, L_s) - C_s \tag{30.1}$$

Then

$$k_s' \equiv \frac{C_s'}{Y_s} = (1 - \alpha) \tag{30.1a}$$

Alternatively, one may compute the internal rate of return above costs. Thus, the only variable input by definition is labour. Hence we write profits π as

$$\pi_s = (1 - \alpha)\, Y_s - (1 + \rho_s)\, \bar{W}l_s. \tag{30.2}$$

Here $\bar{W}$ is the subsistence wage earned by a landless labourer. Setting $\pi = 0$, we get the rate of return earned by the sharecropper ρ_s in terms of the share of wages in output.

$$\omega_s = \bar{W}l_s /Y_s = (1 - \alpha) /(1 + \rho_s). \tag{30.2a}$$

Equations (30.1a) and (30.2a) define the income output ratio as

$$k_s' = (1 + \rho_s)\, \bar{\omega}_s. \tag{30.3}$$

Equation (30.3) defines in principle the advantage of the sharecropper over the landless labourer as being $\rho_s \omega_s$, the extra income he has due to access to land. It is then straightforward to see that the zamindar's power vis-à-vis the sharecropper lies in his ability to fix α' such that $\rho_s = 0$. A value of $\rho_s = 0$ would define maximum zamindar power. Then $C_s' = \bar{W}l_s$. This gives

$$\alpha' = (1 - \bar{\omega}_s) \tag{30.4}$$

The advantage of (30.4) is that it defines the maximum share purely in terms of the land leasing relationship independently of transactions in other markets such as money (grain) lending.

The *tenant* starts with enough grain stocks to hire labour as well as feed his household. Let h be the proportion of hired labour and $(1 - h)$ family labour. Then parallel to equations (30.1) and (30.2), we have

$$\Delta G_t = Y_t\, (I_t,\, L_t) - R_t\, (L_t) - hWl_{ht} - (1 - h)C_t, \tag{30.5}$$

where l_t is all labour $(l_{ft} + l_{ht})$ R_t is rent paid on L_t land, and Y_t is output.

$$k_t' = C_t'/Y_t = \frac{(1 - \gamma) - h\bar{\omega}_{ht}}{(1 - h)}, \tag{30.5a}$$

where $\gamma = R_t/Y_t$ and $\overline{W}L_{ht}/Y_t = \bar{\omega}_{ht}$

$$\pi_t = Y_t - R_t - (1 - \rho_t)\overline{W}l_t \qquad (30.6)$$

$$\bar{\omega}_t = \frac{(1 - \gamma)}{(1 + \rho_t)} \qquad (30.6a)$$

then

$$k_t' = \frac{(1 + \rho_t)\,\bar{\omega}_t - h\bar{\omega}_{ht}}{(1 - h)}. \qquad (30.7)$$

If the zamindar is all powerful, he will be able to extract that rent which leaves the tenant only subsistence wage. That maximum rent γ' can be derived from (30.6a) as before:

$$\gamma' = (1 - \bar{\omega}_t) \qquad (30.8)$$

Thus γ', α' are the maximum shares of net output extractable by a zamindar. If he can extract such shares, the zamindar is indifferent between own cultivation with hired labour, sharecropper leasing, or tenant renting. Just to keep our accounts complete, we can define landlord's income and rate of return as

$$\Delta G_z = Y_z\,(l_z,\,L_z) - Wl_{hz} + \gamma Y_t + \alpha Y_s - C_z \qquad (30.9)$$

Then

$$k_z' = C_z'/Y_z = (1 - \bar{\omega}_{hz}) + \gamma Y_t/Y_z + \alpha Y_s/Y_z \qquad (30.9a)$$

The landlord's profits arise from own cultivation as well from leasing land. So we get

$$\pi = Y_z - (1 + \rho_z) - Wl_{hz} + \gamma Y_t + \alpha Y_s. \qquad (30.10)$$

The internal rate is then

$$\rho_z = \frac{(1 - \bar{\omega}_z) + [1 - (1 - \rho_t)\bar{\omega}_t]\,\lambda_t + [1 - (1 + \rho_s)\bar{\omega}_s]\lambda_s}{\bar{\omega}_z} \qquad (30.10a)$$

λ_t and λ_s are ratios Y_t/Y_z and Y_s/Y_z respectively and in (30.10a) we have substituted for α and γ from equations (30.2a) and (30.6a). The most powerful landlord will only allow $\rho_t = \rho_s = 0$ and hence $\bar{\omega}_t = \bar{\omega}_z = \bar{\omega}_s = \bar{\omega}$

$$\rho_z' = [1 - \bar{\omega}]\,(1 + \lambda_t + \lambda_s)/\bar{\omega} \qquad (30.11)$$

There are thus two equivalent ways of looking at the economic power of the zamindar *vis-à-vis* his 'clients'—tenant, sharecropper, and landless labourer. If the *actual* income of these clients defined as maximum sustainable consumption does not exceed subsistence consumption, then the landlord is most powerful. The distance between actual consumption and subsistence consumption (equal to subsistence wage) is thus one measure of the relative power of the client *vis-à-vis* the zamindar. A second measure is the gap between the rates of return earned by the different parties, i.e. the gap between ρ_z and ρ_s, and ρ_z and ρ_p, etc.

Power measured as a distance is also relative to another party. Thus the distance of the sharecropper from the zamindar is

$$d_{sz} = (\alpha' - \alpha) = (k_s' - \bar{\omega}_s). \tag{30.12}$$

When $d_{sz} = 0$, the sharecropper has zero power *vis-à-vis* the zamindar.[10]

$$d_{tz} = \frac{(\gamma' - \gamma)}{(1 - h)} \quad (k_t' - \bar{\omega}_t). \tag{30.13}$$

The distance of the landless labourer from his employers–tenant or zamindar is measured symmetrically by the gap between actual wage and subsistence wage.

$$d_{ht} = (\bar{\omega}_{ht} - \bar{\omega}_{ht}) \tag{30.14a}$$

$$d_{hz} = (\bar{\omega}_{hz} - \bar{\omega}_{hz}) \tag{30.14b}$$

We now can drivel the total power of a tenant *vis-à-vis* the zamindar as well as the worker he hires as

$$d_t = \frac{d_{tz} - h d_{ht}}{(1 - h)} \tag{30.15}$$

Thus if the landless labourer can claw back some surplus from the tenant in the shape of a higher wage this can only come from what the tenant has clawed back from the zamindar.

The other measure is in terms of the rates of return ρ_j. This of course cannot be applied to the landless labourer. But the ρ_j expressions can be derived by setting $\bar{\omega}_j = \bar{\omega}$.

$$\rho_s = (1 - \alpha - \bar{\omega})/\bar{\omega} \tag{30.16}$$

$$\rho_t = (1 - \gamma - \bar{\omega})/\bar{\omega} \tag{30.16a}$$

$$\rho_z = \frac{(1 - \bar{\omega})(1 + \lambda_t + \lambda_s) - \bar{\omega}(\rho_t \lambda_t + \rho_s \lambda_s)}{\omega} \tag{30.16b}$$

when $\rho_s = \rho_t = 0$, $\rho_z = \rho_z'$ as given in (30.11). Thus the antagonism of the power relationship is brought out clearly in these formulae. The zamindar has what the others do not have. This is not surprising since we have equated economic power with shares in net output.

The rates of return measures are all derived on the assumption of subsistence wage and hence they are in some sense conditional upon a powerless group of landless labourers in case of ρ_t, ρ_z. Any deviation of $\bar{\omega}_h$ from $\bar{\omega}_h$ will alter ρ_t and ρ_z.

---

[10] The distance $\alpha' - \alpha$ may not be directly observable. There may, for example, it be historically established norms about shares, say, α^*. The zamindar may be compelled, say, by social pressures, to distinguish $(\alpha' - \alpha)$ as being $(\alpha' - \alpha^*) + (\alpha^* - \alpha)$. If, however, economic circumstances persistently justify a share higher than the norm, the landlord may be able to extract an equivalent return in other services or the average norm may break down. Jan Breman's analysis of the Hali tenure with the Anavil zamindars of South Gujarat immediately comes to mind f as an example of how norms can often be unprofitably binding on zamindars but which then can be done away with over time.

Another way of sustaining the norms would be for the zamindar to denote part of the surplus $(\alpha' - \alpha^*)$ he could claim to ritual expenditures—temple donations, etc. David Ludden's essay in Desai et al. (1984) bears on this question.

Interlinked Markets and Measures of Power

Having established a baseline in the case of only land and labour contracts, we can now look at the complications caused by interlinked markets on measures of power. While interlinkage can spread across all input markets, attention has been focused in some recent work by Bhaduri on the tie-in between credit and land. Thus, Bhaduri assumes that the sharecropper not only leases in land for payment of a share to the zamindar but that he also borrows from the landlord grain to tide him over the production cycle.[11] The sharecropper has some grain stocks but they only furnish a part of his consumption needs. He borrows a proportion σ of his consumption needs C_s. The zamindar charges a rate of interest ρ_{sz} on this. Then we can rewrite (30.1) as

$$\Delta G_s = (1 - \alpha)\, Y_s - (1 - \sigma)\, C_s - \sigma\, (1 + \rho_{sz})\, C_s$$

$$= (1 - \alpha)\, Y_s - (1 + \rho_{sz})\, C_s \qquad (30.17)$$

$$k_s'' = (1 - \alpha)/\,(1 + \sigma\rho_{sz}). \qquad (30.17a)$$

The presence of grain loan does not affect the internal rate of return ρ_s in any way. So we can see that in presence of a grain loan, the highest rate of interest a zamindar/lender can charge so as to leave $k_s'' = \omega_s$ is

$$\rho'_{sz} = \rho_{ss}/\sigma. \qquad (30.18)$$

We have labelled the internal rate of return ρ_{ss} to make it clear that the parties to this interest rate are the same. Equation (30.18) makes clear that when all grain is borrowed $\sigma = 1$, then the landlord can recoup the difference between α' and α by charging an interest rate equal to ρ_{ss}. In Bhaduri's model, it is assumed that σ is equal to or even *above* one. This would then mean $\rho'_{sz} < \rho_{ss}$ since the maximum a landlord can extract in share and loan repayment is total net output Y_s. An alternative way of seeing this is to write (30.18) as

$$(\rho'_{sz} - \rho_{ss}) = (1 - \sigma)\rho'_{sz}. \qquad (30.18a)$$

Now α' represents the maximum the zamindar can extract by virtue of his ownership of land. The source of power behind α' is access to land which the landlord has and by assumption the sharecropper does not have. In (30.18), we then add a dimension of landlord power due to grain loaning activity—the source of power now being access to grain stocks. Thus, even when there is no grain loan, i.e. $\sigma = 0$, the power measure we have proposed shows the relative power of the zamindar over the sharecropper. A new composite measure of power embodying these two sources then is

$$d''_{sz} = d_{sz}\,(L_s) + d'_{sz}\,(\sigma). \qquad (30.19)$$

[11] Bhaduri's description has been questioned on grounds of descriptive accuracy as to Bengal agrarian relations by Bardhan and Rudra (1980b). Srinivasan has questioned some restrictive assumptions of the Bhaduri model (Srinivasan 1979; Bhaduri 1979). My concern is to make my scheme comparable to his without delving into these issues.

Here $d_{sz}(L_s)$ indicates that the source of power is land ownership and $d'_{sz}(a)$ that it is indebtedness of the sharecropper.

Since d'_{sz} arises from indebtedness, it is quite possible (but I do not know how likely in actual fact) that the sharecropper may choose a high C_s (i.e. $C_s \geq \overline{W} l_s$) and thus may put himself in the zamindar's thrall. This is then partly a behavioural matter. As we shall see below when we analyse uncertainty, a sharecropper may choose to be in debt as a way or generating a secure level of consumption. In such a case, a measure of power would give a misleading impression since a sharecropper is choosing a high C_s which implies a high a and in exchange for the entire output Y_s gets C_s. The result being a high C_s/Y_s ratio despite seemingly low power.[12]

The behavioural aspect alluded to above can be clarified by using (30.1a) and (30.17a). The reduction in consumption due to indebtedness is given by the difference between k'_s and k''_s. Call this μ_s, then

$$\mu_s = \sigma \rho_{sz}/(1 + \sigma \rho_{sz}) \qquad (30.20)$$

Now if ρ_{sz} were decided independently of σ then the sharecropper can minimize μ by choosing a high σ since $\partial \mu / \partial \sigma = \rho/(1 + \sigma \rho)$.[12] So a zamindar (or any other lender) would make ρ_{sz} an increasing function of σ

Dynamic Consideration

What we have obtained so far are simple measures of power on the assumption that net output is so disposed so as to leave grain stocks at their previous level. We improved them a bit by introducing rates of return of the different parties. We need now to discuss dynamic considerations of our measure. Some of them are implicit, i.e., reproduction of the sharecropper relationship by renewing the loan contract at the same level when $\Delta G_s = 0$. But output may grow and this means that proportions such as k'_s and $\bar{\omega}_s$, etc. will change over time. Before we do that let us examine the process whereby power is exercised.

Of the three aspects of power that we defined above, *access* to resources is measured by access to land and size of initial grain stocks. The landlord has land to lease out as well as stocks of grain to loan. The sharecropper has no land except what he can obtain from the landlord and he has limited stocks of grain ($= (1 - \sigma) C_s$). The tenant by assumption has enough grain stocks to hire labour and feed his family during the production cycle ($h C_{ht} + (1 - h) C_{ft}$). He needs to lease in land from the landlord.

The aspect of *control* only enters in the share-cropping contract for the landlord has no control over the labour process of the tenant. This control is

---

[12] To see this, let us go back to the measure of power suggested at the very outset—the ratio of grain stocks to subsistence consumption. We can then decompose this ratio $G_s/\bar{C}_s$ into four parts

$$G_s/\bar{C}_s = (G_s/C'_s)(C'_s/Y_s)(Y_s/C_s)(C_s/\bar{C}_s)$$

The first part G_s/C'_s is the 'wealth–income' ratio in terms of grain, C'_s/Y_s is the share in total output of the sharecropper, Y_s/C_s the actual consumption output ratio, and $C_s/\bar{C}_s$ the relative affluence of the sharecropper *vis-à-vis* the landless labourer. These four components may move in different directions.

exercised by the landlord because having given a loan of σC_s, he has no guarantee that the sharecropper will put in enough labour to be able to have output which can repay the loan. While our measures are in terms of proportions of output, total output is so far left indeterminate. Having secured enough grain to survive the production cycle, what incentive does the sharecropper have to put in labour, especially if his indebtedness is very high?

Having given σC_s as a loan and land L_s to the sharecropper, the landlord wishes to make sure that the labour input will be enough to ensure output which will at least repay his debt. Thus let $Y_s = Y_s(l_s, L_s)$. Then he wants

$$Y_s \geq \bar{Y_s} = \frac{(1 + \rho)\, \sigma C_s}{(1 - \alpha)} \tag{30.21}$$

(I drop the subscript sz to the rate of interest since the context is clear.) But of course he will want higher output as well since he gets a of each additional unit. The control over the labour process is the way the landlord makes sure he recovers his investment. He will extract labour input from the sharecropper until he gets the same amount as if he was hiring labour at subsistence wage. Thus the minimum labour he wants is l_s' and of course the landlord expects that

$$Y_s(l_s', L_s) \geq \bar{Y_s} \text{ where } l_s' = C_s / \bar{W}. \tag{30.22}$$

The sharecropper wishes at least to leave his grain stocks unchanged at the end of the production cycle. He wishes to have output which will give $\Delta G_s \geq 0$, so he wants

$$Y_s(l_s', L_s) \geq \frac{(1 + \rho\sigma)\, C_s}{(1 - \alpha)}. \tag{30.23}$$

If the sharecropper finds at l_s'' that the marginal product of labour is still positive, he will work more. This is because every additional unit of grain can be used to provide for future consumption. This will then reduce future indebtedness. This is what provides the linkage between current labour input, current output, and future indebtedness. The sharecropper will maximize, output since additional output can be used to reduce the next period's indebtedness. (Of course, it can also be used to increase consumption and the choice will depend as usual on intertemporal considerations involving ρ. We take it, however, that ρ is sufficiently high for him to maintain current consumption low and reduce debt.)

Let us then say that the sharecropper in the current period (labeled o) has borrowed $\sigma_o C_o$ at interest rate ρ_o. He then puts in enough labour so as to maximize output for the given size of land. Let this output be Y_o. Then the surplus grain ΔG_s left over after repayment of loan can be expressed as proportion of subsistence consumption. (We omit the sharecropper subscripts unless it is likely to lead to confusion.)

$$\Delta G_s = \beta_1 \bar{C_1} = (1 - \alpha)\, \bar{Y_o} - (1 + \rho\sigma_o)\bar{C_o} \tag{30.24}$$

In eqn (30.24) we label the exchange period which begins the new cycle 1 and the initial period 0. Now β_1 is the proportion of surplus to subsistence consumption.

Ignoring once again any saving or dissaving in the exchange period, we can relate β_1 to σ_1 indebtedness in the new period since $\beta_1 = (1 - \sigma_1)$. Thus, we get taking $C_o = C_1$

$$\sigma_1 = 1 - (1 - \alpha)\bar{k}^{-1} + (1 + \rho_o\sigma_o). \tag{30.25}$$

The simple dynamics of the sharecropper situation captured in eqn (30.25) says that higher output will reduce the potential indebtedness of the sharecropper since at constant consumption level C, more will be left over for storage and future use. This also shows the incentive the sharecropper has for maximizing expected output, thereby putting in more labour than static profit maximization would predict. This is because every additional unit of output has to be valued in terms of its impact on future indebtedness.

The higher output from share-cropping sets up a problem for the landlord. Out of each additional unit he gets α but he loses $\rho_1\Delta\sigma_1$ of future loan interest from what remains with the sharecropper. His net gain depends on whether

$$\rho_1 \geq \alpha/(1 - \alpha). \tag{30.26}$$

If ρ_1 is greater than $\alpha/(1 - \alpha)$, then the landlord's loss from future interest reduction will be greater than his gain of the extra a in output. If the shares are typically equal, then this means that if interest rates are below 100 per cent the landlord will get more grain from extra output than he loses in future interest receipts. Of course, extra output by increasing d_s makes the sharecropper relatively less dependent while giving the landlord larger grain resources. Thus, the Bhaduri proposition that landlords have no interest in productivity gains depends on landlord monopoly of lending and some exceptionally high interest rates

The share-cropping situation then consists of an interlinked relation involving land leased for a share of net output, a grain loan at a stipulated rate of interest, and control over labour input. It will be reproduced from one period to the next as long as indebtedness is positive, i.e. $\alpha > 0$. But it will be reproduced in a modified form from one period to the next if the relative distance changes. Otherwise it is reproduced exactly.[13]

In the absence of the indebtedness element, the only difference between share-cropping and tenancy relates to uncertainty since rent is fixed irrespective of final output and only the share is fixed in share-cropping. To reduce uncertainty and moral hazard, the landlord undertakes supervision of labour input. We shall look into uncertainty a bit more in a later section. For the present we can end this section with a few concluding remarks.

The dynamics in the tenancy relationship also depend on the course of output. Since the tenant is assumed to hire labour, he cannot maximize output but with fixed rent, he would wish to maximize surplus above rent and wages. He may overutilize family labour but he will not use hired labour beyond the surplus maximizing point. The higher the output the smaller would be γ_1' and ω_t'. This will lead to obvious changes in d_t which need not be spelt out.

---

[13] Note thererore that reproduction does not imply unchanging distance or any other comparative static equilibrium situation or even a steady state. It only requires that there be an outcome of period t which will lead to a renewal of the relationship in $t + 1$.

III

Measuring the Power Structure

In the previous section, I have proposed two simple measures of power. These measures take the form of distances and are in terms of consumption levels or wage levels, In *principle,* we can measure these distances. But measurement is only a step toward providing a theory, so we must pursue the matter a bit further.

Our measure of power has two prongs. First, we say that if the landlord who controls allocation of land and grain loans can so extract the surplus from land under various tenures that the other party to the contracts—share-cropping, tenancy, labour hire—are left only with subsistence consumption, then we say that the landlord is most powerful. This implies in our terms that the relevant distances are zero. We state this condition as

$$d_{sz} = d_{tz} = d_{wz} = 0. \tag{30.27}$$

What our d measure then represents is a world in which competition among demanders of land for cultivation and for jobs enables the monopolist controller of land to extract maximum surplus. There is no coercion—no extra-economic compulsion needed to secure $d_{jz} = 0$ (for all j). There is implicit a lack of alternative opportunities and this needs to be spelt out.

The second prong of our measure is in terms of differences in rates of return. Thus in a neo-classical competitive theory, rates of return on different tenures and in different activities (moneylending/agriculture) will be equalized, From this point of view a situation of zero power would be $\rho_z = \rho_t = \rho_s$. We could further refine such measures by relating these ρ_j to riskless return in the economy as a whole.

The ρ_j measures therefore say that inequality in rates of return represents an ability on the part of one agent to secure a higher rate of return than another. These two measures tell two inter-related parts of the same story.

We can now look at the *structure of power* in terms of our measures. Notice that the condition $d_{jz} = 0$, $j = s, t, w$ already incorporates a world of one landlord and many competing tenants/sharecroppers/labourers. But we can adopt a measure of a landlord's power over the set of sharecroppers, tenants, and workers contracting with him by looking at the distribution of d_{jz} for each category j for a single z.

An all-powerful landlord will again be able to have $d_{sz} = 0$ for all his sharecropper, $d_{tz} = 0$ for all his tenants, and $d_{wz} = 0$ for all his workers. This immediately suggests that for a particular landlord one should be looking at the *mean* (in general, the moments of the distribution) of d_{jz} for each category. Thus, take a landlord z with S_z sharecroppers. Then

$$\bar{d}_{sz} = \frac{1}{S_z} \sum_{S=1}^{s_z} d_{sz}$$

is the mean distance of the landlord over all his sharecroppers. Some sharecroppers will be at $d_{sz} = 0$, others at $d_{sz} > 0$. The lower the mean, the more powerful the landlord. Also for each landlord, one can similarly define the mean distance over tenants $\bar{d}_{tz}$ and variance and mean distance over workers $\bar{d}_{wz}$ and variance.

The distribution of the d_{jz} singly or jointly then summarizes the power relation of a single landlord with all his 'clients'. The lower the mean and variance we conclude that the more powerful is the landlord. The higher moments of distance d_{jz} can also be similarly studied.

An extension of this idea to cover many landlords is straightforward. Within a given regional area, for each landlord one can *in principle* look at such distributions. Not all landlords will be equally powerful *vis-à-vis*, say, sharecroppers nor will a landlord be equally powerful against all clients.

How can one use the information in these distributions? Later on, I wish to sketch a theory of the determinants of the mean/variance of these distributions in a way which will illuminate the data gathered in village studies. But before that, we can illustrate some uses of the distance distributions.

Take the case where in a particular region there are many landlords as well as many sharecroppers, tenants, and labourers. Now if the landlords were of roughly equal size in landholdings and were to *compete* with each other, the client groups could improve their positions, i.e. their d_{jz} would increase. This would lead to high mean of individual landlords distributions as well as high mean over all landlords. This would be the beneficial type of competition much expounded in economics textbooks.

If landlords were to collude, then sharecroppers' conditions would be similar across landlords. The distributions would look similar and will have low means and low variances.

The *power structure* can then be defined as the degree of cohesion/competition among landlords as well as the distance between landlord and his clients and distances as between landlords. Landlords will be strong or weak relative to each other as well as relative to their clients. Thus a sharecropper working for a weak landlord may be better off than one working for a strong landlord, though sharecroppers as a group may be quite badly off. If we could measure these distances for a village or a relevant size area, then looking at distributions singly and as a group will be a major step toward understanding the power structure.

Notice that the data required for such measures are on outputs, wages, rent, consumption levels. These are not impossible to gather. What the discussion so far does is to show how to put such information in a systematic way to extract the power information.

IV

Reproduction of Social Relationships

A major problem confronting all theories of power in economic theory is that since we deal with voluntary contractual arrangements, it is hard to explain why any party would enter voluntarily into an exploitative arrangement. Having once entered such a contract, say by accident, why should anyone *renew* the contract or, in other words, why should such relationships be *reproduced*? This is the major stumbling block, for example, in economists' willingness to accept the Marxian theory of exploitation. Marx himself tried to combine a world where at the

phenomenal level voluntary exchange rules but structural class relations reproduce these arrangements which are unequal but not always perceived as such by
the participants. To the economist, on the other hand, it is sufficient to show that
it is in the interest of both parties to a contract to enter into it. The division of
benefits of trade may be unequal but neither party can be worse off than they
would be without the trade.

In the previous sections, I proposed a measure of power in terms of the
difference between actual and subsistence consumption in the static case or in
terms of the evolution of the unavoidable (in the sense that consumption is kept
at subsistence) proportion of indebtedness over time. Neither of these measures
involve any involuntary elements in behaviour. But we need to discuss in some
more detail as to why sharecroppers renew (reproduce) sharecropping arrangements.

Consider first the choices facing the sharecropper. To make matters easy,
assume that $\sigma \leq 1$ and $C_s = \bar{C}_s$. Thus at the beginning of any production cycle, he
does not owe anything to the landlord and may have a small stock of grain.
Typically this stock will be insufficient to feed him (and his household) over the
production cycle, i.e. $0 \leq \beta < 1$. He has a choice between re-entering into a share-
cropping contract and borrow $(\sigma - 1)\bar{C}_s$ at a high rate of interest or to work as a
hired labourer. The choice is between a guaranteed level of consumption over the
production cycle and perhaps no net surplus (or no addition to the stock of grain)
and finding work at subsistence wage.

Now uncertainty is important here. First, the sharecropper cannot guarantee
that he will find enough work at sufficient wage to provide subsistence since
typically there is insufficient work in the slack season though 'full employment' in
the busy season. So he has to compare the expected wage income as a hired
labourer with guaranteed consumption at $\bar{C}_s$ but with unknown value for future
indebtedness.

The value of future indebtedness σ_1 is unknown since output is unknown. By
taking a loan he incurs a fixed repayment charge of $(1 + \rho_o)\sigma_o \bar{C}_s$ against an
uncertain income $(1 - \sigma)\bar{Y}_{s,o}$. He knows the amount of land he will get and let us
say that he is willing to put in enough labour to maximize *expected* output. The
uncertainty in this case is due to weather and hence unrelated to any power
consideration and hence to any variable controlled by the landlord. Let us say that
θ is the random error with zero expectation and the production function for the
year τ is,

$$Y_{s\tau} = Y_s (l_{s\tau}, L_{s\tau}) + \theta_\tau. \tag{30.28}$$

So his future indebtedness is, from equation (30.25),

$$\underset{\theta}{E} \sigma_1 = 2 + \rho_o\sigma_o - \frac{(1 - \alpha)}{C_s} \underset{\theta}{E} Y_{so} \tag{30.29}$$

where E is the expectations operator .

Compared with this, the expected wage income is a product of the wage rate
and the amount of work available. The wage rate, one may take it, is impersonal
or at best depending on village-wide conditions but the probability of finding
work will depend not only on conditions such as weather which will affect
sowings, harvesting, etc. (θ_τ), but also, for any sharecropper, it would depend on

his personal relation with his landlord and the other landlords. If landlords competed with each other, then the probability of finding a job will be similar for sharecroppers across landlords and the uncertainty will reduce purely to the natural factor. If landlords colluded (as members, say, of a *jati*) or were of unequal power but dependent on some particular landlord, then it will matter very much who the sharecropper worked for and the relation of his landlord to the power structure. Thus, he may be denied employment by any other landlord in the area if they all collude or if his landlord is the most powerful amongst the landlords.

Now this personal element in the expected income will differ across different individuals, landlords, and villages. But this is exactly what d_{jz} captures. We have to think of d_{jz} as consisting of systematic components (of which more below) and a random component. The relation of an individual sharecropper to the structure can be looked at as

$$(d_{sz} - \bar{d}_{.z}) - (\bar{\bar{d}}_{..} - \bar{d}_{.z}) = \eta_8 .$$

(30.30)

The first part is the relation of an individual sharecropper to the average sharecropper *vis-à-vis* his landlord and the second term is the mean distance over all landlords less the mean for his landlord and measures his landlord's power relative to other landlords. Thus η_s is the individual sharecropper's personal component which will enter into his chances of getting a job.

Thus, his expected wage income will be

$$E(w_\tau l_{s\tau}) = (\bar{\bar{d}}_{wz} + \bar{w}) \underset{\theta_\tau \eta_s}{E} l_{s\tau} .$$

(30.31)

E is again the expectations operator and the expectation is now over two random variables θ_t and η_s.

Thus at the beginning of each production cycle, a sharecropper has to compare the certainty of consumption $\bar{C}_s$ and future expected indebtedness $E\sigma_1$ against the expectation of wage income $E(wl)$. What makes a sharecropper reproduce the relationship is then the way he views his chances of alternative income given the power structure. Thus the weaker he is *vis-à-vis* his landlord (low d_{sz}), then not only will he pay high ρ_0 and perhaps ρ_1 but his expected wage income may also be low. Thus he is led to reproduce the share-cropping relationship 'voluntarily', but saying that does not imply that power relationships play no role in his decision.

If η_s captures the individual component in the power relationship, the systematic components $\bar{d}_{.z}$, $\bar{\bar{d}}_{..}$, $\bar{d}_{wz}$, and $\bar{w}$ will be related to factors at the village and economy level. The sort of factors which enter here are well known: availability of irrigation, extent of double cropping, concentration of land ownership, the ratio of cultivable land to active labour force, availability of non-agricultural employment in the area or within a proximate distance, existence of credit facilities, extent of unionization among workers, and of collusion among zamindars, the nature and enforcement of legislation concerning minimum wages, tenure arrangements, etc. To list such factors is easy, but as we all know it is the quantitative importance of these various factors which is difficult to obtain.

One way to implement the proposed measures and correlate them quantitatively with these factors would be to compute for each village on which we have data (e.g. in the village studies bibliography produced by the Institute of

Development Studies, Sussex)[14] measures of power such as $\bar{\bar{d}}, \bar{\bar{d}}_{wz}$. Then we have to explain the within village variations in $\bar{d}$ measures and across village variations in $\bar{\bar{d}}$, using the information available on related factors. There will of course be tremendous inter-village variation but this is precisely what we want in order to be able to construct an explanatory equation for power. To some extent we can draw on work already done by Biplab Dasgupta and his associates on the village data using principal component analysis.

Another use of these measures is in designing future village studies. If the account presented here is useful, then studies ought to be designed which can collect for as many individuals as possible the raw data which go into making up the distance measures. The moments of the distribution of these measures will give an indication of the *cohesiveness* of the power structure.

It is perhaps worth arguing that measures of mean and variance (and other moments) of, say, the power of zamindars as a group in a village will also throw light on the nature of political power. By and large, I have concentrated on the economic dimensions of power and have taken a fairly abstract picture. But even here if the variance of power among the zamindars is low and the mean as well is low, then the politics of such a village will be more dominated by zamindars than in a village with high mean and variance. Thus though the clients may be in a majority compared to the landlords by a simple head count, when weighted by their relative power, these two groups may show different strengths. Thus, take a village of landlords and landless labourers. Suppose there are n landlords and N (much larger than n) labourers. Their power measure, however, is

$$P(z) = \sum_z \sum_h (1 - d_{hz}),$$

$$P(h) = \sum_z \sum_h d_{hz}.$$

$P(z)$ is the power of zamindars summed over all labourers working for each zamindar and then summed over all zamindars. $P(h)$, the power of hired labourers, is the remainder. When zamindars are all powerful, $d_{hz} = 0$ for all h and z; hence

$$P(z) = N, P(h) = 0.$$

The measure

$$P(z) = n, P(h) = N,$$

i.e. the head count assumes $d_{hz} = 1$. Now $\bar{d}_{hz} = 0$ when $\bar{w}_{hz} = w_{hz}$, i.e. when workers' share of output is that given by subsistence. One can say $d_{hz} = 1$ when workers get all output except for some share for landlords reflecting, say, competitive rates of return.

The head count measure can then be seen as one idealization of the power structure. The maximal measure $P(z) = N, P(h) = 0$ embodies the extreme feudal notion that dependents are completely controlled by their masters. There will of course be room for strategic coalition forming in different situations. Thus if one were to have village level basic democracy as the unit of election, then landlords in

---

[14] Clair Lambert (1976), Institute for Development Studies, University of Sussex, Falmer, Sussex.

each village may be able to exert much power. Parliamentary election over a wider area will give political parties a chance to mobilize those with low power but numbers on their side. By bringing in support from others outside a village, the hands of the powerless may be strengthened. Of course, zamindars may also use political networks to seek alliance with forces outside the village which will support the power structure. Actual outcomes are not predictable in general but one may be able to predict likely patterns if one knew more about the intra-village and inter-village variations in the distance measures.

V

Much of this chapter has concentrated on devising concepts and measures of power by using and extending the simple Marxian notion of economic surplus as a source of power. I have deliberately kept to questions on which an operational measure of power could throw some light. Reproduction has been incorporated into the scheme and at various points I have illustrated how 'voluntary' reproduction of social relationship does not preclude the notion of power. There is much further work to be done in extending this measure to more realistic situations. Thus multiple cropping, technological change, institutional reform in land and credit distribution, political alliances—all these factors need to be thought out in terms of this scheme. I hope to have made a beginning which others may find of sufficient interest to follow.

REFERENCES

Bardhan, Pranab K. (1979), 'Agricultural Development and Land Tenancy in a Peasant Economy: A Theoretical and Empirical Analysis', *American Journal of Agricultural Economics*, February, pp. 48–57.

—— (1980), 'Interlocking Factor Markets and Agrarian Development: A Review of Issues', *Oxford Economic Papers*, March, Vol. 32, No. 1, pp. 82–98.

—— (n.d.), *Labour-tying in a Poor Agrarian Economy: A Theoretical and Empirical Analysis*, Berkeley: University or California.

Bardhan, Pranab, K. and Ashok Rudra (1980a), 'Terms and Conditions of Sharecropping Contracts: An Analysis of Village Survey Data in India', *Journal Development Studies*, Vol. 16, No. 3, April, pp. 287–302.

—— (1980b), 'Type of Labour Attachment in Agriculture: Results of a Survey in West Bengal, 1979', *Economic and Political Weekly*, 30 August, pp. 1477–84.

Bell, Clive (1976a), 'Production Conditions, Innovation and the Choice of Lease in Agriculture', *Sankhya*, Vol. 38, Series C, Pt. 4, pp. 165–90.

—— (1976b), *Some Tests of Alternative Theories of Sharecropping Using Evidence from North-East India*, Development Research Center: World Bank.

Bell, Clive and Pinhas Zusman (1976), 'A Bargaining Theoretic Approach to Cropsharing Contracts', *American Economic Review* Vol. 66, September, pp. 578–88.

—— (1977), 'Sharecropping Equilibria with Diverse Tenants', *Economie Appliquée*, Vol. XXX, No. 3, pp. 391–412.

—— (1979), *New Approaches to the Theory of Rental Contracts in Agriculture*, Development Research Center: World Bank.

Bhaduri, Amit (1973), 'A Study in Agricultural Backwardness under Semi-Feudalism', *Economic Journal*, March, pp. 120–37.

—— (1977), 'On the Formation of Usurious Interest Rates in Backward Agriculture', *Cambridge Journal of Economics*, Vol. I, pp. 341–52.

Bhaduri, Amit (1979), 'A Rejoinder to Srinivasan's Comment', *Economic Journal*, June.

Braverman, Avishay and T.N. Srinivasan (1979), *Inter-related Credit and Tenancy Markets in Rural Economics of Developing Countries*, Development Research Center: World Bank.

Desai, Meghnad (1970), 'The Vortex in India', *New Left Review*, May–June.

—— (1975), 'India: Emerging Contradictions of Slow Capitalist Development', in R. Blackburn (ed.). *Explosion in a Subcontinent*, Penguin. See Chatper 2.

Desai, Meghnad, Susanne Hoeber Rudolph and Ashok Rudra (eds) (1984), *Agrarian Power and Agricultural Productivity in South Asia*, University of California Press.

Lambert, Clair (1976), *Village Studies: Data Analysis and Bibliography*, Bowker/IDS.

Srinivasan, T.N. (1979), 'Agricultural Backwardness under Feudalism', *Economic Journal*, June.

—— (1980), Comment on Meghnad Desai's paper, SAPE, unpublished.

Index

access, to resources in agriculture 374, 379, 384

accumulation 8, 27, 31, 145, 223, 266, 282, 341
  coefficient 144
  Marx's analysis on 120

adult literacy 156

Advani, L.K. 181

Afghanistan, and Taliban revolution 265
  war in 85

Agarwal's model, of macro econometrics 338, 340–52, 357

Agrarian Power and Agricultural Productivity 7

Agricultural Price Commission, recommendations of 32, 126

agriculture (al)/agrarian, backwardness 126
  bourgeoisie 127–8, 130
  capitalist mode of 28, 377
  change in 88
  cropping pattern in, control over 379
  development 272, 273
  economy 373
  exploitative relations in 112
  government policy on 27, 29
  growth 121, 128, 194, 280
  income 343
  investments in 126
  kisans in 32
  maliks in 32
  mazdoors in 32
  mode of production in 27–8

negative tariff on 139
  neglect of, in plans 142
  as occupation 29, 32
  -oriented policy 164
  output 164
  at partition of India 271
  poverty 119
  production (function) 23, 131, 345–7
  productivity, low 112, 119, 120, 127
  relations, power and 373–92
  resources 99
  in South Asia 280
  success in 196
  surplus, and impoverishment of peasantry 125
  tax on 128, 130, 187
  unrest in Telengana 35
  see also Green Revolution, landlords

Ahluwalia, Isher x

Akali Dal, Punjab 167

Ali, A. Yusuf 213

Ali brothers 241

All India Radio 315

All India Trade Union Congress (AITUC)

Allies, India's position on, in Second World War 213
  winning the War 248

Ambedkar, B. 66, 242, 246, 248

American Social Science Research Council (SSRC) 7

Amery, Leo 244

Anderson, Benedict 302
Anglo-Saxon legal tradition, in Europe
    301
Anna Dravida Munnetra Kazhagam,
    Tamil Nadu 167
Anti-Corn Law battle 131
Arya Samaj 225
    movement 239
Aryan invasion, of India 202, 225,
    226
Ashok Mehta Inquiry Committee 88,
    119, 125
Asian Clearing Union (ACU) 292, 293,
    294
Asian crisis 294
Asian Relations Conference 76, 85
Asian Tigers, success of 150
Assam, riots/violence in 89, 235
Associated Chambers of Commerce and
    Industry of India (ASSOCHAM)
    183
Attlee, Clement 249
Australian Congress of Trade Unions
    (ACTU), and CRA 178
Australian National University (ANU)
    94
Austria, war with Prussia 206–8
Ayodhya events 95, 162
    see also Babri Masjid
Azad, Maulana Abul Kalam 214, 241,
    311
Aziz, Sartaj x

Babri Masjid/ mosque, 257
    demolition of 10, 52–366–7, 162,
        220, 235, 236, 258, 259
    issue 252
    and 'shilanyas' for Rama temple in 9
backwardness, cause of 126, 131
Bagchi, Amiya xi
Bahujan Samaj Party (BSP) 52, 81
    BJP's support, in Uttar Pradesh 179
Bailey, 16
balance of payments 20, 22
Balogh, Thomas 108
Bandaranaike, Solomon, assassination of
    308
Banerji, Kalyan x
Bangla Congress, CPU and, in West
    Bengal 39

Bangladesh, 200, 216, 218, 269, 271,
    291, 300
    agriculture in 273, 275
    Bangladeshis, religion, language and
        formation of 228
    creation/establishment of 21, 234
    development in 285
    endowments in 277
    growth rates in 273, 277–9
    GDP of 278
    Indira Gandhi and liberation of 221
    land ownership in 283
    Muslim and Bengali identity in 308
    politics in 291
    poverty in 275
    refugees from 43
    struggle 43
    violence in 284
    war 230
banking system, in India 283
    in South Asia 283
banks, nationalization of 26, 27, 88, 256
Baran, Paul 134, 150
Bardhan, Pranab 5, 70, 127, 155, 166
Basu, Jyoti 40
'Battle of Plassey' 202
Bengal Famine 70
Bengal renaissance 237
Bengal partition movement 239
Bengali identity 308
Bengali Muslims 218
Benn, Wedgewood 243
Berlin Wall, collapse of 302
Béteille, André x
Bettelheim, Charles 32, 108
Bhaduri's model, on credit and land 383
Bhagwati, J. 124
Bharatiya Janata Party 76, 92, 103, 162,
    163, 170, 173, 235, 236, 265, 310
    decline of secularism and rise of
        257–8
    economic liberalization and, in the
        1996 elections 176–82
    economic policy of 52–61
    election manifesto of 1991 53, 54,
        58
    and globalization 82
    governments in states 52
    -led coalition government 259, 261
    -NDA coalition government 80, 84

in the 1999 elections 90
and Parivar 259
policies of 60
as right-wing nationalist party 53, 54
on rights of Kisan 58–9
rise of 77
-Shiva Sena government, and Enron
    case 179
trade policy of 58
Bharatiya Vidya Bhavan 252, 253, 264
Bhatt, R.S. 193
big business, inquiries and control of
    26–7
BIMARU states, growth rates in 284
Birlas 27
Bismark 200, 204, 205, 206, 208, 219
black money 74
Board for Industrial and Financial
    Reconstruction 172
Bofors 166
Bolshevik Revolution 149
Bombay, development of trade and
    education in 34
Bombay Club 162, 187
Bombay model 142–4
Bombay Plan, of 1946 54, 95, 113, 115,
    272
Bose, Subhash 113, 122, 156, 229
bourgeoise class 26–9, 44, 45, 48, 90,
    131
    definition of 32–3
    and economic growth 88
    failure of Indian 86
    non-agricultural 33
Brahmanand, P.R. 2, 144, 145
Brahmo Samaj 225
Bretton Wood system, collapse 136, 151
Britain/UK, macro econometric models
    for 337
British occupation, of India 202
    of South Africa 299
British imperialism, Marx on India and
    223–4
British textiles, demand for 320–2
    export of, and impact on Indian
        handicraft sector 6, 320, 321,
        326
    manufacturing, and labour cost 333,
        334
    and price of imported 332–4

price/value- quality relationship of
    323–9
and supply shift 323, 332–4
Brockway, Fenner 239
Bruton, Henry 3
Buddhism 299, 301, 313
budget, of 1991 101
    of 1992–3 162
    of 1994–5 163, 169
    deficits 73, 89, 102, 162, 163, 169,
        170
    gap, financing the 348
    problems 130, 131
buffer stock supply 73
Bukharin Plan 144, 145
bureaucracy, in South Africa 283
Byers, Terry xi, 4

Cabinet Mission 101, 215, 221, 249,
    251, 302
    proposals 9
cable TV networks 315–16
Calcutta, development of trade and
    education in 34
    industries and population in 39
Cambridge 3
capital, accumulation 342
    movements, regulated 137–9, 184
    stock data 344, 347
capitalism 5, 20, 21, 121, 135–7, 157,
    223
    renewal of Indian 7–11
    'socialism and Indian Democracy' 9
    socialism and Indian economy 149–
        58
    success of 151
    versus socialism 149–52
capitalist development 49, 130, 225
Cargil Seeds office, opposition to 180
caste, division in India 311
    mobility 16
    system 87, 98, 240
    and untouchability problem 86
    'wars' 102
Chakravarty, Sukhamoy 9, 70, 122, 124,
    127, 129, 130, 134, 137, 138, 139,
    155, 166
Chamberlain 244
Chandra, Bankim 238, 239
Chandra, Bipan 319, 320, 323, 332

Chandra Shekhar 101, 160
Chakravarty, Sukhamoy x
Chatterji, Bankim 225
Chauri Chaura incident 241
Chidambaram, P. 91, 177
child mortality rate 156
China, backwardness in, and tackling of
126
Deng's pragmatism in 100
economic power of 307
Great Leap Forward of 126
human development models in 298
war with India (1962) 20, 100, 164,
229–30
Choudhury's model, of macro economet-
rics 338–51
Christianity 299, 301
Churchill, Randolph 244
Churchill, Winston 211, 243, 247, 248
on India 244
civil rights 260
civil services, inflation and 71
Clark, Kenneth 295
class, structure, in India 32–4
struggle 35
Coal and Steel Communities, Europe
300, 306
coalition governments/politics 81, 102,
103167–9, 175, 179, 291
Cobb-Douglas production function
345
Cold War 3, 276, 284, 285
Cole, DDH 114
Colombo Plan 276
Comintern 36
Commonwealth, India and 85
communal riots 65, 234, 236, 254, 255
communalism 10, 232, 234–8, 251, 261
or constitutionalism 259–60
'secularism and Indian nationhood'
10, 232–61
communist movements, in India 35, 36–
9
Communist Party of Great Britain
(CPGB) 36
Communist Party of India (CPI) 2, 36–
9, 235
and Bangla Congress 39
and Congress Party 5
on Pakistan and Kashmir issue 36

split in 38
support to Indira Gandhi 165, 167
Communist Party Marxist (CPM) 5, 21,
36, 38, 39, 50, 165, 167, 235
Political-Organization Report of
1968 41
-led United Front, in West Bengal
21, 22, 41–4
Communist Party (Marxist-Leninist) 21,
43
and Naxalbari revolt 40
Communist Party of Soviet Union
(CPSU) 36
Confederation 216
Germany and 201
Congress of Vienna 200, 203
Congress party 5–8, 15–18, 36, 46, 48,
57, 78, 80, 92, 156, 160, 162, 175,
233, 241, 242, 291
and British India's entry into the War
247
decline in dominance of Indian
politics 63, 95, 101, 258, 309
and economic reforms 10, 161, 174
electoral defeats of 165, 168
formation of 238
hegemony 81, 89
High Command/ leadership 168,
169
Indira Gandhi reshaping the 22
and Left 7
majority, in Central Legislature 215
and Muslim League 246
and Muslim vote-banks 246, 247,
260
-National Left Front government
179
in 1967 elections 256
on partition of India 249
political dominance of 9
and secularism 235
split in 21, 165, 167, 169
in state elections 71, 163
victory in 1967, 1971 elections 20,
21
winning provincial elections 246
Congress Agrarian Reform Committee
273
Congress Socialist Party (CSP) 36
Congress 'Syndicate' 165

Conservative Party, in Britain 211
Constituent Assembly 62, 66, 96–8,
    103, 213, 215, 216
Constitution of India 63, 64, 66, 79,
    216, 227
    amendments to 66–8, 80, 256
constitutional monarchy 203
constitutional reforms, in British India
    237
consumption function 341–3
corporate and non-corporate organiza-
    tions, profits of 343–4
corruption, in politics 195, 295–6
cottage and village industries 142, 144
cotton textiles, demand for, in 19th
    century India 319–36
    industry 28
    manufacturers, in Britain 323, 326
    see also British textiles
Cripps, Stafford 248
Cripps Mission 248
currency convertibility issue 280, 292–3
Curzon, Viceroy 238

Dalit(s) 7, 81, 90
    militancy 95
    movement 92
Dalmia-Sahu-Jain business houses 27
Dandekar, V.M. 152, 156
Danes occupation, of India 202
Dantwala 2
Das, C.R. 250
Das, Veena x
David Glass Memorial Lecture 133
Davos Conference 162
'Death', democracy and decline 84–93
    'Democracy and Development' 10
debt, burden 158
    external and internal 29, 161, 281
    foreign, problem of 56, 58
    internal 56, 57, 58
defence, budget 20, 69
    expenditure 307
    policy 96
deficit financing, and inflation 69
Delhi School of Economics 3, 4
Delhi Sultanate 201
democracy 82, 102
    and communal relations 265
    'and development' 10, 94–104

in India 63, 67, 76, 86, 169
    in India and Sri Lanka 309
Desai, Morarji 128, 130, 145, 146, 151
Desai, P. 124
developing countries, 57, 185
    economic strategies of 150
    industrial growth 153
development, democracy and 94–104
    perspectives 141–6
    in South Asia 285–6
'Development Perspectives', and
    Mahalanobis 9
Directive Principles of State Policy 66
disguised unemployment 143
Dobb, Maurice 120
Dravida Munnetra Kazhagam (DMK),
    in Tamil Nadu 37–8, 167
Dravidian movement, in South India
    226
Dutch occupation, of India 202
Dutt, R.C. 116, 117, 120, 238
Dyer, General 241

East Asian economies, growth of 134
East European economies 167
East India Company 234, 236, 301
    British manufacturers exports to
        territories of 326
    Charter of 224
East Pakistan, liberation of 256
    see also Bangladesh
Eckaus, R. 108
economy (economic), crisis of 1991 257
    development 17, 18, 77, 261
        growth 22, 122, 223, 231, 265
        fall in 254
    liberalization 134
    measuring of 317
    nationalism, economics of 53–9
    planning 134
    policy 95, 175, 186, 340
        of Bharatiya Janata party 52–61
    radicalism, social conservatism and
        88, 98–9
    reforms 10, 52, 81–2, 90, 91, 96,
        102, 157, 160–75, 185, 193,
        285, 291
    relations 22–32
education system, growth of 34–5
1857, events of 237, 239

elasticity of demand curve 321, 322, 335
elections, 64–5, 90
    of 1937 and 1946 244
    of 1967 20
    of 1971 21
    of 1977 165
    of 1980 165
    of 1989 166
    of 1991 101
    of 1996, economic liberalization and
        BJP 176–82
    First , in British India 17, 211
    Second 17
    State 162–3
Ellis, Howard 2
Emergency, Internal 6–7, 46–51, 78,
    165
employment, growth in 142
    index in agriculture 345
    in industrial sector 23
    in organized sector 87, 152
    problem of 144–5
    in public sector 152, 156
Engels 135, 151, 223
Enron case 179, 180
entry policy 172–3
Ershad, President 283, 285
Europe, balance of trade with South Asia
    298
    Single Market 314
European Central Bank 314
European Community 151, 313, 314
European Economic Community 300
European maritime countries, and trade
    201–2
European Monetary Union (EMU) 292,
    293, 314
European Union 289, 292, 300, 314
Eurotom, Europe 300
Exchange-Production-Exchange cycle
    378
Exim Bank lecture 9, 149
exit policy 171–2, 178
expenditure, government 169, 177, 195,
    349
exploitation, Marx's theory of 388
    of workers, in capitalist countries
        151
exports, India's 177, 185, 272
    -oriented policy 278

famines 20, 88, 277
Farm Management Committee 273
Farm Management Survey 340
federalism, economic growth and
    economic stagnation 15–19
federation /federal 211, 243–5, 303, 304
    India as 243–4
Feldman, Girgorii Alexandrovic 108
Feldman model 144
fertilizer, subsidies to 130, 169
film industry 316
financial and banking sector 192
    see also banks
fiscal deficit 72–3, 155
Five Year Plans, First 276
    Second 8, 49, 87, 95, 119, 142,
        144–5, 163, 178, 276
        resource crisis of 186
    Third 88, 95, 107–9, 126–7, 146,
        164, 254, 350, 351
    Fourth 22, 49, 88, 108, 110164, 254
    Fifth 134, 127, 139–40
    Sixth 128, 134
    Seventh 137
    Eighth 137
    Ninth 134
food/food grain, aid, from USA 273
    availability 23, 24, 274
    imports, from US 29
    output 21–5, 30, 45
    prices 73, 348
    scarcity/shortage 87, 119, 276
    sector 369–70
Ford Foundation 2, 3, 7, 88, 119, 125,
    126
foreign aid/ borrowings 22, 29, 100,
    125–6, 142, 146, 155, 186, 276–7,
    279
foreign capital, entry of 28, 29, 57, 58,
    60, 161, 162, 179, 180, 181, 188
foreign debt crisis, of 1991 146
foreign direct investment (FDI) 102,
    137, 172, 173, 185, 194, 195, 281,
    286
foreign exchange, constraint 145
    crisis 164
    reserve 160, 161
foreign policy 229
foreign portfolio investment 137
France, war with Germany 306

Franco-Prussian War of 1870–1 207
Frank, Andre Gunder 124, 134
Frederick William IV, of Prussia 204
free trade 58, 275–6
    doctrine of 223, 224
French Republics 68
French Revolution 103, 201, 203
Frisch, Ragnar 108
Fuller, Christopher xi
Fundamental Rights 66

Gadgil, D.R. 116, 117
Galbraith, John Kenneth 108
game-theoretic approach 376, 377
Gandhi, Indira 5, 7, 9, 63, 77, 80, 88,
    90, 127, 128, 164, 165, 167, 169,
    175, 186, 193, 221, 234, 279
    assassination of 236, 308
    and Congress party 22
    and crisis of secularism 254, 256–7
    and Emergency 6, 46, 47, 100
    'garibi hatao' of 178, 256
    position of 21
Gandhi, Mahatma (Gandhian) 55, 77,
    79, 86, 115, 117, 232, 239, 248
    Dandi march of 242
    economics 53, 115
    and experience in South Africa 250
    and Indian nationalism 241–2
    -Irwin Pact 242, 247, 249
    and Jawaharlal Nehru 245
    on Jinnah's theory of nationality 250
    model of economy 114
    and non-cooperation movement
        209
    and partition 249–51
    and popularization of Hindi 226
    Quit India campaign of 248
    Ram Rajya of 55
    at the Round Table conference 303
Gandhi, Rajiv 9, 80, 90, 95, 101, 121,
    154, 155, 160, 175, 315
    death of 257, 308
    policy under 165–6
Gandhi, Sonia 259
Gaekwads of Baroda 1
Gender Development Index (GDI),
    India's 76
General Agreement on Tariffs and Trade
    (GATT) 58, 171, 173–4, 188

general equilibrium theory, neo-classical
    375, 376
German nationalism 203
Germania to Germany 203–8
Germany(German) confederation 201,
    203
    creation of Reich in 200, 207
    imperialism 201
    and India and nation-states 9, 199–
        219
    planning in 192
    war with France 306
Ghosh, Jayati xi
Gladstone 238
globalization 10, 56, 77, 82, 96, 181,
    183–4, 257, 293, 294, 298, 313
Gokhale, G.K. 77
Goldsmith, R.W. 70, 71
Gorbachev 134
Government of India Bill 1935 78
Government of India Act 1935 50–1,
    62, 64, 66, 201, 211, 216, 243, 245,
    303
Gowda, Deve 81, 90
grain loan, by landlords to labour, and
    power 383–4, 386
Grameen Bank, Bangladesh 291, 312
Great Depression 149
Green Revolution 6, 22, 29–32, 45, 88,
    95, 99, 100, 112, 121, 127, 142,
    153, 164, 168, 178, 187, 189, 273,
    274, 277, 312
    and high food output 110
Greenaugh, Paul 120
Gregory, Theodore 191
Gross Domestic Product (GDP), of India
    60, 73, 90, 103, 111–13, 153, 154,
    156, 157, 161, 162, 166–7, 169,
    194, 195, 270, 276–9, 285, 286
    of Bangladesh 270
    of Pakistan 270
    planning and 134
    of South Asia 286
Grossdeutch solution 204, 205, 207
Grossindische solution 215
Group of 77 173
growth performance/rate 89, 99, 111,
    113, 123–4, 137, 19, 140, 153, 154,
    162, 168, 188, 286, 350
    and inflation 71

planned and actual 135
rates in South Asia 274–5, 277–9,
290
Gujral, I.K. 81, 90
Gujarat and its Bhasmita 10, 264–6
riots/ violence in 10, 179, 265, 266
Gulati, Ashok 139
Gulf countries 314
remittance from 278
Gulf War, and liquidity squeeze 161

Habsburg empire 203
Halden, G. 155
handloom, industry, problems of 336
production, India's 319, 323
Haq, Khadija x
Haq, Mahbub ul 11, 289, 294
Haq, Zia ul 279, 285
Harappa 298
Harriss, John xi
Harrod-Domar model of planning 108,
114, 123
Hasan, Mushril 240
Hasina, Shaikh 285
Hayek, Friedrich 3, 191
Heston, Alan 3
Heyman, Daniel 69
high yielding variety (HYV) seeds 30,
126
Hind Swaraj 114
Hindi, popularization of, as national
language 226
Hindu Code Bill 253
Hindu culture, and society 201, 282
Hindu Family Law, Nehru on 98
Hindu fundamentalism 312
Hindu Mahasabha 252, 246
movement 234
Hindu-Muslim riots/ clashes 232, 233,
236
Hindu nationalism 52, 225, 239
Hindu population 209, 210
'Hindu rate of growth' 95, 166, 193,
194, 256, 279
Hindu religious identity 309
Hindu religious symbols 259
Hindu revivalists, Nehru and 252–3
Hindu vote-bank 100, 265
Hinduism 299, 301
and Hindu society 201, 257

reforms in 225
Hindutva, and BJP 52, 53, 77, 220, 235,
257, 258
Parivar, and rise of 95
revival of 10
history, and Indian nationalism 225–6
and religion 222
Hitler, Adolf 200
and Nazi Germany 302
Hobsbawm, Eric 136
human development, record of, in South
Asia
Human Development Index, India 76,
85
Human Development Report, Pakistan
289
Hyderabad, status at partition 249

Illbert Bill 1883 238
Imperial War Cabinet 241
imperialism 282
import(s) 73, 154
of capital goods 344
liberalization 165
-substitution industrialization
strategy 95, 272, 273, 279
income, in Bangladesh 269
emerging contradictions, and
capitalist development 20–45
expenditure models 338, 341
growth 70, 194
in India 269
in Pakistan 269
quality and value of British imported
cloth 323–9
unequal distribution 282
indebtedness 56, 60
of sharecroppers 384–6, 389
India, agriculture at partition 271,
273
and China war 49, 230, 254, 277
crisis of 1991 101–3
dominion status to 214
end of first republic 10, 62–8
and Germany and nation-states 199–
21
and globalizing world 183–90
industrial economy 270
and Pakistan 85, 293
wars 230, 251, 254, 272, 277

as republic 62
Soviet-style of planning 185, 186
a syncretic vision of 220–1
and USSR 284
see also partition
India Investment Centre 193
Indian Army, in Bangladesh 44
defeat of, in Indo-China war 230
role in reconstruction of national
unity 230
Indian Council for Research on International Economic Relations (ICRIER)
183
Indian Council for Social Sciences
Research (ICSSR) 7
Indian Institute of Managements (IIMs)
186
Indian Institute of Technology (IITs) 186
Indian National Congress 209, 210, 211,
213, 219, 211, 213, 219, 225–7,
271, 302
in the 1937 elections 245
see also Congress party
Indian nationalism 208,
communalism, secularism and 232–
61
Gandhi and 241–2
origins of 224–6
Indian politics 1947–66 15–19
Indica 10, 220, 221
to South Asia 208–18
see also India
Indo-Bangladesh Accord of 1997 315
Indo–Sri Lanka Trade Pact 292
Indus Valley civilization 251
Industrial Commission 1916 240
Industrial Revolution, England 119, 301
industrialization 86, 87, 115, 121, 122,
145, 164, 229, 271–3, 275, 279
industry (ial) 98–9
deregulation 165
development of 34
government policies on 27, 29
growth 187
in South Asia 280–1
at partition 271, 275–6
policies 27
production 23, 25
in South Asia 282
stagnation 88, 89, 153

strategy, of Nehru-Mahalanobis 127
inequalities 99, 224, 282, 283, 310
inflation 20, 21, 69–75, 167, 170, 175,
190, 274, 343
impact on political parties 71
and money supply 71
in Pakistan 278
Information Technology (IT) sector 91
Institute of Economic Growth 6
Intensive Agricultural Development
programme 29, 126
International Commodity Agreement 4
International Monetary Fund (IMF) 89,
95, 123, 128, 129, 137, 153, 154,
162, 178, 193, 279, 285, 307
International Tin Agreement 4
investments 144, 341–3, 344, 348
foreign 29
Iranian Revolution 265
Islam 301, 313
Hinduism and 299

Jainism, in Gujarat 266, 299
Jalianwala Bagh incident 241
Jan Sangh 7, 42, 54, 165
Janata government 7, 53, 95, 100, 128,
178, 257
Janata party 79, 163, 165
Japan, development wave in 298
per capita income of 153
Jayakar, 246
Jayalalitha, J. 101
Jayaprakash Narayan 3, 71, 78
Jayaraman, T. 53
Jharkhand, controversy on 62
Jinnah, M.A. 78, 80, 201, 209, 212–14,
219, 233, 240, 244, 245, 247, 248,
304
demand for Pakistan by 246, 249
mass mobilization by 249
Johnson, Lyndon 73, 127, 193
Joshi, Ram 2
Joshi, Vijay 69–71, 73
Junagadh, status of, at partition 249

Kadekodi, Dr. 133
Kaldor, Nicholas 119, 125
Kalecki, Michael 108
Kamaraj Nadar 88, 126
Kanshi Ram 81

Kargil conflict 306
Karunakaran, K. 168
Karunanidhi, M. 101
Kashmir, accession to India 249, 305
    armed conflict in 216
    confrontation between India and
        Pakistan on 251
    issue 62, 89, 272, 305
    separatist movement in 227
    violence in 257
Kautsky, Karl 120
Kentucky Fried Chicken (KFC),
    agitation against 180–1, 186
Keynes, 184
    growth theory of 136, 282
    models for underdeveloped countries
        341, 342, 246
Keynesian macro-economics 70
Khalistan, movement 62, 78, 89, 100,
    200, 218, 227, 228, 235, 236, 247,
    257, 304
Khan, Aga 240
Khan, Ayub 276, 277
Khan, Nusrat Fateh Ali 315–16
Khan, Saiyad Ahmad 210, 237, 301
Khan. Mohammed Zafrullah 213, 244,
    246
Khan, Yahya, Chinese support to
    43–4
Khilafat movement 241
Khruschev, N. 150
Kisan Mazdoor Praja Party 252
Kishwar xi
Klein, Lawrence 3, 4, 337
Klein-Goldberger model 352
Kleindeutsch programme 204, 207, 208,
    218
Korea, manufacturing output by 153
Kosambi, Damodar 2
Kripalani, J.B. 252
Krishnamachari, T.T. 125, 164
Krishnamurty, K. 6
Krishnamurty's model, of macro
    econometrics 338, 345–50, 352,
    361–6
Krishnamurty-Choudhury's model, of
    macro econometrics 339, 343, 345,
    352, 363–4
Krishnavarma, Shyamji 79
Kroptkin, Peter 114

Kulturstaat movement, Germany 203
Kumar, Dharma x, 6

labour, input in agriculture 379, 380
    landless labourers 27, 32, 40, 274,
        373, 379, 380
    land to 31
    migration in South Asia 300
    process, control over 384–5
Labour Party/government, Britain 8,
    213, 214, 218, 248
Lahore Resolution 243
Laissez-faire 146, 150, 223
Lakdawala 2
Lal, D. 124
land, benami 40
    leasing relationship 380
    reforms 8, 27, 28, 42, 119, 123, 125,
        126, 271, 273, 275
landlords (zamindars) 373
    economic power of 381, 387–8
    income/ profits of 381
    and sharecroppers 376, 378, 390
Lange, Oscar 108
languages, in India 233
    -religion, and nationhood 217–18
Laski, Harold 94
Latin America, economies of 167
    inflation in 69, 70
Lefber, L. 108
Leiffer, Michael xi
Left nationalism 146
Left parties, in Indian politics 5, 165,
    235–6
Leijionhufvud, Axel 69
Lenin, VI 151
Lewis, W.A. 114, 143, 341
Lewis model 342, 352
Liberal Party, Britain 240
liberalism, and nationalism 222, 223
liberalization 52, 96, 137, 147, 153,
    155, 187, 189, 191–6, 274, 316
    as escape route 128–9
    and growth performance of India
        124
    and low inflation economy 74, 75
Liberation Tigers of Tamil Eeelam 307,
    308
    see also Sri Lanka
life expectancy 156

linguistic states 16, 17, 27, 34, 37, 227, 228
Linlithgow 246, 247
List, Friedrich 115, 223
literacy 98
    adult 156
Little, Ian 69, 70, 71, 73, 108
loan *melas* 169
Lokayan 7, 78, 80, 88
London School of Economics (LSE) 4, 5, 191
Lucknow Pact 240
Ludden, David x

Maastricht Treaty, Europe 300
MacDonald, Ramsay 242
macro econometric models 139, 337–51
Madan, T.N. x, 218
Maddison, Angus 298
Madras, development of trade and education in 34–5
Mahalanobis, P.C. 79, 108, 134, 164
Mahalanobis Committee 128, 156
Mahanalobis plan/ model 2, 85, 108, 112, 114, 121, 123, 142, 229, 272, 276
Maharaja of Bikaner 245
Maharaja of Kashmir 305
Mahbub-ul-Haq x
Mahmud of Gaznavi 251
Malaviya, Madan Mohan 246
Mammen's model, of macro ecnometrics 338–9, 343–52
    real model 364–5
Mandal Commission 259
    recommendations 95, 101
Manmohan Singh Festscrift 9
Manne, Alan 108
manufacturing sector 8, 196, 370
Maratha Empire 238–40
Maratha history 217, 226
markets 189, 190, 377
    economy 157
    globalization and 184
    imperfections 375
    interlinked, and measure of power 383–4
    oriented policy 191, 194
    in South Asia 295

Marshall lectures 3
Marwah's model, of macro econometrics 338–50, 353, 366–71
Marx, Karl 3, 114, 120, 135, 151, 378
    on India and British imperialism 223–4
    notion of economic surplus 392
    political economy of 1
    theory of exploitation 388
Marxism, and Indian government 6
Marxists, and Congress party 5
    on Green Revolution 6
    influence of 3, 150
Masani, Minoo 3
Mazumdar, Charu 21, 43
Menon, Krishna 229
Mexican Peso crisis 294
Minhas, B. 156
minorities, population in India 179, 209, 210, 304, 305
    rights of 256, 260
Mitra, Ashok 6
Mizo nationalism 235
modernity/modernization 79, 81, 87, 96, 301
Mahajir Qaumi Movement (MQM), Pakistan 308
Mohanjo Daro 251, 298
monetary sector, and real sectors 348, 349
    see also banking system
money, markets, deregulation of 163
    supply, and government budget 348, 349
    supply and wholesale price index 71–2
Monnet, Jean 300, 306
Montague-Chelmsford reforms 1917 241, 243
Morley-Minto Reforms 239–42, 260, 261
Morris, Morris David 6, 319, 320, 322, 323
Most Favoured Nation status 58, 174, 188
Mountbatten, Louis 232, 249, 305
Mughal Empire 238–40, 301
Mukherjee, Ajoy 39
Multi Fibre Agreement 189, 293
multiculturalism 2

Munshi, K.M. 252, 264, 266
Muslim League 210, 215, 217, 226–7,
  233, 245, 251, 271, 272, 303
  in elections 212–13
  Lahore session of 214
  Morely-Minto reform and 239–41
Muslim nation, demand for 217, 248
Muslim personal law 98, 253
Muslim population, Congress and 247
  and demand for reservation 211,
    212, 214
  fundamentalists 265
  identity 308
  in India 217, 233, 253
  as minorities 209–11, 213, 239
  national consciousness 240
  role of, in nationhood 237
  separate electorates for 239, 240
  and vote-bank 100, 265
  women's rights 78, 101

Naga nationalism 235
Nagaland, guerilla movement in 227
Nagar, A.L. x, 6
Naicker, Ramaswamy 246
Naidu, Chandrababu 81, 101
Naoroji, Dadabhai 77, 115, 116, 120,
  238
Napoleon 201
Napoleonic wars 200, 201, 203
Naqvi, Khaliq x
Narasimham model, of macro
  econometrics 338, 339, 342,
  353, 371–2
Narayanan, K.R. 94
Narayanan Oration 94, 95
nation, building on Nehruvial model
  78–9
  definition of 202
  and identity 197, 316
  and nation-state 218
  -states, birth and death of 199–219
national consciousness 237
National Council of Applied Economic
  Research (NCAER), data on savings
  343
National Democratic Alliance (NDA),
  and economic reforms 82
National Development Council 18
National Front government 81

National Planning Committee 8, 113,
  114, 117, 122, 123, 156, 229, 271
National Renewal Fund 172
National Sample Survey (NSS) data, on
  consumer expenditure 340, 343
nationalism 201, 261, 302
  and liberalism 222, 223
nationality 222, 235, 315
  constructing 222–31
  on religious lines 226
nationalization, of banks and insurance
  companies 164, 165, 256
nationhood 9, 10, 77–8, 82, 103, 199,
  215, 217, 221, 250–2, 258–9, 237,
  261, 304, 310
  varieties of 238–9, 249
Nav Nirman Morcha, Gujarat 71
native/princely states 209, 210, 244
  accession to India 211, 216, 305
  during partition 249
  and formation of federation 303
Navanirman Andolan 78
Naxalbari region, unrest /revolt in 40,
  41, 234, 284, 307
Naxalite movement/revolts 5, 21, 35
  in West Bengal 43–4
Nayar, Deepak xi
Nehru, Jawaharlal 1, 9, 10, 46, 77, 79,
  94, 97, 100, 113, 156, 169, 227,
  232, 234, 242, 261, 277
  and the Congress party 245, 252
  and discovery of India 220
  economic programme of 258
  foreign policy of 229
  and Gandhi 245
  and Hindu revivalist 252–3
  Mahalanobis model/strategy 56, 57,
    60, 76, 117, 122–7, 130, 131,
    153, 155, 158, 161, 164, 178,
    180
  and national construction 228–9
  and Indian nationhood 251, 252
  on planning 114, 117–18
  and reforming Hindu family law
    86
  and secularism 221, 253
  and theory of nationhood 258
  on underdevelopment 117
Nehru Report 1928 240, 242
Nehruvian socialism 9, 260

Net National Product (NNP) 123, 343, 346
new economic policy, of 1991 141
   of 1992, political economy of 122–31
Nicholas, Ralph x
Non-Aligned Movement 49, 77, 85, 95, 100, 103, 229
non-cooperation movement, and Gandhi 209, 241
non-plan expenditure 170
non-resident Indians, borrowings from 58, 89, 95, 137, 155
non-tariff barriers (NTBs) 190
North-East India, violence in 257, 308
nuclear level arms race, between India and Pakistan 306
Nurkse, R. 143

October Revolution of 1917, in Russia 302, 311
oil shock, of 1970s 184, 278, 279
Oldenburg, Philip x
Oldenburg, Veena x
organized sector, employment in 152
   benefits to industrialists from tariffs and subsidies 189

Pakistan, agriculture in 271, 272
   balance of payments crisis in 274
   Bengali Muslims' demand for regional autonomy 216, 217
   break-up of 200, 201, 216, 217, 218, 234, 269, 275, 277, 284, 291, 300, 302, 304
   demand for 213–14
   developments in 285
   economy of 291
   formation/creation of 200, 201, 210
   fundamentalist movement in 311
   GDP of 85, 278
   Growth rate of 277–9
   and India 85, 293
      wars 21, 22, 230, 251, 254, 272, 277
   industries in 271, 272
   inflation in 278
   and International Monetary Fund 279
   as Islamic republic 233, 251
   military dictatorship in 292
   nationality problem in 235
   planning in 272, 276
   population growth in 274
   terrorism and 84
   and United States 284
   violence in 284, 308
Panchamukhi, Professor 133
Pannikar, K.M. 253
Pant, Gobind Vallabh 86, 246, 252
Pant, Pitambar 134
Parekh, G.D. 2
parliamentary democracy 63, 64
Parry, Johnny xi
Partei Kammunist Indonesia (PKI) 42
partition, of India 9, 10, 77, 97, 200, 227–8, 230, 261, 269, 300
   and after 227–8
   Gandhi and 249–51
   issue 214
   and refugee settling 271
   and riots/violence 232
   World War II and 244–9
Pata Padshahi, revival of 238
Patel, I.G. xi
Patel, S.J. 153
Patel, Vallabhbhai 245, 252, 264
patent law 173
Patil, R.K. 126
Patil, Shivraj 65
Pattnaik, Prabhat xi
Pawar, Sharad 174
Pay Commission 91
peasants, revolts/ guerrilla movements 21, 34
   uprising in Telengana 37
   see also tenants
People's Plan 113
per capita income 23, 109, 135, 137
permit-license-quota raj 59, 89, 91, 95
perestroika 130, 154
PL 480 73, 127, 273
planning, in India 6, 8, 22, 26, 111–21, 153, 192, 350
   criticism of 124
   and economy 112
   holiday 193
   in a new perspective 9, 133–40
   by numbers 107–10
   for an open economy 137–8

role of State in 122, 123
Planning Advisory Board 113
Planning Commission 107–9, 121, 127,
   129, 130, 142, 145, 152, 195, 276
   reorganization of 22
Plant, Arnold 191
Pokhran nuclear test, and sanction
   against India 193
political economy 7, 13, 49, 122–31,
   144–5, 167, 376, 377
   of South Asia 281–5
politics(al), and corruption 195
   corruption in South Asia 295–6
   and crime 265
   developments in 1950s 95
   developments of South Asia 280
   and killings in South Asia 309
   party 17, 18
   problems of, in South Asia 290–2
   and violence 102
Popular Front policies 36
population, of Bangladesh 269
   engaged in agriculture 32, 120
   growth in South Asia 274
   of India 20, 269
   living below subsistence level 108
   of Pakistan 269
   problems of rising 115
portfolio capital 188
Portuguese occupation of India 202
poverty 99, 140, 142, 156, 157
   anti-, programme 156, 177
   in Bangladesh 270
   causes of 116
   in India 270
   in Pakistan 270
   reduction in 187, 188, 193–5
   in South India 120
'power and agrarian relations' 7, 373–92
power, definition of 374
   structure, measuring 377, 387–8
   of zamindars 381, 391
Praja Socialist party 2, 17
Prasad, Rajendra 86, 98, 246, 253, 252
Premadasa, Ransainghe, assassination of
   308
Preobrazhensky, E. 143
President's Rule, in states 64, 67
price level, role of 346, 347, 375
privatization 91, 130

and liberalization and growth 136
property rights, Marx on 120
protectionism, policy 189, 190238
public sector 99, 129–30, 150, 168, 193,
   194, 265, 282
   contribution to GDP 152, 154
   earnings of workers in 171
   employment /labour in 26, 156, 178
   reforms 178
   stand on private sector 59
public space, erosion of 80–1
Punjab, and confrontation between India
   and Pakistan 251
   unrest in 166
Prussia, war with Austria 206–8

Quit India agitation/campaign 213, 248

Radhakrishnan Memorial Lectures 124,
   134, 139
Rahman, Shaikh Mujibur 43, 273, 308
Rai, Kalpanath 168
Rai, Lala Lajpat 238
Rajagopalachari, C. 86, 214, 249
Ramakrishna movement 225
Ramjanmabhoomi temple issue 78
Ranadive 37
Rao, P.V. Narasimha 90, 160, 162, 170,
   171, 188, 190, 309
Rashtriya Swayamsevak Sangh (RSS) 92,
   173, 181, 234, 252, 257
   anti-globalization stand of 82
   on Gandhi 55
Rathenau, Walter 136
Reddaway, W.B. 108
Reformation 299
reforms, anti-, enemies of 170, 171
   and business performance 173
   movements 237
   of 1919 303
regional development, uneven 33–4, 45
   in South Asia 284
regionalism, movement for 19
   problem of 33–5
Rehman, Zia ur 283
religion(religious), and caste 235
   fundamentalism 311, 312
   identity 236
   in India 220–1, 225
   and nationhood 218

of South Asia 299
   state on 234
reproduction, of social relationship 374,
   377, 384, 388–92
Reserve Bank of India 163, 181, 190
   data on investments 340
revolution of 1946–9 96–8
rice, growth rate of output of 30–1
Robbins, Lionel 191
Robinson, Joan 3
Rockfeller Foundation 127
Roman Empire, dissolving of 203
Rosenstein-Rodan, Paul Narcyz 108
Rostow, Walt 3, 150
Round Table conference(s) 10, 201, 211,
   242, 243, 245, 249, 258, 302, 303
   First 78, 100–1
Rowlatt Act 241
Roy, Bimal 87
Roy, M.N. 2
Roy, Raja Rammohan 259, 301
R S Bhatt Memorial Lectures 9, 191
Rudolph, Lloyd x, 128
Rudolph, Suzanne x, 7, 121, 128
Rudra, Ashok x, 7
ruling class 48–50
rupee devaluation 20, 22, 88, 127, 158,
   164, 193, 273
rural areas, employment in 174
   population 32
   poverty in 116
   unemployment in 28
Rushdie, Salman 265
ryotwari regions 33, 120

Samajwadi Party (SP) 52
Sangh Parivar 52, 259, 260
Sanyal, Kanu 43
Saraswati, Dayanand 301
Savarkar, Veer 79, 257
school enrolment rate 156
Schuman, Robert 300
Schumpeter, J.A. 3, 150, 151
Schwarzenberg, Chancellor 204, 205
Sectoral model, for food grain sector
   366–7
secularism 1, 2, 77, 95–7, 99, 103, 234,
   252, 260, 261
   communalism and Indian nation-
      hood 232–61

decline of, and rise of BJP 257–8
   Indira Gandhi and crisis of 254,
      256–7
   in practice 253–4
   problem of 220
Selbourne, David 46, 47, 48, 51
self-employed population 33
self-sufficiency 49, 87, 95, 137, 145,
   146, 273
Sen, Amartya x
Sengupta, Arjun xi
September 11, aftermath of 84
Servants of India Society 92
Seton, Marie 79
Shah, K.T. 113
Shah Bano case 9, 78, 87, 95, 101, 253
Shamlal 2
Shantaram, V. 87
sharecroppers/sharecropping 27, 31, 32,
   373, 376, 378, 383–5, 389, 390
   and indebtedness 385–6
   and landless labour 380
Shastri, Lal Bahadur 88, 127, 164, 193,
   221, 230, 254, 257, 27
Shiv Sena 89
Sikhism 299
Simon Commission 201, 243, 244,
   245
   Congress response to 242
   Report 243
Singh, Arjun 168
Singh, Charan 119, 126, 128, 129, 273
Singh, Manmohan 90, 91, 133, 146,
   160, 177, 179, 186, 272
   New Economic policy of 141
Singh, V.P. 81, 101
Single European Act 314
Sinha, Satyaendra 241
Sinha, Yashwant 91
Sivasubromanian 70
Smith, Anthony xi
Smith, Adam 223
Smith, F. E. 243
social backwardness 86, 91, 311
social relationships, reproduction of
   388–92
social reforms 10, 86, 224
social structure 32–3
socialism 1, 7, 26, 49, 95, 100, 103, 180,
   290

capitalism and Indian economy 149–58

capitalism versus 149–52

crisis of 7–11

Socialist Eastern Europe, collapse of socialism in 150

Socialist party 165

socialist revolutions 150

Socialist Unity Center, West Bengal 39

South Asia, defining a new vision for 297–316

economic problems of 10–11, 269–86, 289–96

new vision for 297–316

political economy 7

society in 299

violence in 284

South Asian Association for Regional Cooperation (SAARC) 292, 301, 316

South East Asia, economies of 187

South Korea, growth rate in 290, 294

Soviet Union, collapse of 8, 85, 151, 302

India and 49, 145, 284

planning in 111, 136, 192

Sri Lanka, civil war in 257

planning in 295

religious disturbances in 312

Sinhalese majority in 304

Sinhala-Tamil division in 310, 312

Tamil Tigers insurgency in 89, 307, 308

Srinivas, M.N. 16

Stalin 86

state, formation on linguistic lines 227, 234

role of 135, 136, 158

sector, growth of 26

sale of equity by 171–2

State Finance Corporation 193

stock exchanges 186, 191

Subhan, Rehman x

subjecthood, theories of 239, 241, 243

subsidies, government 155, 187, 195

Subramanian, C. 126

sugar production, scam in 168

Sukhamoy Chakravary Lecture 9, 133

supply constraints, role of 346, 347

surplus, extraction from rural sector 124, 131

problem of 126

share of 377

transfer to Britain 115–16, 124–5, 131

Suzy Paine Lecture 130, 133, 134

Swadeshi policy 55, 56, 60

Swaminarayan movement 225

swaraj, demand for 209

Swarajists 242

Swatantra party 3, 18, 28, 53

Tarapore Committee report 294

tariffs, imposition of 17, 18, 119, 161, 281

taxes/taxation, on income, expenditure and wealth 164, 177, 281, 282

indirect 343

reforms in 125

Tebhaga movement 273

'Tehelka' incident 84, , 92, 194

Telengana, agrarian unrest in 35, 37, 86, 234, 256, 284, 307

Telugu Desam, Andhra Pradesh 167

tenants/tenancy, 373

output and, relationship 386–7

power of vis a-vis landlords 382

territoriality, and nationality 226–7, 230

textile industries, during British rule in India, 28, 224, 225

Thapar, Romila 253

Thatcher, M. 8, 80

Tinberg-Klein model 337, 338

Third World 85

Tilak, Bal Gangadhar 77, 238, 239

trade, deficit 57

liberalization 184

policy of BJP 58

in South Asia 293–5

trade unions 38

two-nation theory, of Jinnah 217, 249, 251–3, 261

two-sector growth model 339, 341

Ulyanov-Lenin, Vladimir Ilyich 120

underdevelopment 112, 114, 117, 124

unemployment 28, 87, 108, 144, 151, 274

disguised 143

in underdeveloped economies 342

Unit Trust of India 193

'United Front' government 37, 39–42, 81, 285
United Nations (UN), India's role in 85 observers in Kashmir 305
United States of America (USA), aid from 164
  hegemonic position of 151, 213
  hostility to India 186
  macro econometric models for 337
  'open door' policy, and migration to 315
  and Pakistan 284
untouchability, practice in India 98, 242
universal adult franchise 211
Upadhayaya, Deen Dayal 53, 55
Uttarkhand, controversy over 62

Vaishnavism, in Gujarat 266
Vakil, C.N. 2, 69, 72, 74, 75, 141, 142, 144, 145
Vakil-Brahmanand plan 144, 145
Vanaik, A. 128
Vasco da Gama 299
Versailles Treaty 208
Varshney, Ashutosh 265
Viceroy's Council 246
Vidyasagar, Ishwarchandra 301
Vietnam war 4
violence, and instability, culture of 308–13
Vishwa Hindu Parishad 257
Vivekanand 301
Voters' League for Reform, USA 93
V S Desai Memorial Lecture 8

Walrasian General Equilibrium model 138
Wavell, Lord, Viceroy 248–9

Weimar Republic 68, 208
West Bengal, and Bangladesh struggle 43–4
  President's Rule in 40
  United Front experience in 39–42
Westminster Constitution 63, 67
Westminster tradition, in Britain 80, 96, 97, 304
Wheat, growth rate of 30–1
Whittlesey, Charles 2, 3
wholesale price index (WPI) 70–2, 74
Williamson, John x
women, right to vote 97
World Bank 56, 156, 186, 193, 286, 298, 307
World Development Report of 1990 156
World Trade Organization (WTO) 190, 286
World War, First 209, 302
  Second 302, 303
    and partition of India 244–9

Yadav, Laloo Prasad 101
Yadav, Mulayam Singh 101
Yahuda, Michael xi
Youth Congress 50

Zamindar(i), abolition of 42
  powers of 381, 391
  province, agriculture and population growth in 120
  and sharecroppers 378–9, 382
  in West Bengal 33, 39
Zetland 244, 246
Zhdanov 36
Zia, Begum 285
Zollverein treaty 205